Ian C. Macdonald

News and the Southams

News
and the
Southams

CHARLES BRUCE

1968   MACMILLAN OF CANADA   TORONTO

© Charles Bruce 1968

Printed in Canada by Southam • Murray
for The Macmillan Company of Canada Limited
70 Bond Street, Toronto

Contents

Illustrations

Photographs (*between pages 132 and 133*)

The Southam Brothers in 1927
The Southam Family in 1905
Mercy Neal Southam
The Presidents of the Company
  William Southam
  F.N.Southam (William Notman and Son)
  Philip S. Fisher (Ashley and Crippen)
  St. Clair Balfour (Karsh)

Illustrations in the text

News and the Southams

The Family and the Company

Early in 1877 a thirty-three-year-old printer moved from London, Ontario, to Hamilton and with a partner took over a fading newspaper – the *Spectator*. For more than twenty years in London he had worked for the *Free Press*: carrier boy, printer's apprentice, printer, job-room foreman; finally plant superintendent with a small share in the business. Now he had sold that small interest and scraped up enough money here and there to take a chance as a newspaper publisher on his own.

This was William Southam. Under his direction the dying *Spectator* revived, picked up prosperity and power. Its purchase was the first of many steps, unforeseen at the time, towards a modern company with mass communications and printing interests across Canada.

That was far in the future.

In the 1880s Southam and his partner, William Carey, set up printing plants in Toronto and Montreal. In 1897 Southam bought the Ottawa *Citizen*, another daily then fighting for survival. His sons had begun to come into management of the properties. The idea of a family company began to form.

In March of 1904 Southam Limited was chartered as a Dominion company. Its authorized capital was $1,000,000 and its shareholders were William Southam, his wife Wilson, and their six sons and one daughter: Wilson, Fred, Richard, Harry, William James, Gordon, and Ethel. It was in every respect a family firm, a holding company designed to enclose the moderate wealth the elder William and his offspring then possessed and to grow with whatever new adventures, investments, and speculations they might undertake.

Its chief assets were a half-interest in the *Spectator* (which did not become wholly owned until 1925), the *Citizen,* and the commercial printing plants in Toronto and Montreal, in which the Carey share had been bought from the estate of William Carey, who died in 1890. This was active wealth, a core of properties run directly by the Southams. In its vault the company also held a mixed bag of investments including stock in Hamilton industries that William had shared in founding or developing.

When Southam Limited was succeeded in 1920 by William Southam and Sons (still a family affair) its assets figure had increased five-fold, in some degree reflecting a lessened value of the dollar but largely through expansion. In the intervening years the Southams had bought majority interests in two more newspapers: the Calgary *Herald* and the Edmonton *Journal,* both of which had grown and prospered. In 1920 they bought the Winnipeg *Tribune,* and in 1923 a controlling share in the Vancouver *Province.*

By then it was obvious that their main interest was newspaper publishing. A further reorganization in 1927 emphasized this. Late in that year they set up The Southam Publishing Company Limited as a holding company for the six newspapers. Other properties (real estate, investments in non-publishing industry, and at that time the commercial printing plants) were left with a revised version of William Southam and Sons.

Up to this point, though Southams owned most of the stock in the individual newspaper companies, others, including senior employees of the newspapers, held varying amounts. Southam Publishing now acquired this scattered stock and issued its own securities in exchange. Thus the central Southam company was no longer strictly a family concern. Men from outside the family, whose lives were linked with its associated newspapers across Canada, became shareholders and members of its board. At the same time it outlined publicly the principle of territorial home rule for the newspapers that had developed from their earliest days.

Later developments enlarged the pattern. As the Southams got rid of non-publishing interests and William Southam and Sons moved toward dissolution, the printing plants came under the wing of the central corporation, which then (in 1938) was renamed The Southam Company, a title it kept until 1964, when it took the name Southam Press Limited. Meantime in 1941 it took over the assets of its subsidiaries, henceforth to be called divisions, and became technically an operating rather than a holding company. The final step to open ownership came in 1945 when stock was offered to the public and listed on exchanges in Toronto, Montreal, and Vancouver. At this time the company re-emphasized the policy of local editorial independence, the principle that 'newspapers are essentially community services' and must be published and generally administered in their own regions.

The problems of newspaper publishing are many: not the least of them, the fact that any newspaper worth the name must be a business, must make money, to preserve independent life; and yet must recognize that the service that justifies its existence is essentially social rather than commercial. Ownership of a group of papers multiplies the problems and raises a further hazard: the suggestion of centralized power.

Perhaps because of the nature of Canada and of the family, the compulsion to personal power, which in a larger sphere was ingrained in men like Hearst, Northcliffe, and Beaverbrook, never really touched the Southams. For one thing, there were too many of them, each with a mind of his own.

The Southams of the early and middle years were noted for their closeness, their sense of family: William, the shrewd and robust founder; Fred, who as 'F.N.' headed the company for more than twenty years; Wilson and Harry, the idealists at Ottawa; Richard, the laconic printer; Bill, brilliant and erratic, the weaver of schemes; Gordon, the youngest, already a voice in company affairs before he was killed on the Somme. They could, and did, argue to agreement on questions of business. This was certainly a key in the door of success. But when they talked at times in the early years of common editorial policies, nothing much resulted. No one of them could have imposed a concerted editorial course on the rest. Nor were the men who worked with them, and shared in shaping Canadian newspaper life in a quickening time, the sort who would fit easily into a mold.

Since 1945 the company has added two newspapers – the Medicine Hat *News* and the North Bay *Nugget* – and a host of specialized trade journals, and has extended its printing business. It has interests in radio and television and minority shares in three newspapers apart from the wholly owned group: the London *Free Press,* in which its quarter-interest dates back to 1907, the Kitchener-Waterloo *Record* and the Brandon *Sun.*

The brothers are dead. The old close relationship has dissolved. The family and the company continue. The 'family' now includes scores of men and women two and three generations removed from William, some active in management of the company or its divisions; a few in the news or printing business at other levels; many following different ways of life altogether and, from a company point of view, scarcely distinguishable from the general public. More than 2,500 of the Canadian public share in company ownership.

The old family company has taken a shape that William certainly could not even have guessed at when he scraped up $6,000 to buy the *Spectator* with partner William Carey in 1877 – nor even when Southam Limited was founded twenty-seven years later and he began to pass more and more responsibility to his sons.

Some things persist. Notably the color and verve and flair of human events, and public interest in them. The narrative that follows is

THE FOUNDING GENERATIONS

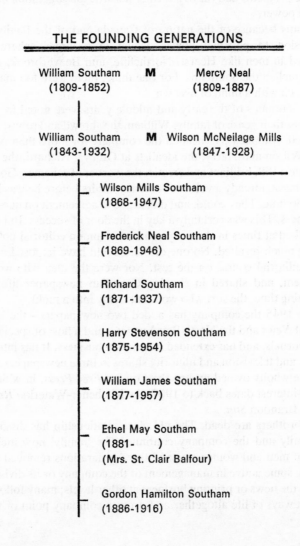

| William Southam | **M** | Mercy Neal |
| (1809-1852) | | (1809-1887) |

| William Southam | **M** | Wilson McNeilage Mills |
| (1843-1932) | | (1847-1928) |

Wilson Mills Southam
(1868-1947)

Frederick Neal Southam
(1869-1946)

Richard Southam
(1871-1937)

Harry Stevenson Southam
(1875-1954)

William James Southam
(1877-1957)

Ethel May Southam
(1881-   )
(Mrs. St. Clair Balfour)

Gordon Hamilton Southam
(1886-1916)

designed to tell something of the Southams, of the people who worked and work with them, and of the newspapers and printing plants and the company. Inevitably the story from time to time finds itself interlaced with aspects of that unpredictable thing, transient but inexhaustible, with which they were and are chiefly concerned: the shared flow of living, the day's news.

1
William and
the *Spectator*

To the stonemason from Kingsthorpe it must have been one of those times in a man's life when even the present is touched by a special light. There is a hint of laughter in a letter that reached him at Lachine from the old town, the life forsaken but still the heart of his experience, in England: 'I congratulate you on the birth of a son. I think it must be Billy Southam again.' And then the sly reminder: 'You used to say you should save money then.'

For two generations the family had run to girls. William Southam, the immigrant father, already had four of them. He himself was the only son among six children born to Richard Southam, a bacon dealer of Kingsthorpe on the northern outskirts of Northampton. Richard had died in poor circumstances in 1819, when William was ten years old.

What William had when he landed in Canada was the skill of his hands, the remarkable woman Mercy Neal, whom he had married in St. Giles' Church, Northampton, in December 1834, and the four daughters: Ann, approaching her eighth birthday; Elizabeth, six; Hannah, who would be five next Christmas day; and Lucy, three years old. And, of course, the prospect . . . 'You used to say you should save money then' . . . even that might be possible. Certainly he had believed in the chance of a better living for Mercy and himself and the family, or he would never have given up the pinched but established security of English village life and spent what he had on the Atlantic passage.

But for the time being, in that fall of 1843, his mind must have played lightly at times with just the present fact: it was indeed a son, a second Billy Southam, who had interrupted the family's journey to get himself born on August 23, at 'Upper Lachine Road, near the

Toll Bar, Montreal, Canada', as the address on the letter from home
had it.

It is to be hoped at least that William had his moments of satisfaction in the simple present as well as in hopes for the hidden future.
As things turned out the promise of time was to be delayed at least a
generation; he would not be there to see it.

Like most families who move into a new land (except for those of
the governors and the major-generals) the Southams were little concerned with records. It was not until two generations after the first
William's death that grandsons, themselves already aging, would begin to wonder; and by then anything from those early years but the
barest facts – birth notices, marriage records, and dates cut in cemetery stone – were obscured by time. William worked at his trade in
various places. The next child, Mary, was born in Buffalo, on January 12, 1847. By the time a second boy, Richard, arrived in 1848
the Southams had settled down in London, Canada West. On June 9,
1849, eleven-year-old Elizabeth died. Sarah was born in London in
the summer of 1850. And there on January 28, 1852, William died.
He was forty-three years old.

From that point on, except for whatever of William would appear
unrecognized in inherited traits of personality, the family story is that
of Mercy Neal Southam, their children, and the generations that followed. Notably the boy – 'Billy Southam again' – who was not yet
nine years old when his father died, and the family eventually born
to him and the Scottish girl he married.

At the stonemason's death there were seven children of whom Ann,
tall and handsome at sixteen, was the eldest. Mercy had the tenacity
that often runs with gentleness. Sometimes as an aging woman she
would talk with grand-daughters about the hard times of early widowhood, when she took in washing to keep the family going, but by
then the hard years were a memory. When she died on November
26, 1887, at the age of seventy-eight her sons and daughters (except
Ann, who died a spinster at thirty-nine) were married or otherwise
settled in life. She would be remembered by daughters of her children
as a loving woman and by grandsons who would establish scholarships in her memory as the founder of a family. A photo taken late
in life shows wide-set eyes touched with humor and shrewdness, a
mouth firm but perhaps masking some inner amusement. There is in
the face a suggestion of qualities that developed in less subdued form
in her firstborn son.

When young William was twelve years old, in 1855, he quit school and went to work as a carrier boy for the London *Free Press*, which had just started issuing a daily edition. The paper had been founded by a young Scot named William Sutherland in 1849 as a Reform weekly. A bit over-ambitious, Sutherland tried daily publication briefly in 1852 with little result but debt. Meantime Josiah Blackburn had come out from England in 1850 and gone to work for the Paris *Star*. At the end of 1852 he bought the $500 mortgage Sutherland had placed on the *Free Press*. Two years later he went daily, continuing to publish weekly as well, and this time the venture paid off. The four-page, eight-column morning paper was an immediate hit. Late in 1857, in the savage depression that followed the Crimean war, Blackburn pulled in his horns and went to twice-a-week, but the protests of his readers (backed by increased advertising from London merchants) was immediate. He was back on a daily basis in a month.

William Southam was one of four boys delivering the daily – it had a circulation of about 500 at the start – and collecting the subscription money of twelve and a half cents a week. Early in 1859 he went a step further and signed up with the *Free Press* as an apprentice to the printing trade. The next five years laid the foundation of his future. He learned the craft of printing and he read his way through the library of the Mechanics Institute. When the Blackburns (Josiah had brought his brother Stephen out from England to join the business) handed William a memento of his completed apprenticeship in January of 1864 it was a volume of Scott's poems. A little later they appointed him foreman of the job department. To the end of his life William was to remember warmly his years on the *Free Press*.

The brief tension of the Fenian Raids enlivened the early summer of 1866. It also made news. For a day or two the Blackburns wondered whether they would get it into print: ten of their staff were in the militia units called to the front. Among them were William Southam, an ensign in a rifle company, and his younger brother Richard, an assistant pressman and spare-time artilleryman. The London units didn't see action, and William's chief recollection of the experience was an altercation he got into with superiors on the journey back for refusing to turn his men out of a railway car reserved for officers.

By this time new competition had appeared in London in the *Evening Advertiser,* founded by John Cameron, who had been a fellow-apprentice of Southam on the *Free Press*. The *Advertiser*'s political persuasion was Clear Grit. For some time the *Free Press* had been swinging away from its Reform policies towards independence. The appearance of a competitor hastened the move towards the Conservatism that the *Free Press* later embraced and also brought into being – at Southam's suggestion – an evening edition.

The year of Confederation was a big one for William. Apart from the excitement of the union itself, which pulled into the beginnings of a nation the more than 3,000,000 people of four provinces, there were personal matters of importance. Stephen Blackburn took a job as registrar of titles at Glencoe and wanted to sell his share in the paper. Southam was one of a group of three (the others were John K. Clare and Henry Mathewson) who bought it.

Meantime he had fallen in love with a nineteen-year-old girl named Wilson Mills. The Mills family were Scots, from Ayr. James Mills, a cabinet-maker, reached Hamilton with his wife and children in the summer of 1854 to take a job with a furniture dealer, arranged for him by a former Ayrshire man in the lake shipping business. They lived in Hamilton only a few months, moved on to Galt for a brief stay, and thence to London, where James settled down at his trade at just about the time Billy Southam was starting his morning deliveries of the *Free Press*. William Southam and Wilson McNeilage Mills were married at St. Paul's Church November 14, 1867, the day before Wilson's twentieth birthday.

On October 2, 1868, the first boy was born. He was given his mother's first and last names – Wilson Mills. The 'Wilson' was a traditional name for girls on the Mills side. Being suitable also for boys it continues to crop up as a first or second name for Southam descendants of both sexes.

Years later William would say of this first of his six sons: 'I brought up Wilson, and Wilson brought up the rest.' The statement was probably made with a touch of laughter. There is little evidence that either Southam parent delegated much of the bringing-up process. But Wilson's studious and tolerant approach to life undoubtedly had its influence – a moderating influence, perhaps, among a crew of boys with widely different personalities and, later on, combined with a shrewd (almost paradoxically so) business sense, among a group of individualists pounding out family agreement with the hammers of their difference.

All that was in the future. For the present William had his work as superintendent of the *Free Press*, his name on billheads at the bottom of the list of proprietors, and $1,200 a year. Life in London was busy and pleasant. William's enduring interest in sport had its beginnings there. His younger brother Richard played for and later managed the Tecumsehs, a notable London ball team in those days of gloveless players and cricket-like scores. William himself appeared at times in the Tecumsehs' line-up. A surviving account shows Richard scoring ten runs, William seven, in a 70-43 victory over Hamilton Maple Leafs in August of 1869.

And of course there was the growing family. Fred, Richard, and Harry were born in the seven years following Wilson's birth. A fifth son was on the way when, early in the winter of 1877, there was news from Hamilton. The *Spectator* was on the rocks. Its owners and others concerned for the survival of a Conservative newspaper there were looking for a buyer. Josiah Blackburn wasn't interested; but William Southam was.

The *Spectator* had an honorable history reaching back to 1846. In that year a group of moderate Conservatives in Hamilton decided they needed a paper to fight the party's battles. Edwin Dalley approached Robert Smiley, a young Kingston printer of Irish parentage, then working in Montreal. Smiley had a little money of his own and a fund of independence and ambition. He came to Hamilton at Dalley's invitation, picking up a second-hand press for $150 on the way, and set up shop on the second floor of a building housing the Dalley and Stevens wholesale drug house 'nearly opposite the Market'. The first issue of the twice-a-week Hamilton *Spectator and Journal of Commerce* appeared Wednesday, July 15, 1846, a four-page paper in eight-column format.

First-column position went to a seventy-two-line Ode to Queen Victoria. Other front-page material included a discussion of post office inefficiency (better and cheaper postal facilities were to be a crusading subject for the early *Spectator*), news of the corn bill debate in the House of Lords (received via the steamship *Britannia*, which had arrived at Boston 'on Saturday week'), a column from the London *Times* on the state of Europe, and a gory description of animal fights staged as entertainments in India, written by a travelling bachelor of divinity named Rev. Robart Caunter. His style was graphic and explicit:

> I witnessed at one of these sanguinary exhibitions a contest between a buffalo and a tiger. The buffalo was extremely fierce. . . . It commenced the attack by rushing towards its adversary, which retreated to a corner of the arena, where, finding no escape, it sprang upon the buffalo's neck, fixing its claws in the animal's shoulder, and lacerating it in a frightful manner. It was, however, almost instantaneously flung upon the earth with a violence that completely stunned it, when there appeared a ghastly wound in the belly, inflicted by its antagonist's horn, from which the bowels protruded. The conqueror now began to gore and trample upon its prostrate enemy, which it soon despatched.

And so on for three columns, including the main go between three wild dogs and a bear, won by the bear on a TKO.

Hamilton's population was 7,000 and its incorporation as a city was set for January 1, 1847. Smiley, starting from scratch, got into other interests as well as the *Spectator*, including real estate and a woollen mill at Ancaster. He died well off, while still a young man, in 1855.

Meantime the paper had begun daily publication in May 1852. At Robert Smiley's death it went to his brother John, who sold a half-share to William Gillespy, an editorial writer, and soon thereafter the other half to Alex Robertson, the book-keeper. The paper lost ground in the depression of the late 1850s, particularly severe in Hamilton, where a population of 27,500 in 1858 fell off to less than 20,000 in three years.

In 1864 Thomas and Richard White bought the *Spectator*. During the Whites' six years of ownership (between their operation of the Peterborough *Review* and their purchase of the Montreal *Gazette*) the paper regained its position and influence. These were the lively times leading up to Confederation, which the *Spectator* strongly favored, and on into new problems of infant nationhood that followed. When the Whites went to Montreal they sold the *Spectator* to Alexander Lawson, David McCulloch, and Alexander Mars, operating as Lawson, McCulloch and Company. It was reasonably prosperous for two or three years, until depression struck again in the middle 1870s. By 1877 it was broke, and the stage was set for Southam.

He took his cue after some hesitation. Life in London was pleasant and secure, and family responsibilities were growing. There was also the question of how to raise the money.

William's problem and decision live in the family legend. Sixty-six years later one of his sons writing to a nephew put it this way: 'You have probably heard that your grandfather Southam started his newspaper career by putting up the huge sum of $6,000 to buy the Spectator. His salary at the Free Press was $1,200 per annum with which he had to support a wife and five children. His limited income was probably why he made the venture, and for a few years after he bought the property he was very worried that he would not be able to put it over, in which case he would have to start all over again minus the cash and the $1,200 per annum but with the five children.'*

At about the same time another son, writing to a brother in a dif-

---

*F.N.Southam to Gordon T. Southam, October 4, 1943.

ferent context, recalled an incident to which he attributed the creation of 'the famous family motto': 'When Bill Vallance said to Father, "If I thought you had the hearts, Southam, I'd make it three no
trumps," and Father replied, "Take a chance, Bill, take a chance,"
and they got through with three no trumps, game and rubber, and
let out a roaring laugh.'*

The three-no-trumps story belongs to a period far later than the
1877 move into Hamilton, but something of the spirit of it must have
worked in William while he thought about the *Spectator* – that and a
related Southam characteristic: a careful calculation of the odds.

At the urging of Alex Gillies, salesman for Buntin, Gillies and
Company, from whom he bought newsprint for the *Free Press,* William went to Hamilton on a winter Saturday with Gillies and studied
the plant. On the way back to the railway station he asked a sudden
question: 'Alex, do you think it is a good buy?' Gillies said, 'William, if I didn't think so I wouldn't wish it on a friend.' William was
convinced. But he couldn't swing it alone.

A close friend in London was William Carey, who had been
brought to Canada as a boy from his Irish birthplace and now was a
partner in a book-selling firm. Carey also was willing to take a
chance. The articles of partnership they signed on March 20, 1877,
called for the contribution by each partner of $4,000, with an addi-
tional $1,000 each within a year if mutually agreed upon.

By now the various members of the immigrant family were reasonably well settled. Three of the girls were married: Hannah to George
Gibson,† Mary to James Reid, and Sarah, the youngest, to Jack
Mills, William's brother-in-law. Lucy had stayed single and was on
the way to becoming London's leading dressmaker, an imaginative
craftswoman who attended balls and receptions to see the effect of
her creations and pick up ideas for new ones. When William got together his share of the money to put the *Spectator* on its feet, a loan
from Lucy was part of it.

Early that spring he sold his small interest in the *Free Press* and
moved into the Royal Hotel in Hamilton, not far from the building
at MacNab and Market that then housed the *Spectator*. For the time
being Wilson and the boys remained at London.

In August the Spectator Printing Company was chartered with authorized capital of $20,000. The original shareholders were Southam

---

*W.J.Southam to F.N.Southam, April, 1941.

†George (Mooney) Gibson, catcher for Pittsburgh Pirates in their winning
world series of 1909, and later manager of the club, was the youngest son of
this union.

and Carey, at $5,000 each, and five other Hamilton men: Alexander Turner, John Calder, Donald McInnes, James Turner, all merchants, and James Walker, manufacturer. Stock held by the five totalled $2,300. Eventually more than a dozen other individuals and business firms subscribed for small allotments under agreement to sell to Southam and Carey when the principals could afford it. They included Buntin, Gillies and Company; John Riordon, the paper-maker; and Adam Brown, railway promoter and politician, who had been born in Scotland in 1826 and would live on to die in his 100th year. Within a few years all stock had been redeemed by the partners. They held the $20,000 in equal shares.

The Paper and the Party

Southam and Carey took over a property that was in bad shape as a business and at that stage uninspiring as a newspaper. Wages were long past due. Printers and newsmen needing shoes and groceries took orders on merchants against advertising accounts. Jimmie Allan, who had joined the paper as a messenger in 1870 and went on to head the advertising staff for half a century, recalled that he got an order on an undertaker to bury his father. Several printers had quit and left town. Of the paper's eight front-page columns (it was still at four pages) advertising filled six. A serial story and reprinted features used up the other two. Inside, no one tried to dress the copy with even the label headings of the time. LATEST BY TELEGRAPH was good enough.

The new owners put their pooled resources into straightening out the business and brightening the paper. William Southam was a trained printer with an all-round newspaper man's interest in men and events and a sense of what people would buy to read. That spring and summer he transformed the *Spectator*, widening the format to nine columns, confining front-page ads to the two left-hand columns, and filling the other seven with solid news: not only the wars and famines of Europe and Asia but the politics of Ottawa, Toronto, Quebec, and Halifax, and the life of Ontario's growing towns. Russia was fighting Turkey in the fall of 1877. The *Spectator* carried detailed reports, but the fall of Kars shared space with Brantford, Collingwood, Owen Sound, Port Dalhousie, Belleville, Ameliasburgh, Kinmount, and Watford.

Human interest got play, and the *Spectator*, as the custom of the time was, sometimes mixed its editorial advice with the news. TERRIBLE OUTRAGE! introduced a local story narrating the ordeal of a

Mrs. Williams, who had been attacked by two toughs: 'The ruffians threw her down and the intention evidently was to ravish her person. However at this juncture footsteps were heard' . . . just in time . . . and the miscreants fled. 'It is high time', the *Spectator* said in a final paragraph, 'that the Police Commission got through their wool the importance of appointing more policemen.'

Probably the paper's strongest feature at the time Southam and Carey moved in was page two, the editorial page. David McCulloch, an eloquent early protagonist of a protective tariff, stayed on staff to shape some of the *Spectator*'s most effective editorials. A former upholsterer for the Great Western Railway, the studious McCulloch had been hired in 1864 by the Whites. He was clear and persuasive with pen and paper, but his years as part owner, after the party his paper supported slid into eclipse, had been frustrating at best. Now, as the Conservatives fought their way out of the shadows of the Pacific Scandal assisted by dissensions and indecision among Alexander Mackenzie's Reformers, McCulloch was a reasonably happy warrior.

The *Spectator* took the view that the real Tories in the old bad sense of the word were Premier Mackenzie and his fellows, while the real Liberals (in the good sense of *that* word) were the moderate Conservatives:

> The premier is not a Conservative, but a Tory of the ancient school, and dubbing his Toryism with the name of Reform does not in the slightest degree change the essential quality of it. The progress made since the days when his political opinions were moulded he is unable to understand. Since that time the real Conservative Party has developed into a party which is progressive in its tendencies and liberal in its ideas, neither clinging blindly to the present nor rushing madly into wild schemes for the future; this is the conservatism which Mr. Mackenzie does not understand and a great many workingmen do.
>
> Mr. Blake belongs to a slightly different type of ancient Toryism from Mr. Mackenzie. . . . Mr. Blake is wholly destitute of sympathy with the people. . . .
>
> Mr. Cartwright, before he joined his present party, was considered a Tory of the old school, and he seems to have fallen among congenial companions.

Through the summer and fall of 1878 the *Spectator* met the first test under its new ownership of reporting a federal election campaign and fighting its party's battles in such a contest. It went into both phases of this responsibility with obvious zest. The paper daily front-paged stories from across the country, as the old pros of both parties stumped the circuit. At the head of its editorial column it carried a line-drawing of the Canadian ensign flowing in the breeze and the heading 'Our Battle Cry: Protection to Home Industries'. Between full-dress editorials it ran single paragraphs in bold-face type highlighting the issues and warning against the 'tortuous course' of its rival, the *Times*, which had once supported protection but now damned it as 'a snare set by knaves to catch fools'. As election day approached, the *Spectator* ran a list of Grits who had been disqualified or unseated for corrupt practices after the 1873 election.

Win or lose, the election itself was the news story of the year. The *Spectator* announced it would stay open election night and bulletin results. Crowds gathered early at the lighted building.

In the previous November William Southam had started a morning edition. It came off the press Wednesday, September 18, 1878, carrying the national election returns with as much exuberance as the single-column headings of the period could hold:

VICTORY!

Splendid Triumph for the National Policy.

Probable Defeat of the Government.

LARGE GAINS IN ONTARIO.

Quebec Does Her Duty Nobly.

. . . and so on.

In Hamilton itself Conservatives won both seats.

A short editorial, headed 'The Spectator's Share of the Work', 'modestly acknowledged' complimentary references to the vigor of its campaign. For the paper the result was a twofold victory. It had done a solid job of news coverage, and the party of its heart was back in power.

There were rugged years ahead. There were debts to pay off and stock to buy back. But in 1878 the *Spectator,* as a newspaper property, had begun to rise from the trough of the wave.

Plans and Growing Boys

By the early 1880s the *Spectator*'s pages reflected the upbeat of a city. In 1879, spurred by National Policy protective duties, the iron founders from Ohio had moved in; names like Doolittle and Wilcox became Hamilton names. The newcomers leased the old plant built by the Great Western Railway to reroll worn rails and got into the manufacture of wrought-iron bars and cut nails. This was a project that would grow and merge a generation later into the Steel Company of Canada, an enterprise that with infusions of Canadian men, money, and plant would absorb the Americans rather than the other way round. It was also a signpost. Other industries of Canadian and United States parentage were on the way. The city's population had reached 35,000.

William Southam may have looked ahead to a time when he would get into industrial promotion, but for the present he threw his energy into the newspaper and printing. The one expansive step he and Carey took was to set up as general and railway printers in Toronto, in the new building that housed the *Mail*.

In his own field he was already a familiar figure among the Hamiltonians, a tribe of hard-headed realists. They knew him as a shrewd man in the news and printing business, restless and jovial, a sharp competitor in two of their favorite pastimes, poker and curling. President of the Thistle Club in 1884, in mid-January he curled on one of four rinks that defeated Toronto by a total score of 80-62.

He joined when he could in fishing and gunning expeditions with his sons, but for the most part gave them a loose and easy rein. In 1880, after brief periods on Market Street and Bay Street South, he had rented the house on John Street North that the older boys remembered as the centre of a kind of golden age – a house with a high stone wall, a carriage gate, an orchard, and a peacock. And briefly, a cow. The brevity of this animal's tenure resulted from an event soon woven into family legend. A small neighbor boy had the job of driving it each morning along Barton Street to a pasture across the railway tracks. One morning the cow's arrival at the crossing coincided with that of a freight train. Shortly thereafter the herdsman appeared at the kitchen door and announced to the mother of the family: 'Please ma'am the cow's dead. But here's the horns.' It was too much for William. What helped to keep the memory green was the sound of his uninhibited laughter.

From the beginning Wilson, Fred, and Dick practically lived their Hamilton summers on the bay or at the beach. In the early years they would take the little passenger steamer from the foot of James Street (return fare for children: five cents) across to the piers flanking the canal connecting Hamilton Bay with the lake. Sunfish, perch, and rock bass swarmed round the foot of the timber piers. After the move to John Street, William leased a boat. The boys would walk four miles out to a creek in West Hamilton with cheesecloth minnow-net to trap bait, lug it back in a water-filled pail, and get up before sunrise to row three miles to a fishing spot at Brown's wharf. 'Then', Wilson recalled, 'we usually with a small frog or minnow for bait landed one or two five-pound black bass which well repaid us for our walk the day before.'

By early 1884 William had plans for the *Spectator* and for the family. He himself was just into his forties. Wilson was in his sixteenth year and soon to spend some months at the Toronto plant. Fred was fourteen and about to start setting type in the *Spectator*'s job-room. Richard was twelve, Harry eight, and young William James six. Ethel, first of the family to be born in Hamilton, had reached her second birthday in November.

Editorially the paper was reasonably strong. H.F.Gardiner had left the managing editorship in 1880 to go to the *Times* and David McCulloch had dropped out two years later to become collector of customs, but at the time of these departures the *Spectator* already had on staff an able editorial man in Augustus Toplady Freed, who succeeded Gardiner as managing editor. And in the early 1880s it hired John Robson Cameron.

A boy from nearby Beamsville, Freed broke in as a printer's devil on the Dundas *Warder*, went on to Harcourt Bull's Hamilton *Gazette* (later absorbed by the *Spectator*) fought in the Civil War with the 27th New Haven, worked on papers in Albany, New York, and Chicago, and returned to Hamilton in the 1870s.

Cameron's career was at least as colorful. Born in Lanark county, he also had learned the printing trade, worked for the Sarnia *Canadian*, gone to Arkansas and thence to the Detroit *Free Press* and on to Winnipeg with the Wolseley expedition. There he had been associated with John Luxton in founding the *Free Press* and served as an alderman. After reporting for the Minneapolis *Tribune* he came back to Canada, first to the Guelph *Herald*, then to the *Spectator*.

Freed wrote easy-going verse as an avocation. Cameron built a reputation as a paragrapher without peer. He did not fear the pun. At a time when some newspapers were terming 'shameful' certain references to Sir John A. Macdonald's nose, Cameron's comment was: 'Shame! It's more than a shame! 'Snoutrage!' When the Buffalo *Express* suggested that 'Canada should have enough sense to come in out of the reign Victoria,' Cameron shot back: 'Canada prefers the reign Victoria to the hail Columbia.'

The *Spectator* building at MacNab and Market, leased from an estate, was really two joined buildings: one of brick, the other stone, each with four storeys and cellar. The *Spectator* was scattered: newsprint in the cellar, business office on the ground floor, stockroom on the second, folding-room on the third, with the chief operating departments on the fourth. Here were engine-room and pressroom, bindery, job-room, ticket-room, editorial, reporters', and composing rooms. The place held more than a dozen tenants, including a fire insurance company, a couple of laundries, a lawyer, a seed merchant, an oil merchant, a coal-oil and crockery store, tailors, a whip-furl manufacturer, and a shoe-last manufacturer, a firm of painters and the hall of the Uniformed Patriarchs.

Up top, the various newspaper rooms opened by separate doors off a long corridor. Back and forth along this hallway William Southam paced when he had something on his mind. One decision he came to was that the Spec must move. He arranged to shift the plant that coming summer of 1884 to a building owned by John Proctor on James Street just south of Main. As things happened the paper was forced into an earlier move.

At 3:30 in the morning of Wednesday, January 23, George Bread, heading home from his night-shift job as a silver-plater at Copp's foundry, glanced across Market Square and saw flames behind the *Spectator*'s stockroom windows. He shouted and ran to turn in an alarm.

Up on the fourth floor night pressman Robert Ferguson had just begun to run off the morning edition when the smell of smoke startled him and assistant Bob Locke. They ran to the job-room. Smoke poured through cracks in the floor. Flames turned them back from the elevator shaft. They made for the stairs. Safe on the street they stood back to peer up at a scene thus described by the *Spectator* that afternoon:

> Around on Market Street they saw a young man named Johnny Munro, the 'folding feeder' . . . getting out of his window. Munro sleeps on the premises so as to be ready to put the morning edition of the paper through the folding machine.
>
> He took a rope he had and tied it to the bedstead, threw it out of the window and let himself down by it, after having first thrown out his mattress and bedclothes to fall on. . . .
>
> As he passed the stockroom window the flames were bursting fiercely out and as the young man shot through the lurid mass his face, hands and hair were burned, though not much.

Firemen got there quickly but, though the stone walls stood, they could save little. From the stockroom flames shot up the elevator shaft and along the corridor. Sparks fell down the shaft and set fire to the newsprint. Ferguson's press on the fourth floor, carrying two pages of type, crashed through to the floor below. The second 'side' – the local and telegraph pages – was saved and rushed over to the *Times* where the morning *Spectator* was issued in half-sheet form.

The afternoon edition, also produced on *Times'* presses, carried a column-and-a-half description of the fire, including a suggestion of incendiarism. Detail was thorough, right down to the fact that Ferguson lost his hat, coat, overcoat, and vest (with watch in pocket). The heading was GONE UP IN SMOKE.

For several days the *Spectator* put out a single edition daily from the *Times,* but by February 1 had bought out the *Tribune,* a paper then in liquidation after a brief existence. For several months it issued from the *Tribune*'s old location on James Street North.

Loss in the fire was $29,000 of which $20,000 was covered by insurance.

The mechanics of moving didn't slow up the *Spectator* in its practically continuous debate with esteemed contemporaries. Early in February the Toronto *Globe* charged the Spec with various offenses: It had 'shouted itself hoarse' in 1878 in pointing out the iniquities of the Liberals, and it had claimed that 'no workingman would henceforth walk the streets for lack of employment'. The *Spectator* replied that it could find no special charges on its books for throat medicaments. As to the statement about the workingmen: 'We deny it. . . . But it is true that the number of working people employed in Hamilton today is at least 2,000 in excess of the number employed in 1878.'

It then went on to a *Spectator*'s-eye view of the industrial situation:

> We are charged with having said that 'tall chimneys would throw clouds of smoke to the heavens in every city, town and valley of the Dominion.' We plead guilty to the tall chimneys, but not to their wide diffusion. Every place is not suited to tall chimneys. . . .

Blandly the Spec suggested that, judging by the cries of the *Globe* and the London *Advertiser,* Toronto and London were in the not-suited class. Hamilton was different.

> In Hamilton and other towns the tall chimneys have risen in great numbers. Here we see the chimneys of the rolling mills, the clock factory, the Meriden works, seven new foundries, the chandelier works, the forge works, the cotton mills, the glass works and a host of others

built or reopened since 1878; and at the present time fourteen new factories, or immense additions to the old ones, are about ready to begin operations. We plead guilty to the tall chimneys.

Perhaps it was a relief to Freed a couple of days later to get out of the political ring for a little. Alfred Tennyson had just accepted a title and stepped into controversy. The *Spectator* termed the criticism 'senseless clamor'. But, for all that:

> We confess we would rather he had remained Alfred Tennyson. . . . It would be pleasanter to think of Alfred Tennyson the poet than of Baron Tennyson. At the same time there is no line in the poet's writings which Baron Tennyson could wish to blot. . . . If Tennyson carry to the House of Lords the spirit which animates most of his writings he will be of great value there. . . . We shall see if his views have changed since 1852 when he took the Upper House to task for too much subservience to Louis Napoleon . . .

>> My lords, we heard you speak: you told us all
>> That England's honest answer went too far;
>> That our free press should cease to brawl,
>> Not sting the fiery Frenchman into war.
>> It was an ancient privilege, my lords,
>> To fling whate'er we felt, not fearing, into words.

In June the *Spectator* settled down in the Proctor Building as planned, for a run in that location of fourteen years. And no one could charge that it or its esteemed contemporaries permitted any abatement of the 'ancient privilege'.

Family in Business

They were vivid years. The *Spectator* faced new and sharp competition. The Southam newspaper and printing interests spread to Montreal and Ottawa, and the older boys moved out from Hamilton to run them. Industry continued to raise its chimneys; William Southam put money and effort into more than one. A hint of the future appeared toward the end of the century in the beginnings of hydro-electric power. A sixth Southam boy was born on February 7, 1886, and named Gordon after the hero of Khartoum.

By then the Southams had moved from John Street North to a double house on Bold, shared with the family of St. Clair Balfour, a wholesale grocer and curling-and-poker companion of William's. Further moves took them briefly to Markland Street and then in the early 1890s to Pinehurst, the stone house on the south side of Jackson Street West that would remain the home of the elder Southams for forty years.

In January of 1889 William sent Fred, just past nineteen, to Montreal to set up a ticket-printing shop in the railway capital of the country. Five years later Richard went to Toronto to manage the printing
plant Southam and Carey had established there in 1881.

In the summer of 1889 the Harris brothers and E.D.Cahill, a lawyer, launched a third daily in Hamilton – the *Herald*. The *Spectator*
for August 2 welcomed it with this editorial note:

> The Hamilton Herald is the name of a journal which made its appear-
> ance in the city yesterday, under the management of Mr. John M.
> Harris, recently connected with the Hamilton Evening Times. The
> new paper looks well, has an able advertisement editor and an able
> press, thinks a good deal of itself, makes the customary promises to
> be the best paper in the country, claims a big circulation and fills a
> long felt want. It gives about half the reading matter for a cent as the
> Evening Spectator gives for 2 cents. For a cheap paper it is a very
> good one, and is quite creditable to the management and enterprise
> of Mr. Harris. Here's hoping you may never regret it, Johnny.

The *Herald* at times sounded a refreshing note of independence.
As civic elections in December of 1889 approached, it commented:
'The biggest streak of fun lies in the fact that the organs are in dead
earnest. The Spec does not make grimaces when it leads forth the
little Tory puppet, nor does the Times smile as it brings out the little
Grit monkey.' Its independence, however, often had a Grit tinge.
John M. Gibson was the chief Grit power in Hamilton; about the
only satisfaction the *Spectator* could take from the new situation was
a chance to refer to its two competitors as Gibson's 'senior and junior organs'.

More important than the *Herald*'s politics was the fact that it hit
the street as a one-cent paper. The *Spectator* eventually cut its price
from two cents to meet the threat and dropped its morning edition to
strengthen the evening. The new competition, together with general
business slackness through the 1890s, lightened the *Spectator*'s till.
In 1889 the paper made $12,600. In 1890 the net was down to
$5,000. Not until 1898 did it reach the $12,000-a-year mark again.

Already in the 1890s old Hamiltonians were described as 'having
seen the growth of the city from an insignificant town to the chief
manufacturing centre of the Dominion'.

Sport was news. Hamilton and London played in an international
baseball circuit that included a team from Bay City–Saginaw, referred to as the Hyphens. Major league results were front-page stuff.
Pneumatic-tired safety bicycles thronged the roads, and cycle race-
meets rated detailed reports running up to two columns.

In May of 1890 William Carey died at the age of forty-six; he had never fully recovered from a spine injury suffered in a fall two years before. Wilson Southam was then in his twenty-second year; he had picked up some business experience in the drygoods firm of Knox, Morgan and Company as office boy and later travelling salesman. Soon after Carey's death he joined the *Spectator* as secretary-treasurer.

For more than a year in the late eighties he had been away. A suspicion of heart strain as a result of pulling an oar in the Leander crew caused the doctors to advise a sea voyage. The trip, south from Halifax aboard a lumber vessel fitted with auxiliary steam power, lengthened into an Odyssey in which he just missed shipwreck when the cargo shifted, crossed the isthmus of Panama on muleback, travelled slowly up the continent through Mexico to California, and eventually reached headquarters of the only family he knew of in the Northwest Territories – the remarkable McDougalls: the two Johns, who were Methodist missionaries, and David, the trader. There at Morleyville on the edge of the Stoney reserve he mulled over the possibility of settling in the West. William called him back to Hamilton.*

By day he learned the business at the *Spectator*. Outside working hours he strove for self-improvement, apparently with some thought of politics later on. 'I find everybody can do something to entertain others except myself,' he wrote after an evening out in 1895. 'I am a drone in the society hive and must really try to find out some point wherein I can by study or practice qualify myself to bear my share of entertaining others. Fortunately my health seems sufficiently good lately to enable me to take up some study. The question is, what would be most profitable?'

Geology, he confided to his private notebook, would be of great service 'if I should, as I hope, take a trip to the mountains again.' English and the art of conversation were necessary 'to a newspaper man with political aspirations'. Finance was the subject he had least inclination to study – 'and perhaps the one I have most need of: as without the pecuniary means an honest political life is almost an impossibility.'

A month later he was encouraged by improved conversational

---

*As recalled by Wilson's son, John D. Southam, the end of the story was this: 'He was out in the West when he wrote to his father saying that he had $1,800 and would like to borrow $2,000 more from his parent so that he could start a sawmill to cut wood for Calgary. My grandfather wrote back: "You had $500 when you started from Halifax. Now you have $1,800. You must also have a brain. So come home." That is the story as I remember my dad telling it to me when I was a young fellow in my teens.'

powers (though 'sadly conscious of many shortcomings yet to be remedied') and enthusiastic about the educational effect of a girl acquaintance who talked well and whose 'society life is so different from mine that we can each strive to reach a ground that will interest the other and usually meet on an impersonal topic such as our views on certain ethical questions.'

Wilson's self-questioning did nothing to blunt a developing business sense. His seven years at the *Spectator* – in modern terms he acted as business manager and executive assistant – fitted him for the next family venture as if it had been planned that way.

In the fall of 1897 William bought the Ottawa *Citizen* and put Wilson in charge. Harry had graduated from Trinity College (Trinity University as it then was) and gone to the Montreal plant for experience. He joined Wilson at Ottawa – the beginning of a remarkable union of faiths and ideals, allied with a keen eye for business, that was to last for half a century. At the same time young W.J., who was through school and had gone to work in the Bank of Hamilton, came over to the *Spectator*.

If William felt that he had hoisted the take-a-chance motto in the *Citizen* purchase he may have had some slight cause for it. Despite the falling off in returns from the *Spectator* he had planned a new home for the paper and bought property next door to the Proctor Building which the Spec had occupied since the year of the fire. With English money borrowed at four per cent he put up the six-storey structure at 36 James Street South that was known as the Spectator Building long after the paper had outgrown it and made its last move in 1921 to King Street East. The James Street building, said to have been the highest in Hamilton or Toronto at the time, was well on the way to completion when Wilson went to Ottawa to run the *Citizen*. On Monday, January 31, 1898, the *Spectator* was issued from the new building. The paper then was running eight six-column pages.

That winter of 1898 was a newsy period. Under the heading WITH THE DEATH WATCH the *Spectator* carried from Cayuga on January 8 a story that began:

Man's mercy alone can now save Mrs. Olive Adele Sternaman from death. They put the death watch on duty yesterday morning and from now until she goes to the gallows on January 24 sharp eyes will watch her every movement. . . .

A rumor was rife for a time that an unexpected and surprising event personal to the prisoner would intervene and arrest the arm of death because the law would be punishing the innocent with the guilty. The rumor was finally set at rest. . . .

Mrs. Sternaman had been convicted in November of doing away with her husband George by means of arsenic, and there was evidence that a previous husband had expired in the same way. Nevertheless, the *Spectator* said, she was 'not a whit different in appearance from the general run of women.'

The Sternaman case was one in which new developments kept popping daily as the fatal date approached, with defence counsel W.M.German of Welland in the role of Perry Mason. Several jurymen gave affidavits that if they had known their recommendation for mercy would be disregarded they would have found Olive not guilty. David Thompson, the Cayuga coroner, raised a potent point. At the trial a doctor had testified that the post-mortem on George Sternaman's exhumed body had shown the thoracic cavity dry, thus scotching contentions that the body had been embalmed, a process that would have accounted for the discovery of arsenic. Dr. Thompson now came up with the information that he had been on hand at the post-mortem and had seen 'a quantity of serous fluid in the thoracic cavity'.

German travelled to Ottawa with a final plea. A cabinet committee went into the evidence and on January 18 ordered a new trial. The *Spectator* quoted Mrs. Sternaman: 'When I wakened this morning and looking out of the window, saw all the trees drooping in white, and the sun shining on them, and knew that I shall some day be out among it again, it seemed the most beautiful day of my life.' So it proved. The second trial cleared her.

The Klondike rush was on and along with stories on the nondescript thousands gathering at Dawson City, Fort Yukon, Skagway, Dyea, and Lake Bennett, the *Spectator* published a map showing 'What Mackenzie and Mann will get if the Yukon [railway] deal goes through.' The proposed land grants equalled in size the area of nine Ontario counties. This particular proposal of Bill and Dan died in the Senate.

But the chief political story was the Ontario provincial campaign with election day coming up March 1. Gibson was the *Spectator*'s main target. The veteran capitalist had said he wanted one more term, then would be content to retire. 'Why another term?' the *Spectator* asked. He had feathered his nest fairly well. Wasn't he satisfied with a 'competence he never could have made but for the good nature of the Hamilton Grits and Tories who have kept him at Toronto'? How many more big companies did he want to get into, on the ground floor? And what had he done for the voters who had stuck to him? 'He has given them smiles once every four years and an Alaska stare during the rest of the time.'

A few days later the *Spectator* summed up in one sentence (which seems to bear the stamp of John Robson Cameron) its view of the two Liberal candidates in Hamilton: 'It is high time that Mr. Gibson were retired to his law office and Mr. Middleton to his tombstone factory.'

On March 2 the paper was able to report victory in Hamilton: 'Carscallen snowed Middleton under and Colquhoun left Gibson out of sight.' But its early headline on the general result – IT'S CLOSE BUT WHITNEY HAS IT – was too optimistic. The Liberals won, 49 to 44. The Spec would have to wait until 1905 to celebrate a province-wide Whitney victory.

Early in April it reported an event that might have been taken as foreshadowing a changing future. Hamilton's first horseless carriage, a Winton one-lunger imported by John Moodie, rolled down Main Street. 'It looks like a heavy phaeton and has pneumatic tires,' the paper said. 'It is very quick, and makes little noise, except when the brakes are applied. It does not frighten horses, and costs a thousand dollars.'

By 1899 William was variously involved in Hamilton's industrial life. In July the Hamilton Steel and Iron Company (progenitor of the Steel Company of Canada) took out a Dominion charter. The Hamilton and Fort William Navigation Company was set up in November. Southam was among the founders and first directors of both.

The World, the Empire, and the Third Main

The *Spectator* has had its sedate periods, including a stretch in comparatively modern times when no local story, unless it ranked as national news, could force its way to the front page. The era in which Victoria's reign closed and the world moved into the present century was not one of them. The world, the Empire, and the home town vied for display in a lively paper.

In 1900 strange names marched in its headlines – Bloemfontein, Burghersdorp, Dewetsdorp, Wepener. Lieutenant Eddie Morrison, who not so long ago had been the Spec's city editor, was out there with the guns. Waves of imperial purpose surged through John Robson Cameron's paragraphs. Gus Freed, now an inspector of weights and measures, but still writing for the paper, turned out occasional productions in verse:

Rough John, tough John, bluff John Bull
With a heap of human nature underneath his scanty wool –
The cheeriest, beeriest, stoutest carl upon this earthly ball,
For old John Bull is the daddy of them all. . . .

The Hamilton Spectator

GREAT FAMILY JOURNAL

HAMILTON, CANADA, THURSDAY, MARCH 1, 1900.

NUMBER 52.

LADYSMITH RELIEVED

Lord Dundonald Led the Relieving Force

ENTRANCE OF BRITISH FORCE WAS UNOPPOSED

Boers Are Reported to Have Deserted the Country Between Lyttleton's Headquarters and Ladysmith, Leaving the Course Clear.

Buller's Army Successful on Their Fourth Attempt to Relieve the Garrison—Their Task Was a Difficult One, Much Fighting Being Done.

Gen. Littleton's Force Now Moving on Nelthorp—How the Glorious News was Received in London and Other Parts of the Empire.

Colesberg and Colesberg Junction Now Held By the British Troops—Repulses For the Boers, Who Make Attacks on Mafeking.

LONDON, march 1—The War Office has received the following dispatch, dated Lyttleton's Headquarters, March 1: "Gen. Dundonald, with the Natal Carabiners and a Composite Regiment, entered Ladysmith last night. The country between me and Ladysmith is reported clear of the enemy. I am moving on Nelthorpe."

GEN. BULLER.

DISPATCH FROM GEN. BULLER.

LONDON, MARCH 1, 6.55 p.m.—Gen. Buller wires from Nelthorpe, under to-day's date, that he has just returned from Ladysmith. The whole country south of that place is clear of the enemy.

BULLER'S VICTORIOUS MARCH.

But early that spring a Hamilton story broke that almost pushed the war in South Africa off page one. Or at least forced it to shove over, and gave the Spec a crack at the type of local coup it loved – a political exposé.

The ratepayers voted March 14 on a by-law authorizing the city to lay a $200,000 water main to Barton Street and Sherman Avenue and enlarge the filtering basin at the beach. The *Spectator* opposed this proposal: Hamilton was cursed with officials ignorant and afraid, the voters hadn't been assured that this third main was necessary, and the price of iron just then was too high. This view did not take. The by-law passed by 1,322 to 824. For one day the *Spectator* contented itself with expressing disappointment at the turnout (5,000 were eligible) and a suggestion that while a third main might be useful in a year or two, the proposed enlargement of the filtering basin shouldn't go on; any available money should be spent on an intake pipe with its outer end beyond the mudline. 'But the people who manage these things for Hamilton got into a rut years ago. . . . Because our forefathers drank water alive with wrigglers from the breeding place in the filtering basin, we, it seems, must go on doing the same thing.'

Then an unemployed baseball player named Marr Phillips was arrested for impersonating an absent ratepayer at the polls. The *Spectator* scented blood. On Saturday, three days after the vote, it published names of the 120 voters recorded as having marked ballots in the second division of Ward Five. It stated its object as twofold: To show which ratepayers were interested enough to vote 'and as a means of proving or disproving charges of personation and plugging to secure the success of the by-law.'

Over the weekend the word trickled in. On Monday the Spec reported that at least three of the supposed voters were dead, two lived in Toronto, one in Montreal, one in North Dakota, and one in Wyoming. In an accompanying editorial it charged the existence of an impersonating gang and claimed it had been used by the Liberal party in past elections, a claim promptly ridiculed by the *Times*.

On Tuesday the paper disclosed the names of eleven more ratepayers who apparently had marked ballots in absentia or after death. City council authorized an investigation and county court judge Colin Snider started hearings. Phillips the ball-player told all at the investigation, pleaded guilty in court, and got a month in jail as the 'tool of others'. A deputy returning officer drew six months.

The Snider investigation (hampered a bit when several key witnesses flitted to Buffalo) rolled on. It was brought out that $5 was the price of a vote cast on behalf of the dead or absent. Also that $125 had passed from an iron-pipe manufacturer to an alderman to help get out the vote, and thence through a chain of individuals to some of the boys marking the ballots. The judge found that there had been fifty personations in one division, a few elsewhere. Not enough to account for the by-law's majority, but enough to establish the substance of the *Spectator*'s exposé.

Twelve years later Hamilton got around to extending an intake pipe beyond the mudline and the wrigglers.

On January 22, 1901, the *Spectator* published a black-bordered extra, its pages filled with the story of Victoria's life and times. Gus Freed mourned in elegiac verse the 'heavy tidings of sad verity that our good Queen is dead'.

A special turbulence marked early years of the Edwardian era in Ontario. A Liberal government had been in power since Edward Blake toppled the Sandfield Macdonald administration in 1871. In the way of old and long-successful party machines, the organization had grown first ruthless and then careless. George W. Ross won again in the spring of 1902 but with a margin of only two or three seats. Charges of corruption flew like hail. The *Spectator* and other Conservative papers (and such rare independents as the Toronto *News* under John Willison) took grim delight in exploiting breaks like the Gamey charges and the cruise of the *Minnie M*.

Robert Gamey won Manitoulin for the Conservatives in 1902 and faced a protested election. On January 30, 1903, the Toronto *Globe* quoted him as saying 'Manitoulin is my politics' – he planned to support the government.

On March 11 the story blew open in the legislature with the first of successive bangs that enlivened front pages for years. The *Spectator* next day carried 'Gamey's Story in Brief' on page one and devoted most of page five to the details. The story was that his support had been bought by a promise to let his election stand uncontested and by a package of money left on a smoking-room table. His purpose, he said, was to get evidence that would convict someone in the government of bribery. He handed the money-package on the floor of the house to opposition leader Whitney. 'The wily tricksters', the *Spectator* said, 'had to be met by trickery in order to convince the people of their identity and their guilt.'

When a royal commission of two judges cleared the government and cast doubt on Gamey, the Spec observed: 'The redeeming feature of the judges' decision is found in the fact that it is so very much astray from the facts upon which it is supposed to be based that it is nothing short of ridiculous. It will be brushed aside by the great thinking public. . . .'

In its 'Current Topics' column it asked: 'Who owns the money?' It was a good question. No one knows yet where it came from. Eventually the $2,000 Gamey had placed in Whitney's hands went to the Hospital for Sick Children in Toronto.

The affair of the *Minnie M* involved transport of a load of characters from Michigan (equipped with whisky, beer, and cigars) who disembarked on the Canadian side long enough to take a special train to Helen Mine and Michipicoten Harbor and vote in a Sault Ste. Marie by-election.

The *Spectator* had its share of hard-hitting fun during these years. But it never forgot that it was a home-town newspaper. In the summer of 1903 Old Home Week brought back hundreds of former Hamiltonians. The *Spectator* published a 126-page magazine supplement celebrating the history of the city and its industries. City editor John Wodell dreamed up a feature: a story describing Hamilton in the year 2003 illustrated by wash drawings from the brush of local artist J.R.Seavey – tall buildings, sweeping terraces, giant masts with moored dirigibles. William Southam saw the pictures lined up around the baseboard of Wodell's office and shook his head: 'It's a crazy thing, Wodell.' Relating the incident a half-century later, Wodell recalled that in the conduct of the paper he had never had a direct order from William Southam. On publication day for the Old Home Week supplement, William couldn't get through the crowd clustered round the front of the building to buy the *Spectator*. He went in the back way and climbed the stairs to congratulate Wodell, laughing.

Merriment, a thigh-whacking delight in life, was one of his characteristics. There were times when worry beset him as he watched the business operations of his sons and times when rage overtook him at some aspect of *Spectator* management. Such storms passed quickly from the surface of a nature remembered as essentially tuned to mirth.

Southam Limited

William now was sixty years old, still keen minded and fit, but ready to go a long further step in turning over direction of Southam affairs to his sons. Fred in Montreal, Dick in Toronto, and Harry and Wilson in Ottawa all managed properties that were separate in a business sense except for William's ownership. In Hamilton W.J. was

deep in the *Spectator* and soon young Gordon would move in somewhere. No central clearing-house existed except in William's head.
Furthermore, what would be the shape of things when he himself was
gone? Wilson brought into the open the question of an arrangement that
would preserve both family and business relationships. He had been
reading about the Rothschilds and their progress from generation to
generation in Europe. 'The idea occurred to me', he wrote more than
forty years later, 'that the Southam family should pattern itself after
the Rothschilds and stick together as a family. . . .'* Presumably
family solidarity was the limit of the imitation he had in mind. He
could scarcely have seen much likeness between the business activities of the two clans. There is plenty of evidence of the Southams' respect for the dollar, but it is hard to imagine them as merchants of
money as money, on however grandiose a scale – least of all, perhaps, the gentle and studious Wilson. On the other side of the coin, it
is arresting to think of the Rothschilds producing devoted single-tax-
ers and converts to Social Credit.

Wilson talked it over with his father and got Glyn Osler's advice.
Osler, a former fellow-student of Harry's at Trinity, was then practising law in Ottawa with the *Citizen* as one of his clients – the start
of a lifelong association with Southam company affairs.

Osler suggested a joint stock company. The Southams hadn't considered anything quite so formal, but there seemed to be no other
way of doing what they had in mind. Southam Limited came into
existence on March 4, 1904, with William, Wilson, Fred, Richard,
Harry, and Bill as directors, all described in the letters patent as
journalists. William was president at $4,000 a year to start, Bill sec-
retary at $2,000. The others got a dollar a meeting and expenses. The
by-laws provided for a vice-president at Montreal, recognizing Fred's
activity there as manager of the printing plant and in other pursuits –
largely real estate – on behalf of the family. Authorized capital was
$1,000,000 divided into 10,000 shares at $100 par.

The procedure then began of turning in stock of the various Southam enterprises and investments to Southam Limited. By the end of
1904 the *Citizen*, the Montreal printing plant (under its new name of
Southam Limited Montreal), the Mail Job Printing Company, and the
Southams' half of the *Spectator* all showed on the new company's list
of assets, along with stock in Hamilton industries that William had
shared in founding – Hamilton Steel and Iron, Hamilton and Fort

*W.M.Southam to P.S.Fisher, April 20, 1946.

William Navigation, and the Pure Milk Corporation. A mixed bag of other interests ranged from such solid investments as Cataract Power to speculations like Canadian Gold Fields Syndicate. The total assets figure was $899,538.55.

Thus was set up the first stage of a family-in-business oligarchy. Eventually it would evolve, through growth and change across half a century, into a public company of far wider scope, in which the family element would remain – not as the entire fabric, but as central and sometimes colorful threads in its weave.

This however was far from the Southams' minds as they worked out a plan to ensure a sharing in decisions touching the company's welfare and in the results of what William and his sons had already achieved or hoped to. In effect William distributed his assets and grouped them in a manner that ensured the family acting as one in a business way for that generation at least.

Of 3,605 shares in Southam Limited issued before the end of 1904, William held 1,400 and each of the seven children (Ethel and Gordon were brought in as shareholders that fall) 315. William converted his 1,400 to the same number of preferred and transferred 800 to his wife. Later on Ethel's 315 shares of common were converted to 700 preferred.

The reasoning, from William's point of view, seems to have been that the active heads of Southam properties should benefit from expansion through ownership of common – and also take the chance of loss – and that Ethel, to whom he later transferred an additional 800 preferred, shouldn't be subjected to any take-a-chance tendencies the boys had inherited. Recalling the circumstances later, Fred noted 'a feeling on Father's part that we were a rather speculative lot', a judgment that he felt was vindicated on several occasions including 'the Rea mess, the trouble we were in on our Calgary place when war broke out, and the Baynes Carriage Company complication'.*

In practice, though a by-law provided that 'William Southam personally shall have full power and authority to invest the funds, assets and moneys of the company in such manner as he in his unfettered discretion may see fit', the company undertook no deal without full discussion and, if possible, full agreement.

For instance when in the spring of 1907 William had a chance to buy for $13,000 a quarter-interest in the paper on which he had grown up, the London *Free Press*, he wrote the away-from-home boys for their views. Fred and Dick saw no point in a minority inter-

*F.N.Southam to Glyn Osler, July 27, 1925.

est unless it could be useful in getting full control, though they raised no real objection. Wilson and Harry approved of the quarter-interest buy. William went ahead. When the Southam Publishing Company took over this quarter-interest in 1929 the price arrived at was $315,000.

As to speculative tendencies, the fact is that profitable deals, returns from sound investments, and expanding newspapers and printing plants far outpaced whatever was dropped on the lemons. But some lemons there were – often of a smallish variety. The take-a-chance element and the lure of what lay underground found their way to the books in such entries as Cobalt Mining Company, Big Creek Natural Gas Syndicate, Gowganda Mining Syndicate, and Last Chance Mine. Although the Southams made some money on one or two Cobalt propositions at the height of the silver boom, most of these ventures were simply written off.

Last Chance held a special interest because one of the family took a hand in operation. William's brother Richard, the one-time young artilleryman of Fenian Raid days, now in his early sixties, was at a loose end when, in January of 1910, Wilson wrote his father about a Mr. Jones. Mr. Jones would be along to see him at Hamilton; he had a 'little hydraulic gold mine proposition in the Cariboo country' and needed $7,600 by September for ditching and sluicing. Southam Limited put up the money and Richard went out to oversee the works.

On an August day in 1911 two telegrams arrived at Hamilton. One was from Richard. It said: 'Dismiss Jones.' One was from Jones. It said: 'Beg to resign.' A harassed bank manager at Quesnel found himself in the middle. Appealed to by W.J. for a neutral opinion on what was going on, he reported that Jones was a good mining man but spent too much time in the barrooms of Barkerville. The bank man begged that anything he said be kept confidential as 'too many men here would drop me very quickly if they thought I made a practice of communicating direct with the eastern investor.' Another neutral asserted that some old hands wouldn't work for Richard. In the end both managers stayed on. In 1912 the eastern investor put $3,500 into developing one of the three claims involved. The return in gold was twenty and a half ounces worth $400. Shortly thereafter Last Chance disappeared from the Southam list of assets.

Of the larger schemes that failed to ripen perhaps the sourest were 'the Rea mess' – an attempt at a department store merger that proved costly – and the Baynes company.

The promoter of the carriage business was James Bibby Baynes of

Buffalo. When the company set up shop late in 1905, William South-am was one of the principals. Baynes built a factory on the Hamilton waterfront and ran into trouble, including the long credit terms expected of carriage-makers by their customers, and later the impact of the motor-car. Southam was no devotee of the automobile; despite the Russells and Pope-Hartfords driven by his sons and the Rolls in his own garage, he was on record as believing such machines were for women and invalids. But he recognized the signs and did his best to get Baynes into the motor-car business. In 1910 a proposal to sell out to a Detroit firm fell through and tribulations continued for the shareholders. Eventually the firm closed and sold out to the Brant-ford Carriage Company. A schedule of Southam Limited's securities at the end of 1918 showed its investment in shares and cash advances in the Baynes company at $88,378.69. Actual value of this asset was listed in realistic terms: $1.00.

The flops were exceptions. Through the company's middle years surpluses were growing on its profit-and-loss account; also growing was the proportion of publishing and printing properties, including the buildings housing them, on its list of assets. In 1909 these amounted to less than half the asset-figure of $1,678,000. By 1913 they accounted for more than two-thirds of a $3,000,000 total. The Southams still occasionally went into industrial and real estate prospects. Canada Crushed Stone Corporation (a quarry at Dundas) and McKittrick Properties, which developed into the Hamilton district of Westdale, were two. But they were turning more and more towards preoccupation with what they knew best – the printing press, its products, and its services.

Just here the company ran into a sticky period through the financing of two new buildings in Calgary. These were started in the prosperous times of 1911-12 and completed in the tight-money period of the pre-war depression. With the war's outbreak in August of 1914, bank credit came to a standstill for weeks. Business fell off and tenants couldn't pay. The growth of Southam Limited's surplus slowed, though the difficulty was mainly a lack of ready money rather than shrinkage in actual wealth. At one point William cut his own presidential salary, which had been raised to $12,000, to $2,000. In the spring of 1915 the brothers decided to sell investments and pay off banks, to 'reef down tight' as F.N. put it. With some unwillingness William saw his pet stock, $50,000 worth of Pure Milk Corporation, go on the market. In May, F.N. in Montreal was getting rid of Steel of Canada preferred at 69 to 70 and common at 12 to 13. By November, the preferred sold at 91 and the common at over 40. William figured the boys had kicked away $100,000 and wasn't slow to say so, at which F.N. commented: 'Father certainly has it on us. He has the further advantage of reaching his decision several months after ours.'

Normal dividends continued. Preferred paid its flat six per cent throughout the life of the company. Because Southam Limited had been organized as a growth proposition as well as a holding apparatus, and all male members of the family drew salaries from the individual businesses, profits from the first four years went into an accumulating rest account. By 1908, however, with the sons building or about to build houses (none of the Southams ever went in for small rose-covered cottages) and some of them bringing up families, the question came up of dividends on the common – taking out some of the accumulating profit.

Writing his father that August, Wilson mentioned that he had been opposed to dividends for two reasons: 'One, that Southam Limited would have no surplus to invest or at least a reduced surplus; and the other that if we had the extra income individually our wives would spend it with no particular increase of benefit to the family.' This last he admitted wouldn't hold water as most of them arrived at the same result by over-drawing their company accounts, and the only reason that didn't apply to himself as it did to Fred and Dick was that his wife had $4,000 a year of her own. He added: 'I am willing to take mine with the rest though it will undoubtedly check the growth of Southam Limited to some extent.'

In December of that year a bonus from surplus gave the sons $96,000 split in various amounts. In 1909 the company declared its first regular common dividend at six per cent of par, a modest figure considering actual value of the stock. The disbursement grew periodically until, in 1912, each of the brothers drew $9,450 a year in dividends, which at this stage was more than any of them got as managers of the properties.

Issuance of additional stock in later years brought the company's capital finally to 3,500 preferred at a par value of $350,000 held variously by the parents, Ethel, Harry, and Wilson; and 5,670 common at a par of $567,000 (worth six or seven times that much) equally held by the five surviving brothers and Gordon's estate.

By the end of 1919 the company's net worth was more than $4 million. In a sense Southam Limited had outgrown itself. It was reorganized in 1920 as William Southam and Sons.

Gordon and the Tigers

In the spring of 1907 Gordon Southam graduated from University College. He was twenty-one years old and a topflight athlete. The family talked over where he should begin to train for a lifetime in the business. Fred wanted him in Montreal. Dick wanted him in Toronto. His mother wanted him at home. Her opinion carried and Gordon went into Molsons Bank at Hamilton, following the pattern of Wilson, Dick, and Bill of picking up outside experience before joining the family firm. This decision was important to at least one establishment outside the family – the Hamilton Tigers.

Youthful exuberance was still strong in the heartbeat of Canada in that year of 1907, its pulse tuned to good times and the optimism of the opening West. Panic in Wall Street might tighten up money and shake some nerves under the broadcloth of St. James and Bay. (SMASH GO THE SAVINGS BANKS read a *Spectator* headline on October 24) but the Dominion saw not much to fear. Rudyard Kipling was in the country and an unnamed versifier whose words were reprinted in the *Spectator* felt independent enough to take issue with his emphasis on Canada's winter weather – and incidentally to breathe something of the country's spirit:

> A nation spoke to a poet
> A people sent word to its bard:
> Come in my season of fruitfulness
> You that have judged me hard;
> Gaze on my endless acres
> That a wealth of gold disclose,
> When the wheat flames o'er the prairie
> Of our Lady of the Snows.

In Hamilton sport made more than its usual grist of news that fall. Tom Longboat the Onondaga, who had won the Boston marathon in April, was in his heyday. Trying to establish a record for the forty-four miles from the Waldorf hotel in Hamilton to the Queen and Yonge corner in Toronto, he set too fast a pace, stopped to bathe his feet in whisky at Oakville, slowed to a walk at Etobicoke, and quit just east of the Humber.

But the really hot topic was football. The Big Four was set up that year, putting Montreal, Toronto, Ottawa, and Hamilton into a regular schedule. Dick and Harry had both played in the Tiger backfield in earlier years. Now the club wanted Gordon, who had starred at Varsity for the team captained by Casey Baldwin, a young man whose name would soon become legendary in the history of early aviation.

After the Tigers lost to Montreal, 10-2, at Hamilton on October 12 he agreed to play.

Trouble marked the season's start. All hands got branded as professionals by the Canadian Amateur Athletic Union. There was no suggestion that football players drew money, particularly in Hamilton, where years later one stalwart would complain that he couldn't even get replacements for bicycle tires worn out riding to practice. But Montreal had a halfback named Ernie Russell, who, it was claimed, played pro hockey. The Big Four teams played against him and were thus contaminated. The label of technical professionalism stood throughout the season.

Harry in Ottawa was a little perturbed. 'I learn from the Hamilton papers that Gordon has consented to play with the Tigers,' he wrote his father. 'I do not see how he could have avoided it very well, but it seems a great pity that he has had to sacrifice his amateur standing.'

He went on to put across a small lecture on newspaper ethics. Frank Nelson of the *Globe*, a C.A.A.U. official, had issued a statement from the Union's standpoint. This the *Spectator* carried under the heading A PREJUDICED VIEW.

> A heading [Harry wrote] is supposed to reflect the body of the article. This heading reflects the sporting editor's opinion on the views of the article. . . . Sport in Canada is getting down to a very low ebb. Sporting editors of most of the daily papers are holding it down. On the corner lot, in the schools, and in the college teams to some extent, and to a lamentable degree in the city teams, the main desideratum is victory. Evade the rules whenever possible, if you are sure the officials are not watching you, seems to be the slogan of most Canadian teams. . . . We encourage dishonesty and hypocrisy in the sports of the youth, and yet we wonder at the graft in Canadian public life.

Whether Harry's little sermon had any immediate effect on *Spectator* headings is doubtful. In any event Gordon played spectacular football for the Tigers. The Canadian game at that time still retained some of the characteristics of English rugby, including the four-point drop-kick from the field. Gordon's artistry in this manoeuvre was unique, as he had proved at Varsity.

The *Spectator* at this time was running a contest that called for completing limericks by adding final lines. Entry fee was ten cents (which could be applied to want ads or subscriptions) and rewards ranged from a $15 first prize down to fifty boxes of candy. With a touch of laudable opportunism and dubious verse, the *Spectator* produced four-fifths of a limerick in mid-season:

With the Tigers a-playing the game,
Not posing on last season's name –
What think you will be
The result we shall see? ...

While the Tigers played out the schedule Spec readers labored to complete this minor classic.

On October 26 at Montreal, Gordon displayed his drop-kicking ability in spectacular fashion. After missing by inches on his first try, he kicked one in the first quarter to put Tigers ahead 4-0. In the second quarter Hamilton scored a single, but Montreal went out in front on a touchdown, scored when a kick went over the line, hit an electric-light wire, and dropped in position for Percy Molson to fall on it. In the third quarter Southam dropped one from thirty yards out, at an angle, to put Hamilton ahead 9-7, and the Tigers withstood Montreal's attack to the end.

He repeated the two-goal performance a week later against Ottawa, but dislocated an ankle and was out for the last of the season. Montreal eventually won the league title.

Miss Laura Bowron of Victoria Avenue won the limerick contest with a line based on the Tigers' colors: 'They'll yell-o till black just the same.' The *Spectator* admitted the contestants seemed to have had trouble with this particular limerick.

In January Gordon got back his amateur standing in time to captain Hamilton's hockey team.

By the fall of 1908 he was in the business. He had left the bank and gone to Ottawa for a period of tutelage with Harry and Wilson at the *Citizen*. In November he went into the *Spectator*'s business office to start a career eventually cut short by war.

Girls and Circulation

In 1908 the fight with the *Herald* for first place in circulation pulled the *Spectator* into a rousing stunt to settle the question. Late in March it announced it would send 'the 10 most popular women in Ontario on a five-week tour of England, Ireland, Scotland, France, and Germany'.

An examination of the announcement disclosed that the basic index of popularity would be ability to induce the residents of Hamilton and near-by areas to subscribe to the *Spectator*. True, candidates could amass votes by having readers fill in the names of their favorites on coupons published daily, but this was a one-at-a-time procedure (except on Saturdays when each coupon was worth five votes), whereas one paid-in-advance yearly subscription racked up a thumping 3,000. Qualification was simple. Candidates must be female, at least sixteen years old, and nominated by some responsible citizen.

In a period when travel for pleasure beyond the cruising range of excursion steamers, railway locals, and the horse and buggy was scarcely thought of by the mill-run of people, this chance at moonlit seas and strange lands was sensational. By April 6 the *Spectator* reported that 'a wave of interest is sweeping over Hamilton and the province of Ontario unequalled in the history of Canada'. Fifty-four girls had been nominated – twenty-three in Hamilton and thirty-one from the surrounding district. The battle for ballots was on.

Not unexpectedly, considering the newspaper climate in Hamilton at the time, the contest drew caustic comment from the *Spectator*'s chief rival. The Harrises had reasons of their own to be burned. The professional promoter who dreamed up the scheme had offered it first to the *Herald*. Turned down, he took it up street to the *Spectator* where Bill and William thought it over and decided to take a chance. The *Herald* ran a sour editorial suggesting the contest was keeping subscription money out of the pockets of newsboys with widowed mothers.

The Spec had a ready-made riposte. It called attention to the fact that during the previous year one of the *Herald*'s business-office girls had won a voting contest run by the Toronto *World* and that the *Herald* had hailed her victory in an editorial. 'Do not everlastingly knock a competitor showing a little more enterprise than you do,' the *Spectator* advised. 'The Spectator promises not to publish mean insinuations about any legitimate effort you may put forth to build up your business.'

The newsboys seemed unworried. In fact they had to be stopped from clipping ballots and voting for their favorites (or possibly peddling the ballots) and then selling the ballotless papers, thus disfranchising the buyer.

One other complication developed – from a bargain-day stunt of slipping in ballots good for twenty-five votes. They had to stop it; on bargain days it was impossible to buy a Spec in downtown Hamilton after 6 P.M. and longtime readers complained they couldn't get a paper.

Meantime the candidates and their friends plunged into the business of selling the Spec and clipping coupons for the ballot boxes set up in the business office. On April 13 the first standing was announced. Lily Gowland, a Hamilton salesgirl, led in the city with 161,911 votes. Ethel Smith of Burlington headed the poll in the district with 149,463. A week later these two still led, but on April 27 Evelyn Peachey passed Ethel Smith in the district, and at May 18 Lily Gowland had dropped to fifth place in the city. On June 8 Willa O'Dell passed seven others to lead in Hamilton, and Kate Dowser of Grimsby jumped from fifteenth to third in the district.

The *Spectator*'s boast of the wave of interest that swept over Hamilton may not have been far wrong. Certainly the contest built circulation indirectly through its transient news value as well as directly through subscription sales. The paper's progress stories on the vote rivalled its coverage of the provincial election campaign that ended June 8 with the return of James Pliny Whitney's government.

By June 15 it was running standings daily. By then the original list of entrants was down to 35 as tail-enders dropped out. On Saturday, June 20, the final count began. Wednesday's *Spectator* carried an eight-column line:

FIFTEEN SPECTATOR GIRLS GO TO EUROPE

The paper had increased the number of European travellers from ten to fifteen. In fact it had decided to reward all hands. There were thirty-two finishers. In Hamilton Lily Gowland had made a comeback and finished first. She and seven others from the city would tour Europe. Edith Allen of Waterdown led the district and she with six others from outside Hamilton would also get to cross the Atlantic. The seventeen other girls who stayed in to the finish got trips to Montreal or up the Saguenay. The Spec had a field day with the results – pictures of the ballot-counting, pictures of the girls, and interviews.

The girls left Hamilton on Tuesday night, June 30, aboard the steamer *Dundurn* for Prescott, there to entrain for Montreal where the Europe-bound would board the liner *Lake Manitoba*.

The *Spectator* made the most of the departure with a parade to the waterfront, brass bands, and fireworks. The excursion steamers *Macassa* and *Turbinia*, crowded with the young of Hamilton, accompanied the *Dundurn* out on the lake. The *Spectator*'s luck lapsed. Rain fell. Fog rolled in. Heading back into harbor the *Turbinia* thumped into the piers of the Burlington canal. Backed off and hit the piers again. She finally docked at 7 A.M. to caustic comment by worried parents. If the language at that time had been debased by one of our modern clichés it probably would have been said that the rain, the fog, and the *Turbinia* had damaged the Spec's public image, a little.

But circulation was up. It rose from 12,299 in 1907 to 16,905 in

1908, the year of the contest. In the main this circulation was held (not always so of contest-won readers).

Although the trip-to-Europe stunt was an unusual expense in 1908, the paper's net profit for the year at $30,000 was only $5,000 less than the figure for 1907. In the years ahead it would move up.

And the girls had a good time. The Olympic Games were on in London, and they saw fellow-townsman Bobby Kerr win his preliminary heat in the 100 metres. He finished third in the final and won the 200.

John Wodell had become managing editor when John Robson Cameron died in 1907. Wodell and his wife accompanied the contingent to Europe. Shepherding fifteen high-spirited girls around London and Paris was an experience for Wodell. A comparatively small man, he returned to Hamilton weighing eight pounds less than usual.

'The Home Concern'

At about this time also the *Spectator* locked horns with a local version of manifest destiny – the invasion of Hamilton by publicly owned power.

The circumstances that set the scene for this fight went back to the previous century. In 1896 John Patterson, developing a radial railway from Hamilton to Burlington, got the idea of turning waste water from the Welland Canal into power. The Five Johns (Patterson, Gibson, Moodie, Dickenson, and Sutherland) and James Dixon set up for this purpose the Cataract Power Company. Under a succession of names, but always known as 'The Cataract', this company from 1897 on delivered electricity to Hamilton. It was a pioneer in North America in such long-distance transmission.

Imagination as well as money went into Cataract. Canal water, drawn off in a succession of lakes where Beaver Dam Creek descends the Niagara escarpment, swept through penstocks to a power station 265 feet below. Lord Kelvin had claimed that twelve miles was the limit of transmission. Cataract power flowed into Hamilton from thirty-five miles away. It became a key force in a new industrial surge. Ten years after the company's first switch was thrown, as the Dominion Power and Transmission Company, it was pouring power into most of Hamilton's industries and five street and radial railway systems.

By that time a new prospect stirred Ontario: the promise of power and light 'unloaded by corporation tribute' as one report put it, for its towns, villages, and farms. Ontario lacked coal. What it had in

quantity was the white coal (as the papers began to call it) of cas-
cading water. Apostle of the new order was Adam Beck, a son of
German immigrants, who had made money manufacturing wood ve-
neer, become mayor of London and a Conservative member of the
legislature. Beck's patrician face and rigid jaw proclaimed an inner
passion. As chairman of the Ontario Hydro-Electric Power Commission from 1905 on, his consuming purpose was to develop to the full
the Whitney Conservative government's policy of publicly owned
power. Beck's toughest battle was with private interests in Toronto.
In Hamilton he had an entrenched opponent also in The Cataract.

When the lines were drawn the *Spectator* picked the unpopular
and in the long run the losing side, largely it seems through a sense of
respect for a successful local industry. This despite one aspect that
was obviously embarrassing. Early in Cataract's history William
Southam invested in it. Southam Limited's assets in 1904 showed
$15,000 in the power company. In 1907, with Beck's plan looming,
it had $34,000 in Cataract. Earlier, Wilson had sounded a caution-
ary note: 'I do not see that Whitney's scheme will interfere with the
success of this stock – at least for years to come. But Harry and I
have for some considerable time thought it inadvisable to hold stock
in any concern that has a public franchise, solely for the reason that
as newspaper publishers it would often be the duty of the newspapers
to criticize the company . . . and where we did not criticize it our
good faith would be open to suspicion.'

This had in it the seeds of a policy gradually arrived at many years
later and eventually explicitly stated: exclusion of the Southam company from any interest outside mass communications and printing
and of executive personnel from party involvement.

On more than one occasion the *Spectator* did sharply criticize The
Cataract. Early in November of 1906 a strike tied up Hamilton's
streetcar system and broke into wild riots, with at least one fractured
skull, before the Ontario Railway and Municipal Board ended it by
ordering the company to recognize the union and the strikers to sign
a three-year agreement. The day the strike started the *Spectator* said:
'The men now have the backing of public opinion. That they have
grievances is admitted on all hands; that they have been patient is
quite plain. . . .' The Cataract had antagonized the people of Hamilton by long neglect: 'It has allowed its rolling stock and track to run
down; its service has been abominable; its anxiety to please the public invisible. It has, we think, foolishly made it a point to fight the
"union" and in various ways it has forfeited its right to consideration
by an impartial public.' Throughout the month-long affair, while

colorful front-page stories detailed the various moves, the editorial line was anti-company.

But on the question of power for Hamilton's public services the paper backed Cataract:

> With competition assured by the hydro-electric lines, which we are told will be gone on with whether this city comes in or not, we are convinced that Hamiltonians would prefer to do business with the local company, prices being equal, if for no other reason than that of civic pride. It is up to the Cataract management to give the people a reasonable chance to do business with the home concern.

The *Spectator*'s case was that Hamilton stood alone in already having abundant power available. Manufacturers had multiplied and prospered because of it. If this could be continued at reasonable cost nothing more could be desired. Why should Hamilton contribute towards an undertaking that would mean 'our ability to attract manufacturers will be shared by Toronto, Brantford, Woodstock – the whole western peninsula of Ontario'?

The Cataract, the paper argued, had undertaken to furnish current at rates to be measured by hydro-electric rates elsewhere. 'Two rival plants in a city the size of Hamilton could only ruin each other's chances for remunerative operation,' the paper said. 'Like the Kilkenny cats, they would devour each other, and sooner or later one concern would have to buy the other out at the price of scrap iron.* Is this fair to the company to which the city already owes so much? Is this business horse-sense on the part of the community?'

The Hydro fight produced a curious line of battle. Central figure in the Cataract company was J.M.Gibson, the veteran Liberal capitalist. The *Herald*, independent with Liberal leanings, supported Beck and Hydro. The *Spectator* backed a company headed by Gibson, its political target for a generation, and found itself on the same side as its old rival the *Times*, which viewed Hydro as 'a huge socialistic scheme'.

The fact that the Southams had money in the power company was meat and drink to the *Herald*, which called the *Spectator*'s arguments 'sonorous nonsense', mounted a personal attack, and claimed William was drawing 30 per cent on his Cataract investment. Writing from Montreal, Fred suggested that 'pretty nearly everything that was said might be taken in a complimentary sense as showing the wonderful business ability of William Southam', and that 'nearly

*When the Ontario Hydro-Electric Power Commission purchased the Dominion Power and Transmission Company in 1930, the price was $21,000,000.

every man in Hamilton would be glad to be pounded for the same reasons.' The only point he thought worth denying was the 30 per cent; six or seven per cent would be more like it. In this he was close to the mark. Southam Limited had $34,189 invested in Cataract at the time. In 1907 it collected dividends of $2,238 or about 6.5 per cent.

For some time the terms 'Hydro-Electric men' and 'Cataract men' divided the political population of Hamilton more effectively than the old party labels. When Mayor T.J.Stewart – a Conservative and a Hydro-Electric man – closed a council meeting to the press in April of 1908, with Beck there to discuss power, the *Spectator* honored four aldermen who opposed the closing by running their pictures. It termed the meeting 'a spectacle that has not been enacted in the régime of any Hamilton mayor since the dark ages'.

Any non-Hamiltonian trying to follow the city's politics at this time must have been more than a little dazed. Wheels rotated within wheels at various speeds and in odd directions. When in the fall of 1908, Conservatives asked Stewart to run as a federal candidate against Adam Zimmerman, the Liberal generally supposed to have West Hamilton in his pocket, the *Herald* saw in this a plot to remove from civic affairs a champion of Hydro: 'It is to be hoped that Mayor Stewart's backbone will prove to be strong enough to resist the pressure. . . .' When Stewart took the nomination (he was subsequently elected) the *Herald* coolly supported Zimmerman, largely on the ground that Laurier was going back in and a Liberal back-bencher would be more useful than a Conservative one. On the other hand it backed Laborite Sam Landers in East Hamilton against Conservative Sam Barker and Liberal J.M.Eastwood of the *Times* (which it called an 'unclean sheet' for sneering at Landers). And it defended its position on Stewart by saying it was not the *Herald* that deserted Stewart, but Stewart that deserted the *Herald*.

The *Spectator*, critical of Stewart as mayor, went down the line for him as a federal candidate. Scorning suggestions that he was being removed from civic politics through latter-day Machiavellianism, it reminded the world that those Liberals who had tried to persuade him he was needed as a strong-man mayor now were charging him with weakness. But 'those admirable qualities which these people admit Mayor Stewart has shown in his position as mayor are his best recommendations for the more important work at Ottawa.'

The exchange of compliments between the papers was up to standard. As the election approached, the *Herald* noted that the *Spectator* had ceased to refer to it by name and was substituting such terms as 'this wolfish Laurier organ disguised in public-rights sheep's clothing'.

By 1912, after various votes by council and the ratepayers and at least one unsuccessful court action by Cataract, Hydro-Electric Commission power reached Hamilton. The *Spectator* continued critical of Hydro matters for another ten years until a new hand in the paper's affairs and a new study of the situation brought about a more balanced view.

The Great Chance

As the year 1909 opened, the *Spectator* sounded a call for unity:

> The temptation toward isolation and separatism must be fought to the utmost – fought as men fight the drowsiness of death in the paralysing chill of the western winter. We must make ourselves familiar with the full facts, and derive from them a degree of sympathetic feeling that will enable us to stand together. Prejudice, arising from any cause whatsoever, must be regarded as nothing short of treason. We must think west and east, and be bounded on either side by nothing short of salt water. We of Canada are one, and on that day when we forget it the great chance will have passed. . . .

It was perhaps a fitting and prophetic introduction to the rest of the century. Within six years this group of provinces called Canada would begin to forge in tragic achievement a kind of nationality – and paradoxically lay bare the long flaw in the metal of the union.

These last years before Sarajevo were active and pleasant for the Southams in their family and business life. On January 22, 1909, the *Spectator* devoted one paragraph in its 'Society, Home and Clubs' column to the marriage of Ethel May Southam to the second St. Clair Balfour, thus recording the culmination of a childhood acquaintance begun in the double house on Bold Street in the 1880s. Gordon, now assistant business manager of the *Spectator*, took time out in the summer of 1910 to captain a Canadian cricket eleven that toured the United States and England. That fall he married Mary McGibbon of Montreal and set up housekeeping across Jackson Street from the elder Southams while building a house on the mountain. There were lively evenings at Pinehurst, laced with talk of politics and the *Spectator* and with William's aggressive bridge play – take-a-chance bidding and the vigorous plaint when set: 'Ruined by Chinese cheap labor!'

In that year also a young New Brunswicker named Max Aitken engineered a merger of Hamilton Steel and Iron, Montreal Rolling

Mills, and other concerns into the Steel Company of Canada, with William Southam as one of its first directors.

In 1908 the Southams had bought control of the Calgary *Herald.* In 1912 they began to build it a new home. That year they gathered in the Edmonton *Journal.*

Meantime, in the summer and fall of 1911, the *Spectator* took full advantage of another chance at all-out political warfare. HOW DO YOU LIKE THIS? asked its editorial-page heading September 1. Under it bloomed a resurrection of Champ Clark's notorious quotation on reciprocity: 'I am for it because I hope to see the day when the American flag will float over every square foot of the British North American possessions clear to the North Pole.'

Throughout the campaign the paper carried a standing feature on page one entitled LIBERALS WHO ARE OPPOSED TO RECIPROCITY, a list replenished with new names from day to day. Newspapers quoted in the Spec as giving the American view with implications of annexation ranged from the Dunkirk *Union* to the Sioux City *Journal.* On September 20 the *Spectator* hoisted to the top of its front page the Union Jack and the Stars and Stripes, with the command to CHOOSE YOUR FLAG. Two days later, with Laurier out and Borden in, it was able to report A NEW ERA HAS DAWNED.

Early in the winter of 1913 William Southam, leaning out from the balcony of the Thistle Curling Club – to josh his old opponent at bridge, poker, and curling, Bill Vallance – fell to the ice. The accident put him in bed for days, but in February he was able to sail on a Mediterranean cruise with his wife, his son Fred, and daughter-in-law Daisy.

The Balkan wars and the home rule bill began to move off the front page. In the first week of July, 1914, the death of Joseph Chamberlain recalled an imperial dream. On Saturday, July 25, the *Spectator* ran reports from Paris, London, Rome, and Berlin under the headline EUROPEAN POWERS NOW FEAR ANOTHER WAR. Three days later it reported Austria's war declaration on what was then Servia, and on August 1:

GRIM-VISAGED WAR NOW
THREATENS PEACE OF
COUNTLESS THOUSANDS

In six years Gordon had become an aggressive man of business at the *Spectator,* a factor in the paper's popularity among the sports-minded, particularly the British immigrants of East Hamilton for whose satisfaction he had arranged to run Old Country soccer scores.

He hoisted the flag of daily circulation on the right-hand corner of the front page. Now his mind was on other things. Soon after graduation he had been commissioned in the 13th regiment, Hamilton's oldest militia unit. With war a fact he transferred to the artillery and began taking field courses. Through the summer of 1915 he organized for active service the 40th battery, the Sportsmen's, and in August was gazetted major commanding. His lieutenants included Conn Smythe who, a quarter-century later, would recruit a new generation of sports figures in another Sportsmen's Battery – the 30th – to fight in a new war.

The battery sailed in February 1916. So now while the *Spectator* recorded the deadly stalemate across the fields of Europe, letters to the family began to arrive, from Bramshott and then Whitley. Some were touched with an ironic humor. 'Knowing the influence that the opinion of one of our Canadian soldiers in a "near front" position will have on you,' Gordon wrote his father in April, 'I am hastening to forward you my opinion on the probable duration of the war. This is based on a close study of conditions in England today, after seven weeks' visit (I might mention that conditions are mostly rain) and numerous interviews with officers on leave. Add to this the reading of H.Belloc's articles in *Land & Water*, and the conclusion is – nobody knows.' He signed off with an allusion to certain characteristics of William and W.J.: 'Don't let this adverse news prevent you from signing whatever Brother Bill, the weaver of schemes and seller of houses places before you.'

Most were addressed to his mother: news of the delayed arrival of a field kitchen she had sent the battery, purchase of a Scripps Booth car for Mary, who had followed him to England, encounters with Hamilton men in the camps.

A note of crisp comment on Canadian affairs sometimes broke through the recital of adventures and events. After personal experience in the Ypres salient in May, Gordon had moved the battery across the channel. By September it had been in France, firing and under fire, for six weeks. He dashed off a program: 'All munitions profits over, say, 20 per cent, to go to the government – tax on land-value – government ownership of CNR, GTP and CPR; municipal ownership of all utilities. . . . A close inquiry into the government land deals and other swindles, and the guilty ones put behind bars; all men disabled in this war to be given some kind of a chance at a reasonable living when they get back home again. A lot of us wouldn't mind fighting for the above-mentioned country. . . . Committees for this would do more for recruiting than their present twaddle.'

On the Somme 'some mysterious new contrivance' had made its appearance (obviously the tank).

In October, after several moves, the battery dug into a forward position on the Somme near Courcelette. All day Sunday, October 15, German batteries centred their fire on the brigade. In mid-afternoon, headquarters ordered all hands to withdraw till the shelling let up. Gordon went forward to see that the gunners were pulled back and under cover. This done, he started back to his dugout with Sergeant-Major Norman Harvie of Orillia. At the sound of a shell overhead they jumped for a shell-hole. Both were killed by the burst.

Next afternoon, eight black horses drew an artillery wagon to the cemetery in Albert, the town of riven streets and the hanging Virgin. All the guns were in action and no gun carriage was available. Those at the graveside included the old *Spectator* and *Citizen* man, Brigadier-General E.W.B.Morrison, and a friend of Upper Canada College days, Major Harry Crerar. 'It was a regular soldier's funeral,' Morrison wrote his old friend, George Allan at the *Spectator*. 'A heavy battery was in action in the next field, the battle planes were circling overhead, and beyond was the constant roar of the continuous battle. . . .'

Mary McGibbon Southam cabled the word of Gordon's death. William had left for the office when the message reached Jackson Street. In some unexplained manner the news was posted at the *Spectator* before his arrival. It was from his newspaper's bulletin board that he learned of the death of his youngest son.

The guns spoke and men died along the Ancre and at Arras and at Messines and Vimy Ridge. At last the United States moved towards war. Russia crumbled to the edge of revolution. And in Canada a single word – conscription – cracked the illusion of unity.

In Hamilton, as elsewhere with few exceptions outside Quebec, the newspapers were united on the basic issue. But there, as in some other areas, a fight grew over who should go to Parliament to put a win-the-war program into effect.

There was no dispute over the Unionist candidate in the eastern riding – Major-General S.C.Mewburn, who had just been appointed Minister of Militia and Defence. For West Hamilton the *Herald* supported Conservative-Unionist T.J.Stewart, whose entry into federal politics it had opposed in 1908. The *Spectator*, which had supported Stewart in 1908 and 1911, came out for the acclamation of soldier candidates, men who had seen war service.

Perhaps the fact that both Gordon Southam and Bill Carey, only son of William's old partner, had died in action lent vigor to the *Spectator*'s stand that where Unionist soldier candidates were available they should be unopposed, that M.P.s in a wartime parliament should be men who knew war. The *Spectator* was not alone. The Toronto *Telegram*, for instance, had sharp comment for 'the party machinists who try to force civilians upon constituencies that wish to elect soldiers'.

At the start of the campaign, the *Spectator* in a front-page editorial condemned Stewart for a verbal attack on Jack Counsell, a prominent Liberal. 'Mr. Stewart stated in effect that Mr. Counsell was a sneak and a coward, and, after donning the King's uniform, had not gone to the front. . . .' the *Spectator* said. 'The attributes of a coward and a sneak could be applied to John L. Counsell just about as fittingly as the instincts and attributes of a gentleman could be applied to an ungenerous enemy who thus takes advantage of his opponent's absence.' The facts were that Counsell had qualified as an artillery officer with distinction, and had suffered a hernia and sciatic eczema in training, the *Spectator* said. 'He is as fit now to go to the front as a man would be to play through a football game with a broken leg, and the thousands here and all over Canada who know Mr. Counsell are aware that he has the heart and the courage to do both.' The *Spectator* suggested that because of this attack alone Stewart should be disqualified as a candidate.

Two Unionist conventions met. One picked Stewart. The other – termed by the *Herald* 'a fake, hand-picked convention got together by personal enemies of Mr. Stewart' – advanced the names of Lieutenant-Colonel William Hendrie and Lieutenant-Colonel John McLaren, Hendrie's entry being tentative in an effort to break the deadlock; he eventually withdrew.

The *Spectator* had opposed McLaren when he ran as a Liberal against Stewart in 1911. It backed him now for endorsation by the Unionists as a man who had served at the front. Bill Mullis, who had succeeded Wodell as managing editor, made a personal pilgrimage to Sir Robert Borden on McLaren's behalf. On November 21 Borden endorsed Stewart. Pressed by the *Spectator* for reasons, he replied: 'In each province a committee of ministers was appointed to report to me upon the endorsement of candidates in support of Union Government. The determining factor in each constituency was the desire to select a candidate supporting Union Government who would have the best prospects of being returned. . . .'

The *Spectator* published the Borden message, deplored old-fashioned 'machine manipulation', and on Saturday, December 15, two days before the election, offered some headlined advice:

FOLLOW THESE, YOU CAN'T GO WRONG
MEWBURN – THE FLAG – MCLAREN

Mewburn had no trouble, but in West Hamilton the *Spectator*'s cause was a losing one. Stewart won, with Laborite Walter Rollo second and McLaren third. By 1921 the paper was back to orthodox lines. It supported Stewart and other Conservative candidates in the Hamiltons and Wentworth.

Meantime there were family events linked with the house on Jackson Street. In the spring of 1918 Captain Eric Harvie, cousin of Norman Harvie who had lost his life in the shell-burst that killed Gordon Southam, was back in Canada after a severe war wound, stationed at Beamsville as an air force adjutant. In Hamilton he met Dorothy Southam, up from Montreal to visit her grandparents. In September of 1919 they were married in Montreal.

It was the second marriage in the F.N.Southam family that year. In July the second daughter, Amy, war widow of Major Eric McMurtry, married Frederick I. Ker.

The future of the Harvies would be part of the future of Alberta. It was not obvious then, but the marriage of Amy Southam and Fred Ker would, indirectly, have much to do with determining the style and tone of the *Spectator* for a period of thirty years.

The Fight for Two Cents

In the early fall of 1920 the *Spectator*'s biggest paper of the week came out on Fridays – 44 pages. 'Some of the outlying corner stores and laundries', Bill informed Wilson, 'are discovering that this much for one cent is a bargain way to purchase wrapping paper. As soon as enough of them realize it, we will go broke through increased circulation.' For thirty years, since the *Herald*'s appearance in 1889, the Hamilton dailies had been selling at a cent.

It was not a situation that anyone at the *Spectator* liked. Jimmie Allan in his review of the 1918 advertising year remarked that while things were in good shape (the paper cleared $55,000 after spending $30,000 of its net on remodelling buildings) it was not seemly to look cheerful: 'Rather should we be clad in the habiliments of woe until the era of two-cent papers is ushered in. When that happens (God wot it may be soon) we can abandon the gravity which $76-per-ton newsprint thrusts upon us.'

By 1920 a newsprint price of $130 was forecast. The *Spectator,* of course, was hardest hit with its more than 30,000 circulation compared to 15,000 for the *Herald* and 5,000 for the *Times*, and more pages a day than either. But the cost-pinch now had brought the *Herald* to the point where its publishers also were at least thinking about that extra cent. The hitch was the *Times*, long since relegated to third place, losing money but stubbornly hanging on.

That summer W.J.Southam had what he called 'a hen on'. Bill's theory was that something should be done to upset the status quo; out of the resultant uncertainty would come a two-cent price for papers.

Working on this belief he had tried one promising but abortive ploy two years before. In October of 1918 he bought, personally, the Brantford *Courier* as a 'bluff and call hand', trading a block of Canada Crushed Stone stock for the paper. As he described this transaction, he had been approached by the main shareholders, 'wealthy Brantford gentlemen who three or four years ago purchased control for political purposes', but who had made no headway against the established *Expositor*. Bill regretfully sent the Brantford gentlemen away, but thought it over in relation to the Hamilton situation, changed his mind, and made a deal.

In a report to Wilson he explained that he had used every argument he could think of with the *Herald* and the *Times* to get them up to two cents, without result. What he wanted Wilson to do was to arrange a transfer of the *Courier*'s Canadian Press franchise (the modern term is 'membership') from Brantford to the morning field in Hamilton. 'By throwing this bomb into the local field,' he wrote, 'I feel fairly confident that from panic and chaos two-cent papers will be speedily evolved if this morning Courier agrees to keep out or get out after starting.' The scheme actually got as far as an application to Canadian Press Limited for transfer of franchise on which action was postponed. By mid-December, Bill admitted that for the time being he was buffaloed: 'The plan is not going to succeed as Bob Harris of the Herald recently told Ferrie of the Times to look out for me, that I was up to some devilment. I heard this of course indirectly. Bob must have discovered my tracks although I thought they were fairly well hidden.'

Bill closed the Brantford *Courier* January 1, 1919, made a small profit by selling subscription lists and goodwill to the *Expositor*, and reported he had had a barrel of fun.

The *Courier* deal served as practice for the larger scheme of 1920. This was to buy the *Times* through a third party, swing it into the morning field, continue as a morning paper if it could break even or a little better, and close it if it couldn't.

The man who undertook to act as purchaser was John M. Imrie, then manager of the Canadian Daily Newspapers Association – the organization dealing with the business side of newspaper life as Canadian Press Limited dealt with the news side. Imrie, Toronto-born son of a Scottish printer, had learned printing with his father and gone on to study production methods and costing and to edit for a time *Canadian Printer and Publisher.* Imrie was well versed in the practical side of publishing. He took on the buying job for Bill with the understanding that he would go on to a career with the Southams – with the *Times* (if it survived) or head office or one of the other newspapers.

By August Imrie was negotiating with the *Times'* owners, with Bill in the background supplying what information he could and the money to back the deal: 'You are to go through to the limit, doing your own gunning and I am to provide the ammunition.' Bill learned that the *Times* had lost $4,000 in 1918, done no better than break even in 1919, and would likely lose $10,000 in 1920 at current newsprint prices. 'The source from which I obtained my information believes there is not much chance of a deal going through at $75,000,' he told Imrie, 'but that somewhere around $100,000 would take the whole box of tricks now that the principals are frightened into a mood to sell.'

The situation was tricky. To preserve secrecy Bill had to operate off the cuff, borrowing collateral from the *Spectator* and Southam Press, the printing company, to back the bank loan Imrie needed to put the deal through. 'While I am not keen on the *modus operandi,*' he wrote Wilson, 'lacking as it does formal directors' sanction and legal blessings, I do not believe we could obtain the results we are after by handling it differently. . . . I went ahead after finding out first that the majority of the board of directors of our different companies approved, and confirmation and legal ratification will and must necessarily follow.'

A hint of the freedom of expression that marked communications among the brothers comes through in Bill's account of a conversation with Dick: 'Brother Dick in a burst of blunt expression termed my methods as crooked, and before he delivered to me a Southam Press note he insisted on a one per cent endorsement fee. I readily agreed to this, but thought in his use of the gift of speech that he showed great lack of diplomacy.' He had not even mentioned the deal to

William. 'While I realize I am taking awful chances, I believe it is much the wisest course to take these chances and leave everybody around here in the dark and let them act perfectly natural and according to their instincts when the news breaks.'

On August 31 the *Times* accepted a cheque from Imrie for $10,-000 on account. The completed deal called for payment of $77,000 for the newspaper and job plants, $18,000 for paper stocks, and $31,000 for book accounts, plus $9,000 for a year's rent of the building. While all this was going on, the fires of curiosity in Hamilton business circles burned with their usual erratic flame. On the day Imrie's $10,000 cheque went through William mentioned he had heard the *Times* was sold. The *Spectator*, he told Bill, now could look for some real competition. Did Bill know who had bought it? Bill's reply was, 'Search me.'

That day also, Bill met on the street General S.C.Mewburn. Mewburn told him all about the transaction and hazarded the guess that Joe Atkinson of the Toronto *Star* was the man behind Imrie. Atkinson's managing editor, John R. Bone, had been seen lunching with Eastwood of the *Times*. Farther down the street the story was that a group from the Canadian Manufacturers Association had forked up the money. No one, at this juncture, seems to have suspected the lanky sauntering figure who stopped on the corners to ask what was new and listen to the gossip.

Imrie's purchase and his application for a morning franchise for the *Times* threw the Hamilton newspaper field into confusion – or at least the appearance of confusion. The *Herald* protectively and the *Spectator* (going through the motions) also applied for morning publication rights. Had all the applications been serious, Hamilton was faced with the startling possibility of six newspapers – three morning and three evening.

Bill explained the unlikelihood of this in a letter to J.F.B.Livesay, general manager of Canadian Press Limited: 'As far as the Spectator is concerned . . . I withdraw their application for a morning franchise . . . mainly because the application was filed for "saw-off" purposes.' If Imrie were granted a morning franchise the *Times* would discontinue in the evening field. 'I would suggest that the simplest, quickest and best way to help clean up the Hamilton situation would be to grant Mr. Imrie's application and lay the other applications over.'

That is what happened.

With the *Times*'s objection removed by the paper's purchase, the Hamilton newspapers went to two cents on October 27. Thus was consummated what was probably the most elaborate scheme ever devised for the purpose of engineering a one-cent price rise.

Though the plan succeeded in its central purpose, in one aspect the plot failed. Bill had hoped for a *Spectator-Times* merger, with a profitable morning *Times*. It soon became apparent that this would not work; if the papers merged the *Herald* would break back to one cent. The alternatives were to run the *Times* as a completely separate entity or to close. The switch to morning publication was made early in November but success was not in the cards. The *Times* ceased publication and Imrie proceeded to sell off the plant.

All this was a sideshow to new moves at the *Spectator* itself.

As early as the middle years of the war it became apparent that the James Street building was out of date. And the paper needed more press capacity; on days when it ran more than twenty pages, late deliveries caused complaints. In 1916 the Southams rented a new site on King Street East and bought land behind it on King William Street. They planned to remodel stores and build a new office on the King Street front and erect a fireproof plant building after the war. By the fall of 1920, work was well advanced. To complete the job the paper needed money.

In so far as it was in his nature to worry, W.J. did so. Apart from the *Spectator*'s immediate situation, he had scented over the horizon the depression of the early 1920s. In a letter to Wilson he couched his feeling in nautical terms (Bill was an active small-craft sailor and sometime commodore of the Royal Hamilton Yacht Club): 'I wouldn't be surprised if the seven-year swing with a possible panic will arrive right on time and it is due in 1921. . . . It looks to me as if it will keep everyone jumping to shorten sail for the squall and then for the long beat to windward in a pockety breeze with several rolling calms, which will be accompanied by sea-sickness.'

The Spectator needed $425,000 to pay off building costs, the *Times* liability, and the business-profits war tax, take over the lease on the King Street property, and buy a new press. The need was met in part by injecting new money into the capital set-up. The Spectator Printing Company's capitalization still stood at the $20,000 of 1877. Now $250,000 in new stock was issued, William Southam and Sons buying $125,000 common and the Carey estate $125,000 in participating preferred. W.J. turned over his leasehold and option-to-purchase on the King Street property for a $75,000 mortgage. The rest was assumed as a liability guaranteed by the parent company.

Stewart Macdonald, the Careys' representative on the *Spectator* board, had a pawky sense of humor. 'When being enlightened as to the necessity of the Times purchase, on top of the other colossal commitments in effect,' W.J. reported to F.N., 'he remarked that my greatest oversight would appear to have been that I overlooked buying the Bank of Hamilton also. Although it is no laughing matter I can't help chuckling.'

The *Spectator* moved to King Street in mid-May 1921, and celebrated with a seventy-fifth anniversary number on June 4.

Bill's conjectured beat to windward, as far as the *Spectator* was concerned, turned out to be nothing more uncomfortable than a close reach. The paper's gross profit in 1921 was $186,000 – within $1,000 of the 1920 figure. The heavy weather was a couple of years away. To meet it the Spec would have a new man aboard. Frederick I. Ker took on the job of assistant manager and secretary at the time of the move to King Street. He would just have time to learn how the ship handled before she headed into what came to be known as the 'War with Herman'. It was no pockety breeze.

2
The Printers

In January of 1889 a young man from Hamilton arrived in Montreal. He brought with him two ticket presses from the *Spectator*'s jobroom, a hand cutting-machine (years later he would describe it as a hand-cutting machine), and $1,500. He set up the equipment on one floor of a wooden building on Craig Street, got together a crew of seven (two pressmen, two compositors, a boy, a girl, and himself), and opened for business. Fred Southam, nineteen years old and homesick, thus became the first of the Southam sons to run one of the family properties on his own – as manager of Southam and Carey, Railroad Ticket Printers.

A time would come when, for a period, commercial printing would outrank any other Southam activity, until overtaken and passed by the craft that became their chief occupation – publication of newspapers. It would hold a substantial place in over-all operation even after that, as it does today. But perhaps an element in the printing picture that turned out to be as important as any to the future of the Southam enterprises was an indirect one. Fred's boyhood move to Montreal placed him in a business climate that favored young ambition. The interplay of climate and ambition would push his horizons well beyond the limits of the printing business. In this environment developed the F.N.Southam who came to head the company a generation later, when daily newspapers had become its chief concern, and to hold that post for more than twenty years. At the time, however, such possibilities crossed no one's mind at all. The objectives were immediate and practical.

The *Spectator*'s publishers were already established in the printing business in Toronto. Early in 1881 they had set up a plant in the new building housing the *Mail*, the newspaper some ambitious Conserva-

tives had founded in 1872. The *Mail* had fallen on lean times during
Alexander Mackenzie's Liberal administration and been taken over
by John Riordon, the St. Catharines paper-maker, its chief creditor.
Heartened by Sir John A. Macdonald's return to power in 1878, the
Mail's new owner built new quarters: the four-storey brownstone
with tower that remained a landmark at King and Bay streets until
merger of the *Mail and Empire* and the *Globe* left it to the wreckers'
hammers in the late 1930s.

The *Mail* did no job printing. But it had space to spare. Southam
and Carey bought out a printing firm called Bingham and Taylor,
moved the equipment to two floors of the newspaper building, and
operated under the name Mail Job Department. The business was a
partnership established May 16, 1881.

A Hamilton printer, George McKay, took charge as manager.
Early in the 1880s the eldest Southam son, Wilson, came to the Mail
Job for experience – a foretaste of Southam practice. In this instance
it didn't take. The other Wilson, mother of the growing family, didn't
like having a fifteen-year-old away from home, even though he lived
with uncle Jack and aunt Sarah Southam Mills. He went back to
Hamilton within a year. It was the third son, Richard, whose life was
to be linked with the Toronto plant.

No doubt government business came to the Mail Job, but patronage was never much of a base to build on and the link with the *Mail*
was no advantage by the late 1880s; the newspaper turned its coat
and went into opposition, though it later recanted (and incidentally
absorbed its rival the *Empire* in 1895). The plant prospered on general commercial printing, particularly railway time-tables, folders
and time-bills, and theatre work. In 1890 it reorganized as the Mail
Job Printing Company.

With the Toronto plant well established the logical next step was
Montreal, the railway capital of the country. Things went well for
Fred and his ticket presses from the start, as railway building moved
toward its period of most lavish expansion and young towns grew into cities and laid miles of streetcar tracks. In the 1890s, in addition to
bales of tickets for the railways, the plant turned out tickets and
transfers for streetcar lines in Montreal, Toronto, Cornwall, Hamilton, Winnipeg, and as far away as British Guiana. Fred himself
adapted and fitted with numbering apparatus the first press he used
in streetcar ticket production, a contraption known around the shop
as 'The Elephant'.

He showed a first-year profit of $4,302.53. Ten years later the
yearly margin had grown to $15,000. Summarizing for William in

1901 the first twelve years of operation, Fred could add up a total net for the period that was forty-five cents short of $112,000. His plant had long outgrown its original quarters and moved three times – to a second location on Craig, then to the Herald Building on Beaver Hall Hill (where it was burned out in March of 1893), and again to three floors on Notre Dame Street.

Fred himself at the time of this 1901 report, was a married man and a father and on the threshold of more wide-ranging business affairs.

Nearer home, Richard had come over from Hamilton to manage the Mail Job at Toronto. Limping from a football injury sustained in the Tiger backfield, Dick entered the plant on a fall day in 1894 and settled into a career in printing that was to last forty-three years.

This was the time of the travelling vaudeville and stock companies, long before moving pictures had even begun to squeeze the living theatre into shallow pockets of big-city nightlife. Until the stock companies died the Toronto plant was one of the best-known producers of posters and general theatre printing in Canada. Johnnie Norman, who had kept books for Bingham and Taylor and continued with the Mail Job (he later became secretary of the company) combined the duties of book-keeper, canvasser, and collector, and somehow found time to pal around with travelling agents and managers. 'Not only to greet them on arrival,' an old-timer recalled, 'but to watch closely for their departure.'

The orders were sometimes unusual. Alice Mae Sullivan, who came to the Mail Job in July of 1903 for two weeks' work as a relief stenographer (and stayed forty-five years), had an ear for stories from the firm's Bay Street days. She recalled hearing of managers sending in a hurry for reams of chopped-up paper to create snowstorms over the heads of wayward daughters in the melodramas of the time.

As business grew, both Fred and Dick felt the urge to get out of rented quarters. In Montreal, Fred's ticket-printing plant moved to Donegana Street in 1904, but the site was due to disappear with erection of the CPR's new Windsor station. In the summer of 1906 he bought for $17,500 a lot fronting on St. Alexander Street and made plans to build – five storeys and basement in reinforced concrete to cost $120,000.

Financing raised some problems. Southam Limited at the time had a curious mixture of obligations. The elder Southams were moving spirits in the Health Association that made Hamilton the first city in Canada to care for tuberculosis patients in a local sanatorium started and operated by local subscription. Early in March, Bill wrote Fred that the company owed the bank $56,000 and would have to find $15,000 for the Hamilton and Fort William Navigation Company. Other commitments included $10,000 for the consumptive hospital and an Easter donation of $2,000 to Christ Church Cathedral. In addition to which Bill himself wanted to borrow $8,000.

Writing his father a month later, Fred noted that the bank overdraft had been reduced to $43,000 and the Easter donation paid. But meantime he had spent $35,000 on his building and would need $90,000 more. Dick needed $6,500 for new machinery, Wilson $2,000 for a linotype and he himself $4,000 to pay off a note on his new house. He figured total company and family requirements at $140,000 and remarked 'this is a lot of money.' However, he had arranged for a loan on his building of $75,000, and the printing plants and the *Citizen* would produce some cash as they went along. Everything would straighten out by September 1; William could then approach the bank for $30,000 or so: 'You could then buy in some more Cataract preferred if you wanted to. Dick and Wilson could blow in what they need for new machinery, and you would have enough left over to take all your grandchildren to Atlantic City next spring.'

By October 24 he was able to report the new building almost finished. Tenants were moving in. As usual with Southam communications, this report moved easily from business to family matters: Harry planned to come over for Saturday's football game. How about Ethel coming down with Gordon? She did so. The game they saw, incidentally, on that Saturday in late October of 1907, was the one in which Gordon drop-kicked a field goal in the third quarter to pull out a 9-7 victory for the Tigers.

Fred moved his plant to two floors of the new building early in December.

An odd byplay that year was an offer that might have taken the Southams out of printing. The American Bank Note Company approached Wilson with a view to buying both plants. Fred, though he was already building in Montreal, was ready to sell if the price was right. He suggested about $500,000, but recognized that, while there were arguments for selling in Montreal, there were advantages to staying in business in Toronto. In Montreal it was all tickets; some of the large street railways were thinking of printing their own, and no one could tell when somebody would butt in on the railway ticket business. Dick on the other hand had a large diversified business. Fred suggested taking a casual position, an attitude that 'we are willing to discuss things, and might possibly entertain an offer as our tastes lie more for the newspaper field.' Dick, who regarded nothing in life as outranking commercial printing, opposed the whole thing. No price that anyone would pay could possibly be right. In the end the proposal petered out. So did Fred's apprehensions about the street railway ticket business. Within a year or so he signed new long-term contracts with the streetcar lines in Toronto and Montreal.

The Toronto plant had bulged out of the *Mail* in 1900 and moved to a building at York Street and Millstone Lane. Southams bought a lot at Duncan and Adelaide in 1905 and in 1908 Dick began to build. Early in 1909, the Mail Job Printing Company was reorganized as Southam Press Limited and on July 1 moved to the new building. Nearly half a century later, Tom Saunders recalled that the move was made without a hitch – presses, forms, and all their related furniture.

Saunders was the archetype of long-service printers. Born in Kent in 1868, he came to Canada at eighteen and worked in three plants before joining the Mail Job in 1900. Fascinated by railway printing, he began taking folders and workbills home for study. When the Grand Trunk and Canadian Northern merged in the Canadian National system in the early 1920s, Saunders worked out the master time-table with traffic experts of the road. The job took seven weeks. Compositor, proof-reader, at one time superintendent of the plant, he went on working into his late eighties.

The presses had not been rolling in the new building long when their crews began to wonder if they had boarded a sea-going printing plant. With certain combinations running, the building vibrated, not unpleasantly, as if propelled by reciprocating engines. Richard called in a firm of engineers, who hung their plumb-bobs and duly reported: 'We should be surprised to find that the vibration would seriously injure the building at least for many years, but in the absence of any more data than are at present available, we cannot say that vibration will not cause deterioration.' What, Richard wanted to know, did they mean by 'many'? Three or four years or fifty or sixty? The engineers replied that what they had in mind was fifty years or more, but they really couldn't say. The best Richard could get out of them was that if anything untoward were to happen, there would be plenty of warning. Fifty years later another generation of engineers found no deterioration and no danger. The building still simulated at times a 20,000-tonner on a Mediterranean cruise in sunny weather.

Two developments occurred during this building period that had a bearing on the future of the Montreal plant.

In November of 1907 Fred bought the Canada Tag & Label Company – $30,000 in plant and $10,000 in paper and book debts at the reserve price of twenty-five cents on the dollar. This put the Montreal plant into the many specialties in addition to tickets that were to become a sizable part of its business.

In the following February, Will Southam joined the Montreal business. William Waugh Southam (Will or Willie Waugh to the family) was a son of the elder William Southam's younger brother Richard. Richard, like William, had learned printing at the London *Free Press* and later established a printing and lithographing business of his own at London. He is said to have been the first printer to do four-color work in Canada. Now he was selling out. Will was on the lookout for a job, and Fred welcomed him in Montreal. Will Southam wanted to get into general printing. Fred told him to list what he needed and go ahead. Will did so. He also sent for Roy Coghill, who had worked with him in his father's London plant and as an artist on the *Advertiser*. Thirty-eight years later, when Will Southam retired as general manager of the Montreal plant, Roy Coghill succeeded him.

By 1911 general printing accounted for a third of the Montreal plant's business. Tickets, however, were still the mainstay. Whether it was an eight-gallon can of milk going from Lachute to Mile End, an immigrant travelling from Montreal to Vancouver, or an excursionist on the Ha! Ha! Bay Railway, chances were that Southams had printed the tag or ticket covering the journey.

In 1912 figures for the preceding seven years showed total net earnings of $275,000 at Toronto and $279,000 at Montreal. These figures were cited in connection with a development that was something of a milestone in this period of Southam history. From January 1 of that year, the two printing plants were consolidated in one company – Southam Press Limited – to facilitate a bond issue of $750,-000. Proceeds were to pay off mortgages on the Toronto and Montreal buildings and to provide for additions and 'further development of our other enterprises' as Fred put it in a letter to a Montreal investment house that was looking into the possibility of raising the money in England. The 'other enterprises' included two buildings then going up in Calgary, one of them as a new home for the *Herald*. The English money wasn't forthcoming. Eventually Dick raised it through a firm in Chicago.

Least known to the public of all the brothers, Richard Southam with his heavy dark moustache and saturnine appearance was a usually quiet man, who could be at times notably unconventional. The house he built on Teddington Park Boulevard in 1913 was the scene of many a party, planned or impromptu. Richard is known to have telephoned around in search of a piano-player at 3 A.M. Over in Hamilton, W.J., whose occasional activities drew such adjectives as 'unorthodox', 'erratic', and 'eccentric', complained mildly in later years that he didn't quite see why his operations raised more eyebrows than Dick's.

Unconventional or not, Richard built a reputation for business judgment. The Toronto plant had been the big money-earner for several years, Fred noted in a discussion with Wilson in 1915; furthermore, if Dick's advice on investments had been followed, 'the liquid condition of Southam Limited would compare favorably with the London mint.'

In its promotional brochure for the bond issue, the Chicago firm noted the current financial position of the Southam family: 'These bonds are guaranteed . . . by the joint and several endorsements of Messrs. William Southam, William J. Southam, Gordon H. Southam, Wilson Mills Southam, Harry Stevenson Southam, Richard Southam, and Fred Neal Southam. The aggregate net worth of these guarantors is in excess of $2,000,000.'

The Southams continued building. Back in 1907, with completion of the plant on St. Alexander, Fred had begun to think of an outlet through the block and a building fronting on Bleury Street, the two to be joined back to back. It was not until June of 1912 that he got the lot-owner tied down to a deal: $60,000 for a fifty-foot frontage on Bleury. The new ten-storey Southam Building on Bleury began to rent space to tenants on May 1, 1914.

That fall, wartime uncertainties hit the printing business. But from 1916 on, with the return of confidence despite the war, both plants increased their output. By 1924 each was doing more than $1,000,-000 worth of printing. In 1928 they went back to operation as separate companies. By this time each plant employed more than 300.

Fred and Montreal

When Southam Limited came into existence in 1904 its by-laws called for one vice-president, to represent it in Montreal. Fred of course was the man in mind.

His first responsibility, as it had been for fifteen years, was the printing plant, which now dropped the Carey name (the Carey interest had been bought out in both Montreal and Toronto) and became simply Southam Limited, Ticket Printing Department. But his activities soon took him well beyond that. Will Southam's arrival early in 1908 began to free him from detailed plant routine. Montreal was the money centre of the country, it was growing fast, and Southam Limited's profit-and-loss account was receptive to accruals from many kinds of business.

At this time the brothers were considering propositions ranging from land at Prince Rupert to mines in Mexico. Fred opposed all that. In his opinion there were better bargains and more certain returns in real estate that was near enough to look at.

On January 13, 1909, he wrote his father: 'I have purchased the corner of Guy and St. Catherine streets for $225,000.' The terms were $25,000 cash and the rest in instalments. Total cost of the property, the northeast corner of Guy and St. Catherine, rose to $293,000 counting building improvements. Later events tell something of the atmosphere of the period in Montreal. A year after the purchase an insurance appraiser valued the property at $335,000. In early October of 1911, Fred sold it to alderman James Robinson for $500,000. Robinson owned the adjoining corner. Fred reported: 'He suggested to me a year ago that one of us buy the other out, that a good way would be to put a price on both corners and then toss up as to who would get the whole block.' And, with a dig at W.J., 'This would have appealed to your son William, I am sure.'

Most deals were smaller than that, few if any as profitable. One block of property bounded by St. James, Desrivières, and Glackmeyer streets stayed on the books of successive Southam companies for thirty years. But most were undramatic and reasonably profitable turnovers.

Of all the brothers, Fred at this period expressed his views most often and positively in the round of family letters. It might be a plan for a Southam takeover (to use a term not then in use) of Hamilton Steel & Iron, which was not pursued, an opinion on the advisability or otherwise of buying into another newspaper, comment on *Spectator* or *Citizen* editorials, or a run-down on stock market possibilities. He read the family's two newspapers critically, usually with more concern for quality of presentation than editorial doctrine. Writing W.J. in June of 1908 he admitted not knowing enough to be either a free-trader or a protectionist, but blasted the style and arguments of *Spectator* 'red hot adequate-protection' articles. However, writing on the same day to Harry, who also had pitched into the *Spectator*'s editorials, he noted that 'Our respected father's adequate-protection views may do as much for the country in these strenuous times of competition as free trade would have. . . . The old man's horse sense is very sound.'

Since copies of letters went to everybody, they provided opportunities for occasional needling. Writing his father in the last week of 1910, Fred combined some investment advice with an appraisal of family business tendencies as seen by himself: 'At the present price of Detroit United you can get out of both it and your American Locomotive at a profit and I think you are making a mistake not to do so. Incidentally it would be a good example to Wilson and Bill. Bill is essentially a speculator and the only difference between him, and you and Wilson, is that you think you are investors; whereas Dick and I, while extravagant, are the only two of this type in the family.'

The sense of family now had new implications. In 1894 Fred had married Agnes Linton (known from childhood as Daisy), daughter of Robert Linton, a dry-goods dealer. Their three children, Dorothy, Amy, and Margaret, were growing up. Early in the century Daisy had had to take lung treatment at Saranac Lake; in 1905 Fred moved the family from Mackay Street to the clearer air of the Westmount slope, buying and remodelling a house on the newly opened Belvedere Road.

The quality of Southam family meetings of this period comes out in the off-the-cuff agendas F.N. frequently included in his letters of invitation, as when in May of 1912 he suggested W.J. come down: 'We can have a final chat on the Calgary business plans, look over the Montreal real estate situation, have a game of golf, a few rubbers of auction and talk over the Vancouver proposition with the assistance of Harry and Wilson whom we will endeavor to get down here for a day or two.' The Vancouver proposition was a suggestion, not acted on, that they buy the *World*.

In these years of his early middle age F.N. was becoming well known in the business community of Montreal. (Suggesting a modest bonus for him in 1910, Wilson noted that 'he has been travelling with a set of multi-millionaires for some time.') Success in the printing business and elsewhere had come to him through insight and the instinct for making friends, a quality intensified by a liking for the games businessmen play. A cricketer in early life (he and Wilson toured Ontario with a Hamilton junior eleven in the summer of 1887) he had become a good curler and golfer.

At the same time, events conspired to stir a growing interest in Canada apart from the familiar communities of the Lakes and the St. Lawrence. When purchase of the Calgary *Herald* first came up Fred thought 'Calgary is too far off for any of us to be particularly interested in it as a newspaper field.' Five years later he was putting much of his time into the two buildings that, along with the *Herald*, signalized the company's expansion in western Canada.

The Printers and the Newspapers

In 1937 F.N.Southam wrote his nephew Bill,* then running the Toronto printing plant: 'I do not think the write-up you suggest, wherein you emphasize the connection between the printing plants and the newspapers, is advisable. This will apply to any advertising which either of the press companies might get out at any time. It has always been our policy to keep the publishing company quite separate and distinct from the printing plants, and I think we should continue to do so.' Early in 1938 Philip Fisher also wrote Toronto Bill: 'As an organization we have definitely set our faces against printing sales-talk reinforced by the suggestion that we also publish newspapers.' Both statements were made in turning down drafts of promotional copy drawn up at the Toronto plant.

The position stated by the latter-day F.N. might have puzzled the Fred of a quarter-century before, who once remarked to Wilson that 'we have gone to considerable trouble in years past to associate our newspapers with our printing plants.' It would also have caused some regretful head-shaking by Richard who in 1915 stated bluntly, also to Wilson: 'The original idea in buying a chain of newspapers was that they should all work together for the common good of Southam Limited – the common good now, as for years past, being the boosting of the printing business.'

This statement of Richard's was not precisely accurate. The Southams were certainly in business to make money, but there is nothing to suggest that their idea of the common good was limited to the printing business or that newspapers were acquired to assist that enterprise. However, Richard's point of view was one he probably never relinquished, though he came to recognize that other members of the family didn't share it and that as far as company operations were concerned it was long out of date. Twenty years after his letter to Wilson, in sending F.N. a clipping of a Winnipeg *Tribune* editorial that criticized a milling company, he noted that this company in the preceding year had bought $40,000 worth of printing from the Tor-

---

*William Wallace Southam, Richard's son. The number of Bills and W.W.s in the Southam connection takes some sorting out. In addition to William Wallace there were two other W.W.s: William Waugh Southam in Montreal and William Watson Southam (W.J.'s son, who was and is known as Peter), then in Vancouver.

onto plant, and remarked philosophically, 'Things like this I suppose cannot be helped.'

The modern Southam company practice of considering commercial printing as a business completely separate from newspapers is a natural follow-through of the local independence principle, which had been recognized even before The Southam Publishing Company was set up as a newspaper group in 1927. Other things probably came into it – including the trend of newspapers generally away from influences of this kind. In 1954, because the term 'press' traditionally identifies the newspaper world it was removed from the titles of the commercial plants, which henceforth were known as printing companies.

All this is a long way from the attitude Fred expressed to his father in 1908, just after the Southams had bought in at Calgary and when the question of going into Edmonton was first raised: 'I know you don't like to have it suggested to you, but the moral effect of the ownership of these two western papers would be a very valuable adjunct to your general printing business, both here and in Toronto. Toronto Railway contract has not been settled yet, but I am quite satisfied that Mr. Mackenzie would have it attended to very promptly if he was aware that we controlled newspapers in Calgary and Edmonton.'

However, when it came to news handling, any comment by F.N. even then on treatment in the newspapers of printing-plant customers was usually based on an expressed desire for fairness rather than favoritism.

A lively example occurred during the federal election campaign of 1908 when transportation was the chief issue. The talking point was construction cost and the political nature of it, specifically cost of the National Transcontinental (being constructed by the Laurier government for lease to the Grand Trunk Pacific) from Moncton to Winnipeg, and of the GTP proper from Winnipeg to Prince Rupert, built under what amounted to a government guarantee. Fred as a railway ticket printer didn't like some of the stories that were getting into print – aimed at the government, but reflecting on the GTP enterprises – and wrote his father in a cautioning vein. His mood was not improved by the fact that William turned his letters over to W.J. and Jimmie Allan for reply.

As election day (October 26) approached, reports appeared in Hearst's *New York American* and a sheet called the *Boston News Bureau* about the 'political spoils system' in Canada. Liberals claimed these stories were engineered by a hatchet-man in Conservative pay. Fred spotted a *News Bureau* story in the Calgary *Herald* and sent it to his father with an explanatory letter. The *Boston News Bureau*, he said, was known as the mouthpiece of a group of interested capitalists who used it largely for stock-gambling operations. The Southam papers had carried a great deal of just criticism of the Grand Trunk Pacific as coming from Robert Borden. This criticism, made by a responsible politician, was legitimate news. The papers should confine themselves to that. Otherwise 'we might just as well go out of the railway printing business.'

At the time Fred was behind with his reading of the *Spectator*. He got to his back numbers on November 5 and found staring up at him from the front page of the October 21 issue a *Boston News Bureau* story headed GOVERNMENT RAILWAY WAS BADLY BUNGLED. He thereupon wrote brother Bill a letter in which his capacity for sarcasm, usually fairly good-natured, got free rein.

> I would respectfully submit for your consideration that we at present have invested in hard cash, or will have in the near future, close on to $500,000 in our two printing plants in Montreal and Toronto. A large part of this investment has recently been made in order to avoid the heavy business loss which we might incur through fire. About two-thirds of the income of Southam Limited comes from these two plants and about 40 per cent of their business from the railways. I mention these facts because I think the stake is sufficiently large to have you take such precautions as will absolutely do away with what is a ten-times-greater risk than that of fire, *viz*: the publication of what I can only describe as stupid guff about the railways with the idea of helping (?) the party from whom, by the way, we get neither thanks nor tuppence. In my humble opinion not only is it poor politics but bad business, to say nothing of the morals which would excuse such a position. Knowing as I do with what facility you are at all times ready to crawl under the bed in order to oblige an advertiser or dodge a five-hundred-dollar libel suit, I have thought that possibly the facts I have mentioned in the foregoing might appeal to you on your only vulnerable side.

W.J. was more inclined to admire literary style than to worry over critical content. He sent a copy to Bert Woods marked 'This is good in spots.' Woods took it more seriously. The *Herald* was in the midst of a build-more-railways campaign. There would be competition for charter rights and bond guarantees. Was he expected not to discuss railways at all? This was hardly possible.

Fred undertook to straighten out the record:

> The position I take is that governments (Grit or Tory) and railways should get the same kind of a deal as any private individual or corpor-

ation. Because they are in politics and not given to libel suits is no reason why they should have untruthful reports or doubtful news items printed about them. . . . In so far as I personally am concerned none of the papers we are identified with need ever consider the job-printing interests of Southam Limited provided you give everybody, railways included, a fair deal. Neither the Spectator nor the Herald did so in the items complained of, hence my kick.

He added a pungent P.S.: 'Permit me to add that any printing we secure from either railways or business concerns is given us in open competition because either our price or our service is best, probably both. Judging from the treatment our customers sometimes get, I should say we secure this business not because of but in spite of our newspapers.'

The relationship, or lack of it, between newspaper policy and the printing business came in for some further soul-searching a few years later, just after the *Citizen* had moved into a position of political independence.

The federal Conservative party, at the time Fred remarked that Southams were getting neither thanks nor tuppence, should have been able to say a thank-you now and then, but tuppence was beyond it. It had been out of power since 1896. The Southams could expect none of the work farmed out by the King's Printer while Laurier ran the country. After 1911 they looked for better things, and things were not as good as they expected.

Dick blamed the *Citizen*'s whacks at the government. Wilson didn't agree: though government printing at the Toronto plant had fallen off to nothing, it had increased at the Montreal plant; the trouble was that Dick wasn't going after the business. Government printing by the Montreal *Gazette* had jumped from $25,000 in 1913 to $148,000 in 1914, and Wilson believed the chief reason was the *Gazette*'s establishment of a special bureau in charge of its parliamentary representative, 'a brilliant newspaper man and a chap who seems to be thought of very highly by all ministers'. This was John Bassett.

Dick wasn't impressed. He came back with his remark about the common good being the good of the printing business, said the increase in Fred's government volume was largely in tickets, Fred being the only Conservative who had a ticket plant, and added the admission that he hadn't been going after the business. What was the use, considering the way the *Citizen* was acting?

Fred had studied the figures and he came up with a conclusion of his own, closer to Wilson's than to Dick's, but carrying a kicker. 'There is only one way by which we can get our share of what is going,' he wrote, 'and there is really not much use my going after it unless I am assured of our newspaper backing.' By newspaper backing he meant just about the opposite of what Dick meant. He meant a show of independence rather than unqualified support for the government party. The *Gazette*'s printing increase, he surmised, had followed a threat by the *Gazette* to withdraw support because of a post-office deal, part of the proceeds of which 'were known to be going to the Montreal *Mail* who are competing with the *Gazette* in the morning field.' He concluded that 'when Gordon has shown Father the figures I am sure he will not be satisfied with the treatment we have been getting, and if he is willing to kick hard enough, or permit me to do it for him, we will get our share. Otherwise we will not.' He planned a trip to Ottawa to start a campaign.

This letter of Fred's perturbed William, who fired off a telegram of protest. Fred backed up a little. He hadn't intended to suggest any change of policy, particularly for the *Spectator*, without further consultation. However, legitimate pressure could be brought to bear. He made several trips to see Bob Rogers, the lord of patronage, to press his point: all government printing should be done by the bureau at Ottawa. If this were not possible such amounts as could not be handled there should be distributed to the various plants pro rata.

Getting the business, however, was tougher than pulling teeth. In 1917, with Rogers's hostility now in the open, Toronto plant manager Adam Lewis reported to W.J. in Hamilton: 'Our difficulty there has been that, owing to the attitude of the *Citizen*, the Hon. Bob gave instructions to the printing bureau that nothing must be given to Southam.'

In August Bob Rogers resigned from the government. In October the Southam Toronto plant was asked to receive and ship all publicity for the First Victory Loan and to handle some of the printing. The staff publication *Team Work* recorded: 'We printed 8,500,000 pieces of literature, made 1,350,000 impressions, made 10,350,000 folds, gathered 5,886,000 pieces, inserted into 1,962,000 envelopes, and used 15,000 square feet of floor space.' The Victory Loan job however seems to have been a one-shot order. Little government printing went to Southams in the years that followed.

In any event, by that time Fred had gone into war work as an unpaid member of the Imperial Munitions Board, established to speed production in Canadian shell factories, a job that from late 1916 to the end of the war left him only a day or two a week to attend to Southam business.

And the Toronto plant was busy with a job that put government printing in the shade – production of catalogues for a national mail-order house.

Through the early 1900s the Toronto plant developed considerable catalogue printing. Early in 1916 it got the biggest such job it had ever undertaken – Simpson's. New color presses and binding equipment to handle it cost about $100,000.

By this time the mail-order houses had become countrywide general stores. Mail-bags on rural routes bulged with their wares. A man could consult a catalogue and outfit himself from the skin out with a balbriggan undershirt at 65 cents, drawers at the same price, a white cambric shirt plus two collars and two ties (one each in white and sky blue) for $1.19, the best suit in the store – a blue English worsted – at $24 or a cheap tweed at $8.95, three pairs of socks for $1.00, calf oxfords at $3.69, a topcoat for $12.00, a boater at $1.50. To set all this off he could purchase a French briar with vulcanite mouthpiece for 29 cents.

Prices for ladies' wear were comparable – from switches of genuine human hair in all shades of brown and black (no greys) at $1.65 up, to bust confiners of white batiste (hooked front and back and admirably boned) for 55 cents. Children's goods on the toy pages in 1917 included such games as 'Hunting the Huns' at 35 cents. The musically inclined could buy a 31-stringed instrument combining the sweet music of guitar and zither for $3.69.

The Simpson job forced expansion of printing operations from three to six floors at Duncan Street and raised problems of personnel as well as equipment. Monotype composition, make-up, proof-reading, printing, binding, were assigned to what amounted to a staff within a staff.

Charlie Keates, who had left Southams earlier to study color in New York, took charge of the four-color inserts. Keates is another name in the list of old-time printers. Billy Keates worked as a pressman for the Mail Job in the early Bay Street days. Charlie joined as messenger in 1895 and not long thereafter learned presswork from his father. A time came when the plant was short of pressmen with a poster order to be rushed through. Dick Southam walked in and found young Keates, aged twelve or so, in charge. He said: 'If I were you, Charlie, I'd put on long pants when you supervise a pressroom.' A second Billy Keates, brother of Charlie, signed on as a press feeder in 1912, became a foreman, and retired in 1963.

Production of the mail-order catalogue by Southams continued until 1931 when Simpsons made other arrangements.

3
Ottawa:
The Early Years

Wilson Southam caught some sleep on the floor of his new office that Sunday night, but well before 3 A.M. he joined the crew in the basement pressroom to see the forms come down. This cold Monday morning – November 29, 1897 – would be a time to remember. The plate for page four – the editorial page – carried an announcement: 'This journal is now the property of the Ottawa Citizen Company, limited, of which Wilson M. Southam is the managing director, the company having acquired the property by purchase from the late owners, the Messrs. Shannon. . . .'

There was more to it than a simple change of ownership. In the month since William Southam had bought the Ottawa *Citizen* for $9,000 and a promise to collect book debts for the Shannons, Wilson and a small crew of craftsmen from the *Spectator* had worked hard and secretly, with a final spurt in the forty-eight hours since Saturday's paper. This had been produced from the *Citizen*'s old location at 71 Queen Street, where its front door faced a livery stable. One of the new owners' first decisions was to move to the front street. In two days they had moved the five old Rogers typesetters and other equipment to new quarters with a lane to Queen but the main entrance on Sparks, between Metcalfe and Elgin. In a 40'-by-20' basement there, the erectors had set up a new Goss web press that printed from stereo plates. It was a high-speed job for those days, built to turn out 10,000 eight-page papers an hour.

The immediate job was to get Monday morning's paper rolling. But that afternoon was to see the birth of the *Evening Citizen*, a one-cent paper conceived to compete with the *Free Press* and the *Journal*, both selling at two cents.

For a few shaking moments it looked as though neither the old morning nor the new evening paper would reach the street that day. In the rush to install equipment, no one had found time for test-runs. Now as the pressmen hoisted in the newsprint they found that the chucks on the new press wouldn't hold the iron cylinders of the newsprint rolls. They didn't fit, and nothing the erectors tried, with time flying, would make them hold the rolls fast.

Among the onlookers, the stereotypers, typesetters, reporters, and carrier boys assembled to see the fast press run, was Fred Southam, down from Montreal to help start the new family enterprise. Fred by now had a good deal of experience in making press machinery work, and he was wearing overalls. He stepped up and held his shoulder against the roll. At slow speed the press started, the papers began to fall. John Robson Cameron, over from Hamilton to backstop the new venture editorially, interposed his 250-pound bulk to relieve Fred. Still in slow motion, the 2,000 or so copies of the morning edition rolled off the Goss. By press-time for the new evening paper the erectors had fixed the chucks. The *Evening Citizen* emerged, in Wilson's words, 'smoothly and noisily as a lusty infant should'.

Thus occurred the most notable development in the *Citizen*'s history and a key move in the branching out of the Southams. Founded by William Harris in 1844 as the *Packet*, while Ottawa was still Bytown, the paper had gone through several changes of ownership in its fifty-three years of existence. It had become the Ottawa *Citizen* in 1851 (four years before Bytown changed its name), had gone twice-weekly in 1859, and daily in 1865. Originally Reform, it had swung to Conservatism. Charles Mackintosh, who became principal owner in 1877 after some years on the staff, supported Sir John A. Macdonald, served as mayor of Ottawa, was elected to Parliament, and finally through his interest in western development became Lieutenant-Governor of the Northwest Territories in 1892.

Robert and Lewis Shannon of Kingston took over. By 1896 with the federal Conservative party in disarray, and with the Laurier victory in that year and the expected end of government advertising and printing patronage for their paper, they were ready to call it a day. William Southam's success with the Hamilton *Spectator*, regardless of what party ruled at Queen's Park or Ottawa, was already well known to the trade. The Shannons approached him in 1896 and caught his interest, but changed their minds. They were back a year later, after losing $3,700 in the meantime, and this time they sold. Robert Shannon, the cultured, spinsterish bachelor who edited the paper, went back to a law practice that would eventually take him to Saskatoon. Lewis, the manager, a militia major with a waxed mous-

tache and described as 'more handsome architecturally' than his
brother, joined the permanent force.

With an agreement of sale signed, Wilson Southam moved to Ottawa October 27, 1897, took a room on Maclaren Street, and went
to work. In November Harry joined him after playing out the football
season with Montreal. The *Citizen* had experienced its last change of
ownership and come into hands that began at once to widen its scope
as a business and would eventually lead it into new and exciting and
controversial ways as a newspaper.

For the time being, however, the only suggestion of change concerned production: 'The new management has introduced certain
mechanical novelties which we venture to hope will somewhat improve the appearance of the paper.' Politically, party followers had
nothing to fear: 'The change in the management will have no effect
whatever upon the Citizen's policy. Conservative it was born and
Conservative it would die, if such a thing as death were possible for
the Citizen. . . .'

This resounding declaration (which would stand up fairly well for
a dozen years or so) was backed by an editorial, entitled 'The First
and the Last', on the theme that the first Reform government of Canada had foundered on the Rock of Broken Promises, and that the
current one was headed the same way, having already thrown overboard its cargo of Free Trade and Retrenchment and Reform.

Page one of the morning edition on that cold November Monday
carried a column and a quarter on a speech at Toronto by former Finance Minister George E. Foster on behalf of O.A.Howland, Conservative candidate in a Centre Toronto by-election (which he lost);
a London report on Lord Mount Stephen's marriage in St. Margaret's to Miss Giana Tufnell in the presence of Lords Wolseley,
Strathcona, Clanwilliam, Clifford, Selbourne, and Waldegrave, and
assorted ladies ('The bride's responses were clear and distinct while
Lord Mount Stephen's were low and apparently feeble'); the fall of
an Austrian government after riots involving a few broken skulls;
and a roundup on lynchings in South Carolina, Georgia, Florida, and
Alabama.

A dispatch from the New York *Times* described Sultan Abdul Ha-
mid's distress over Russian demands, and increasing activity among
those pashas who were known as the war party and who 'are understood to have an idea, where obtained none knows, that Germany is
about to enter upon a career of conquest in which it will be the function of the Turks to occupy the attention of Russia while William
over-runs France.'

The whole period, apart from the somewhat localized South African war and the Spanish-American conflict, was one of 'incidents'. In 1898 the *Citizen* would carry a heading PREPARATIONS FOR WAR on a story of Anglo-French quarrels at Fashoda on the Nile. In succeeding years Germany's exercise of what later came to be known as brinkmanship would be reported from spots like Tangier and Agadir, until at last the headlines of July and August 1914 marked the end of incidents and 'splendid little wars' and signalled a four-year descent into hell. All that was comfortably in the future as Wilson and Harry dug into the job of building up the *Citizen* from a total morning and evening circulation of 3,700.

A long partnership in thought and action was forming. Wilson had experience and a studious cast of mind. Harry, when he joined the *Citizen*, was in his twenty-third year, big and handsome (of the Southam brothers, at a full six feet, he was second only in height to the six-foot-four W.J.) and a notable athlete. After daytime work building up the paper's want ad section (he originated the slogan 'two papers are better than one'), fall evenings found him practising with the Rough Riders, a football team that commanded considerable civic pride. Reporting Southam activities while retaining a semblance of modesty was sometimes a problem. After a 27-3 victory over Osgoode Hall in 1898 the paper resorted to quoting the Toronto *Globe*: 'Southam is the pick of the halfbacks. His punting and running were away ahead of the standard.'

The young *Evening Citizen* put before its readers every aspect of Ottawa life, sometimes with a relish that would have been frowned on in later years when reporters and deskmen came to refer to the practices governing handling and play of questionable stories as the 'Sunday School Act'. When in the fall of 1898 Nellie Christopher charged Dr. Emile Lambert with rape, as the result of an event that seems to have occurred step by step from the fitting of an elastic stocking, the *Citizen* gave it full front-page treatment, including reduction of the charge to common assault, its elevation to indecent assault, and the doctor's final acquittal.

Though its new managers were also new to Ottawa, the *Citizen* pitched into editorial opinion on local events without hesitation. In the civic vote at the start of 1899 it favored Sunday streetcar service, which won out, but its pick for mayor finished last in a field of three.

Possibly as a result of full involvement in local affairs, the *Citizen* in its first year under Wilson Southam ran into a series of libel suits. At least two of them illustrate some peculiar hazards of newspaper publishing.

On the night of March 28, 1898, young Charlie Bishop, still in his first year as a *Citizen* reporter, met detective Robillard of the city police near the Russell Theatre and asked what was doing. Robillard told him a girl named Eva Gourdeau was under arrest for theft from a home on Daly Avenue. Bishop went along to the station, picked up the details, and wrote his story. A deskman devised from this account a bulletin for window-posting.

The ink was scarcely dry on the morning *Citizen* before lawyers for Major François Gourdeau, deputy minister of marine and fisheries, and former commandant of the Princess Louise Dragoon Guards, sued for libel. The sum asked was $5,000. The major had a daughter Eva. Furthermore, he told the court when the case came on in October, his family had been in Canada since 1624 and no other family in the country bore his name. The major implied that if the *Citizen*'s deskmen didn't know who the Gourdeaus were, they should; the names of his wife and daughter had often appeared in the paper's society column, a feature headed 'Ottawa's Vanity Fair' and carried under the byline 'Frills'.

Robert Shannon, acting for his old newspaper, read the story in court – it identified the arrested girl as a domestic from Janesville – and drew from the major the admission that no one reading it through would think it referred to his daughter. However, the window bulletin had lacked the detail that made it clear the girl couldn't have been the Eva of Ottawa society, and on that aspect of the matter the case went to the jury. Its verdict cleared the *Citizen*.

In the second instance the *Citizen* lost what might be referred to in prize-ring terms as a newspaper decision. The affair had its comic aspects as a piece of infighting marked by the acrimony then common in competitive newspaper towns.

In October of 1898 an itinerant clairvoyant calling herself Madame Mathieu blew in from Halifax and set up shop. The *Citizen* carried her ad. The *Journal* attacked her activities as illegal, said it had refused to print her advertising, and chided the *Citizen* for doing so. The *Citizen* came back with a charge that the *Journal* was persecuting the lady because she hadn't advertised in it. The *Journal* served the *Citizen* with notice of intention to sue.

At this stage the *Citizen* repeated its suggestion of the *Journal*'s motive for attack and published an affidavit from Madame Mathieu's agent in which he claimed he had been quoted a price on an ad by the *Journal* and had turned it down. It went into a bitter review of the newspaper situation in Ottawa as seen from its standpoint:

> Ever since the *Citizen* began business under its present management, the two local evening papers have conspired to injure the paper and its business. Their advertising agents combined in a campaign of

falsehood against us until the Citizen was driven to issue a circulation challenge to vindicate itself to our advertisers. Then both the Journal and Free Press hunted their holes and shut up like jack-knives. Then in conjunction they reduced their prices one-half in an attempt to freeze out the Citizen. . . .

If the Ottawa reading public had any special curiosity about the outcome of this small civil war, it wasn't satisfied for nearly six weeks. On December 12 the *Citizen* capitulated. It had now been made clear that the Mathieu affidavit had told only part of the story, 'the fact being that before seeing the advertising man at all, the clairvoyant's agent had made a visit to the Journal office and his advertising had been refused unconditionally by the business management.' The *Citizen* therefore withdrew its imputation as to the *Journal*'s motives though 'maintaining there was strong provocation. . . .'

In its opposition role on the federal front, the *Citizen* in common with all Conservative party papers had hard words for Laurier and his ministers. Criticism of Clifford Sifton, as minister of the interior, for administration in the Yukon under gold-rush conditions, was just then particularly fashionable. When the London *Times* sent a reporter named Flora Shaw to Dawson City, the *Citizen* played up her report that Klondikers had to pay through the nose to get claims recorded and even to get letters from the post office. (The Liberal Ottawa *Free Press* commented: 'Miss Shaw has evidently been primed up, and her Arctic goggles colored for her by some artistic hand.')

The position of Liberal free-trade journals since advent of the Laurier government – which had done little to lower tariffs – opened a natural field for editorial gibing. In Toronto the *Mail and Empire* suggested that the *Globe* 'indulges in the folly of talking free trade, preaches the doctrine of Cobden, and shows the advantages of a protective tariff.' Obviously 'it does not know where it is at and neither do the Liberal leaders.' The *Citizen* in an editorial entitled 'Organs Out of Tune' claimed the mix-up was even worse than that: 'The question now is not whether the government leaders know where they are at, but whether the government organs know where the government or each other are at and whether the government knows which is its organ and where its organ is at.'

But news as news was the glittering stock in trade. Mafeking and Ladysmith, the Canadian contingent on the veldt, and nearer home the day-to-day happenings from which, every now and then, would break the unexpected.

Biggest local story of the era broke on the windy afternoon of Thursday, April 26, 1900, when a frame building in Hull took fire.

The flames blew into west Ottawa, where they cut a swath nearly three miles long from the Chaudière district to Dow's Lake. The *Citizen* of April 27 lined HULL AND THE CAPITAL'S GREATEST CALAMITY over a deck that reported 'Fifteen Million Dollars Damage . . . The West End of the Capital and the Greater Part of Hull Wiped Completely Out of Existence.'

For days the paper carried the eight-column line HE GIVES TWICE WHO GIVES QUICKLY. Sir Charles Tupper with $100 headed the *Citizen*'s list of givers. Lily Langtry appeared at the Russell Theatre May 16 and turned over the night's receipts – $1,000. Reconstruction started quickly. Some of it was transitory; fire swept much of the same ground again in 1903.

The Morrison Touch

Men whose names would live in the weave of *Citizen* history are linked with the period of the Southam purchase. Charlie Bishop, later dean of the press gallery and finally a senator, came up from Bear River, Nova Scotia, and went to work for the Shannons in September of 1897. A year later D'Arcy Finn, a teen-ager from Ottawa South, joined staff as a copy-holder, the beginning of a lifetime with the paper. And in 1898 a remarkable editor-in-chief took over. Cameron had gone back to Hamilton after a few weeks. Hugh Clark came down from his weekly at Kincardine to write editorials, but soon went back and got into politics. The man who followed him was Edward Whipple Bancroft Morrison.

Morrison was thirty-one when he came to the *Citizen* after several years on the *Spectator*. His title at Ottawa was editor-in-chief: a position described by Finn, looking back many years later, as 'about 36 degrees higher' than that of a modern managing editor. He wrote editorials, ran the news staff, drew pen-and-ink illustrations, rode horses, and painted water-colors.

Morrison – somewhere he had picked up the nickname 'Dinky' – set up Sunday afternoon classes in news work. Bishop recalled them thus: 'He would proceed to give an instructive lecture about some phase or other of the business: how to get a story, how to phrase and arrange it. . . . Of all things, he would say, "Be sure of your facts – take no chances." He would talk about political writing and musical and dramatic criticism and the ethics of journalism and maybe the philosophy of life at large.' Morrison's phrasing was often original. To a young reporter who kept inserting the word 'we' in his copy, he said: 'There are only two people in this business entitled to use "we" – an editorial writer and a man with a tapeworm.'

A notable example of the articulate man of action, Morrison went off to the Boer War as a lieutenant in one of three batteries that sailed from Halifax January 21, 1900. A detachment of infantry sailed first – a disappointment to the gunners. But in December, 1899, word came of Buller's defeat at the Tugela with the loss of twelve guns. The Canadian force of three batteries from Kingston, Ottawa, and Quebec mobilized its volunteer militiamen and got ready for sea in less than three weeks. 'If an Imperial gunner knew that we took out six-horse teams of crazy horses which had never been together . . . and galloped in column of route, he would have fainted,' Morrison wrote. 'But the world has yet to know that the Canadian soldier can go anywhere and do anything.'

Utterly given to his job with the guns (he commanded the left section of D battery for seven of its ten months on active service), Morrison still felt the reporter's urge. From the first he sent back to the *Citizen* and the *Spectator* newsletters vivid with a sense of life. Writing from Ste. Flavie, Quebec, as the batteries headed east for embarkation, he noted that 'since crossing into this province, there has been nothing in the shape of an ovation or send-off for the troops by the people in the towns passed.' It was different in New Brunswick where crowds gathered at Campbellton, Bathurst, and Newcastle. Even at obscure crossings in the night the troops could hear the fading sounds of cheering as the train ran through.

Morrison had an eye for the fantastic and a fairly biting wit. Three days out of Halifax, he reported, D battery's seasick monkey escaped from its cage, invaded Major W.D.Hurdman's cabin, and tore the book of Ecclesiastes from a handsome Bible presented to the major by the Ottawa Ladies Auxiliary. From somewhere near the Cape Verde Islands he speculated on what principles citizens could have used in presenting reading matter to the batteries. He questioned that the average gunner would take much interest in *Titus, a Soldier of the Cross*, the *Boy's Own Paper* and the *Young Ladies' Magazine*, the *Traveller's Guide from Death to Life*, and the *Gospel Trumpet*. 'The ocean from here to Halifax', he reported, 'is strewn with literature.'

His letters to the *Citizen* and the *Spectator* continued throughout his service in the field, spiced frequently with touches of tart originality. One individual whose characteristics can be deduced became 'a statistical gentleman in the ammunition column with a plate-glass window in the upper left-hand corner of his face'.

One of his last and most graphic bits of correspondence, written in late November, raised an international furore. Boer irregulars were fighting a shoot-and-run war (which included wearing khaki and luring British troops into rifle range) and sheltering between-times as peaceful farmers in their houses, which they also used as ammunition laagers. After issuing a warning, Smith-Dorrien put on a house-burning expedition by British troops, covered by Canadian artillery, that Morrison described as 'like the old-time forays in the highlands of Scotland two centuries ago'. He wrote it with no pulled punches, but in the context of its cause. The Canadians 'had a little account to settle with our old friends the enemy up there and we would not have been quite satisfied if we had gone home without wiping it off the slate,' he wrote. Two Canadian dragoons had been killed by Boers dressed in khaki. 'It was a terrible thing to see,' he reported of this trek through the Steilpoort Valley, 'and I don't know that I want to see another trip of the sort, but we could not help approving the policy. . . .'

The *Citizen* ran the letter January 2, 1901. Five days later a chopped version appeared in the New York *Sun* under a lead that said 'The Canadian troops in South Africa, according to recent reports, are evidently not much in sympathy with the harsh measures now being enforced against the Boers. . . .' The background of reasons for the 'burning trek' had been removed. So had anything else that might serve to justify the expedition. In this form the Manchester *Guardian* and other anti-war papers in England published the story. It got into a stop-the-war pamphlet. An uproar at Westminster ensued.

The London *Chronicle* ran Morrison's original *Citizen* letter in parallel columns with the *Sun-Guardian* version to illustrate omissions and distortions. Morrison himself wrote an editorial, a summary of which was displayed in England, pin-pointing some of the alterations. Eventually the *Sun* and the *Guardian* ran the full letter.

Some months after his return, Morrison was decorated with the Distinguished Service Order for helping to save the guns at Lillefontein. Partisans of his said it should have been the Victoria Cross and would have been if he hadn't written the piece about burning the Boer houses. This is questionable; Smith-Dorrien's recommendations were made in November, 1900, well before the storm over the letter occurred. In four cases he recommended V.C.s. For Morrison he recommended 'some special mark of Her Majesty's favor'. In a letter to Wilson Southam from Pretoria, November 26, Morrison himself suggested this would possibly be the D.S.O.

In any event the incident didn't cure him of writing what he saw, even when on military duty. From England in 1902, as a member of the Coronation contingent, he had some caustic comment about British junior officers. As a lieutenant-colonel in France early in the First World War he wrote long descriptive letters to his wife – designed for publication in the *Citizen*. They didn't affect his career; he went on to command all Canadian artillery as a major-general and took a knighthood in stride.

Drumbeats and Ballots

'The whole result is to be deplored,' the *Citizen* regretfully noted, 'especially at the present situation of imperial affairs. . . .' The date was October 21, 1903. Currents of imperialism had picked up strength that year. The *Citizen* and other Conservative papers found inspiration in Joseph Chamberlain's vision of an empire linked by preferential trade. But now – the Lord Chief Justice of England had just handed the United States a great slice of land along the Alaska-Canada border. In Vancouver a theatre crowd howled down the national anthem.

The question turned on which line of mountains was meant in a vague old Russian-British treaty, a matter unsettled when the States bought Alaska from the Russians in 1867. Canada argued for a line confining the panhandle to a width of five or six miles. The Americans wanted a line along the heads of the inlets thirty miles back, thus cutting the Yukon off from direct access to the sea, and they got it. The final bitter pill was that they also got two of four islands, on which there seemed to be little doubt of Canadian ownership, in a channel at the lower end of the territory. Their position in relation to Port Simpson, then the proposed terminus of the Grand Trunk Pacific (later established at the new town of Prince Rupert) caused some alarm. 'To Canada the cession of Sitklan Island means as much as if the United States had secured a strategic position commanding the entrance to Vancouver Harbor and the straits of Juan de Fuca,' the *Citizen* said.

Of three British members of the tribunal, headed by Lord Alverstone, two were Canadians – Sir Louis Jetté and A.B.Aylesworth. They refused to sign the award. This made no difference in its effect but stood as a symbol of Canadian feeling. Lord Alverstone took an editorial drubbing. The *Citizen* accused him of nothing worse than stupidity in the face of American avarice:

> The whole incident as outlined in the dry phrases of red tapedom is eloquent of the unprincipled characteristics of one great branch of the

Anglo-Saxon race on the one side; the well-bred unsuspecting credulity of the other party to the case, and Canada in the pathetic role of the perfectly sophisticated unwilling but dutiful sacrifice.*

By next day Morrison was taking a realistic view and expressing it in his usual brisk way: 'Friends, Romans and country-men: there's no use grousing. What we need to do is to get busy and accumulate a Canadian population of about 25 millions.' As a footnote to the times it is recorded that out in Winnipeg Sanford Evans of the *Telegram* suggested that Canada should establish a department of external affairs.

By the summer of 1904 the boundary dispute, if not forgotten, was at least fading before the imminent prospect of a federal election. During this campaign, particularly in the matter of the Lord Dundonald affair, the *Citizen*'s trumpets blown by Morrison sounded loud and clear.

The hero of Ladysmith had been in command of the Canadian militia for the past two years. On June 4 at a military banquet in Montreal he charged political interference, citing as an example the fact that Minister of Agriculture Sydney Fisher (acting for the absent minister of militia, Sir Frederick Borden), had struck the name of Sweetsburg's mayor (a Conservative) from the proposed roster of officers for an Eastern Townships regiment. In the midst of the storm Dundonald was fired – by telegram to London, Ontario, where he had gone to inspect a militia camp. Conservatives claimed this haste in dismissal was planned to prevent an ovation at the camp. In any case, ovations there were; plus a kind of triumphal progress through Toronto, Ottawa, and Montreal. Verbal sabres clashed in Canadian and British Parliaments. (The young member for Oldham, Winston Churchill, thought Dundonald might have been right in protesting, but that his present position wasn't defensible.) Meantime Dundonald had been told by the British government to quit talking and come back home.

In the Canadian house Fisher said that far from acting politically in striking off the mayor's name, he had acted to *prevent* politics in

*In Vancouver, under the heading 'How Far Shall We Trust?' the *Province* commented: 'With a few more arbitration decisions, in which our territory is reft from us, and our trade injured, Great Britain will realize Canadian sentiment more quickly than is now anticipated, but the sentiment will then be very different from that which we have hitherto entertained, and which we have been desirous she should appreciate. . . . What a delightful role the parent plays, who to satisfy the greed of a grasping neighbor is able to give away a few acres or a few dollars which belong to his sons.'

the militia; the original list of officers looked like a Tory compact. Sir Wilfrid Laurier signally failed to smooth matters when he used the word 'foreigner' – quickly corrected to 'stranger' – in referring to Dundonald, thus setting off not only a new burst of true-blue imperialism but also a discussion of English-French semantics.

The *Citizen*'s hopes were high. As the November 3 election date approached it ran day after day at the top of the editorial page a cut of the flag with disembodied hands holding it aloft and a quote from the general: 'Keep both hands on the Union Jack.' Finally it organized a Dundonald Day for November 1. Although 20,000 to 40,000 (depending on which paper you read) had lined the streets for Dundonald's departure, July 26, the November 1 demonstration was not a great success. One reason may have been that, three days previously, Liberal candidate N.A.Belcourt at a public meeting read a document dated back in May and signed by Lord Dundonald. This unfortunate piece of paper recorded the general's view that Ottawa would have to wait for a new armory because other places were worse off.

The morning *Citizen* just then was using a curious front-page make-up on days when the news justified relegating want ads to inside pages. Three-column lines in heavy type balanced each other. On November 4 the paper's left-field headline reported CANADA ACCLAIMS LAURIER. Its righthand companion flared the ultimate disaster: OTTAWA HAS GONE LIBERAL. A couple of sober editorials analysed the result, but Morrison's refusal to take himself too seriously came through in two brief entries in the comment column: 'The Citizen rooster is unable to be out this morning. He is troubled with a frog in his throat.' And: 'Has anybody any smelling salts?'

The *Citizen* now occupied a home of its own. By the spring of 1903 the Southams had built circulation to over 10,000, more than half accounted for by the evening edition with its emphasis on local news. Apart from the daily, a twice-a-week edition, later named the *Central Canada Citizen*, reached 7,000 country homes.

After losing $5,500 in 1898 and $3,800 in 1900, the paper had gradually picked up until it showed a profit of $9,300 in 1903. Early in that year William borrowed $60,000 from a Hamilton estate and, as building progressed on a Sparks Street site a block west of the old leased premises, threw in $50,000 of his own. The *Citizen* met some construction costs as it went along. The building was completed in June of 1904. Sixty years later, after various extensions and remodellings, the *Citizen* still published from this site.

Early in the new year of 1905 the *Citizen*'s hopes for a Laurier de-bacle revived, sparked this time by signs of the government's internal breakup: 'Tarte, Blair, and now Sifton. . . .'

On the plains of the North-West, Alberta and Saskatchewan were coming into being as provinces. As usual in every aspect of national development back to Confederation and beyond, a note of furious acrimony ran through the march of events. SCHOOL FOR MINORITY TO SHARE PUBLIC MONEY was the *Citizen*'s line February 22 over its story of Laurier's bills to erect the new provinces. The white-plumed knight, with his minister of the interior away, had included a provi-sion for separate schools. The *Citizen*'s position (and that of other opposition papers and of the Toronto *Globe*, which deserted Laurier on this one) was that the forms of education were matters for the provinces to decide, not something to be imposed by the Dominion.

A full-scale upsurge of religious vituperation ensued, complete with related side-issues, including the presence in Ottawa of a new papal delegate, Donatus Sbarretti. Msgr. Sbarretti was suspected of trying to influence the federal government to restrict Manitoba to its postage-stamp dimensions unless an expanded province would pro-vide for separate schools. Over in Hamilton the *Spectator* called the Prime Minister 'a puppet in the hands of this foreign dignitary who makes and unmakes provinces as he pleases'.

On March 1 Clifford Sifton, whose immigrants in sheepskin coats populated large areas of the new provinces, resigned his cabinet post in protest. But when, later in the month, Laurier introduced a com-promise amendment to the school provisions ('a mere remodelling of the verbiage', the *Citizen* said) Sifton found it satisfactory and drew the sorrowful editorial assessment: 'Another Aureole Faded'. The *Citizen* would have to wait six years for a Sifton move that would help defeat Laurier – ironically at a time when its own views were almost at the point of swinging away from the Conservative party line.

The Idealists

The first ten years of the new century saw the development of ideas in the Ottawa Southams that would determine their approach to exis-tence as long as they lived, and through this, indirectly, the shape and form and voice of their newspaper. One of these was a conviction of the rightness of Christian Science.

The light came first to Harry and through him reached the mind of Wilson.

A young friend, Richard Fudger, wakened Harry's interest in the teachings of Mary Baker Eddy. Long afterward an incident of the time remained in the memory of Harry's sister Ethel. In the winter of 1907 she and Harry visited California and, on at least one occasion, attended a Christian Science church with Dick Fudger and his wife. After the service, men and women of the congregation came up and spoke to them in a friendly way. It was, apparently, a new experience for Harry. Along with the emotional and intellectual appeal of the faith itself, he found in Christian Science a warmth he had missed in the Anglican church.

The habit of joint study, when one of the brothers found himself concerned with a new idea or faced with a business decision, was already formed. In these years Wilson usually acted as spokesman for the *Citizen* in discussions with his father at Hamilton or Fred in Montreal. His letters almost invariably expressed a shared view: 'Harry and I think . . .'. Their closeness grew in a personal as well as a business way under the circumstances of their lives in Ottawa. In 1899 Wilson had married Henrietta Cargill, daughter of the Conservative member of Parliament for South Bruce. By 1909 there were four children – Margaret, Bill, Jean, and John. Harry lived with the family.

It is apparent that the brothers' new sense of personal direction – whether it resulted from their devotion to Christian Science or from a developing quality of mind of which this was a manifestation – had much to do with the conception of the responsibilities of publishing that now moved them. A strong sense of conscience broke through in a discussion by letter that Harry carried on with W.J. in the summer of 1907:

> The newspaper is able to do a lot of good, and it is doing some good even without trying. All newspapers do a tremendous amount of harm – some of them maliciously and some of them through ignorance. I think the conscientious publisher will try to minimize the harm his paper does, and endeavor to offset what harm he must do by doing the maximum good. . . . I do not wish to be interpreted as meaning that the Citizen is less blameworthy than the Spectator in this regard, but I do claim that the Citizen is trying to be less blameworthy than it used to be. I may be wrong, but I do not think the Spectator, even if they thought about it, could make a similar claim.

Already Wilson and Harry had put on record in a memo to news editor and staff the kind of paper they wanted. Dated May 16, 1907, it read:

> A reputation for *reliability* and *fairness* in the news columns of the Citizen is the management's ideal which every member of the staff

should keep consistently before him. We wish to have people think and say: 'If you see it in the Citizen it's quite likely to be so.' A newspaper of such a character would have a tremendous influence in its constituency and its material prosperity would be greatly enhanced. Of equal importance is it that the Citizen should have a reputation for printing, if not more, at least as much news as its contemporaries. Its reports should be complete and fair and free alike from bias on account of the reporter's predilections and the Citizen's editorial opinions. Each heading should reflect the sense of the article with *absolute fairness*, especially so when controversial matters are concerned. The correctness of every item should be verified when at all possible. The 'other side' of every story should *invariably* be given. Unconfirmed rumors when of sufficient importance to print should be designated as such. Accuracy should not be sacrificed for effect, and exaggeration of facts should always be shunned. Padding is an unnecessary and expensive practice and should be avoided in news items. A manifestation of enterprise in the development and exploitation of news is commendable and essential, but sensationalism or 'unsavory' news unfit for home reading should be eschewed. The morbid and unattractive should be kept down while the uplifting and helpful should be paraded.

An accompanying memo to out-of-town correspondents added this note of guidance:

> Although politically the Citizen supports the policy of the Conservative party, correspondents should not allow this to interfere with their giving the Citizen impartial copy dealing with political matters. The Citizen is not the organ of any political party or of any politician; but is striving to be a high class, fair and reliable *newspaper*.

The job of putting the Southams' journalistic ideas into effect went to a mixed but competent crew led by Morrison. The *Citizen's* news and editorial staff had grown to twenty, including several men whose names would live in the annals of the craft. Bill Noakes, who would build a long career in Brandon, was news editor. The veteran Bob MacLeod reported from Parliament Hill. Tommy Gorman, the later entrepreneur of hockey and horses, bossed the sports page. D'Arcy Finn ran the night desk. Charlie Bishop handled city hall, Fred Davy edited the twice-a-week edition, and out on the beats were Dr. Peter Mellon, the non-practising physician whose services ranged from sports reporting to editorial writing, and R.K. (Andy) Carnegie, later press gallery chief for The Canadian Press.

In their notes on treatment of unsavory and morbid news – the beginnings of the 'Sunday School Act' – Harry and Wilson put into practice their personal convictions. This went considerably further than care in handling news. Both became teetotallers; the *Citizen* began to campaign against the liquor traffic. Both viewed with distaste some aspects of patent medicine advertising. As early as 1906 the *Citizen* had declined to sell further space to something called Pure Virgin Oil of Pine because wording of the proffered ad made it appear that the paper, rather than the medicine company, asserted its curative powers.

The personal testimonial technique (brought to the ultra in refinement by men of distinction forty years later) sold millions of pills and rivers of liquid. In the year after the Southams bought the *Citizen*, Emile Zola (believed to be hiding in the Austrian Tyrol) was in the news in connection with the Dreyfus case. He also appeared in an ad for Vin Mariani (the wine that makes the weak strong). So did Sarah Bernhardt and Victorien Sardou. In 1907, for another product of which the effects can be deduced, this type of salesmanship reached a height that has never been surpassed:

SENATOR COSTIGAN
SAVED FROM DEATH

Practically everyone in Canada has heard of Hon. John Costigan – statesman, orator, M.P., cabinet minister, and now senator, from New Brunswick. For over 30 years this prominent man was a martyr to Chronic Constipation. Leading physicians of London, Paris, New York, and Ottawa treated him in vain. It remained for a wonderful Canadian discovery to cure him – and in only three months, too. . . .

Apart from what they regarded as the repellent and deceptive quality of some medicine advertising, the Southams also saw it as based on fear – written to scare people into swallowing the stuff. On January 1, 1909, the *Citizen* appeared without patent medicine and liquor ads, a policy that was to last for more than forty years. Never a newspaper to hide its virtues, it reported in March 1911 that in the last thirty months it had refused more than $10,000 worth of objectionable linage.

By this time Wilson and Harry had begun a personal program that broadened their interests as citizens of Ottawa. They built houses. Wilson outlined the plan in a letter to his father early in November of 1909. 'Certain circumstances have happened of late that make Harry think he should have a home of his own,' he wrote. 'The most desirable location for such a home in the Ottawa district is adjoining Rockcliffe Park. He did not care, however, to go so far away from his friends unless we would join him, and build alongside him.' Chief among the 'certain circumstances' was Harry's engagement to twenty-one-year-old Lilias Ahearn, daughter of Thomas Ahearn, Ottawa street-railway owner. They were married December 1.

The brothers bought land in Rockcliffe and built their houses side by side – Wilson's Lindenelm and Harry's Casa Loma. The closeness of thought remained; a shared receptiveness to new ideas, perhaps a kind of restless searching for them. From now on the *Citizen* would back unorthodox causes when they felt like it.

Arguments within the wider circle of the whole Southam family over the *Citizen*'s course would naturally develop. To these Harry and Wilson had a double-edged answer. They felt they were right. And apart from that, circulation sprouted in the reader-interest aroused by departure from the traditional and the staid; it was good business.

Toward Independence

In the spring of 1908 Harry Southam spent six weeks in England and while there fell in with the single-tax doctrine of Henry George. After he and Wilson studied the subject the *Citizen* embarked on a crusade for tax reform that was to last through the lifetime of the brothers.

A modification of the single-tax idea, in the form of taxing land values to the limit and exempting improvements partly or wholly, had already been adopted by local governments in New Zealand and some parts of Australia and was being introduced in the Canadian West. Protagonists saw it as an encouragement to builders and a check on land speculation.

Harry and Wilson talked up tax reform with the family, wrote editorials, and pressed Premier Whitney of Ontario for an amendment to the Assessment Act to allow application by municipalities of the site-value system. Many Ontario municipalities petitioned for it. Whitney could see no real demand for such a change, but agreed that A.E.Fripp, Conservative member for West Ottawa, should introduce a private bill to draw discussion. Ontario enthusiasts set up a Tax Reform and Direct Legislation League and elected Wilson Southam president. Many newspapers supported the movement, including – for a while – the Ottawa *Journal*. In 1911 even the *Spectator* came a certain distance into the fold, suggesting that Whitney allow Ontario municipalities the same privilege as those in the West; if it proved valueless no one would be hurt.

Meantime the *Citizen* fought for Robert Borden through the 1911 federal election campaign. Wilson and Harry had no doubts about Borden, but as free traders they showed some reluctance to dive into the stream of opposition to reciprocity. When Finance Minister W.S. Fielding explained the proposed treaty to the Commons late in January the *Citizen* noted that 'the present developments look favorable for the future relations of the two countries.' As discussion developed it disagreed with those who saw reciprocity as a menace to the imperial tie.

When in mid-February Champ Clark made his remark about the American flag flying clear to the North Pole, the *Citizen*'s heading was CLARK'S REMARK SEMI-JOCULAR, an attitude backed up by wire stories from Washington. Laurier also gave it light treatment when Sam Hughes raised it as evidence of a drive for annexation. 'If some nefarious intention of the kind . . . should be put into action', he would call on Hughes as a gallant soldier to dispose of it. Sam said he'd be glad to.

However, as it became obvious through that spring and summer that reciprocity was a party issue, the *Citizen* began to revise its view. By July 27 it was arguing that the scheme was, after all, an experiment: 'No one knows how it will turn out. . . . What will result should reciprocity ensue between two nations each owning half a continent can only be decided by actual test.' Therefore, the real question was not whether it would be good or bad, but whether Canada was prepared to take a chance. The prudent position for the opposition was not to try to prove the unprovable, but to warn the Canadian people that this was a gamble and insist that they have the opportunity to say whether or not they would accept the risk.

Two days later it warned the Conservatives not to let the Liberals narrow the issues down to this one thing. What about the naval question? ('Though three years have gone by, Canada has nothing to show for even its tinpot navy but His Majesty's Canadian tinpot Niobe.') There were plenty of other alternatives: dredging scandals, departmental corruption, extravagance, and graft. Were these to be sidetracked, the opposition to be enticed into the field to 'tilt with the white-plumed knight to save our sweet Lady of the Snows from the ogre, reciprocity'? There was no necessity for any action on reciprocity except insistence that it be referred to the country – 'Reciprocity is a mere matter of referendum.'

That afternoon Laurier dissolved the House, and regardless of anything the *Citizen* could think or say, reciprocity was the issue on which he would stand or fall.

Bobby Leach went over Niagara Falls in a barrel and emerged alive. J.A.D.McCurdy barnstormed Ontario in a flimsy affair that flew. In England, reform of the House of Lords was under way. (The *Citizen* believed that 'this advance in liberty, the greatest since the 18th century, is the work not so much of the Liberal party, or even of the radicals of Great Britain, as of the Henry George men.') And on Saturday night, July 29, the night of Parliament's dissolution, H.M.C.S. *Niobe* hit a shoal off Cape Sable Island and holed her star-board engine-room. She had been at Yarmouth as an old home week attraction, left harbor for sea-room when a sou'west gale blew up, and got lost in the fog – leading inevitably to the crack that the Can-adian navy had run aground while attending a farmers' picnic.

But the hard developing headline news that summer was reciproc-ity, with Sifton and scores of other Liberals peeling off from their party. Like it or not, the *Citizen* had to deal with it. By August 1 it was chiding Laurier (who said he wanted the treaty in effect quickly so the fall crops would get the benefit) for undue haste, for running a get-rich-quick scheme. By mid-August it saw signs in the States of an impending war between big business and an 'artificially inflamed public opinion that is determined to deal as relentlessly with the trusts as the trusts have dealt with the people'. Was this the time for Canada to go into partnership with a country subject to depressions and on the brink of conflict? Late that month it produced figures to show that farmers in Pennsylvania and New York weren't doing so well and that Boston's consumers were paying more than Ottawa's. On September 20, the day before election, the *Citizen* declared: 'The safe course is to vote against it. There is no hurry, no rush. Therefore the proper and prudent course is to turn down the reciprocity of the United States, if only until we know more about it.'

On the tax-reform question Whitney remained unconvinced. During the 1913 session of the legislature he grew peevish with the publish-ers of the *Citizen*. It was a bit cool, he suggested, for men who 'worked for Sir Wilfrid Laurier in the fight for reciprocity until all chance of victory had vanished, and who do not believe in anything that other people believe in – like vaccination for instance – to undertake to tell the government of the province along what lines they shall shape their course.'

The remark widened a developing breach. On February 26, in 'A Reply to Sir James', the *Citizen* termed absurd the inference that 'no newspaper whose views do not coincide with the premier's is quali-fied or justified in advising the provincial government.' It added that the Premier had mis-stated the paper's stand on reciprocity and on vaccination. The *Citizen* and other independent Conservative pa-pers, it said, had supported reciprocity at first because they conceived it to be in the interest of consumers. The *Citizen* had, however, done its utmost to secure the election of Borden and his Conservatives. But this duty to the federal party didn't obligate the paper to a similar attitude toward the Whitney government:

> In the opinion of the Citizen it is more important – especially now that the Conservative party under Premier Borden is in power at Ottawa – that Ontario municipalities be granted local option in local taxation, than that the Conservative party under Sir James Whitney be continued in office. This statement is made in the full belief that Sir James Whitney is the best premier Ontario has ever had.

It would be impossible for the paper, if he continued to oppose tax reform, to support Whitney in the next election. Reorganization of the opposition under capable, honorable, and aggressive leadership 'would make the Citizen's anticipated action less difficult.'

As for vaccination the *Citizen* believed in individual liberty of choice in that 'and indeed all medical treatment'.

The drive for tax reform was one aspect of an attitude that was growing in the minds of Wilson and Harry, with some support from Fred. Back in 1909 he had written: 'While it is desirable that we should retain our connection with the Conservative party, the more independent you are and the further you are ahead of that party in advocating certain policies for it, the more I will be personally pleased.'

On the 1911 day of triumph for Conservatism, William wired Wilson congratulations on 'a great day for Ottawa and the Citizen'. Since then the *Citizen* had been expressing views that sometimes differed from those of the party and the *Spectator*. So much so that in the fall of 1912 William cut off his home subscription, an act that incidentally caused Fred to comment:

> I understand you have landed a solar plexus blow on your Ottawa representatives. This is really too bad. In my humble opinion it was the only high-class editorial sheet being delivered at 163 Jackson Street West. Your education is going to suffer as a result, and as for poor mother, it is simply a shame that she should have to sneak down to the Spectator office or up to Gordon's house to read her favorite newspaper. You must have been thinking of our bank overdraft or some other depressing circumstance.

Whatever William may have thought and sometimes said, it is apparent that he never *ordered* a line of policy for Wilson and Harry. It is interesting to speculate on what might have happened had the Southam-owned *Citizen* been under management other than that of two Southam brothers when it began to deviate from orthodox ways.

In any event the move towards new positions on public affairs was under way, accelerated just at this point by changes in the paper's editorial force. Morrison, senior to the Southams in years and experience and a natural conservative, joined the permanent army. Charles Casson, a Unitarian minister, moved into the top editorial spot. And in February of 1913 the *Citizen* hired Charles Arthur Bowman, a young Englishman trained as an engineer, who had been fired from the Department of Railways and Canals, largely it appears for having criticized waste and patronage in a prize-winning draft plan to reorganize the government's technical services.

In Bowman, a Northumbrian brought up in Gladstonian Liberalism and in personal sympathy with British labor movements, the Southams found a man equipped by skill and temperament to make the swing away from orthodox politics. It was not long before the *Citizen* was off government patronage lists – nothing new, since it had never been on them during the Laurier regime – with Bowman firing his missiles of dissent at just about any target he chose.

However, while it may be that Wilson and Harry looked ahead to something beyond Fred's idea of independence with party links, for the time being at least they seemed content to ravel rather than cut. In January of 1914 Wilson tried to explain things to Borden. The occasion was a rumor that federal Conservatives were so irked at the *Citizen* that they planned a new morning paper in Ottawa backed by the government. The Montreal *Herald,* Hamilton *Herald,* and Ottawa *Journal* published the tale. Wilson thereupon wrote Borden:

> In view of the whole-hearted support that we are giving your administration in the Edmonton Journal, Calgary Herald and Hamilton Spectator ... and in view of the further fact that the Citizen has not neglected to reiterate that it has no use for the hypocritical Liberal party, we have given no credence hitherto to these reports; but as they have been more pronounced of late we thought we were justified in asking you if there was any truth in them.

The letter went on to set out the *Citizen*'s position. It was unable to be in entire accord with all administration policies, but had been in agreement 90 per cent of the time. The Southams felt that 'the loyal support the Citizen gave the Conservative party from 1896 to 1911 entitles us to a very considerable freedom from party trammels' before party leaders would be justified in taking exception to its attitude. For months the *Citizen* had not received government advertising and was satisfied to do without it 'if the price is to be the reducing of the Citizen to the ranks of the inane party organ that seems to be the desire, if reports are true, of some of your colleagues.' But it was rubbing it in a bit strong for them to foster the launching of another paper in a field like Ottawa.

Borden replied that the rumor hadn't reached his ears. Nothing came of it. Wilson reported to his father that he proposed to tell Borden 'just what we are trying to make of the Citizen, that it is not antagonistic to his administration but on the contrary ... the semi-independence of the Citizen is one of the best safeguards that his administration has.'

Whatever their position federally, the Ottawa Southams by the spring of 1914 had decided that they couldn't back Whitney in the province. The question now was whether to get into the fight for the Liberals under Newton Wesley Rowell, who had endorsed tax reform and undertaken other crusades that appealed to Wilson and Harry – including a drive to 'Abolish the Bar'. Or just to remain aloof. They set out their position in a letter dated June 15 to Stewart McClenaghan, president of the provincial Liberal-Conservative Association, in which they reviewed the history of their tax-reform efforts. They had reached the conclusion that as Rowell stood for several progressive measures advocated by the *Citizen*, including local option in taxation, 'we have practically no option but to support him and his campaign, unless the government can give us a definite public assurance that the Fripp Bill will be passed through the legislature at the next session even though it be restricted to cities of 100,000 or over.'

Even so, they moved only after consulting the family.

As you know [Wilson wrote his father] we believe the taxation of land values is the most important question bearing on the prosperity of the people of this province. . . . With this belief, and the family's permission, we would like to give Rowell a straight support in this campaign, provided the Whitney government do not accede to the reasonable suggestion we have made. . . . This request will come, no doubt, as a shock to you and the rest of the family, but Harry and I have been getting accustomed to it for the last 10 days as we saw how things were shaping. Even with your permission we may not decide to support Rowell very strongly, but we want to acquaint you and the family with the lines we have been thinking on, and would be glad to have the various members write us their opinion as fully and frankly as they care to.

The Southams in Hamilton sent their comments by wire. 'Stick to your principles but don't go back on the party,' said the mother of the family. 'Of the two they are the best.' The senior William's telegram was succinct and caustic: 'Go as far as you like. Your support is all that is needed to keep the other party out of power for the next 10 years.' W.J. added a characteristic note of mockery: 'The old guard here although deeply hurt have been sympathetic with you in

Citizen's forced revolt from the grand old party because of your convictions. Today however we have been thrown into a panic and stampeded by a rumor that Citizen is about to advocate the adoption of Mohammedanism to be taught in the schools as the universal religion. How about it?'

From Montreal, Fred wrote: 'I do not see any particular reason why the Spectator should not pursue its present policy and you one that is directly opposed to it. As a matter of fact the Spectator expresses the views of Father while the Citizen expresses yours and Harry's. . . .'

News of the letter to McClenaghan leaked out, inevitably. The *Journal* asked – and answered – a question:

> Will it be believed that the Citizen . . . which stigmatizes the Whitney policy as advocacy of 'the barroom' and 'the rum traffic', has within a week made a formal proposition to the Conservative leaders to support the Whitney policy – or, in its own phrases, to support the barroom and the rum traffic – provided the Conservative leaders would promise to take up the Single Tax? Such is the case.

To which the *Citizen* replied that it had promised no such thing. It had stated that lacking public assurance of local option in taxation it would support Rowell. Which it did. The *Citizen* for Tuesday, June 23, carried a variety of news: stories on the investigation into the *Empress of Ireland*'s sinking, the Prince of Wales's twenty-first birthday, amendments to the Home Rule bill, unseating of the Ottawa board of control, a mock battle at Petawawa. On page two it told the story of its own political switch.

Under a boxed heading THE CITIZEN AND TAX REFORM it carried the text of the letter to McClenaghan, along with the information that McClenaghan had sent it to Whitney, 'who replied that the government was not in favor of tax reform, nor is it in favor of local option in taxation.' Under the circumstances 'its readers will understand why the Citizen prefers to place principles before party, just as so many hitherto Conservatives are placing principles before party on the great moral issue of Abolish the Bar – and supports Mr. Rowell in this election.'

The subsidiary engagement with its rival continued. Two days later it quoted from a 1913 *Journal* editorial: 'If Sir James Whitney is going to maintain his present attitude against tax reform, we think that the province can afford to retire Sir James Whitney from power.' Harry and Wilson were both cricketers, but the *Citizen* added this footnote: 'The foregoing is from an Ottawa Journal editorial of January 9, 1913. Subsequently the Journal leased four floors of its new building to the Federal Conservative Government.'

Liberal abolish-the-bar and tax-reform candidates won the two Ottawa seats from Conservatives in the June 29 election. But Whitney carried the province.

The decision to back Rowell was the *Citizen*'s most startling move of the period, but there were battles also on other fields. The liquor traffic might share the spotlight with tax reform in the province; in Ottawa itself the question dividing the ratepayers was not rum but water.

In 1911 typhoid cast suspicion on the Ottawa River. On the ground that no one yet knew enough about the source of pollution, the *Citizen* opposed a scheme to pipe from McGregor Lake in the Gatineau hills, which was defeated in a by-law vote. Typhoid broke out again in 1912 and was traced to breaks in the intake pipe – which leaked sewage into the drinking water, a fact dramatically disclosed by an engineer named Noulan Cauchon, who traversed the pipe with two companions stretched on hand-wagons.

The city and its council split over two schemes – to pipe water from Thirty-one Mile Lake, a high-cost proposal (favored by the *Journal*) or to set up a rapid sand-filtration plant (backed by the *Citizen*). The paper carried stories from scores of centres – from Fredericton to Little Rock – on the virtues of filtration. Looking back on this jousting later, D'Arcy Finn remarked that 'Wilson Southam was the protagonist of filtered water on our paper, and for those two or three years the business end was run by Harry and W.M. and I did nothing else but run the propaganda end of the paper on filtered water.' After a two-year tangle of votes, injunctions, and vituperation, filtration won a ratepayers' vote on January 5, 1914 – and was disapproved by the provincial Board of Health. War pushed the question into the background. For fifteen years heavy chlorination met the health problem. Then in the late 1920s, without controversy, filtration plans were revived. When the Lemieux Island plant opened April 30, 1932, the *Citizen* celebrated with a special edition.

Early years of the First World War set up a variety of targets for the *Citizen*'s barbed darts.

The muddle over shell manufacture, until the formation in 1916 of the Imperial Munitions Board, was a favorite theme. The *Citizen* urged that the government's own machine-shops be mobilized to make shells at cost. It missed few chances to pepper profiteers. At one point it printed figures showing contributions of munitions firms to the Patriotic Fund (a wartime charity) and compared them with the investments of these same firms in war loans. The editorial was headed 'The Superpatriots'. 'In the eyes of the munition-makers patriotism is a matter of 5 per cent and plenty of kudos,' the paper said .'Why not call the subscriptions of the profiteers to the next loan the Superpatriotic Fund?'

But the paper's best-remembered wartime ploy was not an editorial but a news beat – though one that undoubtedly came to it because of the climate of its editorial page. On a May evening in 1916 Frank Carvell, New Brunswick Liberal, spotted Bowman in the press gallery and called him to his office. What he had to show him was a letter from Lieutenant-General E.A.H.Alderson, commanding Canadians at the front, about the Ross rifle.

No issue of the time raised greater heat than the Ross, the history of which went back to 1902 and a contract made by the Liberal government of that time. The Canadian-made rifle had its enthusiasts and critics in both political camps. As early as 1908 the Hamilton *Spectator* commented: 'It requires no great effort of imagination to picture what would happen if, in the event of sudden hostilities, the Canadian soldiers were placed in the field equipped with the rifle. There would be a slaughter of the innocents.' But Sam Hughes, the Lindsay rifleman who organized the launching of Canada's first big adventure in full-scale war, was a passionate backer of the Ross. By 1915 Canadians were in the field with the rifle. Stories drifted back from the front of its poor performance in trench warfare, of hands torn by jammed bolts, of men throwing it away and arming themselves with Lee-Enfields left by British dead. Tests continued, reports were made and pigeon-holed. Eventually the 1st Division got Lee-Enfields. The 2nd, 3rd, and 4th remained equipped with the Ross.

Against this background Carvell handed Bowman the Alderson letter. The name of the person to whom it was addressed had been clipped off. In part, it read:

> I may say that very soon after we got out here with the 1st Division I found that the men were picking up the Lee-Enfields whenever they could and throwing away the Rosses. I issued an order that this was not to be allowed, and prior to the 2nd Battle of Ypres that order was carried out. The experience of the battle showed that the Ross jammed so badly that I was obliged to let this order die a natural death. When the division was re-armed with the Lee-Enfield the men cheered loudly on hearing the news and it was found that there were already more than 3,000 of the rifles in the division.

It went on to report on a test that showed the Lee-Enfield's superiority in rapid fire with various kinds of ammunition.

The *Citizen* ran the story May 16 with a rather diffident lead to what was, under the circumstances, an explosive piece of news: 'In view of the fact that the War Office report on the Ross Rifle . . . has never been made public, a great deal of interest attaches to a letter from General Alderson, commander-in-chief of the Canadian forces at the front, in reply to a communication from Ottawa on the subject. . . .'

Considerable steam broke loose in the House next day. The old Liberal warrior Frank Oliver remarked that he couldn't conceive such a report would be allowed to stand for an hour without being contradicted 'if it could be contradicted'. Members wanted to know who wrote it, to whom, and why. There were suggestions that it gave information to the enemy and thus breached censorship. Conservative wheelhorse Robert Rogers, who had suffered from some of Bowman's thrusts in the past, remarked that he wasn't surprised that 'that paper would be guilty of publishing this letter, or anything else by which they could hope to create excitement.' He suggested that 'the individual who would be guilty of publishing this letter in the form in which it is published – the proper place for him would be in the tower of this building.' He had apparently forgotten that since the fire of February 2 that destroyed the Parliament buildings the House had been meeting in the Victoria Museum. Reminded by Liberal William Pugsley that no tower now existed, Rogers promised to provide one if the miscreant could be found.

Bowman had the impression that the letter had been addressed to the Governor-General, the Duke of Connaught. He has recorded that Lord Richard Neville, the Duke's military secretary, came to the *Citizen* and confirmed its substance. Actually the extracts published by the *Citizen* are word-for-word from a letter written by Alderson in February to Major-General W.G.Gwatkin, British-born chief of the Canadian general staff at Ottawa, in response to a query from Gwatkin. The full text of this letter, which Hughes had seen soon after its arrival, eventually appeared in 1938 in Colonel A.F. Duguid's unfinished history of the Canadian forces. Alderson assured Gwatkin that he was stating facts and nothing else and that, therefore, he did not mind to whom Gwatkin might show it. Just how it reached the Governor-General's office – whether as a copy of the letter to Gwatkin or as a separate communication using exactly the same words – remains obscure.

Publication of the letter coincided with behind-the-scenes moves apparently already under way that would eventually end the history of the Ross as a combat weapon. The record seems to indicate that the published story and the reaction to it may well have speeded the process. During House discussion May 17 on the *Citizen*'s action, Sir Robert Borden said that 'about three days ago' a message had gone to the Commander-in-Chief (Haig) asking for new tests and leaving all questions having to do with the rifle to his judgment. The message he referred to was a cable addressed to Sir Max Aitken, then Canadian government representative at the front. It read:

> Have consulted with General Hughes and we are prepared to leave matter to judgment of Commander-in-Chief after he has had all necessary tests of both rifles under such conditions as are experienced at front. Men making tests should be of like experience. Please impress on Commander-in-Chief the unfortunate results of any action or criticism by British officers in Canadian service which might unnecessarily displace confidence in our rifle. It is only arm we are equipped to produce in Canada at present and we believe it effective if properly used. Minister informs me that reports just received of recent official tests in England thoroughly demonstrate efficiency of our rifle.

This message went on May 15, the day before the *Citizen*'s Alderson story appeared. Four days later Borden followed up by sending copies of the May 17 debate to Aitken and Sir George Perley, acting high commissioner. A further message to Aitken June 5 noted: 'It is imperatively necessary that our men shall be armed with an efficient weapon and that they shall have confidence in it. For this reason we suggested tests under direction Commander-in-Chief as results so obtained if satisfactory would naturally maintain or restore confidence; on the other hand if unsatisfactory then rearming would necessarily follow.' Finally on June 8 in answer to messages from Aitken and Perley, Borden cabled: 'We leave question of rearming our troops entirely to judgment of War Office. If they decide that no further tests are necessary or advisable we are prepared to accept and support their judgment.'

In the final event Haig recommended that Lee-Enfields be issued to all Canadian divisions and this was done. Alderson's removal from field command at about this time, incidentally, was generally attributed to Hughes's resentment over his position on the Ross, but was later shown to have resulted from personality clashes within the corps. By mid-November Hughes himself was out of office having finally exhausted even Borden's remarkable patience.

The Pooled Field

In a letter to his father early in 1913 Wilson Southam reported the previous year as the best in the history of the *Citizen*. He added that

EXTRA The Citizen EXTRA

R NO. 130   OTTAWA CANADA, MONDAY, NOVEMBER 11, 1918   PRICE TWO CENT

PEACE!

'ORLD WAR ENDS; ARMISTICE SIGNED; KAISER IS OUT; GERMAN REVOLUTION

MISTICE SIGNED AT MIDNIGHT TAKES EFFECT 6 A.M. TODAY; NEWS IS OFFICIAL

**OUS ANNOUNCEMENT FLASHED
M WASHINGTON AT THREE A.M.
S MORNING; TERMS KNOWN LATER**

(Associated Press Despatch.)

ASHINGTON, Nov. 11.—The world
ill end this morning at 6 o'clock,
ington time, 11 o'clock Paris time.
rmistice was signed by the German
sentatives at midnight.

is announcement was made at the
Department at 3 this morning.
ms not issued till 8 o'clock today.

ASHINGTON, Nov. 11.—Armistice
have been signed by Germany, the
department announced at 2.45
k this morning.

department's announcement
said: "the armistice has been

is announcement was made verb-
y an official of the state depart-
n this form:

e armistice has been signed. It
igned at five o'clock a.m., Paris
d hostilities will cease at eleven
k this morning, Paris time.

ABLE TERMS OF THE ARMISTICE

terms of the armistice, it was announced, will not be
de until later. Military men here, however, regard it as
at they include:

diate retirement of the German military forces from
Belgium and Alsace-Lorraine.

ning and demobilization of the German armies.

pation by the Allied and American forces of such strat-
n Germany as will make impossible a renewal of war.

ery of part of the German high seas fleet and a certain
f submarines to the Allied and American naval forces.

masent of all other German warships under supervision
French mine, which will guard them.

ssion of the principal German naval bases by sea forces
torious nations.

er of Allied and American soldiers, sailors and civilians
ners in Germany without such reciprocal action by the
governments.

KELY ORDERED TO SIGN BY WIRELESS

was no information as to the circumstances under which
tice was signed, but since the German courier did not
an military headquarters until ten o'clock yesterday
French time, it was generally assumed here that the
rmys within the French lines had been instructed by

GREAT ARMY CHIEFS WHO DOWNED THE HUN!

Never will men cease to sing the praise of this matchless five: Foch, the supreme military genius from the ancient Basque tribe of the French Pyrenees, and his four generals, who saw to it at the death of kaiserism—Pershing (top, left) of the United States, Petain (top, right) of France, Diaz (bottom, left) of Italy and Haig (bottom, right) of Great Britain.

**Returning Austrian
Troops Are Killed.**

(Associated Press Despatch.)
INNSBRUCK, Austria, Mon-
day, Nov. 9, via Basel, Nov.
10.—Austrian troops have
occupied the railroad stations
here.

Austrian troops are returning from the former front in
swarms, clinging to the cars
in wherever they can get a foot.
Many have been crushed or
decapitated by the cross-pass-
ing through tunnels. Besides
to the number of 171 were
picked up on a single day on
the railroad tracks near Innsbruck.

Make Germans Pay.

LONDON, Nov. 10.—A party of American headquarters and unquestionably
several hours were necessary for the
examination of the terms and the decision. It is regarded as possible, however,
that the decision may have been made at
Berlin and instructions transmitted from
there by the German government.

PRESIDENT WILSON GOT THE NEWS FIRST.

Germany had been given until eleven o'clock this morning,
French time six o'clock Washington time, to accept. So instill
we will and at the hour set by Marshal Foch for a decision by
Germany for peace or for continuation of the war.

The momentous news that the armistice had been signed was
telephoned to the White House by representatives of the President
a few minutes before it was given to the newspaper correspondents.

**PUNISH EX-KAISER
IF LAW ALLOWS**

(Associated Press Despatch.)
MILWAUKEE, Wis., Nov. 10.—
International law, in the form of
the fundamental rule, still may be invoked to punish William Hohenzollern, ex-kaiser of Germany, for
his crimes if Holland will surrender him, former President William
Howard Taft said tonight, when he
came here to open the United War
Campaign tomorrow.

"As long as there are extradition
treaties in force between Holland
and the principal nations among
the Allies, I do not see any reason
why Holland should not be forced
to give him up for punishment and
probably do so, but that is for Holland to decide.

**MAD DESIRE TO
DOMINATE WORLD
IS ALSO TOPPLED**

(Associated Press Despatch.)
NEW YORK, Nov. 10.—The
Associated Press tonight issued
the following war review:

The German people, for a generation obedient and submiss-
ive servants of their war lords,
for more than four years the
pliant instruments in ravaging
the world, have spoken a new
word, and the old Germany is
gone. From the confused, som-
times conflicting and often delayed advices from Germany in
the last two days it can now be
non-apparent that William, emperor and king, has been strip-
ped of his power. He is now
plain William Hohenzollern, a
fugitive in Holland. With him
fall toppled into with William's
mad design to rule the world.

**OTTAWA BEGINS
CELEBRATE ANEW
ALLIED VICTORY**

Immediately the News Was
Flashed to Capital Citizens
Thronged Streets and
Organized Parades.

The peace celebration was
any immediately after the fina
flashes of the electric lights a
ranged by The Citizen carried the
news.

Hotels, railroads, fire stations and
all places with people on sight duty
got the glad news first and their
shouts of hot won revolve stores
in nearly places. Night watchmen
in buildings and dwellings were
covering all lads got the light sig-
nals and immediate telephones the
good news to those who were not
asleep. Then came the call for the
strike and the announcement was
made over the telephone lines, and
soon the joyous peal was sent over
through the telephone from the
official announcement stations the
few moments after the announcement which tolled to the city.

Then there was a rush of people
to The Citizen office to see the news
in bulletin form. As they came all
manner of noise was a feature as
who had been sleeping down the
players from all Ottawa's factory
Pipe Band had their pipes all ready
they played among the other way to
arouse and waked up more than
those.

In less than half an hour an im-
menae crowd had gathered in front
of The Citizen office, cheering and
shout. They generally confined to the
south for out of town, was met on
the street and was caught up by the
Citizens, generally carried in the
south for out of town, was out on
the street and was caught up by the
Citizens, generally carried in the
south for out of town.

**"PEOPLE'S GOVERNMENT" HAS
TRIUMPHED IN GERMANY, MOST
OF COUNTRY ENDORSES CHANGE**

Workmen's and Soldiers' Council and Socialists in Co-
operation with Social-Democrat Deputy Ebert as New
Chancellor. Cities All Over Empire Swi . 'nto Line
Behind New Regimes.

(Associated Press Despatch.)
LONDON, Nov. 10.—According to despatches from Ams-
dam and Copenhagen, the revolution in Germany is extending
rapidly, but in most places the desired effect is being achieved
without violence or serious disturbance. In some places, notably in
Anhalt, Mens-Darmstadt and Mecklenburg-Schwerin, the princely
house are co-operating with the reforming parties in establishing
a new order of things.

Complaints already have been heard in Berlin that the press
censorship is being exercised as arbitrarily by the new as by the
old regime.

REVOLUTION SUCCEEDS; GENERAL STRIKE

(Associated Press Despatch.)
AMSTERDAM, Nov. 10.—A Berlin despatch received here
says:

"The revolution here has been brilliantly. There has
been an almost entire absence of bloodshed. Strikes have resulted
in a complete cessation of all work. Various regiments have gone
over to the Soldiers' and Workmen's organizations in quick succession. Apart from some insignificant cases of shooting, there
has been complete quiet.

"Order prevails and the military patrols already have been
withdrawn. Great jubilation and enthusiasm reigns throughout
the city.

A despatch received from Karlsruhe, says that Grand Duke
Friedrich has issued a proclamation declaring that the constitution
will be summoned November 15 to change the constitution.

"Another despatch from Stuttgart says the King of Wurttem-
burg announces in a proclamation that his person shall never serve
as a hindrance to the development of the wishes of the people.

"The Soldiers' and Workmen's Council has been established
at Dusseldorf and has issued a proclamation that plunderers will
be shot and that no strike will be permitted. The revolution here
has passed without disturbance.

(Continued on Page Five).

**KAISER ABDICATES,
FLEES TO HOLLAND
WITH MILITARISTS**

Once Mighty Despot a Fugitive. Signed Abdication at
Grand Headquarters Saturday. Crown Prince Also
Has Renounced Succession.

(Associated Press Despatch.)
LONDON, Nov. 10.—(Midnight)—Both the former German
emperor and his eldest son, Frederick William, crossed the Dutch
frontier Sunday morning according to advices from The Hague.

GENERAL STAFF WITH THE FUGITIVES.

LONDON, Nov. 10.—(12.35 a.m.)—The former German emperor's party, which is believed to include Field Marshal von Hin-
denburg, arrived at Eysden, on the Dutch frontier, at 7.30 o'clock,
Sunday morning, according to Daily Mail advices.

Practically the whole German general staff accompanied the
former emperor, and ten automobiles carried the party. The automobiles were bristling with rifles, and all the fugitives were armed.

The ex-kaiser was in uniform. He alighted at the Eysden
station.

(Continued on Page Two)

**BRITAIN SLOWING UP
IN MUNITION WORK**

(Associated Press Despatch.)
LONDON, Nov. 10.—In consequence of
the message was telephoned to the
Ottawa Electric Company and the
announcement was received. No report
were fire to respond, giving out four
times. Almost immediately after the
Ottawa Electric Company lights were
out, in an instant there was left
light aglow in the building, but the
people in the all night restaurants
and other night workers and the
celebration of the greatest event in
the world's history since the cruci-
fixion.

On the corner of O'Connor and
Sparks str., soon excitement was visible and there was a rule. The Rev.
Dr. Cummings and others were
rushing to the lane behind Bryson
Graham's stores, which at five o'clock
cent, pushing cases and oil boxes
were taken and thrown out into the
middle of the street, merely significant of the enthusiasm of the people

THE WEATHER

TORONTO, Nov. 10.—Showers
have occurred today in Eastern
Quebec and the Maritime provinces.
Otherwise the weather in Canada
has been generally fair.

Forecasts:
Ottawa and St. Lawrence Valley
fair and cold.

Citizen Extras
will be issued from
time to time as the
news developments
warrant.

'on account of our policy initiated three years ago of spending our entire revenue on broadening and solidifying the foundations of the newspaper, our net surplus is small' (it was only $3,800). But he felt the *Citizen* was in a stronger position than it had ever been.

Wilson's optimism suffered a dampening in the clouded business weather of 1913. In that year the *Citizen* took its first loss since 1900 – about $8,000. He proposed some economies, but nothing drastic. W.J. commented from Hamilton:

> The governor agrees with you that it is better business to trim out only such features as would not affect your prestige, even though it has resulted in a deficit.... With Father's congratulations I am offering my condolences ... in view of the fact that in spite of the constant and strenuous efforts and admirable ethical code which you have used and adopted in your recent pursuit of the fickle goddess of fortune, she has not been surprised and startled to a sufficient degree to cause her to drop in your path sufficient gold to enable you to carry on your good works and still make each end meet the other.

Though the paper got back into the black by $6,000 in 1914 (total revenue was running at over $200,000), the prospects were not particularly bright.

By this time costs had made it obvious that with three English-language papers in the Ottawa field, there wasn't much possibility of a reasonable profit for anyone.

The background to this is curious. In 1905 the owners of the *Free Press*, a Liberal paper founded in the 1860s, decided they had had enough and looked around quietly for a buyer. The Southams and P.D. Ross of the rival *Journal* bought it and installed, as general manager, Ernest Norman Smith, then city editor of the Toronto *Globe*. Word of the sale leaked out. The Southams (as operators of a Conservative organ) and Ross (publisher of a paper then nominally independent with Conservative leanings, and himself a Conservative and close friend of Borden) found themselves in an uncomfortable position as the known owners of the only Liberal paper in town. To merge the *Free Press* with either *Citizen* or *Journal* would have opened the way for a new Liberal party paper. The logical thing was to sell. On January 1, 1907, Norman Smith bought a majority interest in the *Free Press*, largely with interest-bearing notes to the Southams and Ross.

It seems apparent that in a business sense, whether or not the Southams and Ross realized it, nothing from their point of view was really solved. If the old paper failed, political money would raise a new one. If it succeeded, it would eat further into the possibilities of the Ottawa newspaper field. As it happened, Norman Smith, who had gained varied news experience in the dozen years since he had come out from Fleet Street, produced a competitive paper. War costs, finally, convinced all hands there wasn't room for three. And by that time the *Citizen*'s swing to independence and beyond – a swing so pronounced as to make establishment of a new Liberal paper unlikely – had cleared the way to absorption of the *Free Press* by the *Journal*. The *Free Press* went out of existence as an entity December 31, 1916, and appeared next day as a morning edition of the *Journal*, under the name *Journal-Press*, with Norman Smith as vice-president and editor. Two years later the word *Press* was dropped from the title.

Thus the Ottawa English-language field became the preserve of two newspapers, each with morning and evening editions. Norman Smith's consideration for the *Free Press* was one-fifth of the *Citizen* and one-fifth of the *Journal*, the paper with which his working life would be identified for the next forty years.

More than a simple sale of the *Free Press* was involved. In a business sense, the *Citizen* and the *Journal* went into a kind of partnership to end cut-throat competition. A Wilson Southam memorandum written in November 1919 records that for a brief time Southam Limited held two-fifths of *Journal* stock and Ross held two-fifths of the *Citizen*. This arrangement was ending at the time Wilson wrote his memorandum; but some of its business effects were preserved for years in a series of working agreements.

Most important and longest lasting of these was the Ottawa Newspapers' Subscription Bureau, a joint set-up that took over circulation of both papers.

An advertising agreement, even more unusual in form, provided that in any year when one paper's linage exceeded the other's (excluding the *Journal*'s patent-medicine ads) they would split the net surplus revenue. Each reported progress to the other in statements that took no Hawkshaw to decipher despite coding – Green for *Journal*, Purple for *Citizen*. 'If Purple's total linage exceeds Green's total linage,' a Harry Southam memo ran, 'then the surplus carried after a deduction is made for the cost of same, is divided equally; and if Green's total linage exceeds Purple's total then the surplus (excluding proprietary medicine advertising) is divided equally after a deduction for carrying charges. The idea of this division of surplus was based on the assumption that the paper with the larger circulation would attract the larger linage, and the division was intended as a sort of balance wheel.' In practice the split had little significance.

Over fifteen years the difference amounted to less than $7,000: Green rebated $3,271 to Purple, Purple $10,080 to Green.

It was probably from this close business co-operation that some public suspicion of common ownership arose. This was unfounded. Even E. Norman Smith's personal one-fifth interest in the *Citizen* had disappeared, as a direct interest, in 1932 when he sold his *Citizen* stock to The Southam Publishing Company for Southam company securities. In fact each paper guarded its position warily. The point of view of both is probably fairly presented in a memorandum from Harry Southam to P.D. Ross in 1934:

> It is . . . because of the temporary nature of our agreements that we have felt justified in doing our best to sell the Citizen to both national and local advertisers, even though we realize that if we get more than our share of the advertising the excess of revenue over 50 per cent is divided equitably.
>
> The Citizen (or the Journal) in the future, near or distant, might be acquired by a new owner, and we felt that we should be careful not to do anything, or leave anything undone, which would tend to depreciate the value of the Citizen.

The situation was thus a kind of armed truce with neither paper, understandably, willing to drain its moat or spike its guns despite their peaceful alliance.

In news-gathering the traditional rivalry persisted regardless of the nominal business truce, though a newsprint shortage or a drop in ad linage might result in deals to keep news columns within stated limits.

In practice matters were not wholly peaceful even on the business side. Agreements banned the use of comparative statements of circulation and ad linage in promotional work of all kinds. But *Citizen* salesmen couldn't resist the space-selling argument that the *Citizen* went into more city houses than the *Journal*. Their *Journal* counterparts undertook to demonstrate that their paper circulated among more readers of a certain class. Result: eloquent memos of protest between the Southams and P.D. Ross or E. Norman Smith.

On the news side a royal visit, a tough parliamentary session, or a war would push one paper up to two or three columns a day more than the other, whose senior desk men would of course respond in kind.

Over the course of years the memoranda that flowed back and forth at intervals between the generals were fairly aggressive, as were sometimes the news and ad tactics of the horse and foot. But while they lasted, the agreements saved both papers money that would otherwise have gone into competitive promotional effort.

'That Petty Little Sheet'

The *Citizen*'s simmering war with Robert Rogers came to a boil in the winter of 1917. This particular flare-up illustrates the kind of complication that could spring from the Southams' business activities outside publishing; and incidentally casts light on occasional moves at this time toward concerted editorial action.

Throughout 1916 Judge A.C. Galt, acting as a special commissioner for the T.C. Norris Liberal government in Manitoba, had been investigating scandals in the construction of an agricultural college – part of the general situation that had toppled the provincial government of Sir Rodmond Roblin. One of the witnesses was Rogers, one-time minister of public works for Roblin, who had moved up to the same position in the federal cabinet. Galt examined Rogers sharply. Rogers in turn denounced the commissioner for acting as such while a judge and called him a grafter for taking pay. The bite of Galt's strictures as felt by Rogers was not lessened by the fact that Galt himself had been a Conservative, appointed to the Manitoba bench by the Borden government. On January 30, 1917, Galt brought down a report in which he refused to accept various statements made by Rogers and held him responsible for the increase in a certain contract price.* Rogers replied with a declaration that the commissioner was manufacturing Liberal ammunition for Norris.

On February 1 the *Citizen* came out with an editorial under the heading 'Hon. Robert Rogers Found Guilty'. The burden of it was that Borden should fire Rogers: 'Hon. Robert Rogers must not be allowed longer to degrade the Crown by holding a position as minister in Canada. . . . The Prime Minister's sense of personal honor must compel him to protect the Crown, by retiring Mr. Rogers until he has cleared himself of the verdict of guilt brought by Justice Galt.'

On February 7 it again inserted the needle:

> It is a week since Mr. Justice Galt of the Manitoba Supreme Court indicted Mr. Rogers for the part he played in the increasing of a government contractor's bid . . . and for the unlawful passing of an order-in-council falsely stating the amount of a contractor's tender to have been $68,929 when Mr. Rogers knew it to have been $60,229.
> Why is Mr. Rogers allowed to remain a minister of the Crown?

That afternoon Rogers rose in the House. After referring to the Galt report as one 'that carries with it in every line unmistakable evi-

---

*In July a two-man board appointed by the federal government came to a counter-conclusion: 'That the evidence does not sustain the findings of Mr. Justice Galt in so far as they reflect upon or prejudicially affect the honor or integrity of Hon. Robert Rogers.'

dence of animus, temper, and misrepresentation', he continued:

> ... If the Citizen was the pure sheet that it would like its readers to believe it to be, then it would undoubtedly be obliged to support me, for the simple reason that the owners of the Citizen newspaper had the very best of reasons to know that the affairs of my department are honorably and honestly administered in the public interest. Heaven knows, the owners of the Citizen know, and I know, that I have not the support of that petty little sheet today simply because I would not yield to pressure and become a party to the purchasing, for a post-office site in Montreal, of a lot which the Southams were most anxious to sell to the government at a cost of $400,000; a site that was not suitable and not in the public interest to purchase.... I have not been prepared to despoil the administration of my department for the personal gain of that compact. If I had, I would today have their full and devoted support. ...

Fred had in fact tried to sell the St. James Street property to the government three years before, when he heard that purchase of a post-office site was planned. On February 17, 1914, he had written Rogers offering the full 37,000 square feet for $400,000 or the easterly part of it for $250,000 and followed this up with both written and verbal arguments that the land was more suitable for the government's purpose than the Hotel Carslake property that was eventually bought.

It may be assumed that the *Citizen*'s attitude would have been cited by Rogers as an obstacle to the purchase, and that F.N. would have countered with reference to party support given by other Southam papers. In a letter to his father reporting that prospects for the sale didn't look bright, he remarked that he was sending a representative to Ottawa 'to put it up to them ... tactfully and plainly ... just what we have done for the party in the past through our newspaper connection and what we may or may not do in the future.' In the same letter he reported on a previous conversation with Rogers and added ironically: 'He then gave me to understand that a more sympathetic attitude on the Citizen's part would possibly result in the purchase of our block, a title for you, and a senatorship for all your sons.' That there was any promise of *Citizen* support as a quid pro quo appears unlikely. Apart from personal ethics, F.N. was not in a position to commit the *Citizen*. No brother of Wilson and Harry would go out on that particular limb. Looked at closely, Rogers's statement did not say in so many words that such support was offered. But much was implied.

The *Citizen* carried the full Hansard report of Rogers's attack and invited 'the fullest investigation of the incident referred to by him'.

It denied 'his entire charges and miserable insinuations' and asserted: 'His facts are improperly presented and his assertions are false as a perusal of the correspondence which should be on file in his office will show.' It then quoted Fred's letter tendering the land in which he had said an independent valuation would confirm his quotations and that he would not go on record as having sold this property at the price named 'unless after investigation they were satisfied that it has equal or greater advantages than other property under consideration.'

'What is there in the above to justify the accusation that Mr. Rogers is being attacked because he was not prepared to despoil the administration of his department for the personal gain of that company?' the *Citizen* asked. It suggested 'an official investigation of all the circumstances relating to the negotiations and final purchase of the post-office site in Montreal.' It challenged Rogers to repeat his statements outside the protection of the House 'in order that the courts may be evoked to decide in the public interest and in justice to the Citizen and its proprietors whether the charge is a slander or simply a political attack.'

Over in Hamilton, under the heading HON. ROGERS WRATHY, the *Spectator* ran a straightforward account of the Rogers charge and a separate story quoting the *Citizen*'s reply. It made no editorial comment, but on February 9 William allowed his feelings an outlet in a wire to Borden:

> The Hamilton Spectator, from its very inception, has been strongly Conservative. From deep conviction it is still, on the whole, in thorough accord with the Conservative party. But it is a great strain upon our fidelity to find one of your ministers, the Hon. Robert Rogers, without the slightest basis in fact, imputing unworthy motives to the Ottawa Citizen and the Southam family.
>
> I look to you for protection against the action of Mr. Rogers in taking advantage of his position in the House of Commons to besmirch the name of my family. You know what should be done in fairness to me and mine, and my confidence in you is such that I believe you will give the matter your personal attention at once, now that this direct appeal has been made to you.

The Prime Minister was a patient man, but the mood in which he considered this wire may have been sharpened by the fact that he had to digest at the same time another *Citizen* editorial. After referring to Premier W.A.Martin's action in Saskatchewan in expelling from the legislature certain members found to have extorted money and accepted bribes, it regretted that the federal Prime Minister did not seem to possess the same kind of moral courage.

Borden's written reply to William was crisp. He said he would not have taken the course Rogers took, but 'not only the minister of public works but many members of the government have been subjected to a great deal of attack and misrepresentation from the Citizen for more than three years.' The motive for this he couldn't conjecture. Personally he had neither the time nor inclination to concern himself with such attacks, but different men had different temperaments and 'those who indulge in such attacks must not be surprised if persons suffering from this species of warfare sometimes hit back.' He wouldn't justify any untrue or unfair statement by a minister but Rogers had asserted his statement was well founded. 'I thoroughly appreciate your long and loyal service to the Conservative party,' Borden wrote, 'and indeed the attitude of the proprietors of the Citizen has prevented me from giving to that service the recognition which I greatly desired. . . . I hope that the principles of that party may receive your support in the future as in the past; but if that support is contingent upon members of the government remaining silent under a continued stream of misrepresentation and abuse I am unable to guarantee that such silence can be maintained.'

Meantime W.J. had wired Bert Woods suggesting that the Calgary *Herald* and Edmonton *Journal* might take the stand that 'on account of the Galt findings Sir Robert Borden should point out to the Hon. Robert that his greatest act of kindness would be to sing a swan song to the mutually long-suffering public and then step down and out.'

Woods went after Rogers in the *Herald*, apparently welcoming the chance. 'Even apart from his attack on the Citizen, which is of itself sufficient,' he wrote Bill, 'he [Rogers] has a bad influence on the Conservative party. . . .'

In Edmonton, Bob Jennings, without prompting, had taken a cool and moderate line. The Rogers attack was naturally crackling ammunition for rival newspapers in cities where the Southams published. The Edmonton *Bulletin*'s two-column heading ran:

TORY FAMILY ROW AT OTTAWA, ROGERS ACCUSES SOUTHAMS OF AN ATTEMPTED HOLD-UP

In case any Edmonton reader didn't know the *Journal* was a Southam paper, the deck under the main heading informed them: 'Minister of Public Works Asserts Newspaper Men Who Own Number of Newspapers, Including Edmonton Journal, Endeavored to Sell Him Unsuitable Piece of Land for $400,000, and He Refused to Allow His Department to be Despoiled.'

In the *Journal* of February 9, Jennings undertook to make the *Journal*'s position clear: Its policy had nothing to do with that of the *Citizen*, which was 'the recognized exponent in the capital of the views of the Liberal opposition'. The *Citizen*'s criticism of Rogers was exactly in line with that of other Liberal newspapers, and no proof had been submitted that its position had been dictated by any such motive as that ascribed to it. In any case, the people Rogers attacked could look after themselves. As for the *Journal*, its only desire was 'here and now to make its position plain and it can do nothing more than repeat that its course is not and has never been dictated by any person or persons outside of its own office. . . .' In supporting Conservatives it had done so out of belief, not obligation: 'It has sought no party favors and cannot be accused of being a party hack. . . . It is not affected in the slightest degree by what Mr. Rogers charges and the attempt of its local business rival to make it appear that it is will not deceive anyone who is acquainted with its history.'

Writing Wilson, Jennings said that frequent attacks by the *Bulletin* 'and the occasional outbreaks of restless criticism on the part of old-line Conservatives' made it desirable for him to issue such declarations of independence from time to time. Wilson wired him that the editorial was well handled, but added: 'We are not however a Liberal newspaper.' The *Citizen* in its masthead line described itself as independent.

Woods remarked in a letter to William:

> I have been strongly tempted to send a wire to Sir Robert Borden on behalf of the Herald and Journal, letting him know that these two papers cannot feel sympathetic towards the Conservative administration so long as Hon. Robert Rogers is a member of it. However, I did not like to do that as it might imply a concerted newspaper action which might not be in accord with your wishes.

In this, Woods accurately read William's mind; the senior Southam viewed suggestions of concerted action with a cold eye.

The Rogers episode disturbed him, as indicated in a letter February 16 to Dick, to whom he wrote as 'the only member of the family who has not been dragged into the controversy'.

> I have been tremendously wrought up and been mad as a hatter for most of this week, but what can you expect, Dick, with the bunch I have around me at home and elsewhere, especially in Ottawa. . . .
>   My present bust was started by the Rogers, Galt, Citizen and Southam family controversy. . . . Those damn fool sons of mine in Ottawa and elsewhere would like the Spectator, the Calgary Herald and the Edmonton Journal to join in the attack because they hope

with this far-flung battle-line to force Rogers out and thus purge and
purify the government.

At most times I am a rational lovable father and husband, but the
rest of the time I am Conservative and the Spectator has always been
a Conservative paper. Even if the Spectator joined in the attack I
don't think we could 'get' that grafting braggart Rogers. Personally
I don't want it done. I may be wrong and I should like to know what
you think about it.

After the usual 'Yours affectionately, W. Southam,' a postscript
noted that 'I still think as I always thought that you are the brainiest,
safest and sanest of our freak nut family, present company not ex-
cepted. . . .'

The racy style of this missive bears some resemblance to that of
W.J. It may be that he concocted it for William's signature. W.J.
used to claim that Dick adopted a Napoleonic attitude toward his
mail: leave it alone and it answered itself. There is no record that he
ever gave an opinion on paper about bringing the *Spectator* into the
fight.

Six months later Rogers broke with Borden and resigned, thus removing one of the obstacles to union government – a movement in
which Borden had the *Citizen*'s support along with that of most English-language dailies (with a few exceptions like Frank Oliver's Edmonton *Bulletin*) of whatever political hue.

The Progressives

Back in 1913 the *Citizen* had commended Arthur Meighen for his
opposition to letting lobbyists for big business – 'the ramparts of
gold' – appear before the banking and commerce committee. It suggested him for solicitor-general, the post he got. By 1920 with Borden ill and about to retire (Meighen succeeded him in July) it held a
less favorable view. It ran a series of editorials on why Meighen
wouldn't do. And while it agreed with Mackenzie King that the union
government no longer represented the people, it found no special en-
chantment at the moment in the man who now led the Liberals.

A new movement had caught the eye of the Southams and Bowman. Ernest C. Drury was running Ontario with a government of
United Farmers. From Carleton in New Brunswick a farmer member came to the Commons in a by-election. On March 5, 1920, Dr.
Michael Clark referred to the cross-benchers (largely western members led by T.A. Crerar who had left the government on the tariff issue) as the National Progressive party. Next day the *Citizen* hailed
the party and the name: a change of heart was coming over Cana-

dians; they were breaking away from 'old party-fund politics'.

As the election finally approached in 1921 the *Citizen* backed the Progressives. 'Mr. Mackenzie King', it said editorially, 'would be well pleased to have organized labor, farmers, and ex-service men link up with the Liberal organization. But when they prefer to co-operate in the Progressive movement independent of old party politics, Mr. King is just as ready as Mr. Meighen to try stirring up class prejudice against the new national development.' Old party followers were mistaken in calling the Progressives faddists. 'The Progressive movement springs from the soil. To call those who have to do with the soil faddists or opportunists is to mistake the inherent character of the movement. It is also drawing to its support those in the urban areas who are slightly weary of the make-believe of yesterday.' Though the *Citizen* and a couple of weeklies were the only press support the Progressives got in Ontario, the province elected twenty-four of that faith, and with sixty-odd across Canada the party held the balance of power in the house. But in Ottawa itself their candidates got nowhere.

The Southams struck up friendships with Progressives like Henry Spencer, George Coote, and William Irvine, men interested in proportional representation (one of Wilson's pet studies) and in the workings of money and banking.

Since 1920 Bowman had been reading and passing on to Wilson and Harry, and promoting in the *Citizen*, the theories of C.H.Douglas, the Scottish engineer who had come up with some ideas for making purchasing power equal production through the credit of the state. This left the *Citizen* open to a few shots from its rival. The *Journal* took pleasure in April of 1922 in reproducing from the *New Statesman*, which hitherto – at least so the *Journal* said – had been one of Bowman's bibles, a devastating analysis of the Douglas credit scheme. In an accompanying editorial, the *Journal* reasoned in a tongue-in-cheek way that 'if the thing weren't nearly insane, economically, the Citizen wouldn't have pounced on it so riotously.' Nothing like that fazed the *Citizen*'s publishers or editor. When in the spring of 1923 the Progressives wanted Douglas to come over and appear before the banking and commerce committee the Ottawa Southams paid his way.

Six or seven years of prosperity were ahead. It would be ten years or more before the eruption of Social Credit as a faith and a passion in the West. By then the idealists among the Progressives at whose instance Douglas first came to Canada would have drifted out of their original loose grouping – some into the Liberal fold, some into the

Co-operative Commonwealth Federation in a new attempt to reconcile the farmer's aims with those of the industrial left. It would take a
new breed of politician to make the name Social Credit familiar in
Canada.

Billy, Wilson, and Harry

Meantime the *Citizen* modified its view of the federal scene. By the
time the election of 1925 came round, it saw hope for the Liberal
party's escape from ancient shackles. 'There is far more advanced
Liberal thinking in this part of Canada than people in the western
provinces appreciate,' it said July 15 in comment on Vincent Massey's joining the cabinet (a brief excursion into politics that ended
with defeat in Durham). 'The old order is passing: of necessity it
must, to hold the Dominion together. The old guard of bygone party
politics has held on tenaciously. It has almost destroyed the Conservative party. The admission of younger leaders into Liberal councils
can do much to revitalize public life in Canada.'

Regarding the Progressives (then under Robert Forke) it developed the theme by suggesting that 'without definitely linking up with
the Liberals, the tendency is in the direction of closer co-operation,
rather than trying to organize another party.' It was absurd for Liberals and Progressives to split the vote with so little difference between them. 'The effect is to let in Conservatives, who represent
minorities only, as in the last provincial election [Howard Ferguson
had ousted Drury in 1923] while majorities are deprived of their representation.*

About all it could say for Meighen was that reactionary interests
in Montreal were trying to oust him as Conservative leader. His prospects for election on a high-tariff platform in a western farm seat
were about as promising as those of a free trader in Hamilton. In this
forecast the *Citizen* proved wrong. Meighen won Portage la Prairie
that year and as leader of the largest group came close to over-all victory; so close that the *Citizen* on October 30, the morning after election, appeared to think he would form the government. By next day,
however, when it was apparent that King would carry on, the paper

---

*Later the view was somewhat different. In February of 1942 (a period when
it was critical of Mackenzie King) the *Citizen* in an editorial entitled
'Farmers Need to Get Together' suggested of the Progressives: 'They could
have become the official opposition, but they were badly served by an element
whose tactics were to capitalize on the farmer vote by steering it into the
Liberal party.'

agreed there was no urgent reason for his resignation pending a test of strength.

The *Citizen* took the conventional Liberal party line on the constitutional issue of 1926, which overshadowed scandals in the Customs Department and saw Mackenzie King consolidate his power. To the *Citizen* the thing was black and white: 'The function of the King and his representative is to accept the advice of his Prime Minister, good or bad. If it is bad, the Prime Minister will answer to the people.'

As for the customs scandal, the *Citizen* had no doubt that serious abuses existed under the King government and previous governments, that it was right that attention should be drawn to these, and that the machinery of administration needed to be strengthened. 'But it is one thing to admit the imperfections of human nature and another thing to create the impression, as some of the Conservative stumpers are doing, that the government is blackened by the exposure. . . . There is no reason why Canadians should be ashamed of their government, no matter how they may blame certain officials who misused their positions.' Bowman was adroit at recalling past sins and relating them to present assumptions of virtue: 'If he [Meighen] seeks to make the public believe that his own party is wholly pure and undefiled, he will fail. The memory of the scandals of the war is too fresh. . . .'

The middle and late 1920s – Mackenzie King and the Southams were now on a Billy, Wilson, and Harry basis – were probably the years in which the *Citizen* under these two Southams came closest to a strict Liberal party line. By the 1930s, though the paper stayed with King when the chips were down at election time, the old impatience with traditional parties, particularly on monetary matters, broke through again. The editorial page rang with it: 'Bank of England Imperialism' . . . 'Social Credit and the Banks' . . . 'Golden Image in Retreat'. . . .

4
Western
Adventure

In the summer of 1906 J.H.Woods travelled west from Toronto for a holiday, taking his wife along for a look at the old territorial districts that had become provinces of Canada the year before. In the ranch town of Calgary he met and talked with John J. Young, who owned and published the *Herald*. Later Young came east, looked up Woods, and asked him to come out and manage the paper. On April 24, 1907, he took over as editor and managing director. The time, the man, the place, and the paper were well met.

James Hossack Woods (nicknamed 'Bert' for no known reason) combined varied newspaper experience with drive, durability, and flair. A smallish man who would become rather rotund, physically and mentally a bit chesty, already in his fortieth year, Woods brought to Calgary a boyish enthusiasm and a generous share of native acumen. His personality and his years on the news side at the Toronto *Mail and Empire*, in the business office of the Toronto *News*, and as manager of his own advertising agency were ideal qualities to throw into the competitive, the sometimes cut-throat newspaper life of the opening West.

Calgary was then less than a generation old, an outgrowth of a log fort set up by the North West Mounted Police in 1875 and the coming of the CPR eight years later. In the year of the railway, population rose to around 500. Tom Braden, a Peterborough school-teacher, and Andrew Armour, a printer from Barrie, set up a hand-press in a tent on the banks of the Elbow. The first issue of the Calgary *Herald, Mining and Ranche Advocate and General Advertiser* appeared August 31, 1883. Mackenzie Bowell, the Belleville compositor and politician who would later become a controversial Prime Minister of Canada, happened to be in town. He helped to get the first *Herald* out.

Changes of ownership followed. Hugh S. Cayley (who was once jailed for printing his opinions, later prominent in Territorial politics, and eventually a county court judge in Vancouver) tried daily publication in 1885, the year of the Northwest Rebellion. He sold out in 1886 and by 1893 the new company was on the rocks, the paper appearing twice-weekly, weekly and 'off and on'. Young and Charles A. Magrath bought it in 1894 and again went daily. Magrath, destined for political prominence, soon sold out to Young, who worked his way through the hard times of the 1890s and got the paper on its feet. A capable journalist and a versatile man, Young had edited Nicholas Flood Davin's Regina *Leader* and the Moosomin *Spectator*. He sat for three years as a member of the Northwest Territories legislature, played the organ in church, and led a choir. The trade paper *Printer and Publisher* for July 1905 characterized him as 'a fine example of what can be made in Canada of an Englishman who is caught young'.

Though a natural Conservative, he had run the *Herald* with some independence, coming out against party lines for the provincial legislature and viewing as of lesser importance the separate-school issue that kicked up such a furore in the East. 'Rival gangs of politicians are shouting themselves hoarse in Ontario over the educational affairs of Alberta,' he wrote. 'It is just possible that Alberta would be more thankful to these enthusiasts if they would urge more even-handed justice for the West in the way of distribution of the natural resources of the country....'

At the time of Bert Woods's arrival the city had reached a population of 20,000. The first tides of immigration had washed to the Rockies and beyond. New waves of colonists were coming from the East and Europe and up from the States. A Territorial population of 65,000 in 1901 reached toward the quarter-million mark in the new province. A crop area of 152,000 acres in the first year of the century had grown to 900,000 in half-a-dozen years. Someone had already coined the term 'world's bread-basket' for the Canadian West. Along the western edge of the basket, colorful with hard wheat, cattle, railroad branch-lines (and a sprinkling of remittance men), Woods found his spiritual home.

He also found that Young, who had branched out into real estate and mining, needed money and wanted to sell the paper. Within six months Woods had a five-year option on a half-interest in the *Herald* and a free hand to sell the property on Young's behalf. In September of 1907 he wrote Dick Southam, whom he had known in Toronto, recalling that 'your company has wanted to come into Western Canada' and suggesting the Southams might like to buy. The figure quoted was $80,000 for the paper and job plant. The first suggested deal called for a Southam purchase of a half-interest plus help to Woods in financing the other half. The Southams turned it down. Fred, Wilson, and Harry all saw Calgary as too far away for the family to keep in touch with local sentiment. And with a new building for the Montreal printing plant nearing completion and one planned for Toronto, money was tight.

Just after Christmas, Woods came back East with a new proposition. The price had dropped to $60,000 and he thought $50,000 would buy the business if $15,000 could be available at once in cash. He still wanted a half-interest, deferring his own payments; and he could arrange a deal covering the newspaper only, excluding the job plant.

Again the Southam family conferred by mail and telephone. Since September they had heard a good deal more about the *Herald* and Calgary. Conservative M.P. Maitland McCarthy talked with Wilson at Ottawa and gave him a sales pitch. 'Calgary is now larger than Edmonton and in his opinion Edmonton will never catch up,' Wilson reported. And the *Herald* was the only Conservative paper west of Winnipeg. Charles Ussher, western traffic manager for the CPR, gave Fred much the same picture. Fred now thought 51 per cent of the newspaper (excluding the job plant) wasn't a bad proposition. But at least 51 per cent it must be.

In the end the deal was made early in January in the Hamilton home of Henry Watson, banker friend of William Southam, and father of Wilfrid J. (Bill) Watson and of Annie Beatrice (Dimps), who had become young Bill Southam's wife in the previous May. Bill Watson, then twenty-six and not in the best of health, had spent six years in the Merchants Bank. He wanted to go west.

They bought the newspaper for $30,000, represented by $22,000 in cash and notes and the balance in assumed liabilities for equipment on order. Authorized capital of the new Herald Publishing Company was $100,000 of which $30,000 was then allotted in $50 shares – 301 to Southams, 199 to Woods, and 100 to the Watsons. Woods put up $3,000 in cash. Southam and Henry Watson took notes for the balance of his interest. William Southam was president of the company, Woods vice-president and managing director, and Bill Watson secretary-treasurer.

Years after that evening gathering at Hamilton, Bill Watson would tell a story of the morning after. He came downstairs to breakfast, his mind running on the western adventure, and found his father dumping the contents of a decanter. Bill expressed some natural surprise. 'This stuff cost me thousands of dollars last night,' the senior Watson said. 'I'm getting rid of it.'

Wilson Southam's doubts were less dramatically expressed: 'We do not imagine there will be any returns from this investment for many years as the profits will likely have to be turned in to the business to develop it. . . . I don't imagine that this proposition will be of so much use to the present generation as it may be to some of our sons.' He was right in his assumption that profits would be ploughed in for a while, along with new capital. But it did not take a generation to produce a ripening crop. The *Herald* was fertile soil.

Owning a newspaper in Western Canada was new and exciting to the Southams: their first move outside the central provinces and the first newspaper venture in which they left management to other than family hands. William wondered whether the new ownership should be publicly acknowledged and his own name used in connection with the *Herald*. All the boys thought so. On other points agreement was not so general. Fred thought Harry should keep a close eye on the *Herald*'s editorial policy. Dick suggested this was a pretty long-range proposition and that the paper would be safe in Woods's hands.

Wilson brought up a point. The *Herald* had come out flat-footed and said that any political party that suggested a higher tariff wouldn't elect a corporal's guard west of Winnipeg. He and Harry inferred that it opposed any such increase, and they thought this proper. But that wasn't the *Spectator*'s view and some contemporaries 'might point out that you are advocating one trade policy in the *Spectator* because it suits that particular constituency, and a different trade policy in another of your papers because it suits that particular locality . . . in this way laying yourself open to the charge of inconsistency.' He then injected a note of friendly persuasion. Perhaps William could agree with the policy advocated by the *Herald* – which, incidentally, 'Morrison, without any suggestion or hint from us in any way, at one time stated was the attitude of the *Citizen*. . . .'

Here Fred got into the discussion again. Local control was all right in local matters, but in his view (which would change with time) the three Southam papers should express the same general policy on national affairs. He was inclined to agree with Wilson and Harry on the tariff, with this modification: 'That as the bounties on steel are reduced a protection of 20 or 25 per cent should be substituted.' Tongue in cheek, and obviously referring to the Southam interest in Hamilton Steel and Iron, he added: 'This of course affects our own pockets and for that reason the Ottawa contingent will readily agree to support it.'

Without making a point of the inconsistency that he himself implied was beginning to exist between the *Spectator* and the *Citizen*, Wilson touched on a question that would resolve itself eventually through the evolution of the company – and its dissociation, as a company, from the editorial positions of its newspapers.

Despite theoretical discussion, no one seems to have worried much about the specific nature of the *Herald*'s political attitude just at this time. Woods wrote to W.J., however, that the Conservatives were nervous. 'I told them quite plainly', he wrote, 'that the Herald was in no sense their organ, but was an independent newspaper, entitled to express its own views. . . . At the same time I let them know that the Herald intended to support M.S.McCarthy in the coming election, thus satisfying them as to our course, while retaining our independence of action.' The question would come up nearly two years later in sharper form. Meantime Woods put the *Herald* into an enthusiastic and persistent campaign for provincial development.

Railroads in Big Letters

On Thursday, August 27, 1908, the *Herald*'s travelling correspondent Jess Dorman set out on a crusade.

The page one line that day read: THE HERALD'S RAILWAY POLICY FOR PROVINCE OF ALBERTA. In a mixture of news and persuasion the story said:

> The Herald's staff correspondent . . . left Calgary today on horseback to accomplish a trip which ought, at this stage of the game, to be done in a palace car. The present trip is being undertaken for no other purpose than in the hope of hastening the day. . . .
>
> The course the rider will pursue runs in a northerly direction, out past Carbon, Ghost Pine, Three Hills, and other points on toward Vermilion.
>
> The land department reports that practically all the homesteads in the territory to be traversed are taken, and it is said that the settlers are there, a great many of them actually working their claims, awaiting with the true pioneer patience the coming of the road that will make their land valuable, and enable them to obtain at least some of the comforts of life their enterprise and fortitude have so fully deserved. . . .

These people had come to Alberta on the assurance that the railroad would soon pass their doors. They were out there waiting for it 'and the Herald man is travelling out to call upon them, to see how they are faring and to tell its readers.'

The Herald's purpose is RAILROADS in big letters. Its motive is not political; it is not undertaking to say by whom or by what means, or upon what basis, the roads should be realized; but it is going out to demonstrate the crying need for them.

For the next month Dorman's travels got front-page play: 'Rich Knee Hill Country Anxiously Looks for Roads', 'Put in 25,000 People from Here to Red Deer', 'Advantage of Fertile Alberta Compared with the Dakotas', 'Farmers Away Ahead of Railways and No Sign of Their Coming', 'Correspondent Follows the Buffalo Trails to Crooked Lake'. Examples of progress forged by railroads studded the stories: 'Three years ago the first nail was driven in Stettler, following the advent of the little branch railroad, and today the city has close to a thousand people, and an assessed valuation of over half a million dollars.'

At least once Dorman tapped a remarkable vein of pathos: 'At Hardisty the other day they brought in one who had lost track of the path of reason entirely, the result of his long solitude. The fatal moment struck when he was building a ladder, and always as long as there is life in his body he will be building ladders, no doubt to climb high upon, to look across the prairie and see if he can discover the approach of someone to break his solitude.'

The culmination of this campaign came November 24 when the *Herald* ran as its top line a single word: RAILWAYS. The story reported Premier Rutherford's announcement of a provincial Department of Railways. If the federal government couldn't be induced to assist immediate construction the province would take up the task. 'The Premier has closely followed the development of the Herald's railway policy,' the story said, 'and cites instances which have been given in this paper as evidencing the need for the action which he proposes to take.' The *Herald* didn't claim its campaign had been exclusively responsible, 'but it does believe that the course it has pursued, namely the furnishing of concrete information showing the necessity for branch-line extensions, was the proper way to go about this vital matter. . . .' It again disclaimed any political motive: 'In this matter the Herald knows no party politics. Its policy is and will continue to be RAILWAYS in large letters and it will lend its utmost assistance to every legitimate project having that object in view, whether its source be Liberal or Conservative.'

This cozy attitude towards the Rutherford government on railways, incidentally, was not to last indefinitely. In 1909 a first-class tangle developed after Rutherford guaranteed the bonds of a company formed by a Kansas City promoter to build the Alberta and Great Waterways line from Edmonton to Fort McMurray. The *Herald* actively attacked the contract. Charges of rake-offs and graft flew freely. After a party split, Rutherford's resignation, and Arthur Sifton's succession – and a long round of litigation – the line was finally built during First World War years. In 1929 it became a part of Northern Alberta Railways, jointly operated by CNR and CPR.

The Troubled Conservatives

Late in 1909, party dissatisfaction with the *Herald* came to a head. In December, Woods reported to William Southam that the Calgary Conservatives planned a new daily paper. The rumored starting-date was March 1.

The discussion that developed casts a lingering light on two subjects only indirectly related: early efforts of the Southams to arrive at a workable relationship with a manager far from home base, and the particular quality of political life in the Alberta of the early 1900s.

> There are in this country two kinds of Conservatives [Woods wrote to William], one the ordinary kind of independent Conservative voter, and the other the machine politician, headed by Senator Lougheed, R.B.Bennett, Dr. Brett of Banff, and similar people. These latter are, in my opinion, a most unfortunate bunch of politicians. Individually they are decent well-meaning men, but they never seem to play the game of politics rightly, and they always get licked by whatever they go up against.
>
> They would like us to write Conservative politics from year's end to year's end. What they would like is a kind of fool Conservative paper the Mail and Empire has been and they would not care an atom whether such a course was wise, either from a commercial or a political point of view, as long as they could read its editorials and feel that they were hot stuff.

Woods said Albertans liked a spice of independence in political editorials. At election time the *Herald* had fought strongly for the Conservatives, but this wasn't enough for Lougheed and his group. As for the new paper, it was more likely to go broke than anything else and he didn't plan to approach anyone about it:

> With your approval I would let them go right ahead with whatever plans they have, and if they bring out a paper of their own I would propose to turn the Calgary Herald into an entirely independent paper

without any party affiliation whatsoever, either implied or expressed,
a paper that would fight Western battles and criticize either political
party with equal freedom. That is the kind of paper I would like best
to run and I believe it is the kind that will pay best in this country.

The Southams did not share Woods's nonchalance. They had experience in competitive fields and certainly Calgary was already competitive. Liberals read the morning *Albertan* and the *News* (said to have
been founded by Liberal money to counter Bob Edwards's attacks on
Clifford Sifton and the Laurier government in the *Eye-Opener*),
which chopped away at the *Herald* in the evening. A new Conservative paper would narrow the *Herald*'s field. The Southams thought
Woods should do everything he could to head it off.

The question of who had final say in the paper's operation now got
into the discussion. 'We agree with Fred that Bert Woods desires to
make the Herald his personal organ,' Harry wrote. 'We think this
ambition should be nipped in the bud and he should be given to understand that the Herald is Father's personal organ.' In view of Wilson's earlier worry about inconsistency, there is a certain Olympian
tone to Harry's conclusion that, because 'the Herald is published in a
new country', personal control by William 'should not prevent it
from being really independent, if not radical.' He added: 'Wilson and
I would prefer the latter.' This however was apparently a course to
be considered only if the new Conservative daily actually got going.

Woods assured Bill in a letter written January 3, 1910, that he was
not treating the proposed new paper lightly. He went on to picture
the background:

> Regarding the Conservatives, there is no particular Conservative wing
> that is dissatisfied with the Herald. The Conservative party in Alberta
> is badly disorganized. . . . For years it has been a regular hotbed of
> mutual treachery. Both Lougheed and Bennett detest McCarthy, who
> cordially reciprocates their sentiment. The other members of the
> party neither admire nor respect Senator Lougheed in his political
> capacity. As to Bennett, he certainly possesses what Whistler used to
> call 'the gentle art of making enemies' and it is hard to find a Con-
> servative in town who is his personal or political friend. He dominates
> the situation to some extent by his intellectual strength.

Back of these were some well-meaning politicians who would like a
paper to pound politics into its readers every day in the year. They
had told him, Woods said, that they would rather see the *Herald* out-
and-out Liberal than have it a paper they couldn't depend on to promote their views. One trouble, however, was that their views were
not much good.

Woods didn't think he, himself, should approach Lougheed or any of his following. However, Wilson might see the senator in Ottawa and suggest that the starting of a new paper would be unfair to the Southams, 'who are supporting the Conservative party in the East'.

A couple of weeks later McCarthy and Lougheed talked with the Ottawa Southams on separate occasions. From these discussions Wilson and Harry gathered that, so far, there was nothing but talk in the idea of a new paper, though the Conservatives were dissatisfied with the *Herald*. Anyway, Wilson deduced, it would be difficult to please everyone: 'Bennett and Lougheed quarrel between themselves on political questions and from this fact we would judge that it would be a practical impossibility for anyone to have their entire goodwill.'

In reporting to his father on the Lougheed conversation Wilson produced one nugget of curious information: 'He said that the year before we came there, his partner, Bennett, and himself had the opportunity of buying a 49 per cent interest in the Albertan, expecting at that time to get a few more shares and secure the control. The control did not materialize, so that they are in the position of being Conservative leaders financing the leading Liberal organ.'

By early February the crisis seemed to be over. Woods talked with R.G.Brett, president of the Alberta Conservative Association (and later lieutenant-governor). They reached an informal understanding: the *Herald* would devote more attention to politics on behalf of the Conservative party, and the party would use its organization to boost *Herald* circulation and would abandon its attitude of distrust and forget about setting up another newspaper.

However, in advising Woods what he had told his party *confrères* about this, Brett mentioned 'making the Herald the outstanding paper in the province, with you as business manager, devoting your time to that, and a first-class cracker-jack of an editorial writer.' He also said that he had been instructed to place the position before the Alberta Conservatives at Ottawa, and the party leaders had suggested it might be arranged that William Southam meet them there.

Woods reacted characteristically.

I am, as you know [he wrote Brett], the managing director and editor of the Herald, and this company would not be agreeable to any change which expressly or by implication altered that position. I would not care to appoint an editor . . . nominated by the Conservative party, as I propose to remain the editor. All I look for is that with increased prosperity and a larger business in which the members of the Conservative party can substantially assist, I would be able to en-

gage a man who could devote himself to editorial writing under my
direction. . . .

These matters, as you know, are all matters of evolution. The Herald is today in effect an independent Conservative paper, and it will
remain so hoping to be a more useful factor in independent Conservatism than your people have thought it to be in the past. But its general
management and editorial control must necessarily remain exactly as
they do at present.

The situation might have remained in this state of balance had it
not been that Brett and a delegation including McCarthy, Charles
Magrath, and John Herron, all Alberta M.P.s, called on Wilson and
Harry at Ottawa and declared they faced three choices: to get
'straight conscientious intelligent support' from the *Herald*, to start
a new paper, or to go out of business as a party in Alberta.

In his report to William, Wilson wrote:

They admitted that they had probably been wrong in their attitude
toward the Herald, but gave as an excuse that Mr. Woods and Attorney-General Cross were close personal friends and that Sydney
Woods [Bert's brother] was the deputy attorney-general and the brains
of the Liberal aggregation in Edmonton and that they thought on that
account Mr. Woods's sympathies were really Liberal, and therefore it
would be more or less useless to appeal to him. We pointed out that
this certainly was not fair to Mr. Woods and that possibly the trouble
was really principally on their side. Though they all felt very strongly
on the question of the Herald's non-activity in supporting the Conservative party, yet they were extremely fair and were not blaming us
or Mr. Woods or the Herald particularly, but just that they wanted
that condition of affairs changed if we could see our way to doing it
and, if not, nothing would be left but to look elsewhere for support.
Mr. Magrath pointed out that being independent Conservative was all
right in Ontario, where there were so many papers of each party stripe
that were straight party organs, but in Alberta conditions were quite
different; that there were only three Conservative papers in Alberta:
the Herald, the Edmonton Journal, and some weekly down in southern Alberta. These Conservative papers posed as independents, while
all the other papers were straight Liberal.

The two Ottawa Southams came up with a tentative program. 'We
would suggest', Wilson wrote, 'that Bert engage a good Conservative editorial writer, and, while calling themselves Independent Conservative, to be really a straight Conservative party organ, fight the
Conservative battle on every possible occasion, but always in a high-
class non-abusive way; this editorial writer of course to be entirely
under the direction of Bert as editor-in-chief; that party leaders be
encouraged to come in and offer suggestions as to editorial policy,

but while strongly Conservative editorially, that the news columns should be absolutely free from bias.'

This, he said, was only a suggestion. Woods might decide that he could give the party the assistance they were asking by continuing as his own editorial writer. However, though he and Harry were the real editors of the *Citizen*, they found time to write an editorial only about once a month. They thought Woods would find that things would work out better if he adopted the same practice.

William sent Wilson's letter off to Woods with a covering note and drew a stiff reply. Woods was never a man to underestimate his own powers or position. What burned him was that the Conservatives had gone over his head in a situation he thought he had smoothed out with Brett, and that the Southams had listened to them. And the politicians had had 'the impertinence to refer to the fact of my brother's position, and my personal friendship with Attorney-General Cross. . . .' He offered to resign or buy out the Southam interest in the *Herald*, and in doing so again defended his position vis-à-vis the party men: The *Herald* had fought in Dominion and provincial elections 'about as hot a party fight on behalf of the Conservatives as any paper could – hotter than good newspaper work justified.'

When the proposal for the new daily appeared, he had decided it was nine-tenths bluff. He had met Dr. Brett and made a friendly informal arrangement that 'if the Conservatives would do us good we would do them good, and that we might start in by giving them, from then on, a generous support.'

'This we have been doing,' Woods wrote, 'and as a matter of fact the entire attack on the government at Edmonton is based on the discovery by the Herald of the flaws in the Alberta and Great Waterways Railway contract, a discovery which we published in the Herald and with which the Conservative leaders had nothing to do, except to take advantage of it.'

He went on to review the paper's progress during the two years of Southam control and Woods management. Circulation would reach 10,000 that year. Advertising was up. The *Herald* was beginning to make money. 'I am prepared to assume the full responsibility for the future development and success of this business,' he wrote, 'but must ask you to believe that we know the field here and know the Conservative party, and also know the temperament of this western public. . . . The men who saw Wilson in Ottawa have only one object, and that is to get an organ in Alberta as cheaply as they can and as fully under the control of their party as they can secure. We have only one object, and that is to make the Herald a success.'

If it were considered by anyone in Calgary that a group of politicians could go to either Hamilton or Ottawa and get the sympathy of
the investors in the *Herald* to anything approaching a dictation of
policy, his own usefulness to the paper would be gone. In his arrangements with Southam Limited he had understood the company's
interests were purely commercial, that it was entrusting him with an
investment:

> It is in the defence of that investment that I must entirely refuse to ac-
> cept the suggestion made in Wilson's letter to you. The Herald pro-
> poses to continue to the Conservative party the support that it has re-
> cently been giving, and to wait for a generous length of time for them
> to reciprocate by doing something for us. Even if they did nothing for
> us, the feeling of the Herald is in that direction, but to make the Her-
> ald a straight Conservative paper, strongly endorsing Conservative
> views, etc., I would not do it in this country, nor would we consent to
> any Conservative politicians or anyone else being able to come back
> here and say that they were able to influence the policy of the Herald
> from any source outside this office.

At this point Woods informed the Southams for the first time that
he had taken on other newspaper interests in the West. The Conservatives had mentioned to Wilson that there were only three Conservative papers in Alberta, the Edmonton *Journal*, the Calgary *Herald*,
and a weekly.

> The Edmonton Journal does not pose as an independent. It is a
> straight Conservative paper and its policy is controlled by me. The
> only objection the Conservatives have to it is this same feeling of dis-
> trust and a desire to dictate to it. . . . The Lethbridge News has been
> for some years a struggling weekly. It is right in Mr. Magrath's own
> constituency and town, but he, though a rich man, has let it go to seed
> for lack of financial support, just as the Conservatives in Edmonton
> let the Journal go to seed for the same cause. I, acting for some
> friends, secured the Journal in Edmonton and it has not changed its
> policy one atom. Recently, acting for some friends here in Calgary
> . . . I secured the Lethbridge News, and it will be started as a daily
> next month. If the Conservatives of Alberta wish to buck the Herald
> they will have other troubles as well. We do not want them to buck it,
> nor to buck them, but propose as between the two that the Herald will
> be on top and not the party.

Woods still owed money on his stock interest in the *Herald*. None
the less he concluded on a note of some confidence. He would not
want to lose the Southam connection and friendship. However, 'If
. . . your confidence does not extend to the limit defined in this letter,
I will be glad to consider with you a rearrangement financially of this
business on such terms as will be agreeable to you.'

William sent the correspondence round the family and sent a reply drafted largely by Wilson. In a mild and slightly ironic manner, it suggested that Woods hold his horses; he might not be entirely infallible. He himself had suggested someone might see Loughheed – the violence of his reaction to 'the ordinary business courtesy' of the talk at Ottawa seemed hardly justified. Wilson had made it clear that the Southams felt the *Herald*'s lack of co-operation was the Conservatives' own fault. As for the suggestion that Woods hire an editorial writer, it was also made clear that this writer would be under Woods's direction. Finally, 'it was plainly stated that these were only suggestions and that the decision was entirely in your hands.' The one point Woods might take exception to was the Conservatives' reference to his friendship with Cross and his brother's position. Under the circumstances – since Woods himself had freely expressed his opinion 'of the different gentlemen who are interested in the Conservative party in Alberta' – perhaps he was a bit hypersensitive about that.

The letter went on to say that the Southams liked Woods's management of the paper, though they couldn't agree that he had absolute say as to its editorial direction, or that the Southam interest was purely commercial. He could rest assured that if the Conservatives or others came up with suggestions, they would be told, as they had been in this instance, that 'we would consult you in the matter with full confidence that whatever you decide will be in the best interests of all concerned.'

Since Woods now controlled two more newspapers and had offered to buy the Southam interest in the *Herald*, perhaps he might be reminded – the letter suggested – that there was still opportunity to assist in financing the *Herald*. In view of the paper's showing 'and also because of the liking we have for and confidence in the managing director and secretary-treasurer' Southam Limited had no intention of parting with its interest. 'As my son Bill expresses it,' the letter said, 'with you at the helm we certainly get action for our money in more ways than one.'

It noted also that since Brett's talk with Woods, the *Herald* had been giving first-class support to the party.

On one central point, however, this soft answer was unequivocal: 'To avoid future misunderstanding I think it is necessary that we should make it quite clear that I have the final say as to both editorial and business management.' The general effect of the wordage that surrounded this clarifying statement was to express confidence that Woods's judgment was good and to imply that as long as it stayed that way no prerogative would be applied.

Woods replied: 'I thank you very much indeed for the tone of your letter, with which I heartily agree in its reference to the relation of the president of The Herald Publishing Company to the company. We here will always wish to recognize the entire right of our president to an ultimate decision on all matters affecting this company; only we did not exactly feel that it was the president who was deciding them in the instance referred to.'

This last was a dig at Wilson (who commented mildly that Woods had sidestepped the fact that when William forwarded Wilson's letter he had done so as an expression of his own views). Much of Woods's correspondence indicates that had his mental agility been transmuted into the physical he would have made a remarkable defensive boxer with a superior left jab – sometimes thrown while going away.

He added in a P.S. 'regarding those other papers' that he had no financial interest in them at present but did have 'a potential interest and exercise control over them.'

The rumored party organ in Calgary never got going. And after various vicissitudes and changes of ownership and political alliance, the *News*, which became the *News-Telegram*, finally expired as the Calgary *Canadian*. The *Herald* and the *Albertan* remained as rivals in the field.

The Buildings

In the fall of 1911 the Calgary *Herald* shared in a news development that was typical of the city and the time. On Wednesday, October 4, under a map of the downtown area it ran a story on the latest land sale:

BIG REAL ESTATE DEAL MEANS THAT
THE HERALD WILL HAVE SPLENDID NEW
HOME IN BUSINESS HEART OF CALGARY

The story reported that Southam Limited 'the well-known newspaper publishers and investors of Hamilton' had bought two corners at Seventh Avenue and First Street West, one from Senator Lougheed, the other from Theodore Revillon, at a total cost of $327,000. On these it would proceed to build.

As Wilson had forecast, more had gone into the *Herald* in these early years than had come out of it, as Southam Limited guaranteed a line of credit and advanced money for plant. But Henry Watson's sacrificial libation proved needless. The paper, under brisk management, grew with the town. In its first year the new Herald Company barely broke even – a net profit of $718.50 on revenue of $70,000. Two years later, with doubled revenue, it cleared $9,000.

By 1911 it had outgrown its old rented quarters at Centre Street and Seventh, which had been roomy enough when the building was erected for Young in 1903. Various propositions were considered and discarded. Finally in August a Southam expedition went West – William, Fred, Bill, and their wives. From this visit grew the deal announced October 4.

That day's *Herald* might well be taken to illustrate the forward thrust of the Calgary of its time. The eight-column line went to another story. The CPR held its annual meeting in Montreal that day. Three locations, Calgary, Bassano, and Medicine Hat, had fought for the railway's western shops. Woods had a man posted at the meeting-room door. At noon his three-word message arrived: 'You get shops.' The *Herald* sold 1,200 copies of an extra in twenty minutes.

The paper ran twenty-four pages in its regular editions that Wednesday. A brief on the killing of a man by an automobile in far-off Hamilton rated front-page space. A sports-page piece speculated on effectiveness of the three Ms – Mathewson, Marquard, and Meyers – for the Giants in the forthcoming world series with the Athletics. A story from Cape Town headed TROUBLE CAUSED BY PROBLEM OF COLOR quoted General Hertzog: While 'the native should be allowed to rise as high as he could in his own circle, there should be no equality with Europeans.' The Empress, advertised as the only picture-house in Calgary, was showing 'a beautifully pathetic drama' called 'Hungry Hearts'. Over at the Lyric, 'In Old Kentucky' featured six thoroughbred horses on the stage.

By then the Southams were back East, stimulated by a deal that had in it a mixture of the urges that seemed particularly to appeal to them: development of a property plus a bet on the future of a town.

In one respect a pay-off on the bet would be long deferred. Growth of the *Herald* as a newspaper was hardly in question. But low cards would soon begin to fall in the game of real estate and business generally. Some close-to-the-vest playing was in prospect.

They picked the Lougheed corner for the *Herald*'s home and put up a ten-storey building with the newspaper housed in lower floors and basement. Excavation began in August of 1912, but it was not until Saturday, December 13, 1913, that the paper moved. The *Herald* ran an eight-column cartoon across the top of page one showing the procession of staff and machinery.

Woods took great pride in the new building, particularly the large second-floor newsroom with its light-colored walls. But newspaper men have never been particularly reverential. Shortly after the move, a number of staffers, working in the newsroom late one night, were joined by a colleague known as Major Light. The major arrived in from a religious ceremony, but had stopped off on the way; he was comfortably loaded. Standing on a desk he began to re-render one of the sermons he had heard. Torchy Anderson, then a junior on the paper, recalled the denouement: 'The Herald then operated a Sunshine Club and the lone society editor had to carry on this charitable activity. Donations in kind were frequent and on her desk that night somebody had left a dozen eggs. . . .'

The major fled at the first volley. He was unscathed. Not so the walls. When Woods arrived next morning silence fell as he stalked through to his office. Managing editor Jack Cairns answered a summons and emerged with an announcement: 'The staff is fired!'

'But', he added, 'don't go away. We have to get a paper out.'

No one went away.

Meantime work went ahead on the Revillon corner. The Southams had agreed to erect a six-storey-and-basement building for the Calgary Furniture Company under a twenty-five-year lease agreement.

The furniture company moved into the new store – the Southam Building – early in 1914. The real-estate boom had already faded to a whisper. Wartime uncertainties put business further on the downbeat. By November, Bill Watson had to report that the furniture dealers hadn't paid their October rent and were still behind on September. The rental figure of $54,000 a year was cut to $42,000, but a year or so later the company failed. The lease was cancelled, Southam Limited taking over some bits of real estate that had been pledged by the furniture company's principals.

The value of this collateral may be gathered from a report by Woods, who went to look at some of it. One forty-acre lot in North Vancouver had been valued at $20,000. Woods didn't reach it, since he estimated the climb up Grouse Mountain would take five hours. He reported to Bill Southam: 'I found one live real-estate man in North Vancouver, all the others having been dead since the boom. He said that the only possible use to which the property could be put in his opinion would be as a pasture for mountain goats, but that we would have to tie the goats to the trees in order to keep them from falling off the land onto our neighbor's lot.'

The Southam Building had a checkered career for years, housing a succession of stores on lower floors until the Calgary post office moved in for a stay that lasted until 1932 when the *Herald* itself moved across the street and the buildings switched names.

Neither building turned a profit in the early years. In November of 1914 the ten-storey Herald Building showed annual revenue of only $60,000 from $105,000 of rentable space. As late as February, 1917, W.J.Southam noted ruefully in a letter to Woods:

> Last week brother Fred was up here and among other things he mentioned that our Calgary buildings after taking care of operating expenses were approximately just paying the taxes, insurance, and mortgage interest and that in other words one million dollars of our money was lying out there in bricks and mortar without giving any return excepting in an artistic sense, which at this distance we miss entirely, although Father sometimes gets his money's worth by orating after looking at the photos of the buildings, which are hung on the walls of his office.

The *Herald*'s position as a tenant developed one nagging point of contention between F.N.Southam and Woods. Of the Herald Building's construction cost, $10,000 had been charged to the paper for a press pit and other extras. Woods thought it was too much. The *Herald*'s rent was fixed rather casually at $12,000 a year, later raised to $15,000. Fred thought it was too little. Since the financial interest of Woods and Watson was in the newspaper only, it was to their advantage to keep *Herald* costs down. At the same time they were in effect western representatives of Southam Limited whose interests embraced both the building and the newspaper.

The problem was settled in 1919 when the *Herald* bought the building for $685,000 in seven per cent preferred stock created in an increase in capital of the Herald Company. Of the new preferred, $40,000 was distributed to minority shareholders as a sweetener. The purchase had the effect of establishing a single company interest among all *Herald* shareholders – and also protecting the *Herald* to some extent from excessive payments of profits tax.

Death in a Prairie Arena

A scene remains in the mind of Bruce Boreham, who was sports editor of the Calgary *Herald* in the days of seven-man hockey and white-hope heavyweights: a hotel room, a glance through a window, and a big awkward prize-fighter suddenly pale as death; an incidental moment in a spring day that put Calgary into the record books as the site of an event that was tragic, macabre, and bizarre.

After his demolition by Jack Johnson, former heavyweight champion Tommy Burns (born Noah Brusso in Hanover, Ontario) came to the lusty cowtown in two capacities – as haberdasher and fight promoter. A civic element contended that prize-fighting was illegal in Calgary. Backed by a real-estate man, Burns built an arena outside the city limits. There, on May 24, 1913, a Saturday, 7,000 flocked to see Luther McCarty and Arthur Pelkey fight ten rounds.

McCarty, an ex-cowboy from Nebraska hailed as 'white heavy-weight champion', had lived and fought in Calgary a couple of years before and gone on to meet the top white battlers of the time – Carl Morris, Jim Flynn, Frank Moran, Jess Willard. Burns lured him with a purse of $5,000 to fight his protégé Pelkey, a native of Chatham, Ontario, billed as a local boy.

Peculiar omens preceded the bout. At one stage of training Mc-Carty pitched off a horse and fell on shoulders and neck. The Nebraskan made friends with an Anglican minister, Reverend William R. Walker. The two became inseparable. At main-bout time on that May Saturday, the crowd looked on in some bewilderment as Walker, in clerical garb, climbed into the ring. His purpose was to warn the fighters not to forget in their pursuit of fame that they had a Creator and to prepare to meet Him.

The fight lasted one minute and forty-six seconds:

> The bell rang. Both shook hands with referee Ed Smith. Then they faced each other and the match was started. There was nothing to it for the first minute. Both exchanged light taps to the body. Then while coming together Pelkey sent his left to McCarty's jaw and his right to the body. The blow hit in the vicinity of the heart. Luther stood there for a second, then he reeled and describing a half-circle, fell to the floor, never to move again.

Thus Boreham wrote in the *Herald* after the fatal result was known. No one realized at the moment that what had happened was more than a simple knockout.

Pelkey and Boreham left the arena through a yelling crowd while McCarty still lay unmoving.

More than half a century later the sports editor remembered: 'Pelkey lived at a little two-storey hotel in Calgary. I drove back with him to get a first-hand story from a man who could claim he was the new white champion. We were sitting in his room talking and looking out the window when one of those long black undertaker's vans drove by. Pelkey turned to me and he was white as a ghost: "Gosh, I hope Lute McCarty isn't in that thing." He was.'

Pelkey gave himself up to police. Boreham hurried to the *Herald* to help Jack Cairns round up a crew to get out an extra – with hand-set type since the lino pots were cold.

On Sunday night the Burns arena burned to the ground.

An autopsy attributed McCarty's death to a dislocated neck and resultant haemorrhage, whether caused by Pelkey's fists or an old injury aggravated by blows, no one knew. A coroner's jury cleared Pelkey, but pressure forced his arrest on a manslaughter charge. He went to trial, defended by a young Calgary lawyer known in those days as 'Sports' Smith and later as Arthur L. Smith, M.P., and won quick acquittal.

Burns, also charged, was never tried. He took Pelkey on a tour of the States. Brief reports came back to Calgary: Gunboat Smith knocked him out in San Francisco; Carl Morris kayoed him in Tulsa. Eventually he died of sleeping sickness. Tommy Burns turned to religion, organized a group in northern California, and filled occasional letters to Bruce Boreham with quotations from the Bible.

Imbroglio in Oil

Real estate was dead by 1913, but a new excitement soon hit Calgary. Early days of the oil boom involved Woods and the *Herald* in a situation that lacked only a cloak and a couple of daggers to rank with anything then touring the playhouses of the West. In a metaphorical sense even these props were there.

History had already developed in Albertans a high sensitivity to the smell of oil. Early explorers reported seepages from the sands of the Athabasca. Workmen drilling for water in CPR construction days struck natural gas north of Medicine Hat and by 1904 the Hat used it for heat and light. In the following year A.W.Dingman incorporated a gas company and drilled near Calgary. Early in 1913 Dingman and others began to sink a hole for oil about thirty miles southwest of the city.

On Thursday, October 9, the *Herald* reported: 'The Herald is informed that a first-class quality of oil has been struck at the well of the Calgary Petroleum Products Company, on the south bank of Sheep Creek, near Black Diamond. . . . The oil is said to be almost pure gasoline.' Next day the paper carried a letter from Dingman in which he confirmed the fact that 'oil of a very high specific gravity has been struck', but cautioned that this didn't prove commercial values. An accompanying story set the tone of things to come: 'The Dominion land office was besieged this morning by a clamoring mob of applicants struggling to file for oil leases on lands as far as from Priddis on the north to a line parallel with Claresholm on the south, and extending over a belt from 10 to 20 miles in width, west of the fifth principal meridian. . . .'

The *Herald*'s leading editorial sounded a warning. There had been previous oil showings but not in commercial quantities. Everyone would hope that things would be different this time. But . . . the *Herald*'s advice was crisp: 'Do not speculate in oil lands unless you have so much money that you are financially able to throw it out over the Bow River and bet whether it will fall into the water or not.'

The preliminary flow in the Dingman well was cased off; drilling continued.

From this core of fact, rumor, hysteria, and stock-selling schemes proliferated. Reporting to the Southams, Woods noted that the people connected with the Dingman enterprise were 'all first-class, spending their own money'. But in Calgary, company after company set up shop to sell stock in the oil potential of vast stretches of gopher country.

On October 24 the *Herald* front-paged a WARNING TO THE PUBLIC. 'The day of the oil promoter is with us,' it said, 'and unless something is done to stop him the seller of fake oil stocks will reap a harvest in Calgary. Also will he carry the name of this city far and wide as a place of stock boomers where cupidity reigns instead of conscience.' Woods followed this up with a series on 'The Flotation of Oil Companies' in which the paper detailed the capitalization methods of several companies by name.

Counter-attack was inevitable. In an editorial October 29 the *Albertan* charged that 'the principal and only object of the Herald is to keep the small investor out and let the big man make more money'; to which the *Herald* replied that 'no one with a soul much larger than that of a flea would be so despicable as the Calgary morning paper.'

Three weeks later an advertisement in the *Albertan,* signed by an oil man, asked the question: 'Is Standard Oil paying for the front-page knocks in the Herald?' The *Herald* replied to the ad (for which, incidentally, the *Albertan* apologized) with a front-page box headed DENIAL OF A SLANDER.

But Woods was taking no chances of being caught unaware. He tipped William Southam: 'Among other things I understand they are hunting up investments of Southam Limited in eastern Canada with a desire to trace some Southam money to stock in the Imperial Oil Company. If they can do this they can claim that the attitude of the Herald is dictated by Standard Oil interests through Southam Limited.'

W.J. assured him that Southam Limited had no money in oil stocks and went on light-heartedly to record that their only venture into oil had been a losing one: 'There is an item showing on our books which totals up to some $15,000, which was sunk in drilling for oil in British Columbia. The promoter of this venture sent to brother Wilson at the time he was tapping our bank account a book on how to discover where oil should be. This book is all we had to show for our $15,000.'

Woods went on with his dissection of stock-promotion methods. On November 20 the *Herald* published a curious story. A weekly devoted to oil news, it said, had planned to run a libellous article about the *Herald* and those connected with it. Woods had heard of it and warned the printer, who insisted the article be deleted. S.E.Beveridge, an oil man, had gone to the printing office and urged its publication, undertaking that if the printing company were held responsible he would pay any loss incurred. 'Mr. Beveridge is a respectable citizen as far as the Herald knows,' the story said, 'and yet he was inciting another man to commit an offense just because he is angry with the Herald for spoiling the sale of his particular oil stock.'

The sequel to this was a *Herald* story November 27 headed EDITOR OF HERALD IS SUMMONED FOR LIBEL, the charge being based on the *Herald*'s statement that Beveridge's action was 'inciting to commit an offense'. On December 3 Woods wrote W.J.Southam: 'The case came up in police court today and judgment is reserved by the magistrate. . . . We have had a good story out of it today, as we took advantage of the preliminary investigation to ask the complainant a number of awkward questions. . . . If the magistrate should refuse to commit, we will then be at liberty to comment on the evidence.'

It didn't work out that way. On December 5 someone dispatched a telegram to William Southam at Hamilton. Signed simply 'Alberta Oil Men', it read: 'Woods committed for trial defamatory libel. Why persist in error?' Woods made a story out of even that. The anonymous message, the *Herald* said, was 'promptly wired back to the Herald office by Mr. Southam together with his emphatic endorsement of the Herald campaign and his hopes that it would be maintained until wildcatting had been stopped.'

In a letter to the elder Southam, Woods reviewed the situation. He did so with considerable nonchalance, probably justified by existence of under-cover activity of which there is internal evidence in his report:

> From a newspaper standpoint this is a very interesting fight. The facts are that as soon as a seepage of oil was discovered in the Dingman well, a lot of people here began organizing oil companies. The country for 100 miles by 50 was blanketed with applications for oil leases

entirely irrespective of any geological knowledge or indication and in
addition to hot speculation in the leases themselves, about 50 companies prepared to go after the small money of the general public. . . .
It happens that the men who have been promoting oil companies
are the same people who used to sell subdivisions. The real-estate
business is dead and they thought they saw a chance for easy money
in oil stocks.

As for the libel action, he did not think they could succeed in a
higher court, and he wasn't much worried. There were other aspects
to the campaign:

They have formed an oil association here which consists almost entirely of oil-stock promoters and real-estate agents. These people have
subscribed money and opened offices and are busy hunting up evidence to injure the Herald. . . . Please understand that I am fairly well
informed concerning their movements, and that there is not much real
danger in anything they do. . . .
Meanwhile we have our own plans under way which we will use if
necessary. We do not propose to make ourselves a bore to our readers
talking about oil, but will continue our campaign with moderation and
dignity as occasion demands, and I have little fear but that in the end
we will have increased the Herald's standing and prestige a good deal
at some expense for law costs, etc. . . . Of course there is one feature
we have to be careful to discount, namely the fact that those who are
really drilling are likely to strike oil, in which event the situation will
necessarily be altered. . . .

Woods reported further on December 19. He thought the scrap
was about to end:

The oil men met on Tuesday night and a better element took hold of
the association, and they are now negotiating with us for friendship.
They say that they are prepared to promote the oil development in a
sane and reasonable way, and they want to be assured of fair treatment from us. I have told their secretary today that we have every
desire to assist the industry, and have much respect for a number of
the men now identified with it, but naturally they cannot expect very
cordial relations with us as long as their vice-president . . . continues
to industriously try to put the editor of the Herald in jail. I understand
that the rest of the promoters will probably induce him very shortly
to voluntarily abandon his action.
We are still paying some money for investigation purposes but I
think before long it will be all over.

It wasn't quite curtain-time. A letter was drafted, designed to go to
William Southam, detailing the perfidies of J.H.Woods. On December 29 Woods wired Bill: 'Understand letter to Mr. Southam was
mailed yesterday. Please return it to me after perusal, preserving
carefully envelope and postmark. Wire when sent.'

This confused Bill a bit. No such letter arrived.

Woods explained in a note, in which there is further evidence of a helping hand in the enemy camp: 'The letter it was proposed to send you never went. They could not get anyone to put his signature to it. I secured a copy of it and enclose it herewith. You will notice that it contains one or two very distinct libels on me personally. I wanted to make sure that while they were writing the letter they wrote a good one, so I secured the insertion of those references.'*

The libel charge was withdrawn on December 30.

For a while, with no further news from the Dingman well, excitement slackened. An English geologist named Cunningham Craig published a cautious report from which the *Herald* drew the conclusions that oil in commercial quantities existed in Alberta, that much of the exploratory work so far done had been futile, but that 'within three months or thereabouts Calgary should have a pretty fair idea as to whether or not it is to be the business centre of a large oil market.' The paper continued to urge caution 'until actual developments assure the presence of a real commercial oil field.'

Other news, as usual, was plentiful and varied. Admirers presented the aged Father Lacombe with a new Ford car. Sam Hughes threatened to withdraw Canada's Bisley team if peep sights were banned. Lord Strathcona died. Mrs. R.R.Jamieson became a commissioner of the Calgary juvenile court, the first woman judge in Canada. In Savannah, Georgia, builders completed the Batson flying ship, designed for trans-Atlantic flight, and in London Claude Graham White proposed to fly the ocean in 1915.

On Thursday, May 14, 1914, the *Herald*'s top line went to R.B. Bennett's protest in the Commons against leaving the Canadian Northern in Mackenzie and Mann's hands – the historic speech in which he stigmatized Arthur Meighen as a gramophone for the company. The *Herald* termed his arguments forceful and fair, but not convincing.

Late that afternoon, with the drill down to 2,718 feet, the Dingman well blew in.

The story broke for morning papers but there was plenty of fresh drama for the *Herald*. At 11:40 A.M. Friday, the eighty-four-foot derrick caught fire at the top. Drillers Dinsmore and Horndyke

---

*In *Saturday Night* for February 23, 1952, D.M.LeBourdais, who worked in Calgary during the 1913-14 oil boom, related that he had been told years afterward that the secretary of the oil association – a new man – was a Pinkerton detective obtained for Woods by Alfred Cuddy, then Calgary chief of police. LeBourdais's informant was Cuddy.

The Southam brothers in 1927

F.N. (Fred), Richard, W.J. (Bill), Wilson, Harry

The Southam family in 1905

Seated: Mrs. William Southam, Ethel
Standing: Harry, Gordon, Wilson, William, Fred, Richard, William J.

Mercy Neal Southam
(1809-1887)

William Southam
1877 to 1927

F.N. Southam
1928 to 1945

Philip S. Fisher
1945 to 1961

St. Clair Balfour
Since 1961

The Presidents of the Company

climbed it with pails of water and doused the blaze. For its late edition the *Herald* had pictures of Calgarians crowding the sidewalk in front of oil company offices, waiting to buy stock. The oil boom was on again.

The *Herald* now relaxed its advertising practice: 'As you are aware,' Woods wrote F.N.Southam, 'the policy of the Calgary Herald since the false start of last fall has been that it would not take oil-stock advertising into its columns until oil had been discovered in commercial quantities. On Friday, after the strike had been verified, we opened our columns to oil advertising. . . . Meantime our editorial policy continues conservative and we have advised our people against going excitedly into speculation. . . . Speaking with due care, I really think we are on the eve of a very considerable oil development, which will of course have its dangers and disadvantages in excessive speculation but which will in the end add new industries and forms of enterprise to the city and district.'

To his discussion of all this Woods brought a reporter's eye: 'The crowds in front of the offices, the unreasoning way in which people have rushed to put in their little bits of money, and the incidents of men who a week ago were borrowing money for their household necessities, and who now want to know what motor is more expensive than the Napier or the Pierce-Arrow – as long as one can view them philosophically they are certainly interesting.'

Writing to William Southam late in May he reported the situation as gradually quieting, noted that most if not all of the companies 'will at least honestly spend in development the proceeds of their treasury stock' and added that 'in the seven issues up to last Saturday night the Herald carried about $10,000 worth of oil advertising.'

Few if any Napiers or Pierce-Arrows accrued to Calgarians who bought oil stock indiscriminately. Most of the new companies folded up. Dingman's – Calgary Petroleum Products – survived, deepened its discovery well, and added two more. Imperial Oil organized Royalite, which took over the Dingman company; thus the well that blew in on May 14, 1914, became Royalite No. 1, first producer of the Turner Valley field. The valley would eventually have more than 300 producing wells, developed in an orderly manner by well-backed companies. But meantime war had come, for the time at least depressing booms, businesses, and newspapers alike.

In June of 1914 the *Herald* front-paged a 'panoramic view of the big military training camp in Calgary'. Between 2,000 and 3,000 militiamen were there. The 23rd Alberta Rangers marched out for musketry. The Army Medical Corps went afield for practice in their particular line of work 'such as gathering up the wounded and giving first aid'.

The practice was soon to become reality.

A variety of wartime experience came to Calgary itself. During one riotous night in February of 1916 soldiers in training, urged on by civilians described by the *Herald* as 'flyspecks of humanity', smashed up two restaurants owned by someone who was said to have fired a returned soldier and hired an Austrian. On the next night they demolished the interior of a hotel, apparently in the belief that it was owned by a man named Poffenroth (who had, however, previously sold it to an Englishman).

By then most of Woods's staff were overseas or headed there, including advertising manager Leigh Spencer, sports editor Bruce Boreham, and Torchy Anderson.

Woods himself reported a little wistfully to W.J.Southam in June of 1916 that he now had 'the full title of private' in a reserve militia battalion that trained two nights a week. He was then nearing fifty and no candidate for military glory. Six years later, in 1922, he was appointed honorary Lieutenant-Colonel of the 10th battalion, Calgary Highlanders, a distinction he particularly prized.

Edmonton

In 1909 J.H. Woods undertook to revive the Edmonton *Journal*. In that year John P. McConnell, publisher of the Vancouver weekly *Saturday Sunset*, got an option on the *Journal* and turned it over to Woods, who brought Milton Robbins (Bob) Jennings out from Toronto as managing editor. Jennings, originally from upstate New York, had worked on Ontario papers for ten years or so. He brought to Edmonton an engaging personality and a background of realistic experience.

By the end of 1910 Woods was heavily committed personally in both the *Journal* and the Lethbridge *News*, which he had converted from weekly to daily publication. What he had in mind was a central company – Canadian Newspapers Limited – to operate the *Herald*, the *Journal*, and the *News*. The principals would be the Southams and himself. The Southams were not interested in putting the *Herald* into any such proposition; it was doing all right as it was. Nor did they think much of the Lethbridge prospect. But the *Journal* was something else.

This was not the first suggestion that they go into Edmonton. Early in 1908 Harry Evans, a friend from Hamilton days, then setting up an investment business in Edmonton, tipped off Wilson that he thought the *Journal* could be bought. Evans knew something about newspapers. He had once managed the Winnipeg *Telegram,* edited by his brother Sanford. The *Journal,* he wrote, had been doing well until a current real-estate slump but now was in a tough spot – badly managed and five weeks behind on its payroll.

At the same time W.A.Griesbach (later a major-general and a power in western Conservatism) wrote Wilson saying it was rumored that Southams were interested in western newspapers – apparently word of the Calgary *Herald* deal reached Edmonton quickly – and suggesting they buy out one of the largest shareholders for $6,000 or so. Another $4,000 or $6,000 would put the paper in good shape.

Wilson told Griesbach the Southams were not in a position to think about it just then. His response to Evans was less negative. He sent him the Griesbach correspondence and commented: 'We are naturally anxious to assist the Conservative party wherever possible, as at present we think they are the party of purity, and we are not averse to getting a bargain in any business proposition if we could raise the funds.' He asked Evans to appraise the plant.

Woods also got in on this 1908 discussion, advising W.J. that the *Journal* would have a hard time for a while 'as Edmonton has not any body of Conservatives worth counting on, the town being politically owned by Frank Oliver'. But the future was assured.

The paper then was less than five years old. In November of 1903 John Macpherson, John W. Cunningham, and Arthur Moore, all of Portage la Prairie, had set up in opposition to the *Bulletin,* the paper Oliver had founded with a press dragged into Edmonton by ox-cart in 1880. Edmonton, with a history of more than 100 years as a fur-trading post, still had only 4,000 people in 1903. But the railways were coming. The CPR's branch from Calgary had been there since 1891, though it ended at Strathcona, across the deep cleft of the North Saskatchewan. The Canadian Northern came in 1905 and the Grand Trunk Pacific was on the way. The paper started by Macpherson, Cunningham, and Moore was moderately Conservative. Starting with a daily circulation of 1,000, it grew and made money for a while but, by 1908, as Evans informed Wilson Southam, its position was precarious.

Evans got access to the plant and sent Wilson an inventory. Wilson wired an offer of $5,000 cash and up to $10,000 in assumed liabilities. The *Journal*'s owners turned the offer down.

No further proposition was made to the Southams about Edmonton until Woods came up with his three-paper-company idea, but as early as May 1911, it was rumored around Calgary that they had the *Journal*.

In April of that year Max Aitken, the boy wonder who had just pieced together several industrial mergers in Canada, tried to buy the Calgary *Herald*. His motive was to further the political fortunes of fellow New Brunswicker R.B.Bennett. Apparently the future Lord Beaverbrook was a little leery of the future Viscount Bennett's business diplomacy; on April 4 he wrote Bennett: 'I have explained to Southam that I need the Calgary Herald on account of my interest in Canadian politics, so be careful not to interfere with the negotiation proceedings.' Bennett replied: 'I have not even mentioned the matter for I was afraid that they would suspect that I had some interest in the transaction. As a matter of fact they control a paper at Lethbridge and Edmonton as well and the combination would prove very powerful if properly managed.'

Woods at that time 'controlled' the *Journal* and the Lethbridge *News* in one way or another, but the Southams had not yet put any money into them. Presumably Bennett's reference was based on his knowledge of Woods's association with the Southams in the *Herald*.

As far as Aitken's efforts to buy went, Southams simply refused to sell. The *Herald* of course backed Bennett in the federal election that fall, in which the future Prime Minister won the Calgary seat.

Woods had put $6,500 into Lethbridge stock and was optimistic even though the city had had a hard time for a couple of years with crop failures and coal strikes and already was served by a daily paper. Back in 1905 young W.A.Buchanan had come west from St. Thomas and bought the weekly *Herald*, which he turned into a daily in 1907 at the start of a bright career as prairie editor and Liberal politician. Oddly, Woods saw Buchanan's early success as an augury for the prosperity of a second paper rather than as competition that would make things tough. He figured the *News* needed $25,000 to $30,000 to build it up to 'something better than the Herald' and visualized cutting the Calgary *Albertan* out of the morning field in southern Alberta and the Crow's Nest Pass country.

The Southams were dubious about Lethbridge. 'The News looks to be a very lame duck indeed,' Wilson noted in December 1911, when plans were coming to a head. 'I wouldn't touch Lethbridge,' William scribbled in the margin of a letter from Fred. But Woods was personally involved for several thousand dollars and felt the paper could be made to pay. In the end the Southams went in; Woods was entitled to a run for his money and perhaps the *News* would pay its way. In any event the move would put them in a strategic position in regard to the *Journal*. At a meeting of Southam Limited January 2, 1912, they recorded their decision:

> On the understanding that the Lethbridge News would be merged with the Edmonton Journal, through both properties being absorbed by Canadian Newspapers Limited, and that the shares in the News would be entitled to the same exchange basis as shares in the Journal, this company agreed to subscribe at par to $30,000 of stock in the Lethbridge News Co., and $20,000 in the Edmonton Journal.

In February John Wodell arrived in Lethbridge to take charge, fresh from a month in Bermuda, provided by William Southam as reward for a strenuous year on the *Spectator* in which three elections – Dominion, provincial, and civic – all turned out the right way.

It soon became apparent that the Lethbridge duck was indeed arthritic, with small chance of cure in the current business climate. Early in 1913 Lethbridge Conservatives, alarmed at the prospect of a fold-up, moved to approach the party hierarchy at Ottawa for support. Fred, Wilson, and Harry stepped in with protests. 'If the paper is to be carried on as a charity . . . then the Conservative party should take it over from us and run it themselves,' Wilson wrote his father. 'If the town is not good enough . . . to support this paper, then the only self-respecting course as far as Southam Limited is concerned is to pull out.' That is what they did. The *News* published its last daily edition July 31, 1913. It ceased as a weekly in December. Wodell moved to the Calgary *Herald* where he continued until retirement in 1945 after fifty-five years on Southam newspapers.

In two years of operating the Lethbridge *News* something more than $30,000 went down the drain. But the picture at Edmonton was different. The *Journal* had begun to thrive.

At about the time the Lethbridge experiment expired, Southam Limited put a further $30,000 into Canadian Newspapers Limited on behalf of the *Journal*. From early 1912 on they retained control of this and successive *Journal* companies. Woods held a sizable personal interest and executives of the paper also shared in ownership. Several Albertans including Griesbach and Magrath held a few shares.

Both the paper and the city had come a long way since 1908. Prospective colonists read of central Alberta as 'The Land of Big Crops and Rich Pastures'. Edmonton hoisted an inviting slogan: Come and Grow With Us. The city had reached across the river to absorb Strathcona, where the new university stood. Population was close to

50,000 and 15,000 or so were buying the *Journal*.* From 1912 on, though there were depression years when things were close and others in which competitive rate-cutting chopped profits to a sliver, the *Journal* never lost money.

A curious sidelight on the times is that late in 1913 Harry Southam proposed that both the *Journal* and the Calgary *Herald* be sold. He and Wilson, while they had favored going into Edmonton, were never enthusiastic about it. Harry's view as relayed by Wilson when the proposition was reaching its final stage late in 1911, seems to have been somewhat equivocal: 'Harry looks at the buying of further newspapers as a mistake if our object is to make money. He believes that we can make it more easily, more quickly, and with less risk, in real estate. But if our object in buying newspapers is to make money, and to preach reforms, such as single tax, then he is in favor of such a policy.'

Fred's feeling, expressed at the same time, differed: 'As we are in the newspaper business I think it will pay us in the long run to continue branching out in this line within reasonable bounds. . . . I am firmly of the opinion that the Edmonton proposition within the next five years can be made one of the best newspaper propositions in Canada.'

In December of 1913, apprehensive of uncertain business weather ahead, Harry came up with a definite recommendation: 'I favor, if we can get a reasonable price, selling our western newspapers. . . .' He thought Senator Lougheed or Robert Rogers, or both, would be glad to buy. He added a prediction that must have caused him some wry reflection later: 'I believe that our Calgary real estate will bring in bigger returns for all time, or at least for many years, than these two newspapers put together.' During the five years 1915-19, when the Calgary buildings scarcely made fixed charges, the *Journal* showed net profits ranging from $13,000 to $63,000 a year; at Calgary the *Herald*'s net for the period totalled more than $200,000.

W.J.'s characteristic comment on Harry's suggestion was that Lougheed and Rogers, dropping barrels of money through their current ownership of the Calgary *News-Telegram*, would probably try to get him into a matching game in the hope he would take it off their hands. And from Montreal, Fred came in with what amounted to a veto.

If there was a key point in the early history of the Southams at

*In 1966 Edmonton's population reached 400,000. The *Journal*'s net paid circulation was 135,000.

which their central purpose was defined, consciously or not, as the publication of newspapers, perhaps this was it. They were selling industrial stocks at this time to ease a position strained by depressed conditions and the Calgary construction. They neither sold nor tried to sell a newspaper.

Edmonton's growth as a city made prime local news. In May of 1912 first classes graduated from the new University of Alberta. Of more practical interest, perhaps, to more people, was the opening of the Hudson's Bay Reserve, the vast acreage on the northern outskirts owned by the ancient company.

Speculators converged on Edmonton. Hotel registers, the *Journal* said, showed that they came 'from all parts of the Dominion as well as from all corners of the province, from little-heard-of spots on Vancouver Island and equally remote villages in the Maritime provinces, from practically all the chief centres of the United States, and no insignificant number from the United Kingdom.'

On the night of Sunday, May 12, the lines began to form for the draw on Monday afternoon – at a church building on 103 Street – of numbered tickets that would give the applicant the right to buy selected lots.

> There were millionaires and laborers in the line. . . . Before midnight 500 people had gathered on Third Street and Athabasca Avenue and gradually the line stretched along Second Street to the Castle Hotel. By six o'clock this morning it began to go westward and near noon had reached Sixth Street, and practically 1,500 people had formed in the stretch of humanity. . . .
>
> The places in line were held last night as if the very life of the holder depended on the result. Many places were sold to those who did not arrive at the scene early and in many cases as high as $100 and $200 was paid. . . .

The irony was that those first on hand at the draw had no guarantee of the low-numbered tickets that would give them first crack at preferred lots. As the *Journal*'s headline reported Monday: HUNDREDS WAIT ALL NIGHT AND THEN DRAW POOR NUMBERS . . .

When low numbers turned up they were often promptly auctioned. And there was a further irony: Balmer Watt, who wrote *Journal* editorials from 1912 to 1945, recalled that the man who drew ticket No. 1 refused $26,000 for it. Along with that of others, his land eventually came back to the city for taxes as the current boom died.

Edmonton's expansion would resume with the end of the First World War. But for a period hard times threatened the city's credit.

The situation had an incidental by-product in a brief embarrassment involving the Ottawa Southams and Bob Jennings.

The *Citizen* for years had been preaching from the text of Henry George and the single tax. Wilson and Harry, if they had not entirely converted William and the others, at least seem to have persuaded them there was no harm in it. What appears to have been the only specific editorial 'policy' request ever made by Southam Limited or its successor companies to its newspapers was a resolution passed April 16, 1917:

> That it is in the interest of Southam Limited as a publishing and general business concern; as well as in the interests of the farmer, manufacturer, transportation and general trading and producing classes of the country, that business and improvements be untaxed until at least the community-created value of land be taken in taxation for municipal, provincial and federal purposes:
>
> Be it therefore resolved that our associated newspapers be and are hereby requested to use their editorial columns and influence to further this policy, and to oppose any departure from a tendency toward this system of taxation.

Edmonton was a single-tax city. Throughout the summer a move grew among its businessmen to impose a tax on improvements and a business tax to save the city's credit. Land abandonment had become general. To tax privately owned land high enough to cover defaulters and civic running expenses would cause abandonment on such a scale that revenues wouldn't begin to meet the need.

Wilson and Harry wired Jennings an expression of shock at any suggestion of departure from the principle of taxing land only. Jennings, an active and influential member of the Edmonton Board of Trade, did his best to explain: after six months of investigation by committees the board was just about unanimous that new taxes had to be imposed to dispel the shadow of receivership.

'This departure from traditions of civic development is unique,' he wired Wilson, 'in that businessmen are deliberately taxing themselves to place themselves on a sound financial footing. At a conference today [November 23] the only safe candidates for mayor and council refused to run without including the need of emergency taxes as the essence of their platform. The Journal could not desert these men in the present crisis.'

The candidate for mayor was the Southams' old friend Harry Evans.

Harry and Wilson were not convinced the emergency could not be met by raising the mill-rate rather than changing tax-raising methods, but wired Jennings that 'considering all the circumstances', which included the fact that Edmontonians hadn't been properly educated in single-tax principles, probably he couldn't do otherwise than support the businessmen's plans.

Evans, with *Journal* support, won the election. The business tax passed. The proposition to tax improvements on an assessment of up to 25 per cent of value lost by a narrow margin. But soon thereafter Edmonton swung away from the strict land-value system and began to tax buildings.

Early in 1921 the *Journal* moved into its new building at 101 Street and Macdonald Drive, where after two expansions it still published forty-five years later. Its first home had been a fruit store, its second a one-storey building of its own erected in 1905 and enlarged in 1910. Jennings, managing director through twelve years of the city's and the newspaper's growth, did not live to see the move. He died February 16 in Victoria, at the age of forty-six, of heart and blood complications tracing to service in the Spanish-American war.

John Imrie moved out from Hamilton later that year. For twenty years Imrie's name would be linked in the public mind with that of the *Journal*. Like most eastern-born westerners he became a dedicated protagonist of the high plains. Unlike many, he could see the meaning of sectional questions in national perspective.

Imrie's régime at the *Journal* was to cover the second great transition in the West. The first had come with the railways and general settlement. Now, from the early 1920s to the early 1940s, came the time of change from the horse-drawn binder to the gasoline-driven combine. It was the beginning of the age of pitchblende and the further opening of the North. It saw the coming of the bush-fliers, and it saw them move on – to airfields in the English Midlands and the blazing night sky over the Ruhr. It saw a hint, in the extension of Turner Valley oilfields, of larger things to come. It encompassed the grey years of blowing dust and thirty-cent wheat. It echoed to a court-aired sex scandal that wrecked a premier's career. And what was perhaps the strangest story of all – the rise of a high-school teacher and biblical explicator to be premier of his province through preaching strange evangels: government-created credit and a dividend for living.

The Bombing of City Hall

In the 1960s Southam Press produced a twelve-page brochure, *A Career for You in Daily Newspapers*, designed to outline for aspir-

ants the rewards and requirements of the craft. At one point, listing
the qualities of a good reporter, it noted that 'journalism still has its
characters and rugged individualists and even mild eccentrics, which
is one of the things that make the newspaper world so fascinating.'
The Calgary *Herald* had one just after the First World War who was
certainly fascinating. But far, far from mild.

On the morning of Wednesday, March 29, 1922, Mayor Sam H.
Adams sat in his office with commissioners A.J.Samis and Angus
Smith, city-solicitor Leonard W. Brockington, treasurer J.H.Mercer,
and Ralph Wilson, city-hall reporter for the *Herald*. The officials were in troubled conference. Unemployment worried Calgary,
touched here and there with violence and whispers of Communist
plots. Just yesterday a brick had come crashing through the glass of
the mayor's office door, the miscreant escaping down a stairway.

It was in this nervous atmosphere that the city executive met. Not
even Wilson could have guessed at the mischief fermenting in the
mind of a *Herald* colleague, set to bubbling by reports of the mayor's
smashed door and the general sense of foreboding.

This time there was no brick. The door opened and revealed a
crouching figure with a handkerchief tied round its face. It pushed
a small black satchel into the room. Protruding from the satchel was
a sputtering fuse. Wilson leaped for the door to an inner office and
collided with the flying figure of Samis. Mayor Adams and Brockington took cover behind the mayor's desk. Smith crashed through two
layers of glass – window and storm – to the ground twelve feet below. Mercer tried to follow and stuck in the frame.

The fuse burned down . . . to an empty satchel.

That afternoon the *Herald* front-paged a story in which were combined the news and its regret thereat. It was headed AN APOLOGY:

> Wednesday morning, B.C.Long Lance, a reporter on the staff of the
> Herald, opened the door of Mayor Adams's office at City Hall and
> placed inside a bag, which had the appearance of an infernal machine,
> with fuse attached and burning.
>
> All present thought that some person with a grievance planned to
> blow up the City Hall, and there was an immediate rush to escape
> from the room. The thought was natural in view of the fact that
> threats against city-hall officials have lately been heard and consider-
> ing that a rock was hurled through Mayor Adams's window Tuesday.
>
> Commissioner Smith, in attempting to open a window to escape
> from the room, was badly cut about the hands and face.
>
> The Herald deeply regrets this occurrence and that this indignity to
> His Worship Mayor Adams and to the commissioners and other offi-
> cers of the city was suffered by them through the act of a member of

its staff, and tenders its sincere apologies to Mayor Adams and to the other city hall officials affected by his conduct.

This incident marked the final day's employment on the *Herald* of one of the West's most flamboyant characters. Brockington and Adams pleaded for him, but editor Charlie Smith was adamant. Chief Buffalo Child Long Lance must go.

Go he did . . . to the Winnipeg *Tribune.*

The great city-hall bombing was just one escapade in the Long Lance career. Ten more years of free-wheeling were in the cards.

Born Sylvester Clarke Long at Winston-Salem, North Carolina, in 1892 of Cherokee, white, and Negro blood, Long Lance studied at Carlisle, attended St. John's Military Academy, failed the exams for West Point (deliberately, he claimed, in order to get into the war), and enlisted in Montreal in 1916. In France he was twice wounded. Discharged in Calgary July 18, 1919, with the rank of staff sergeant, he applied to the *Herald* for a job, got it, and held it until the incident of the sputtering satchel. The Calgary years of this athlete, poseur, and cavalier-in-the-rough included some colorful moments. Among the highlights were a wrestling appearance with boxer Jack Dempsey, and the evening when the erstwhile staff sergeant, having been commissioned in the militia, appeared in the *Herald* news room in full kit but with spurs on upside down.

From Winnipeg he went to Banff as a railway public-relations man. There he ran into typical trouble when the houseman of a lady friend refused to serve him a drink. Long Lance went to hospital with razor slashes, the houseman with a fractured skull. Both recovered. No one brought charges. But Long Lance was once more unemployed.

He returned to Winnipeg and from there drifted to Hollywood and moving pictures. On the morning of March 20, 1932, he was found dead in the home of Anita Baldwin, daughter of gambler Lucky Baldwin. A revolver lay on the floor beside him. His death was ruled suicide. No inquest was held.

That year Long Lance made the *Canadian Annual Review.* Its list of notable deaths recorded:

Lance, Chief Buffalo Child Long, Indian author and journalist – at Los Angeles, Cal., U.S.A., on March 20, aged 36 years.

The Farmers' Party

'The ease and rapidity with which the western provinces adopt radical legislative methods is a source of wonderment to our more conservative eastern brethren who are skeptical of anything and everything that sounds or looks different,' the *Herald* remarked in a 1916 editorial. 'Commission government for municipalities, single tax, provincial prohibition, the initiative and referendum and other equally advanced legislation has come in the West, where for many years the East has done nothing more than think about it. And now there is coming equal franchise for women. . . .'

This approval of the West's experimental spirit was typical of J.H. Woods and the *Herald*. So was a close interest in the prosperity of the grain growers and stock raisers who made up much of the paper's rural reader constituency. But the paper and its publisher viewed as little short of disastrous the farmers' move into direct action as a political party.

A key by-election was set for November 3, 1919, in which Alex Moore of the United Farmers of Alberta challenged a Liberal in Cochrane. The *Herald*'s chief target was the group government and representation-by-classes theory of Henry Wise Wood, the U.F.A. president. If Moore had been nominated on behalf of the people of Cochrane and in opposition to the Liberal government, the *Herald* said, it would have supported him. But it was evident that his was 'purely a class candidature, directed and controlled by a corporate organization and devoted solely to the interests of that organization and its members, whether or not they might conflict with the general interests of the people of Cochrane riding.'

As for Wood, the *Herald*'s apprehensions had been confirmed by a recent speech:

> . . . in which for the first time in Canada, he advocated the erection of social groups or classes . . . each intended to further the interests of its own group in public affairs, even though by so doing it might commit injustices to the balance of the community: with the result, as Mr. Wood frankly stated, that group would have to rise against group and interest against interest, each fighting like a Kilkenny cat for supremacy, until his theoretical millenium might be achieved.

Wood's theories, the *Herald* contended, were 'half-baked and indigestible'. It opposed Moore's election on such a platform and would 'prefer even to see elected the nominee of a government of which it is very critical.'

Not for the first time it found itself at odds with R.B.Bennett, who wrote Moore wishing him well. The *Herald* noted that this came as no surprise: 'It has been predicted that Mr. Bennett would line up with a farmer's party when one was organized' – a remarkable prediction in the light of future events.

Moore won a close election and the Farmers were off and away.

Some U.F.A. officials at about this time raised the old cry of 'eastern influence' – sinister voices from the East had determined the *Herald*'s position. In this there was a touch of irony; the Southams' Ottawa *Citizen* was all out for the farmer in politics.

Another point of attack on Woods was a rumor that Liberals and Conservatives planned a coalition to foil the Farmers, with the *Herald* publisher promised a cabinet post. Woods scotched this just before Christmas in a front-page editorial. Alberta would stand no coalition for party gain:

> The Herald opposed the suggestion that the United Farmers should combine together to dominate the government of this province. The Herald is equally opposed to any suggestion that political parties should join together to protect themselves from the United Farmers. It is just as vicious that politicians should coalesce in opposition to the farmers as that the farmers should coalesce in opposition to other classes in the community. In fact, of the two evils the farmers would be the lesser.

What Alberta needed was a government of unselfishness, a government that would not be 'tied to the chariot wheels of Ottawa organizations'. It was a later version of Young's forgotten plea in 1905 to erase partyism from provincial affairs.

As the July election of 1921 approached, the *Herald* faced an odd situation. A mixed bag of Liberals, Conservatives, United Farmers, Independents, Laborites, Independent Farmers, and Socialists were in the field. But only Liberals and United Farmers nominated enough to elect a government and the paper disliked both. All it could hope for was 'a definite opposition and a government strong enough to carry on without needing to resort to intrigue'. In Calgary itself the thing was simpler. Five Conservatives were running there, members of the party that 'protested and fought against giving away the natural resources of this province in 1905' and against 'the railway adventures of the Liberal administration'.

In Edmonton the *Journal* held the same view as the *Herald* on class government but expressed it less vehemently. Coming up to the 1921 election it commented: 'We are convinced as completely as we ever were that the farmer's political movement is on a wrong basis. But we cannot shut our eyes to the fact that it is sweeping the rural parts of the province. . . .' Like the *Herald*, it urged election of Conservatives in the cities to form a 'coherent group' in a confused situation. But the paper was realistic. Two days before the election in a headline over grouped stories from the constituencies, it carried a frank forecast: FARMERS LIKELY TO HAVE LARGEST GROUP IN NEW LEGISLATURE.

The *Herald* had arranged an elaborate system to bulletin results – a lighted screen on the Southam Building across the street for details, and a masthead light to flash the over-all verdict: red for the Liberals, green for the U.F.A. The five Calgary Conservatives fell before Labor, Liberal, and Independent ballots. The five in Edmonton lost to Liberals. Over-all the green light went up: to signal the birth of a new provincial régime that would last fourteen years until its fall in a contest even more spectacular.

The one comfort the *Herald* could take was that its hope for a government with a solid majority had been fulfilled. The Farmers themselves had outrun Henry Wise Wood's dream of government by a collection of groups. They were in as a majority political party.

Outspokenly critical of the U.F.A.'s direct role in politics, the *Herald* backed the farm body's executive in its function as a practical farm organization. In 1923 the paper served as a kind of ignition system for the movement that brought the Alberta Wheat Pool into existence.

Returned to the free market after control by a federal board through wartime years, wheat had sunk from $2.21 a bushel in 1919 to sixty-five cents in 1923. Efforts to go back to the board system or organize voluntary pools had stalled. But in August of that year Percy Woodbridge, a former U.F.A. secretary, dropped in to see Charlie Hayden, the *Herald*'s managing editor. Just at that time Aaron Sapiro, a California lawyer who had organized fruit, tobacco, and wheat growers into marketing groups in the States, was working toward the same end in the Okanagan orchards of British Columbia. Woodbridge wanted to get Sapiro into Alberta to put some fire into the pool movement. Hayden took him to Woods and the three worked out a telegram inviting Sapiro to come to Calgary and address a public meeting with the *Herald*'s backing. In Edmonton the *Journal* also got into the campaign. Sapiro's oratory, buttressed by his practical experience in co-operative marketing, led to a quick decision by farmers and business men to organize an Alberta wheat pool. Chairman of the meeting and of the pool's first board of directors was Henry Wise Wood, the *Herald*'s old opponent on political principles. R.B.Bennett and John Brownlee were among the lawyers who drew up the documents. The pool got going by late October and in that first year handled the crop from more than half Alberta's acreage, providing initial and interim payments to spread the grower's income. In 1924 Saskatchewan and Manitoba followed Alberta into the pool system.

Though the depression of the 1930s, when wheat prices dropped even lower than in the early 1920s, called into existence a new Canadian wheat board as the central selling agency, the pools remained dominant at the handling end, a continuing power in prairie agricultural life.

Co-operation in such measures didn't affect the *Herald*'s view of the U.F.A. as a political party. 'What a spectacle it is!', the paper remarked when Brownlee succeeded Herbert Greenfield as Premier in 1925. 'This group of farmer politicians, who have always claimed to be more pure than those of other parties, who claimed possession of higher ideals than ever before guided political parties, throwing their leader to the wolves in the hope that they may save their own skins!'

The *Journal* frequently took a rather more urbane view. 'It must be admitted their record is far from a poor one,' it commented during the provincial campaign of 1926. Chief objection was still the class character of the movement. Other events rather overshadowed local politics that summer, anyway. It was the year of the British general strike and the disappearance and resurrection of evangelist Aimee Semple McPherson. In June a California portrait painter named Blanche Potter turned up in Edmonton and a wave of speculation rolled through the city: could she be Aimee? The *Journal* arranged a confrontation between Mrs. Potter and one Zelma Argue, a Los Angeles revivalist who happened to be in town, and killed that particular rumor. It was also the year of Canada's most spectacular clashes on the federal scene: the customs scandal and the Byng-Meighen-King entanglement. On provincial election day, June 28, most eyes were on Ottawa. The *Journal*'s headline was THERE IS NO GOVERNMENT IN CANADA TODAY. In Alberta the Farmers went back without much trouble.

5
A Voice in
Winnipeg

In the spring of 1920 a veteran newspaper publisher decided to sell his paper. This publisher was Robert L. Richardson. For thirty years, half his lifetime, the Winnipeg *Tribune* had been his developing creation, his livelihood, and in a sense his voice.

Its history went back to the early weeks of 1890. The *Free Press* had just absorbed the *Sun* in a city then known as the graveyard of newspapers. Richardson had been for seven years the *Sun*'s city editor, having come west after breaking in on the Toronto *Globe*. He and Duncan McIntyre, brought up on adjoining farms in the eastern Ontario county of Lanark, got together $7,000 and bought the vanished paper's flatbed. On January 26, 1890, from the *Sun*'s old quarters on Bannatyne Avenue, the *Tribune* appeared. The paper would be independent, Richardson promised, but 'by independence we do not mean neutrality.' The qualification was an understatement.

Robert Lorne Richardson – Bob or Rich to his intimates – was a Canadian blend of Sir Galahad, Little John, and Don Quixote in proportions that depended on the eye of the beholder. The master machinists of both orthodox political parties certainly saw him at various times (depending on whom he was independent against at the moment) as a pestiferous maverick on whose hide no brand would take. Richardson was remarkably consistent in his beliefs. He fought for whichever party came closest to them. When none did, he fought alone. Public ownership, free trade, and 'national' schools were the tallest plumes on his helmet and he wore them with pride and flair.

The Manitoba School Question – still a question in the 1960s and thus perhaps the longest-lived provincial issue in Canadian history – overshadowed everything in Manitoba in 1896, the year Richardson first ran for office. It was, of course, far more than a provincial issue in that year, with Tupper's federal Conservatives committed to the so-called 'remedial' legislation that would have overridden the province's stand against separate schools. The country would pronounce on that and other matters June 23. Meantime, a preview was in the works, a provincial election set for January 15.

Richardson took himself and his paper into the fray for Thomas Greenway's Liberals with all the invective typical of the time. Standing features included a listing under the heading THE NOBLE SIX: 'Here are the names of the noble six Oppositionists, who despite all pledges voted in favor of coercing Manitoba and forcing separate schools upon this province at the bidding of the French hierarchy of Quebec. Let no elector forget their names.'

The *Tribune* hired the Lyceum Theatre for election night, hooked in telegraph wires to keep the crowd informed, and whipped out an 8:30 P.M. extra to celebrate Greenway's victory: MANITOBANS STAND FIRM.

It took the *Tribune*'s muse a couple of days to come up with a ballad in the style of William Aytoun's 'Edinburgh After Flodden', detailing the rout of the 'coercionists' seat by seat. On January 18 the paper front-paged 'Toryboro After Floggin':

> Roblah took from out his satchel
> Doc Mikfadden's* old felt hat
> Saying 'This is all I bring you
> From the place where we are at.
> Boys, I charge you keep it safely
> Do not let its rim be reft,
> For its owner, Doc Mikfadden
> Is the only one that's left. . . .'

And so on.

Richardson himself shared the triumph of the main event June 23, winning the federal seat of Lisgar for the Laurier Liberals. But he could never be a party man, and within a couple of years was in bitter conflict with Clifford Sifton and disillusioned by federal Liberal tariff and railway policy. By the time Greenway went to the polls again in December of 1899 the *Tribune* was in a difficult position. Hugh John Macdonald, whose election to the federal House in 1896 it had bemoaned, now led the provincial Conservatives and his policy of government ownership of railways was also the *Tribune*'s and Richardson's. The paper urged voters to elect candidates as individuals and insisted public ownership was the issue. Since Hugh John and the

---

*Conservative D.H.McFadden sat for Emerson. 'Roblah' was apparently a play on Rodmond P. Roblin's name.

Conservatives were the public-ownership men the implication was plain. When Greenway lost, the *Tribune* chalked up his defeat to his being misled by Sifton. By 1900 Richardson had been kicked out of the Liberal caucus at Ottawa. He rode out in Lisgar as an Independent and won – only to be unseated for corruption on the part of his agents – an action that drew suggestions some of the agents had been planted for the purpose.

One point on which his enemies lost was an effort to bar him from running again. For years this privilege had doubtful value. He lost to a Liberal in Lisgar in the by-election that followed the unseating action. In the next dozen years he would lose four elections. In 1904, when he supported Borden's railway policy ('a government-owned railway rather than a railway-owned government'), Clifford Sifton beat him in Brandon. In 1907, fighting Rodmond P. Roblin's provincial régime, he lost in Killarney. In 1908 he ran as a Borden backer in Assiniboia with the same result. The *Tribune* came out for reciprocity in 1911, and in 1912 a Conservative beat Richardson when he ran in a Macdonald by-election with grain-growers' support.

Despite these personal political vicissitudes Richardson and his editor John J. Moncrieff contrived to issue a bright newspaper. The *Tribune*'s pages recorded the growth of the city and the West. On January 11, 1902, its first industrial development section appeared – thirty-two pages on the city's industries. In that same year it ran its first columns on labor and union affairs. On September 7, 1904, under the heading THE HARVESTERS OF THE SEASON, the paper front-paged the fact that 15,000 workers from eastern provinces had reached the prairies. These were the travellers of the Harvest Excursions, the seasonal adventurers, largely all-purpose Maritimers brought up to handle a boat, a horse, or a pitchfork with equal ease, who helped to reap and stook and thresh the wheat of the West until tractors and combines displaced them.

A couple of weeks later it gave building figures through the first eight months of the year for the cities of the continent. Winnipeg topped them all, its $7,242,000 out-pacing even New York.

This booming prosperity had offshoots that sometimes made startling news. On a May Sunday in 1905, Rev. C.W.Gordon (better known as novelist Ralph Connor, creator of upright heroes and sinless heroines) at St. Stephen's Presbyterian Church 'sternly arraigned the social sets of Winnipeg for their responsibility in the decay of virtue and alarming growth of lust.' The preaching novelist denounced in scathing words 'the flirtations of single men with married women, the lavish serving of intoxicants at social functions, the selfish indulgence of young girls at the unfair and oftentimes theft-producing expense of their admirers, the indecent and gambling amusements of young men, and all the lusts attaching to luxurious living induced by the accumulation of wealth. . . .'

What really shook the pew-holders and news-readers (and brought them to church in droves through pouring rain for the second instalment) was the fact that Gordon poured his wrath chiefly on the married women: 'It is said that the young men are to blame who are found dangling after the married women as their lovers. No man would dare, by any act of his, to suggest what is improper toward a married woman unless she gives the first invitation. . . .'

In his second sermon Gordon went after the men with almost equal vigor. It behooved the upright to refuse to associate with those 'lured by their bestial lust'. But before long he was whacking again at the wives. He had been told there were not ten 'genuine homes' in existence among the fashionable of Winnipeg: the mothers were out gadding. 'The husband may find his way to the club – or elsewhere. Where are the girls? Where are the boys? The mother has no time to look for them. She is too busy with her own men, God forgive her!'

The *Tribune* promoted Gordon from page three to page one for this pronouncement and gave it a column and a half.

Through these years the *Tribune* faced tough competition: in first place, the *Free Press*, owned by Sifton and edited by J.W.Dafoe; on more even terms, the *Telegram*, edited from 1905 to 1913 by Mark Edgar Nichols, who had learned the craft on the Toronto *Telegram* and Toronto *World*. The city had its quota of newspaper men whose names would live for various reasons; among them such diverse practitioners as Garnet Clay Porter, the Kentucky colonel rumored to have reached Canada on the run from vengeful guns; and Arthur Ford, who came to the *Telegram* and the *Tribune* from an Ontario parsonage and would move on to editorial eminence with the London *Free Press* without losing the reporter's urge.

Rivals for the local scoop and the advertiser's dollar, wielders of broadsword and battle-axe in political war, the three papers worked together to frustrate monopoly in world news. Around them, with the help of other western dailies, grew up in 1907 the Western Associated Press, forerunner of The Canadian Press, the country's co-operative news service. When the W.A.P. held its first annual meeting in Winnipeg in 1908 Nichols was elected president and Richardson vice-president.

All three had grown with the city. By 1913 Winnipeg's population reached 200,000, compared with the 24,000 of 1890. The *Tribune*, not a big money-maker, was yet prosperous enough to establish a new home. Back in 1901 it had moved from its old site on Bannatyne to a renovated three-storey brick building – the old Grand Theatre – on McDermot and installed stereotyping equipment and a Hoe rotary. Now Richardson put up the six-storey steel and concrete building at Smith Street and Graham Avenue (where the paper still published in 1968) and installed a new Hoe sextuple that could turn out 24,000 twenty-four-page papers an hour.

The pistol shots at Sarajevo had not yet been fired. In June of 1914 it was news that Robert Borden had been knighted in the birthday honors. Ty Cobb could make the front page by socking a butcher who argued with his wife. A couple of months later bigger and blacker type darkened the paper's face: AERIAL BOMBS WRECK NAMUR . . . POLAND SEES LIGHT, CZAR BREAKS SHACKLES . . . KAISER TRICKS TURKS. Tucked away on page three of a Saturday issue (August 15) a one-column head recorded an event fateful in the future of Winnipeg, the harbinger of prairie wheat-trains turning west: PANAMA ZONE IS CELEBRATING THE CANAL OPENING.

In the spring of 1915 the guns still spoke across Europe. Casualty lists began to lengthen . . . LOCAL MEN FALL ON FIELD. On lesser fields Jess Willard and Jack Johnson trained for the April 5 headline: JOHNSON IS KNOCKED OUT IN 26TH ROUND. In Manitoba events moved toward revelation of corruption in construction of the new legislative buildings and fall of the Roblin government. The *Tribune* on April 1 double-lined the pivotal development:

ROBLIN ORDERED BY LIEUT. GOVERNOR TO NAME COMMISSION TO PROBE CASE

Its accompanying editorial blamed both parties – and both party newspapers. There was no inherent difference between the parties. Their deeds were equally evil. A crime had been committed against the people of Manitoba. Partisanship was responsible.

The paper took a somewhat lighter line four days later in criticizing plans to spend $8,000 on pictures for the building. The editorial was captioned R.PEE'S ART GALLERY.

The peace that followed war was an uneasy peace in Winnipeg. STRIKE COMMITTEE GOVERNS CITY, the *Tribune* headlined May 15, 1919 – '67 Labor Unions Join in General Walkout; Industry Paralysed'. It was the last paper Winnipeg would see for nine days. As the strike approached, the paper took a moderate line, and when it was called off late in June credited this to 'calm-minded labor leaders and the rank and file of the older and more experienced organizations' as well as to 'the stand of that most influential and potential of all leaders, the General Public'.

Meantime in 1917, when he was fifty-seven, a renewal of personal political success had come to the crusading independent. Richardson won Springfield for the Union government and sat again in the Commons. But he was tired now, in 1920, and perhaps touched by premonition (he was to die in the fall of 1921) ready to shed responsibilities and put his paper in other hands.

'I Think We Should Buy The Tribune . . . '

Richardson approached M.E.Nichols as one who might arrange a purchase. Nichols had joined the government's department of information in 1917 after four years bucking competition in Montreal with a new paper – the *Mail* and its evening edition the *News* – which were now no longer in existence. At about the same time Richardson talked to Wilson Southam.

In the particular newspaper climate of that time – most Canadian dailies were strained by wartime costs, and costs were still rising – Nichols could find no one interested in taking on a paper that would need new capital before an owner could count profits. Wilson was more optimistic than the possible buyers Nichols talked to. And 'if we buy the *Tribune*,' he told Nichols, 'we want you to go to Winnipeg and manage it.' For Nichols, as he related the circumstances later, 'the sun seemed to be rising again.' It rose with provoking slowness. Under Southam practice the purchase was up to family opinion. Holidaying in Massachusetts, Harry expressed indifference. F.N. was good-naturedly neutral. On the basis of these views Wilson felt he wasn't justified in going ahead. Just about then, however, the sphinx-like Dick wired from Toronto a characteristic message without argument or explanation: 'I think we should buy the Tribune.' This was enough. Within a couple of days Nichols headed for Winnipeg to look over the *Tribune*'s plant and assess its goodwill. Bert Woods also stopped off on his way to Calgary from an eastern meeting.

They found the position favorable. The *Tribune* now was a strong second to the *Free Press*, having profited from decline of the *Telegram*, which had fallen off after Nichols left it seven years earlier, and which he now reported 'appears to have no consequential paid circulation'. Morning and evening editions of the *Free Press* sold 71,-

000. The *Tribune*'s circulation (then evening only) was 33,000. In 1919 it had managed to scrape through on the right side of the ledger by just under $7,000. The paper was well thought of, though some readers criticized an American tendency in make-up and news selection. 'Injection of Canadian spirit and ideas appears to offer considerable promise of increased prestige and influence,' Nichols wrote.

The Southams paid The Tribune Publishing Company (of which Richardson was principal owner) $50,000 in cash and $190,000 in preferred stock of a new firm, the Tribune Newspaper Company. For the time being the old company kept the building. When the Southams bought it in 1927 they paid $400,000 for the structure and the preferred stock issued to Richardson at the time of the original deal. In October 1920 the *Tribune* absorbed the moribund *Telegram* for $100,000 (much of which came back through sale of its equipment), and Winnipeg became a two-newspaper town.

The Southams put new capital into the business in the early 1920s as Nichols followed a development program based on his June assessment. In the first six months of the new ownership the paper lost $22,000. Thereafter, except for a lapse in 1924 – the period was not an easy one in the West – it kept out of the red.

The Hydro Fight

What the *Tribune* needed, Nichols felt, in competition with the august and able *Free Press*, was something that would give it character, identity as a voice. The *Free Press*, resonant with the pronouncements of John W. Dafoe, was pre-eminent in national politics and international affairs, but largely neutral in lesser matters. The *Tribune*, in Nichols's phrase, sought to be 'a fighting newspaper on all issues upon which we were reasonably sure of our ground'.

Promising ground soon turned up in civic politics, with which the question of public or privately owned power was then entangled. Early hydro battles were past when the Southams bought the *Tribune*. Both the Winnipeg Electric Company and city hydro served Winnipeg, the private company from Pinawa on the Winnipeg River and the city from Pointe du Bois.

On October 12, 1920, the *Tribune*, perhaps in an unconscious overture to coming events, offered a mild salute to OUR HYDRO ELECTRIC SYSTEM: 'The proposal to construct it was fought vigorously by the interests, but it has since been recognized by all citizens that no enterprise on which the city has embarked has been so wise, so prudent, and of so much value as our Hydro-Electric scheme. It resulted in cutting the rates to a third of what they formerly were. . . . It has saved the citizens many millions of dollars. . . .'

The showdown came two years later in a fight between a mayoralty candidate favorable to hydro and one the *Tribune* saw as unduly influenced by the electric company.

In time for the battle (which Nichols called 'our first big fight, the most adventurous, the most successful, and the most far-reaching') Wilfrid L.(Biff) MacTavish joined the *Tribune* as an editorial writer after varied experience at Kingston, Ottawa, and in the West. Nichols himself wrote vigorous and lucid editorials and enjoyed doing it; MacTavish, who wrote with strength and charm, would be his editorial mainstay on the *Tribune* and would eventually follow him to Vancouver.

On November 2, three weeks before the civic election, the *Tribune* came out against one of the two candidates for the mayoralty. It set the situation up this way:

> The problems which confront the city are primarily those which pivot on our public utilities. These utilities are partly owned by the public and partly by private interests. To do justice to the one without doing an injustice to the other is a task which can only be discharged by a mayor combining the convictions of an adherent of public ownership with a dispassionate consideration for the rights of private capital.
>
> The Winnipeg Electric Railway Company, whose enterprise has created the Manitoba Power Company, with its illimitable possibilities of industrial expansion in Winnipeg, deserves a square deal. In the judgment of the Tribune, formed from a close study of his public record, the influence of alderman J.K.Sparling would be exerted in the direction of giving the Winnipeg Electric Railway interests a great deal more than a square deal and the Winnipeg Hydro a great deal less than a square deal.
>
> Winnipeg's main objective lies in the development of its municipally owned light and power business. The security of this property, in which millions have been invested by the city, should have first consideration in the choice of men for the administration of the city's affairs. . . .

The situation was delicate in that Seymour Farmer, the alternative candidate, was a Labor man – and politically Winnipeg still flinched from the effects of the 1919 general strike. The *Tribune* took the ground that this situation had been engineered, and advised Labor to soft-pedal class appeal:

> They are trying to force him [Sparling] down the throats of the people of Winnipeg on the purely negative argument that the goblins will get them if they vote for his opponent. . . . Clever planners and schemers

deliberately prepared a situation in which the people would be placed on the horns of a dilemma. The city was to be asked to choose between Sparling and Labor. . . . Labor should be able to commend its candidate to the thinking electors on the basis of his public qualities and the force of his program . . . not for one class but for all classes.

Years later Nichols looked back on this campaign with reminiscent affection as a sort of winning of spurs in the face of some danger:

> The Tribune took a merciless barrage of abuse. It was branded as a Red. 'Stops' came thick and fast. Some friends came to me when resentment of the Tribune's campaign appeared to be overpowering, urging that we qualify our position. We declined to do so. It seemed to me to be more perilous to wade back than to push through. What a mighty relief election night brought to frayed nerves when it became evident that the Labor candidate had won. . . . Victory dissolved all resentment against the Tribune.

Hydro battles were by no means over in Manitoba. City hydro opened the Slave Falls plant in 1931 and the *Tribune* published a special section to celebrate. But at the same time it grew peevish over the Bracken government's handling of hydro in the province, arguing that provincial hydro was becoming a mere broker, buying power from a private company at one end of a transmission line and selling it to a private company at the other.

Eventually at the close of 1952 the provincial government bought out Winnipeg Electric. Thereafter, except for a couple of points in the north, all electric power in the province was publicly produced and distributed.

The *Tribune* and the Progressives

Western farmers swung into direct political action just as the *Tribune* came under its new ownership. The paper's view of the Progressives as expressed during the federal campaign of 1921 was that the movement lacked leadership. Any such movement 'drawing its nourishment from roots deep in the heart of the people' and aiming at 'a complete remodelling of the policy and administration of the country' should produce leaders with an authentic message. Where were they? All the party had was Thomas Crerar, a man borrowed from traditional politics.

The *Tribune* faced a difficulty common to all western papers whose sympathies lay with a party tagged with the high-tariff label. It pitched into the issue from a couple of angles. Canadian producers were being offered as a panacea a tariff policy that would cheapen

Canadian goods, 'based upon the old and exploded nostrum that the way to cure destitution is to make things cheap'.

> The official leaders of the Progressives overlook the fact that the essential trouble lies not with the price to be paid but with the power to buy. Even to its tariff panacea, safe and sane Liberalism attaches a string. It says that free trade would cure the farmer's ills but that it cannot apply the remedy. It is like a doctor advising a trip to Arizona to a patient who has not enough money to pay his way to Selkirk.

And:

> We have heard nothing but the tariff, the tariff, the tariff. But when it comes down to hard political facts, there is no party or group before the country which proposes to interfere with the tariff in any important or material particular.

This point of view and its various angles the paper developed from time to time: both major parties supported a tariff but the Conservatives talked too much about it; the Liberals took advantage of the climate thus created and held manufacturers' support while winning rural areas by pointing to Conservative high-tariff talk.

The *Tribune*, in that curious campaign of 1921, defended the Progressives against Mackenzie King when the Liberal leader threatened them with isolation: 'In attributing a sectional animus to the West and coupling this with a threat of punishment for contumacy, Mr. King has trespassed far beyond the limits to be tolerated even from a party politician in the throes of a general election.' But in general it held to the view that Progressive leadership was less than a positive force. After noting that Meighen as a loser had 'earned the respect of every fair-minded man who admires courage and candor', but that his government had outlived its usefulness and functioned, although in an honest and painstaking way, out of touch with the people, it put the question to the Progressives in an editorial headed 'And Now, Mr. Crerar':

> It has been widely and openly alleged that Mr. Crerar was in reality shepherding the Progressive movement, quite as separate from and hostile to the Liberals as to the Conservative party, into the Liberal fold, so far as practical administration is concerned. . . . Mr. Crerar must emphasize its differences from the Liberal party, and force things to an issue when matters of principle are involved. If he does not do so, but compromises on support to an administration headed by Mr. Mackenzie King, he will not show good faith to his own followers and will leave the Progressive movement in the air.

When Crerar retired from the Progressive leadership a year later (he would come back in 1930 as an old-fashioned Liberal) the *Tri-*

bune regarded these forebodings as all too well borne out:

> The western farmer is in the grip of a grain-marketing system under which his wheat is degraded and the price artificially depressed for the benefit of multi-millionaires in the grain trade. . . .
> The western farmer asks for light on the processes which are filching from him the profits of his industry and he gets injunctions. He asks for a wheat board and he gets a gold brick.
> The western farmer has got nowhere in the great fight he has been making in the past 15 years for the economic marketing of his grain.
> . . .

Crerar and the Progressives had possessed the power to force action; they hadn't done so. Crerar had made all such things subordinate to Canada's position in the British Empire: 'For the present, unless and until Canada's relations with the mother country are remodelled to meet the aesthetic tastes of Sir Clifford Sifton and his small but noisy menagerie of empire-busters, other business should be allowed to stand.'

The *Tribune*'s crack at the empire-busters was a recurrent theme. Those who professed a larger loyalty to the League of Nations should 'square up to the task of proving that the League is equally solid and enduring and able to render better service than the Empire', which 'in friendly relationship with the United States, is the world's best guarantee of peace.'

Toward the Progressives who won control of the Manitoba legislature July 18, 1922, the paper took a philosophical tone. In a post-election editorial it remarked that the ability to bestow good government lay not in names or occupations. The Conservative and Liberal parties had fallen into disrepute not because of their labels, but because they 'tended to subordinate public service to party service and sought no longer men of brains and independent character as their standard bearers, but pliable men, ready to serve the interests of the party.' The machinery of politics had taken over.

Again it regretted that the Farmers movement in Canada had developed no great men at the top. In Manitoba it was frankly leaderless. 'A very great deal depends upon whether leaders worthy of the name emerge. If they do, then by whatever name they are known, the Farmers will continue to govern because they are worthy to govern. If they do not, the Farmers will soon discover that a farmer can be just as inefficient as a lawyer, a banker, or a manufacturer as the ruler of a province. . . . The beauty and fragrance of the rose are the things that count. . . .'

Two days later the Manitoba Progressives found an acceptable rose in the president of the Manitoba Agricultural College. Of John Bracken, the *Tribune* said: 'They could not have made a wiser choice.'

The Mysterious Stranger

Some time in the pre-dawn darkness of Saturday, June 11, 1927, city editor Fred O'Malley of the *Tribune* woke to the ringing of his bedside phone: Edgar Whitehouse calling from the night desk. Out in Elmwood a department-store clerk had found his wife's strangled body under the bed. It sounded routine to O'Malley. He dozed for a moment, then came awake with a start and a sense of premonition, phoned Whitehouse back to call in a crew, and reached for his clothes. That morning's headline – ELMWOOD WOMAN STRANGLED TO DEATH – was the first in a series that recorded Manitoba's most spectacular manhunt.

Back in December of 1913 a bandit named John Krafchenko had killed a banker at Plum Coulee, escaped to Winnipeg, was arrested and jailed, broke out of a third-floor cell and roamed free until mid-January when the legal trail to the gallows began. The Krafchenko sensation excited Winnipeg. But nothing before or since produced the wave of imaginative fear evoked by 'The Strangler'.

The body in Elmwood was that of Emily Patterson. Her husband, William, found her body as he put his children to bed. He also found the killer's discarded clothes. His own spare suit was missing.

Saturday's story with its description of the clothes sent a thrill of recognition through Mrs. John W. Hill, who kept a boarding-house on downtown Smith Street. On Wednesday evening a quiet stranger had taken a room there. He hadn't been seen since Thursday; but those discarded clothes . . . she sent her husband to the cops. Mrs. Hill's sense of horror was only beginning. She had straightened up the stranger's room and noticed nothing. But on Sunday afternoon, one of her roomers glanced into it from the stairs and saw something under the bed: the naked body of fourteen-year-old Lola Cowan, missing since Thursday night.

Police converged and put the Smith Street house – just down street from the *Tribune* – under guard. O'Malley edged his way through the crowd and round to the back. A porch door stood ajar and unwatched. He reached the kitchen and found Mrs. Hill, who described for him her missing roomer – how he had talked and acted, his request for a quiet room 'in which he wouldn't be disturbed in his religious reflections', and the events leading up to discovery of Lola's body.

It was now apparent that the mysterious stranger had strangled Lola Cowan on Thursday night, Emily Patterson on Friday. A macabre and irrelevant side story became known: a railway conductor visiting friends in the Smith Street house had mistaken his room and slept Saturday night, all unknowing, in the bed under which Lola's body lay.

One thing was now comparatively clear. For months United States police had followed a killer's trail: from Seattle down the coast through Portland, Oakland, Stockton, San Francisco, Fresno, Santa Barbara; across to Council Bluffs, Kansas City, Philadelphia; up to Buffalo; back west to Detroit and Chicago. The trail was marked by the bodies of twenty women, Winnipeg police put twenty and two together and cast a living net for Earle Nelson.

In Winnipeg the word spread. After Monday morning's headline – 14-YEAR-OLD LOLA COWAN SECOND VICTIM OF MAD KILLER – hardware stores sold out their stocks of door-bolts, chains, and locks. Night streets were bare of life. Out on the railway lines hoboes huddled in their jungles. Something like 1,200 were reported picked up. Police chiefs and detectives from American cities, homeward bound from a convention in Windsor, added their advice. The *Tribune* reported their belief that 'the man is the same one whose hands murdered 18 or more women in the United States and whose tactics earned for him the name of The Gorilla.' Animal lovers protested this insult to the tribe of apes.

Tuesday's headline was THOUSAND CLUES FOR STRANGLER FAIL. Nelson changed his wardrobe as he went. A champagne-colored hat was his trademark for a while as he hitch-hiked west, but not for long. Five changes in six days made descriptions quickly obsolete. The trail led to Regina, then toward the border.

On Wednesday night a vagrant was spotted in a slough at Wakopa and surrendered quietly. By 10:40 P.M. – unidentified – he was lodged in Killarney jail, sixteen miles north, his shoes and socks removed. The policeman on duty left his post briefly and returned to the sound of a slamming back door. His prisoner had picked the cell lock with an old nail file.

An overheard comment was the tip that Winnipeg police thought the vagrant at Killarney was it. Reporter Orton Grain was in chief-of-detectives George Smith's office when a late call came through. Smith put down the phone in bitter disgust: 'Damn it all! They had him and they let him go!' Smith loaded a special train with cops and headed for Killarney. (Grain got aboard, armed with expense money hastily gathered from the *Tribune*'s night staff.) When it rolled into Killarney early Thursday Earle Nelson crawled from under a platform, apparently believing it to be a freight on which he could leave town, and was captured without difficulty. On his feet were skating boots, stolen during the night, from which he had knocked the blades.

The *Tribune*'s normal circulation at this time was 30,000. Radio had not yet ended the day of the extra. That Thursday the Trib's distribution reached 62,000.

Earle Nelson had spent time in a California asylum. His record of insanity did not help him. He was hanged in November.

O'Malley's piece of enterprise in the Smith Street kitchen, incidentally, served as the seed of a glorious myth that grew up around his person: he had slipped into the house through the coal-chute and been damned near gunned down by the cops as the strangler. It is almost too good a bit of tradition to disturb, but O'Malley, perhaps a little regretfully, insists that he got his story by no such dramatic means; the kitchen door was open.

6

Vancouver: The *Province*

On a September day in 1901 F.N.Southam waited in the outer office of Sir Thomas Shaughnessy, president of the Canadian Pacific Railway and a director of the Royal Trust Company, in Montreal. His errand was to check with the newly knighted Shaughnessy on a possible deal for the Vancouver *Province*, then in its fourth year as a daily paper. An acquaintance of Hamilton days reached the presence ahead of him. This was George McLaren Brown, the railway company's Vancouver manager, a son of the venerable Adam who had helped finance the *Spectator* a quarter-century before. When Southam got in he found the door to the Coast already closed; on Brown's recommendation another acquaintance, Walter C. Nichol, now owned the *Province*. The completion of F.N.'s errand was twenty-two years and a continent away.

The news however could hardly have surprised him. Two years earlier Nichol had bought half the paper's issued stock from founder Hewitt Bostock for $10,325. He had run it for Bostock since 1897 and converted it from a weekly review in Victoria to a daily newspaper in the vibrant young city on the mainland. Now the remaining paid-up stock was his for $18,825, payable over seven years to the Royal Trust.

Bostock, who first issued the weekly *Province* from an abandoned tabernacle in Victoria in March of 1894, was a young Englishman, already sitting as Liberal M.P. for Yale-Cariboo, when he met Walter Nichol, then editing the Kaslo *Kootenaian*. A Goderich boy, Nichol was thirty-one years old, with a background of newspaper experience in Hamilton where he had worked on both the *Spectator* and the *Herald*, and in London and Toronto. A story survives that William Southam let him go from the *Spectator*, giving the opinion that he would never make it as a newspaper man – a remarkable departure from usually shrewd judgment if the tale is true.

The weekly *Province*, not a newspaper in the strict sense of the word but 'a journal of critical comment and a vehicle for the expression of independent thought', had achieved a reputation but made no money. It claimed to have no politics but naturally reflected Bostock's views, including a belief in absolute free trade. 'To ask a British Columbian to vote for the tariff because it is going to benefit some hot-house monopolist two thousand miles away', it said in an early issue, 'is like asking a man to sand-bag his mother in order that the undertaker in the next street may swell his bank account from the profits of the funeral.'

At first more scholarly and dignified than its tariff analogy might indicate, the *Province* took on a brighter tone with Nichol's arrival. D.A.McGregor, who joined the paper in 1910 for a forty-five-year stint and found time to study its early days, remarked in an outline of its history that Nichol 'was not infrequently the small boy with a pea-shooter.' Usually he hit lightly, 'but he hit repeatedly with a puckish persistence not untouched with malice.'

The political game on the Coast was unpredictable. Provincially there were no parties, only factions. The man who could swing a majority formed the government – a situation that produced some strange bundling by unusual bed-fellows.

As a result British Columbia was on the eve of utter political confusion when the *Province* first reached its public as a Vancouver daily on the afternoon of Saturday, March 26, 1898. On that day, however, a good deal went on elsewhere. Gladstone was dying. Oxford beat Cambridge in the fifty-fifth boat race. Washington moved towards war with Spain. The Prince of Wales practised bicycle riding on the Riviera. There was gold news from the Yukon, including a premature report on the ouster of Soapy Smith from Skagway, and agitation to establish a mint in B.C.

It was said of Nichol that he took more interest in politicians than in politics. The *Province* at this time, while supporting Laurier Liberalism at Ottawa, opposed introduction of party politics provincially. The solution it saw for local confusion was importation of a strong-man. The one it had in mind was Joseph Martin, the 'Fighting Joe' of Manitoba and Ottawa. In May of 1898 it began printing front-page petition forms, with spaces for signatures, headed BRING MARTIN OUT. At about the time Joseph Leiter was trying to corner the wheat market in Chicago (the *Province* front-paged a box-score of his deals), Joseph Martin hit the British Columbia scene. Dominion Day fireworks preceded Jake Gaudaur's victory over Bob Johnson on Burrard Inlet for what was billed as the sculling championship of the world. They could not compare with the display set off by a provincial election a week later, and subsequent events in a government with the Liberal Martin as attorney-general and Francis Carter-Cotton, a Conservative and owner of the Vancouver *News-Advertiser*, as minister of finance.

The fact was that Martin, this storm-bird of Canadian politics – the only man to sit in two provincial legislatures and both the Canadian and the British House of Commons – could get along with no one. In January of 1900, less than two years after its campaign to get him into British Columbia, the *Province* forsook him completely in a devastating editorial entitled 'An Ishmaelite of Politics'. After relating the story of the fellow who couldn't get past St. Peter and was banished by the devil and given a scuttle of coal to start his own hell, the editorial suggested that 'Mr. Martin's political domain should be on an uninhabited island where he could be monarch of the sea gulls and mud turtles and where no profane voice would dare to question his supremacy.'

Martin's vagaries left the *Province* without a political hero. But one was in the wings. On February 24, 1902, a memorable scene occurred in the legislative chamber at Victoria when Martin contended in tug-of-war fashion (during prayers) for the opposition leader's chair occupied by Richard McBride, the personable young lawyer from Dewdney who had recently sprung into prominence. The *Province* suggested 'the childish affray . . . had better be passed by in silence.' Its own observation of this suggestion consisted of 1,500 words, front page, double column. McBride's emergence had already foreshadowed a new era in British Columbia politics and spotlighted a man who could spark the enthusiasm of Nichol, the editor more interested in politicians than politics. It took a while, however. The *Province* still argued for non-party government when McBride came to the premiership in 1903 and formed an all-Conservative cabinet.

Through the early years of the century the paper quoted often from the mythical *False Creek Record*, a periodical existing in the mind of an imaginative reporter named Shad Farron (after the manner in which Bob Edwards in the Calgary *Eye-Opener* lifted some of his best stuff from the equally mythical *Midnapore Gazette*). On June 3, 1903, two days after McBride's appointment as premier, the *Province* quoted from the *False Creek Record* some lines sent in by 'an esteemed contemporary named Macaulay':

Then out spake brave young Dickey,
The captain of the gate:
'To every man upon this earth
Death cometh soon or late.
And how can man die better
Than facing fearful odds
For the good of his own party
And the temples of his gods?'

However, by the time McBride began to campaign three years later for the next election, his personality and the trend of events had won the *Province* over. The day after Christmas of 1906 it gave him credit for conducting provincial affairs efficiently and urged his government's return. In fact it cast McBride in the role of a champion of British Columbia.

By now Nichol and the *Province* were soured on Ottawa, at least as represented by the Laurier Liberals, and saw McBride's Conservative government as a defender of B.C.'s rights. If a Liberal government sat at Victoria as well as at Ottawa, the paper suggested, 'we might have to resort to rafts and push off into the Pacific Ocean as the only possession left to us.'

In the federal election of 1908 the paper endorsed the Conservative candidate in Vancouver (who won) and described the Liberal as 'the apologist for 12 years of federal misrule', a defender of 'the refusal of Sir Wilfred Laurier to give British Columbia reasonable financial terms, and to keep out oriental invasion.'

Although Nichol's political bent was still described as 'Independent Liberal' in biographical reference books, the *Province* came out against Laurier again on reciprocity in 1911. The country was prosperous so why gamble? It was much the same argument as that arrived at by orthodox Conservative papers, including the Ottawa *Citizen*.

Shortly after Walter Nichol became sole owner of the *Province* he wrote a signed article on trends in publishing under the title 'Newspapers From a Business Point of View'.

In the past, he wrote, the newspapers' business as purveyors of news had been kept in the background by their roles as political instruments, party weapons, which had lent them standing and furnished financial support. Nichol produced a theory as to how this had come to be: lack of communication – that is, lack of news – had left them nothing to print but politics.

But this was a new age. 'Unthinking loyalty to a mere name is gone. . . . All this is due chiefly to the means we now possess of knowing, daily, what is occurring in the great world, and the increasing interest which is being stimulated in the mass of mankind in matters other than their petty local affairs.' Some large newspapers were discarding political obligations entirely. Some were even discontinuing editorial comment and publishing views of the various parties side by side in columns reserved for such matter.

'It is a question if such a daily newspaper would not answer in a much more thorough manner than the present one the needs of the people,' Nichol suggested. 'Would it not answer all their requirements? If controversy is wanted, it could be found in the "unattached" editorial columns or in communications, and the energies of the newspaper itself could be devoted more exclusively and unrestrictedly to the recording of events.'

Furthermore, advertisers wouldn't have to use a whole flock of party papers to reach their customers. 'With the partisan feature eliminated . . . and with enterprise, accuracy, and reliability made the *sine qua non* by the public, only the best and most intelligent would survive, and those which hang onto existence through drafts on the party pap-bottle would have to succumb.' Wouldn't everybody be better off? 'One thing is certain,' Nichol wrote; 'it would be business in the completest sense of the word.'

He obviously viewed this trend with approval. In some respects his implied forecast would prove accurate, in others not. Party obligation and hidebound fanaticism would almost disappear in the next half-century. But something of political *tradition* would remain, coupled with a tendency to break with it now and then and a growing realization that freedom from party obligation does not preclude the free statement of a point of view. Few men in charge of newspapers would feel comfortable in the utterly bland position that seems implied in Nichol's article. As far as the *Province* itself was concerned, some of Nichol's associates came to feel that in his later years prosperity had softened him, that he was too much concerned about business aspects, that the paper was too careful, too cautious. Though there was a good deal of fence-sitting, it never quite reached the point of complete and extended withdrawal from editorial conviction.

Nichol's business approach to publishing was evident from the first. He drew circulation with news, and advertising with circulation. At the time of the move to Vancouver the intention was to run four pages Monday to Friday, eight on Saturday. Within a week he told his readers that advertising volume was so heavy he was shortly going to eight a day through the week. Soon a ten-page paper was usual.

Within a month the *Province* claimed a circulation larger than that of its two competitors (the evening *World* and morning *News-Advertiser*) combined, and soon began to run a standing offer of $1,000 to charity if its paid circulation did not exceed that of any other daily paper in British Columbia, $500 if it wasn't double that of the *World*, and $500 if it wasn't double that of the *News-Advertiser*. Half a century later Frank Burd, advertising manager of the *News-Advertiser* in the early 1900s, said that while owners of the two rival papers never took up Nichol's challenge, he did so personally, armed with figures, and that Nichol sent $500 to a hospital. Burd joined the *Province* as business manager in 1903 and stayed with it until his retirement as publisher at the end of 1935.

In any case circulation rose steadily in the growing city. By July of 1899 it was over 5,000. Six months later it showed at 6,300. In 1907 it crossed the 14,000 mark. That was the year in which Louis Taylor, then owner of the *World* (and later for many years mayor of Vancouver), sued the *Province* for libel. Taylor, who had handled *Province* circulation under contract before falling out with Nichol, started a campaign against the *Province* claiming it was owned by the CPR. Nichol came back with a thrust at the *World*, largely based on circulation claims. Taylor sued and lost when he failed to prove actual damage.

The early *Province* passed up few chances to assert its British Columbianism. When in the summer of 1899 mail-order houses began to infiltrate the market, it noted that old-timers had once called newcomers from the East 'North American Chinamen'. The operations of certain eastern firms, the paper said, might justify a revival of the term: 'It may be suggested that the departmental stores of Toronto cut just as badly into retail trades of this province as the Chinamen do into the labor market. . . . It seems almost incredible that people living in Vancouver, where everything that fancy would suggest or wealth purchase is kept in stock, will deliberately send away to the other end of the Dominion to buy goods merely on a catalogue description. . . .'

But the accent was on news – comprehensively reported and often racily displayed. One report of a politician's speech appeared under the heading WINDY WALKEM TALKS. A House of Commons criticism of the penitentiary system was labelled JUMPS ON OUR JAILS. In July 1899, the assassination of President Ulysses Heureux of San Domingo (after several attempts) drew the conclusive caption FIXED HIM AT LAST.

Two days after its first issue as a daily, the first long-distance telephone instrument in Vancouver went into operation at the *Province*. Early in April the paper installed 'a complete quick-process engraving plant' and began to run drawn illustrations, chiefly head-and-shoulders shots of people in the news, and occasionally maps.

Its pages carried the lusty record of a growing city and province – politics, labor (Oriental and otherwise), coastal shipping, railway-building, mines, orchards, timber, and the mills. And now and then the off-beat, startling event that shatters the pattern of the usual.

The Quiet Mr. Edwards

One such event occurred on the night of Saturday, September 10, 1904.

Late that night engineer J.N.Scott of CPR No. 1 pulled up at the Mission City watertank. He was away within two minutes; his train was running late. A little later as he rolled at full speed through fog and darkness toward Vancouver a hand gripped his shoulder. A voice said: 'I want you to stop this train.' Scott turned and faced a masked man with a raised revolver. Two more climbed down over the tender, armed with a rifle and a shot-gun. Scott stopped the train.

Thus began what was later billed as Canada's first train robbery. A neat job it was. One robber stood guard on Scott while the other two escorted fireman Freeman back to uncouple mail and express cars from the passenger coaches, threatening to blow off any head that appeared at door or window. Back in the cab, they forced Scott to haul the front-end cars a mile ahead and stop while they rifled them. This done, they ordered Freeman to uncouple the engine, herded Scott and the fireman into the cab and rode two miles to the Whonnock mile-post, where they dropped off and vanished into the night with $6,000 in gold dust from the Cariboo and $1,000 in cash.

The *Province* had a man aboard the police train that left Vancouver at 2 A.M. Sunday in response to a message from Mission and 'just touched the high spots' in getting up to the robbery scene at Silverdale Crossing. The paper dressed his story with a map and made the most of it in five columns. It included a word-picture of passengers in the detached coaches tucking their valuables into shoes, socks, and hat-bands ('the majority of the women passengers resorted to the usual hosiery receptacle'), anticipating a raid by the robbers (which didn't occur) after they had sacked the mail cars. One passenger was Judge Bole of New Westminster. He appeared in Monday's *Province* in two capacities: as an incidental figure in the robbery story (ROBBERS CROSS FRASER, ESCAPE TO UNITED STATES) and as the presiding judge at a hearing into misdemeanors of another sort (PAID $5 EACH FOR 'TWO FINE GIRLS').

As indicated in the *Province*'s headline the search for the robbers turned south to the international border eleven miles away. Rewards were offered. Arrests were made. All were false alarms.

Meanwhile at Aspen Grove in the Princeton area, a comparative newcomer named George Edwards, a mild little man with a sweeping moustache, continued to attend the dances; a friendly and helpful soul, who once preached a sermon at the schoolhouse when the minister didn't arrive.

Twenty months after the affair at Silverdale Crossing, history conducted a rerun. At 11:15 P.M. on May 8, 1906, engineer Joe Callin at the throttle of the westbound Imperial Limited had just glanced out the window near Ducks, a few miles east of Kamloops, when a hand fell on his shoulder. With the train stopped, two men searched the mail car and departed on horses held at the trackside by a third. This time the loot was light.

Settlers around Aspen Grove and Merritt got a shock when the boss robber, tracked to a hideout in the Nicola valley and arrested there with his henchmen, turned out to be Mr. Edwards. They were due for a second when a visiting California police official took a look at the grizzled little man and said: 'That's Bill Miner!'

Bill Miner it was. A tattoo-mark of a dancing girl confirmed the fact that here was the fabled Kentuckian who had turned road agent as a boy more than forty years before. His first stage holdup was said to have brought him $75,000. Later stories, perhaps romanticized, pictured the period as one of 'Miner versus the Wells Fargo Express'. In any case, after a long stretch in San Quentin, he found himself loose in 1903 with the stage-coach days gone and only trains to rob.

Now, caught after his second enterprise in British Columbia, Mr. Edwards drew a life sentence. But he was by no means through. On August 8, 1907, while working in the brickyard at New Westminster pen, he ran to the fence, scuttled through a hole concealed by rubbish, on through a gate with a broken lock, and away. On February 18, 1911, three men held up a Southern Railroad train near White Sulphur, Georgia. One was a quiet old fellow who went by the name of George Anderson. He protested innocence, but again the little dancing girl betrayed him. Milledgeville State prison held him for a while, but not for long.

Bill Miner's British Columbia years in his double role as small-time rancher and big-time bandit have lived so long in legend, hashed over in the memories of those who knew or claimed to know him, that it is almost impossible (and perhaps not overly important to the spirit of the ballad) to separate myth from fact.

He is said to have first hit British Columbia while hiding out from a robbery in Oregon in 1903, the year of his release from San Quentin. Other versions say he first appeared as Mr. Edwards *after* the 1904 robbery at Silverdale Crossing. Unconfirmed stories circulated about an $80,000 bearer bond supposed to have disappeared in that one. The little dancing girl appears on different parts of Bill's anatomy. Some accounts say he died in prison. One, that he drowned in a northern river. And one . . . that no one knows.

'A White Man's Country'

Asiatic labor raised passions of varying intensity in just about every British Columbia labor leader, politician, and newspaper for half a century. The question flared often on news and editorial pages through the *Province*'s early years.

The paper had never been pro-Oriental. No one who expected popularity in B.C. could afford to be. But on occasion it took a fairly moderate line. In 1903, the year the Chinese head-tax went up to $500, Nichol suggested that Chinese might be let in without paying it if confined to certain work: 'All menial and scrub work of which there is a great deal to be done in a new country could be performed by these people, and they would be only too glad to have the opportunity of doing it.'

By 1907, though no laborer born east of Suez could consider himself popular in B.C., the main thrust of feeling was against the Japanese, coming in by the boatload. On the eve of the provincial election the *Province* charged Laurier, a local Liberal, and the Grand Trunk Pacific with a conspiracy to bring in 50,000 Japanese laborers.

That spring the legislature passed unanimously W.J.Bowser's bill requiring of immigrants the ability to read and write in English or a European language. There was nothing really new in this. Acts of the same kind, all aimed at Asiatic exclusion, had been passed at Victoria before – and disallowed at Ottawa, largely because of an imperial treaty with Japan, which Canada herself signed in 1906, that gave residence privilege in each country to citizens of the other. Lieutenant-Governor James Dunsmuir accordingly withheld assent to the Bowser Bill and got himself burned in effigy in front of Vancouver city hall in the prelude to a night of violence. Dunsmuir's popularity was not enhanced by the fact that his collieries employed Japanese.

Emergence that year of J.P.McConnell's weekly *Saturday Sunset* added a new voice to the anti-Oriental chorus. The Asiatic Exclusion League came into being August 8 at the Labor Hall with McConnell in the chair. More meetings followed, climaxed on Saturday night, September 7, when the League held a mass meeting at city hall. Thousands couldn't get in and looked for diversion elsewhere. First they burned the straw-stuffed figure of Dunsmuir. Then, as the *Province* reported it: 'While the orators of the anti-Asiatic meeting were counselling moderation from the platform the mob of violent spirits ... cast about for some vent for its feelings, which was found when some youngster tossed a brick through a window of a Chinese store on Carrall Street. . . .'

Bricks and stones flew there for a while but the mob soon left the Chinese quarter and headed for Japtown. It was the spirited defence put up by the Japanese that finally cooled things out:

> Armed with sticks, clubs, iron bars, revolvers, knives, and broken glass bottles, the enraged aliens poured forth into the streets as soon as the limit of their patience had been reached. Hundreds of the little brown men rushed the attacking force, their most effective weapons being the knives and bottles, the latter being broken off at the neck. . . . The broken edges . . . made the weapons very formidable, and many a white man was badly gashed around the arms, face and neck.
>
> Armed only with stones, the mob could not stand before the on-slaught of knives and broken bottles propelled by the Japanese while they made the air ring with 'Banzais'. Many of the Japanese went to the ground as stones thumped against their heads, but the insensible ones were carried off by friends, and the fight kept up until the mob wavered, broke and finally retreated.

Monday's atmosphere was tense. The Chinese made the headlines by openly laying in an arsenal while the Japanese fortified rooftops:

> The Chinese of Vancouver armed themselves this morning as soon as the gun-stores opened. Hundreds of revolvers and thousands of rounds of ammunition were passed over the counters to the Celestials before the police stepped in and requested that no further sale be made to Orientals. . . .
>
> Few Japanese were seen buying arms but a bird's-eye view today of the roofs of boarding-houses and stores in the Japanese district dis-closed the fact that the Orientals are prepared for a siege.
>
> Hundreds of bottles are stored on the roofs of the houses, and these with stones, clubs and bricks, will be hurled at the whites in the streets below should any further trouble occur.

Most of the *Province*'s front page went to angles of the dust-up along with much of four inside pages. Another Monday development was a general strike by the Chinese. 'Hotels, restaurants, saloons, private houses, steamers, logging camps and shingle-bolt camps, railways and other institutions employing Chinese are without their boys today,' the *Province* reported.

Chinese employed in homes of the well-to-do were called out by telephone or walking delegates. A certain comic element entered into this and the *Province* didn't miss it:

> In the west end of the city, where hundreds of Chinese are employed in private houses, there was great dismay when it developed that the kitchen help had decamped. Housewives to whom the kitchen is an unknown quantity were forced to roll up their sleeves, don their old clothes and prepare breakfast. Husbands fumed and fretted but had to make the best of the situation.
> Five o'clock tea parties have been cancelled, days at home are being wiped from the slate, and calling lists placed in the stove in order that the ladies may have time to attend strictly to business at their homes.

Editorially the *Province* deplored the lapse into mob rule: 'The first consideration is that we in Vancouver must show that we are prepared to deal with this element: that we simply will not have lawlessness on any account whatever. . . .' Having dealt thus sternly with the weekend violence it went on to the Asiatic immigration issue in general and the faithlessness of Ottawa:

> We are all of the opinion that this province must be a white man's country. We hold it in trust to preserve it for our race. . . . We are, as has been well said, an outpost of the Empire, and that outpost we have to hold against all comers. . . . Our constitutional methods have been met with cynical indifference. Act after act passed by our Legislature with a view to the limitation of Oriental immigration has been disallowed. If the Federal government adopts this attitude with reference to the legitimate and constitutional means we employ to enforce our opinions, it takes upon itself a grave responsibility. If it treats constitutional agitation with contempt, it lays us open to the dangers of the unconstitutional.

Apparently this was not strong enough for the violently exclusionist *Saturday Sunset*. Early in October it characterized the *Province* as 'a servile, spineless laggard behind popular opinion, a jellified adapter to the conditions in which it and its alleged proprietor may find themselves.'

Gradually tension relaxed. The firepower gathered by the Chinese that Monday morning never came into concerted action. Mill-hands and houseboys returned to work. Ottawa apologized to the Japanese Emperor and forked up $9,000 to pay for broken glass. Laurier sent Rodolphe Lemieux to Tokyo to work out a gentlemen's agreement on emigrants, and a young deputy minister, Mackenzie King, to Vancouver to look into such things as the doings of the contract-labor companies. Next spring Bill Bowser's Bowser Bill again passed the legislature. And again was disallowed.

Seven years later violence in another setting again injected the Asiatic question into headlines. This time the unwanted were British subjects.

Immigration from India – there were already 5,000 Hindus in British Columbia – was halted in 1913 by federal orders-in-council that barred the landing of unskilled workers in British Columbia ports because of the current condition of the labor market. In April of 1914 a Sikh agitator named Gurdit Singh chartered the Japanese ship *Komagata Maru*, took aboard more than 350 of his countrymen and steamed across the Pacific to test the law. From May 2 to midsummer the *Komagata* lay in Vancouver harbor with her human cargo while Gurdit Singh's lawyers argued without success. Deportation was the order. The climax began on Saturday afternoon, July 18.

That day Captain Yamamoto, complying with written orders of federal officials, tried to get up steam and leave for Shanghai with the frustrated Sikhs. Foiled by Gurdit Singh's men, he went ashore and applied for police help. Plans were laid: police would board the *Komagata* and protect the captain while his men got up steam. After which the tug *Sea Lion*, carrying armed immigration officers, would escort the ship to sea.

This sounded simple enough. Soon after 1:15 A.M. Sunday, the tug set forth with 120 policemen and forty special immigration officers aboard. Also H.H.Stevens, M.P., and an assortment of lawyers, doctors, and newspaper men. As the tug reached the darkened *Komagata* an immigration man switched on a searchlight. This revealed that the expedition promised to be no lark:

> Crowded along the rail were the swarthy Hindus, wearing their multicolored turbans and picturesque raiment, but it was seen that none of them were wearing any surplus clothes. . . . As they blinked in the glare of the searchlight, the serious-looking faces and fanatical yelling spoke eloquently of the impending trouble. Hardly a word was spoken on board the tug as the two vessels touched, the *Sea Lion's* main deck 15 feet below that of the *Komagata Maru.* The blue-coated stalwarts looked up in silence at the seething hoard of brown men, and each man grasped his baton. High above the din could be heard the five priests aboard the immigrant ship, screeching, exhorting, praying and singing battle songs. . . .

A grappling iron arched up from the *Sea Lion* and the battle of the *Komagata Maru* was on.

Constables sprang from the tug and tried to catch stanchions along the *Komagata*'s rail. Hindus armed with bamboo poles stabbed them back and followed up with a hand-thrown barrage of miscellaneous hardware.

A *Province* man aboard the tug described the defensive ordnance and its effect:

> These spears were made from bamboo poles 10 or 12 feet long, with a sharpened knife bound to the end. The first piece of coal was followed by a perfect rain of missiles of all kinds, and the shattering of breaking glass could be heard on all sides above the hoarse shouts of combat and the cries of the wounded. Bricks from the boiler settings in the stokehold, scrap iron and pieces of steel plate with sharp and jagged edges, sticks of wood and other heavy things were thrown, and almost every missile found a mark on the crowded foredeck of the *Sea Lion*.

'Nearly every man aboard the *Komagata Maru*', he wrote, 'had seen service under the British flag in India, and they brought their knowledge of warfare into good use. . . .'

The *Sea Lion* carried a load of potatoes and cabbages to supply the *Komagata Maru* on her trip back to Asia. Police now began to transfer these with a different intent. But it soon became obvious that constables throwing vegetables *up* were no match for enraged Hindus throwing coal, rocks, and bricks *down,* augmented by such weapons as bamboo spears and a flat-iron wired to a slicer-bar. Chief McLennan and Inspector McIntosh rigged a hose to the tug's pumps, but couldn't clear the rails of the embattled Sikhs. And a new danger arose:

> This was the possibility of the *Sea Lion* capsizing. Unable to secure a foothold on the *Komagata Maru* and having to withstand the rain of missiles from above, the constables and specials sought the shelter of the outer or starboard side of the tug, causing it to list dangerously. The rail was almost under water and the sea poured through the ash chutes into the boiler-room and stokehold.

The cops righted her by returning to the fray. But misfortune followed misfortune. A brick between the eyes knocked Captain Robertson from the wheel. Detective Peter McArthur fell overboard from the top deck. Detective Ricci dropped senseless when hit by a hunk of coal. A 'big black turbaned pirate' threw an axe at constable Duncan Johnson that cut through his helmet and opened his scalp. Someone aboard the *Komagata* fired three shots, apparently at immigration inspector Hopkinson. A friend, fearing Hopkinson would suffer the fate of Nelson at Trafalgar, whipped the inspector's gold-braided cap off and replaced it with a straw hat. It became apparent that the police could make no headway without using guns.

Fortunately they were under orders not to fire. One special drew a revolver but was stopped by H.H.Stevens. Fifteen minutes from the start of hostilities the tug drew off and returned to her pier. She had forty injured. Casualties aboard the *Komagata* were not enumerated.

Over in Victoria harbor the cruiser *Rainbow* – half the Canadian navy – lay at anchor, waiting her turn to patrol the Bering Sea. On Sunday night she got new orders: proceed to Vancouver and get the Hindus out of there. Divers scraped the sea growth off her hull. On Tuesday morning she steamed into Vancouver harbor while hundreds watched from waterfront rooftops. The *Province* reported a slight panic on the hurricane deck of the Spencer building when someone suggested the cruiser might start to shoot. However: 'While almost everyone expected to see 352 Hindus jump overboard from the *Komagata Maru* nobody fell off a single roof in town so far as can be ascertained.'

There was no shooting. At 6:30 P.M. the *Province* was out with an extra: after a series of conferences, ultimatums, and negotiations, it was agreed that 'the dupes of Gurdit Singh' would go peaceably, provisioned for the voyage. Two days later the *Rainbow* escorted the *Komagata Maru* from Burrard Inlet and saw her off on the long Pacific haul.

Newspapers across the country carried some caustic comment while the melodrama was at its height and the *Province* quoted them freely. The Montreal *Mail* suggested that in one way the Hindus had done Canada a good turn: 'By their exhibition of militancy they have afforded the government an opportunity to use the Canadian navy in the service of the people of the country for the first time, since its use at political picnics has gone out of style.' The Ottawa *Citizen* had some customary remarks about machine politicians: 'It has been painfully evident that the petty politicians, both provincial and federal, were out of their depth. The latest exploit of sending a tug laden with police and armed gunmen to deal with the Hindus at 2 o'clock on a Sunday morning is surely the limit of comic opera government.' It would take something more than the statesmanship of Sir Richard McBride and H.H.Stevens to get Canada out of the muddle the Dominion and the Empire were in over this incident, the *Citizen* suggested. To use a British-Canadian cruiser against British Indian subjects 'would seem to be the height of inconsistent Imperialism.'

All such muddles were shortly to be submerged by events that were far from comic opera. At 4:30 P.M. on August 4, twelve days after the *Komagata Maru* headed back across the Pacific, the *Province* ran another extra: BRITAIN AND GERMANY NOW AT WAR.

End of an Era

Both coasts of Canada, in the days before space weapons made land-mass irrelevant, looked nervously seaward in wartime. With reason: Nova Scotians heard the gunfire of German raiders in 1917; sub-marines sank shipping in the St. Lawrence and Japanese shells fell on British Columbia in 1942.

On August 5, 1914, the *Province* carried a story from Seattle: 'The *Iquique* and *Antafogasta*, the submarines constructed at the Seattle Construction and Drydock Company ... for the navy of Chile, have been sold to the Dominion of Canada, and are today, practically, in service to protect the west coast against possible attack from German ships of war.' An Ottawa dispatch next day explained: 'The purchase was made quietly a few days ago before the actual declaration of war and the boats are already at Esquimalt. Steps are being taken to man them with naval reservists within Canada.'

An editorial noted that the Dominion government had acted with discretion – the subs were bought and apparently in Canadian waters before Britain declared war; there was no violation of neutrality. 'Guns and searchlights at Esquimalt, Point Grey, Point Atkinson, and on one or two of the islands should render Victoria and Van-couver fairly safe,' the paper said.

This account of the sub purchase, it became evident later, was not wholly accurate. Naval authorities at Esquimalt, with the sale hang-ing fire, couldn't get a quick decision from Ottawa, which in turn was trying for a 'yes' or 'no' from the Admiralty. In a burst of patriotic decision, McBride bought the subs with $1,150,000 of the province's money. For three days, until Ottawa approved the deal, British Col-umbia had a navy.

Prosaically renamed *CC1* and *CC2*, the two subs, hastily manned by Canadian and British seamen, bolstered the Coast's defences while two German cruisers (later sunk at the Falklands) roamed the Pacific.

By the closing months of 1915 the monstrous routine of war over-shadowed everything. The *Province* published Kipling's naval com-mentaries on pages crowded with news of the gigantic stalemate. Serbian armies retreated into Albania and Montenegro. Bulgarian troops halted at the frontiers of Greece. News from Germany slipped through neutral countries: Copenhagen reported a zeppelin explo-sion at Tenden, Amsterdam a riot in Berlin. Henry Ford set up his peace mission and predicted a general strike of soldiers by Christ-mas. Canadian girls on Lemnos nursed the wounded from the Dar-danelles. On the home front war-loan sales boomed; and jewellery

stores sold little plaster busts of Kitchener and Jellicoe for a dollar
each.

Civilian news ran like an undertone. Sir Charles Tupper died, and
Halifax ministers protested that only Anglicans and Roman Catho-
lics got places at the state funeral. In Vancouver a young engineeer
named C.D.Howe proceeded to build the city's first grain elevator.
The CPR sheds at Golden burned, and a railway fireman fought his
way through flames to run two engines clear.

Now and then a non-war story had impact enough to make the
headlines. One such marked the beginning of the end of an era in
British Columbia. On December 15, his forty-fifth birthday, Sir
Richard McBride resigned the premiership to become the province's
agent-general at London, and W.J.Bowser formed a government.
Nine months later, just before the September 14 election of 1916, the
Province said of Bowser that his 'careful and businesslike planning
for the future' deserved general approval. The voters did not agree.
A revived Liberal party led by Harlan C. Brewster came in for a
twelve-year run of power.

Woven into the campaign that led to Bowser's fall were tangled
aspects of an enterprise McBride had sponsored with characteristic
optimism more than four years before. On February 21, 1912, the
Province led the papers with details of a railway-development program announced by the premier. Its chief feature: 'Construction of
a railway from Vancouver and North Vancouver to Fort George via
Howe Sound, Pemberton Meadows and Fraser River by the Pacific
Great Eastern Railway. . . .' The almost unimaginable difficulties –
geographic, financial, and politically scandalous – that beset the
building and operation of the line thus forecast are part of the history
of British Columbia. Its early years clouded by charges of kickbacks
to both parties, it would come into provincial possession in 1918 and
lie for years among the mountains like a headless and severed snake.
Nearly a half-century must pass before the PGE could at last fulfil
McBride's dream of 1912.

Almost coincident with the beginnings of the PGE a new daily newspaper appeared in Vancouver. When the 1911 federal election sent
only Conservatives to Ottawa from British Columbia, the Liberal
party blamed lack of newspaper support. From McConnell's *Saturday Sunset* it evolved a morning daily. The *Sun* rose on February 12,
1912.

And at the *Sun*, before long, a new and different personality
bloomed in the B.C. newspaper climate. This was Robert James

Cromie. Born in Scotstown, Quebec, of Irish ancestry, Cromie had come west as an eighteen-year-old in 1906, gone to business school and joined the firm of railway builder Colonel (later General) Jack Stewart. When Stewart took control of the *Sun* in 1917 after a period in which it was headed by politician F.C.Wade, Cromie was the man in charge. Eventually he took the paper over. In September of that year the *Sun* absorbed the *News-Advertiser*. The old *World* – now owned by a group headed by John Nelson – remained the competition in the evening field. The *Province*'s leadership in circulation, advertising, and news enterprise was unquestioned.

As an incidental result of this shifting in the field, the *Province* gained the man who for the next seven years would write its editorials, sometimes perhaps with mental reservations. Snowdon Dunn Scott was a born Conservative who regarded a fence-rail as no place for a man to sit. Long ago he had come off a Nova Scotia farm, worked his way to college as a blacksmith's helper, and emerged a Master of Arts from Mount Allison and an addict of Greek and Latin classics. After years of editing papers in Halifax and Saint John and reporting from the Ottawa press gallery, he moved west in late middle age to the *News-Advertiser*. When the *Sun* absorbed the old Conservative morning paper Scott moved to the *Province*, influenced, it is said, by two considerations: he couldn't see himself working for a Liberal paper and his latest *News-Advertiser* cheque had come back marked NSF.

Brown and the *Princess Sophia*

The surge of the Pacific, its commerce, its storms, and the traffic of its coastal waters, has always touched with its own drama the news of British Columbia.

Early in the history of the *Province*, office-boy Lew Gordon won promotion by 'borrowing' overnight the log of a tramp steamer from Alaska and writing the story of her adventurous voyage. Half a dozen years later, in January of 1906, Gordon produced an exclusive by a kind of journalistic dead reckoning.

A ship hit the rocks between Cape Beale and Carmanah Point on the west coast of Vancouver Island, too far off to identify and unreachable through crashing breakers. Gordon retired to a quiet room to search all reported ship movements in an effort to give the wreck a name. Study narrowed the possibilities to a few, and finally to one. The steamer *Valencia* had headed north out of San Francisco for Seattle a few days before. Weather reports showed she would have been beset by fog from Cape Mendocino north. One final check: had the *Valencia* arrived at Seattle or been heard from there or at any other point inside Cape Flattery? She had not. Gordon took his findings to a staff conference. On his evidence the decision was to go; the *Province*'s final edition reported the wreck of the *Valencia.* Some nervous hours later Gordon's reckoning proved correct.

But the wreck of the *Princess Sophia* remains the classic tragedy; and Roy Brown's first report of it (a thing of small significance in the shadow of enormous disaster, but notable in its own way) the classic newspaper exclusive of its time and place.

Brown joined the *Province* in May of 1901. On the night of September 12, 1898, when fire almost wiped out New Westminster (GONE UP IN A HELL OF ROARING FLAMES, the *Province* headlined) he had been a young reporter for the *World* and is said to have scooped the *Province* on the extent of property loss. On the *Province* where he worked for thirty-seven years, winding up as editor-in-chief, he came to know just about everyone who might be considered a news source in British Columbia.

In common with most of the world, Vancouver thrilled to the excitement of coming victory in Europe (LUDENDORFF DISAPPEARS BUT KAISER CLINGS TO THRONE) in the closing days of October 1918. The Second Victory Loan was just getting under way, the drive for $25,000,000 in British Columbia handicapped by Spanish flu. The epidemic cancelled public meetings. On Friday, October 25, the *Province* carried Mayor Gale's appeal to the people for help to deal with flu victims falling sick by the score.

Far to the north that day the 245-foot CPR steamer *Princess Sophia,* southbound from Skagway, lay fast on Vanderbilt Reef in the Lynn Canal, one of the long fjords slicing through the Alaska panhandle. She carried 275 Yukoners and Alaskans bound out for the winter, and a crew of sixty-eight. Captain Louis Locke, a veteran soon due for retirement, commanded the *Sophia;* he had not apparently considered the situation particularly serious when the ship grounded. Aid was on the way from Juneau, a couple of United States government boats stood by. The *Princess Alice* headed north. So did the salvage steamer *Tees,* with pumps and salvage gear.

Then the wind and snow struck.

Some time around noon on Saturday a telephoned tip came to Roy Brown. The *Province* that day came out with an exclusive story under the shocking line: PRINCESS SOPHIA IS LOST WITH ALL HER YUKON PASSENGERS. The hastily written story recounted the facts of a two-day ordeal in weather too rough to transfer passengers –

though the ship seemed solidly grounded and not in imminent danger – and ultimate tragedy as the storm drove her across the reef and the sea engulfed her. It included the ironic fact that when she sailed from Skagway she left behind nearly 100 prospective passengers for whom there was no room aboard.

On Monday the follow-up stories began. 'The steamer *Cedar* picked up the bodies of 17 men and one boy which were found floating in an oil patch near the wreck,' the *Province* said in the course of a grim dispatch from Juneau. 'The fact that the bodies of some women were discovered on one of the *Sophia*'s life rafts indicates that an effort was made to save the women and children first.'

Brown never disclosed, at least publicly, the source of his Saturday tip.

Less than two weeks later he exercised his judgment or his intuition in another way. Over the wire from Seattle on November 7 came Roy Howard's erroneous armistice bulletin. While the *World* sold extras all round them, Brown and the *Province* sat tight waiting for Associated Press confirmation. That Howard's report was four days premature is a part of newspaper history.

Southams Move In

Late in 1920 Walter Nichol moved to Victoria as Lieutenant-Governor of British Columbia. In twenty-two years he had built the *Province* from a tiny weekly into the best known and probably the most prosperous daily west of Winnipeg. Victoria and government house life were pleasant after strenuous and profitable years. He was still under sixty, but the incentives were no longer there; and his son Jack who had joined the paper after war service had not developed the interest and aptitude necessary to take over.

From time to time he offered his business manager at the *Province*, Frank Burd, a chance to buy the paper. Burd hesitated; there were people he could go to for the money but the responsibility shook him a little. In Montreal in 1923 M.E.Nichols took him to see F.N.Southam. On his return to the Coast he told Walter Nichol the Southams would like to buy the *Province*.

An attempt at evasive action flavored the deal. Nichol told Burd to ask Southam to come to Victoria by way of Seattle – to avoid any tip-off to inquisitive Vancouverites – and register under an alias. F.N. laughed these instructions off and arrived openly, accompanied by his son-in-law Philip Fisher. Out of their meeting with Nichol at government house and later bargaining at Vancouver came the *Province* purchase, completed in August.

The price was $2,000,000 for four-fifths of an enterprise thus valued at $2,500,000, subject to an agreement that a $100,000 interest go to Burd. Nichol kept one-fifth (later converted to Southam Publishing Company stock and purchased by the company for redemption after Nichol's death late in 1928). A fair slice of the $2,000,000 could almost be called an exchange of money for money rather than for plant, real estate, and goodwill, since the *Province*'s reserves included just over $1,000,000 in cash and war loans. Circulation at the time was 62,000.

In its quarter-century in Vancouver the *Province* had overflowed from its original building on Hastings Street into one next door, but roomier and more impressive quarters were needed now. The Carter-Cotton Building at Hastings and Cambie and the Edgett Building just behind it were for sale. This was a traditional newspaper corner. The Carter-Cotton Building had once housed the weekly *Herald* and what was now the Edgett Building had been the home of Carter-Cotton's *News-Advertiser*. The *Province* paid $350,000 for the buildings, spent another $150,000 on alterations, including a connecting bridge and tunnel and moved in at the beginning of 1925.

The Vancouver newspaper situation was fluid and full of excitement. Charles Campbell owned the *World*, having bought it in 1921 from the Nelson group. Campbell was best known then as owner of a storage and warehouse business, but from this time on his life would be linked with newspapers; already in 1912 he had helped organize the *Sun*. Cromie, restless, imaginative, and ambitious, bought the *World* in March of 1924 and converted it into an evening edition of the *Sun*. Indirectly, and in a way that reflected personal rather than business interest, the new owners of the *Province* had a hand in completion of the deal. Cromie owed Campbell $135,000 with a deadline to meet. The story goes that Campbell threatened to close him out and take over the *Sun* in default of payment. Cromie made an emotional appeal to F.N.Southam who was visiting Vancouver at the time. The upshot was that F.N., impressed by Cromie and his growing family, agreed to advance the money. For a couple of years the *Province* held third-mortgage bonds on the *Sun*.

Less than three months after selling the *World*, Campbell brought out a new evening paper, the *Star*, which he shortly sold to General Victor Odlum. This crowded the evening field with three papers and started something of a price war. But the trading was not over. Early in 1926 Odlum's *Star* took over, from Cromie, the morning *Sun*'s circulation (that edition going out of existence) and moved into its field. The *Sun* added the *Star*'s abandoned evening readership to its own. Vancouver newspaper publishing thus settled down to a situation that, with a break here and there, would become its pattern for a generation: one morning and two evening papers.

This however was the only respect in which it did settle down. Cromie's drive, imagination, and eccentricity made the *Sun* a newspaper that might at times offend certain fringes of the more eventempered *Province*'s readership, but was very seldom dull. The *Province* itself was never the least of its rival's targets and now its 'eastern ownership' set up a new point of attack. But the *Province*, urbane and reasonable – too urbane and too reasonable, its critics said – would hold its lead for twenty years, until circumstances outside its own control left it open to crippling attack.

No special shake-up followed the Southam purchase. Frank Burd continued to run the paper. The branching out was in buildings and machines – eighteen new linotypes on a floor three times the size of the old – and establishment in 1925 of a Sunday edition under a young Englishman, Lukin Johnston.

The paper continued its moderate line. In 1924 considerable political uproar stirred British Columbia. The Provincial party organized by Conservative A.D.McRae had forced an investigation of the PGE and entered the lists as a third force with the avowed purpose of turning out Honest John Oliver (successor to Brewster) and keeping out William J. Bowser. All three parties, the *Province* said, had nominated men of high standing. None had pointed a way out of the PGE morass. Summing up: 'It is for the electors to say whether they wish a new administration altogether or whether they think the elimination of some of the reckless spenders from the Oliver government and a thorough housecleaning will meet the situation and entitle the premier to a new lease of power. ... The Province has done its utmost to provide the fullest facilities for publicity and discussion. It is now for the electors to decide.' Oliver squeezed in.

7
The Company

By the early 1920s the Southam name meant newspapers and printing. Paper and press of course had been at the heart of the matter since 1859, when William signed up as a printer's apprentice at the *Free Press*; perhaps even earlier, when as a twelve-year-old he delivered the paper to the households of London. They had been more firmly rooted there with the *Spectator* purchase in 1877. Across the years between, in the brisk business climate of a growing country, William and his sons had reached out also to other things: blast furnaces in Hamilton, steamers on the Lakes, corner lots in Montreal, milk and ice companies and department stores, gold mines and oilholes. Always with a view to swelling the surplus account of the family company. But the central interest remained and gathered strength and found expression in the newsrooms and pressrooms of a growing group of newspapers across the country and the printing plants on Duncan Street and St. Alexander.

The holding mechanism now was William Southam and Sons, a company set up in the summer of 1920 as a reshaping of Southam Limited and capitalized at $5,000,000 – five times the figure set in 1904 for its predecessor. It was still strictly a family concern. William, seventy-seven years old that summer, continued as nominal president with Wilson and F.N. as vice-presidents, Wilson acting as chief executive from his office at the *Citizen*, where Harry had taken over much of that newspaper's management. F.N., after strenuous years with the Imperial Munitions Board, at this time looked forward (or said he did) to a life of comparative leisure.

This prospect was not to be realized. Whether he was ever really serious about it is questionable. It was scarcely in his nature, as a vigorous man in his fifties, to be satisfied with prolonged vegetation.

There was, of course, the printing business, which he liked. But his cousin Will had run the plant during F.N.'s years of munitions work; he had no wish to relegate him to a lesser position. And now a new alternative appeared as the company grew. The Southams bought the Winnipeg *Tribune* in 1920. It was F.N. who travelled west each year to keep contact with managers in the western cities. Wilson suffered a temporary set-back in health. As long before as 1919, after handling executive work during F.N.'s time with the munitions board, he had noted that his tendencies were 'quite in other directions' – the study of social and political movements that could be reflected in the *Citizen*. When Southams bought the Vancouver *Province* in 1923 the company's expansion led Wilson to make the definite suggestion that F.N. take over as chief executive. In 1924 he did so, as managing director, and the work began of setting up a central office in Montreal.

Over the years a sort of transition had taken place in F.N.'s business life: from printer to printing company executive – with increasing general business interests and responsibilities – and on to operating chief of a company in which newspaper ownership had become the central fact.

One other event important to the company's future occurred at the beginning of 1924. A young man named Philip Fisher came on staff as assistant to the vice-presidents. Fisher had behind him the contrasting backgrounds of the wild haphazard days of early air warfare and the Montreal business world. As a McGill student just past his nineteenth birthday he had gone to an Ithaca, N.Y., flying school in the spring of 1915 to qualify as a seaplane pilot, since the Royal Navy had let it be known it would grant probationary commissions in its air service to pilots already trained. A year later he was flying anti-submarine patrols out of Dunkirk (sightings were reported back to base by carrier pigeons) in two-seater seaplanes that doubled at night in bombing raids on the Zeebrugge-Bruges canal and sub base. Plane-to-plane fighting in Sopwith baby seaplanes and land-based Pups followed, and finally command of a flight of the legendary Sopwith Camels. Fisher's score of enemy planes shot down was two or three. It was while leading a flight of five Camels in a dogfight over Dixmude (a 'general action', his citation for the Distinguished Service Order called it) that Fisher got a tracer bullet in the left knee in September 1917. He reached base, working the rudder with his right leg, but spent the rest of the war in hospitals.

Back in Montreal early in 1919 he suggested to a friend that the first thing he wanted to do was meet some attractive girls. The friend arranged tea at the Ritz Carlton where he met Margaret Southam. Fifteen months later they were married.

Except for that Ritz Carlton tea and its consequences, Fisher might never have made contact with the Southam company. But at that time there was no suggestion that he work for it. It was not until several years later that circumstances combined to bring this about.

During the first years after his return from overseas he worked in real estate (his father Roswell C. Fisher and his uncle Sydney, who had been Laurier's minister of agriculture, both held a good deal of it), later in the statistical department of a securities company, and then on administration of his father's and uncle's estates. He and his father-in-law got on remarkably well together; lacking a close business associate, F.N. often talked about Southam problems in his presence. So that Fisher already knew something about the company when, at lunch one day in June of 1923, his father-in-law told him of a planned trip to Vancouver to bargain with Walter Nichol for the *Province*, and suggested he go along to lend a hand. He did so, and while F.N. handled the negotiating, did such chores as checking figures with the auditors before the deal got down to definite terms. The trip proved to both that they could work together effectively and it came at the right time. Fisher's family affairs were cleaned up. The Southams needed a strong central office and a man to help run it, both of which facts Fisher had observed with interest and anticipation. At the end of the year he joined the company formally. Henceforth his business life would be concerned entirely with its developing affairs.

The Southam Publishing Company

These affairs centred now, more and more, on the curious and strangely exciting world of newspapers. For years the Southams had been edging out of their secondary business interests.

But there were snags in the way of developing this preoccupation and exploring fully the possibilities of group newspaper ownership. Though the chief assets of William Southam and Sons lay in its massive blocks of shares in the six newspapers and in the printing plants, a miscellany of left-overs from the speculative days remained on its books. And about the six newspaper companies themselves, there was a certain awkwardness. William Southam and Sons owned most of the shares in each, their active managers had smaller interests (some of them in more than one paper), and in some of the companies non-newspaper people held shares as well. They were in effect water-tight compartments. There were thus two spots of difficulty. The central company must still concern itself with a clutter of matters having nothing to do with newspapers; and the newspaper companies themselves lacked the flexibility needed for such things as transfer of executives from paper to paper and co-operation in news-gathering and advertising sales.

In the mid-1920s an idea began to form. Why not set up a new central holding company whose sole concern would be the news-papers? Let the operating companies continue but buy up all their stock, exchanging it for shares in the new parent company. Such a move would open the water-tight compartments, create a common pool of ownership and remove the snags.

In December of 1927, the Southams and their publishers estab-lished The Southam Publishing Company on that basis. A condensed version of William Southam and Sons retained the miscellaneous properties and for the time being the printing plants. The Southam Publishing Company emerged as a corporation founded on a com-munity of interest in one thing – newspaper publishing.

The business life of the Southams had started as a one-man show. It had grown into a family business with Southam Limited and Wil-liam Southam and Sons. Now, in its most important aspect, it had be-come a business family that included the active publishers of all the newspapers and, as shareholders, a scattering of senior newspaper staff. Though the Southam family owned most of the stock by far, shareholders totalled about 100. In a corporate sense a step had been taken towards the development of 1945, when Southam company stock would go on public sale.

However, it was the immediate and the practical that concerned directors of the new company when they first met in Montreal on February 2 and 3, 1928, after the organizational formalities had been cleared away. The originals were the five Southam brothers, with F.N. as president; Philip Fisher, secretary and assistant to the president, Ker of the *Spectator*, Nichols of the *Tribune*, Imrie of the *Journal*, Woods of the *Herald*, and Burd of the *Province*. Walter Ni-chol was added at the first meeting. They plunged at once into some of the questions the company had been formed to tackle. Committees were set up to look into co-operation in news-gathering and advertis-ing representation.

By midsummer Lukin Johnston of the *Province* was established in the *Times* office in London, and Charles Smith of the *Herald* in Washington. Paul Reading of the Toronto *Star* came on staff to write economics from Montreal. A year later Charles Bishop of the *Citizen* (the lad who had come up from Bear River in 1898 and would retire to the Senate in 1945) took over as group representative on Parliament Hill. These were the beginnings of Southam News Services.

The advertising side took a little longer, but late in 1929 under the guidance of Bill Watson, who had come down from Calgary as an assistant to the president, the company set up national sales offices in Toronto and Montreal with John C. Hogan and C.A.Abraham in charge.

Soon after its organization the company outlined in a series of advertisements the way in which it had come into possession of six newspapers and its philosophy of group operation. 'The Southam structure is singular in the fact that it has grown out of no design to establish a group of newspapers,' the first of these promotional ads said. 'It very largely represents a natural and casual gravitation of individual newspapers to a family long-established in the newspaper business in Canada.' The circumstances in which the newspapers were acquired were reflected in the manner of their operation: executive heads accepting basic standards of journalism (which in the case of the Southams forbade 'entanglements, business or political, which would prevent the free exercise of the newspaper's influence in any question of public policy') in all other respects had a free hand. It was a system of 'territorial home rule supported by a background of group strength'.

This, the advertisements carefully asserted, was simply strength in the business of publishing:

> The Southam newspapers were not acquired with any thought of creating or exercising a power in politics, finance, or any other domain foreign to a newspaper's normal and proper sphere of public usefulness. No such power has been assumed or considered over the long course of years in which the group has grown. . . . The acquisition of the six newspapers, one after another, has no significance other than as evidence that a family strong in newspaper aptitudes have been sufficiently successful as publishers to expand their business and over a period of nearly fifty years to carry it into six important Canadian cities.

London Assignment

Of the news bureaus set up by the group in those early days London was the prize. Lukin Johnston made the most of it. English-born, Johnston had reached British Columbia as a youth, joined the *Prov-*

ince in 1909, edited the Cowichan *Leader*, and worked for the Victoria *Colonist*, gone overseas and come back a major. He had rejoined the *Province* in 1919.

To the London assignment Johnston brought experience, ambition, and an easy style. He could write knowledgeably from Geneva on the League, from London on Britain's departure from the gold standard, and make an entertaining column from a summons for parking in Berkeley Square. (The magistrate 'entered through a small door in the paneling like a tiger being let loose on unsuspecting Christians.')

In the fall of 1933 Johnston toured Germany, writing what he saw and pulling strings for an interview with Hitler. The call came on Wednesday, November 13, and that evening Johnston questioned the dictator for half an hour and produced 'the first statement of Germany's future policy made since Sunday's monster referendum constituted Hitler absolute master of Germany'. He telephoned the story to A.C.Cummings, his assistant, and got ready to leave for home.

On Saturday, Reuters News Agency reported: 'Major Lukin Johnston, Canadian journalist stationed in London for some years, was reported missing today from the London and Northeastern steamer *Prague* while en route from the Hook of Holland to England. . . .' Five months earlier a Royal Navy commander had vanished from the same boat. Some London newspapers saw sinister hands at work. But the evidence pointed to simple accident. Johnston had gone on deck shortly after midnight on the Friday morning to rest in a deck chair. At some time after 2 A.M. the chair was seen to be unoccupied. Investigation turned up the fact that he had fainted in his Berlin hotel four days earlier and had seemed unwell aboard the steamer. The assumption was that he had gone to the rail, possibly seasick in the heavy weather, suffered a weak spell, and pitched overboard.

Round the Circuit

In the days when five Southam brothers dominated the directorate of The Southam Publishing Company discussion often veered from company affairs as such to business matters as related to the family. Non-family directors and managers and editors present by invitation sometimes found themselves fascinated auditors of a crossfire that primarily concerned the Southams alone. From one such meeting in Montreal a newcomer once emerged in a state of shock, observing in shaken disbelief to Philip Fisher that he had never thought to see the breakup of the Southam brothers. Fisher merely laughed. He had been through it all before.

The habit of arriving at a course of action by a hammer-and-tongs version of open diplomacy originated far back in family history. It flourished briskly in the days of Southam Limited. In those days William, though he had handed operation of papers and printing plants over to the boys, was no silent figurehead. Writing W.J. from Montreal in the summer of 1912 about a forthcoming meeting in Hamilton, F.N. suggested Bill tell the president: 'We will all be extremely disappointed if he does not give very forceful expression to his general views of the crowd he is doing business with. I also think we should have Mother and Ethel present in case we should decide to take any personal actions for damages. Ask him not to waste any of his steam on the junior members of the firm but to hold it until we are all on hand to see the explosion.'

In this case the explosion had a delayed fuse. One of the questions to be settled concerned arrangements with Woods and Watson at Calgary. William argued against the suggested settlement but had to rush off to another meeting and told the boys to do what they liked. They did so and later F.N. told Woods what had been decided and asked for confirming letters signed by William. William disagreed with certain details and refused to sign W.J.'s drafted documents. 'The discussion', W.J. informed F.N., 'closed with much heat on Father's part and a hurried retreat to the Thistle.'

Whereupon F.N. wrote his father a five-page letter concluding: 'I have most decided objections to being given definite instructions and then being told to swallow myself. As I find it necessary to retain some slight portion of my self-respect, I won't do it, nor while I am a member of the board will Southam Limited do it.' William wired his answer: 'Letter received. Thanks. As you appear to be willing to run Southam Limited I am resigning in your favor.' To which F.N. replied: 'Your wire received. Would suggest by way of compromise that the directors run it with the president's assistance.' The message has survived the years and remains in the files, bearing on its margin in William's racy script the record of his melted resistance and a suggestion of the laughter that was never far away: 'I have now rushed to the Thistle rink.'

The habit of hammering out agreement in talk and by letter and telegram usually followed mellower lines, but it is a central fact in the business history of the Southams.

There was one area of operation, however, in which the conclusion was *not* to establish family-made decisions.

In early years the talk often turned to the policies of the papers. When they bought the *Herald*, F.N. had given the opinion that the three Southam papers (*Spectator*, *Citizen*, and *Herald*) should agree editorially on national affairs. He still thought so in 1914, perhaps in a more limited sense and certainly with a stated proviso.

'I wish you and Wilson', he wrote Harry, 'would try to think of some method whereby the Citizen and the Spectator would keep more closely in touch with our two western papers, with the idea of eventually getting everybody in line on some policies. . . .' But if they were going to spearhead some kind of national front they would have to get out of Ottawa and study the country: 'It is an absolute impossibility for you to get the western point of view in any other way than by a personal investigation. . . . Of recent years, or since you and Wilson have been developing your ideas along radical lines, you have hardly been out of Ottawa.'

Harry and Wilson however obviously felt they could set a proper example from the capital. A situation that had in it a touch of paradox was forming. Wilson and Harry, in breaking the *Citizen* away from traditions held in common with the *Spectator*, had sharply reinforced the idea of editorial home rule originally raised by the Calgary *Herald*. But now they looked towards what was in effect a reversal of the process: they sought to impose their own policies, by example, on the other papers of the group.

This view came into the open in July of 1915 when the *Citizen* published an exchange of correspondence with an unnamed Winnipeg man. This letter-writer proposed that the *Citizen*'s publishers buy the Winnipeg *Telegram*, since its current owners were running it as an adjunct to a political machine (the *Free Press*, he said, was no better, and the *Tribune* not a force), and give Winnipeg a decent newspaper, free from liquor ads and nostrums and party obligations. The *Citizen* replied, in print, that it was flattered but had enough on its plate for now:

> We have not yet demonstrated that the people of the Ottawa Valley in particular, and Canada in general, are ready for an independent, clean newspaper for the home. When we have demonstrated this fact, as we surely will, we still have the Hamilton Spectator, Calgary Herald, and Edmonton Journal, all of which are conventional party organs with advertising policies which differ not at all from those of the Winnipeg papers. . . . When we show that an independent clean newspaper can be a profitable one as well, we expect to have our other papers follow our lead.

There was more in the same vein, a vein of pure gold for the Calgary *Albertan* and the *News-Telegram*. For years Bert Woods had been stung by jibes of these competitors that the *Herald* and *Journal* were 'foreign-controlled' and reflected the opinions of eastern money. Now, here in this published correspondence, was outright admission not only of eastern control of the *Herald* and the *Journal*, but a boast that the *Citizen* hoped to lead these two western papers into its own path. The *Albertan* and the *News-Telegram* made the most of it. Woods wrote plaintively to W.J. Bill undertook to cheer him up:

I was watching a ball game yesterday afternoon between Hamilton and St. Thomas [he wrote]. Dutch Schroeder was pitching for Hamilton and after the smoke of battle had cleared away he won his game – 2 to 0. In the second inning, however, the first man up for St. Thomas was presented with a base on balls by Dutch. The next man up placed a safe bunt and the third man did likewise, thus filling the bases – no outs. The fourth man had three balls to his credit and no strikes. I wish you could have been here to see the confidence displayed at this point of the game by Dutch. It was delightful. The conditions which you are operating under in Calgary along with such worries as you outline are mere trifles compared with the hole Dutch found himself in. On the next ball pitched the batter knocked out a fly to short centre which our centre-fielder grabbed and by a perfect throw to the plate cut off the man who was trying to get home from third before the throw. This made two out and the next man up knocked a long fly to right and the side was retired. I presume Dutch was a bit worried but he didn't show it. Keep on pitching the same kind of ball as you have been in the past and it's a pipe that you will win out with as much apparent ease as Dutch Schroeder. . . .

Hamilton did beat St. Thomas 2-0 in a game in the old Canadian League on July 18, 1915. W.J.'s account of the second inning differs only in detail (permissible for dramatic effect at that distance from Calgary) from the *Spectator*'s.

It is doubtful that the Schroeder story comforted Woods much. And F.N. remarked: 'If your friend Dutch had been the active head of any of the papers referred to . . . and had the vocabulary of only an average ball-player, his remarks on the publication of the correspondence would have been even more interesting than the thrilling innings you describe.'

Discussing the published correspondence with Wilson, Woods suggested its effect on the other papers might have been considered, and went on diplomatically:

I believe that it is very difficult for anyone to say that just because in a certain environment and in certain conditions a certain policy has succeeded, therefore in other environments and in other conditions not only would that policy succeed, but that it is the only policy that would succeed. . . . I admire the Citizen very much but I would not go so far as to say that it is the only kind of newspaper I admire.

Any serious attempt to set up a common editorial front would have run into some curious anomalies. At one time or another nearly everyone took a hand. In May of 1915 Gordon, who often blasted the *Spectator* for hidebound Conservative attitudes, lit into Harry for an editorial backing the Liberals in England and opposing a coalition there. 'A partisan shriek worthy of our best efforts,' he wrote, and proceeded to demolish the *Citizen*'s arguments.

Despite their obviously individualistic approach to political matters (except perhaps for Wilson and Harry who seemed to think as a unit), with the transition to William Southam and Sons in 1920 the brothers got round to talking again about something like a united front.

Two Southam papers were then taking opposite stands on a matter of public interest. The *Citizen* hammered for an early Dominion election. The Calgary *Herald* urged that the new Prime Minister, Arthur Meighen, continue with the job in hand.

Wilson wanted to write Woods about aligning editorial policies, 'thus', as W.J. expressed it, 'creating the strength of a giant but not using it as a giant unless necessary.' He advised Wilson to take a soft approach:

> Suggest that he confide in you as to his future aims and ambitions because you might like to assist him. . . . Possibly mention 'My country, 'tis of thee' and not 'Me and my party' is to be the national anthem, that the great unwashed are to be lifted up – and those in high places are to be pulled down so that others who learn to wash the speediest can continue the everlasting circle of working towards – nobody knows what except Harry and you and our editors.

At an October meeting in Montreal the brothers actually got down to studying a proposed 'unified editorial platform' that Wilson had drawn up. Its fate is reported in two letters from W.J. to Wilson.

> When at Jackson Street upon my return from Montreal I mentioned the purpose of our meeting there, and while Mother was strong for whatever the Citizen advocated, I wasn't able to discuss details as Father started right in to warm up, contending that we could think for ourselves and run our own show. (October 25)
> Copy of Bert's letter arrived this afternoon and, believe me, he shoots some ultimatum when he says that he would rather work for the street-car company as a motorman than for the Herald unless J.H. Woods guides the Herald. (November 6)

Bill's suggestion was 'that we table these matters of policies for verbal discussion later'.

A verbal discussion did take place in April of 1921, when five directors of William Southam and Sons (the five Southam brothers) set out to determine the policy Calgary and Edmonton should adopt on a liquor vote in Alberta. They split three to two on the policy itself and then reached a unanimous decision: to leave it to the western management. Thereafter references to editorial stands took the form of nothing stronger than friendly persuasion, or more frequently simply discussion.

This discussion, of course, was not confined to editorial content. Having trained as a printer and spent more than half his life as head of a printing business, F.N. Southam had a keen eye for newspaper appearance: typography, ad composition, make-up. Writing Jimmie Allan at the *Spectator* in 1933 he noted improvement in ad composition 'from which it is quite evident that some of your old job-printers are again coming into their own as against the rule-twisting horse-bill group that were temporarily in control. . . . We are now going after the Province.'

But editorial pages held F.N.'s consistent interest. Editorials he liked went 'round the circuit' as examples. Sometimes he disagreed with an approach – not always convincing the editor concerned. His chief purpose was usually to illustrate the virtues of moderation rather than to push a specific point of view. 'From the manner in which from time to time I take exception to extreme partisanship in any form,' he wrote Imrie in 1933, 'you will understand, and I hope bear with me, if I take advantage of every opportunity which presents itself to stress this particular, and to my mind, most important matter.'

Writing Harry in the spring of 1935, F.N. noted that local autonomy had become so highly developed in each unit of the group that it was difficult to take exception to any practice or point of view the local management wished to take. That was all for the best. 'My only justification for butting in as I occasionally do is that even subscribers are sometimes allowed to differ with your editors.' The butting in F.N. was doing at this time consisted chiefly of arguments with Harry and Wilson over the repetitiousness and bitter tone of Bowman's Social Credit editorials.

Something of his philosophy is evident in discussions with others, as well as editors and members of his own family, in those depression days. Sir Joseph Flavelle, his old chief at the Imperial Munitions Board, blamed everything on war debts, speculation, and selfishness: 'Is not our problem first an inquiry as to the spirit in the hearts of the human family, whereby we have lost faith in one another?' F.N.

agreed but suggested selfishness was inherent: 'May it not be that we are dealing with a fundamental biological factor which Old Mother Nature in her wisdom (or should we say folly) decided was essential for our creation and future climb toward the heights? While at the moment we seem to be making an awful mess of it . . . it is just possible that the Old Lady has us running on schedule and that some day by the grace of God we will reach the promised land.' The bite and laughter in F.N.'s letters often came out in postscripts. The afterthought on his letter to Flavelle read: 'About that promised land. Do you think editors Cromie and Bowman will be there? If so, good Lord deliver us to a happy Hell.'

The human factor was the one no one could outguess. Quite possibly the Douglas plan, or something else equally radical, would come into the foreground soon, he wrote Harry in January of 1935, acknowledging *The ABC of Social Credit*, which Wilson had sent him with an invitation to discuss it. 'It is also quite possible, indeed very probable, that good old human nature . . . will ball it up just as effectively as it has done with other reforms.' The Southam family's own increased prosperity of a few years before 'certainly got balled up for fair' in the depression years, he reminded Harry. As for *The ABC of Social Credit*, he had studied it and wasn't sure whether the book or his diet had brought on the appendicitis attack that sent him to hospital on Christmas morning. In any event he declined Wilson's invitation: 'A debate with him on . . . monetary and economic reforms would be about as profitable, so far as I am concerned, as a religious discussion with Fred Ker. It is impossible to score against a man with a hobby or religious convictions.'

Nevertheless, a discussion of the *Citizen*'s continued emphasis on monetary theory went on for years, accelerating with events. When the Aberhart campaign brought on a kind of emotional civil war in Alberta, F.N. found himself on the one hand taking pot-shots at Harry and Wilson and on the other urging on the Calgary and Edmonton newspapers the need to be reasonable – on the other side of the question. 'You are dealing with very explosive and difficult problems', he wired Leigh Spencer, 'and while fully meeting your responsibilities to your public you should lean backwards in your efforts to be fair and impartial. . . .'

Philip Fisher also occasionally exchanged ideas with publishers and editors, often on questions of economics as related to the human condition. In mid-depression, commenting to Imrie on a *Journal* editorial lamenting that lack of demand caused unemployment, he put forth the view that 'unemployment is not based on a lack of demand for goods, but on the ability of the economic system, as at present thrown out of gear, to translate the desire for goods into terms of purchasing power to pay for the cost of their production.' While he agreed that 'we should have a managed currency and credit structure controlled in a final analysis by a governmental agency in the interests of the community at large,' he could find no logical solution in the monetary reform theories then being advanced.

Fisher's lifelong connection with organized welfare work through Montreal's federated charities and the Canadian Welfare Council sometimes colored his comment. When the Beveridge report came out in Britain late in 1942 he sent copies to all Southam publishers, admitting to being thrilled by it as a plan for providing social security without removing the work incentive. Writing to H.S. Southam in 1943, after publication of *Make This Your Canada* by the C.C.F. enthusiasts Frank Scott and David Lewis, he noted that some of his business friends confessed the book made their blood run cold. 'I am hoping', he added, 'that after their blood thaws out they will do something to really warm it up a bit,' a sentiment with which H.S. heartily agreed.

Fisher once expressed the company's operating philosophy concisely in a letter to a former Southam editor. Charlie Hayden, who had gone from the Calgary *Herald* to a farm magazine in British Columbia, suggested in 1943 that the group study Canada's anticipated postwar problems and come up with a concerted plan to meet them. Fisher wrote:

> The six Southam newspapers are headed by six able publishers, backed by six able editorial staffs; and if they each write obeying the promptings of their respective judgments, I think in the long run they will do more for the country than if they tried to reach a synthesis, and perhaps place themselves in the position of supporting something that might appeal to their collective minds but which did not quite equally touch their hearts.

The fact is that from the beginning the newspapers never followed similar editorial policies except through adherence to similar traditions or when the men responsible happened to think alike.

A glance at positions taken on some of the controversial issues of their time reveals some interesting comparisons.

On November 16, 1925, Arthur Meighen made his statement of principle that in the event of another war 'it would be best . . . that the decision of the government . . . should be submitted to the judgment of the people at a general election before troops should leave our shores.' Comment by the Southam papers on this dictum – destined to become a classic point of friction in the Conservative party – reflected various angles of view and degrees of emphasis. Of the four that reacted at the time only one agreed with it.

Meighen spoke at a Hamilton dinner. Three weeks earlier he had come out of a federal election with the largest party group but short of a majority and with only four seats in Quebec.

The *Spectator* noted that though Parliament was responsible for Canada's war effort, 'upon Mr. Meighen is saddled the onus of conscription and everything else which is obnoxious to our French-Canadian compatriots.' It felt that his promise of a general election, and his exposition of the position at the time of the World War, should set the matter at rest and 'serve to remove the bandage from the eyes of prejudiced voters, wherever they may be'.

In Ottawa the *Citizen* made no comment immediately, but when Meighen repeated his principle in the Bagot by-election campaign a few days later, the paper termed it pathetic, bordering on the absurd: 'It is possible that the Conservative publicity bureau would carry on with business as usual, telling the people to vote for Tweedledum while bombing squadrons were saturating London or New York with poison gas. But it is hard to imagine Mr. Meighen delivering an election speech at the Auditorium to an audience in gas masks.'

In Edmonton the *Journal* in a scholarly discussion questioned Meighen's conclusion. Wouldn't it have been sufficient to say that he would hold an election only if extensive opposition were manifest?

Most forthright of all was the Winnipeg *Tribune*. Its editorial was headed 'Play The Game or Get Out' and its blast was patterned to pepper a few hides besides Meighen's:

> Holding a general election in advance of the dispatch of Canadian troops to participate in an Empire war is a formula closely harmonizing with the views of men like Sir Clifford Sifton, Henri Bourassa, and John S. Ewart, K.C. It comes strangely from the lips of Rt. Hon. Arthur Meighen. . . .
>
> What a picture Mr. Meighen has presented to the British Empire and to the world. . . .
>
> While other parts of the Empire were fighting, Canadians would be voting. Bullets flying in the battle front and ballots flying in Canada. Battles with other parts of the Empire participating and stump speeches on the Canadian hustings.

The *Tribune* returned to the theme after the Conservatives failed in Bagot a few days later: 'It is likely soon to become evident that he has lost in this political misadventure ground which can only be regained by frank and speedy disavowal of a policy.'

Far from disavowing anything, two years later Meighen threw the Conservative leadership convention of 1927 at Winnipeg into disorder with a defence of the speech. In Vancouver the *Province* remarked that its resurrection would have to be reckoned a singular persistence in error: 'It amounts . . . of course to confirmation of a great deal in the popular estimate of Arthur Meighen. All his courage emerges in this Winnipeg utterance – and all his unforgetting obstinacy.'

The *Spectator* remained loyal to Meighen: 'It was as a private citizen that Mr. Meighen addressed the convention, and as such he had the right to make the personal explanation of his Hamilton speech which he considered necessary, in view of the misunderstanding of it which prevails. One may not agree with the speech, nor believe in the feasibility of the policy . . . but that does not justify the imputation of low political motives.' Premier Ferguson of Ontario had accused Meighen of bad taste. Dispassionate observers, the *Spectator* suggested, would not exonerate Ferguson of a similar charge. 'The occasion did not call for this venomous onslaught on a former great chief.'

To a League of Nations committee on November 2, 1935, Walter Riddell of Canada suggested an oil embargo as one of the sanctions against Italy, then invading Ethiopia, and a month later was repudiated by his government: the idea was his own, Canada was taking no initiative.

It was unfortunate, the *Province* said, that the government 'should have chosen this moment for an announcement which, whatever it meant, must have given courage and comfort to Mussolini.' Canada had gained prestige through Riddell's suggestion. She would lose far more than she gained through the government's disclaimer. In Edmonton the *Journal* produced a rather equivocal editorial suggesting Canada would probably go along with whatever the League ordered, since Canadians believed that 'the League is the most potent instrument yet devised for the preservation of world peace.' The Calgary *Herald* suggested that, whether Riddell was acting on instructions or on his own, nothing but undesirable publicity could follow the pointed repudiation.

Again the *Tribune* was blunt. Its editorial headed 'More Weaseling at Ottawa' took a swing at the Bennett government, which before its defeat in October had confined the statement of its position at Geneva to general terms. Then it went into the Riddell tangle: 'It is humiliating to all Canadians. . . . Are we to assume that all these years Canada has been giving mere lip-service to the League and the collective system? The League is engaged right now in its first and vitally important effort to establish the rule of law . . . and Canada of all countries is the one showing least concern and doing most to weaken and betray the cause.'

The *Spectator* disbelieved the statement that the Riddell suggestion had not been government policy. It attributed the repudiation to pressure from Quebec, and argued that Mackenzie King 'should either have taken a passive stand at Geneva in the first place or, having adopted a vigorous policy should have stood by his guns.' The *Spectator* thought the vigorous policy the right one. Rather presciently, the paper suggested that the only worthwhile peace would be one in which Mussolini met defeat: 'That is the only kind of language men of violence understand. Generosity they mistake for weakness.'

The *Citizen* backed the government. Canada was subscribing to collective measures as agreed upon, but would incur heavy responsibilities if she took the lead. The Canadian people would almost certainly refuse to engage in war abroad as a result of economic action. Bowman, in fact, managed to turn the situation into a reflection on the previous government: 'During the five years since 1930 while intensified economic war has tended to push nations everywhere into new military preparations, Canadian defence has been sabotaged under the policy of deflation and disaster economy. . . . Canada is more defenceless than Ethiopia at this moment.'

In May of 1940 the Rowell-Sirois Commission recommended federal take-over of provincial debt, unemployment relief, and the income-tax and succession-duty fields. Eight months later the premiers of British Columbia, Ontario, and Alberta broke up a conference called to work out plans based on the report. The *Citizen* backed the rebels, contending there was no time for such things with a war on, and arguing that the report contained the seeds of too much centralization. All other Southam papers took an opposite view. The *Province* (going in for shorter editorials with more bite since M.E.Nichols's advent) was the most vehement: 'Canada's three saboteurs are Pattullo, Aberhart, and Hepburn. Their emblem is the parish pump, rampant.' They were out to blast 'the first constructive attempt made in three generations to bring the Canadian national setup into conformity with the needs of the time'.

The Company in the Thirties

Early in the company's history members of the Southam family began to think ahead, some of them perhaps no more than casually, to the question of future control. There was no urgent cause for misgiving, but eventually settlement of estates would open the probability of stock dispersal to meet succession duties. Some of it might fall into questionable hands. The company reorganized in 1931 to settle this problem for the time being at least.

The original capital set-up in 1927 authorized $7,000,000 in six per cent preferred shares at $100 par, and 700,000 no-par common shares allotted at the outset at $10 each. Shares actually issued amounted to about $4,500,000 in preferred and the same amount in common (at the $10 figure). This arrangement had been almost immediately altered by converting preferred to debentures in a move to forestall double taxation.

In the 1931 reorganization the company split the existing no-par-value common (which in that year changed hands at $15) so that each holder of ten old shares became the owner of one new $100 preference share and ten new common. Dividend returns remained unchanged. Division of the common into two classes, with only one share in five having voting rights, ensured control. All voting shares were vested in a new companion company, Southam Securities Limited. Its only shareholders were the inner circle of family and company directors – the Southams and the experienced hands on the papers and at head office: Burd, Nichols, Woods, Ker, Spencer, Imrie, Fisher, Watson. Shareholders of this company thus controlled the publishing company. Southam Securities also served as a trading-agent for odd lots of publishing-company stock and debentures that came on the market from time to time.

Depression hit the company and its newspapers with a series of descending thuds. At the end of 1931 its list of investments, on the books at $1,397,000, had dropped to a market value of $320,000. Soon after incorporation, with newsprint price increases in prospect, it had bought newsprint company stocks as a hedge. Newsprint prices fell. So did newsprint company stocks, along with everything else. In the first six months of 1929 the six newspapers had rolled up a net profit of $735,000. For the first six months of 1932 the figure was down to $347,000, with worse to come. That fall the company passed its common stock dividend. It was not restored until 1936. Head office executives, publishers, and the rank and file took successive pay cuts.

Even the smallest ray of light was welcome. In September of 1933 Imrie reported from Edmonton that in August, for the first time in forty-three months, the *Journal* had shown an increase in advertising linage. The increase was one-tenth of one per cent.

Over at Hamilton the irrepressible Jimmie Allan, then in his sixty-third year with the *Spectator*, frequently commented on the papers' advertising records in verse. Toward the end of the depression of the early 1920s he had resorted to Cowper:

> Ye fearful saints, fresh courage take
> The clouds ye so much dread
> Are big with mercy and shall break
> In blessings on your head.

Now as some signs of betterment began to show in this longer and deeper depression he hailed his opposite numbers cheerily:

> Congratulations, Billy Russell,
> Who daily uses wit and muscle
> To linage gain in far Vancouver
> By every scheme he can manoeuvre. . . .
> Long may you serve 'neath Province walls
> Before the final curtain falls.

The company never actually lost money. Throughout it maintained a margin over the preferred stock dividend and applied it to cutting debt instead of paying dividends on the common. The result was an increase in value of common stock. Given an attributed value of $6.00 at the time of the 1931 reorganization, it dropped to a low of $2.00 in 1932, rose to $6.00 in 1936, and to $8.50 in 1938.

Merger and a Change of Name

In 1938 the publishing company bought the stock of the Montreal and Toronto printing companies and the Southam Building in Calgary, three historic properties in the Southam business story. At the same time, since printing is not publishing, it changed its name to The Southam Company.

For ten years the printing plants had been the chief assets of William Southam and Sons – the company holding the family's non-newspaper assets. Through the depression, with real estate hard put to meet carrying charges, they alone of the various properties in this company had made any money.

Now those members of the family who had stayed with the tradition of publishing and printing had edged out of nearly all their other business interests. And Richard Southam, the brother chiefly concerned with printing, was dead.

The publishing company had been established on the basis of a community of interest between the various newspapers and their publishers. Obviously this did not apply to printing plants. But in the ten years since its establishment the publishers had come to know the plant managers and to feel that company ownership of a couple of printing plants would not affect their editorial independence. The plants needed sound administration. So the deal was made. (In 1948 the Southam Building would be sold, and in 1958 the printing business would be reorganized as a subsidiary, The Southam Printing Company.)

Though the plants had managed to stay in black ink there had been ups and downs. Loss of the Simpson catalogue business in 1931 hit Toronto hard. But some years earlier the plant had begun to produce wrappers for the Quaker Oats companies in Peterborough and England. Restrictions on imports of United States magazines brought helpful business in magazine-runs for the Canadian market. This in turn disappeared under a new trade treaty in 1935.

Now again came the jolts of wartime economy.

A glance at Southam plant history makes obvious one problem in the commercial printing business – that of adjusting work to equipment and equipment to work. Big jobs often call for special machinery. In changing and competitive times any given job may vanish. The presses on which it was done remain – to be stored, or sold if there is a market, or put into use again when suitable work comes up. Printing for the English Quaker Oats business disappeared in the wartime need of shipping space for supplies more vital than cereal wrappers. But shortly thereafter, as a conservation measure, Canada banned imports of pulp magazines; the canvas came off the Hoes, installed for this work in the early 1930s but idle since 1935. Throughout the war years runs of pulps were turned out at Duncan Street. This in turn would end.

Meantime in 1940 two men whose careers thenceforward were closely tied to Southam printing joined the Toronto plant. One was W.H.Woolnough, who came in as sales manager from an advertising agency, became general manager in 1941, and held that post until transferred to head office of the parent company in Montreal in 1946. The other was J.F.Hayes, who followed Woolnough as general manager at Toronto.

The war over, American pulps were again free to enter Canada and production of the Canadian runs was lost. However, newsprint was short in the States. Jack Hayes invaded the American market, setting up a deal to print complete North American editions at Duncan Street. A fleet of tractor-trailers rolled down the roads to Chicago and New York, loaded with Canadian-printed copies of such magazines as *Ranch Romances* and *Western Mystery*. This business turned in a profit while it lasted. It didn't last long. Under United States copyright laws, American writers lost protection in their own country when periodicals carrying their stories were printed in Canada only. Magazine printers in the States appealed to Washington. The business vanished overnight. And Hayes ruefully recalled: 'While the American printers were working to prevent these magazines from being printed in Canada, the Hoe people were on my doorstep trying to sell new American-made presses to do the job!'

Although the period 1942-52 was considered in retrospect as one of favorable advance, the margins over costs and taxes were less than lush. In 1945, for instance, the Toronto plant did just more than $1,000,000 worth of business for the first time since 1929. Gross profit was $114,000, but fixed charges and income tax reduced this to earnings of $51,000. Montreal had a turnover of $1,324,000 that year for a profit of $62,000 after tax.

Family tragedy darkened the post-war years.

On Richard's death in 1937, Adam Lewis had become president of the Toronto plant with William Wallace Southam, Richard's eldest son, as managing director. William Wallace joined the firm at the age of twenty-two in 1923, after graduating from Royal Military College and studying typography at Indianapolis. By 1937 he knew its operation, its staff, and its problems. A secondary interest was the army. This moved into first place in September 1939. Shortly after going overseas he rose to command the 48th Highlanders, and as a brigadier led the 6th brigade (Cameron Highlanders of Winnipeg, South Saskatchewan Regiment, and Fusiliers Mont-Royal) at Dieppe. Twice wounded in that action, he was captured and remained in a German prison camp until early in 1945. The Distinguished Service Order marked his gallantry; but he never recovered from the wounds of Dieppe and died in Toronto in April 1950.

In that year his younger brother Kenneth (Bud) Southam became general manager of the Toronto plant. Bud Southam had broken in on the Winnipeg *Tribune* before the war and had gone to work as a printing salesman on his return from service with the R.C.A.F. His career as head of the plant, hailed by old-timers who had worked for Richard and known Bud as a boy around the place, was tragically short. He died of cancer in September 1952, the last of Richard's three boys. The second son, Richard Jr. (better known as Jack), had been killed in a motor accident near Granby July 21, 1929, while on staff at Montreal.

The Public Company

Three years after the 1938 merger the parent company switched
from holding to operating status. Through the 1930s the system of
separate companies, though it had some cumbersome aspects, had
seemed to be the simplest way of dealing most effectively with half a
dozen different taxing authorities. Wartime changes that brought the
whole corporation tax field under the federal government ended one
argument in favor of individual companies.

In the background also were thoughts of a possible public market,
eventually, for Southam stock; investment dealers urged that any
such offering should be that of an operating rather than a holding
company.

There were one or two distasteful possibilities. Competitors in the
West, for instance, might seize on what they could hold up as a new
reminder of 'eastern ownership' – a historic bogy. Actually no
change in the emphasis on local management was involved. Philip
Fisher wrote M.E.Nichols: 'Nothing in all this discussion . . . carries
any implication of change in the practical relationships that have
existed between this office and the operating offices. That relationship has been worked out over many years . . . and the last thing we
have in mind is that any technical change in the structure of the organization should have any effect on our actual habits of operation.'

In the end it was decided that advantages outweighed difficulties.
At December 31, 1941, the subsidiaries transferred their assets and
the technical change was made – largely a matter of consolidated ac-
counting. As divisions rather than companies the newspapers continued to run their own affairs.

Tied in with this reorganization were plans for a financial tidying-
up. Debentures and preferred stock carried dividends of six per cent
at a time when interest rates generally were down. Furthermore, corporation taxes – levied after payment of debenture interest but before payment of preferred stock dividends – had greatly increased,
with the result that the company had to earn $10 to pay the $6 preferred dividend, with a consequently reduced pool of earnings available to the common. Early in 1942 it issued $7,000,000 in new five
per cent debentures.

Questions involved in the whole matter of succession – how to
provide for succession duties and retain family control – were of increasing concern now to the elder Southams. The arrangement of
1931, while it took care of the control angle for the time being, had
not provided a market for any large block of stock that might have to

be sold. Southam Securities, the private company holding the voting stock, had learned from experience that it could not be sure of selling non-voting shares to people already connected with the enterprise. Meantime succession-duty rates had risen. Inevitably, to ease liquidation of estates and, incidentally, to set an unquestioned value for probate (in the early 1940s different provinces set different values on stock held by shareholders who died), the company would soon need a wider field of sale.

In any absolute sense the two objectives – to establish a trading market and assure continued family control – were irreconcilable. Such a market implied some kind of public listing, and in the view of the investment men the only effective listing would be that of voting stock. The plan evolved in late 1944 and early 1945, largely by Philip Fisher with F.N.Southam's concurrence, called for reclassifying the existing 500,000-share issue of stock as all-voting and increasing it to 750,000. Common-share holders would get rights to buy additional stock at a preferential rate, some would be offered to the public with stock-exchange listing to follow, and 30 per cent of the outstanding debentures would be redeemed. Apart from establishing a market, the plan had the virtue of setting a more reasonable balance-sheet ratio of debentures and capital stock.

Opinions were divided and sentiment strong. In Ottawa Wilson at first urged an alternative plan: retention of voting stock by the family and their old close associates, and public listing of an issue that would carry a preference as to dividends but voting power only if dividends failed. His chief argument was the danger of stock-buying by special interests. The investment dealers held out for listing of voting common without restriction. They pointed out that in any event the future of the company lay in Southam hands; perhaps there was more danger in the possibility of private trading (for instance, in case of family disagreement) than in open dealings on the market.

In Hamilton W.J.Southam and Fred Ker raised objections based mainly on the position of debenture holders, who would see part of their investment redeemed for cash, but would get no chance to buy common except at the public price. Technically debenture buyers are people who lend money to a company at a fixed interest-rate and with preferred security, in contrast to those who buy stock and thus share in ownership, take the risk, and merit the profits. In the Southam Company there were historic circumstances that made the position a bit less simple than that. Most of the debenture holders were Southams or descendants of Southams, some of whom had become holders of debentures (rather than stock) through circumstances other than a simple money-lending process. The preponderance of debentures in W.J.'s estate went back to a trust agreement of 1931 when the brothers took over the bulk of his common-stock holdings, at a time when the common-stock future was uncertain, in return for senior securities. Ethel Southam Balfour's position traced to her father's caution in the early days of Southam Limited. Gordon Southam's estate had been converted into $600,000 in debentures, inherited by twenty-six nephews and nieces as they came of age. All this with the aim of safeguarding income to individuals. But the individuals were a varied lot. Many certainly had no connection with the company and would have none. But some would make it their career. From Halifax in that February of 1945, Commander St. Clair Balfour, Jr., in port between convoys, wrote his father in somewhat disillusioned mood: 'The debenture holders are merely loaning money to the company which it no longer needs. . . . But they are direct descendants of William Southam, and they should be given an opportunity to retain an interest in their company. . . .'

In Hamilton W.J., Ker, and the elder St. Clair Balfour expressed their views in a memorandum of which the chief point was that stock should be offered 'to present holders of all securities, either for cash or in exchange for debentures at par on an equitable basis', and opposed public issue through a brokerage house 'except in so far as the unsold residue to present security-holders might be involved'. W.J. also appealed to F.N. independently, arguing that through previous conversions to debentures 'our incomes . . . were seriously affected, and furthermore we were also changed from the position of stockholders in a family company in which we should have and hold this position, into apparently the position of money-lenders to the company.' Now a public issue was proposed and 'we can't have these at a fair price as the common-stockholders must again through rights get theirs.' Later, and again on his own, he went so far as to have an investment house draw up an alternative plan.

Fisher told Ker, in comment on the Hamilton memorandum, that 'you are asking the shareholders to concede something to the debenture holders in terms of stock purchase rights to which the debenture holders have no legal claim whatever, and to which nothing in their past tenure of debentures gives them even a moral claim.' He thought the company owed one moral obligation to the debenture holders: not to proceed with any wholesale redemption simply to get an interest rate below five per cent. But to go further would mean 'asking the shareholders to forego advantages . . . implicit to the ownership of common stock. . . .'

Ker differed with this interpretation of the moral claim. In his view it lay in the fact that 'its (the company's) directors have in the past consistently encouraged the purchase of senior securities when the prospective purchasers had the option of taking or holding common stock, because the preferred and debentures offered greater security to those who needed it.'

Fisher held to his view, replying to all objections on the ground that the company's officers must approach the question in terms of its effect on the company as a whole. If there were adjustments to be made within the Southam family itself, they should be made by family rather than by company action. The family and the company were no longer quite the same thing; had not been, in fact, since 1927. One-third of the shareholders, holding one-fifth of the common stock, were completely outside the family orbit.

In this, incidentally, Fisher stuck to a position consistently taken. Years before in another connection he had written: 'The real meaning of the organization of The Southam [Publishing] Company ... was that, *for corporate purposes*, a Woods or a Burd or a Fisher would be as much a member of the family as a Southam.' It was not possible to believe that any senior members of the Southam family had retained a purpose that 'those shareholders bearing the name of Southam, or perhaps having married persons bearing the name of Southam, should feel free to form a narrower clique.' He was now applying this principle in a somewhat wider sense.

In the background of course was the fact that the family itself was no longer the unit of a generation before. The close-knit group of six brothers and a sister was in process of dissolution. Now there were six sets of cousins, men and women, many of whom had no intention of working for the company, themselves already married and beginning to raise families still further removed. The family element in the company's management would be continued through interest and ability rather than inheritance.

Apart from the family and financial angles there were discussions on what effect public listing would have on goodwill, its possible reaction on the newspapers. Here also there were reservations. Ker didn't think it would help the *Spectator* 'if some unpopular local skinflint could be referred to as a shareholder of the company'. Out in Winnipeg Wes McCurdy drew up a memorandum noting that 'in its highest conception a newspaper is supposed to be a trust reposing in the hands of responsible and public-spirited people,' that all the Southam papers had benefited from this conception, and that some measure of the benefit would be lost if their affairs were to be handled in a pattern evolved by big business.

In the end the plan went into effect largely as originally worked out. The company's issues of 400,000 non-voting and 100,000 voting shares were all classified as voting and increased by 250,000. Common shareholders got the right to buy additional stock at the rate of four new shares at $10 each for each ten already held. A.E. Ames and Company agreed to buy 125,000 at just over $12 for re-sale to the public at $13 (the profit being their fee for establishing a market) on a dividend basis of seventy-six cents a year. Of the $2,-550,000 realized on the new issue, $2,070,000 went to reduce the debenture issue to $4,830,000, the rest into a reserve for pensions.

Public listing followed. Within a few days the stock reached $15. Successive dividend increases brought the yearly return to $1.60 by 1955 with a corresponding rise in share values, and a $3.20 rate in the spring of 1960, when the stock was split four-for-one. (At 1966 market highs, the equivalent of a common share valued at $2 in the depths of the depression in 1932 would have brought about $160.)

The fears of those who recognized necessity, but still disliked it, were somewhat eased by the fact that along with announcement of its 1945 refinancing plans the company made a public statement defining the traditional home rule principle:

> The practice of the company is to leave the direction of editorial policy of each newspaper to the discretion of its local publisher who is an executive officer of the company. The company's objective in all of its newspapers is to preserve complete political independence and to present news fairly and accurately.

This theme was developed in the annual report for 1945, the first after reorganization, in a statement of belief that newspapers are essentially community services and must be published and generally administered in the communities they serve. Subsequent decisions were designed to keep the record clear as regards big business or political influence. The company would have no financial interest outside mass communications and printing. Officers and senior executives would not act as directors of other unrelated firms operated for profit. Officers and those involved in news-handling and editorial positions would take no active part, outside the publications they served, in municipal, provincial, or federal politics.

On October 2, 1944, Wilson Southam's seventy-sixth birthday, his brother Fred wrote him a characteristic note: he had been overlooking this anniversary for years because he believed it wasn't good form in the best Christian Science circles to pay much attention to birthdays, but this time he was going to wish Wilson happiness anyway. He enclosed a reference that tickled him, an extract from an address by the president of Union College about an illustrious predecessor, Eliphalet Nott, who at the age of seventy-two had announced that declining years made necessary his retirement. The difficulty was that Eliphalet had gone on making that speech for the next twenty-one years with unfortunate results for the college. This, F.N. suggested, seemed to point a moral.

In the following May, with reorganization completed, F.N. retired from the presidency to chairmanship of the board and Fisher succeeded him. It was just over sixty years since F.N. had begun his working life as a printer's apprentice at the *Spectator*. Early in 1946 he was stricken with illness from which he had apparently recovered. He was ready to leave for Atlantic City, scene of many Southam family gatherings in earlier years, when on Monday, March 18, he lay down for a nap after lunch and did not waken.

The Company and the I.T.U.

Within a year of the date at which it 'went public' the company met a stiff challenge from the International Typographical Union.

In Winnipeg the I.T.U. local struck the Southams' *Tribune* and the Siftons' *Free Press* when joint negotiations for new contracts failed. The Winnipeg papers continued to publish. The I.T.U., with its international executive advising, then called strikes at Hamilton, Ottawa, Edmonton, and Vancouver to force a switch from local to group negotiation on basic points and acceptance of certain conditions by all Southam papers concerned, and thus recoup the situation at Winnipeg. Calgary was not involved; the contract there had been with another union since the 1930s.

In the background of the Winnipeg dispute, but directly concerned in the extension of the strikes only because it was the rock on which Winnipeg negotiations foundered, was a toughened program of the printers' union. At a convention in Grand Rapids in 1944, the I.T.U. decided on certain new provisions in its general laws. These included a directive that in all contracts locals secure time-and-a-half for all work beyond five shifts in any one week, and for all off-day work whether in excess of five shifts or not. Buttressing these provisions was a sharpened insistence on recognition of the general laws in which they were included, and exemption of these laws from arbitration.

Most contracts between I.T.U. locals and newspapers provided for a joint standing-committee to settle disputes arising out of their operation or interpretation, a committee that could convert itself into a board of arbitration (by adding an independent chairman) whose majority vote was decisive.

The 'general laws' of the I.T.U. had in fact for many years stipulated that they not be subject to arbitration. But application of the principle seems to have been somewhat flexible, agreements frequently specifying that recognition of the general laws apply only in so far as they did not conflict with terms of the contract. Now the union sought their acceptance in all contracts, protected by the flat undertaking 'that local union laws not affecting wages, hours and working conditions, and the general laws of the I.T.U., shall not be subject to arbitration.'

Some contracts (those jointly negotiated in Winnipeg, for instance) called for a regular work-week of five days with the provision that if at any time the union did not come up with enough printers to enable the newspapers to operate for six days on a five-shift-per-man basis, available printers as necessary would work a sixth shift at straight-time rates. Since these were closed-shop agreements the union was the only source of men. The I.T.U. now insisted – under the terms of its general laws – that no one be permitted to work more than five days a week at straight time. It thus set up specific standards relating to hours of work (in the overtime aspect) and armored them against arbitration.

Publishers contended that establishing such predetermined conditions removed from the realm of collective bargaining matters that belonged there. A circular of the Canadian Daily Newspapers Association in June 1945, put it this way: 'It is evident that the entire principle of collective bargaining which has characterized publishers' relationships with their mechanical staff for many years is destroyed if publishers must accept clauses relating to wages, hours and working conditions over which they have no control.'

As matters stood, wage increases were still subject to approval by war labor boards. And labor regulations (PC 1003) required that collective agreements include provision for arbitration of all disputes arising out of their 'interpretation or violation' during their term of existence; a provision, incidentally, included in subsequent legislation also.

The pertinent sections of the legislation read:

17. Where an employee alleges that there has been a misinterpretation or a violation of a collective agreement, the employee shall submit the same for consideration and final settlement in accordance with the procedure established by the collective agreement, if any, or the procedure established by the Board for such case; and the employee and

his employer shall do such things as are required of them by the procedure and such things as are required of them by the terms of the
settlement.

18. (1) Every collective agreement made after these regulations come
into force shall contain a provision establishing a procedure for final
settlement, without stoppage of work, on the application of either
party, of differences concerning its interpretation or violation.

(2) Where a collective agreement does not provide an appropriate
procedure for consideration and settlement of disputes concerning its
interpretation or violation thereof, the Board shall, upon application,
by order, establish such a procedure.

These requirements on their face seemed to establish the I.T.U.
non-arbitrability clause as contrary to the regulations* and this point
became as accompanying argument to the publishers' general objections. This situation was technically rectified, at least in a general
sense, late in January 1946, when I.T.U. international president
Woodruff Randolph and labor department officials agreed on addition to the non-arbitrability clause of the words: 'Except in so far as
such arbitration and the results thereof are compulsory under Canadian laws.'

In the fall of 1945 I.T.U. contracts were coming up for renewal in
several cities where Southam papers published. At all points where
more than one newspaper printed, competitors were also concerned;
I.T.U. practice was to establish one local in each city. In Vancouver
the *Province*, the *Sun*, and the *News-Herald* negotiated jointly with
Local 226 for identical contracts. Winnipeg and Edmonton followed
the same practice. In Ottawa the interlocking was even more pronounced; the *Journal* and the *Citizen* had a single joint contract with
four unions – printers, pressmen, stereotypers, and mailers. At each
point the local Southam publisher negotiated only with respect to the
city in which his paper published.

The regular fall meeting of the company's board of directors (of
which the Vancouver, Winnipeg, Ottawa, and Hamilton publishers
were members) in early October talked about the I.T.U. laws and recorded the result in the minutes:

A general discussion took place on the labor problems at the various
divisions, particularly with respect to the International Typographical

*On December 7, 1945, M.M.Maclean, director of industrial relations, wrote
Randolph: 'Section 17 of the Regulations requires compulsory arbitration of
all provisions of a collective agreement, and the decisions of the arbitrator
are final and binding on both parties to the agreement. Section 18 requires
every collective agreement made after such Regulations came into force to
contain a provision establishing a procedure for final settlement without stoppage of work, etc.'

Union and its demand for recognition by the publishers of its own 1945 laws. No formal action was taken but the general feeling was that the laws referred to were unreasonable and demands for acceptance of them should be resisted.

Obviously there was nothing specific or binding in this. In Vancouver the *Province* and the two other papers signed, on November 2, identical contracts including the unqualified non-arbitrability clause after eight months of negotiations that seemed destined to end in a strike unless they did so.

At other Southam points, references to the laws contained limiting phrases stating that terms of the contract were paramount. It is perhaps questionable that inclusion of such a limitation in any new contract could mean much, since it was unlikely that I.T.U. headquarters would approve a contract that contained terms not in accord with its laws.

The labor committee of the C.D.N.A. reported in the spring of 1946:

> The acceptance of I.T.U. 1945 laws and their exemption from arbitration continued to form the principal issue between publishers and the local unions. All agreements signed have recognized the laws. Modified recognition has been given in most cases, but with full exemption of the laws from arbitration. Your committee has emphasized that modified recognition does not in itself give protection against the laws, but protects the publisher only in cases of conflict between clauses in the agreement and the I.T.U. laws.

At Edmonton in November the Southams' *Journal* and Charles Campbell's *Bulletin* signed identical contracts (including limited recognition) with the I.T.U. local, which eventually repudiated them on advice of an international representative after the Winnipeg trouble had developed. Hamilton and Ottawa (which had varying forms of recognition in existing contracts) were due to negotiate shortly, but the positions they might have taken on this or any other issue became academic. They did not get the chance.

For the rub had come at Winnipeg. There Victor Sifton of the *Free Press* and Wesley McCurdy of the *Tribune* held out against unqualified recognition of union law and the non-arbitrability provision. The I.T.U. held out for it, after having one draft contract disapproved at Indianapolis. Canadian international representative Harry Finch came to town. A conciliator was appointed. And on the night of November 8 the printers stayed away from work.

Winnipeg went without printed news on Friday, November 9. Next day the *Free Press* and *Tribune* got out a joint paper – based on copy typewritten and engraved – and continued to publish. By early December it was obvious they could stay in business, without the I.T.U. if necessary; and the threat of concerted action elsewhere began to appear.

On December 3 Allan Histed, president of the Hamilton local, wired Fisher: 'In view of pending negotiations in Hamilton this union urges your influence be used in securing settlement of Winnipeg lockout of our members by your company. Unified action by all local unions involved contemplated as cannot reconcile acceptance of laws in Vancouver and rejection in Winnipeg by same company.' Similar messages, so closely related in wording as to make it obvious that their form had been agreed on, arrived from Ottawa, Edmonton, and Vancouver December 4 and 5.

Fisher replied at some length, noting that 'there has been no lockout in Winnipeg' where 'the members of the union absented themselves from work while a conciliator appointed by the government was trying in accordance with government labor regulations to settle the matter in dispute.' He repeated the company stand:

> The Southam Company believes that newspapers are essentially community enterprises and must be administered in the city of publication. Details of any labor negotiations are accordingly vested in the hands of the responsible officials of the company in each city. Each newspaper is a separate organization and in association with other newspapers in the same city has traditionally entered into its own contracts with the local typographical union.

This drew from the locals messages expressing the view that 'The Southam Company has control of policies of its agents' and inability to subscribe to 'separate conception of six companies within the parent body'. They concluded:

> The typographical unions producing newspapers for units of the Southam chain have co-ordinated their efforts and have voluntarily vested in the executive council of the International Typographical Union power to order such action as they see fit to bring about a settlement in Winnipeg and consummation of contracts in other cities similar to that accepted by the Southam Company in Vancouver. We urge acceptance of MacNamara effort to bring principals together on collective basis.

Fisher and W.J.Watson did attend a conference with Deputy Minister of Labor Arthur MacNamara and other labor department officials and Randolph and other I.T.U. representatives at Ottawa, January 30. Randolph brought up the question of a standard policy for all Southam newspapers and Fisher stuck to the position that such a policy would be impracticable and unacceptable.

It was at this time that MacNamara and Randolph worked out the formula qualifying the non-arbitrability clause: 'Except insofar as such arbitration and the results thereof are compulsory under Canadian laws.' As late as the last week in June, however, Fisher said he had never been informed of any agreed-upon phrase.

At that point, the end of January, Winnipeg was the only city in which I.T.U. men were out. But events were on the move. Ottawa and Hamilton I.T.U. locals applied to the Ontario Labor Relations Board for intervention, the Hamilton application setting forth that 'We have been continuously in contact with the Federal Department of Labor since December 1945, in an effort to have The Southam Company Limited, Montreal, through their respective heads, meet with our authorized representatives for the purpose of negotiating a chain contract. . . . We have placed the negotiating representation in the hands of our international representatives. The Southam Company . . . refuses to deal on this basis.'

(In fact what the I.T.U. sought was not a 'chain contract' covering everything, but agreement by the company to compel all its newspaper divisions to accept certain uniform conditions – including the non-arbitrability clause.)

The provincial board dismissed these applications on the ground the question was one for the national board, and the scene moved to Ottawa with the international union itself the applicant for group negotiation.

There on May 20 the board heard arguments from both points of view. At one point C.L.Dubin, lawyer for the union, contended that 'unless we can negotiate directly with the president or some responsible officer with respect to a general policy, then one local is played off against the other . . .', to which A.S.Pattillo for the company replied that 'it has been a question of the international union playing one local against the other and playing the whole crowd against us.'

Pattillo incidentally took occasion to express the company's objection to application of the word 'chain' to its newspapers. 'Chain' implied joined links operating together. Each of the company's papers was run by a local publisher in a local community far from the others, none interfering with the operations of any other and not managed by a head office.

Two days later the board dismissed the application in these words:

The union's bargaining rights . . . have been established . . . for local units only. Therefore it is clear that in order to invoke the provisions of the regulations to compel the company to bargain with the applicant union with a view to the completion of an agreement covering newspaper establishments of the company in the several provinces, it would be necessary for the union to first establish its authority to do so by obtaining certification under the regulations as the bargaining representative of the employees in a single bargaining unit extending to all plants involved.

Whether I.T.U. headquarters ever considered trying to set up such a bargaining unit is not on record. It would in any case have been a time-spending process and a quicker way to get results seemed available. On Thursday night, May 30, I.T.U. printers stopped work at the Hamilton *Spectator*, Ottawa *Citizen*, and Edmonton *Journal*. On the night of June 5 they quit at the Vancouver *Province*.

An I.T.U. statement made it clear that the walkouts were designed to force company intervention in Winnipeg: 'Persistent efforts on the part of the officers of the various unions and officials of the federal department of labor to bring the two parties together have been of no avail because of the adamant position taken by the president of the Southam Company Limited that he would not interfere in the Winnipeg dispute.... With the spread of open shop operation our unions could be destroyed piecemeal. We are convinced that this is the aim of the company....'

For the company, Fisher repeated the traditional position: 'It is our conviction that daily newspapers must be administered in the cities in which they are published, and authority to deal with labor relations in the different cities ... has been traditionally vested in the local publisher.' He referred to the May 22 decision of the national board and concluded: 'Ever since the Winnipeg strike, the publishers of other Southam newspapers have been quite prepared to continue amicable relations with their respective local typographical unions, and if the difficulties which originated in Winnipeg have spread to other cities, the blame must rest completely upon the shoulders of the International Typographical Union and the several local unions which have submitted to its instructions.'

At this point Fisher asked the company's directors what they thought about a special meeting. Was there any point in it, unless the company were to consider retreat from the home-rule principle? Could directors who were also publishers be spared from their struck newspapers to come and talk about it? Only one of fifteen directors, a non-publisher, favored a meeting. None was held.

The Edmonton *Journal* (jointly with the *Bulletin*) and the *Spectator* continued to publish without interruption. The *Citizen* managed a curtailed edition June 5 and built up from there. Only at Vancouver were the presses stilled for a significant and serious length of time.

On June 21 F.W.Maxted, Canadian vice-president of the International Printing Pressmen and Assistants Union, came to see Fisher in Montreal. The position of such mechanical unions (none of which had joined in the I.T.U. demand for group negotiation) was uncomfortable and confused. Pressmen and stereotypers had gone back to work in Winnipeg after a short period of refusing to cross I.T.U. picket lines. At the moment the stereotypers were out in Vancouver, Hamilton, and Ottawa, but not in Edmonton. Pressmen were out in Edmonton and Ottawa, but not in Hamilton and Vancouver.

Maxted thought the I.T.U. might be willing to discuss a settlement under which the Winnipeg situation could be by-passed or accepted as a *fait accompli*, so that talks could be centred on reconciliation at the other four points. Fisher said arrangements for settlement at individual cities were up to the publishers, but that he would act as intermediary if it was just a question of opening lines of communication. A letter from Randolph led him to doubt that the I.T.U. head was prepared to by-pass Winnipeg, and a long-distance telephone conversation confirmed this view. The two agreed however to get together and did so in Toronto on June 28.

Nothing really came of it. As afterward stated by Fisher: 'Mr. Randolph enunciated most clearly the policy of the International Typographical Union which was that no contract would be signed by any local with any Southam newspaper unless each and all of the five Southam newspapers affected were prepared to sign a contract in form satisfactory to them, which form would include a clause incorporating and recognizing as inarbitrable the general laws of the I.T.U. now in effect, subject only to such limitations as might be imposed by the labor laws and regulations of Canada and its provinces.' To go along would have meant not only departure from traditional practice, but repudiation of the Wes McCurdy–Victor Sifton stand-together agreement in Winnipeg, where the papers now were publishing with new composing-room crews who had been promised continued employment. The position was deadlocked.

Statements were sometimes confusing. On June 8 Finch issued one at Winnipeg asserting that arbitration was not an issue since 'this union agreed to arbitration as required under the Wartime Labor Relations Regulations.' The Winnipeg publishers rejoined that 'he fails to state that no offer of arbitration was made at any time to the publishers of the Winnipeg newspapers and . . . he fails to define the limited arbitration which he claims to have offered in other quarters.' They then recalled the fact that when negotiations bogged down they had suggested that the drafting of a new contract be referred to a board of arbitration, which the union had refused.

Finch in his statement obviously referred to the generalized wording agreed on by the labor department as meeting legal objections
to the non-arbitration clause, a development not reached until nearly
three months after the Winnipeg walkout. The publishers, in referring incidentally to the fact that they had suggested an arbitration
board draw up a contract, were citing a procedure that might have
worked if agreed upon, but was not compulsory under the regulations, which provided that agreements must contain machinery for
arbitration, but did not compel the application of arbitration to *negotiation* of contracts. It seems apparent that sometimes, when publishers and I.T.U. officials batted 'arbitration' around, they were swinging at different balls.

The dispute came in for some needling in the House of Commons.
On June 19 Stanley Knowles of Winnipeg North Centre (himself a
card-holder in the I.T.U.) asked about the *Tribune*'s objection to the
non-arbitrability clause. Was there anything new?

Labor Minister Mitchell replied that in the provinces where wartime labor regulations applied to printing establishments, all the
terms of collective agreements were subject to final and binding arbitration, as provided in sections 17 and 18 of the regulations. Since
the typographical union insisted that its general rules must become a
part of the collective agreement, and one of their provisions was that
such rules were not subject to arbitration, 'it will be seen that the
union law in that respect is in conflict with the provisions of the wartime regulations.' All of which gave Finch a chance to take issue on
the ground that the legal angle had been satisfied by the clause as
amended.

A Vancouver development kept alive a semblance of contact between the company's central management and I.T.U. headquarters.
Early in the strike there Leigh Spencer applied to the B.C. department of labor for a conciliation board to go into the dispute between
the *Province* and Local 226. This became a federally appointed industrial disputes inquiry commission under Brigadier Sherwood
Lett. The Lett Commission found no labor dispute in the ordinary
sense of the word, attributed the origins of the strike to the Winnipeg
situation, and suggested that 'the persons capable of settling the issue
are the principal officials of the International Typographical Union
and The Southam Company Limited.' Since neither the I.T.U. nor
the company had shown any disposition to move from their respective stands in the course of a six-months stalemate, the recommendation that the minister bring them together 'for the purpose of resuming their discussions with a view to reconciling their respective

policies' could hardly result in anything more than another round of talks.

However, Labor Minister Mitchell asked Justice S.E.Richards of the Manitoba Court of Appeals to do what he could, and after preliminary discussions Judge Richards in September was appointed a commissioner 'to investigate and report upon matters at issue between The Southam Company Limited and the International Typographical Union'. Fisher pointed out that legally there could be no matters at issue between the company and the International, since the relationship was between the divisions and the locals, but agreed to meet Randolph again to hear any representations he might make on behalf of the Canadian locals. Randolph and Fisher met with Judge Richards in Montreal on October 23 and 24, and on November 28 Richards reported to the Minister that he was unable to bring about a settlement.

Results of the strikes varied with circumstances in the divisions. Eventually the compositors at Hamilton who replaced the strikers joined the pressmen's union. Winnipeg and Edmonton organized their own training plans and continued open-shop operation. At Ottawa the *Citizen*'s new printers became the Ottawa Printing Crafts Union, an affiliate of the National Council of Canadian Labor. When The Southam Company bought the Medicine Hat *News* in 1948, the *News* was an I.T.U. shop and remained so. After a relaxation of the International's position that no contract would be signed with a Southam newspaper unless satisfactory agreements were signed with all, the *Province* returned to the I.T.U. fold in November, 1949.

8
Hamilton:
The *Spectator*

Any vital newspaper published in a city close to a bigger neighbor tends to project with special emphasis the character of its own community. The *Spectator* has always been unmistakably Hamiltonian.

Under the circumstances it is notable that the man who joined it in 1921, and would come to set its tone until mid-century, was neither a Hamiltonian nor a newspaper man; and not surprising that he quickly became both.

Frederick Innes Ker was a construction engineer, a 1909 graduate of McGill, with ten years of canal digging and railway building behind him, topped by two years as manager of a pulp and paper company at Port Alice, on the west coast of Vancouver Island. Various circumstances combined to get him into the newspaper business. Gordon Southam had understudied W.J. on the *Spectator* and in the natural course of events would have followed on. But Gordon was dead on the Somme. John Imrie filled in briefly after dissolution of the *Times*, but Imrie was destined for Edmonton. There was no question of Ker's dynamism and managerial ability. And he had married Amy Southam. F.N. had a great affection for his daughter Amy, and Port Alice was far, far away.

Ker came in as assistant to W.J., who was then vice-president and general manager of the Spectator company. Moving from the world of track and tunnel and pulp machine did not daunt him at all. Few things did. While still in his twenties and working for railway-builder Harry McLean (noted a generation later as the Mister X who handed $100 bills to wounded veterans and tossed banknotes out hotel windows) he had been placed in charge of construction of the Georgian Bay and Seaboard line of the CPR and double-tracking of the Sudbury-Cartier subdivision. At thirty he had been pulled out of the army to build the Montreal aqueduct power canal. He had never been in a pulp mill in his life when at thirty-four he went out to manage the mills at Port Alice. News work would be new, but tackling something new was no novelty.

In fact Ker would have brought the same thrust to anything he tried. It was almost by accident that he got into engineering – he won a McGill scholarship given by the Grand Trunk Railway, for which he later worked. There had been some suggestion of the Church as a career – his father was an archdeacon – and it is a reasonable conjecture that in his choice of engineering the Anglican Church lost an eloquent and aggressive bishop. He has confessed that one of the things uppermost in his mind in entering McGill was the chance to continue playing hockey and football.

Although he had never thought of newspaper work before his move to the *Spectator,* he had the urge to write and the ability to express himself clearly and with force. His engineering background brought authority to the *Spectator*'s editorial page on three subjects of unusual interest in Canada: power, waterways, and railways. He believed in personal observation. In the 1930s in his yawl *Dayspring* he navigated the channels and harbors of the St. Lawrence system from the head of Lake Ontario to the Saguenay.

Long before that, however, he had changed the *Spectator*'s course on one of the subjects most familiar to the grasp of his mind: power. The *Spectator* had reached a circulation of 30,000, far ahead of its competition. Nevertheless, Ker sensed a weak spot in its public relations through its long opposition to Beck and the Ontario Hydro project. He went to see Beck. The Hydro giant at first refused to see him but relented on learning of his background as an engineer.

Early in 1922 W.S.Murray, a United States engineer employed by the privately controlled National Electric Light Association of America, reported critically on Ontario Hydro's Chippawa project, belittling public ownership and claiming American consumers got power at lower rates than those charged in Ontario. The *Spectator* promptly entered the lists on Beck's side, challenging the association with a statement that cost of electric light in fifteen principal towns of the Ontario Niagara district was less than half the rate in any fifteen towns in the Niagara district of New York.

Meanwhile Ker had spent months studying Hydro. On sheets of drawing paper gummed together and stretched on tables he worked out the first composite balance sheet and breakdown of the commission's operations and those of its various regional systems. His campaign culminated in a 106-page Power, Trade and Farm number,

September 7, 1922, the announced intention of which was 'to set forth the very advantageous position of the Hamilton-Niagara district in the possession of the greatest supply of low-priced hydroelectric power available for industrial development and domestic use in any part of Ontario.'

This special edition undertook to give 'a complete and authentic history of the development of our electric resources' both public and private. Treatment was balanced and objective. Beck and E.P.Coleman, general manager of Dominion Power and Transmission, each contributed articles. Ker's balance sheet took up a full page. Profusely illustrated, the issue showed, for instance, by diagram the annual coal-pile equivalent of all Ontario Niagara power plants. The pile was ten times as big as the great Egyptian pyramid of Cheops, a photo of which the paper displayed for comparison.

In one of the articles Ker named W.H.Merritt, who was responsible for the first Welland Canal, John Patterson of Cataract, and Sir Adam Beck as the three men who would stand out in the modern history of Ontario.

Somewhat urbanely, in view of its past position on Hydro, the *Spectator* gave the opinion that it should 'clearly and comprehensively present the situation to those whose understanding might have been clouded by careless and imperfectly expressed statements by parties more or less biased and selfishly interested.'

The special number was, as the Toronto *Star* commented, 'some bulk of a paper for two cents'. In later years Ker looked back on his 'straightening out' of the Hydro situation as one of the important things, from a public relations point of view, in the *Spectator*'s ability to withstand the competitive threat that faced it a year later.

The War with Herman

'Mr. Herman will take possession tomorrow.'

For years the *Spectator* and the *Herald* had enjoyed a reasonably peaceful co-existence, with top spot long since conceded to the Spec. A brief announcement on the *Herald*'s editorial page of Tuesday, November 13, 1923, gave notice that this condition was at an end. It ushered in a year of strife that made old-time Hamilton circulation wars look like teatime at the ladies' aid.

John M. Harris, leading spirit of the small group who founded the *Herald* with $8,500 in 1889, died in 1922. His brother Robert took over. But late in the summer of 1923 emissaries with marked cheques arrived in Hamilton. The November 13 announcement recorded the result:

> Pressure of other business which demands his attention has induced Mr. Harris to dispose of his controlling interest and the Herald has come under new control and proprietorship.
>
> The purchaser is W.F.Herman, publisher of the Border Cities Star of Windsor, one of the best equipped and most successful of Ontario newspapers. The negotiations for the purchase of the Herald were consummated last Saturday. Mr. Herman will take possession tomorrow.

Wilberforce Herman was both an entrepreneur and a successful operator of newspapers. Born in the Nova Scotia south-shore town of Lunenburg, he had gone to Boston as a boy and learned the printing trade. As a young man he went west, bought the Prince Albert *Herald*, turned it into a daily and sold it. Later deals at Saskatoon where he bought the *Capital* and renamed it the *Star*, and at Regina where he bought the *Province* and turned it into the *Post* (both eventually to become components of the Sifton-owned Saskatoon *Star-Phoenix* and Regina *Leader-Post*) made him a known figure in the Canadian newspaper world.

In 1918 he had bought the Windsor *Record* and launched it into lively prosperity as the *Border Cities Star*. Now from the established bastion at Windsor he took over a beachhead at Hamilton – apparently believing, from published circulation figures, that the *Herald*'s penetration of the territory was much more extensive than it was. 'Fresh capital, new ideas, new methods, an abundance of fresh energy', the new owner promised, 'will produce visible effects, satisfactory alike to Herald readers and advertisers.'

The visible effects were at once apparent. A nameplate in the Old English affected by the *Border Cities Star* supplanted the chaste label of the old *Herald*. Eight-column lines (BRITISH PARTIES OPEN ATTACK ON BALDWIN, the *Herald* shouted on take-over day) replaced the reticent one- and two-column Harris make up. Italics and a generous touch of razzle-dazzle brightened inside pages. Pictures caught the eye. Comics increased to a full page daily, with a four-page colored section on Saturdays (Mr. and Mrs., Pa's Son-in-Law, Betty, and Bringing Up Father). Boxed congratulations to the new ownership, signed by personalities ranging from the mayor of Windsor to Arthur Meighen and W.S.Fielding, ran across the foot of page one. Full-page editorials in heavy type startled Hamiltonians on Saturdays: 'Bring McMaster University to Hamilton', 'Plea to Check Motor

Deaths and Injuries', 'An Appeal to Canadian Youth', 'Forward Canadians!'

Reporters, advertising salesmen, and circulation crews moved in from Windsor. Letters assured advertisers that 'The Herald covers Hamilton like the Heavens.' Letterheads carried the claim in red that 'The aggressive and progressive policies of the Herald since the change in ownership are bringing 1,000 new readers a week.'

Over at the *Spectator* the counter-moves got under way. The paper met the *Herald* on comics, organized a rotogravure section for Christmas, started a sports extra and a six o'clock edition (on which it had to raise the price to five cents from two because readers began to drop the Home edition to wait for the Final). Herbert Gardiner, retired one-time editor of the *Times*, one of whose joys had been editorial baiting of William Southam, agreed to write historical features. Reporters were hired. Bills for picture engraving rose from $300 to $1,200 a month. Composing-room cost was up by $4,000 a month for November and December, and newsprint by $9,000.

Billboards proclaiming the virtues of the rivals went up all over Hamilton.

The old warrior Jimmie Allan in his report on *Spectator* advertising for 1923 noted: 'Freighted with a precious cargo gathered from many marts our good ship was just touching port last November when the Pirate from Windsor was sighted. . . . Since then we have been decimating each other with silver shot. The casualties to report are two shattered cash boxes. The end is not yet.'

On February 23 in a letter to M.E.Nichols, Ker said it was hard to say what progress Herman was making. 'He is giving everything away but his plant. . . . He is making us, or we are making him, whichever way you like to take it, spend a pile of money. I estimate his monthly cash loss conservatively at from $15,000 to $20,000.'

All this, of course, with the objective on the *Herald*'s part of increased circulation, the key to advertising. And on the *Spectator*'s, to protect what it had – which meant, in practice, grasping what was there to grasp lest the enemy move in.

While editorial and news and feature content are the final determinants of circulation, there are other avenues that may bring in masses of temporary buyers and (possibly) get some of them in the groove of permanent readership: direct canvass, prizes to newsboys, puzzle contests for readers, and straight premiums. It was in this field that much of the battle blazed.

'Last week Herman went in strong for free photograph premiums – a photograph for 13-weeks subscription at 15 cents a week,' Ker reported to F.N.Southam in mid-January. 'On this basis he wrote up quite a lot of subscriptions. . . . On Monday we learned through divers channels that he had passed a consignment of 600 mama dolls through the customs. . . .'

Wholesale vendors who called themselves 'publishers' representatives' and 'upbuilders of newspapers' turned to Hamilton as a lush field and as a sales example to others. Sewing sets and shopping bags were among the inducements offered housewives for signing up with the *Herald*. 'The needle-book they have used so successfully', one Chicago supplier reported to prospective customers, 'is our No. 7 Dandy, price is $42.40 per gross, only 29½ cents apiece. . . . These are all English needles. We can give you the same style of book but fitted with Czechoslovakia needles at $32.75 per gross or 23 cents apiece.' Catalogues listed the range of premiums available: hot water bottles, cook books, scissors, billfolds, watches, schoolbags, axes, roller skates, adjustable stilts, pocket-knives, pens and pencils, hammers, screwdrivers, wrenches, air rifles, flashlights, dictionaries, baseball gloves, pedometers, and vermin-proof bond boxes.

The *Spectator*'s position was a bit curious since probably twenty-four of twenty-five Hamilton newspaper readers already read it. And still did so, despite the *Herald* offensive. Early in February Alex Muir, the tough little Scot whom Ker had brought from Port Alice – and who would be the Spec's money watchdog for a generation – reported there had been only 437 *Spectator* 'stops' since November and that readers had just about stopped 'stopping'. Nevertheless, to a man of Ker's Celtic temperament, attack was the best defence.

One field more open than the city itself existed in surrounding towns, where little promotion had been carried on since the newsprint restrictions of the 1914-18 war. Out-of-town agents got money prizes for circulation. Carrier clubs were set up at points as far away as Kitchener and a four-page paper – THE SPECTATOR CARRIER – reported their activities. Boys could win a scout haversack or a flashlight for one new six-months subscription; three were good for a catcher's mitt; six would produce boxing gloves; forty, a bicycle. Fast delivery by *Spectator*-owned trucks replaced the mail on some rural routes. 'Nothing but death or migration', noted circulation manager Len Britton, 'removes from the lists a rural reader so served.'

The *Spectator* was not a premium newspaper, having little faith in circulation won by salesmen who emphasized the premium rather than the paper. But there were other gimmicks. Back in 1921 it had put on a contest in which the entry fee was a subscription, the problem to arrive at an elephant's weight by counting the maze of figures that delineated its bulk, and the prizes sizable chunks of money – with theatre tickets as consolation to all non-winners.

Now it embarked on another of the same kind, brought up to date by setting up the puzzle in the shape of King Tut: the answer, his age. And it announced: 'For all contestants who do not get in on the prize money the Spectator . . . has arranged to distribute consolation prizes. Included among these will be cabinet photos of contestant or member of the contestant's family, and large "mama" dolls. . . . Watch for further details.'

A touch of old-fashioned espionage flavored the campaign. On March 21 Bill Mulliss wired Ker, attending a convention in Chicago: 'We have inside information that our friends are about to announce mama-doll stunt. We made an announcement today to wait for the Spectator mama dolls. We stated one thousand are already here. Their plan is one doll for six subscribers for 13 weeks. My suggestion is we make it four subscribers for 10 weeks, cutting it at both ends. . . . Their doll has hair and sleeps but is the same size as ours. Think we should go them one better on this also.'

Ker replied: 'Agree with you we must equal or outdo him in quality and absolutely in terms. Once again our problem is to check him rather than increase ourselves. . . . Suggest you announce tomorrow that thousands mama dolls being distributed after April 1 as consolation prizes King Tut contest and Spectator is going to write contestants who have no children to donate consolation prizes to sick and crippled children as well as to children of unemployed. . . .'

Despite Ker's direction that the problem was 'to check him rather than increase ourselves', the *Spectator*'s net paid circulation rose from 32,370 in 1923 to 38,233 in 1924. About 5,000 mama dolls were given away.

The 'upbuilders of newspapers' continued to haunt Hamilton. In mid-July Ker reported to Philip Fisher that one from New York had been in to see him. 'He came in ostensibly to interest us in a walking, sleeping, talking, singing mama doll with a miniature gramophone in its vitals which grinds out nursery rhymes, prayers, and baby prattle through a diaphragm in the pit of its stomach. Undoubtedly, this doll has it all over other mama dolls – is probably the ultimate in doll development.' Perhaps fortunately (for everybody but the upbuilder) the war was then in its dying stages and this piece of ordnance never got to the firing line.

The *Herald* announced on March 27 that 'as the result of a new standard of comparison 10,551 new readers have accepted the Her-

ald as their home paper', an increase of nearly 100 per cent in four
months to a total of 22,000. But the fact was that these gains had
simply brought the *Herald* up to the circulation figure Herman apparently believed it to have when he bought it.

Advertisers did not respond freely enough to get it out of the red.
As early as March 1 rumors floated around Hamilton that Herman
planned to sue Harris on grounds of misrepresenting circulation at
the time of the sale. As the summer passed, Hamilton war correspondence began to appear in outside newspapers. On July 29 under the
heading CLAIMS HE BOUGHT HERALD ON INCORRECT INFORMATION
the Toronto *Telegram* reported:

> If final court action follows the recent issue of a writ at Windsor, the
> public will be served with an interesting exposition in court of the
> divergences of two newspaper publishers and proprietors, one the
> former owner of the Hamilton Herald and the other the present
> owner. The destiny of the Herald, its building, land, plant, circulation
> and goodwill are also to a large extent involved in the outcome of the
> procedure, the money value of which may run from $400,000 to
> $500,000.
>
> So far there are no pleadings to give body to the narrative, the
> record being that Mr. W.F.Herman, publisher of the Border Cities
> Star of Windsor, has caused a writ to be issued against Mr. R.B.Harris
> of Hamilton, principal former owner of the Hamilton Herald, and
> against E.D.Cahill, K.C., with the short allegation that prior to his
> purchase from 'Bob' Harris in 1923, he was given incorrect informa-
> tion as to how many readers the Herald enjoyed....

The action never got to court. A few days before the *Telegram*'s
story *Spectator* and pre-Herman *Herald* men had begun to meet in-
formally to talk things over, the instigator of these meetings being
William J. McNair, *Herald* editor in the Harrises' time. By September, at the instance of the Southams, McNair had an option from
Herman to buy the business. Terms included return to Herman of
$275,000 already paid on the property, cancellation of notes
amounting to another $200,000 and release of Herman's claims
against Harris and Cahill.

On Saturday, November 15, 1924, a year and a day after the Herman takeover, the *Herald* carried an announcement:

BACK IN OLD HANDS

The Hamilton Herald, which W.F.Herman has owned since November 1923, has been sold by him to a company, which includes the
former proprietors of the Herald and W.J.McNair, former news editor. J.L.Lewis returns as editor-in-chief, Mr. McNair as managing
editor....

One fact omitted was that William Southam and Sons held most of the common stock of the new company, of which Cahill was president and Harris managing director. In 1929 Harris retired and the Southams assumed full – though unannounced – ownership of a newspaper that never after 1923 paid its way.

Estimates of Herman's operating loss through 1924 varied, with $200,000 as the figure most often mentioned.

The *Spectator*'s balance sheet showed a 1924 loss on the newspaper business of $48,500 which was cut to $3,000 by revenue from buildings and investments. It was the only year since 1877 in which the Spec lost money. In 1925 the net was back above the $100,000 mark.

But the *Herald* was fated. By the end of 1930 the Southams' investment (shares in the company and cash advances) totalled $363,-000. Through the next four years the paper lost $295,000. The one saving grace in a direct financial sense, and it was slight, was that *Herald* losses reduced the *Spectator*'s corporation income tax.

Two considerations entered into the *Herald*'s continuance through the worst depression years. One was reluctance to kill an enterprise that employed about 100 people. The other was the theory that the *Herald* as a second newspaper insured the field against invasion. In 1934 Paul Reading came in from Washington to take over the paper for one last effort – not so much in the hope that any sudden conversion could make it self-supporting as to assess the long-term chances. New editorial drive and a price-cut to one cent raised circulation from 9,000 to 14,000. But losses went on. Finally on March 31, 1936, the *Herald* ran its last edition.

Some notable individuals produced the *Herald* in its last years. Writing editorials was Albert Edward Stafford Smythe, poet and theosophist and father of Conn, the hockey master. Ian H. Macdonald, later manager of the Southam advertising office in Montreal, general manager of the Canadian Daily Newspapers Association, and finally deputy-chairman of Thomson Newspapers, ran the business side. Young men coming up in the craft manned the news desks and the beats, among them Burton Lewis, later of the Vancouver *Province*, Prince Albert *Herald*, and Charlottetown *Guardian*; Richard J. Needham, of the Calgary *Herald*, Toronto *Star*, and *Globe and Mail*; E.C.Phelan of the *Globe and Mail,* and the brilliant but unpredictable D'Arcy Marsh.

The circulation and advertising battle of 1924 remains a kind of classic. Ironically, H.A.Graybiel, general manager of Herman's notably successful *Border Cities Star* (which became the Windsor *Star*), cited its result ten years later in opposing application for a Canadian Press membership by interests that planned a second daily in Windsor. At about the same time as the Hamilton war, Joe Atkinson of the Toronto *Star* lost $600,000 in an effort to run the second paper in London, the *Advertiser*, in competition with the *Free Press*. In the light of Hamilton and London experience, Graybiel argued, a new paper in Windsor would have no chance of commercial success. The second paper there never got going.

Indirectly the 1924 excitement had an effect on the *Spectator*'s future apart from the ups and downs of the battle itself and the ultimate fate of the *Herald*.

Earlier the Southams had broached to representatives of the Carey estate (Mrs. Margaret Carey and two married daughters) the possibility of buying out their inherited interest. The war with Herman, together with the need for new money that had risen in 1921, apparently convinced estate representatives that equity stock in the newspaper business wasn't the best possible spot for income investment. Early in 1925 they sold out for $500,000 in bonds. The old Spectator Printing Company became Hamilton Spectator Limited, a strictly Southam concern.

Long retired from any active role in Southam Limited and its successor (though for sentimental reasons he remained nominally president of the family company and the individual newspapers) William Southam kept an active interest in his first newspaper love – the *Spectator*, where it all started.

The old passion for exercise made his morning walk through west-end Hamilton a local event until he was past eighty. On daily visits to the newspaper the habit of economy and a partiality for fresh air would find him turning out lights, opening windows, shutting off radiators. Old age he perhaps resented, but still the laughter came through and at times the irascibility. On his seventy-seventh birthday, W.J. reported to F.N. he 'got madder and madder on receipt of every wire and good wish.' Something of both father and son is reflected in Bill's account of the incident: 'He didn't want to be wished many happy returns, so I went out and bought him a plot in the cemetery. This cheered him up wonderfully. He said it was about the only place I hadn't bought real estate, but he guessed it was one of the surest investments I had made.'

At that time he had nearly twelve years to live, and though his memory had failed so badly that he had given up poker sessions at the Thistle, he enjoyed having Jimmie Allan recall the stirring earlier days: days when the *Spectator*'s circulation was 2,500; the fire; the raising of English money to build on James Street; days when he and William Carey were lured into speculating on margin in barrelled pork futures, and lost a piece of their shirts.

The past, however, was far from all. To the end of his active days the *Spectator* was *his* paper. In his seventy-eighth year he could blast Bill Mulliss on an April day when the *Spectator* came out with the same number of pages as the *Herald*, violating a rule he had set personally many years before that his paper must *always* outdo its rival in size. On this point he forgot economy.

Personal regard for individuals known and liked remained a faith even though fading memory had sometimes erased their names. He talked a good deal with Alex Muir. On one occasion, alarmed at an obvious increase in the number of *Spectator* delivery trucks, he was told that 'Mr. Muir' was responsible. Approaching Alex he demanded, 'Who's Muir?' and added, 'He's got to be fired.' 'I'm Muir,' said Muir. 'Oh,' William said, 'that's different.'

On November 1, 1928, death claimed the girl he had married sixty-one years before. Still he remained active. In the winter of 1930 W.J. had withdrawn to the Boca Raton Club in Florida. Jimmie Allan reported to him there: 'Your father is in the best of health. He makes me shut off the radiator, open the window, put out my electric light, and makes my room so cold that sometimes I am bordering on pneumonia.' But the robust frame was weakening. On February 27, 1932, William died.

The Weaver of Schemes

Early one morning a young teletype attendant on lone duty at the *Spectator* was startled by the apparition through a second-floor window of a tall figure in white tie and tails. W.J.Southam hadn't bothered going home for his office key.

In the middle of an English night the telephone wakened an elderly colonel in Woking, Surrey. The General Post Office had a cable for him. Someone in Palm Beach, Florida, was suggesting that as the King and Queen were coming to Canada that summer (actually they were not) he come too.

In time Hamilton learned not to be startled; and it wasn't long before the Woking colonel wrote: 'I hear *all* the people in Canada know you as Bill Southam; this speaks much for your personality. . . .'

Many things spoke for the personality of W.J. Shrewd business moves for the *Spectator* in his younger and middle years, later deals and gambles that ranged from successful to disastrous, offhand generosities and spur-of-the-moment japeries and calculated masquerades. The stories that grew up around him amount to a kind of canon, a legend that needs no fictional embellishment (though in the way of all folklore it acquired some) because the facts are enough.

Perhaps the essence of W.J. can be distilled in one brief anecdote. One morning early, the rector of Christ Church Cathedral in Hamilton, arriving to conduct a communion service, found him standing on the steps in the rain waiting for the church to open. As they passed in, Bill halted briefly by the poor-box. Since his gift on such occasions was usually a hundred-dollar bill, rector tipped off verger to gather in the proceeds. This time the contribution was a ticket to the races.

Napoleon's query about a brilliant army officer 'But is he *fortunate?*', if applied to Bill Southam could have been answered 'yes' through most of his years as active manager of the *Spectator*. His later business ventures would have brought a 'no'. Early in 1931 – with the depression settling in for its long run – he decided to plunge personally as a hotel builder. Already holding a one-sixth interest in the Connaught Hotel he became convinced Hamilton needed more accommodation and borrowed $400,000 to build a wing.

His formal loan application (one bank had already declined), after listing his assets, continued:

I have an income, which is mostly outgo and then some, of $100,000 annually and I am always hard up. As to my character I am fairly honest and an easy mark for bankers, get rich quick promoters and apple sellers. My habits at times are excellent.... Try as I can it is impossible for me to cultivate that cold, green, Greek banker's eye and dignified, severe manners and deportment, as I realize if I could I would be a great man, or near great, on the surface. But try as I can it is beyond me, so unfortunately for the world I will have to continue to be a simple, kindly, easy to anger, quick to forgive easy mark of a newspaper boy; thank God and my revered and respected ancestors. I don't think a hell of a lot of the ability of my brothers but if anyone else doesn't, look out. I admit that it is mainly through their efforts that the bunch of junk, as outlined above, is still in my possession. My brothers Wilson and Harry are still for prohibition. Fred is inclined that way, especially for me, and as for brother Dick, old John Barleycorn has more or less made him like it. I believe less at the present time than more.

If there is any further information you would desire I would be most happy to break forth again and I will conclude with the remark that any banker who says that the common stock of the Southam Publishing Company is not worth $20 a share is a proper damn fool . . . and this is my opinion of most bankers, especially amongst the higher-

ups, and this leads me to believe that I am qualified to become a bank
director, as I know I couldn't do worse than some of the rest of them.
Now do I get that $400,000?

He got it, and returned to Florida where he had some real-estate
deals going. Later in the year, with the hotel wing well under way
and the Florida real estate gone sour, it became apparent that W.J.'s
personal financial perch was shaky indeed. The family company –
William Southam and Sons – moved in to take over many of his assets and obligations and switch his Southam Publishing Company
interests into a trust based on the higher security of preferred stock.

The same period saw his brief experience in horse-racing as an
owner, as distinguished from a life-long career as devotee and bettor
at Canadian and United States tracks. In the spring of 1930 he
bought from Edward Riley Bradley, of the Idle Hour Farm at
Lexington, three mares in foal named Breathless Moment, Briny
Breezes, and I Win. The price was $10,000. They dropped one filly,
Becautious, and two colts, Bethankful and Big Time. When the get
were yearlings Bill disposed of the mares, colts, and filly to W.E.Bul-
mer of Oakville, subsequently killed in a motor crash. When Bul-
mer's stock was sold in 1933, Bethankful brought top price as a two-
year-old, $620. Briny Breezes went for $65.

In October 1932, W.J. got a bill from Algernon Daingerfield, assistant secretary of the New York Jockey Club: he owed the West-
chester Racing Association $450. The two colts and the filly had
been entered while yet unborn in the 1932 Futurity, won by Lee
Rosenberg's Kerry Patch. As Bill wrote to Rosenberg: 'I was new at
the game and didn't know then that these unborn foals were entered.'
He paid up.

His return on the original investment thereafter consisted of occasional cheques for such sums as $26.25 – five per cent of the purse
– as the breeder whenever one of the three foals won a Canadian-
bred race, which was not often.

His experience as a bettor was varied, sometimes including the
finding of winning tickets in obscure pockets after a meet was over.
Thorncliffe paid off in 1933 on a couple of delayed $10 tickets but
returned four others uncashed. They had been bought in 1930.

W.J. discovered a credit balance after the Belmont meeting of
June 1935, and made it the occasion for a touch of ceremonial criticism:

My one criticism of the Belmont Park race track [he wrote Tom
Bohne, Bradley's secretary] is the lack of display. It is one of the most
beautiful racing plants in the world, but why those millionaires or ex-

millionaires get away with the way they clothe themselves when attending the races beats me. . . . I don't see why the Whitneys, Vanderbilts, and all those birds are allowed to dress like stable hands. . . . I believe the late August Belmont and the old crowd who have passed on are not resting any too quietly in their graves because of the way things are being handled at present. Wonderful horses and racing, but the human element, awful. I'll be seeing you at Saratoga. . . .

Instructions followed – to spend the Belmont credit on a grey Ascot topper at a Fifth Avenue hatter's and present it to Bradley. The colonel thanked him kindly but feared that if he wore it to the track it would cause even greater comment than his arrival at Empire City several years before in an open Model-T.

W.J. retired as managing director of the *Spectator* in 1930 – a move agreed on between himself and the brothers following some typical flamboyancies – and from vice-presidency of the paper after the 1931 hotel venture. Ker succeeded him. The two were temperamentally poles apart but outwardly-expressed differences seem to have been rare.

One flared in 1935 when Premier Hepburn brought in legislation to cancel four power contracts that had been signed in more prosperous years by Conservative predecessors. Ker wrote furious editorials. 'Repudiation by the government of Ontario', the *Spectator* said on April 2, 'would be the dirtiest piece of political business in the history of the province and would put the Liberal party and the people who condone its action in a position not less contemptible than that of a welshing bookmaker at Epsom Downs on Derby Day. The great monument to Sir Adam Beck is being defiled and shattered by his traditional enemies.'

W.J. didn't agree and, mentioning his *Spectator* directorship, which he still held, wrote Hepburn to tell him so. Furthermore, he got a letter into the *Spectator*'s correspondence columns signed 'G.O.B.McL.' (the companies concerned were Gatineau, Ottawa Valley, Beauharnois, and Maclaren) in which he referred to Hepburn, Arthur Roebuck, T.B.McQuesten, 'and their political boss, Arthur Slaght' as 'the four horsemen of repudiation', but asserted they were right: 'An operation without an anaesthetic is painful, but this wholesale one was necessary and successful, and have no fear, the patients will all recover, not excepting the power companies.'

The net result appears to have been some exasperation on the part of various people – including F.N.Southam who scribbled 'Dear Bill: I can't get this point of view; in the latest slang term it's a lousy one' on a copy of G.O.B.McL.'s letter – and perhaps some satisfaction to W.J. at having caused it. The contracts, incidentally, were eventually renegotiated on different terms.

Having created his flurry over the power contracts W.J. sailed for England with his old friend F.D.L. (Frank) Smith, chief editor of the *Mail and Empire*, who had been along with him and other Canadian newspaper men on a 1918 jaunt to England and the battlefields.

As usual with most of W.J.'s activities that 1918 trip had produced some interesting side-effects. In New York before departure Fred Wilson, manager of Hearst's International News Service, called on the group to invite them to dinner with the Hearsts. Since at this time both the news service and the Hearst papers were banned in Canada for anti-British virulence, the party declined. But W.J. and one or two others accompanied Fred Wilson to the theatre as individuals, where Wilson informed him that Hearst's health was suffering by the unkind treatment he was getting from the British and Canadian governments.

A couple of months later Lord Beaverbrook as Minister of Information said farewell to the returning editors with a plea that they do all they could to cement the ties between the Anglo-Saxon races, particularly by helping to erase from the American mind the thought that England was a buccaneer out for world domination. This fermented in the active mind of W.J. Surely one way to cement relations would be for one or two British press lords to buy through a Canadian (preferably W.J.Southam) Hearst's news service and some of his papers, leading to an Anglo-Canadian-American cable and wire service, owned 49 per cent by each principal and two per cent by the Canadians – who would act as umpires. All this he tossed at Beaverbrook by transatlantic mail. The Beaver replied that he could scarcely believe Hearst was ready to sell anything, and that the suggestion might be a peace offensive by which he hoped to establish an armistice while he got his papers back into Canada. Beaverbrook however suggested that Bill dig deeper and let him know the upshot.

Up to this point the one offensive, peace or otherwise, that had been mounted existed only in W.J.'s mind, except possibly for a less grandiose aim that occupied Fred Wilson's. W.J. now sent Bill Mulliss to New York to see Hearst and bring back an assessment. Mulliss, a smallish man of Napoleonic tendencies, who is remembered for idiosyncrasies as well as virtues – an accomplished lightweight boxer, he is said to have wrestled stubborn reporters into subjection – faced the lord of San Simeon one day toward the end of October. It is regrettable that no Damon Runyon was present to record this confrontation. All that remains is Mulliss's report in which he expressed the belief that Hearst was sorry his former prejudices had been too severe, and 'appeared to be sincerely concerned in seeing that the name of Hearst and his newspapers should stand well with those he had thus assailed and misrepresented.' In Mulliss's opinion he would do anything to bring this about.

W.J. forthwith asked Fred Wilson what were Hearst's views about going to England to talk with people like Beaverbrook, Northcliffe, Rothermere, and Burnham. To which Wilson replied that Hearst would go if invited.

In the end all that resulted from this web of correspondence and visitation was an effort on Fred Wilson's part to sign the *Spectator* to a five-year contract for International News Service. The farthest W.J. would go was to accept a two-months' trial.

No side-issue quite as grandiose as that of 1918 grew from the 1935 voyage, but there were some. The main objective of the trip was the King's Jubilee. But as a kind of dividend Frank Smith had set up an interview with Rudyard Kipling, then in London at Brown's Hotel. W.J. entrusted Smith with some copies of Kipling's verses to be autographed, and then decided to accompany him in person. However, he was given, as he later expressed it in a letter to the master himself, 'the frosty mitten' by Mrs. Kipling.

> I went downstairs from your suite and felt so hurt that I wrote a note to Frank Smith and sent it up to your rooms. In this note I mentioned that I felt sure that if it had been in the time of Bill Shakespeare he would not only have received me but would have come to my party. I was giving a dinner for Canadians at the Empire Ball that night at Grosvenor House and invited you and Mrs. Kipling to join us. After I sent the note up I left Brown's, and later Frank Smith told me that you would receive me but I had flown.
>
> However, it was very good of you to sign *The Glory of the Garden* for me and one for Frank Smith and four copies of 'If', one each for my young sons and one for me.

Typically, W.J. promptly gave away one of the autographed 'Ifs' to a chance acquaintance for her eleven-year-old son. And on the *Duchess of York* coming home he presented another to R.B.Bennett for Bennett's nephew Harrison.

Plans were under way for a new Federal Building on John Street in Hamilton. Back in February, W.J. had urged on Bennett the advisability of widening John Street to make a better setting for the building. Aboard ship on May 13 he followed this up with a written argument for adding a couple of storeys, which could be used for a city hall and a civic art gallery.

Bennett, thanking W.J. for the copy of 'If', wrote in his best platform manner that he was sure his nephew would 'in some small degree realize the true spirit and implications of the immortal lines of
one whom I greatly admire not only as a great writer of prose but the
true poet laureate of Empire whose vision, seeing far beyond the
horizon, beheld what, alas! statesmen could not discern until too
late.' He added, just before a sign-off sentence: 'I will do my best
regarding the other matters of which you wrote.' As excavation proceeded with no sign of street-widening and no word of extra storeys,
Bill wrote R.B. at Ottawa: 'I am enclosing a copy of the classic you
wrote me at sea aboard the Duchess of York. Is the second-to-last
sentence meant or is it nothing but words, words, words?'

By this time the matter was in the hands of Public Works Minister
H.A.Stewart who reported the suggestions couldn't be accepted. Bill
replied with an argument for at least one additional floor – for the
art gallery. With his plea he sent Stewart a picture of Sir John A.
Macdonald, who stands in bronze back to back with Queen Victoria
– at a distance of several hundred feet – in the middle of King Street.
One of his incidental arguments for the John Street widening had
been that this would afford a better view of Sir John. Stewart's thanks
for the picture was all Bill got out of this campaign. He closed the
correspondence by suggesting the government add the extra storey
anyway 'with the thought of using it to store away politicians who
are dead from the neck up'.

He had more success with Kipling. Having given away some of his
autographed copies he wrote wondering whether he might mail over
some more for signing. Kipling replied from his home at Burwash,
Sussex, that he'd be glad to sign. This response drew from Bill a typical letter in which he listed the people to whom he proposed to present the additional copies, including Bennett and his new nephew
William Herridge, Jr., and Colonel E.R.Bradley, 'the greatest race-
horse owner in America'. He added that he hoped to get back to
England to have tea with Mrs. Kipling whose bark, he understood,
was worse than her bite, and wound up with a postscript explaining
that he was not really an autograph hunter: 'This is only my second
offense. The last time was when Jack Dempsey knocked out the Wild
Bull of the Pampas, Luis Firpo, in 1923. I saw the fight in New York
and it was between super-gladiators. Dempsey appeared next day at
the Belmont race track and I got him to sign my race program. His
greatness and fame faded but yours will never die. But, oh boy!
Dempsey at his peak was as quick as a tiger. . . . He had the wallop
with his fists that you have with the pen.'

Bill Southam stories have a polish of their own, each with its recognizable twist. There was the time he asked Harry Greening, who had bought Gordon's house on the mountain, for a contribution to a charity, and was told: 'Bill, I haven't even got my coal in yet.' That night Greening came home to find a pile of coal on his front lawn. Or the time his wife, wakened in the small hours, found one of his drinking companions who was unknown to her comatose in the living-room and dispatched him by taxi to an address supplied by Bill. Next morning a family of strangers discovered the white cargo, still comatose, in *their* living-room. Or the time Bill applauded in the middle of a sermon, offered the rector – after the service – a case of champagne if he would assemble his notes for copying and distribution, and sent him one bottle as a down payment.

The classic incident – which happened to be fairly well documented in news stories – was that of the great cockfight. In certain sporting strata around Hamilton there was considerable interest in the gamebirds at that time. Bill himself, who had been introduced to this form of entertainment in Florida, subscribed to *Grit and Steel*, described as 'the world's foremost game fowl journal'. Late in January 1937, while he waited to take off for a usual winter foray in the south, he conceived the idea of holding a 'main' at his old summer place at Port Nelson. Workmen set up a three-tier plank grandstand in the house; Bill sent out invitations and had a supply of beer, gin, rye, and sandwiches laid in. When Burlington Police Chief Lee Smith led a raiding party of provincials into the house at 1 A.M. Sunday, January 24, two men were in the pit, one holding a bird. Eighty or so men, some in evening clothes, and a few women occupied the amphitheatre.

The story broke in the Toronto *Telegram* next day under a heading HAMILTON ELITE QUIZZED AFTER COCKFIGHT RAIDED: 'Panic reigned at a Port Nelson summer home early Sunday, when police raided a cockfight and barred all avenues of escape to the 130 men and women . . . of Hamilton's smart set.' Twenty-six gamecocks were seized.

W.J. appeared in court February 1, pleaded guilty to maintaining a cockfight, and was fined $100 and costs. At this time he turned over to the *Telegram* (the *Spectator* having refused them) pictures taken by a Spec photographer. The *Telegram* caption reported:

> Shortly before the raid a Hamilton Spectator photographer, on instructions from Mr. Southam, whose family owns that newspaper, took photographs of the festivities for Mr. Southam's private collection. After the case was disposed of in court yesterday, Mr. Southam

gave two photographs to the Evening Telegram representative at Burlington. Above photograph shows two bird-owners introducing game-cocks to each other, preparatory to a battle of spurs and beaks in the arena.

The case was far from 'disposed of' at that point. Eighty charges of 'frequenting' had been laid, and though many found-ins had given names borrowed from the pages of history, others continued to trickle into court to plead guilty and pay $25 fines. By March 2 the Crown had collected $877.50 in fines and costs.

The laughter that followed this elaborate escapade was spiced with speculation. Had W.J. himself tipped off the cops? Was there more to it than appeared? The Port Nelson place was one of the assets taken over in 1931; its legal owner was Herald Securities Limited, one of the Southam subsidiary companies, of which B.B.Osler was president. This fact came out in evidence and appeared in news stories. Was the whole thing a W.J. ploy to poke fun at what he sometimes called the Bleury Street brain trust? Such small mysteries are part of the legend.

When W.J. died in 1957, having outlived all his brothers, the *Spectator* said: 'His well-developed if at times somewhat eccentric sense of humor was only another facet of a character that will not be easily forgotten. Many of his friends have said of him that only one person could competently write a biography of him – Bill Southam himself.'

With this W.J. probably would have agreed. From time to time he did put certain things on paper to keep the record straight. Writing Bradley on June 24, 1935, to congratulate him on Black Helen's victory in the American Derby at Chicago, he took occasion to correct the colonel's recollection of an episode in the sales ring at Saratoga. The true and correct version, according to Bill:

I strolled into the party where everyone was correctly clad in evening clothes. Not having mine with me, I wore my commodore's uniform. That year I was commodore of the Royal Hamilton Yacht Club, one of the two Royal yacht club charters in Canada. When I first entered I walked up behind the auctioneer's block and deposited a fancy French boudoir doll there, which at the moment I happened to be carrying, and then went to the back of the auction room and in was led the Man of War colt and they started bidding. After they had warmed up a bit and reached a price of $3,000 I said, like Marks, the lawyer in Uncle Tom's Cabin: 'And seventy-five.' The price moved up slowly to $3,800 and occasionally I would interject 'and seventy-five'. At this stage the auctioneer warned me that this was a serious business and to govern myself accordingly. I kept quiet for a few moments and when the price reached $4,000 I couldn't resist and came out again with 'and seventy-five'. At this stage they allowed me to collect my doll and under the guard of honor, consisting of a couple of jolly policemen, I was led from the auction sale to my taxi, when I went to a restaurant and got one of the colored singers to sing some of my favorite songs, one of which I like particularly and sang with gusto. It is called 'Old Black Joe': 'Gone are the days when my heart was young and gay; gone are the friends from the cotton fields away', etc. I presented one of the colored lady singers with the French doll, went back to my hotel, had an hour's sleep, changed and at 5:47 A.M. went down in the elevator with you to have breakfast with you at six. You said, 'Bill, I would have bet one million dollars you wouldn't turn up this morning.' The night previous I was pretty near starting for home, peeved because the auctioneer didn't treat my bids and me with proper respect and because George O'Neil, an Irish friend of mine, didn't show proper respect for the King's uniform I was wearing when I saw him at the hotel. However, Thomas S. Bohne, your capable and efficient secretary, cooled me out and persuaded me to stay on for another day to appear with you again in the afternoon at the races as the best-dressed man in Saratoga.

In another letter to Bradley, Bill mentioned that his sister had couched an appraisal of him in a note: 'Bill, you would be a great man if you weren't such a silly ass. Lovingly, Ethel.' He followed this up with a few more illustrations:

I believe it is such things as taking the kiltie band to Stotesbury's birthday party and passing the collection box of St. Edward's Church at Palm Beach in through your front door – after you had already contributed approximately $100,000 to this church – and other episodes of mine, that have earned for me this erroneous judgment of sister Ethel's, with which other people agree.

The wife of a great friend of mine, Mrs. Jack Counsell, lectured me and her husband some years ago. Hubby and I were in the living-room of their home late one night when she came in from a bridge party, and possibly had lost, because she immediately gave Jack a tongue-thrashing and then to polish it off turned to me and ended her remarks by saying, 'Bill, I would like to have a picture of your stomach.' Next morning I went to the clinic and had my stomach photographed and X-rayed, and sent her the picture and the doctor's report, both of which were perfect. This was some years ago and in May of this year, at a party of more or less strange English people, I hear the story repeated. . . .

He also reported factually to F.N. – though not in much detail – after the Port Nelson cockfight, appending the account casually to a report of an approach by Septimus DuMoulin, the old Tiger football player, for a contribution to Trinity College School:

I told Sepi that you and the brothers hadn't recovered from my Connaught Hotel escapade and some of their own as yet and that the time wasn't opportune for this touch, so you can pass it up without hurting anyone's feelings if you so desire. . . .

I have just finished a three weeks visit to the Preston Springs clinic and have finished up with an operation of one hour's duration on my nose, which was part of my trouble, the rest of the damage to my anatomy being in fair shape and not beyond repair. . . . I was feeling so good that to celebrate I ran a cockfight at your highway place and was pinched by the provincial police with 100 of my friends of all walks of life from north of the bridge to financial and industrial leaders. It was a thrill and fun but it will cost me a couple of hundred. . . .

F.N. sent the letter to the brothers to get their view on the contribution to T.C.S. (they finally settled on $1,000) with no reference to W.J.'s cockfight until well along in the correspondence when he suggested 'he take the jail sentence and subscribe the amount of the fines to the school', an idea that obviously did not appeal to W.J. who by then was off to Florida.

Frank Smith once wrote: 'You have Dr. Jekyll and Mr. Hyde beaten a mile.'

Back in 1917, when Bill's schemes were working out, his brother Wilson suggested: 'You are really a Napoleon of finance, masquerading as Bill Southam.' Fifteen years later, when the luck and the judgment and the business climate had changed, Wilson regretfully concluded that Bill was subject to 'fits of irresponsible optimism'. But affection remained. On one occasion Wilson, concluding a plea that W.J. remount the water wagon (a vehicle on which he took periodic excursions), signed himself 'your very loving but discouraged brother', took a second look at this sentiment and amended it in a follow-up letter: 'Your very loving but *never* discouraged brother.'

In many ways he was the modern equivalent of the 'projector' of Restoration England. He might have stepped from the pages of John Aubrey's *Lives*, casting off doublet and surcoat for white tie and tails; or possibly the checkered overcoat he'd had tailored from Man O'-War's blanket.

The Strike . . . and Evelyn Dick

At mid-afternoon of Thursday, May 30, 1946, business manager Alex Muir learned that I.T.U. printers on Southam papers in Hamilton, Edmonton, and Ottawa would walk out that night. In an effort to get all possible copy set, composing-room foreman Albert Waite ordered overtime that day. This the printers refused to handle; it was obviously for Friday's and Saturday's papers. There would, they said, be no *Spectator* on those days. Their forecast was wrong.

Although the *Spectator*, along with others in the group, had hoped that the 'unified action' threatened in December as a result of the Winnipeg situation would not come down to this, it had not taken the possibility lightly. Clair Balfour, then executive assistant to Ker, had gone to Winnipeg to learn details of the typing-and-engraving technique that had kept the *Tribune* and the *Free Press* rolling through the tough early days of their strike the previous fall. When the printers went out a rough plan was ready. With engraved pages, pre-set type and lavish use of pictures, the *Spectator* brought out a twenty-six-page edition on May 31. Through Thursday night and Friday, Albert Waite worked alone in the composing-room, completing forty hours on his feet. By Sunday night the paper had three men on the floor – Waite, his son Jack as assistant foreman, and an operator from Winnipeg. The *Spectator* board-room became a dormitory.

As usual in such crises, editorial, advertising, and business-side people found themselves doing strange jobs. When the stereotypers went out three days after the printers, foreman Jimmie Lithgow pulled in five recruits from other departments, including Balfour, David Ker (son of the publisher), Frank Sercombe (a former apprentice who had joined the news staff), a driver, and a janitor. They manned the casting boxes until the stereotypers returned, which they did before long.

Ker was in England at a Commonwealth Press Union conference. Chief direction of the paper's defence fell to Muir. The little Scot met his responsibility with resolution and sometimes a touch of wry humor. When Ker cabled that a hundred years of *Spectator* men stood behind the loyalists who were getting the paper out, Muir remarked that he would trade the ghosts for one good printer. Reporting to Ker by letter in the early days he described managing editor Jim O'Neil – a notably slender and courtly man – as 'a shadow of the shadow he formerly was'.

Gradually the paper got back into conventional type, some set in its own composing-room, some at weekly shops in nearby towns. For weeks Balfour ran a curious courier service. Leaving the plant for the day at 4 P.M., he would return later to pick up working printers and drive them home. What the pickets presumably did not know was that on his afternoon departure, his car carried bulk type-metal for the weekly shops, and that on his evening return to pick up the printers he delivered galleys of set type. No one interfered.

Violence might well have been much greater than it was. This was a lively time in the labor world. The *Spectator*'s headline in its first improvised issue, May 31, read: OPERATORS REJECT LAKE STRIKE TRUCE. Steel men, electrical workers, and rubber workers went out that summer, and sometimes joined picket lines at the *Spectator*. Of eight men arrested August 1 in the one serious melee at the building – a truck was overturned and the driver attacked – only two were printers.

The pressmen's union remained at work, though for one brief period it was touch and go. On the Tuesday after the walkout, striking seamen and steelworkers joined the picket line. When the pressmen left for lunch their return was uncertain. Muir and Balfour reached their international president, George Berry, by phone at union headquarters in Tennessee. Berry in turn got the Hamilton local secretary at home and emphasized the terms of the contract. Lunch over, the pressmen went back to work as usual.

On June 11 page one was back in type and on Saturday, June 15, only two and a half pages of engraved copy were necessary. By that time the *Spectator* had eleven men in the composing-room. By early September it had become obvious that the I.T.U. was adamant in refusing to negotiate with individual newspapers and the company equally determined to stick to the principle of local management. The *Spectator* sent discharge notices and vacation pay to the striking printers and began to recruit a new composing-room staff in earnest.

The paper's circulation had been clipped. In March of 1946 it had touched 71,000. At mid-June, having dropped its 6,000-plus final edition when the strike started, still struggling with mechanical problems, and feeling the effects of a propaganda campaign, it was down to 61,000. But that spring and fall events occurred that re-emphasized the effect on circulation of a newspaper's reason for being: the news.

Back on March 16, a Saturday, ten weeks before the printers walked out, the *Spectator* carried a line on its local page: 'Murder Indicated in Torso Found on Mountain'. That morning five children hiking along the Mountain scenic drive had made the discovery near Albion Falls, south-east of the city.

Violent crime in Hamilton has always seemed to have a special flavor. On the afternoon of February 25, 1909, a stranger called at the Herkimer Street house of school principal Thomas Kinrade and demanded money. Two Kinrade daughters, Ethel and Florence, were at home. Florence rushed upstairs for a $10 bill, heard shots, rushed down again. The stranger snatched the money and ran. The body of Ethel, shot dead, lay on the floor.

A prolonged inquest was that spring's sensation in Hamilton as the Crown lawyer's intensive questioning of Florence gave it almost the aspect of a criminal trial. At one point, pressed on the question of whether she knew the killer (which she denied), she fainted on the stand. The coroner's jury returned a 'murder by person or persons unknown' verdict. No one was arrested or tried. Florence went on to marriage and the stage.

The Kinrade case remained Hamilton's classic murder mystery. Then one dark night in 1930 Bessie Perri disembarked from the car of her husband Rocco, king of the bootleggers, and was shot dead. Fourteen years later, on April 23, 1944, Rocco himself complained of a headache, took two aspirins, stepped outside, and vanished. It was generally accepted that gangsters' guns had done for Bessie; she had been an efficient helpmate in Rocco's rise. The funeral was spectacular. Rocco's obsequies were of course held in camera. He is believed to lie at the bottom of Hamilton Bay, shrouded in cement.

Discovery of the body by the scenic drive, head, legs, and arms missing, opened a series of events that eclipsed anything previously recorded in the annals of Hamilton crime. A gang killing was at first assumed. At least five disappearances (including that of Perri nearly two years before) were on record. Not on this list was a driver for the street railway, John Dick. Dick, married to a photogenic brunette named Evelyn MacLean the previous October and later separated, had been missing from his lodgings only since March 6. Three days after the discovery a relative of Dick's identified the torso.

Sensations followed: a borrowed automobile with blood on the slip-covers, a blue-striped shirt with arms cut off at the point where Dick's were severed, bones that could have belonged to missing limbs, teeth sifted from furnace ashes. And, in Evelyn Dick's attic, inside a trunk, the body of an infant encased in cement.

By April 15 four persons had been charged with murder: Evelyn and her parents and a one-time oarsman, for the killing of Dick; Evelyn and the oarsman, for death of the child.

The mother was quickly discharged. Eventually the oarsman went free also, with nothing against him but the company he kept. The father got five years as an accessory after the fact (a pair of Dick's shoes, one of them blood-spotted, turned up in his cellar) and a concurrent fine for amassing a modest fortune by stealing streetcar tickets.

But the central figure was Evelyn. Her trial opened October 7, 1946. Into evidence went five somewhat contradictory statements she had made to police, and into the *Spectator* and other papers columns of question-and-answer testimony and pictures of the good-looking twenty-six-year-old. On October 16 she was convicted and sentenced to death.

Into the case on appeal came Toronto lawyer John Robinette. A stay of execution, an appeal hearing, and direction for a new trial (the appeal court found her statements inadmissible) kept Evelyn Dick in the news. On February 24, 1947, she went on trial for a second time. On March 6, a year to the day from the time John Dick was last seen alive, a jury found her not guilty of killing him.

The murder charge for the infant's death remained. On this she drew a manslaughter conviction and a life sentence. Even in the women's prison at Kingston she made news. Early in 1949 word leaked out that she had appeared as an angel in the Christmas play. She was released in 1958.

At September 30, 1946, the *Spectator*'s circulation stood at 64,-500, down about 4,000 from the year before. By the end of the first quarter of 1947 – the period of the second Dick trial – it had added 3,000. At the end of the year it approached 70,000.

It was of course a fact that the *Spectator* had no effective competition identified with Hamilton, though Toronto papers were fairly widely read there. These, incidentally, froze their Hamilton city-proper circulation during early days of the strike. With no competing daily actually published in the city, Hamilton differed from Ottawa where the *Citizen* made a slow but successful recovery from strike paralysis, and from Vancouver where the *Province* lost ground it could never regain.

Soon after the walk-out the striking printers brought out a small throwaway four-pager called *Classified News*, which developed into the thrice-weekly Hamilton *News* published by Unitypo Incorporated, an I.T.U. subsidiary. But it was not until 1954, thirty years after the 'War with Herman' (and ignoring the period in which the *Spectator* supported the *Herald* as a kind of poor relation) that the *Spectator* faced direct daily competition in Hamilton. This occurred when brewer Andrew Peller bought the *News* from Unitypo and turned it into a morning daily with, for a time, an evening edition. It reached a circulation of 18,000 and lasted seventeen months. At the time the *News* ceased operations in February of 1956 the *Spectator* was up to 92,000.

Modern Pressures

Safely out of the strike crisis the *Spectator* in 1947 had a record year and one that foreshadowed unusual problems. In that year on four occasions it printed editions of fifty-two pages; on twenty-six days it ran to forty-four or forty-eight. These were big papers; they strained press capacity and delayed deliveries. Purchase of four second-hand press units eased the pinch for the time being.

Some publishers at this time thought newspapers were about as bulky as they could get. But when Balfour took over from Ker in 1951 brisk business with resultant pressure for advertising space was still pushing up the size of individual papers – in 1950 the Spec had to run more than fifty-six pages on nine occasions. At the same time growing population combined with the pull of the paper to push up circulation.

All this posed some interesting questions. For instance: should size of papers be held down by sharp increases in advertising rates? It was perhaps a choice that faced most newspapers, but it had a rather special importance for the *Spectator*. Technically in a one-paper position, but only forty miles from the power of the Toronto evening papers, the Spec had always remained in character a *local* newspaper. Balfour felt that sharp rate increases would drive out some of the smaller advertisers who had been the paper's strength. The result would be a loss in diversity, a concentration of advertising by a group of powerful merchants, with the vulnerability that this would imply.

Sixty-four pages seemed to be about the ideal top limit. By the last three months of 1953 the *Spectator* consistently ran sixty-four on Thursdays and Fridays, the traditional heavy days for advertising aimed at weekend shopping. Equipment to make this possible in straight runs – on one set of press units – was on order. Still the pressure grew.

Should the line be held at sixty-four? If so, the rationing or refusal of offered advertising would automatically create competition, turn customers to other outlets. Balfour had advertising manager Roy Davis survey United States metropolitan papers by letter. How often did they exceed sixty-four pages on weekdays? What was their experience with these large papers from the readers' point of view and the advertisers'? Of fifty-eight newspapers that replied forty-one ran more than sixty-four pages fairly regularly. They believed that the larger the paper the greater the circulation – and consequently the happier the advertiser. Of the seventeen that did not exceed sixty-four all but one wished they did. All of those whose size was limited by press capacity were installing more units. The *Spectator* had confirmed that in facing the pressures forcing it into larger papers it was certainly not alone.

It was not, however, possible to follow the old principle of relax-and-enjoy-it when faced with the inevitable. Growth forced an almost continual remodelling of the Spectator Building. While its front on King Street East remained virtually unchanged, interior rejigging and extension doubled the space for a staff that had grown from 198 to 450 in twenty years. Auxiliary buildings in the rear for plant, paper storage, and truck garaging also grew.

All this was still in progress in 1955 when Tom Nichols took over from Balfour, who was then moving up in the head office echelon as managing director of The Southam Company. Nichols, a son of the former publisher of the *Tribune* and the *Province*, and a *Spectator* man since 1934 except for wartime naval service, remained convinced of the *Spectator*'s role as a specifically Hamilton institution. It wouldn't want the type of make-up used by a couple of other Southam papers which he considered 'strained and anything-for-novelty' – all right for their constituencies but not for the Spec. Nor would it mimic the streamlined Toronto metropolitan papers: 'I would almost say it should be our first aim to be as *unlike* them as possible, and to create a habit that makes the Spectator a familiar family face. . . .'

Now and then there would be a twist to the tense business of running a newspaper – 'too big and complicated a business mechanism to fly by the seat of one's pants' as Philip Fisher once said – that Nichols couldn't resist passing on to head office. In 1957 a circulation canvasser, checking on 'stop' orders, reported that one family had 'used it for starting fires in their stove but have now acquired an oil furnace.'

The *Spectator* remains Hamiltonian. Metropolitan in size and in its approach to general news coverage but never forgetting the local touch. By 1965 its press capacity had grown to 50,000 ninety-six-page papers an hour. Its circulation was reaching toward 120,000. It still ran homey little items packed with names and, somewhere back of the national politics and international acrimony and the unforeseen Acts of God, pictures by the page of local brides and grooms, actual and prospective.

9
Ottawa:
The Later Years

'There should be a general election in Canada this year,' the *Citizen* said on May 1, 1934, 'but it is hard to discover any reason for turning out one conservative party to put in another.'

The text was familiar. Bowman had preached from it in 1921: 'Both old parties . . . are fighting desperately to stem the forward movement. . . .' He would still be getting mileage out of it in 1939: 'The Liberals are the Conservatives in this country; there is no difference between the parties. . . .' And in 1944: 'If ancient shibboleths are offered in the place of radical action, both conservative parties may very well be defeated. It will serve them right.'

Stodginess, patronage, and party funds had centred the target of political delinquency in the past. They rated now as inner rings around the black bull's-eye of orthodox finance.

The prosperous 1920s had given place to the hungry cantankerous 1930s and the sprouting violence that would run wild across the world at the end of them. In Canada, in April of 1930, Mackenzie King proclaimed his refusal of so much as a five-cent piece to Tory provincial governments and suffered for it. R.B.Bennett threatened to blast his way into world markets and suffered for that and other things. Hitler came to power and stole Austria; beer parlors opened in Ontario that summer of 1934 and a dark brew was nicknamed for him. At Geneva in the fall of 1935 a Canadian proposed cutting off oil to Italy, a step that might have foiled the conquest of Ethiopia and halted Fascism, and was repudiated by his government. Franco moved to take over Spain and the English king gave up his throne for a woman. In the lesser area of provincial politics Mitchell Hepburn hit front pages flamboyantly and often.

The *Citizen*'s castigation of both federal parties had a kicker in it.

At least at election time the Liberals were merely erring members of the family, the Conservatives the bad boys from down the road. For Bennett in 1933 the paper had kind words: 'No fair opponent can gainsay that the Canadian prime minister's dearest ambition is to serve the Canadian people. He is demonstrating it daily in a life of courageous endeavor.' But, a fortnight before the 1935 election: 'Mr. Bennett can conceivably win. But he should not be permitted to win. He has had his opportunity and has failed. . . . The only choice for the great majority of Canadians is to give Mr. King another chance. He may be bold enough to depart from outworn practices and try something genuinely effective. He must, to make good. But he should be given his chance – for it may be the last.' As for H.H.Stevens and his Reconstructionists: 'His remedies fall far below his analyses.'

The *Citizen*'s habit of swinging at both parties did not prevent offers of government appointments to the Southams from both sides of the fence. When Vincent Massey was about to leave Washington Mackenzie King suggested to Harry that he take the ministry. And on an autumn Sunday in 1931 Hugh Guthrie telephoned Wilson; he had a message for him from R.B.Bennett. The message, it developed when the two met that afternoon, was an offer of the lieutenant-governorship of Ontario. To the relief and under the gentle persuasion of their wives the brothers turned the positions down.

However, Harry did accept one appointment. It could hardly be termed political. Early in his lifetime he had been caught by the magic of paint on canvas. Gradually the house in Rockcliffe began to display a notable collection: Matisse, Picasso, Van Gogh, Gauguin, Pissarro, Monet, Courbet, Daumier. And at a time in the early 1920s when most Canadian critics were treating the new Group of Seven like barbarians, Harry Southam hailed their work as new and significant.

One day in 1929 the Governor-General, Lord Willingdon, dropped in to see the collection. Shortly afterward Mackenzie King appointed Harry chairman of the board of trustees of the National Gallery. Six years later, in recognition of his services to Canadian art, he appeared in the birthday honors list as a Companion of the Order of St. Michael and St. George – at the instance of R.B.Bennett. Woods of the Calgary *Herald* was similarly honored and F.N.Southam noted with a customary chuckle: 'Apparently Mr. Bennett was quite impartial in the matter of economic affiliations, for otherwise he could hardly have included Bert and yourself in the same list.'

In the abdication crisis of December 1936, the *Citizen* had sympathy for Edward VIII and something else for the journalistic analysts who undertook to judge him. Beverley Baxter wrote in a current magazine: 'The challenge of the King was not to the rights of parliament but to the moral standards of the nation, and parliament, as the nation's spokesman, closed its ranks. . . .'

In an editorial entitled 'Scribes Without Sin Among Them' the *Citizen* mentioned the 'virtuous freedom to condemn' assumed by some commentators, and said:

> However virtuously the ranks of parliament may have been closed, to include scribes, pharisees and hypocrites, as well as righteous members like Beverley Baxter, it may be doubted whether the final answer has been given to the king's alleged challenge. On a former occasion, recorded in the most enduring book of history, when the scribes and pharisees demanded the stoning of the sinner, they were challenged first to make sure they were without sin themselves.

When Hepburn took over the provincial Liberal leadership in 1931 the *Citizen* hailed him as having 'the daring, the buoyancy and sometimes the indiscretion of youth'.

On some things it could not go along. It condemned his removal of Conservative publisher P.D.Ross from the Ottawa Hydro-Electric Commission in 1934: only ignorance of Ottawa feeling could have prompted such an action by Toronto. And when Hepburn kicked Arthur Roebuck and David Croll out of his cabinet in 1937 because they disagreed with his opposition to the Committee for Industrial Organization in an Oshawa strike, it called his conduct 'more akin to that of a proverbial bull in a china shop than of a responsible Liberal statesman'. It opposed as 'the ruinous method of repudiation' his 1935 legislation to cancel power contracts – and incidentally got in a whack for its favorite cause by suggesting that a better way to settle the financial difficulty would be 'to restore industrial activity in Canada by reversing the policy of deflation'.

This was its favorite ground. When any public question offered a chance to discuss the money supply the reader could count on finding it – the *Citizen*'s particular King Charles's head. The paper's campaign for change in the valves and channels of buying power was to be a long and colorful crusade.

'Events Are in the Saddle'

On September 10, 1935, Wilson, Harry, and Bowman entertained at luncheon William Aberhart, the new premier of Alberta, and J.W. Hugill, his attorney-general. Next day Harry wrote his sister Ethel:

'I have a feeling that the economic salvation of the world is going to be staged in Alberta and I feel too that a large number of Social Credit candidates from the West will be elected to federal Parliament next month. Events are in the saddle.'

Three weeks earlier the western province's people, bruised by the hardest of hard times, had reached out for the new world they glimpsed in the Aberhart doctrine. It was not exactly the doctrine according to Douglas; shortly before the election Wilson expressed doubt to John Imrie that Aberhart's version of Social Credit was sound or workable. But it was a departure from dependence on what the Ottawa Southams (and they were not alone) saw as an antiquated monetary system that had broken down. Perhaps out of the Alberta experiment would come the ideal equation in which the power to buy equals the power to produce.

The depression had brought Wilson and Harry back to the particular phase of economics – money and credit – involved in Douglas's first appearance in Canada in 1923. Bowman was the expositor of monetary shortcomings to the general public through the *Citizen* in acrid editorials aimed at 'the vicious credit monopoly', Wilson (with help from Harry) the legate to the Establishment. Early in 1932 Wilson was already urging Douglas Social Credit on R.B.Bennett, on E.N.Rhodes, his minister of finance, and on H.H.Stevens, his minister of trade and commerce.

He sent Rhodes a copy of Douglas's new book *The Monopoly of Credit* and suggested drawing on 'the national credit' under Douglas principles to help the coal industry in Cape Breton and the West. Rhodes replied with an openness unusual in finance ministers: 'I must admit . . . that when I start to delve into the realm of currency, exchange and credits, I find myself a bit bewildered, especially when one realizes that so many who are regarded as authorities . . . differ so widely. However as rapidly as my work, which is somewhat pressing these days, permits, I propose, as best I can, to secure a grasp of at least the fundamentals.'

While Bowman flashed his editorial rapier Wilson and Harry pressed their points on a wide variety of individuals. Responses varied. Converts were few. Early in the long campaign Wilson called Sir Joseph Flavelle's attention to a *Citizen* editorial. Flavelle responded with a ten-page letter tracing the world's troubles to war debts and lack of principle. Bankers who supported the adventures of financial filibusters were wrong, but 'an attempt to tinker with existing systems through inexperienced agitation will only add to the disorder.' Liberal party economist R.J.Deachman was more colorful.

A little red schoolhouse in Huron County blocked his understanding. 'There I was taught that 2 plus 2 equals 4. Now when the advocates of Social Credit tell me that 2 plus 2 equals 9⅞ I simply do not believe them.'

Early in 1933 Bennett asked Wilson to serve on the Royal Commission on Banking and Currency, presumably as one who would represent the unorthodox point of view. He declined but continued to press the *Citizen*'s monetary suggestions. When the Commission's recommendations resulted in Bank of Canada legislation early in 1934, he and Harry wrote Bennett a warning that 'if the governor of the bank is a nominee of the Bank of England . . . the result will almost certainly be that the international money power, represented by Sir Charles Addis on the commission and by Montagu Norman in England, will be riveted (even more firmly than it is now) on the Canadian people.' They suggested a Canadian, perhaps Arthur Meighen or John Brownlee.

Bennett replied that any suggestion he had had from Norman could not have been made by any man who thought of regarding the institution as a link in an international chain. He sometimes thought the international money power was an international myth; he had seen no evidence of it. A Canadian, Graham Towers, was in fact appointed governor with a Bank of England man as his deputy.

Over in Montreal F.N.Southam, as president of The Southam Publishing Company, read the *Citizen*'s editorial page with interest and mixed feelings. Late in 1933 while expressing the hope that 'neither you nor Wilson will feel that I am interfering with the freedom of your editorial comment', he suggested to Harry a lighter hand. His comment sprang from a *Citizen* page with seven articles marked for attention. 'Even in enthusiastic quarters,' he wrote, 'there is a wide variety of opinion as to how much-needed reforms are to be brought about, and for that reason, in my judgment, it is poor salesmanship for either a newspaper or an individual to emphasize too frequently or too persistently his own particular remedy.'

Harry replied: 'If you saw some of your family in a boat . . . drifting toward a cataract which would inevitably destroy them, and you knew or at least felt you knew of some way of awakening the occupants to their danger and at the same time could show them the only way by which they could escape destruction, I think you would keep shouting to them from the shore – not occasionally or spasmodically or even frequently but continuously.'

F.N. assured 'both Wilson and yourself and that doughty warrior Bowman' that he had no quarrel with the *Citizen*'s advocacy of the

Douglas way of salvation. What he disliked was the 'bitterly partisan' nature of the editorials and their repetitive nature: 'If some crazy cook were to send to the table for every meal pea soup and rice pudding, after a few days the only possible use for either dish would be to throw it at your wife, or preferably, Bowman, if he was within range.' But neither Wilson nor Harry could laugh at any aspect of Social Credit.

By the winter of 1935 the *Citizen*'s Economic Research Committee – Wilson, Harry, and Bowman – had got on paper a plan based on Social Credit principles to end unemployment in Canada. In a sense it was a plan to *shift* unemployment, taking out of the labor market wage-earners of an age to be determined, paying them a pension drawn from the national credit, replacing them with young unemployed, and establishing a commodity price-discount, also to be financed by interest-free charges against a 'national credit account'.

Wilson sent it to Mackenzie King in February with a plea for its adoption as Liberal party policy. Later he sent 'My dear Billy' an emotional appeal to his sense of history: 'You will be different from all of your forerunners . . . if you but realize the opportunity. . . .' There was no written answer from the Liberal leader until May 27 when in a long and typically Kingish letter he explained that his immersion in affairs had delayed a reply. He was not enamored of *plans* as a means of arriving at reforms: 'The application of fundamental principles in one direction or another, finding for political purposes their expression in policies rather than plans, is, to my way of thinking, the surest method of bringing about beneficial and enduring results.' While ends were all-important, means were equally so in practical politics and 'the means include not only the necessary enactments but the understanding and support of both houses of Parliament and of the country.'

There was small comfort in this. In any case the Southams had already heard from inner circles that the plan would not get Liberal support and had laid it before Bennett, just back from Jubilee celebrations in England. They had talked it over with W.D.Herridge, generally believed to have been the architect of the New Deal program Bennett had broadcast in January. For which, incidentally, the *Citizen* had hailed the Prime Minister's courage while criticizing the program itself as 'leading along the Socialist path of the corporate state'. Bennett replied that he couldn't see the method outlined as effective. The national credit-account idea would defeat the processes of recovery because it would 'destroy confidence in our monetary unit'.

A couple of friendly postscripts to this exchange were written in October after the election. Wilson wrote 'My dear R.B.' that though he had done what he could to defeat the government he had got no pleasure out of it 'because of a certain admiration which I have acquired in recent years for some of your personal qualities.' Both he and Harry were pleased that 'toward the end of the last session, through Bill Herridge, we at least offered you an election-saver in our plan to enable you to fulfil your promise to end unemployment.'

Bennett came back with a philosophical reply. He had no personal regrets or complaints, but was disappointed from a party standpoint: 'For I cannot help but think that, with the Liberals having 170 members in the House sent there by less than 50 per cent of the electors who voted . . . we are facing a very serious situation.' Every now and then the people had to express their resentment against conditions by blowing off steam and 'now that my employers, the people of Canada, have discharged me, I certainly accept their dismissal with equanimity.' As to the plan: 'I still believe that on mature consideration you will realize your suggestions for ending unemployment are not possible in practicable application to the conditions of this country.'

Obviously Bennett would never be a Social Crediter. But Wilson found a crumb of comfort. Opposite the reference to the voting figures he noted: 'Perhaps he is favorable to proportional representation as an electoral reform.'

Meantime, having failed to get the plan sponsored by either major party, Wilson and Harry brought it to public notice through the *Citizen* and other newspapers. William Ward, an English Social Crediter, happened to be in Ottawa that summer promoting his League to Abolish Poverty. He let his name be used. As published in the *Citizen* August 31 and a dozen other Canadian papers (the *Citizen* mailed out proofs), it was prefaced as 'sponsored by William Ward, founder of the League to Abolish Poverty and honorary president of the World Brotherhood Federation'.

The Ward plan as detailed in seven columns of newspaper type suggested retirement of all enfranchised Canadians of fifty or more and payment to them of a 'national dividend retirement allowance' of $60 a month to age seventy when the old-age pension would be effective. Cost of this part of the plan, estimated at $337,200,000, would be financed through a national credit account 'written up as a credit on the ledgers of the Bank of Canada and backed by the same national wealth, public and private, which backs all the present public debt.' In two years the national income would be stepped up to the 1929 level. Thereafter the government should hire a Social Credit engineer to draft a plan for a price discount to prevent inflation.

Wilson pressed on, urging King to reconsider the proposals as now condensed and revised. A couple of touches of sly humor lightened King's comment in January, 1936. 'I do not think that either you or I would agree that men of over 50 should be grouped as a new class of unemployables,' he wrote. And on the suggestion that Douglas be called in to advise: 'I should not like to risk becoming a third party to the trans-Atlantic interchanges now taking place between Major Douglas and Mr. Aberhart.'

At the time, Douglas was furious with Aberhart for calling in R.J. Magor, a Montreal financial man, to help straighten out Alberta's finances. 'All the initial advantage has been lost', he wrote Wilson, 'by this absurd refusal to recognize the impossibility of co-operation with the banking system in a policy designed to weaken the banking system.'

The *Citizen* Social Crediters themselves professed no enmity to private banking. In 1932 Wilson asked Douglas to confirm that his credit proposals 'could be grafted onto the present banking system . . . with little or no change from the way things are done at present.' Douglas said there was no theoretical reason why not, but all the great banks seemed to have become instruments of a certain policy – more concerned with retaining the power the financial system gave them than with mere business profits. It was hard to see how a policy that attacked this aspect of finance could be put through without 'putting these people out of control of the mechanism'.

The *Citizen* however stuck to the line that the banks were useful instruments and did a good job of financing production, that the trouble was with a banking *system* that fell down on the job of providing means of distribution and consumption. Tied in with this was a concept of economic nationalism calling for highest possible use of goods within the producing nation by increasing internal purchasing power, and complementary trade between nations to take the place of extinct trade based on foreign investments.

While there was an implied difference of view between the Ottawa Southams and Douglas on the possibility of getting the banks in line, and though the Southams would come to have reservations about Douglas's attitude on some other questions, they did not waver in allegiance to his theories on money. When in 1936 a clergyman at Fitch Bay, Quebec, submitted plans purporting to 'simplify' Social Credit, Harry wrote him: 'I have to confess that I am not interested in any variation or alleged simplification of Douglas Social Credit unless such is evolved and offered to the world by Douglas himself because, as I see it, he is the only man in the world who has examined every angle of our economic problem.'

In the same letter he referred to his disbelief in the C.C.F. position on monetary matters. Shortly thereafter the *Citizen* expressed its opinion of C.C.F. solutions in a scornful editorial on Angus Mac-Innis's resolution regretting that the government had done nothing to 'lessen the inequalities of income by increased taxation on the larger incomes and by a levy on large accumulations of capital for the reduction of national debt.' 'Without being exactly old crusted Toryism, such proposed measures . . . are just about as bewhiskered,' the *Citizen* said. Woodsworth and MacInnis held the same conservative views about 'sound money' as Bennett or Dunning.

From the date of the Alberta election an element of paradox must have troubled the *Citizen*'s publishers – fully sold on Douglas but doubtful of Aberhart, and, like Douglas, opposed to setting up Social Credit as a separate political party. But what alternative was there to supporting the Alberta experiment as the only monetary reform effort being made in the world? Aberhart, as Wilson suggested later, 'was at least awakening the public to many of the imperfections of our debt-creating system.'

One hope lay in the prospect of providing Aberhart with better advice – if he would take it. In the fall of 1936 Halliday Thompson, an English Social Crediter, suggested John Hargrave, leader of a political wing of the movement, as a good man to go to Edmonton. Wilson and Harry agreed to put up $600 toward expenses. Hargrave's visit and departure after disagreement with the Alberta premier soon became a brief chapter in the fantastic story of the early Aberhart years.

Disillusionment with Aberhart and faith in the system were both strong in a letter Harry wrote John Imrie in February 1937. If Aberhart could be replaced by someone earnest in the desire to carry out the will of the electorate, this might still be done even in the face of opposition by the Calgary and Edmonton newspapers, though he professed now not to be much concerned about Alberta at all. There was a larger view: 'I still have a feeling that antedates my doubt in regard to Aberhart that events are in the saddle, and that Alberta, or New Zealand, or the United Kingdom, or even the United States in the not too distant future, will have to revise its monetary system via the Social Credit route or be shoved into Fascism or Communism – more probably the former than the latter.' He had hoped that Alberta would lead the way out but had been doubtful in view of the attitude of the *Herald* and the *Journal* about Douglas's discovery. 'I had a sneaking hope', he told Imrie, 'that you might have led the Journal into support of Social Credit.'

In August of 1935, Imrie had replied to Wilson's observation that Aberhart's 'so-called Social Credit' didn't appear workable with a reminder that this was the position the *Journal* had taken: 'But we have been careful to point out from time to time the various differences between it and the Douglas system and to emphasize Major Douglas's point about the nature of the area in which alone his system could be in his opinion successful. Thus far the Journal has taken no definite stand either way on the Douglas system as applied to the national field.'

Meantime Aberhart's fight with the press, about to be climaxed by his Act to Ensure Accurate News and Information (with Douglas's blessing), scotched whatever charm Alberta's newspapers might possibly have seen in either theory in any field. Wilson and Harry made no converts among the publishers. When, years later, the Edmonton *Journal* and Vancouver *Province* did on occasion back Social Credit governments, the monetary reform aspect of the movement (the core of Wilson's and Harry's conviction) had largely given place to practical politics.

Obviously, Aberhart's move against the press placed the *Citizen* in a curious position. In an editorial September 23, 1936, when licensing was threatened, it opposed such a step but managed to base its opposition not only on the stand that the proposition was undemocratic but that it was un-Social Credit:

> It would be contrary to the whole philosophy of Social Credit, which is against bureaucracy or state interference with the liberty of the subject. There is a profound need for better relations between the newspapers and the government of Alberta, but anything in the nature of a licensing threat is calculated to involve democratic forces in a distracting fight over a side issue. . . .

(Later, after Douglas had advised Aberhart to 'pass press act', F.N. suggested in correspondence with Harry: 'Just at that point, I think, in the interests of the newspaper publishing business, the Citizen, which has on occasions a very heavily shod boot for the other fellow's point of view, should, with a generous swing, have applied it to that part of the prophet's anatomy which is so well designed for its reception.')

By early 1938 it was obvious that Aberhart's delayed efforts to put his version of Social Credit into effect provincially could get nowhere against disallowances and court decisions. Very well, said the *Citizen*, it's up to the Dominion. Once again Bowman quoted a 1935 utterance (a favorite of the *Citizen*'s) by Mackenzie King: 'Usury, once in control, will wreck any nation. Until the control of the issue of currency and credit is restored to the government and recognized as its most conspicuous and sacred responsibility, all talk of the sovereignty of Parliament and democracy is futile.' Nothing was being done to apply the sovereignty of the Dominion over money power. Nothing to safeguard Canada against another depression.

The Ottawa Southams' hopes now centred on W.D.Herridge. In 1938 he had proposed to the national Conservative convention, unsuccessfully, a resolution that the party 'undertake whatever economic and monetary reform may be required to stabilize production upon its maximum level and to raise purchasing power to that level.' When Herridge in 1940 launched his New Democracy platform, with which federal Social Crediters aligned themselves, the *Citizen* backed it. Wilson and Harry paid for reproduction of a supporting editorial in several dailies as a *Citizen* advertisement.

A sidelight is that at least three Southam papers – the *Province*, the *Herald*, and the *Journal* – exercised their right to refuse advertising and turned it down. It was, Nichols of the *Province* explained, the fact of *Citizen* sponsorship that led to his decision: 'Political advertising properly sponsored is acceptable to the Province. If sponsored by New Democracy or Social Credit, the Citizen's article would have a clear road to our advertising columns.' But one Southam newspaper paying for an expression of its opinion in another Southam newspaper? No.

The *Citizen* could have been under no illusions that New Democracy would get far but its view of Mackenzie King in 1940 was hardly stronger than recognition of a lesser evil: 'While there is little genuine enthusiasm over the present government's performance, there is less over the prospect of a Manion government.' The best that could be hoped for was a stronger opposition.

Some things about Douglas were beginning to disturb Harry and Wilson. They had never given up on the idea that people could be convinced by exposition of problems and answers. Douglas differed. Back in 1936 he had written: 'The idea I am so anxious to make clear is . . . that a sufficient degree of education upon monetary matters cannot be imparted to the general population on such a scale as to make voting upon such matters effective. . . . It is only possible to convey the general idea and to obtain voting upon an emotional basis.' Now his obsession with a world plot troubled them. His articles in *The Social Crediter*, studded with terms like 'the Jew-kept press', elaborated the theme.

Any kind of internationalism appeared to the Social Credit Secretariat as linked to a plot that went far beyond money-getting. Now, in developing this line, the secretariat attacked one of Wilson's long-held convictions and one of his new enthusiasms. Late in 1940 an article by Tudor Jones, deputy-chairman of the secretariat, cast aspersions on the Christian Science movement. Wilson ignored it. A second article, by another writer, attacking Clarence Streit's 'Union Now With Britain' campaign, drove him to protest in a letter to the editor, a copy of which he sent Douglas.

Citing both articles, he suggested the acceptance of Social Credit would be made easier 'if you would first induce Social Credit advocates to close their ranks; secondly, cease senseless and provocative attacks on others' religious beliefs, and then work for the adoption of a free monetary plank in the "Union Now With Britain" provisional constitution if and when one is set up.' He concluded with a plea for 'a turning-back from the blind alley which the two articles of which I complain seem to show you have already entered.'

The Social Crediter made a non-committal reply. Commenting, Douglas wrote Wilson an essay on the brilliance of Tudor Jones, and went on to say that he, personally, drew a sharp distinction between Christian Scientists as individuals and the Christian Science organization. As for Union Now:

> I have always realized that, so far as I could see, you had not grasped the nature of the real problem. . . . You condemn 'senseless and provocative attacks on others' religious beliefs' because you do not, I think, grasp that the groundwork of all policy must of its very nature be a religion – a philosophy. The philosophy which is attacked, and mortally attacked by us, is exactly that of the coercive organization. If you can't solve your provincial money problems because the federal government won't let you, why do you expect an Anglo-American Federation to let you? . . . The short answer to the 'sink your differences and get together' complaint is that in subtle matters the majority is always wrong, and only a minority can be right. . . .

Wilson's reply was, for him, unusually sharp. Tudor Jones was undoubtedly a brilliant scholar but 'I should judge he is suffering from such an educational superiority complex . . . that he is quite incapable of understanding the simple, spiritual, provable truths taught by Jesus.' As for the money problem, there was no solution 'short of its understanding by a sufficiently large and influential body of people to make the so-called political leaders bring in the necessary legislation to free us from the monopoly of credit by international finance and the debt-finance of the bond-selling fraternity.' The fight for freedom from credit monopoly could be carried on just as effectively in Union Now as under separate sovereignties. He added what amounted to a declaration of independence from belief in Douglas's infallibility: 'As you know, my brother H.S. and myself and Charles Bowman are staunch admirers of you personally and of your Social Credit system, but it does not follow that we can accept blindly some of your strategy or tactics. At the moment we are particularly at variance with your attitude to the United States.'

Douglas came back with a repetition of his suggestion that Wilson was an innocent in a Satanic world:

> Your objection to the line taken by the Social Crediter reinforces my opinion that you cannot, up to the present, visualize clearly the nature and potential of the forces which have to be brought to bear, as a dynamic, not a static problem. . . . The essential point to bear in mind is that the money question is not only not the ultimate question, but is made to be of decreasing importance. It has been a ladder by which international plotters have risen to power, and, by means of rationing, licensing, 'planning' and so forth, it is being kicked away so that it cannot be used to reach them. World hegemony is the goal, and it would appear so obvious that Union Now is merely an opposite number to Hitler's New Order, that I am genuinely surprised that you should take it at its face value.

Wilson let it rest there, but a little later Douglas sent him a mimeographed copy of some notes on the Jewish world plot. 'What confuses me,' Wilson commented, 'is that there are probably as many gentiles as Jews seeking world domination through finance – Montagu Norman being an outstanding one – and I fail to see how we can blame the Jewish partner and not the gentile one as well and equally.'

Things were hard to pin down, Douglas replied, because 'the elaborate organization which has been built up over many centuries' was expressly designed to make it most difficult to identify the key men. 'I am fairly satisfied that Brandeis was near the centre and I think I know one or two others. I agree with you completely that there are very many gentiles concerned, but that does not, unfortunately, dispose of the matter.'

By that time many matters were in process of being disposed of on many fronts. The *Citizen* continued to blast the 'international money power', which it saw as crumbling under the war's impact, and while it urged support of war loans it grumbled at the orthodox policy of borrowing financial credit from private sources when the nation could simply lend itself national credit. There were, however, other things besides monetary policy on which to take a stand.

Throughout its depression-born preoccupation with the monetary system, the *Citizen* had never forsaken certain earlier battle-grounds. Since the early 1930s it had hammered at lack of defence preparation and harked back to the iniquities of other days, as in this editorial comment on August 27, 1934:

> Absolutely nothing has apparently been done to safeguard against another orgy of war profiteering in the event of Canada being again called upon to mobilize national resources for national defence. Much sentiment is being published in Canada about the rapacity of international munitions interests, but nothing is being done about it.

When the contracts providing for private manufacture of Bren guns came under critical scrutiny, it recalled its First World War campaign for munitions manufacture in government machine-shops, and demanded assurance 'that an end has been made of the rotten state of political patronage as it has evidently been operating under the policy of awarding contracts to people with an inside track into the public treasury.'

Early in 1939 Bowman followed up with a series of editorials on campaign funds and patronage that brought down on his head the wrath of both old parties. Conservative leader R.J.Manion suggested the *Citizen*'s editor be brought before the bar of the house 'and required to give, what I know he cannot give, one tittle of evidence. . . .'

In the midst of the squall, incidentally, one small echo of a sort of subterranean family feud reached the surface. Without reference to the *Citizen*'s strictures on patronage, Frank Ahearn placed a couple of questions on the order paper: Did Southam Press of Montreal receive orders for tickets, time-tables, and folders for the CNR? How many contracts were awarded to Southam Press from 1922 to 1938? What were the amounts?

Ahearn was Harry Southam's brother-in-law, a son of the founder of the Ottawa street railways. The *Citizen* stood for public ownership of such utilities. Back in 1925 Ahearn had brought a libel suit against the *Citizen* on behalf of the Ottawa Hockey Club (which he controlled) for an editorial by Bowman in which, among other things, he referred to spectators watching 'what they believed to be genuine contests.' Bowman said in court he merely meant that some boys playing for Ottawa and other teams were not natives of the cities concerned. Ahearn won the suit and damages of $100. However, when he entered politics in 1930 as a Liberal candidate, the *Citizen* ignored past and private differences and noted that his decision to run had been 'received with general acclaim throughout the city'.

Ahearn got little change out of his questions on printing. Transport Minister Howe replied that Southam Press did get Canadian National orders, but that the railways took the position it was not in their interest to make detailed information public. King suggested it would do no good to call Bowman before the bar: 'Make a martyr of anyone, whether it be a newspaper publisher, or editor, and you begin to serve probably the greatest purpose he may have in view. . . .'

Now with war a fact, the *Citizen* plugged for an all-out Canadian effort, called for conscription, castigated the government for lethargic leadership. Finally, a couple of years after Mackenzie King's refusal to martyr Bowman, out of the gadfly editor's persistent needling came an incident that recalled the old Rogers threat of a non-existent tower.

The Bren Gun Affair

On January 9, 1941, Grant Dexter of the Winnipeg *Free Press* strolled into the department of munitions and supply to check a query. What was new in the matter of Bren guns? The answer he got was that more than two months before – on October 31, 1940 – new contracts had replaced the original deal with the John Inglis Company of Toronto. The firm now was making Brens under a straight management-fee arrangement rather than the cost plus ten per cent of the 1938 contract. In effect, the government had taken over the plant and hired the company to run it. As the first Bren contract had sparked a political war from early 1938 until shooting started in Europe, this was indeed news.

Bowman made this development the occasion of an editorial – 'At the Business End of the Bren' – in which on January 11 he reviewed the history of the contracts, fired a volley from the *Citizen*'s old position condemning patronage in war supplies, and invoked a mild curse on both sides of the House for past sins. Two storms blew up out of this editorial.

The first, and least violent, was simply a bit of bickering within the trade. Dexter's story was an exclusive. After getting it away to the *Free Press* he had given the facts to the Ottawa *Journal*. Through a swapping arrangement it also reached the Vancouver *Sun* that day. Most Canadian dailies including the *Citizen* were out in the cold till next morning. In the ancient language of the craft, they were scooped. Without making much of a point of it, Bowman slipped into his editorial a suggestion that 'The Free Press has doubtless an exceptional source of contact with government information on contracts for army ordnance.'

As Victor Sifton, publisher of the *Free Press*, was then in Ottawa as master-general of the ordnance, this reference raised some eyebrows. Dexter protested that Sifton hadn't even known about the new contract till Dexter told him about it. That, in fact, Sifton's presence was a source of embarrassment since 'one must be careful not to publish any item which might be regarded as coming from him or arising out of the business with which he is concerned.'

The *Citizen* made amends. Under the heading WINNIPEG PUBLISHER BLAMELESS, it disclaimed any intention of suggesting improper behavior. At the same time it criticized departmental action that favored one newspaper or group of papers at the expense of others – an attitude, incidentally, with which most newspapers, particularly in competitive cities, heartily agreed. The slight unpleasantness of all this blew over quickly.

Until weeks later no one seems to have paid much attention to the concluding sentence of Bowman's editorial: 'When the lads come home from overseas, after some years of service at the real business end of the Bren gun, they may know better where to shoot than Canadian veterans did in the years of debt and privation after the last war.'

No one, that is, except M.J.Coldwell. At some time or other, the C.C.F. leader sent the editorial to Justice Minister Ernest Lapointe. On February 27 – more than six weeks after publication of the editorial – Coldwell brought this into the open in the Commons. His point was that treatment under the Defence of Canada Regulations differed according to the person concerned. For instance the R.C.M.P. had seized a pamphlet issued by left-winger Dorise Nielsen of North Battleford, though it contained nothing but extracts from speeches made in the House. Coldwell invited comparison of this 'with statements that were made, let us say, in the Ottawa *Citizen* of January 11.' He then read Bowman's 'know better where to shoot' sentence and continued: 'I believe in the freedom of the press and the freedom of speech, but the government adopted regulations under which men have been prosecuted and interned for far less than this. . . . What has been done by the attorney general of Canada to whose attention I drew this article?'

Lapointe answered: 'My honorable friend sent me that article not very long ago. I may tell him that he is right. . . . It was a subversive article. . . . And I may tell him that they will have to answer for it before the courts of the country.'

On March 1 the *Citizen* published a long explanatory editorial. Of the sentence in question it said:

The Citizen's quoted words meant only that the returned soldiers after this war may know better where to shoot *with ballots* – in other words, use their votes and influence more effectively – than Canadian veterans did in the years of debt and privation after the last war. The concluding comment had no other purpose but to express confidence in the ability of the Canadian men when they come home from overseas to be more discerning in the way they vote.

The words *with ballots* could well have been included to prevent the Citizen's position from being misrepresented. Nowhere, however, in the editorial columns of this newspaper through the years has there been one instance of inciting Canadian veterans or anyone else to violence or any form of subversive action. The Citizen has long advocated reform measures, but never along any but constitutional and orderly paths.

It reprinted the January 11 editorial in full because Coldwell had quoted only the concluding words 'when he misrepresented the whole editorial purport of this newspaper.' And it suggested none too subtly that the motive for Coldwell's attack might be found in some comment the *Citizen* had made about him. On January 22 the paper had said: 'M.J.Coldwell, M.P., has come to the aid of Mr. Ilsley, Dominion minister of finance, in an attack on Prime Minister Hepburn. It is not surprising to find Mr. Coldwell seizing this opportunity to associate himself with the right people. He has been steadily making the grade since the veteran Socialist, James S. Woodsworth, withdrew from active leadership in C.C.F. politics.'

The *Citizen* was charged – on grounds that the editorial was 'prejudicial to the safety of the state or the efficient prosecution of the war' and 'likely to prejudice the recruiting, training, discipline or administration of His Majesty's forces'. Magistrate Glen Strike heard the case March 19 and dismissed the charges in a written judgment April 2, accepting the *Citizen*'s defence that the 'where to shoot' reference was metaphorical.

The measure of Harry Southam's sense of injury may be judged from a letter he wrote Mackenzie King while the case was pending:

For the government of Canada to hale the Citizen – with whose record of public service you have been acquainted for at least 40 years, and whose integrity, sincerity and independence you have known during the same period – before the courts on a charge of publishing a subversive editorial, is of course a matter of grave concern; but to have the minister of justice preface his acceptance of the proposal of the leader of the Socialist party in the House of Commons that the government proceed against the Citizen with the statement that the complained-of article was subversive – that is to say, pre-judge the case – is surely anything but judicial. . . . Even if the Citizen had permitted to slip into an editorial a sentence that might be construed as subversive if read literally instead of metaphorically (as it was intended to be read) the attitude of your government towards this paper would be, I think, in view of the Citizen's standing and record in the community, difficult to justify.

He suggested the Prime Minister would hardly expect him to remain as chairman of the board of trustees of the National Gallery in view of the government's attack, tendered his resignation, and closed with an expression of regret that this decision 'has to be presented to a much loved and trusted friend of so many years'.

Something like consternation hit officials of the Gallery on learning of this letter. Director H.O.McCurry told Walter Turnbull, King's principal secretary: 'From our point of view his retirement would be something of a calamity. No chairman of the National Gallery board has ever served the institution so wholeheartedly and disinterestedly. No chairman has ever won the confidence of the Canadian art world so completely. . . .' Furthermore, it was known to be Harry Southam's intention to leave an art collection valued at $250,000 to the Gallery, and this would probably be lost. Could the Prime Minister 'in his usual tactful and friendly way' bring about a reconsideration? This Mackenzie King evidently did. Harry Southam remained chairman of the board of trustees until Vincent Massey took on the job in 1948, resumed the position in 1952 on Massey's appointment as Governor-General, and remained in the post until 1953, the year before his death.

He continued, however, now and then to let his feelings show. Six months after the trial, in making a rate concession to Finance Minister Ilsley for war-savings advertising, he reminded him that the government in laying its subversion charge 'did something which may perhaps be not unfairly described as despicable.' It obviously gave him a certain satisfaction to be able to say that 'notwithstanding this attack by the government, or perhaps because of it, the circulation of the Citizen since the trial has increased to a greater extent than at any other time in the history of this newspaper.'

He did not leave his art collection to the National Gallery. Toward the end of his life he sold paintings by Matisse, Picasso, Van Gogh, Gauguin, and the impressionists Monet and Pissarro. There has been spoken and published speculation that resentment at the prosecution of the *Citizen* resulted in this change of plan. This assumption is questionable. He continued to serve actively as chairman of the board of trustees and between 1943 and 1950 presented the Gallery with a dozen pictures by a wide range of painters, from Canadians A.Y.Jackson, Prudence Heward, and his protégé Henri Masson, to the Frenchmen Courbet and Daumier, and made possible by a money gift the purchase of a Paul Gauguin. These do not seem like the acts of a man bent on revenge. Motives are sometimes mixed, but it seems apparent – considering the increases in income-tax and succession duties since the years when he had considered such a bequest – that the reasons for dispersal of the collection were chiefly economic.

Criticism and Crisis

Its experience in court did nothing to check the *Citizen*'s sharp and sometimes rather querulous criticism.

At this particular time it viewed with approval the attempted re-emergence of Arthur Meighen as a political force. In November of 1941 Meighen accepted the Conservative leadership, demanded non-party government, and came up with a policy of compulsory selective service on all fields and fronts – a program close to the *Citizen*'s. His presence in the House of Commons again, the paper said, would help to raise public confidence in Parliament. Meighen's by-election loss to the C.C.F. erased that possibility.

The *Citizen*, in a February editorial, called Mackenzie King 'the last of the appeasers'. The honorable way to free the government of the limitations of King's promises to Quebec against conscription, 'the traditional way of statesmanship, is for the Prime Minister to resign,' it suggested after the April 27 manpower plebiscite. 'This recourse of statesmanship should have been taken in the first instance without putting Canada through the humbug of the plebiscite. . . . It is within the power of the members to rise above party, as the Canadian people have done in the plebiscite, to form a war government entirely free from past commitments or party limitations.'

Some disgruntled Liberals cancelled subscriptions. Now and then, in the course of half a century with the paper, Harry Southam would make such an event the occasion for a letter restating his philosophy as a publisher. To one defector in August of 1942 he put the question: Should a newspaper's editorials be intended to meet the approval of its subscribers or to express its sincere opinions and convictions on public matters? He thought what the reader had a right to demand was honesty in expression of opinion and presentation of news, 'courage and independence and of course incorruptibility'.

The reader had a perfect right to *try* to influence the *Citizen* by cancelling his subscription, but 'I question whether what you are doing is in the interests of the freedom of the press in this country – a freedom which by the way is not something that has been gained and maintained in the interests of the publisher but in the interests of the reader.' He went on to say that the *Citizen* was a liberal paper that had been supporting the Liberal party for years and had supported King in 1940. It had criticized him and his government while supporting some members (notably C.D.Howe) and would continue to do so until the government 'leads Canada into an all-out war effort, something it has failed to do thus far'.

In his reminiscences* Bowman tells of a change of heart. War production under Howe showed no sign of the old 'business as usual' mentality. Credit should go to the responsible head of government. With the agreement of Harry and Wilson Southam, he went to King to admit a feeling of having been unfair. The Prime Minister, he records, 'expressed appreciative relief' – after years of starting the day with *Citizen* editorials he had found the recent going difficult. Thereafter Bowman found opportunities to print a few kind words.

By the time the conscription crisis of 1944 stirred the country, the *Citizen* had come to the view (November 4, 1944) that 'at the present time there is no other leader than Mr. Mackenzie King in sight.' The parties were equally responsible for the home-front situation. The government's war record had been meritorious – except in its failure to give leadership 'along the path of collective national service, as in the other great democracies'.

In the midst of the crisis the *Citizen* blamed most of it on General A.G.L.McNaughton, successor as minister of defence to Colonel J.L.Ralston, forced out for his insistence on conscription. In a speech to the Canadian Legion, McNaughton said he believed 'the man who comes forward voluntarily and shoulders the obligation of honor to fight for his country is a better man and better able to fight than the conscript.' This was, the *Citizen* said, the most disturbing speech made by a cabinet minister since Canada declared war. 'It is mischievous to have the Canadian minister of national defence declaring in effect that the Canadian soldier is a better man and better able to fight than the British or American soldier. The only difference is that the government of Canada left it to the Canadian soldiers to volunteer individually while the British and American democracies volunteered collectively. . . .'

Ottawa Editor, Gray's Publishing Limited, Sidney, B.C.

When, finally, the government decided to take the responsibility of sending trained reinforcements overseas by the national selective draft the paper conceded that 'democracy is operating in Canada.'

The *Citizen* had always thought highly of Ralston, the man who had been shelved for insisting on a policy eventually adopted. It saw him now as one who had placed loyalty to Canada first, 'above party interest or self-interest' and who would be honored in history as a Canadian patriot.

The World of Wilson

On June 13, 1941, the *Citizen* came out with an editorial 'For Union Now to Maintain Freedom' in which it looked with favor on Clarence Streit's proposals for 'Union Now of the U.S.A. and the six British Democracies as the Nucleus of a World Government'. It suggested Canadian M.P.s take Streit's book *Union Now With Britain* home to read. With his usual methodical persistence Wilson arranged with agents of the publishers to give any interested M.P. a copy at his expense.

The United States was still neutral but some of the gloom that made June of 1940 the darkest month in modern history had lifted. War tools were moving from the States.

In that previous June when the one cause for thanksgiving was Dunkirk, even the hope of those tools had gone into precarious balance. As an incidental sidelight on the times it may be noted that W.D.Herridge had taken the Southams into his confidence about a plan he had evolved out of a haunting fear, the fear of American withdrawal into isolation. Early in that June of 1940 he had written O.D.Skelton, under-secretary for external affairs, a letter for Mackenzie King's attention: it was time for Canada to suggest an allied mission to Washington to persuade the American people of the British and Commonwealth intention to fight on. Given a favorable reply, Canada should take it to Britain. King sent the proposal to Cordell Hull, Roosevelt's foreign secretary, and on June 20 Skelton relayed to Herridge Hull's wired reply: '. . . I am impelled to state that in my opinion purposes and objectives which the proposed mission would have in view can be, and are being, accomplished through the existing agencies and channels.'

What Herridge foresaw had occurred. With the fall of France, American plans to send planes, guns, and sub-chasers were off. The New York *Times*, in an editorial headed 'Life and Death of a Policy', complained that while it might be argued that the policy of all help possible had become too dangerous by late June, no such argument had been made. There had been no chance to present the counter consideration: that there were risks in any policy the United States adopted and that complete aloofness might be the most risky of all.

Herridge failed in his effort, which perhaps was a forlorn hope at best. But certain other forces raised counter considerations to restore American hope that the lines would hold at the Channel and in the bombed cities of England. Not some special mission or the 'existing agencies and channels' of Hull's brush-off, but young men in the cockpits of Hurricanes and Spitfires.

Meanwhile – at least until the Commonwealth-American relationship took shape as the Grand Alliance – interest and support for Federal Union grew. It was the kind of idealistic dream that appealed to Wilson Southam and characteristically his mind went beyond the general and immediate into various theoretical possibilities.

For nearly twenty years, with the central company under F.N.'s direction and Harry managing the *Citizen*, Wilson had had time to satisfy his urge to study the social and political movements to which his mind had always tended. Federal Union became one of his enthusiasms. It fitted well with another, which the *Citizen* had been promoting for years: proportional representation. This system called for multi-member constituencies with candidates voted for in order of preference and elected on reaching a quota, with surplus votes distributed according to preference. Theoretically it provides for justice to minorities. Back in 1923 W.C.Good, Progressive M.P. for Brant, moved in the Commons that one or more constituencies be set up to demonstrate the system's workings. His motion failed, with Prime Minister Mackenzie King and Finance Minister W.S.Fielding voting for it, Sir Lomer Gouin and Arthur Meighen against. Later Wilson had taken heart from the fact that Alberta and Manitoba adopted the scheme for city constituencies in provincial elections, and Winston Churchill favored it for city voting in England. Now he saw P.R. as a guarantee of representation for minority groups in whatever set-up might develop from Federal Union. Later he pressed his views by letter on a wide variety of statesmen, politicians, and thinkers, ranging from King Peter of Yugoslavia to Charles de Gaulle, as various schemes for organizing post-war Europe began to flower.

Meanwhile he revived efforts to get the system backed federally in Canada. In December of 1942 the Conservatives were to convene in Winnipeg. Wilson conducted a campaign, which he described in a letter to his son John then overseas with the Canadian artillery:

As there was no one else to work on getting the convention to accept P.R. as part of its future policy I undertook a campaign to educate it to accepting that system. In this I was helped by Mum, Margaret, Roddy, John,* and some of the boys' friends. This group, under my supervision, assembled in the music-room around card-tables and stuffed the already-addressed and machine-stamped long envelopes with four pieces of literature. . . . I sent out about 1,500 to delegates and alternative delegates, as well as writing some personal letters to Arthur Meighen and other Conservative political leaders.

The Conservative convention, chiefly concerned with drafting John Bracken and tacking 'Progressive' to the party name, side-tracked P.R. to a committee. Wilson continued to urge it on people like Sun Fo of the Chinese Republic (in connection with elections in Japan) and Ernest Bevin, Lord Hailsham, Bernard Baruch, Jan Masaryk, the Dean of Canterbury, and the Archbishop of Westminster, chiefly as part of a plan he had evolved with Mrs. Harvey Smith of Syracuse, N.Y., for the post-war absorption of Germany by surrounding countries. This was embodied in a thirty-six-page booklet entitled *No Germany Therefore No More German Wars*, equipped with maps to show how Germany could be sliced up and allotted to Poland, Czechoslovakia, France, Belgium, The Netherlands, Denmark, and Russia. One of the conditions would be that any professed democratic country (this would exclude Russia) would agree to adopt 'The Hare Proportional Representation System in multi-member constituencies' to ensure representation of minorities.

(Sun Fo thought the Mikado would have to be kicked out before elections were held in Japan. Hailsham wrote that he was against 'having inaugurated in our Parliament the group system that has been the ruin of France', felt that P.R. would encourage this, and added: 'I daresay it is an admirable plan, but I am afraid it will not work.')

Wilson stuck to his faith in the principle, but by 1946, after long study and consultation with electoral officers, he had become reluctantly convinced that P.R. would not work for a country as large and thinly populated as Canada. It was generally recognized that under the system, constituencies must elect at least five members each. As an example of the difficulty, this would involve redistributing Manitoba's 17 seats into three. How could a throng of candidates canvass or become known across such vast areas? The alternative would be increasing Commons membership to 900 or more.

*Grandsons Roddy and John Brinckman.

On November 11, 1946, the *Citizen* discussed the problem in an editorial, which concluded that 'in densely populated countries with mixed races, as in Europe, proportional representation would be an ideal voting system.' But 'in Canada with its large but sparsely populated constituencies it would work out satisfactorily only in some urban districts such as in Toronto or Montreal.' This was one of the few questions since reciprocity on which Wilson or the *Citizen* changed direction. Ironically, he had to put up as well-reasoned a defence of its switch on P.R., in correspondence with the British Proportional Representation Society, as he had ever presented for the other side of the case.

The *Citizen*, as it demonstrated, could win battles based on the common and the practical: a civic election or a city referendum. In wider schemes it had to be content with exposition and virtue's traditional reward. It must sometimes have seemed to its readers that its ideal world would have a monetary system modelled on Social Credit, taxation according to Henry George, and governments elected by P.R. No such synthesis was ever in sight. Social Crediters looked on Federal Union as easing the machinations of international bankers. Henry George men warned Wilson that Douglas didn't understand the single tax. He could never get concerted support for P.R.

Part of the country's failure to adopt systems that seemed to him unquestionably right, Wilson attributed by implication to lack of newspaper leadership. When towards the end of his life he set down with pencil on newsprint some of his recollections and conclusions, he regretted what he saw as a lack of interest in public affairs by newspaper publishers and editors:

> It is a lamentable fact, but possibly a natural one, that the great majority of newspaper publishers and editors, no matter how well intentioned they may be, seem unable to take the long view of any question ... even if the public interest and their personal interest run on parallel lines. I attribute this principally to the fact that unless they are natural students – few of us are – they have no time to do anything but what is forced on their attention from day to day: such is the pressure in publishing a newspaper. When any earned leisure comes to them the great majority naturally prefer to seek relaxation of one kind or another – with their families, on the golf course, fishing, gardening, or what not.

He seems to have given little weight to the thought that even a studious man, particularly one of open and skeptical mind, may find it hard to reach the state of ardent conviction that he and Harry were able to attain.

He did not, however, argue for action without conviction. 'Even if I had the power I would not care to insist on them being sympathetic to an investigation of Social Credit unless they had the vision to see something better in it than the present faulty system,' he wrote F.N. in August 1937, commenting on the attitude of the publishers. There was, even, the possibility of error in his own conclusions: 'Their present attitude may be right – mine may be wrong. Local autonomy therefore is an asset to The Southam Publishing Company, which I think should be carefully protected.'

Of Wilson's sons, only John made newspaper work his career – a career eventually cut short by tragedy. The eldest, William, had started in the *Citizen*'s business office, but died in May of 1924 after his car crashed at night into a truck parked without lights near Oshawa. At the time of Wilson's death in 1947, the third son, Cargill, worked in the Montreal printing plant. Hamilton, youngest of the family, was then writing editorials for the *Citizen* after a post-war winter as a reporter for *The Times* in London, but left the newspaper world shortly afterward to go into Canada's foreign service, in which he reached ambassador's rank.

A touch of family continuity, incidentally, marked Hamilton's wartime service. Enlisting in the Royal Artillery from Oxford he was commissioned in May of 1940. Meantime Gordon Southam's old battery, the 40th, which had carried on between the wars as a militia unit, mobilized for active service under Frank Keen, assistant city editor of the *Spectator*. Hamilton applied for transfer and served with the 40th for three years before further transfers took him to other units.

The *Citizen* Strike

At 6 P.M. on Thursday, May 30, 1946, Benjamin Paquin, president of the Ottawa local of the I.T.U., handed *Citizen* business manager Jim Kenney written notice that 'under orders' members of the local 'have to consider themselves locked out'.

Friday's *Journal* reported: 'All compositors employed by the Ottawa Citizen went out on strike on Thursday night and there will be no issue of that paper today. . . .' For fifty years, the *Journal*'s story said, the Ottawa newspapers had had joint agreements with the International Typographical Union without dispute. The latest had expired January 1 and a new one was being amicably negotiated when 'proceedings were stopped on orders from headquarters of the International Typographical Union because of the situation in Winnipeg.'

There was, indeed, no issue of the *Citizen* on Friday. The *Citizen*'s publisher would have been happier had there been no *Journal* either. It did not work out that way.

Joint negotiations in Ottawa were even more closely knit than in other newspaper centres. *Citizen* and *Journal* had a single contract with all four mechanical unions – printers, mailers, pressmen, and stereotypers. As noted in the *Journal*'s story, negotiations were under way towards renewal when on January 23 the printers' local notified the *Citizen* (as in the case of the other Southam papers) that it was through collective bargaining and would not resume except under guidance of its international.

On January 24 – the day after notice to the *Citizen* of cessation of bargaining – the *Journal*'s board of directors met. Minutes of the meeting record that they were 'informed of the invitation of the Citizen that the Journal ought to refuse to publish a Journal alone because of (a) the principle involved in Winnipeg, (b) the tradition of joint negotiation with unions in Ottawa.' The decision the board came to was that the *Journal* 'ought to extend as much co-operation as possible to the Citizen, short of cessation of publication.'

The minutes, which E. Norman Smith sent to Harry Southam when the strike developed, noted that 'while the Journal had earlier assured in a general way the Citizen it would support it in any sympathy strike called in Ottawa, this assurance was given without the knowledge subsequently obtained that Southam newspapers were not united on the issue' – evidently a reference to the fact that some Southam papers had accepted conditions of union-law recognition that the Winnipeg publishers had refused to accept.* The *Journal* had been given no opportunity to approve or disapprove of the decision it was asked to support; there were no local issues; and if the *Journal* ceased publication it would reinforce erroneous local suspicions of joint ownership. The *Journal* would be forcing the equivalent of a lockout, voluntarily depriving the capital of a newspaper. Furthermore, *Journal* stock was on public sale; shareholders would deplore a close-down because of an issue in Winnipeg.

In an accompanying memorandum Smith remarked: 'Like the

*The Ottawa agreement with the four unions, incidentally, included a hedged version. The publishers agreed to respect and observe the laws provided that they 'do not conflict with the terms of this contract which have priority and ... that any changes or amendments ... after the signing of this contract which conflict with the terms of this contract or affect wages, hours or working conditions, shall not become operative ... except by mutual consent of both parties. ...' In submitting desired revisions for a 1946 contract the unions had sought no change in this paragraph.

union I also wonder whether the actions of the Southam units can always be considered apart from the affairs of the central Southam company.' Central machinery was used in provision of news services, selling advertising, and purchase of supplies. 'Apparently one of the disadvantages of such co-operative operation is that the Southam company may be held to share responsibility in the labor agreements of its units. Faced with that responsibility the Citizen now asks the Journal to share with it that responsibility to the extent of closing down if a sympathetic strike is called in the Citizen office. To me that appeal does not seem reasonable.'

Commenting on this position, Philip Fisher took a different view of the principle involved: 'The issue which faced the Tribune and which is now facing other Southam newspapers, is not simply any detail of local contracts, even the very important one of recognition of I.T.U. laws. It is a question of submitting to strike pressure from a union which has broken its contracts, broken labor laws of the country, and refused arbitration. . . .' As for Southam company centralization, the group news services were not directed from head office, and individual publishers had complete autonomy on what their papers published; the ad sales offices did not offer joint contracts and each newspaper controlled the advertising it would or would not accept. There was no joint purchase of supplies.

However, any such discussion had by that time become academic. At a board meeting on May 30 *Journal* directors reiterated that the paper would support the *Citizen* editorially and lend all co-operation within its power, short of ceasing to publish. In an editorial June 1 the paper said: 'It is a pity that Ottawa workers should suffer, and an Ottawa business performing a public service, because common ownership happens to make of the Citizen a weapon the I.T.U. chooses to take up against the publishers of the Winnipeg Tribune.'

Two days later the venerable P.D.Ross expressed a personal view (personal because 'some of my valued associates in the production of the Journal do not wish to share responsibility for my views, or some of them') on the editorial page:

> 'The Journal will benefit at least temporarily by the strike in the Citizen business; more readers will come to the Journal for a time. My personal feeling is that I don't want such a condition to continue; I wish the Journal to flourish purely on its own merits, and I think the Citizen clientele should stick loyally to their own, returning to it when the present trouble is over. My sympathy in the present case is with the Citizen – and with the public. . . .'

That same May 30 board meeting had decided that though the

Citizen had 37,000 readers in the Ottawa trading-zone it would limit extra *Journal* sales to 17,000 daily for the first two weeks, would not accept new advertising from exclusively *Citizen* advertisers, would take no new contract classified, but reserve the right to accept such transient classified as offered.

It also authorized business manager E.S.Planta to check on whether any extra newsprint could be got from the *Citizen*'s quota. This drew from H.S.Southam an ironic response. He was unable to persuade himself that the *Citizen* would be justified in agreeing to release any of its quota 'to help the Journal in its present difficulty – that of supplying Citizen homes with copies of the Journal in its effort constructively to help the Citizen defeat the I.T.U.'s sympathetic strike against this newspaper.' The *Citizen*, in order to reclaim its pre-strike position in city circulation and the want ad business, would need all the newsprint it could get and pay for.

This note of confidence was sounded from a position over which a lay observer might have shaken his head. The *Citizen* tried to get out a photo-engraved token edition that day – Monday, June 3 – and failed. Stereotypers, pressmen, and mailers refused to handle struck work and in effect joined the printers' walkout.

There was one haven to windward, given the canvas to beat up to it. The Ottawa Newspapers Subscription Bureau still distributed both papers. The agreement under which it operated stipulated that 'if the total daily circulation of the Citizen and the Journal differ by more than 5 per cent of the paper of larger circulation the two companies shall co-operate as far as is reasonable and possible to promote the smaller circulation. . . . All special efforts of any description, other than an improved newspaper, to cease, however, as soon as the circulation is brought within 5 per cent of the other.' Thus, once back on the street, the *Citizen* had assurance that through the O.N.S.B. agreement it would have help in recouping. The catch was that to promote circulation you must have some to start with. On June 3 the *Citizen* had none.

Two days later, however, volunteer crews made it, with Dick Malone down from Winnipeg to help. On Wednesday, June 5, the *Citizen* ran a four-page edition, mostly from typewritten and engraved copy, with one large area of front-page space devoted to a five-column picture of Ottawa in the spring, a camera study looking down the river from Nepean Point.

By the next Monday it was up to eight pages with some late news in type. On June 13 it began serving all mail subscribers. On June 17 the paper was up to sixteen pages, nearly all in conventional type, had begun to run advertising, and superseded free distribution with a two-cent charge. (The normal rate was three.)

Setting power from friendly printing shops in surrounding districts and the spirit of editorial, advertising, and business staffs figured largely in the recovery. The *Citizen* set up a private telephone wire to one out-of-town shop and installed a staff reporter, equipped with earphones to take down spot news from the *Citizen* and route it to the printers, whence it was driven back to Ottawa and carried through picket-lines in galleys. Specialists turned their hands to all kinds of jobs: ad man Leonard Gates drove paste-ups to Montreal for engraving; women's editor Jean Logan, brought up on a weekly at Pembroke, doubled on a linotype.

The essential thing was to keep a paper on the street. But news enterprise got its share of attention. Joe Louis met Billy Conn in Yankee Stadium the night of June 19 in the first big post-war ring clash. Bob Southam, managing editor since his return from naval service, sent Fred Johnstone by chartered plane to bring back pictures. Next day the *Citizen* scored a front-page photo beat in an eighteen-page paper.

On June 5, the day the *Citizen* got back into circulation, H.S. Southam addressed a letter to striking composing-room employees. The paper would welcome them back as members of the I.T.U. or a Canadian union. If they couldn't come back as union members, the *Citizen* would be glad to have them anyway 'it being understood that any protection or benefits that they have been receiving from the International Typographical Union may be underwritten by the Citizen.' After June 8 their absence from the composing-room would be considered termination of employment.

This brought no response. On June 10 the *Citizen* began to take in new printers who subsequently formed themselves into a local of the Canadian National Printing Trades Union. On June 15 in an advertisement the *Citizen* said it had broken with unions with United States headquarters, but could still use some ex-employees though not 'unless these men tear up their present union cards and leave the union which has brought the present disaster upon them' – a statement that led to threatened prosecution for unfair labor practices, which eventually came to nothing.

On June 27 the pressmen's and mailers' unions returned to work, and on July 8 the stereotypers. Reviewing the situation August 9, H.S.Southam noted that 'the Evening Citizen is almost as good as ever both as to content and appearance, and the Morning Citizen will, it is expected, reappear in its old format in the near future.' It did so on August 20.

The union put up a brisk propaganda battle through its publication the *Typo Times*, pickets, pamphlets, advertisements, and statements. Picket lines reinforced by *Journal* and government printing-bureau printers paraded at the *Citizen*. To the *Journal*'s embarrassment (it protested to the union without much effect) sandwich boards and panel trucks and one horse-drawn wagon bore signs on which contempt for the *Citizen* was coupled with advice to 'Buy a Fair Journal!' The *Typo Times* reiterated: 'The strike in Ottawa, Hamilton, Edmonton, and Vancouver is NOT a sympathetic strike, but a strike for self-preservation.' A typical cartoon depicted a merry-go-round on which the animals were labelled with the names of Southam newspapers, and in reply to the question 'Are you the proprietor of this outfit?' an obese Southam Company replied: 'No, I just takes in the dough – feller named autonomous owns it.'

The strike cut deeply into *Citizen* circulation for a time. In May of 1946 over-all total circulation for all editions showed the *Journal* at 51,673, the *Citizen* at 52,710. For June the figures were *Journal* 65,192, *Citizen* 38,791 (the *Citizen* at this time had not yet resumed its morning edition, had missed four publication days in June and published limited editions on others). Much of the switch-over occurred in the city itself, where traditionally the *Citizen* had a bulge.

The temporary disparity in over-all circulation caused some difficulty for the Ottawa Newspapers Subscription Bureau. The *Journal*'s discontinuance of its morning edition in July of 1949 (the *Citizen* followed this course four years later) also altered the picture. The joint circulation bureau went out of operation December 31, 1949.

From that point on separate circulation departments took charge at the papers. Old patterns seemed to persist. For the week ending November 10, 1951, the *Journal*'s daily circulation stood at 57,950, the *Citizen*'s at 57,526. Audit Bureau of Circulation figures for the six months ending September 30, 1965, showed the papers still almost neck-and-neck in the over-all race: the *Journal* at 73,199, the *Citizen* at 74,976. In the city zone the *Citizen* had reclaimed its old position.

An incidental postscript: in a discussion by letter of the newspaper business with his brother W.J. early in 1951, Harry Southam regretfully remarked: 'The Citizen was forced to open its columns to liquor and patent medicine advertising by the I.T.U. printers when they . . .

nearly put us out of business; that is to say, as a result of that walkout and the reduction of our operating revenues and the skyrocketing of our operating expenditures, we had to accept copy pretty much from any advertiser who was willing to pay for it.'

Transition

A period was closing. Various circumstances – chiefly his own wish – had combined to keep H.S.Southam at his desk long past retirement age. In 1935 the company adopted the principle of retiring chief executives of the operating companies – the divisions – at sixty-five. Two veterans moved out of active service: Burd of the *Province*, then approaching sixty-six and Woods of the *Herald*, sixty-eight. As a sort of gesture of companionship Wilson Southam, then sixty-seven and no longer particularly active in management but still nominally joint managing director of the *Citizen*, retired as an operating official of the paper.

H.S. would reach sixty-five in 1940. When informal discussion of his retirement arose in 1938 he objected to any such idea. Wilson backed him. Apart from Harry's willingness and ability to carry on, preservation of the *Citizen*'s character as a newspaper, as a forum for liberal ideas, a supporter of unorthodox causes, exercised the minds of both brothers. 'Inevitably the Citizen will express the mental outlook of its managing director,' Wilson wrote F.N. 'With anyone else in our organization in charge we would have, most likely, within a year or two, two Ottawa Journals in a field where one amply takes care of that type of thought.' The fact that the man whom head office had in mind for the *Citizen* succession was John Imrie, then battling Social Credit in Alberta, did nothing to make more palatable to the brothers the idea of H.S. stepping out.

The company position was that a principle had been established; Woods and Burd had been retired under it with some reluctance on their part. The whole set-up of the publishing company implied no special privilege to executives who bore the Southam name. Exhaustive argument developed but events rather sidetracked what might have become a bitter impasse. Wartime emergencies delayed retirement of a non-family executive, Nichols of the *Province*, and removed the possibility of immediate critical comparisons. H.S. stayed on. The printers' strike and the fight for recovery followed. By then H.S. had a successor coming up through the ranks in the person of his son Bob. In June of 1953, just entering his seventy-ninth year, he retired.

He had never lost the habit of questioning rigidly conventional views in any phase of existence. At a time when the Iron Curtain was newly frightening he was 'more fearful of clerical Fascism' as it operated in Spain, for instance, and believed that the best way to halt the spread of Communism was to make Christianity and democracy work. To a business acquaintance in 1950 he suggested people were yielding to the temptation to regard Communism as a dynamic cause rather than an effect, and directing all their endeavors against this effect instead of correcting the flaws and weakness of the free enterprise system 'which tend to breed the disease called Communism.'

He still thought the *Christian Science Monitor* the best newspaper in the world, but didn't hesitate to suggest to its editor that his Washington men now and then were letting editorial opinion show in their factual reporting.

A total abstainer from the time of his conversion to Christian Science, he did not question anyone's right to drink. His view of the liquor traffic in later years, as expressed from time to time in the *Citizen*, was that the federal government should take over distilleries, breweries, and wineries, control imports, and remove the profit motive from the trade.

A keen sensitivity to criticism (real and sometimes imagined) remained. In the course of the family's English genealogical researches, Wilson had obtained the issue of armorial bearings in the name of William Southam and his male descendants. This gave rise to a touch of F.N.'s sometimes rather biting humor. He would, he wrote Wilson, 'have preferred to let Father's and the family record stand without either shield or buckler.' As for the sketch of the armorial bearings, the moosehead on the shield might be replaced by an Ogopogo 'indicating that we are a lot of queer fish anyway.' A second jocular reference to Ogopogo led Harry to assume he was being ridiculed for his monetary views. In an eight-page letter he resigned as a director of The Southam Company – a step rescinded in a postscript as the result of some friendly persuasion before the letter was mailed.

While other members of his generation of the family journeyed to California or Florida, Harry liked the Ottawa winters. For him no southern playground could compare with Rockcliffe, where he could see his grandchildren often, and the *Citizen* office. He had been away from the publisher's desk less than a year when on March 27, 1954, he died.

The Looking-Glass

In 1949, three years after Charles Bowman's retirement, the *Citizen* ran his recollections in seventy-one instalments. He called them 'Through The Citizen's Looking-Glass'. This title, he wrote Harry Southam, could be taken as a concession to the paper's critics: 'I seem to recall that Alice through the looking-glass saw everything upside down. . . .'

The *Citizen*'s present-day looking-glass is less inclined than that of Bowman's day to reveal an unexpected image. But the paper diverges at times from official Liberal positions, and its divergence is usually to the radical side of the road, somewhat in the old tradition. The paper campaigned for abolition of capital punishment and criticized the Pearson government for its failure to make it a matter of policy. It questioned Walter Gordon's style of nationalism but supported most of his views on social welfare.

When Finance Minister Mitchell Sharp in September of 1966 announced a one-year postponement of national medicare the *Citizen* dissented, urged reform-minded Liberals to challenge Sharp and the cabinet. In a signed column, editor Christopher Young noted that the Liberal party had always been, among other things, an alliance of social reformers and free-trade conservatives. One tradition had been dominant under Lester Pearson, the other under Louis St. Laurent and the 'managerial Liberalism' of the 1950s. The *Citizen* has rather consistently identified itself with the social-reform tradition.

Young happens to be a nephew of Mrs. Lester Pearson, who is his mother's sister. From time to time this relationship has been cited in the Commons in attempts to discredit *Citizen* positions. Young replied only once. This was in connection not with an editorial attitude but with the accuracy of a news story.

When working for Southam News Services, Young was one of several Canadian reporters covering the Commonwealth Economic Conference at Accra in September of 1961. Stories attributed to Canadian delegates Donald Fleming and George Hees a leading role in Commonwealth opposition to Britain's bid to enter the European Common Market. These reports eventually brought from government sources charges of misrepresentation and distortion of what had actually been said at the conference's closed meetings. In the Commons in January, Fleming returned to the attack: 'The misrepresentation of what happened at Accra has been enormous. It has been said that Canada led a ganging up on the United Kingdom. Nothing could be further from the truth.' He suggested that Young's stories were slanted to suit the Pearson line because of the relationship.

By this time Young had moved up to be editor of the *Citizen*. In his weekly column he quoted from stories sent by other Canadian correspondents. Direct quotations from the ministers' speeches appeared in the same form in several stories. Had *all* the Canadian reporters at Accra misrepresented and distorted the news? 'Since these electrifying quotes appeared in the dispatches of all the Canadian reporters who covered the conference,' Young wrote, 'it must be obvious to the most cynical that we did not make them up.' He then disclosed where they *did* come from: 'The fact is that we were given these statements by assistants to the two Canadian ministers, undoubtedly on the instruction of those ministers.' The complete text of a speech by Hees had been handed out. Facts on Fleming's came from notes taken by his own assistant.

Young's column concluded with a reconstruction of the denouement:

> Meantime in Ottawa, the Prime Minister was not happy. Reaction in Canada had been unfavorable. Urgent long distance phone calls from Ottawa, I was told later, failed to penetrate the incredible confusion of Ghana's telephone exchange. It was only when the conference was over that the ministers learned about their chief's displeasure.
>
> Then began the effort to rewrite history. . . . Rather than announce a change of policy or admit that he went too far, Mr. Fleming says that the reporters were guilty of 'enormous' misrepresentation.
>
> Besides, one of them was related to a Liberal.

The *Citizen*'s latter-day views on Social Credit – as represented in modern party alignments – were expressed when thirty S.C. members, consisting largely of Réal Caouette's following from Quebec, won their way to Parliament in 1962. Commenting on the possibility of their alliance with the minority Conservative government the paper remarked that 'Social Credit's views on financial policy, as far as anyone understands them, give small ground for confidence that such a deal would be in the best interests of the country.' Later after Caouette threatened to 'overthrow the government' unless it followed policies that won his approval, the *Citizen* remarked: 'Mr. Caouette's arrogance is a measure of the man's personality and, by implication, of his party's character. . . . The public can now see this group in better perspective.'

A newspaper's comment on aspects of civic affairs usually stimulates reader interest, particularly when it takes an unequivocal stand. In

1964 the *Citizen* put up a fight against the choice of Confederation Park as the site for the Canadian Centre for the Performing Arts. The paper favored this centennial project, but argued that construction there would destroy the concept of the park as an area lending a touch of grandeur to the capital, an open space near its heart. And why spend money to increase congestion in an area where millions had already been spent to relieve it? It was a losing fight, however. Ottawa found an added fillip of interest in the fact that the co-ordinator for the Centre was publisher R.W.Southam's cousin and fellow-director of Southam Press, Hamilton Southam.

A longer campaign, and one that promised to continue well into the future, has been that for a children's hospital. Early arguments met a simple 'no' from both Queen's Park and the city under Mayor Charlotte Whitton. The fact that 'Charlotte, Lottie, Dr. Whitton, or just that woman' (as the *Citizen* once described her) had been a *Citizen* columnist, when out of office, did nothing for either the mayor or the paper when she occupied the mayor's chair. They were usually sharply opposed, with the *Citizen* often coming out on the short end. However, when Don Reid defeated Charlotte in 1964, the children's hospital was part of his platform. Two years later the Ontario Hospital Services Commission accepted the idea in principle – but set 1975 as the probable building date.

Perhaps the paper's most notable involvement in civic affairs in recent years, however, was essentially a news story – an exposé of corruption in the suburb of Eastview.

In the spring of 1960 a retired contractor named Oscar Perrier tipped reporter James Quigg that something was doing. The *Citizen* assigned veteran crime reporter Joe Finn (son of D'Arcy), who was told by Perrier that he and other businessmen had formed a Citizen's League, had found shortages in municipal funds, and were drawing up a petition to demand investigation by the province. The *Citizen* took it from there. Toronto sent a police inspector, a commission looked into Eastview's finances, the municipal treasurer (she had apparently pocketed most of the parking-meter revenue) went to jail, and Perrier won the mayoralty in a landslide overturn.

Now and then an old habit of tossing fire-crackers breaks out. One incident occurred early in the flag debate of 1964.

Discussion of a distinctive Canadian flag was nothing new to the *Citizen*. In December of 1946 it had run a series of articles by D.F. Stedman, a student of heraldry, in which he developed a flag incorporating elements of both the Union Jack and the Tricolor. This was an adaptation of the lower left canton of the Union Jack with the

white diagonal of St. Andrew widened to represent the northland and
the Eskimos as its original owners, the red diagonal of St. Patrick
widened to recognize the Indians, and part of St. George's cross and
its edging of white included to represent, with the basic blue background, the Tricolor of France. Stedman dismissed suggestions for
a maple leaf flag because of the limited area in which maples grow.
The *Citizen* printed the heraldic argument and Stedman's conclusions in a booklet distributed to senators, M.P.s, members of provincial legislatures, and newspaper editors.

By 1964 however the paper had other ideas. On Sunday, March
17, Prime Minister Pearson told a national convention of the Royal
Canadian Legion at Winnipeg his reasons for proposing a new and
distinctive flag for Canada and was roundly booed. The *Citizen* had
on its staff Rusins Kaufmanis, an Estonian who had studied drawing
in a Russian prison camp and later in Canada, and whose pictured
line could be as caustic as Bowman's in type. At a *Citizen* editorial
conference Ben Malkin (a one-time sergeant of artillery in the Italian
campaign, incidentally) came up with an idea for Rusins, which duly
took shape: two smirking veterans at a drinking table in a Legion
hall, with Pearson visible through a window, maple leaf flag under
arm. The caption: 'I guess we showed him, didn't we?'

Mayor Whitton, who regarded the proposed flag as 'a white badge
of surrender', made the *Citizen*'s front page next day. She had wired
the Legion expressing 'the chagrin and shame . . . Ottawa residents
overwhelmingly share at the grossly insulting caricature of the
Legion.'

The cartoon along with many and strong views on the flag issue
set off a barrage of letters to the editor that overflowed to a special
page for days.

The cartoon, the *Citizen* said editorially, was a statement against
humbug. 'The Royal Canadian Legion members wear a maple leaf
cap-badge, veterans of World War II possess maple leaf discharge-
buttons, yet the Legion rejects the maple leaf as a Canadian symbol.
. . .' A few days earlier the paper had stated its position: 'The whole
medieval business of heraldry strikes us as a lot of nit-picking, hair-
splitting inconsequential nonsense. . . . Surely a symbol need only be
a means of identification, reasonably pleasing to the eye, and having
a rational link, if possible, with the political, geographic, or occupa-
tional circumstances it is supposed to represent.' As for surrender:
surrender to whom, to what? The maple leaf flag recognized no
element of superiority in any racial group. 'It recognizes only the
nation and the equality of all its parts.'

One of the many letter-writing dissenters was D.F.Stedman. 'The maple leaf', the heraldic expert wrote, 'is used because it is supposed to grow here. True, it does, in six per cent of the country, and has leaves half the time.'

But the maple leaf it was to be.

10
The Urgent
West

The last of the 1920s were expansive years in Canada. The country set up legations in Paris and Tokyo in 1928, extending a practice already established at Washington. On January 28 the London *Times* commented: 'The international position of Canada is now, of course, fully recognized.' Mackenzie King travelled to Paris with Frank Kellogg and on August 27 signed for Canada a document that brought fifty-nine nations into a pact renouncing war. 'A new date in the history of mankind', Aristide Briand called it.

The country's railways set records for freight hauled and revenue earned, employment was at its top, and active stocks on Canadian exchanges were worth – so the indices said – $1,000,000,000 more at the end of the year than at the beginning. Proposed development of a St. Lawrence deep waterway was much in the news.

The West shared a general optimism. In Alberta, crop values were down from the 1927 record but stockyard business was up. Eyes were turned to the North, to the hard-wheat country of the Peace and beyond to the ore lurking in mountain crevices and under the treeless plains of the barren lands.

For a year or two now in that sweep of Arctic and sub-Arctic country the airplane had been tentatively edging in on the canoe and dog team. In 1926 Doc Oakes and friends pioneered at Sioux Lookout in northern Ontario a flying service for mining-men that blossomed into Western Canada Airways. In 1928 Punch Dickins flew into the farther north-west.

If drama were needed to fix continental attention on the North, and the airplane in relation to it, 1929 supplied it.

On New Year's Day a northern mail carrier halted his team at the telegraph office in Peace River town, 300 miles north of Edmonton.

He was twelve days out from Fort Vermilion, nearly another 300 miles down the frozen Peace, and he carried a message for Dr. M.R. Bow, deputy minister of health in Edmonton from Dr. H.A.Hamman at Little Red River, fifty miles beyond that. Written December 18, it was an appeal for help. Diphtheria had broken out at Little Red River. Already the Hudson's Bay factor there was dead. Late in the day the message reached Bow over the wire from Peace River. He appealed to Commercial Airways, which then consisted of Wilfred (Wop) May, Vic Horner, their partner Cy Becker, and one Avro Avian. That night the *Journal*'s radio station, CJCA, broadcast messages to points along the route: get landing places cleared.

Next day the paper front-paged the take-off: TINY AEROPLANE IN RACE AGAINST DEATH TO NORTH. In their open-cockpit, seventy-five-horsepower plane, May and Horner took off at 12:45 P.M. for country where no plane had ever been. They carried a thirty-pound parcel of toxoid and antitoxin, wrapped in rugs and warmed by charcoal. That afternoon they flew through bitter cold under low cloud to a strip staked out on ice at McLennan Junction. Next morning they hopped to Peace River, refuelled, and were off to Fort Vermilion. There, stiff with cold, they were lifted from the plane.

Other flights were in the news that month. The army monoplane *Question Mark* set a record of 150 hours in a refuelling stunt over Los Angeles. Lady Bailey flew around the African continent. In Canada nothing quite touched the May-Horner mercy flight; 10,000 Albertans turned out to welcome the fliers and the little biplane back from the North.

That fall another story of northern flying held the continent in suspense. On the evening of September 8 a party of eight headed by Colonel C.D.H.MacAlpine took off from Baker Lake in two single-engined planes, their object to sweep westward by stages across the barrens to Fort Norman on the Mackenzie. They simply disappeared. Through late September the search-planes fanned out from Baker Lake and Stoney Rapids, piloted by men whose names read like a who's who of the bush and the North: Dickins, Blanchet, Hollick-Kenyon, Brown, Brintnell, Cruikshank, Sutton, Spence. Frost ended the float-plane season and with the freeze-up they were off again.

Then on November 4 a radio operator at Churchill picked a faint message from the air: 'MacAlpine and party found. All well. Located at Cambridge Bay.' Grounded by lack of fuel, they had spent five weeks in a moss-chinked stone hut waiting for the freeze-up, and trekked with the help of Eskimos across Dease Strait to a Hudson's Bay post.

The air search in a sense had failed. It had had its own moments of suspense; at times pilots scanned the tundra for lost fellow-searchers. Two pilots and their mechanics spent a fortnight in the open in bitter cold until brought to safety by dog team. But the spirit of the endeavor caught the public mind. The *Journal* bore down hard on a theme, often repeated in its emphasis on the opening of the North: the need for more radio stations, more emergency landing fields equipped with gas and oil.

Before the year ended, organized and scheduled flying had come to that desolate land with establishment of airmail from Fort Mc-Murray along the 1700-mile route to Aklavik.

The fortunes of aerial prospectors varied. The October market-crash crimped exploration. But one reconnaissance at least had a significance that could scarcely be foreseen. From the air in the fall of 1929 Gilbert LaBine saw orange streaks on the southern shore of Great Bear Lake. Next spring he went back for samples from the rock. Eldorado and Port Radium were on the way.

Early in 1929 a story of another kind caught the interest of Canadians. On the night of January 10 Charles John Perceval, ninth Earl of Egmont in the Irish peerage and Baron Lovell and Holland in the House of Lords, died at his Hampshire seat. The intriguing angle was this: 'Frederick Joseph Trevelyan Perceval, a distant relative, who resides at Priddis, Alberta, succeeds to the title.'

The *Herald* hurried a staff-man to Priddis, twenty miles southwest of Calgary. There Frederick Perceval and his fifteen-year-old son Fred lived in a two-room log ranch-house, with family portraits on the walls and fifty head of cattle and thirty horses on the range. Perceval had left England as a boy, come out to Iowa and up to Alberta. He had married a Montreal girl who died in 1916, leaving him with a son. The *Herald* found the news hadn't thrown the new earl into any ecstasy of excitement: 'On the contrary it may be a moot point, after a residence of about 26 years in the Alberta foothills, which he has learned to love as only an old-timer can, whether he will leave its undulating hills and dales to don a coronet and ermine.'

Frederick Perceval decided to return to England for a year. The year stretched out and the story developed. Others purporting to be relatives entered claims to the title, claims that failed but irritated. The new earl decided to sell out and travel.

In April of 1932 Lukin Johnston reported: 'While he awaits a purchaser for the castle at Ringwood, Hampshire, Britain's loneliest peer lives in his kitchen, his sole companion being his 18-year-old son, Viscount Perceval. The earl does his own cooking, for they have no domestic help, and only half a dozen men are employed to keep in order the estate of 500 acres of pine woods and fields through which the little river Avon peacefully flows. . . .' A month later the tenth earl died after a motor crash.

That summer his son returned to the province of his birth and to happier days; marriage to a Calgary girl, and a new career that would bring him eventually to 5,000 acres west of Nanton. A reticent man with an enviable place in the province's ranching life, in later years he would seldom appear in the news except as host of the local 4H club or the purchaser of registered shorthorns.

Late in that good year of 1929 a political development heightened for Albertans their cheerful sense of progress. At Ottawa on December 14 Alberta and Manitoba took over their natural resources – Crown lands, mines, minerals, and resultant royalties – which had been federally administered since the erection of the provinces. The *Journal* congratulated Brownlee on the Alberta settlement in effusive terms. He and his associates, the paper said, had two great achievements to their credit coming up to the 1930 election: the resources settlement and sale of northern railways to the CPR and CNR. It was a better government than its predecessor. But there was still that 'unsound basis' of class. The *Journal* urged a union government.

Developments were soon to come that in cumulative effect would go far beyond anything mendable by such a course. But in 1930 the U.F.A. had strength enough to hold off the old-line parties and settle in for another round.

The Vast Anomaly

The surging 1920s went out like a rushing fall in the tide of life. By 1932 the level was at its lowest.

Writing to Philip Fisher early in February 1933, Imrie of the *Journal* used a practical example to illustrate the plight of the West:

> Suppose a farmer in the Edmonton district borrowed on January 1, 1930, $2,000 at eight per cent. The principal was the cash equivalent of 1,990 bushels of wheat and the annual interest charge the cash equivalent of 158 bushels. On January 31, 1933, it would have taken 7,107 bushels to repay the principal and 571 bushels to pay the annual interest charges.

The Calgary *Herald*'s front page for Monday, August 1, 1932, reflected the temper of the times. Paraguay and Bolivia were mobilizing. Berlin reported seven dead in the riotous aftermath of Reichstag elections that gave Hitler's Nazis their biggest following yet. On Parliament Hill Commonwealth statesmen talked imperial trade. The top story told of a conference of a different kind. In an abandoned Ottawa garage 700 delegates of the 'national conference of unemployment councils' – many of whom had ridden the rods to get there – had framed their depression demands: cash relief, seven-hour work-days, repeal of taxes and tariffs on life's necessities, exemption of all poor farmers from taxes, debts, and rent.

The account of still another gathering, which would have some continuing significance in Canadian life, appeared on page 9 under a two-column italic heading: *Move to Establish Co-operative State Launched in Calgary.*

> Co-operative Commonwealth Federation (Farmer-Labor-Socialist), an organization for the purpose of establishment in Canada of a co-operative commonwealth, was launched Monday at a joint meeting of Western Conference of Labor political parties and the United Farmers of Alberta. . . .
> On Sunday, a meeting of the Western Conference and the United Farmers of Canada, Saskatchewan section, had agreed to form a commonwealth federation, which will now be merged into the new organization and name. . . .

Elsewhere on the page appeared reports of speeches by J.S.Woodsworth ('Says Statesmen of World Unable to Solve Crisis') and M.J. Coldwell ('Humanity Subordinated to Bonded Interests').

Editorially the *Herald* was a bit curmudgeonly: 'The new organization with the imposing name may be more pink than red at the outset but it is apparent that Russia has provided the inspiration. . . .'

Still, somewhere there had to be an answer to the world's troubles. Bennett of Canada declared international finance had broken down. Bruce of Australia called the position of industry in relation to humanity a challenge to civilization. In an editorial August 20, 1932, the *Herald* noted these views and quoted with approval an Ottawa *Citizen* editorial calling for reform of the monetary system.

> The present situation [the Herald said] is a vast anomaly. Facilities for production, and production itself, have attained an efficiency that should be able to provide a higher standard of living to a greater number of people than ever before; and yet the people perish because they cannot buy and the producer perishes because he cannot sell. Precedent and tradition, along with the entrenched rights of vested finance, hold the world in thrall while somewhere close by there is a formula, involving perhaps sacrifice of previous convictions and sacri-

fice of gain, that would loosen the floodgates of prosperity and bring comfort and happiness to the millions. . . .

Somewhere close by there *was* a formula, soon to enchant most of Alberta's people. In the *Herald*'s view it was not one that would loosen the floodgates of prosperity.

The well-being of newspapers naturally ebbs and flows with the fortunes of their readers and advertisers. Both the *Herald* and the *Journal* were feeling the pinch. In 1929 the *Herald* made $300,000 before taxes. In 1932 the figure was down to less than one-sixth of that.

In May of 1931 the street delivery price of wheat in the Calgary area was thirty-seven cents. The *Herald* came up with a subscription scheme for its farm readers that was in part a gamble, in part a sharing with the farmers of the low buying-power of their chief product. The *Herald* offered a year's subscription for ten bushels of No. 1 Northern (or equivalent in lower grades) delivered at the nearest elevator. Since the cash subscription rate was $8.00 a year, and wheat was well below eighty cents a bushel, farm readers got a bargain. The practice continued for years until higher grain prices ended its advantages.

In the fall of 1933 the *Journal* tried the same scheme for a short but effective period. The circumstances were intriguing. At the end of 1932 the *Journal*'s circulation was just over 30,000 compared to 14,500 for Charles Campbell's *Bulletin*. But by mid-1933 the *Journal* had dropped 1,000, and the *Bulletin* picked up 2,000. Campbell had a theory of newspaper operation in depression times: fight R.B. Bennett, fight the banks, advocate fiat money and debt cancellation and vast public works.

All this appeared to be working for the *Bulletin*. Another element was saturation coverage of a public sensation. Back in the spring of 1931 the Edmonton newspapers reported briefly the fact that Oran L. McPherson, minister of public works in the U.F.A. government, had been granted a divorce from his wife Cora. In July of 1932 he married the former wife of the co-respondent. Early in 1933 Cora McPherson moved to upset the divorce decree, claiming conspiracy and collusion in one of a series of actions that eventually failed. Throughout three weeks in May the *Bulletin* ran the evidence verbatim – fifteen to twenty-five columns a day. The *Journal* carried a condensed report of four to six columns.

Imrie felt the *Journal* had lost ground to sensationalism. He decided to see what a bargain wheat-rate would do. It added 1,532 new subscribers in seventeen days.

The Scandals and the Press

The McPherson case had been spectacular enough. On September 22, 1933, the *Journal* carried a story that outdid it in immediate impact and eventual effect:

BROWNLEE IS CHARGED
IN SEDUCTION ACTION;
PREMIER MAKES DENIAL

The story summarized a statement of claim by Allan MacMillan of Edson and his daughter Vivian asking damages for seduction. As outlined the thing was straight out of Edwardian melodrama. The Premier, the claim went, while being entertained in 1930 by MacMillan, then mayor of Edson, had persuaded Vivian to come to Edmonton and work for the government. He had then seduced her and 'laughed at her old-fashioned scruples' and at various times over the course of years had insisted on her living in his house.

Brownlee was in Ottawa. The *Journal* reached him there for his denial – 'not a word of truth in the allegations' – and his statement that the case would enable him to come to grips with rumors. He would defend the action to the limit and hope to show 'the real cause behind it'.

Rumors persisted. Five days later Provincial Treasurer R.G.Reid at Macleod blasted 'the whispering campaign that has been going on in the province . . . against the moral character of members of the government.'

There were also counter-rumors. Through their lawyers the Mac-Millans denied suggestions that their action was the result of a political plot.

The Brownlee case came to trial next June with day after day of sensational evidence. This time the *Journal* went all out, employing a battery of court reporters and running up to four pages daily. But still with discretion: Imrie's word to the desk was that the stuff should be fit for a twelve-year-old girl to read, but must make clear to adults exactly what happened. These ticklish objectives were apparently achieved.

On Saturday, June 30, the *Journal* got ready to extra. Mechanical crews stood by. At 8:45 P.M. the verdict came in: $10,000 to Vivian MacMillan and $5,000 to her father – a verdict Justice Ives disagreed with and refused to enter pending further thought. That was the hitch that snagged the extra. A senior editor refused to believe in the possibility of this judicial position. While argument proceeded the *Bulletin* hit the street. The *Journal* was twenty minutes late.

The incident raised a fast burn in *Journal* staffers. Legislature reporter Tom Mansell, assistant city editor Don MacDougall, and Homer Ramage conspired. They would come back with a Sunday extra. Based on what? Would Brownlee resign? What Mansell had to do was confirm the intention. He did so from sources unrevealed. The extra ran.

A slight sequel followed. Someone at the *Bulletin* stirred a group of clergymen into charging the *Journal* with breach of the Lord's Day Act. The charge was withdrawn in police court and Imrie distributed $25 bonuses for the enterprise that led to it.

Imrie had come to think highly of Brownlee. The *Journal* commented that after the verdict there was nothing he could do but leave, and added: 'Albertans as a whole must regret keenly the circumstances under which it has become necessary for Mr. Brownlee to vacate his post and at the same time they must recognize the ability and the zeal that he has brought to the discharge of his public duties. . . .'

There were years to go before the end of it. Four days after the jury's verdict Justice Ives finally refused to accept it and dismissed the case. In February 1935, the appellate division of the Alberta Supreme Court dismissed an appeal by the MacMillans. Early in 1937 the Supreme Court of Canada restored the $10,000 award to the girl, a decision eventually confirmed by the Privy Council.

At the time of the MacMillan statement of claim, Brownlee forecast (to Imrie in confidence) drastic changes in legislation covering the rights of the press in such matters. In April of 1935 the government introduced two new bills – one to amend the libel and slander act, the other to regulate the publication of reports of civil cases.

The libel and slander bill as originally drafted, among other things limited privilege (in relation to time of publication) to reports of publicly heard proceedings if published 'in the next issue of the newspaper published after the day upon which the proceedings . . . were heard, or within 10 days thereafter, whichever period is the shorter.'

The act regulating publication of civil matters prohibited all but the briefest facts about marital cases and banned publication before trial in any civil case of 'anything in any statement of claim, statement of defence or other pleading' other than 'names and addresses of the parties and their solicitors; and a concise statement of the nature of the claim or of the defence . . . in general words. . . .'

Though the government claimed the bills had nothing to do with the McPherson and Brownlee cases, it could not erase the conviction that the wide publicity given these sensational suits had brought the legislation into being.

This belief was certainly not lessened by an incident that occurred during discussions by newspaper men with the cabinet and a legislative committee about its implications. After a hearing in mid-April McPherson swung at publisher Charlie Campbell of the *Bulletin* and knocked him down.

Imrie argued that wording of the time-limit provision in the libel and slander act amendment would prevent publication in an afternoon paper of court proceedings that morning. The ten-day limitation would make impossible publication of Privy Council decisions received by mail. The bill was revised to provide privilege if 'the report is published contemporaneously with the proceedings . . . or within 30 days thereafter.'

The government also inserted in the bill regulating reports of civil cases a clause specifying that it not apply to proceedings started before its coming into force – which cleared the way for coverage of future developments in the McPherson and Brownlee cases, both then under appeal. But the restrictive principles remained to affect the future.

The bills passed April 20, probably without rousing much real interest in the general public. For already political ferment of a new kind excited the province. The bills of 1935, as threats to the press, scarcely rated with proposals that eventually would spice the brew.

God's Economy

On Saturday, February 18, 1933, the *Herald* ran on page 3 two-thirds of a column under the heading RECOMMENDS DOUGLAS SYSTEM AS CURE FOR ECONOMIC SITUATION:

> 'Credit Power for Democracy' is the slogan of the Douglas system of economics and this 'is the only system that will pull the province, or the world, out of the present situation,' stated William Aberhart, B.A., addressing a crowd of 1,500 persons Friday evening. . . .
> 'Every citizen should be able to secure food, clothing and shelter from the country he lives in,' stated the speaker, 'and the present economic situation under which we are now living is unable to provide British fair play to those who are living here.'

The Douglas plan, the story continued, 'recommends that the province, or state, be viewed by its citizens as a gigantic joint-stock company with the natural resources of the province behind its credit.' Bona fide citizens would be shareholders 'entitled to basic dividends sufficient to provide the bare necessities of life for each individual and his family.'

Up to this time reports of William Aberhart's activities had appeared mainly in space devoted to church and school. For eight years the principal of Crescent Heights high school had broadcast on Sunday afternoons from the Calgary Prophetic Bible Institute, his personal creation. At about the time in 1932 that James S. Woodsworth and M.J.Coldwell were rallying farmers and laborites to establish a co-operative state, a fellow-teacher converted Aberhart to belief in the theories of C.H.Douglas, and that autumn he had begun to weave them into his religious broadcasts. Now in response to growing interest he was speaking on Social Credit outside the scope of the Institute.

It would have taken a prescient reader to find in reports of Aberhart lectures during that winter of 1933 any hint of the tumult ahead. Even through the following summer as listener-interest fused with his own enthusiasm, and he and a graduate of the Bible Institute, Ernest Manning, spoke through southern Alberta, it seems evident that neither the old-line politicians nor the newspapers sensed the sweep of the movement then gathering. But by January of 1934 Social Credit had reached the front page. Aberhart was called to Edmonton to outline his ideas to the legislature; so was Douglas, on his way back to England from a Pacific tour. On the night of April 7 the British engineer spoke to thousands in the Calgary armories and drew a page and a half in the *Herald*.

The relationship between Douglas's theories and Aberhart's adaptation was already in question, but not the enthusiasm of growing sections of the province's people, or their devotion to the eloquent and evangelical figure whose gospel promised release from poverty. Hunger and debt, scandals that touched their current leaders, the gleam of a new economic doctrine infused with the old-time religion and the magnetism of Aberhart: all combined to roll up marching waves of emotional purpose.

When in January of 1935 a U.F.A. convention refused to include Aberhart Social Credit in its election platform, it fixed the certainty of a Social Credit political party. The *Herald* greeted this development with an editorial criticizing the blending of religion with political appeal and the Aberhart interpretation generally:

The Herald does not believe in the Aberhart Social Credit proposition nor does it greatly respect the manner in which it has been promoted up to the present time. The mixture of religion and politics is never agreeable to the thoughtful observer, and it cannot be doubted that the leader of this movement has used and is using a tabernacle built in the name of religion to promote what is rapidly becoming a political party. . . .

Major C.H.Douglas . . . has worked out what he considers to be at least a partial remedy for the undoubted ills of today. Whether one agrees with him or not one may respect his sincerity and his logic. The Alberta application of his theory seems to be degenerating into a series of political catch-cries by which the voters would be virtually bribed into voting for representatives of a policy which they really do not understand, and the application of which in practical life has never been defined. . . .

Aberhart replied with a continuing attack on the *Herald* that reached its height in a Sunday broadcast April 28: 'Some of the citizens of this province cannot distinguish falsity from truth. I am cancelling my subscription tomorrow. What about yours?' The *Herald* made a point: 'Is everyone opposed to the political opinions and plans of Mr. Aberhart to be boycotted?'

The movement had grown with almost no press support except for the weekly *Social Credit Chronicle*, founded midway through 1934. The Ottawa *Citizen* was far away, its voice scarcely heard in the West. In Alberta the dailies reported Social Credit factually on news pages and did their best to dissect it in editorials. Least critical for a time was the *Albertan*, but as the election campaign gathered strength it pitched in on the Liberal side.

Aberhart continued to blast away at the *Herald* and newspapers generally as tools of the 'Fifty Big Shots' who ran Canada.

The uncertain relationship between Douglas, the original theorist, and Aberhart, apostle of a variation for Alberta that seemed to be his own brand, continued to be a point of attack for critics of the movement.

On April 3, the day before the Calgary Social Credit convention of 1935 opened, the *Herald* printed a letter from the Social Credit Secretariat in London setting forth that this body 'believes that the function of democracy is to demand results, not to indicate methods.' This was Douglas doctrine, under which legislatures would simply appoint experts to carry out the people's will. The letter went further in stating that Douglas was prepared to advise any government that had 'a mandate to deal with the existing financial system' but that so far only one proposal, an interim one for New Zealand in 1933, had carried his authority. This seemed to disapprove both Aberhart's proposals and the direct political action in which Social Credit in Alberta was now involved.

Opportunities to develop this theme increased with Douglas's second arrival in Edmonton, to advise the U.F.A. government on financial reform and on the extent to which his proposals were practical in the province. It has generally been assumed that the government's hope was a disavowal of Aberhart and a statement that Social Credit could not be applied provincially. Douglas himself later wrote to Wilson Southam: 'You will realize that I was fully conscious that my visit to Edmonton . . . was engineered for purely party purposes, and was intended to weaken Mr. Aberhart's position. It did not appear to me to be in the general interest to allow this scheme to mature. . . .'

It did not mature. Douglas wrote a report in which he confined himself to 'possible methods and strategy with regard to the preliminary object, that of obtaining access to the public credit', but felt there was room for 'considerable action on the part of the province without placing the province in danger of the invocation of legal sanctions against it. . . .' He did not mention Aberhart at all.

Social Crediters claimed Douglas's report showed his plan could be operated provincially. Opponents claimed just the opposite. Attorney-General J.F.Lymburn expressed the government's view: The Douglas idea was predicated on the power of a state to issue 'real effective purchasing-power or money', and the government of Alberta had no such power.

In effect, all this was irrelevant. Aberhart had won Alberta before Douglas's arrival. Anything that happened thereafter could only strengthen the emotional bond.

As the August 22 election approached, the *Journal* took a realistic view. The Social Credit proposals were bound to dominate the whole election. Those undertaking to put them into effect would find themselves faced with insuperable obstacles and would be compelled to abandon the attempt. But this was no reason to take lightly the possibility of their winning the election.

After the event, with fifty-six Social Credit members in a house of sixty-three, the *Herald* saw the result as a popular revolt against depression and the old political parties, not wholly inspired by the lure of monthly dividends: 'As a result of almost two years of intensive propaganda, with a hymn as a battle cry and a pulpit as a forum, the new economic gospel fell on receptive ears. It appealed to the discouraged and the discontented, and because of its origin it was believed in by a people wanting to believe.'

Elect Manning, Irwin, Anderson, Bowlen, Gostick, Hugill

Today's Weather
FORECAST—Cloudy and unsettled.
TEMPERATURE—Calgary, 5 a.m. 47,
August 24—Sunrise 6:28; Sunset 7:42.

THE CALGARY DAILY HERALD

5 O'CLOCK EDITION

FIFTY-SECOND YEAR   CALGARY   LOCAL   CALGARY, ALBERTA, FRIDAY, AUGUST 23, 1935   ○ ○ ○ 24 PAGES

SOCIAL CREDIT LANDSLIDE

MUCH GRAIN FORECAST TO GRADE LOW

C.N. Survey Indicates Wide Variation In Yield

WEATHER HOLDS UP HARVESTING

Five Bus. to Bumper Crop Prediction For Alberta

(Special Dispatch to the Herald)
WINNIPEG, Aug. 23.—Cool weather with varying amounts of precipitation has interrupted harvesting operations in many districts, according to the weekly report of the Canadian National Railways.

New Party Registers Overwhelming Win Provincial Election

Alberta to Have First Social Credit Gov't in World — Cabinet Ministers Go Down to Defeat as U.F.A. Administration Routed; Only Hon. J. F. Lymburn Stands Chance of Retaining Seat.

Opposition May Total Four

FLASH

The standing at 1 p.m. was:
Social Credit elected 56
Liberals elected 2
Conservatives elected 1
Social Credit leading 21
U.F.A. leading 1
Total seats 63

(By Canadian Press)
EDMONTON, Aug. 23.—Alberta will have a Social Credit government, headed by William Aberhart, the 57-year-old Calgary founder of the Alberta Social Credit League.

In its initial bid for power, and the first time the electors of a Canadian province have ever been offered a social credit administration, the league candidates made a sweep of the rural ridings. They were also among the leaders in the proportional representation count proceeded at an early hour this morning in the cities.

Premier Reid, head of the U.F.A. government since 1934, when he succeeded Hon. J. E. Brownlee in the premiership, was defeated by social credit in his riding of Vermilion. He has represented Vermilion in the legislature since 1921, the year the U.F.A. defeated the Liberal regime which had held power from the formation of the province in 1905.

Reid Likely To Remain in Power Until Sept. 13

EDMONTON, Aug. 23.—The Reid government will remain in office until the present Alberta legislature is dissolved...

Constituency Figures

LEGEND
U.F.A.—United Farmers of Alberta.
L.—Liberal.
C.—Conservative.
S.C.—Alberta Social Credit League.
Ind.—Independent.
Ind.-Lab.—Independent Labor.
Ind.-Lib.—Independent Liberal.
Lab.—Labor.
C.C.F.—Co-operative Commonwealth Federation.
*Member of Last House.

New Leader at Home

The above pictures, taken this morning show the home of William Aberhart, Calgary, leader of the Social Credit party and his wife. Top left, the large principal political leader is depicted below in the garden.
—Photos by Herald Staff Reporter.

CRISIS LOOMS IN BELGRADE

Gov't Grants Rail Orders

Rush Empire Defences in East Africa

Export Britain Plans Speed Reinforcement Of Troops

LONDON, Aug. 23. (A.P.)—Armed forces...

Ottawa Fears Alberta Economy and Industry Endangered By Scheme

4 SOCIAL CREDIT, CONSERVATIVE AND LIBERAL WIN HERE

Record Vote of 41,193 Cast in City Election As E. C. Manning, Chief Lieutenant for Social Credit Leader, Heads Poll.

Eliminate Labor Candidates

On the crest of the wave that swept through the length and breadth of the province, Calgary section of the provincial social credit party elected four out of six candidates in the provincial elections held Thursday, one Conservative and one Liberal candidate also were elected.

The new M.L.A.'s for Calgary are E. C. Manning, Fred Anderson, Mrs. E. G. Gostick and John W. Hugill, K.C., all members of the social credit party; John Irwin, Conservative, and John J. Bowlen, Liberal.

ALBERTA COAL COMMISSIONER ON WAY HERE

Moose Jaw Quits Sask. Rugby Union

B.C. BANDITS BREAK CORDON

The Weather

Mostly Fair

SOCIAL CREDIT TOUR PLANNED

Don't Wait For a Tenant

You can't afford to waste time and lose money just waiting. Get a tenant now any other people are getting them every day ... with a Herald Want Ad. People are moving now. Don't delay. Call on ad-taker.

PHONE M89

The situation that faced Alberta newspapers was new and troubling. Government hostility to a dissenting press was nothing unusual but here there were special circumstances. No election had ever aroused such animosities. Families were split, neighbor refused to speak to neighbor. And the government elected by 164,000 of 302,000 voting Albertans regarded the newspapers as 'mad dogs in our midst'. It had been elected by people in the grip of a special dedication. Would this spill over into mass anger against the press?

Whatever else the newspapers of Alberta had to lose, their chief danger was loss of public goodwill. The best they could hope to do was report the news impartially and, without deserting principle, discuss government performance in a manner least likely to invite active resentment. This the *Journal* and the *Herald* tried to do. Their discussions of performance certainly did not satisfy the government. But over the long haul the public continued to read.

There were some lighter moments. Leigh Spencer (soon to take over from Woods as *Herald* publisher) called a staff meeting the day after the election. A man with whom the paper had carried on a bitter fight for months was destined to run the province. Did anyone have personal contact? Was anyone *persona grata*? Reporter Fred Kennedy remarked hesitantly that he had a date for breakfast with Aberhart next day. As a member of the separate-school board, he belonged to a committee of which the premier-elect was chairman. This chance circumstance put Kennedy into the press gallery at Edmonton and made him the *Herald*'s liaison man with Aberhart for eight years. It was not entirely a peaceful relationship.

Kennedy frequently phoned Aberhart from Calgary. A story still circulating at the *Herald* a generation later concerns one such call. Aberhart lost his temper and began to shout. Kennedy yelled back. Editor Robert Somerville, drifting into the newsroom, inquired of news editor Gerald Brawn what the commotion was about. Brawn cautioned him: 'Sh-h-h-h . . . Kennedy's talking to the Premier at Edmonton.' 'Well,' Somerville asked, 'why the hell doesn't he use the telephone?'

But in general there was little cause for laughter.

One of the steps recommended by Douglas in his report to the previous government had been provision of 'a news circulation system under the unchallengeable control of the province, particularly in regard to radio facilities of sufficient power to cover a wide geographical area'. Did this mean a government propaganda system paralleling existing news outlets, or government control of the established outlets themselves? Or both? These questions now had become pertinent.

Three days before the election Aberhart had announced that, if victorious, the Social Credit party would get into the publishing field itself. Through the months thereafter reports circulated that a deal was on for Social Credit purchase of the *Albertan*.

Founded in 1902, this property had been run for years by William Davidson, at one time a Liberal member of the legislature, and had come under sole ownership of George M. Bell in 1927. Laboring under the increasing handicaps common to morning newspapers, it had not prospered. In fact from May 1932 to April 1934, under a deal between Woods and Bell, the *Herald* had contributed $2,000 a month to its morning rival to keep the field stabilized: in plainer language, to keep the *Albertan* in the morning field and out of direct competition with the *Herald*. This ended when in May of 1934 Bell switched to evening publication and cut subscription rates. When after seven lean months as an evening the *Albertan* went back to the morning field the *Herald*'s contribution resumed at $1,250 a month under a two-year agreement.

This was the situation when on January 15, 1936, the *Albertan* came out with a front-page headline: PURCHASE OF THE ALBERTAN MADE. An announcement from Bell reported completion of negotiations for sale of the paper and its radio station CJCJ to a new company. The paper would continue to publish in the morning and would 'enjoy the confidence of the government as well as being the official organ of the Social Credit party.'

The arrangement actually was an agreement to sell rather than a completed purchase. A preferred-stock issue of $700,000 was to provide $100,000 for current expenses and $600,000 to Bell for the property, the whole deal to be closed within a fifteen-month period during which Bell would keep control. The hope was to sell enough stock to Social Credit groups and individuals to make it stick. It did not turn out that way,* but the *Albertan*'s switch to Social Credit gave *Herald* circulation-men something to think about. The *Herald* dropped by 900 almost at once, though the loss was soon retrieved.

Though he now had a newspaper that not only reported Social

---

*George Bell's death two months after reaching the agreement did not affect it; but stock-selling efforts failed. At the end of the fifteen-month period about one-sixth of the purchase price had been paid. After various extensions the arrangement lapsed in 1939. Eventually the *Albertan* came under control of George Bell's son Max, as part of a colorful complex of newspapers, oil wells, and horses, and later became a division of F.P. Publications, the group formed by Bell and Victor Sifton.

Credit but backed it on the editorial page, the new premier of Alberta continued to blast the press in general. With political activity now centred at Edmonton, Imrie and the *Journal* were under the gun.

Imrie, long a student of economics and national as well as provincial and western affairs, did his best to cultivate the acquaintance of Aberhart and his ministers, on one occasion at least getting them together with Edmonton businessmen to discuss Social Credit policies. When Aberhart went to Ottawa in December to attend a Dominion-provincial conference, the *Journal* front-paged reports sent by the premier himself.

Attacks on the press continued. Often now they mentioned the possibility of control by licensing. In March of 1936 a brilliant young lawyer, Lucien Maynard, produced a Social Credit plan for caucus discussion that asserted 'it is absolutely important that the newspapers be put "under the unchallengeable control of the province" ' and suggested the only way this could be done was by having all newspapers and newsdealers licensed. 'The license fee', the draft plan said, 'could be a nominal amount only, as the object is not to obtain revenue but to obtain control.' Toward the end of May, Aberhart himself in an address at Edmonton advocated licensing of newspapers as a governmental regulation to compel publishing of uncolored and accurate news.

By August it was fully expected that a licensing bill would come before a special session of the legislature later that month, and weeklies and dailies (except the *Albertan*) met at Edmonton to consider action if this happened. No licensing bill came up but verbal attacks continued. Aberhart's comments varied from promises to 'give the press a ride' to 'Fiddlesticks! I couldn't be bothered', spiced here and there with such offhand remarks as: 'Tell Imrie I'll fix the Journal.'

Possible attempt to control the news was the chief worry, but not the only one. In the background was the effect on newspapers, as business operations, of new business practices. September legislation provided for two experiments: 'prosperity certificates' – scrip kept up to date by adding stamps weekly – and a system for the exchange of goods and services between voluntary registrants through vouchers of 'Alberta credit'. If use of scrip became general, and if registration under the Credit House Act were made compulsory, the newspapers must then almost certainly accept this type of payment for subscriptions and advertising. As matters turned out the scrip scheme lapsed and the Credit House Act died inoperative. The licensing threat remained.

In September the provincial companies operating the *Journal* and the *Herald* reorganized under Dominion charter – North Western Publishers Limited and South Western Publishers Limited – as a possible safeguard.

In his Sunday address at Edmonton October 18, a speech in which the religious motif was dominant – 'people are recognizing that Social Credit is a crusade, an economic movement from God Himself' – the Premier reported a stream of resolutions from study groups urging that the press be licensed.

Alberta division of the Canadian Weekly Newspapers Association wrote the Premier urging him either to stop making general charges or take definite action against newspapers he claimed were telling lies.

On Thursday, October 29, Imrie and his managing editor, Cliff Wallace, spent the afternoon with Aberhart and radical members of his cabinet – W.A.Fallow, W.W.Cross, and Maynard – arguing over the rights, responsibilities, and sins of the press. The conference started badly. All four ministers charged the *Journal* with maliciously misrepresenting them – habitually and as a deliberate policy. Imrie and Wallace denied the general charge, pointed out inaccuracies in some of the ministers' recollections, and, as Imrie reported later, 'endeavored to give them a picture of how news is secured and handled, and some of the limitations, human and otherwise,' that get in the way of absolute accuracy. Imrie pointed out that the *Journal* had never accused the premier of insincerity and suggested that one of the main elements in creating an impression of misrepresentation by the press was the frequency of conflicting statements by ministers themselves. Verbatim reports existed of speeches Aberhart and others had made in the past few months and from these a story could be written setting out in parallel columns the contradictions. In fact a *Journal* reporter had constructed such a story. It had not been used.

In the end an appearance of harmony mellowed the meeting. Imrie reported to F.N.Southam: 'Although press licensing was not mentioned during the conference I cannot believe, in view of the spirit that prevailed throughout its closing hour, that Mr. Aberhart will go ahead with it.' If Imrie really had any illusions that the threat to the press was past they were destined to be swept away, though when the blow fell it would take a form more elaborate than simple licensing. Meantime the newspapers called the shots as they saw them.

The Alberta situation seemed to Imrie to be part of an extreme reaction against circumstances, worsened by depression, to which he and the *Journal* had been calling attention for years – the difference in effect of national policies on various parts of Canada. Back in 1925 he had attended an economic conference in Winnipeg where Maritimers presented a reasoned case for redress of handicaps. At that time the *Journal* discussed one aspect of the relationship between the outlying provinces and Ontario and Quebec: the tariff. The tariff was something that 'a people are willing to impose upon themselves in the belief that its resultant benefits will outweigh its costs.' The *Journal* agreed that this was the effect on Canada as a whole, but the ratio between costs and benefits was not the same in the West and the Maritimes as in Ontario and Quebec. There should be a *quid pro quo*. Canada could not lift the natural barriers and toss them into the Arctic Ocean. But Canada could say to the Prairies and Maritimes and British Columbia: 'From this day on, these natural barriers are Canada's burden – not yours alone.' In practice this would mean federal absorption of all or most of the freight charges over the barriers on Canadian products. The benefits would be to those sections receiving in lesser degree the direct benefits of the tariff.

Imrie was one of a delegation that carried to the federal government a recommendation for a tribunal to examine Maritime grievances – a body eventually appointed and headed by Sir Andrew Rae Duncan – that brought about a series of adjustments.

Now more than ten years later he worked out with Balmer Watt a series of editorials that elaborated the earlier theme and called for 'A Duncan Commission for the West'. The first set the tone: 'Social Credit movements and actual or threatened debt and interest reduction legislation in the West reflect the swing of the pendulum to a far extreme as a protest against an accumulation of grievances; some justified, others psychological. . . .'

The series went into the history of western development, noting that large land areas had been opened for settlement far from railroads and highways and without regard to soil-quality or water supply. Provinces had run up debts with maturities ouside the current period of low interest rates. Prairie debt, and the lack of a system of compensation for provinces hurt by the general tariff policy, and freight costs, were among questions that called for commission study. 'What the Prairie West needs most of all today is a new hope, a new spirit, and a new confidence of its own future,' the *Journal* said. It was the lack of these that had induced Alberta to try the Social Credit experiment.

In February of 1937 Mackenzie King announced plans for a

Royal Commission on Dominion-Provincial Relations, which in some of its aspects would cover more ground than the *Journal*'s proposed commission for the West.

In August the *Journal* returned to the theme. No negative action, such as disallowance of Social Credit legislation, would meet Alberta's need. Let Ottawa speed up its national commission and get busy on a new constitutional plan for refunding provincial debt under federal guarantee.

Such reasoned discussion did nothing to lessen demands of the Alberta government party's left wing for regulation of newspapers. Revolt against failure to get a Social Credit system operating stirred the ranks; and out of the tumult emerged at last – as part of a drive to introduce a specific monetary and credit program – the shape of press control.

Revolt and the Press Bill

Early in December of 1936 John Hargrave, leader of the political wing of English Social Credit, arrived in Edmonton. To look things over, he said, and perhaps write a book. By December 18 he was acting as unpaid adviser to a planning committee including Cross, Fallow, Maynard, and R.E.Ansley.

Hargrave's view of affairs just then, according to a booklet in which he later reviewed his Alberta experience, was this:

> Alberta had a Social Credit premier who had promised $25 a month basic dividend, but who could not now find out how to 'get it back' if he attempted to keep his promise; a Social Credit attorney-general [Hugill] who held that it was illegal to issue any such dividend, whether it was possible to get it back or not; and a Social Credit minister of lands and mines [Ross] who frankly admitted that he was 'not a Social Credit man' and was just going on with his technical work leaving Mr. Aberhart and his colleagues to find out whether anything might be done along the lines of Social Credit.

Despite this, Hargrave said, numbers of Albertans thought Social Credit was already in operation, and so did certain members of the legislature. They had confused a vague conception of social justice, and semi-socialistic attempts to tax it into existence, with the price-income mechanism of Social Credit.

Hargrave would come to be regarded as the catalyst that set off the 1937 revolt of Social Crediters impatient for action, one of the results of which was an attempt at press control. But he himself had none of the animosity toward newspapers that marked Aberhart and

Douglas. He found the premier's implacable hostility 'rather to be wondered at' because 'the newspaper files showed that the attacks made by the press . . . were on the whole very mild indeed.' Also it seemed 'a little extraordinary to be continually girding at the press and yet never to make any effective reply in the semi-official government daily paper, the Albertan.'

When at the end of more than two weeks work he and the planning committee had devised a scheme for Alberta along Douglas lines, it was to the press that Hargrave turned to guard against its being submerged, altered, or suppressed. He allowed a reporter acquaintance – Jack Sanderson of The Canadian Press – to make it public. On Wednesday morning, January 6, Sanderson took his copy to Aberhart and as protection for Hargrave and himself asked the Premier if he would undertake not to deny it. Aberhart made the promise and kept it. That day the *Journal* carried Sanderson's story under a double eight-column line:

11-POINT SOCIAL CREDIT PROGRAM REVEALED; ISSUANCE NEW ALBERTA MONEY BASIC FEATURE

'A new financial system for Alberta,' the story ran, 'which would apply for the first time anywhere in the world the Social Credit theories of Major C.H.Douglas, has been recommended to the Alberta government.' It then went into detail on the plan's provisions, including issue of debt-free money negotiable within the province, the setting up of a central credit-house in Edmonton to function in some respects like a chartered bank, a retail price-discount system, and monthly dividends of $5 in Alberta money.

The *Journal* commented: 'It is difficult to believe that the majority of the cabinet ministers or of the Social Credit members of the legislature will endorse proposals that go to such extremes.' A week previously Aberhart had disavowed any intention of drastic legislation. How did Hargrave come to be chosen as technical adviser? Where did he fit in relation to Aberhart and Douglas?

Douglas quickly made one point clear. He took a dim view. Hargrave's program was premature because 'power to deal with public credit in the province has not been secured.' To put forward such a scheme without first having obtained this power was like starting a war by handing your plans to the enemy. Aberhart rapped this 'dog-in-the-manger attitude' and declared Hargrave was 'efficiently and capably rendering every assistance in this great experiment'.

By the last week in January, however, Hargrave had concluded that his plan would be either set aside or bungled in application, and decided to deliver a shock. On Monday, January 25, the *Journal* again came out with a double line:

HARGRAVE REPUDIATES S.C. GOVERNMENT, QUITS, DECLARING HIS CONFIDENCE HAS BEEN SHATTERED

In a long statement Hargrave claimed the first Social Credit government in the world was not yet committed to Social Credit. Aberhart called him faithless.

Down in Calgary, where the departing expert halted briefly on his way east, the *Albertan* did its best in the general confusion. It headlined: ABERHART COUNTERS HARGRAVE. The *Herald* countered with Hargrave: SOCIAL CREDIT IMPOSSIBLE UNDER ABERHART.

Insurrection sparked by Hargrave's departure broke out when the legislature met in February. In March the back-benchers forced suspension of Solon Low's conventional budget. Before the House adjourned it had passed the Alberta Social Credit Act, superseding previous inactive legislation and providing for a board empowered to get experts to work out a program.

As April ended G.L.MacLachlan, chairman of the Alberta Social Credit Board, sailed to consult Douglas. In mid-May they conferred at Newton Stewart, Scotland, where Douglas agreed to send two men 'qualified to appraise the various factors in the political and technical fields . . . as a basis for future action.' George F. Powell and L.D. Byrne headed for Edmonton.

Thus the stage was set for the Aberhart government's most spectacular performance: the attempt finally to take 'power to deal with public credit' and, incidentally, to control the press. This performance would be accompanied by a concatenation of events – disallowances and court judgments and appeals, imprisonment of two ranking Social Crediters, and, as a sort of side show, threat of jail to a news reporter.

These lively events renewed excited attention in Social Credit journals from Fig Tree Court to New South Wales. In fact discussion in overseas Social Credit periodicals sometimes gave Albertans information they couldn't get at home. It was thus that they first learned of one of Douglas's cabled directions to Aberhart: 'Pass press act.'

However, the four-day session in August of 1937, convened to ripen first fruits of Douglas's re-entry (via Powell and Byrne) into the Alberta drama, did not touch the press. Its main achievements were acts bringing bank business under control of government-appointed committees, denying unlicensed bankers the right to action in civil courts, and blocking action to test legislation except by government permission.

Three of the government's more conservative ministers had long since resigned or been forced out. Now Attorney-General Hugill followed them. The bitterness that marked the times came through in his explanatory speech to his constituents. He asked them to cast off illusions: 'The primary illusion is William Aberhart. The minister of health might very properly now have the psychiatrists examine his leader's mentality, having first satisfied himself of the stability of his own.'

Ottawa disallowed the August legislation and the members headed into their third session of the year. At this, called to pass further credit and banking acts in an attempt to circumvent the federal veto, the publishers' apprehension centred at first on a bill conferring on the Minister of Trade and Industry wide powers of registration and licensing (the Trades and Businesses Act). But it soon became evident that government plans called for a control act aimed specifically at the press. Introduced September 30 it was labelled 'an Act to Ensure the Publication of Accurate News and Information'.

Six days earlier the *Albertan* – still carrying the masthead line 'A publicly owned newspaper supporting Social Credit principles' – printed a front-page editorial that amounted to a sorrowful declaration of independence. After the election, it said, it seemed necessary that at least one newspaper should attempt to present the case of this new legislature aiming at improvement in the economic system. The *Albertan* had assumed this role and still believed that changes must come in the world's economic planning. But there were right ways and wrong ways to do things. It was doubtful that the majority of the people of Alberta wanted 'complete, immediate and wholesale destruction of any Canadian custom or any Canadian institution – just because Major Douglas, thousands of miles away, or Mr. Powell, in Edmonton, are trying an experiment.'

When the press bill was introduced Peter Galbraith of the *Albertan* joined Imrie, Wallace, and Leigh Spencer in an all-night session at Edmonton to work out the beginnings of a counter campaign – an effort that found one reflection before the Privy Council, another in the first Pulitzer Prize awarded outside the United States.

The bill in effect handed to the chairman of the Social Credit Board control of what could be said about the government. It would force publication of any statement furnished by the chairman relating to 'the objects of any policies of the government of the province; the means being taken or intended to be taken by the government for the purpose of attaining such objects; the circumstances, matters and things which hinder or make difficult the achievement of any such object.' It provided also that such statements would be privileged under the Libel and Slander Act. And it forced disclosure of sources: newspapers were required to supply on demand the names, addresses, and occupations of all persons furnishing information and 'the name and address of the writer of any editorial or news item. . . .' Penalties ranged from fines to various prohibitions: prohibition of articles written by certain persons, prohibition of news furnished by certain persons, prohibition of publication itself.

Under the heading 'Goodbye to a Free Press' the *Journal* said:

> Thus the Aberhart government would turn back for more than 200 years the clock of liberty and progress. It would make the press of Alberta a propaganda bureau for Messrs. Douglas, Powell, and Byrne. It would force publication of government-prepared statements and would permit the stifling of news that the Social Credit Board might consider 'unfavorable'.
>
> The machinery of dictatorship and censorship is outlined clearly in the bill.
>
> Any kind of government statement, even one in which individuals and institutions might be maligned and vilified, could be required to be printed in the newspaper's ordinary type to the extent of one page in a daily newspaper and one-tenth of the space in any other publication.
>
> That propaganda of this type is contemplated is suggested by a clause that would make all articles ordered by the Social Credit Board 'privileged' under the Alberta Libel and Slander Act. No matter how false a newspaper knew such statements to be, it would be forced to print them under penalty of a $500 fine for each refusal, with possible forced suspension of publication added. A slandered person would be denied financial redress by the prohibiting of libel actions. . . .

Censorship would be made effective, the *Journal* argued, through clauses compelling publishers to reveal names of writers and sources. The bill, if enacted, would 'place in the hands of a few men such power . . . as no British monarch or government has presumed to assume for the past two centuries.'

The editorial concluded:

> Did many say 'it can't happen here'? It *is* happening here.

The brief worked out on the night of September 30 on behalf of the dailies and weeklies was largely an elaboration of arguments advanced in the editorial.

Between that date and passage on October 4 the government made certain amendments. These limited the nature of any required state-

ment to one having for its object 'the correction or amplification of
any statement relating to any policy or activity of the government'
that had been published within the preceding thirty-one days, and its
length to the length of the statement corrected. Such statements were
to be given 'the same prominence as to position, type, and space as
the statements corrected thereby'.

In the publishers' view nothing was really changed. The term 'amplification' still left the government almost unlimited powers. As a
possibility, Imrie noted, 'It might be held . . . that publication by a
newspaper of certain sentences in quotes from an address by a member of the government was taking such sentences out of their context,
and that there should be such amplification as would comprise the
full text of the speech.' The equal-prominence provision might demand an eight-column line on page one on what the chairman considered a correction or amplification of something published thirty
days before. The possibilities were endless.

As to the question of privilege: protection in the case of honest
error was one thing; and there were times when risks must be taken
in the public interest. To be *forced* to print damaging statements was
something else again. The publishers had not forgotten that two
years earlier Douglas in a letter to Aberhart had advised him not to
hesitate 'to pillory by name either through the press or through the
agency of radio, in every possible way, those who refuse to assist'.

On October 5, Lieutenant-Governor J.C. Bowen reserved assent
on the credit, banking, and press bills and referred them to Ottawa.

Just here a bit of political manoeuvring proved worrisome. Aberhart suggested the bills be referred to the courts. What the publishers
hoped for was immediate disallowance. But in regard to the August
bills Mackenzie King himself had first suggested a court reference;
disallowance followed rejection of this by Aberhart. The Alberta
premier now was asking, in relation to this new legislation, what the
Dominion prime minister had suggested in August. The federal government had little choice. The bills went to the Supreme Court of
Canada.

Imrie worked with the lawyers as they drew up a case attacking the
press bill on many grounds – including the arguments that it was part
and parcel of a plan for a new economic order based on legislation
already found *ultra vires*, and that it sought to deal with a matter of
national rather than provincial interest. 'In effect,' the Alberta brief
said at one point, 'the legislature of Alberta by the press bill has attempted to amend the criminal code . . . and to punish by fine and
confiscation, in Alberta, acts which are now without penal conse-

quence in the rest of Canada.' In March the Supreme Court ruled it beyond provincial powers along with the credit and bank taxation bills, and later in the year the Privy Council referred to it as 'no longer practical in any sense at all'.

Newspaper publishers in Canada and round the world watched the fate of the press in Alberta with more than casual interest. One aspect of this was a quiet investigation by Carl W. Ackerman, dean of the graduate school of journalism at Columbia, into the circumstances of the press-bill fight. On May 2 the announcement came – award of a special Pulitzer Prize for public service in the form of a bronze plaque to the Edmonton *Journal* 'for its leadership in defense of the freedom of the press in the province of Alberta' and certificates citing co-operation of the other five Alberta dailies and ninety weeklies.

Meantime events more immediately exciting than the disputed legislation broke out in a political climate already tense.

On September 29 a one-page leaflet entitled *Bankers' Toadies* appeared on members' desks in the legislature. On one side it bore its title and the following advice:

> My child, you should NEVER say hard or unkind things about Bankers' Toadies. God made Bankers' Toadies, just as He made snakes, slugs, snails and other creepy-crawly, treacherous and poisonous things. NEVER therefore, abuse them – just exterminate them!

AND TO PREVENT ALL EVASION
Demand the *Result* you want
$25.00 a month
AND A LOWER COST TO LIVE

The reverse side listed nine prominent Albertans as bankers' toadies. Those named included Lymburn, H.H.Parlee, president of the Edmonton Liberal Association, Senator Griesbach, and D.M.Duggan, provincial Conservative leader.

Griesbach laid charges. On Saturday, October 2, police raided the Alberta Social Credit League office and seized 2,400 copies of the leaflet. On Tuesday J.H.Unwin, government whip and member for Edson, appeared in police court. Powell appeared the following day. Both were eventually convicted of defamatory libel and sent to Fort Saskatchewan jail – Unwin for three months and Powell for six. Both were released at approximately half-time.

Thus while the contested bills went through decorous legal channels toward extinction, their progress was paralleled by an unrelated series of court appearances, committals, appeals, and convictions affecting two prominent men in the Social Credit movement.

In the emotional climate thus engendered, the Don Brown affair occurred. This was a tangle that in retrospect has some elements of burlesque. No one laughed at the time.

On Wednesday, March 16, 1938, the legislature sitting as committee of the whole considered a bill dealing with workmen's compensation. Discussion developed on an amendment proposed by A.J. Hooke of Red Deer to name specifically chiropractic and osteopathy among treatment methods eligible for coverage. The special committee that had previously considered the bill felt that its definition of a physician as 'a person skilled in the art of healing' covered the point without mentioning various healing professions individually.

J.L.Robinson of Medicine Hat was a chiropractor. On three occasions he stated his agreement with the previous committee (which had opposed naming chiropractic specifically) but qualified this finally by saying: 'Nevertheless, when the vote comes in this, I am going to vote . . . with Mr. Hooke.'

The question did not come to a vote. The committee of the whole agreed on an amendment by Health Minister Cross that did not mention chiropractic as such, but included 'all those who are licensed to practice the art of healing in this province'.

Don Brown, the *Journal*'s legislature reporter, covered the discussion at length in a news story, including Robinson's reference to the fact that he would vote with Hooke, and the final solution through Hooke's agreement to Cross's amendment. Then in his column of incidental chat, 'Under The Dome', he threw in an offhand reference:

> Red Deer's Mr. Hooke made a gallant effort Wednesday to have chiropractors included, specifically, in the provisions for treatment under the Workmen's Compensation Act.
> But found himself opposed by the one chiropractor in the house – Medicine Hat's Dr. Robinson.

Robinson complained that this was inaccurate and moved it be referred to the committee on elections and privileges. On Thursday, March 24, this committee in a report to the legislature declared Brown guilty of a breach of the privileges of the house by 'scandalous misrepresentation' and recommended he be taken into custody by the sergeant-at-arms pending the assembly's pleasure.

Somewhere between the committee and the legislature a further provision got into the report. This was that Brown be committed to

Lethbridge jail. The opposition put up a fight, Conservative leader D.M.Duggan arguing against sending any man to jail 'simply as a protest against his newspaper's policy'. Protests were unavailing. The house approved the report – with the Lethbridge jail addition – 39 to 17.

Overnight, however, the atmosphere changed. Resentment grew over alteration of the committee's report. It was rumored that Speaker Peter Dawson had refused to sign the warrant for Brown's committal. On Friday night when Liberal Gerald O'Connor moved 'that at the close of this present sitting of the assembly Mr. Speaker direct the release of Mr. Don C. Brown from custody' it passed without dissent. Brown never got near Lethbridge jail. He had not in fact been arrested.

The *Journal* noted that as an interested party it did not propose to discuss the case editorially. It simply carried full stenographic reports of proceedings and suggested that citizens read them with care.

The Changing Party

The March election of 1940 gave Social Credit a fairly close brush – something it would not experience in the next quarter-century. Independents elected nineteen and almost matched the government's popular vote.

An incidental sidelight was the move into politics of one who had made a name for Edmonton in another endeavor. Among independents elected was Percy Page, organizer and coach of the best-known group of girl athletes ever developed – the Edmonton Commercial Grads. On June 5, 1940, the *Journal*'s sports page carried a regretful headline: GRADS TO PLAY FINAL GAME IN THEIR HISTORY TONIGHT. Since beating Camrose Normal for the provincial girls' basketball title in 1915, the Grads had won more than 500 games, often against the world's best. Names of their stars were part of the sports lore of Canada . . . Dorothy Johnson, Nellie Perry, Connie Smith, the Mountfield girls, Noel McDonald. Now war had come. Competition had fallen off. It had been a long and legendary day but it was over. They went out that night and beat a Chicago team 62-52.

In this period of the early 1940s new hands took over at the *Herald* and the *Journal*. Leigh Spencer moved to Vancouver and the *Province*, and Pete Galbraith – recruited from the *Albertan* as managing editor in 1940 – followed him as publisher in Calgary. A succession of heart attacks forced John Imrie's retirement late in 1941. This painstaking studious executive died in his sleep on June 18, 1942, at the age of fifty-eight. Walter MacDonald, one-time reporter on the *Province* and since 1937 business manager at the *Journal*, succeeded him.

By 1944 events inside and outside the Social Credit party had begun to change the political outlook. Premier Aberhart died in May of 1943 and Ernest Manning took over. In June of 1944 the CCF established in neighboring Saskatchewan the country's first socialist government.

Alberta was due to vote August 8 and the *Journal* suggested the election would 'turn principally on the determined attempt that the CCF will make to secure control of the affairs of Alberta.' It stood by its past criticism but 'ordinary fairness demands recognition that under Premier Manning the government's record has been such as to warrant much greater confidence in it than during the early stages of its career.' Four years later the paper went the whole way: the choice was socialism or the government. The Independent movement was a spent force. The revived Liberal party wasn't strong enough yet. On its record the Manning government deserved a vote of confidence (which, incidentally, it got).

Down in Calgary the *Herald*, tougher from the first in its attitude, couldn't bring itself to that. It pleaded for a bigger opposition.

By this time further events had raised new signposts on the road to the future. On February 5, 1947, the *Journal* carried a two-column heading: 'Drillers Hit Oil Gusher in Vicinity of Leduc'. The drills on Mike Turta's farm had opened a field richer than Turner Valley and directed a new flow of royalties to Alberta's treasury.

And on Saturday, February 21, 1948, Manning announced at Edmonton the resignations 'on request' of Education Minister R.E. Ansley and L.D.Byrne, deputy minister of economic development, who had remained on staff since the stirring days of 1937.

The *Herald* in an editorial headed 'Kick Them Out: They Believe in Douglas' assessed the significance of this ouster:

> The government . . . has been moving farther and farther away from the party's original platform, doubtless because the possibility of its implementation has become demonstrably more remote. . . . It will undoubtedly pay lip-service to the Social Credit theory so long as it continues to call itself a Social Credit party. But so far as practical politics are concerned it will be an 'old line' party very similar to those it has consistently vilified.*

*The Social Credit position, as expressed in later years by Premier Manning, was that Social Credit is a total philosophy of life; proposals for monetary reform were sound in the deflationary period of the depression, and would be again, given the same conditions. Meantime the country had moved into inflationary times in which proposals for that kind of action were not relevant.

The *Journal* in later years diluted its 1948 support for Manning. In 1952 it disagreed with his gas-export-now policy, fearing a threat to Edmonton's growing petrochemical industries, and in 1955 criticized borrowings from the treasury branches – in effect from the government – by members of the legislature. It saw 'a good chance not only of changing the present administration now but, far more important, of restoring responsible government to Alberta.'

In 1963 it suggested election of the leaders of the three non-government parties with solid followings for each so that they could demonstrate their capacity for providing a good alternative. 'It would not be sensible to claim that Mr. Manning has not given Alberta good government. But this is not the same thing as saying it would not have been much better with a strong opposition to remind it . . . that no one is infallible.' Social Credit elected sixty, Liberals two, Coalitionists one. 'It was', the *Journal* observed, 'just like a rerun of an old familiar movie on the late, late, late show.'

Stunt and Crusade

Good-natured mischief can sometimes make a point. The Calgary *Herald* made one on its front page on Wednesday, July 23, 1941.

A former Calgarian, Viscount Bennett, entered the chamber of the Lords as a peer for the first time that day. Hitler's war machine was thirty-two days into Russia. Japan pressed for bases in Indo-China. From Washington, Bob Elson reported that Sumner Welles had plans for a new world order.

But what caught the eye were pictures of an Indian couple, their team and wagon, and a story:

> After successfully passing through every guard-post between the Sarcee Indian Agency and the boundary of the Indian reserve two miles north of Priddis, and photographing and 'destroying' every bridge and culvert in that area, two 'fifth columnists' were apprehended on the return journey by a patrol of the 19th Alberta Dragoons late yesterday afternoon. . . .

At the Sarcee military camp on the Monday a staff captain had outlined an operational security exercise. Over a sweep of country south-west of Calgary, troops would guard every important bridge and crossroads. Travellers lacking registration cards would be 'taken into custody'.

Fred Kennedy wondered. This was Indian country. Would anyone stop a tribal couple driving casually along prairie trails accompanied by a couple of dogs? He recruited photographer Joe Rosettis, a team and wagon, nondescript clothing, wigs, and a make-up expert. The blond Kennedy became a dark-skinned Indian, Rosettis a convincing squaw. They rattled down the road. Near corps headquarters helmets rose from the grass. They caught the words as a guard yelled back to his mates: 'It's only Indians!'

Hours later, their mission accomplished after several such encounters and stops to roll symbolic bombs under bridges, they decided to return by the same route and report to the last military post. It didn't quite work. Sergeant James Winthringham grew suspicious, commandeered a team from an Indian boy, and gave chase. The infiltration turned into a three-mile race and eventual surrender.

The colonel in charge didn't speak to Kennedy for four years.

This somewhat brash stunt was in the *Herald* tradition. So was a more studied and far-reaching involvement in public affairs that began in 1943, when the paper ran a series of editorials blasting the province's welfare act and its practices in child adoptions. The *Herald* considered resultant amendments inadequate, but it was not until after the war that the situation boiled over.

In January of 1947 that redoubtable Daughter of the Empire Charlotte Whitton, invited by the Order's Alberta chapter, came out to peer at the welfare picture. The *Herald* assigned reporter David Stansfield, and his fourteen articles, produced after seven weeks of study, were largely responsible for the royal commission set up to look into criticism of the child welfare branch.

The Whitton report, used as the basis for a *New Liberty* magazine article 'Babies for Export' by Harold Dingman, flared into another Alberta press spectacular. Almost coincidentally with the royal commission finding (which held that the Whitton report overstated the case, but urged an end to export of babies) Dingman's article led straight to the courts.

On January 5, 1948, the province of Alberta charged publisher Jack Kent Cooke and Dingman with defamatory libel of members of the welfare department and conspiracy to defame the branch and its members.

An intriguing angle lay in the fact that the conspiracy charges were laid under a section of the Criminal Code that forced defendants to travel to Alberta, thus nullifying the right to trial in the province of publication. Miss Whitton faced the same thing later. Eventually the prosecution dropped all charges except one of 'counselling' defamatory libel against Cooke, who was acquitted in April.

The *Herald* was not so fortunate. Though not concerned in the criminal case, it was assessed $5,000 in a civil libel suit brought by an official of the child welfare branch.

John

The *Herald* at this time was under new direction. Back from five years of war – he completed his service as lieutenant-colonel commanding an anti-tank regiment – John D. Southam succeeded Peter Galbraith in December 1946: the first of William's grandsons to reach the rank of publisher and the first Southam to run one of the papers in the West. Except for army service – 'Unfortunately,' he wrote when it was over, 'my most productive years have now been spent in the most unproductive and poorly managed of all professions' – most of his working life had been with the *Herald*.

Fresh from a couple of years at the *Citizen* he had come to Calgary in 1932 as a twenty-one-year-old, just in time to get a quick baptism of business fire. On the weekend of June 18-20 the *Herald* crossed the street. In the late 1920s Woods and Spencer had begun to realize that the Herald Building did not allow for pressroom and mailroom expansion. The Southam Building did. So the switch was made with the buildings swapping names. Once again as in 1914-15 hard times cut into income from the buildings. John spent his first days shifting furniture, thereafter took charge of maintenance and rentals for the paper's former home. A year later Woods appointed him assistant business manager of the *Herald* 'to provide a variation in the present line of succession in our office.'

Apart from his newspaper life John became well known in the foothills and mountain country as a hunter and fisherman and dedicated skier, a founder and first president of the Calgary ski club and active promoter of the sport around Banff.

The stuffily conventional repelled him. Irritated by a resort hotel's insistence on excessive formality by having patrons turn cars over to parking attendants, he once borrowed a power roller from a highway job, drove it up to the entrance, and ordered: 'Park that!'

At the *Herald* he inspired a rugged loyalty, buttressed by a habit of backing his staff in any difference with sources or complaint about news handling.

A mixture of athletic vigor and inner sensitivity, he seemed to have at times almost a resentment at his own position, though he had reached it after years of work and training. But he had come back to the newspaper in preference to anything else. Before demobilization his first wife, a daughter of Philippe Roy, one-time Canadian minister to France, passed on to him a suggestion made by George Hees that he carry into politics his ability to mix with people. John dismissed it out of hand; the minute anyone connected with newspapers went into politics, he wrote, their power for good would be compromised and weakened. At the same time he expressed an almost passionate pride in knowledge of his countrymen:

> My life up to now has been spent in the company of all manner of Canadians from the lobster fisherman and bootlegger of the Maritimes to the farmer, industrial laborer, and salesman of Ontario and Quebec and through the Prairies to the Pacific. I am well acquainted with the Doukhobors and Mennonites, the Ukrainian track-walker and the Icelandic farmer, the descendants of the Texas cattlemen and the Mormon sugar-farmers. I have lived in their houses, shot and fished their acres, and talked to them about their personal problems. . . .

On the afternoon of Sunday, November 28, 1954, he had members of the *Herald* staff up to his house to watch television films of the Edmonton Eskimos' Grey Cup victory over Montreal the day before. John Southam's drinking habits were legendary. That afternoon he was sober and apparently cheerful. Yet shortly after his guests had left the house he was dead, a suicide at forty-five. Motives and mixtures of motives have been ascribed. They are guesswork only.

Alliance and Competition

At night-shift time on May 30, 1946, the printers struck the *Journal*. The pattern was the same as at Hamilton and Ottawa that day and a week later at Vancouver. But at Edmonton the result differed from that in the other two-evening-paper fields. The *Bulletin* stuck with the *Journal*.

Back in November both papers had signed identical new contracts with the I.T.U. As pressure growing out of the Winnipeg strike became apparent, the local repudiated its contract with the *Journal* and on January 19 advised MacDonald that it would not resume collective bargaining except under the guidance and through a representative of the International.

The reply it got was a joint one, signed by MacDonald and Campbell, suggesting it withdraw its letter and join in application to the War Labor Board for approval of wage increases agreed on. Campbell also wrote independently that the *Bulletin* could not be a party 'to your breaking the terms of your contract with the Journal, because it would then cause the Bulletin's contract with you to not be worth the paper on which it was written.' He reminded the local of a long-standing agreement between the papers 'under which either paper will co-operate with the other to publish, for any reason beyond the control of either.'

On the morning of May 31 Campbell placed the *Journal*'s nameplate at the head of page one beside his own. His printers refused to insert it and, when one of his newsmen did so, walked off the job. The paper reached the street as

EDMONTON BULLETIN   EDMONTON JOURNAL

Next day the papers produced a photoengraved, four-page edition and as time passed increased its size. By June 19 page one was back in conventional type, and by mid-July the body of the whole paper was linotype-set.

Production centred at first in the *Journal* plant, the *Bulletin* contributing what it could in composition. Printers trickled in from small-town weeklies. Through one three-week period when the pressmen also stayed away (they returned June 27 on advice from their international) circulation, advertising, and newsmen pitched in as both printers and pressmen. Gradually the papers began to separate their functions. By late August the *Bulletin* was running separate editorial, comics, sports, and women's pages. On September 18 they came out with separate fronts.

MacDonald and Campbell had made a deal to share losses. These were small and soon erased. Early in December, with crisis days passed, MacDonald was able to inject a note of lightness in a report to Philip Fisher. 'Charlie is doing very well out of his alliance with us,' he wrote, 'and has, in addition, the satisfaction of adhering to his agreement. Virtue is sometimes not only its own reward but occasionally can be very profitable.'

Through the next year, while the papers published separately in an editorial and news sense, they ran identical advertising and shared the revenue. It was not a situation that could go on for ever. In October of 1947, faced with complete separation, Campbell decided to sell the *Bulletin*.

Two or three bidders, including the Siftons, were said to be interested. MacDonald urged the Southam company to go after the paper if a Sifton bid failed, and either absorb it in the *Journal* or convert it to morning publication. Viewing with distaste the deliberate creation of a monopoly, the company turned the idea down.

There were three lively years ahead. On January 2, 1948, the *Journal* reported: 'The Edmonton Bulletin and Bulletin Printers

Limited, long owned by Charles E. Campbell, have been sold to a group of financiers headed by G.M.Bell of Calgary, publisher of the Calgary Albertan, at a price reliably stated to be $600,000.'
The new owners promptly signed with the I.T.U. Hal Straight came to Edmonton from the Vancouver *Sun* as publisher, and a newspaper war was on. The *Bulletin* attacked the *Journal* editorially with great frequency, a policy MacDonald viewed as a trap to draw replies and thus get free advertising. He refused to be drawn. The *Journal* avoided mentioning the *Bulletin* in any connection whatever. Its counter attack took the form of a bid for news coverage supremacy. 'Thanks to Don MacDougall,' MacDonald said later, 'we drowned them in local news.'

Neither paper went in particularly for the usual forms of so-called 'promotion', but one skirmish must have convinced Edmonton that its newspapers considered it exceptionally sedentary. For years the *Journal* had placed benches at convenient corners bearing the slogan 'Rest and read The Journal'. Campbell's circulation department had got into the act in 1947. Now Straight followed up with a forest of *Bulletin* benches. And, as MacDonald said, 'for every one he placed we placed two.'

The *Bulletin*'s editorial thrusts often exploited the *Sun*'s old line against the *Province*: eastern ownership. A high point came during the federal election campaign of 1949. H.R.Milner, one of Bell's backers in the *Bulletin* purchase, ran as a Conservative in Edmonton. The *Bulletin*, 'without', as it said, 'deserting its fundamental convictions of Liberalism', supported him because he had stepped into 'the unwholesome journalistic picture' so that 'this community might have at least one newspaper working and fighting for the welfare of Edmonton and Edmonton people.' Until Bell and Milner came along, the *Bulletin* (it now confessed) had been 'a pallid shadow of its eastern-owned pal . . . intent only upon raking in the advertising profits which occurred during the monopolistic bludgeoning of this unholy alliance.'

The *Journal*, traditionally Conservative, calmly came out for St. Laurent and Liberal candidate George Prudham, which drew from the *Bulletin* the charge that 'in petty and petulant spite it changes its moth-eaten political spots overnight.' Prudham won.

Such harpoonery was good fun but ineffective. At the time of the sale the *Bulletin*'s circulation was just under 19,000. It reached 30,-000 thereafter, but never got near the *Journal*, which in September 1950 had passed the 56,000 mark. The *Bulletin* on Saturday, January 20, 1951, carried an eight-column line: THE BULLETIN ENDS

PUBLICATION TODAY. The announcement said that 'steadily rising costs of materials and labor have turned the recent impressive success of the Bulletin into failure to continue publishing.'

To counteract rumors the *Journal* commented: 'The Journal has not bought the Bulletin nor amalgamated with it.' This was technically true. The *Journal* in fact had had monopoly thrust upon it. With the *Bulletin* out of business The Southam Company bought its plant and building under an agreement reached before the fold-up.

The *Journal* Alone

The *Bulletin's* disappearance raised the *Journal's* circulation by nearly 20,000, to 77,000, almost at once. The paper grew steadily with the city. Edmonton's population rose from 160,000 in 1951 to 280,000 in 1961 and kept on going.

It is indicative of the frightening cost of starting new dailies in large cities that no publisher moved into Edmonton to buck the *Journal* despite this expanding market. New dailies tried and failed in Winnipeg and Hamilton. Others would repeat the pattern in Montreal and Vancouver. None tackled Edmonton.

There are two sides to the coin. Rivalry breeds alertness in newsdigging and advertising. On the other hand a free field may provide the profit-margin to produce a better newspaper, if the spur is there.

For the publishers of newspapers that lack direct competition in major cities there is (or should be) a lurking unease: Are we coasting on the slope of monopoly? Do we produce what the city needs in a newspaper? How does the public feel about us? This is one of the spurs. The problem was one that Walter MacDonald recognized. For a brief time he tried to conduct the *Journal* as a newspaper that didn't take sides. This, he found, was not the answer.

> Friends in all political parties confronted me with hopes that the *Journal* would not become a fence-sitter just because we had become the city's only newspaper [he wrote afterward]. I reverted to our previous policy of strong views strongly stated. . . . It was quite apparent that just as men of sound intellect are not much interested in men without opinions, so also an intelligent public would have but little interest in a newspaper void of opinion.

In fact MacDonald had arrived at a philosophy based on the conviction that no newspaper could please everybody. Nor could two or three. So it had better simply be itself.

The responsibilities of publishing in a one-paper city were also much in the mind of his successor. When MacDonald retired early in 1962, Basil Dean came up from Calgary to run the *Journal*. A Berkshire boy, product of the University of London's school of journalism and a one-time assistant on the *Daily Herald* to Hannen Swaffer, the old 'Pope of Fleet Street', Dean came to Canada under an exchange scheme in 1938 and stayed, except for wartime years with R.C.A.F. public relations and a period with Southam News Services in London.

In 1955 he stepped from an associate editorship at Calgary to the publisher's desk and injected his own brand of personal journalism into the paper via an occasional column entitled 'A Publisher's Diary'. Neither excessively bland editorials nor a faceless approach had ever characterized the *Herald*. They did not do so now. Editor-in-chief Dick Sanburn had achieved a pile-driving editorial style. Dean chatted with his readers as Dean, publisher of the *Herald*.

In the spring of 1962, shortly after moving to Edmonton, he set up a new reportorial beat, the Last Frontier. For a half-century and with increasing attention as the airplane drew new trails across the North, the *Journal* had brought news out of the area from correspondents at remote posts, and organized occasional forays by staff men. Now it assigned a full-time man to travel the 1,500,000 square miles of the Yukon and Northwest Territories, a country populated by 41,000 inhabitants, mostly Indians and Eskimos. It could not be called a high-circulation area, though the *Journal* sold 800 a day in the Territories and Dean once boasted that circulation had risen from two to four at Tuktoyaktuk. But it was a vast part of Canada of which the effete south needed to be told. Reporter Bob Hill had been on the beat a year when he fell into the most startling spot break of its kind ever to come out of that forbidding region.

Just before midday on February 4, 1963, Ralph Flores, a Californian who had been working on the DEW line, took off in his light plane from Fairbanks, Alaska. With him was Helen Klaben, a Brooklyn girl hitching a ride. Their announced destination was Seattle. They arrived nowhere. Searchers gave them up for lost.

On Sunday, March 24, Hill happened to be in Whitehorse on assignment. That night Harry Boyle of the Whitehorse *Star* phoned him an almost unbelievable tip. Boyle had just heard from a correspondent at Watson Lake, down by the northern B.C. border; a pilot flying supplies into the Rocky Mountain trench had spotted an SOS tramped in the snow and figures believed to be Flores and Klaben. Hill headed for Watson Lake. By Monday the story of the man and girl who had survived zero weather for seven weeks, most of the time without food, had hit the world's front pages and magazine and newspaper writers were streaming north.

The Edmonton Journal

FORECAST: MILDER | EDMONTON, ALBERTA, MONDAY, MARCH 25, 1963 | FIVE CENTS

Two Alive 50 Days After Crash In Northern B.C.

By BOB HILL
Journal Staff Writer

WATSON LAKE, Y.T. — A man and woman have survived 50 days on a northern B.C. mountainside on two cans of fruit and two cans of sardines.

They were rescued today after being spotted accidentally Sunday.

Helen Klaben, 21, of Brooklyn, N.Y., is suffering gangrene in a broken right foot and has a broken left arm in splints.

Ralph Flores, of San Bruno, Calif., has broken ribs.

First reports of their condition came from the pilot of one of three planes that flew into the mountainous country, about 80 miles southeast of here today.

Jack McCallum said the woman was thin and the pair had nothing to eat since the fruit and sardines gave out seven days after their plane crashed Feb. 4.

The two were on their way to Seattle from Alaska when they disappeared.

'Cried In My Arms'

"She is in good spirits," McCallum said. "She cried in my arms, when we reached them."

McCallum said the couple had moved down the hillside from the crash scene and set up a tarpaulin for shelter.

They had no sleeping bags, no axe and no rifle, he said. Wood for a fire was chopped with a hammer and chisel.

Miss Klaben was carried piggy-back down the hillside to a plane to be brought back to Watson Lake, from where they were expected to be taken to Whitehorse.

Chuck Hamilton, Yukon Flying Services pilot, spotted the wreckage during a flight Sunday with supplies to a big-game guide in the Rocky Mountain Trench of B.C.

It was not known for sure until today whether the two people he spotted waving near the wreckage were the missing couple.

When the plane disappeared it touched off one of the biggest air searches this part of the north has ever seen but it was finally called off.

Since Feb. 4, the lowest temperature recorded here was 42 below, although during a 10-day mild spell, a high of 24 was reported.

Markings Matched

Hamilton said the wing was all he could see of the plane because smoke from a nearby campfire obscured everything but the marking "N588." The Flores plane was marked "N58-856."

An SOS, he said, was tramped in the snow of a meadow about a mile from the crash scene.

Hamilton said two trappers he met Sunday at Aeroplane Lake, not far from the crash scene, set out immediately for the wreckage.

Flores came to the Yukon in October, 1960, to work as a mechanic for a DEW line contractor, Federal Electric Company. He had completed his contract and was flying home when his plane disappeared.

Hamilton described the terrain as rough and "very bad for walking." He said a trapper's trail leads toward the scene from Aeroplane Lake but the trappers he talked to weren't sure whether it went all the way.

Hamilton said "he felt it was a woman" he saw nearest to the plane. "At first I thought it might be an Indian squaw. It was hard to tell."

SAN BRUNO, Calif. (AP) — "Oh, my God, I'm so happy," said Mrs. Theresa Flores, when told here that her husband, Robert Flores, might be alive.

"We had the feeling all along that he would be found alive," she said of herself and their six children.

Miss Klaben, a former employee of the U.S. Bureau of Land Management in Fair-

See VICTIMS Page 2

Verbal Shots Across Border

* * *

PM Raps Stories

By EDDIE KEEN
Journal Political Writer

PINCHER CREEK — Angered by American magazine comment on his election campaign, Prime Minister Diefenbaker has completed a four-day prairie swing after speaking to an estimated 32,000 persons.

And the prime minister was at his fighting best. The huge crowds of the day seemed to stimulate him for night speeches, the longest of the tour given in the final night here when he turned U.S. magazine criticism of him into a critical analysis of the United States.

"We in Canada must determine our own policies. When some nations start to point out to us what we should do, let me tell you this: Canada was in both wars long before some other other nations were. Let that be clear." He was interrupted by applause and then continued: "Let it also be clear that in the last war, for a period of 15 to 18 months, freedom was in the custody of the people of the British Commonwealth. We don't have to be told what to do after our record of service."

HEADS WEST

The prime minister left Alberta Sunday for Vancouver Island and the Okanagan Valley of B.C. He will speak in Nanaimo, Victoria, Vernon, and Kelowna before returning to Vancouver for a major address Wednesday night. Thursday he returns east.

He attacked British and American papers for printing stories last year which he claimed led to foreign investment being pulled out of the country causing the exchange crisis, and labelled several Canadian papers as "not being friends of mine."

HIT MAGAZINES

The American magazines Look, Time and Newsweek also came under fire for their commentary on the campaign, and a front page editorial in the usually Tory Toronto Globe and Mail backing the Liberals brought the comment the east is angry because of what he has done for the west.

The prime minister was at his oratorical best ridiculing Liberal leader Lester Pearson, and he spent considerable time doing this. And many times he compared his whistle-stopping to the trail blazing of Sir John A. Macdonald some 80 years ago.

DIEFENBAKER AT IRVINE, ALTA.
. . . humorous moment in campaign

...And United States Calls For More Aid

WASHINGTON (CP) — A special committee established by President Kennedy has called on Canada and other industrialized countries to increase their foreign aid programs.

A Canadian official, when told of the report, estimated that because of austerity, the Canadian economic assistance total this year dropped by about $7,000,000 from last year's $62,000,000.

Together with long-term export loans, the Canadian aid total would be about $135,000,000 for the year—roughly one-third of one per cent of the country's national production. This would compare with about one per cent for the U.S. and slightly more than one per cent for France.

A committee of the 20-country organization for economic co-operation and development has estimated one per cent of national production—value of all goods and services produced—should be a country's foreign aid goal.

The U.S. plans to reduce its own aid substantially, thus paying less heed to "the varagies of ephemeral world opinion."

CUT PROPOSED

The 10-man committee, headed by Gen. Lucius D. Clay, proposed that the total U.S. aid program — estimated at about $3,900,000,000 for the current year—be cut in the future by $500,000,000 a year or more. The one dissenter, AFL-CIO President George Meany rejected this view, arguing that aid be increased instead of reduced to step up the fight against world communism.

Kennedy sent Clay a letter saying the recommendations would be applied carefully in the government's continuing review. Aides said Kennedy's proposed foreign aid program for the next fiscal year—originally set at $4,900,000,000—may be trimmed by $300,000,000 or more before it is presented to Congress.

But in reference to any $500,000,000 cut Williams Dentzer Jr., executive director of the committee, noted that the committee had not considered some proposed new programs which could add hundreds of millions of dollars to the over-all program, reducing the effect of any cut.

IGNORE CRITICISM

The committee suggested the government pay less attention to possible world criticism and stop trying to do too much in too many countries.

The U.S. had to demand more economic reform from Latin countries. Washington had to show a tougher attitude against countries which use American military base rights as levers to extract more help from the U.S.

Clay said the committee did not want to name specific countries in a critical way but the report also criticized Indonesia.

GREEN SAYS U.S. GIVING ORDERS

VANCOUVER (CP) — Hon. Howard Green, external affairs minister, said Sunday a U.S. committee report urging Canada to spend more money on foreign aid "appears to me to be another case of Americans trying to tell Canada what to do."

In an interview at his home here, Mr. Green said he always wants to see more money spent on foreign aid "but it must all come from the taxpayer's pocket."

"Americans spend great sums on foreign aid to influence the politics of that country.

"Canada doesn't lend money—she gives it."

Thompson Claim Said Unfounded

Premier E. C. Manning termed a report by National Social Credit Leader Robert Thompson as, "wholly unwarranted and without foundation."

Mr. Thompson said Sunday in Vancouver at a press conference that Premier Manning would likely be in the Cabinet if his party won the April 8 federal election.

Mr. Manning told The Journal today, "I am certain Mr. Thompson had no intention of conveying the impression taken from his comments at Vancouver, as we have had no discussion on this matter.

"I have repeatedly made clear that I still regard my first responsibility is with the people of Alberta.

"If the time ever comes however, when I feel an obligation to try and help further Canada's interest in the federal field, I will personally advise the people of this province first of all."

Martial Law

GUATEMALA CITY, Guatemala (Reuters)—The Guatemalan government today declared a state of martial law.

See STORY Page 13

Strike Talks Stalled

PARIS (Reuters) — About 240,000 striking French coal miners today dug in for a long struggle with the government.

Angry union leaders Sunday turned down a coal board pay-increase offer and no date was set for further talks. As the strike which has paralysed France's state-owned coal industry moved into its 25th day, the failure of the negotiations was expected to have repercussions in other branches of nationalized industry and services, already hit by sporadic strikes.

The main issue in the labor disputes is the income lag of workers in nationalized industries as compared with private enterprise.

Paris transport workers were to meet to discuss what action to take over their pay discontent.

The 3,000 workers at the giant natural gas field at Lacq in southwest France said they would not return to work before the miners.

After the breakdown of the miners' talks, Leon Delfosse of the Communist-led Miners Federation urged the men "to reinforce their strike in unity." Leaders of the Catholic and Socialist-led unions also called for stronger strike action.

CLAIMS WAGES LOWER

Delfosse said the miners' wages are 11 per cent lower than those in private industry. However, the miners had been prepared to use an eight-per-cent increase as a basis for negotiations.

Eight per cent was the first assessment of their pay gap by the three "wise men" appointed by the government to report on income disparities between public and private industry. The "wise men" later corrected the figure to 7.4 per cent after learning of a productivity bonus.

Delfosse said the government refused to give the eight per cent immediately. The unions were offered 3.5 per cent now and the remaining 4.5 per cent spread over two years, he said.

Rock Derails Mainline Train

CALGARY (CP)—Three diesel units and a baggage car of the CPR train, The Canadian, were derailed in Albert Canyon, about 240 miles west of here, Sunday night. No one was injured.

HON. PETER DAWSON
. . . dies suddenly

Speaker Dawson Dies, 70

Speaker of the Alberta Legislature, Rev. Peter Dawson, 70, died suddenly in Edmonton Sunday.

Stricken at his chambers in the Legislative Building just after he returned from a speaking engagement, Mr. Dawson collapsed and was taken to the University Hospital. He was attended by Hon. Dr. J. D. Ross, minister of health.

Legislators today were to cancel sittings immediately after the Legislature opened.

Mr. Dawson's health had been good and there was no indication during the current session of the Legislature of any illness.

Mr. Dawson's record as speaker is outstanding in the legislative annals of the Commonwealth. He was appointed speaker of the Alberta Legislature in 1937, serving for 26 years up to the time of his death.

It is believed that Mr. Dawson's total term as speaker of an assembly is the longest in the history of the Commonwealth. His record is matched only by that of Sir Robert D. Nicholls, who was speaker of the House of Assembly in South Australia for 23 years.

BORN IN SCOTLAND

Mr. Dawson was a native of Scotland and a United Church minister. He had represented Little Bow constituency as Social Credit member since the party swept into power in 1935. He was named speaker two years later and in his 25th year had the longest service in that position in the British Commonwealth.

Premier Manning said Mr. Dawson's "sudden and untimely death was a tremendous shock to me personally and to all associated with him."

Arthur Dixon, government member from Calgary, as deputy speaker, will take over as speaker for the remainder of the session, expected to prorogue this week.

Funeral arrangements will be announced later today after a meeting of the cabinet, Mr. Manning said.

Mr. Dawson succeeded N. E. Tanner as speaker. He was born at Slateford, Ayrshire, Scotland, and came to Canada in 1911. He was educated at Garrick Academy, Scotland and St. Stephen's College, Edmonton.

He is survived by his widow and two sons.

Commenting on the death of the speaker, Mike Maccagno, Liberal member for Lac La

See FUNERAL Page 2

Eruption Survivors In Bali Seek Forgiveness Of Gods

KLUNGKUNG, Bali (AP) — Pious Balinese flocked to the white beaches here today to cleanse themselves of sin.

They fear their sins may have angered the gods of the Agung volcano, which erupted last week, killing almost 1,500 persons.

They carried small house temples and the Hindu trinity to the shore and offered sacrifices. Then they entered the South Pacific to wash away their sins.

The cleansing festival takes place every 100 years. The volcano erupted in the middle of it, increasing the fervor of devotees who believe that natural disasters will occur if they fail to purify themselves. There were more than 200 injured and 65,000 left homeless in the disaster area, once lush and green, which now is a vast desert of ash and mud.

The official death toll was 1,478. It is feared this will rise when buried villages are excavated.

This seaside village has become one of the most important rescue centres. Military units, police, Red Cross and government officials face a gigantic task in providing food and shelter.

Airfreight Owner's Home Hit By Rock

Vandals smashed a window Sunday at the home of Dennis Heffring, president of a freight company whose employees daily cross picket lines at Pacific Western Airlines.

Witnesses say two men were involved in the rock-throwing incident early Sunday morning. Two 13-year-old babysitters were sprayed with broken glass.

Mr. Heffring said Reid Oddliefson and Kevin Byrne were uninjured in the incident. He set the damage to the plate glass window at $200. Mr. Heffring said his car radiator had also been damaged by the vandals at his St. Albert home.

PHONED THREATS

He said that for the past few days he had been receiving threatening phone calls during which he was called a "scab." The voices also threatened to "get" him.

His company, Central Western Airfreight, is operating as usual as a freight forwarding agency for Pacific Western Airlines and other customers.

POLICE ESCORT

In another incident Saturday, PWA stewardesses not on strike asked for police escort after they were repeatedly "cut off" by a vehicle while driving home from work.

The incident was not repeated while the girls were being escorted by police.

Officials of both striking unions expressed surprise when told of the two incidents today.

They said that no union members had been involved, as far as they knew.

"We're against any kind of violence. As a matter of fact we were looking forward to the possibility of holding talks (with the company) later this week and this sort of thing isn't going to help anything."

Meanwhile, orderly picketing

See VANDALISM Page 2

Where To Find It

B.C. SCHEME?—Gen. A. G. L. McNaughton, former chairman of the International Joint Commission, charged Saturday that the British Columbia government schemed to downgrade the advantages of the Columbia River power project. (Report on Page 36)

WEATHER

Sunny periods, milder, light winds, low tonight 26, high tomorrow 43. Details on Page 2.

13 Contest Three City Seats

There were no surprises or last-minute rush as deadline for filing nomination papers for the federal election closed at 2 p.m. today.

Four candidates will battle to represent the constituencies of Edmonton West and Edmonton Strathcona while the addition of a Communist Party candidate makes it a five-way race in Edmonton East.

Candidates and their constituencies follow. Members of the last House of Commons are indicated by (X).

Edmonton West

Orvis A. Kennedy, Social Credit; Hon. Marcel Lambert, minister of veteran's affairs, PC, (X); John Motyl, NDP; J. Harper Prowse, Liberal.

Edmonton Strathcona

John Decore, Liberal; Terrence Nugent, PC., (X); S. A. Sorenson, Social Credit; Jan Sowton, NDP.

Edmonton East

Donald Brinton, Liberal; Ivor Dent, NDP; Lucien Maynard, Social Credit; William Skoreyko, PC, (X); William Tuomi, Communist.

An unofficial Canada-wide compilation on the eve of nomination day showed 1,015 candidates already have completed the formalities for nomination or announced their intention of contesting the election.

Some dropouts can be expected before the 2 p.m. local standard time close but since nomination day usually brings a spate of late-filing independents, last year's total likely will be surpassed.

Progressive Conservatives and Liberals have candidates for all 265 seats so there will be no acclamations. The New Democratic Party and Social Credit follow 228 and 224 nominees respectively and may increase these totals slightly. There are 13 Communists and so far 20 independents.

There has been a sharp increase this election in the number of women candidates with 42 nominated so far. There were 27 in 1962 when five were elected.

As a reporter's beat the Last Frontier is scarcely believable to news-editors who deploy staff no farther than the perimeters of their circulation areas. City editor Stan Williams once astonished an editorial clinic at Columbia University. He had to resort to an atlas to prove that when the *Journal* sent a man to Cambridge Bay it was, in distance, like a New Jersey paper sending one to Austin, Texas.

A year later the *Journal* took another step beyond the boundaries of the strictly necessary. Taking as its text a quotation from Adlai Stevenson – 'A democracy is a society in which honorable men may honorably disagree' – 'The Journal for Dissent' appeared opposite the editorial page on May 28, 1963, heralded by an announcement that readers were invited to disagree with the opinions of the *Journal* or with any widely accepted viewpoint.

Dean's consciousness of the pitfalls of publishing in a one-paper city came out in some personal comment:

> Our numerous critics to the contrary . . . this newspaper has always been acutely aware of the responsibility it must carry as the only daily newspaper in the northern half of Alberta. . . . We are, collectively, as anxious as any group in this area that there should be a free and forceful play of conflicting opinions about all the great issues of the day, holding this to be an essential part of the process whereby a democracy arrives at something approximating the truth.

In the first 'Journal for Dissent' a university professor documented a vigorous objection to newspapers building stories on catchy and sometimes irrelevant quotations lifted from their context. The feature grew in popularity though it produced less dissent from the *Journal*'s opinions than Dean would have liked to see.

Basil Dean, a newspaper man whose early promise had been richly confirmed in maturity, died of a coronary in December 1967 at the age of fifty-two.

11
Winnipeg:
The *Tribune*

In pre-Christmas days during the bleak early 1930s certain packing-rooms at the *Tribune* presented a commentary on the times: the packers, stuffing boxes with clothes, food, and toys bought through the paper's 'Empty Stocking Fund', were themselves drawn from the ranks of the jobless. As voluntary help they got two hot meals a day, a $5 Christmas present, and parcels for their families. The Stocking Fund had come into existence in 1918. In the 1930s it almost became big business. Heavily manned by volunteers, working with school attendance officers, hospitals, and welfare groups, it bought shoes and clothes for school children through dreary depression winters.

This was an expansion of an existing welfare effort. The *Tribune*, holding that 'more than any other enterprise a newspaper owes a responsibility to its community', got two new ones going – one directed mainly at shoring up morale, the other at bringing food and clothes to families of the unemployed.

In the summer of 1931 the paper organized outdoor community song-nights. At the final night that year 50,000 came out, including a volunteer choir of 1,000 voices and five bands. More than 60,000 jammed Assiniboine Park for the final night of the 1932 season, when the Governor-General and Countess of Bessborough were there. Community singing continued through the summers of 1933 and 1934.

Meanwhile on September 10, 1931, the *Tribune* asked the women of Winnipeg to form a Friendship League. It asked for 1,000 volunteers to make weekly calls on families of the unemployed and 'do what a friend and neighbor can do during the difficult winter months.' By mid-November 1,000 had enrolled. The paper set up headquarters in its building. Its trucks collected contributions, a clothing exchange was organized, a furniture warehouse opened. Husbands of the 1,000 women helped out. The Friendship League existed for eighteen months and paved the way for a women's auxiliary of the city's unemployment advisory board.

In the light of depression conditions the paper grew impatient with party politics:

> Surely at a time when there are 30,000 unemployed in the province, when the principal industry of agriculture is depressed to an extent never known before, when municipal and provincial finances are subjected to strains never contemplated, a political dog-fight can be avoided and means found to bring about a union of all the qualities of statesmanship the parties possess. . . .

This was the *Tribune* on October 10, 1931, shortly after Progressive Premier John Bracken had issued an invitation to Conservative, Liberal, and Labor leaders to join in a union government to meet the crisis. In the ten years since it had welcomed Bracken to the leadership the paper had 'not found the provincial administration an expression of the ultimate in statesmanship.' In fact it felt the government had done considerable sinning, but surely now reasonable men could arrive at a reasonable agreement with so much at stake.

Conservatives and Labor refused to join the coalition, and when in January of 1932 the Liberals went in with Bracken a bit of the bloom was off the rose for the *Tribune*. It accused the premier of closing the door to union government in Manitoba by introducing federal issues and assailing R.B.Bennett. Nevertheless, it still believed the province's position called for union of parties, and when Bracken's Liberal-Progressives won the June election it saw the result as a denunciation of partisanship.

Federally the paper supported Bennett, though not without exception. In the spring of 1935 M.E.Nichols, chatting casually by letter with F.N.Southam, had some observations to make on circulation as related to political positions. After the 1930 federal election the paper had won 1,500 customers away from the *Free Press*, largely, he thought, because of the rival paper's repetitious slamming of Bennett. But it hadn't been able to hold the gain. Nichols attributed this to the fact that 'while we have not given the Bennett government consistent support by any means, and have at times walked right into it, we have doubtless taken some of the backwash of public disappointment over Bennett's failure to cure unemployment and restore business conditions.' He added cheerfully that the paper was in a much more comfortable position since Bennett and Stevens between them had taken the conservatism out of the Conservative party. The price spreads inquiry and Bennett's broadcasts had caught western ears and 'the Tribune is no longer appalled at the thought of being suspected of Conservative leanings, since Conservative leanings now-a-days are leanings to the left.'

Neither politics nor depression (the depths of it were past but the tide was slow to rise) could dim for Winnipeg the lustre of December 7, 1935. Western football teams had made eleven fruitless trips east in pursuit of the Grey Cup, beginning with Edmonton Eskimos who lost 23-0 to Toronto Argonauts in 1921. The West's worst humiliation had been Regina's 54-0 loss to Queen's in 1923, its best bid another Regina effort in 1930, when the Roughriders held Balmy Beach to 11-6. This time Winnipeg came east loaded with a blond explosive named Fritz Hanson from North Dakota State and an assortment of rugged individuals whose names have become legendary in the lore of Canadian football: James, Fritz, Rebholtz, Kabat, Adelman, Oja, Mogul.

Along with this task force of natives and imports came a twenty-three-year-old reporter who already had toiled five years on the *Tribune*'s sports staff. He was well equipped to record for jubilant readers the cataclysm that turned the Canadian sports world upside down:

> HAMILTON – In the murky shadow of the mountain where the terrible Tigers roared and ruled, Western Canada's 15-year-dream of football empire came true. . . .
>
> Nine thousand looked on and wondered that the gridiron stronghold of the East could fall so helplessly, as the Four Furies of the Winnipeg rugby club swept madly in the wake of an impregnable wingline to an 18-12 victory in the greatest east-west battle of them all.
>
> Almost reckless in its conception, but as sure and cool in execution as the black murder of a Louis was the attack that rocked Tigers back at the first raging charge and shot home three touchdown thrusts before their sad Saturday was done. Deadly, cunning as a Riffian ambush. . . .

Ralph Allen would go on to turn out compelling prose as columnist, war correspondent, novelist, and popular historian. None of it ever grew quite as purple as the rolling periods in which he enshrined the golden ghost of North Dakota and the linemen whose tackles almost jarred the mountain loose.

Weapons and War

In June of 1939, the spring after Munich, the *Tribune* sent associate editor Randolph Patton and photographer E.P.Gibson to Camp

Shilo. In brief illustrated front-page stories under the title 'Canada's Token Weapons', the two demonstrated the curious ordnance with which permanent force and reserve units tried to train. The series opened with a discussion of the two-inch mortar. One photograph showed the actual mortar as supplied to British territorials. Next to it appeared the token weapon used by permanent-force men at Camp Shilo in their exercises and in instructing militia units. They had built it themselves from a board, a piece of drainpipe, and bits of wire. The *Tribune* noted that the Princess Patricia's, in case of need, were supposed to supply instructors for all militia units in Western Canada in the use of a variety of infantry weapons. But, except for a few men who had seen this mortar in England, no one knew anything about it except what they had read. There was not a single specimen of the real two-inch mortar in the West. The series continued through twelve articles – token tanks, obsolete howitzers, ancient machine guns.

In less than three years Winnipeg would become one of the first Canadian cities, in that particular war, to have hundreds of its youth caught up in deadly ground combat.

In October of 1941 Winnipegers crowded in thousands round the station while the Grenadiers pulled away. A battalion with a history. It had fought through one world war as the 78th, been mobilized from militia to active service the day after Hitler struck Poland, spent a year on garrison duty in the West Indies. Now it was off on a mission undisclosed.

On October 27 the troopship *Awatea* sailed from Vancouver. On board were the Winnipeg Grenadiers and the Royal Rifles of Quebec – just under 2,000 men. At mid-November they deployed with British and Sikh troops around the defences of Hong Kong. On December 8 the Japanese attacked. At Christmas they overran the city.

In Canada, while the fate of individuals was still uncertain (eventually it became known that more than 400 died in battle or in prison camps), circumstances surrounding the expedition raised a political storm. In January, campaigning in Arthur Meighen's losing cause in York South, Ontario Conservative leader George Drew (himself a First World War battery commander) rang in Hong Kong, in criticizing the government's manpower practice. 'At the very last moment,' he said, 'a large number of untrained men were attached to the forces . . . in order that they might be brought up to strength. Many gallant young Canadians went into one of the bitterest battles of all history with little knowledge of the weapons they were called upon to use.'

Headlines and editorials bloomed. Under opposition pressure
Mackenzie King appointed Chief Justice Sir Lyman Duff a commissioner. Duff took evidence in secret, with Drew as opposition counsel, and on June 4 brought down a report. It absolved all hands of
dereliction, with the reservation that there had been 'some lack of
energy' in not getting vehicles to Vancouver to accompany the
troops. On the whole, Duff found, the task had been well performed.
He noted that it had been urged by Drew that a change of government in Japan in October – when Tojo and the war party took over
– ought to have led the government into re-examining the question of
policy raised by the United Kingdom's original invitation to send an
expedition. The chief justice had read dispatches that he couldn't
disclose and his conclusion was 'that . . . nothing emerged before the
departure of the expeditionary force on October 27 which could have
been considered to be a justification for the withdrawal by Canada
from the responsibilities she had undertaken.'

Drew promptly commented that he found it 'almost impossible to
believe the summary of the report I have read in the press has any
reference whatever to the evidence given before the inquiry that I
attended,' and called for full disclosure of the evidence. Almost at
once he faced a charge (which was soon dropped) under a section of
the Defence of Canada Regulations dealing with utterances 'intended or likely to prejudice recruiting, training, discipline, or administration'. The furore continued. On July 11 Drew wrote Mackenzie
King a thirty-two-page letter dissecting the Duff report.

On request, King agreed to table this document – then recanted on
the ground that it would violate the secrecy under which the Duff
proceedings were conducted. Publication of the evidence itself, he
said, would assist the enemy. Drew contended the reverse was true:
suppression would help the enemy; only if the facts came out would
people understand the need for reforms in control of the forces.

While all this went on, a 7,500-word partial text of the Drew letter
was in the hands of about 100 daily newspapers across Canada. The
Canadian Press had wired it out, to be released for publication when
tabled. King's refusal to table left news-editors up in the air. Into this
situation the press censors, who had no power to prevent publication,
but whose approval or refusal-to-pass was an accepted yardstick of
what was publishable or not under Defence of Canada Regulations,
were now injected.

They told askers that they would not pass anything that contra-
vened the regulations even if tabled. Faced with the text of the Drew
letter they stamped it 'not authorized for publication' and, while ad-

mitting that some parts of it might be publishable, declined to pass any section at all because it all added up to a reasoned argument.

Editors across the country thus had a piece of prime copy they felt they couldn't safely publish. But they could comment in general terms on the circumstances that put them in this position and many did. The Ottawa *Citizen* for instance printed its opinion that there was nothing in the letter that could impair public morale or be useful to the enemy.

In Winnipeg, editor John Bird and publisher Wes McCurdy decided to do a piece of home-made censorship. On July 17 the *Tribune* ran the Drew letter – nine columns liberally broken by hand-drawn Xs to indicate deletions of material that might breach the regulations.

Despite deletions Drew's main contentions on training and equipment got into print:

> . . . Two battalions of infantry were sent from Vancouver to Hong Kong on October 27. The war committee and the general staff knew that an early attack by Japan was possible. They knew that these men might be called upon to fight a desperate enemy at any time after they disembarked.
>
> Nevertheless units were sent which had never had any firing practice whatever with some of their most important weapons. They had little firing practice with any weapons. They were unready for active service by any standards of training.
>
> And in a war in which vehicles to move weapons are an absolute necessity, they went into action against the Japanese before a single one of their vehicles had arrived in Hong Kong. . . .
>
> If that could happen with this small force, what may happen if hundreds of thousands of men are involved unless steps are taken immediately to reorganize the department of national defence and the headquarters staff? . . .
>
> It should have been the object of the commission to point the way to more effective direction of our military effort. That object has been disregarded. . . .

At one point the letter noted: 'The commissioner . . . emphasizes over and over again that the Canadian government received no warning of increased danger in the Pacific prior to the dispatch of the Hong Kong force. . . . No matter what information may have been conveyed to the war committee, or the cabinet as a whole, you know that this finding of the commissioner is directly contrary to the facts. . . .'

Of the material self-censored by Bird, the most explosive was an elaboration of this point: that the Canadian government had been warned of changed circumstances before the force sailed.

'The evidence is clear', Drew wrote, 'that never from the beginning to the end of the time that this subject was under consideration was there any thought that Hong Kong could be held in the event of war with Japan.' The original British proposal had been made in the light of an *improved* Pacific situation, a lessening of war danger. It called for a small reinforcement of the Hong Kong garrison more as a deterrent demonstration than anything else. Defence Minister Ralston had testified that one of the major factors that influenced him 'was the statement that the situation in the East was bettering to some extent.' But on October 16 the war party had come to power in Japan. One message from the British government, Drew wrote, 'stated in explicit terms that the time had come to reckon with the possibility of an early attack.'

The argument implied in the Drew letter (accompanying specific strictures on sending units short on training and without their vehicles) is that the expedition was planned on the assumption that fighting was unlikely; that subsequently war had become probable; and that, since Hong Kong could not be held in the event of war, the whole thing should have been reconsidered.

A quarter-century later a certain amount of official mystery still clung to the affair. The million words of testimony to the Duff commission finally reached the Commons table in March of 1948. It showed no clear-cut warning. Five secret British dispatches remained undisclosed, on the ground that such telegrams are framed on the basis that they will not be published and the whole system of full and frank communication would be prejudiced if such messages had to be prepared on the basis that this rule might not eventually be observed. In April, Mackenzie King addressed a query to British Prime Minister Attlee, who replied that none of these messages contained any warning that 'early hostile action by Japan against the United Kingdom or the United States was expected.' On which Drew commented that Attlee's message had been drawn by the nature of King's query, which referred to messages the United Kingdom authorities communicated to the commissioner.

There were, he said, others: one from the Admiralty to the British Commander-in-Chief, China, a copy of which had gone to King, instructing an addition at Manila to the *Awatea*'s naval escort because of altered circumstances; and one from the office of Lord Halifax in Washington relaying information forwarded by the British government that the whole situation in the Pacific had changed and that everything should be reviewed in the light of events.

No action, incidentally, was ever taken against the *Tribune* for its publication of parts of the Drew letter, or against the Toronto *Telegram*, which reproduced the *Tribune*'s text – complete with Xs.

Strike at Winnipeg

Winnipeg was without its daily newspapers Friday. Printers in the composing-rooms of the Free Press and Tribune did not report for work Thursday night. Instead they went into continuous session with other members of Local 191, International Typographical Union, at the Labor Temple.

This action was taken while their representatives were meeting the Winnipeg publishers in last-minute efforts to prevent a breakdown of the negotiations for a new contract which have been in progress for more than a month. . . .

Thus began the lead story in an odd-looking publication that reached the street in Winnipeg on Saturday, November 10, 1945. For one day the city's news-stands had been bare and its carrier boys idle. Now the papers had struggled into print with a joint edition under a double nameplate:

Winnipeg Free Press   The Winnipeg Tribune

Its eight news pages were jammed with typewritten copy under pasted-up headlines, the whole production engraved – then stereotyped and printed by volunteer crews.

Most of this paper's front-page news concerned the troubles that explained its existence. The lead story went on to announce Mr. Justice W.J.Major's appointment as commissioner to probe the dispute. In separate stories the joint paper carried the latest from Harry Finch, Canadian representative of the I.T.U., and the publishers: opposing sides in a contest that had stilled the linotypes the day before.

After that idle Friday, Winnipeg would not again miss a daily paper. But the strike that started there would reach out to hit newspapers in four cities across Canada – Hamilton, Ottawa, Edmonton, Vancouver. For the time being however it was a Winnipeg matter, with overtones in Indianapolis.

The I.T.U. had been back under contract with the Winnipeg papers for two years after an eight-year period when the printers had operated as a local association. Negotiations for a new contract had started in September and continued without final result (one draft had been agreed to, but turned down by the international) until November 7, when the publishers – Victor Sifton of the *Free Press* and Wesley McCurdy of the *Tribune* – asked appointment of a conciliator. The printers walked out with conciliation in progress.

The break came over relationship of I.T.U. 'general laws' to the contract.

The expiring agreement, after outlining arbitration procedure, provided for inarbitrability of I.T.U. general laws only in so far as they did not conflict with terms of the contract. The union now sought complete acceptance of I.T.U. laws and their unqualified exemption from arbitration. This the publishers refused to grant. Differences existed both over the principle involved and over practical matters on which newly inserted provisions in the laws touched – notably insistence on overtime rates for all sixth-shift work. However, it was on the recognition-and-arbitration principle that most argument centred. Efforts to settle this issue got nowhere.

Judge Major met with union and publishers through November and early December. At the last joint conference the publishers proposed, in view of failure to make progress, that the job of drafting a new and binding contract be left to a board – one representative of the union, one representative of the publishers, and a third to be appointed by the chief justice of Manitoba. The union turned this down.

In an interim report November 15 the judge noted that 'one of the chief obstacles – if not the main obstacle' was the I.T.U.'s insistence on unqualified exemption from arbitration of its general laws. The publishers, contending that this 'destroys the principle of collective bargaining', had offered non-arbitration of 'the general laws . . . not affecting wages, hours and working conditions'; which the union would not accept.

Mr. Justice Major continued his efforts to December 4 and next day submitted a final report regretting his inability to reach a settlement. His commission required him to set out a specific recommendation. He recommended provincial legislation

> . . . wherein provision is made that all matters in dispute affecting labor relations between employer and employee arising out of any contract, and any dispute in regard to any provision affecting labor relations which either party desires to be included in any new contract, shall be submitted to arbitration under the provisions of the existing Arbitration Act and amendments thereto; that any provision in any agreement, condition, or stipulation to the contrary contained in any contract or bylaw or regulation of any organization inconsistent with this provision shall be null and void; and that every such contract shall be construed or governed by the laws of the province.

The recommendation of compulsory arbitration for 'any dispute in regard to any provision affecting labor relations which either party desires to be included in any new contract' apparently would have extended the arbitration principle to the process of negotiating new agreements, a step considerably beyond the existing regulation that agreements must provide for arbitration of disputes arising under them. In other words, it would have enforced the signing of contracts. No action resulted from the Major report.

Meantime the combined *Free Press–Tribune* continued to publish.

Over at the *Free Press* and just back from war service was Colonel Dick Malone – newspaperman, veteran of the Sicilian invasion, and one-time liaison officer for Field Marshal Montgomery in Italy, where he had founded the Canadian army newspaper, the *Maple Leaf*. As Canadian public relations officer through the Normandy campaign, Malone had helped re-start newspapers with impromptu staffs in liberated Europe. Sifton and McCurdy left general production up to him through the early stages.

Mechanically and in emergency personnel, the *Free Press* was best equipped to produce the joint paper. *Tribune* editor John Bird, news editor Carlyle Allison, and business manager Arthur Moscarella moved over and worked with their *Free Press* opposite numbers, headed by George Ferguson.

Stenographers typed the news on glossy paper between rule lines. Strips of copy went out to the engravers, were reduced to column size and engraved, brought back and stereotyped. Executives helped man the composing-room. Two men gave up their I.T.U. cards and stayed. Ten veterans just out of the army came in to train. For the first week or so this was the total composing-room staff of the combined papers.

There were other snags. Pressmen and stereotypers quit work, then came back on the advice of their international officers. In the interim, editors, executives, boys from the maintenance department, and garage helpers manned the presses and casting-boxes.

On December 14 the publishers delivered to the I.T.U. a letter repeating their offer that the terms of a new contract be settled by an arbitration board and asked a decision by 6 P.M., December 17. The offer could not be held open longer 'since we must begin to make full-scale preparations for the resumption of printed newspapers in Winnipeg.' Up to this time the publishers' doors remained open, the machinery in readiness, and the typographical work to be done indicated, in case the printers returned.

With refusal of the December 14 suggestion the papers began to build up a new composing-room staff, recruited from country print-shops, apprentices, and trainees. Individual printers who returned – and they were few – did so under a severe psychological barrage from the Winnipeg *News*, a twice-a-week tabloid published by the union. They found themselves black-listed on the front page. The printers' paper also published periodically lists of non-unionists accepting composing-room work, cartoon versions of The Southam Company as a paunch-bellied, silk-hatted, cigar-smoking figure reminiscent of early-century depictions of the Trusts, and articles under such headings as 'The Unholy Alliance', 'The Stupidity of the Southams', and 'Who Owns The Winnipeg Tribune, the Siftons or The Southam Company?'

The *News* was a lively production, carrying some general news and some advertising, but largely filled with the virtues of the I.T.U. and the sins of the Southams, the Siftons, and the workmen who continued to get the papers out. Of the pressmen's union, July 30, 1946: 'Judas Iscariot was a happy man in comparison and he took the only sensible way out.'

The joint *Free Press–Tribune* ('the two-headed monstrosity', the *News* called it) grew in size and gradually increased the proportion of its content handled by orthodox printing methods. By mid-January it was up to eighteen pages, eight of which were typeset. Within a month it was no longer strictly a joint paper. On Tuesday, February 19, McCurdy wrote Fisher in jubilant mood: 'Yesterday was a red-letter day. . . . On Saturday each paper had its own title on the front page. Yesterday each paper had its own dress and make-up with different illustrations. . . .'

As it grew obvious that the struck papers could and would continue to publish, the campaign against them stepped up. In January the Winnipeg and District Trades and Labor Council declared them unfair to organized labor. Leaders promoted mass demonstrations climaxed by an outdoor parade as the weather warmed up in early May.

Long before that – as soon as it became apparent that the strike in Winnipeg had failed – the threat of pressure through strikes elsewhere appeared. On December 7 the *News* carried Harry Finch's statement: 'The unions of the International Typographical Union have decided that unified relationship with the various chains involved is the only type of relationship they will recognize in the future.' This was at just about the time the locals at Hamilton, Ottawa,

Edmonton, and Vancouver wired Fisher the threat of 'unified action'.

On February 15 the *News* said: 'The printers of the respective papers of the Southam and Sifton chains will now join the Winnipeg printers and refuse to publish . . . the Edmonton Journal, Hamilton Spectator, Ottawa Citizen, and Regina Leader-Post.' The forecast was accurate except for Regina, where printers of the Sifton-owned *Leader-Post* refused to strike.

One more attempt to settle Winnipeg proved ineffective. On February 1 Labor Minister Mitchell wrote McCurdy and Sifton suggesting a fact-finding board in an effort to reach a settlement. The publishers replied with a review of the fruitless negotiations. They had taken on 'new and binding commitments' and it was no longer possible to 'resume any relationship with the International Typographical Union'. By then the papers had built up a strong composing-room staff. At mid-February they had more than 100 compared to a pre-strike total of 124. Moreover, in view of uneasiness on the part of new men, they had assured them of job security.

However, Mitchell appointed W.D.Card of Portage la Prairie as commissioner, and Card went ahead with a rather thankless job: the publishers taking the stand that they would make the facts available for review (which they did) but would not negotiate for a contract, and the union sticking to its previous position. Card reported May 1, regretting that he could make no useful recommendation. He found the stoppage was 'not a lockout but a strike and the strike was in contravention of law' and that 'the failure of the local union to come to an agreement lies strictly on the shoulders of the executive head of the International Union at Indianapolis.'

'In this particular case,' he added, 'there is a situation in which it seems clear that one of the parties to the dispute sought throughout and still seeks to dominate the other, and unfortunately both parties to the dispute seem to have ignored the interests of the State and the public.' Presumably, as far as it applied to the publishers, this concluding curse-on-both-your-houses dictum referred to their refusal to re-enter negotiations because of their 'new and binding commitments'. Elsewhere in his report, Card suggested they could get rid of their new employees if they wanted to.

Neither the Major nor the Card report had any effect whatever. The union expressed its view in the Winnipeg *News* June 21 in an editorial calling for Humphrey Mitchell's resignation: 'The minister of labor appointed two utterly inexperienced persons to act as conciliators. . . . Both these men are quite competent in dealing with matters pertaining to civil or criminal law – but when it came to delving into the complexity of the technical angles of the dispute they were lost. . . .'

By the time the Card report came down, the Winnipeg papers were well on their way to resuming completely separate entities and normal publication methods. In little more than a month the main impact of the strike would be felt elsewhere.

In Winnipeg there was one interesting outgrowth. In April, the *News* reported canvassers selling $5 shares in the Winnipeg Co-operative Publishing Company organized to produce a third daily paper. Nearly two years later it made its appearance as the morning *Citizen*. On April 13, 1949, it published for the last time, having lost $140,000 in just over 13 months.

The Flood and the Papers

Of all Canadians, Westerners probably take most interest in the general trend of weather. Businessmen and grain-growers look to the sky and the long-range forecasts. How heavy will the run-off be from winter snow to provide early moisture? How will spring sun and rain affect the seed-bed? Will August rain delay cutting till frost nips the standing grain?

In Winnipeg, a city veined by rivers, there is an angle to this interest that has nothing to do with crops: how high will the run-off swell the Red, the historic stream that curls for thirteen crooked miles through the city's heart? Eighteen feet above datum (average winter ice-level) is flood stage. In 1948 it surged past that to twenty-three.

The winter of 1950 was one of deep snow followed by a late thaw and heavy rains. In the first days of April, news of high water began to drift in from North Dakota. Still, as late as April 8, Winnipeg expected no danger. Snow and cold next day, blocking normal run-off, changed the prospect. Though the river was then only 7.1 feet above datum, three days later engineers warned that a flood threat was near. On April 12 the work of shoring up dikes began.

Slowly the river rose round the border town of Emerson, sixty-five miles south of Winnipeg, and the towns and villages along its banks: Dominion City, St. Jean Baptiste, Morris, Silver Plains. Thousands had quit their homes in North Dakota, some taking uncertain refuge in Emerson, which by April 19 was stock-piling food. At this time the Red was still below flood stage at Winnipeg, but five towns to the south were already beleaguered. On April 21 the river rose three feet and left its banks in Winnipeg. A week later 500 people fled from Morris, the river crossed its 1948 peak and families began to move out of St. Vital.

The battle of the dikes was on as the military and thousands of volunteers piled sandbags against the rising Red. On May 5 the last links with towns south of the city went out in a downpour of rain. Next day Brigadier R.E.A.Morton of Prairie Command took charge of flood-fighting and relief.

That Saturday dawned as one of the blackest days in the history of the flood. The Wildwood dike, protecting an area of Fort Garry, collapsed. So did the Riverview, in South Winnipeg. A volunteer drowned in a basement, the one life lost during the weeks of struggle.

Throughout, both Winnipeg papers published. Carriers delivered in hip rubber-boots, sometimes from boats. Though theatres were closed, business at a standstill, and local advertising almost non-existent, city officials and publishers saw the newspapers as important to morale. The army would dike their buildings if necessary. The papers planned to continue anyway. If one building went, they would print jointly in the other. If both went, they would issue a joint edition at Regina, Saskatoon, or the Lakehead: the R.C.A.F. would fly the papers in. On Sundays both published extras, distributed free.

On May 14, when its second Sunday extra appeared, the *Tribune* had a beat. Ross Munro, then in Winnipeg to cover the flood for Southam News Services, heard rumors of a plan to evacuate the city completely if the water rose past a certain point. Munro went to Dick Malone, Victor Sifton's right-hand man at the *Free Press*, now back in uniform as a brigadier to head up emergency planning. Malone confirmed his information, let him see the file, and scrupulously respected the exclusive. The *Tribune* carried the story; his own paper went without it. The plan called for a withdrawal to lines east and west of the city and the setting-up of food depots and evacuation shelters. It would go into effect if the river rose to 32.5 feet.

At that time the Red stood at 30.2, and had stayed at that level for twelve hours. On May 19 it crept up to 30.3. Next day, inch by inch, it began to drop.

On May 18, though water had begun to seep into the basement of its building at Smith and Graham, the *Tribune* ran a sixteen-page special edition – a pictorial record of a flood still at its height. This it sold at 25 cents and turned over the proceeds, $56,000, to flood relief.

The flood cost more than $20,000,000 and led to plans for a flood canal to divert surplus water in future emergencies. In 1966, when

City Flood at Crisis; Army in Control

The Canadian army has been placed in command of all Manitoba flood relief efforts, with Brigadier R. E. A. Morton directing officer.

Defence Minister Claxton has authorized placing military reserve forces on active service to fight the Manitoba floods. Troops will be brought from Shilo and Rivers to join the relief battle.

Dominion Weather Bureau forecast rain and snow for the Red River areas today, but said skies were expected to clear on Sunday.

The city engineer's department has been placed on a 24-hour alert. City records and documents are being moved to higher levels in City Hall after waters poured into the basement of City Hall annex.

Volunteer flood worker Lawson Ogg, 873 Sherburn St., was swept into the basement of a Kingston Crescent home today and drowned. First flood victim in the Greater Winnipeg area, he died when the flood swept through a barricaded door and trapped him.

Houses are floating at Morris where huge waves keep refugees from fleeing to Winnipeg by C.N.R.

Official report from the city engineer's department said the flood fight is lost. Every dike in the city except one has been broken. "The city's resources have been exhausted; no attempt will be made to repair dikes."

Dominion City began its first large-scale evacuation today.

The Weather
FORECAST: Clearing Sunday, Cool

THE WINNIPEG TRIBUNE

FINAL EDITION

61st Year — With colored comics, 10 cents — Price 5 cents

WINNIPEG, SATURDAY, MAY 6, 1950 — 52 PAGES — NO. 108

ALL CITY DIKES BROKEN

Water flows over the approach to Norwood Bridge at the foot of Bell Ave., and Main St., cutting off the bridge. Provencher Bridge to St. Boniface has also been closed.

Victims Flee New Red Tide

More Red River Valley residents fled the flood today as heavy rain threatened a new tide of destruction. Hundreds of people have now been evacuated.

Nearly three inches of rain fell at Grand Forks in 24 hours and the fall was an inch each along the valley.

The first surged six inches higher at Morris, rose 6 inches at Ste. Agathe and swelled at St. Norbert by one foot.

Only at Emerson was the Red dropping this morning. There the level fell less than two inches.

The fury of the river menaced Letellier, hitherto safe behind a nine-foot dike. But today water is seeping through the barricade holding back a 7 1/2 foot wall of water.

At Morris, lashed by wind, rain and flood, 60 evacuees were helped by huge waves from reaching a safer high ground in Winnipeg.

Houses are floating in Morris where water is nearing 10 feet deep in main street.

MORRIS

Red River rose another six inches at Morris. Some homes, dislodged by strong winds and floods, are

(Continued on Page 14, No. 1)

Water is lapping at the windows of Winnipeg's new Princess Elizabeth Hospital, and has run wild, the basement. The picture shows the foot of Oakwood Ave., and Eccles St.

The Red River today flowed over Water St. at the approach to Provencher Bridge. St. Boniface Cathedral can be seen in the background. Note boat on the street.

Tribune Flood Edition Sunday

The Tribune will publish an emergency edition Sunday at the request of civic officials as a public service.

The edition will be published Sunday at or about 12 noon. It will be delivered to Tribune subscribers free.

The edition is designed to circulate government and city instructions to citizens on the increasing flood emergency.

Morton Directs Aid Plan

The army has been placed in supreme command of Manitoba flood relief.

Premier D. L. Campbell announced today the government appointed Brigadier R. E. A. Morton, general officer commanding Prairie Command, to direct relief efforts.

The premier said the flood situation in the Red River valley had deteriorated so seriously that the government has decided to centralize all flood relief efforts.

The provincial government statement said arrangements had been made to evacuate patients in Winnipeg Municipal Hospitals to Deer Lodge military hospital.

Defence Minister Claxton today authorized placing any necessary reserve forces on active service to aid in the flood crisis.

He also authorized moves of military personnel from Rivers and Shilo to the flood zone.

The defence minister said all defence troop-carrying vehicles and men were used in the invasion of Normandy, are being shipped to Winnipeg. They have been standing by on flats at Camp Borden Ont. and London, Ont. armored for this emergency.

Additional sandbags will be made available from Regina and additional pumps from the Royal Canadian Engineer camp at Chilliwack, B.C.

In Winnipeg, the military headquarters would draw on three regiments in the reserve

(Continued on Page 14, No. 2)

BRIG. R. E. A. MORTON
Commands Flood Relief

Trapped Worker Drowns

The Red River flood claimed its first victim in Greater Winnipeg today when a volunteer flood worker drowned this morning in Elm Park.

St. Vital police gave his name as Lawson Alfred Ogg, 25, of 873 Sherburn St.

Ogg was working in Kingston Crescent home at 6:30 a.m. today when the flood tore through the barricaded back door and swept him into the inundated basement.

Ogg was working as a volunteer flood worker at the home of Dr. Albert Johnson, 207 Kingston Crescent. He and others with the Optimist

(Continued on Page 14, No. 3)

Hundreds Flee Suburb Homes

BULLETIN

J. W. Sanger, general manager of Winnipeg Hydro Electric System, told an emergency meeting of city council today that total evacuation of Winnipeg might be necessary.

The Hydro manager said he had already made plans to evacuate some of his staff to Slave Falls and Pointe du Bois.

Mr. Sanger suggested that other employees in Winnipeg make arrangements for evacuation of their workers.

Council appointed a civic official committee headed by City Engineer W. D. Hurst to govern all flood control in Winnipeg.

Greater Winnipeg lost its battle with the Red River today.

Hundreds of square blocks in the city and its suburbs lay inundated after dikes broke under a constant all-night pounding.

The flood claimed one life early this morning. Twenty-five-year-old Lawson "Scotty" Ogg, of 873 Sherburn St., was swept to his death when the flood waters tore a Kingston Crescent home where he was working.

River continued its surging rise today and stood at 26.3 feet above datum at 11 a.m.

This is an increase of 1.5 feet in the last 24 hours.

Here is the flood situation at press time today:

- All city dikes but one have been swept away.
- Widowhood Park area is covered with water. Three hundred families have evacuated.
- Fifty square blocks in West Kildonan is flooded.
- Elm Park is inundated and cut off except by boat.
- Estimated 220 patients evacuated from municipal hospitals.
- Huge section of River—

A few hundred persons fled Winter Park area in St. Boniface & Norwood and Provencher bridges closed by flood waters.

- Five evacuees — Higgins Ave, North Main, Portage Ave, Pacific Ave, Nairn Ave, Rorie St. and Annabella St. covered with water.
- Central heat cut off in many sections but officials say will keep operating.
- In the 24-hour period ending 8 a.m. today Winnipeg received 1.88 inches of precipitation.

City Line Fight

Deputy city engineer A. J. Taunton said today that Winnipeg had lost its battle with the flood.

(Continued on Page 14, No. 4)

Evacuation Race Clears Hospitals

Two municipal hospitals were cleared of almost 200 patients early today just before the Red River burst into Riverview.

The dike raced to the hospitals in to beat at swirling waters over block after block in the district.

Waters may be four feet deep near King George Hospital, in the area.

About 150 patients from King Edward Hospital, in the same district were evacuated at 3 a.m. today. Another 50 fled from near King George Hospital at 5 a.m.

Evacuees from King Edward Hospital have been taken to Lodge Hospital. Most were still

view covered with water.

Shortly after 5 a.m. when workers defending the flood dikes lost their battle. Waters poured into the area.

Families are fleeing homes on Morley Ave. and partial lines in the Riverview area.

(Continued on Page 14, No. 5)

City Jail Moves Prisoners As Floods Cut Heat in Cells

City police Friday night moved to protect 12 prisoners from the effects of the flooding Red River.

Prisoners in Rupert Ave. police station were removed from their cold cells to the two sub-stations in the city because heat had been cut off in the downtown jail.

One official explained there were no blankets available at the central station for those awaiting trial and prisoners Friday night dropped to the point where it was necessary to move the prisoners.

Until heat is restored to the Rupert Ave. jail, prisoners will be held in the sub-stations.

Sandbags Rushed To City By Army

MONTREAL (CP) — Two carloads of sandbags to fight the

Manitoba floods left by fast freight today for Winnipeg.

More than 200,000 bags were in the shipment, a hurried job by the command of the Canadian army, which supplied the bags.

Spokesman said the shipment will be rushed through, checked en route. If necessary, the new bags can be shifted to fast express en route.

Ottawa was working as a volunteer flood worker at the home of Dr. Albert Johnson

Ottawa Orders DUKWS To Manitoba Floods

LONDON, Ont. (CP) — "Dukws" army amphibious trains left London early today for Winnipeg to aid in the evacuation and in patrolling of flooded Manitoba towns.

Dukws were sent from 27 C.O.D. as a request from Ottawa. Officers and men of 27 C.O.D. and No. 1 company R.C.E.M.E. worked all day last Sunday preparing the vehicles when the order was telephoned army headquarters ordered that the equipment might be needed.

Orders to move came Friday night.

Doctor Travels Flood To Deliver New Baby

Dr. Joseph Boucher, St. Jean Baptiste doctor, travelled 14 miles in boat, hand-car and caterpillar tractor Friday night to deliver a baby.

In the flood emergency, this was nothing new to Dr. Boucher.

In addition to these prompt transport he had also recently been attending expectant mothers and the sick.

Police Appeal Here For Loan of Boats

A police co-ordinating service went out today under the direction of Chief Constable Charles Marcher to provide water transport for all flooded areas.

Chief Marcher is co-ordinating individuals owning boats with two boats in operation.

Chief Marcher is fleeing victims and co-ordinating rescue, dispatching rescuers and relief agencies.

(Continued on Page 14, No. 6)

Tribune Carrier Boys Fight Through City Flood

Tribune readers who receive their papers today can understand difficulties of delivery through the water-logged area.

Carrier boys have all reported for duty despite the snarled communication and barriers in getting to their depots. The boys are exerting heroic efforts in making their paper deliveries. Slogging through muddy roads and detours through water-covered areas.

Several of the carrier boys have called upon assistance of friends or relatives to make sure the paper gets through.

In areas where communication is only by water and where residents are still in their homes, a few carrier boys have "hitch-hiked" by boat to deliver The Tribune.

In view of these difficulties Tribune readers are asked to bear with patience any late delivery.

the Red rose again, the canal was still uncompleted. But the river stopped well short of its 1950 high and dikes had been reinforced.

Flavor of a Birthday

On April 6, 1965, the *Tribune* brought out a 110-page seventy-fifth anniversary edition. As usual in such special issues the paper recorded a notable flow of history in story and picture – from the Seven Oaks massacre of 1816 down through the fur brigades and the troubles of 1870 and on to early bush-flying, The Strangler, depression and dust and Bennett buggies, wartime and the flood. What made this one unique was its front page. *Tribune* readers that day were startled by a format that followed the layout of Richardson's first issue of January 28, 1890 – cramped type, one-column label headings, two columns of classified ads on a page from which they had long been banished.

Tribune head-writers, trying to capture the flavor of that early paper, caught a good deal of it. A TERRIBLE NIGHT, topping the story of a Greek earthquake, and MAYOR FLIM-FLAMMED, over an Alabaman's experience in Washington, might well have been scribbled by a desk-man in Richardson's time. His modern counterparts could not quite reach the pathos of SAD END OF A SOPHOMORE, recording an 1890 horse-and-buggy traffic death in New Haven, or the impact of STARK NAKED IN CHURCH, the label on a slight sensation reported from Toronto. But they came close.

Only the substance of the news differed. And even there a subtle likeness breathed. The *Tribune*'s first issue reported forty lives lost from the British ship *Lochmoidart*, wrecked on the Dutch coast. Its seventy-fifth edition printed the story of a passenger-freight collision in Brazil with forty dead. Readers of 1890 would have puzzled over a reference to 'the first Gemini docking and rendezvous mission', but the intelligence from France that 'two lovers wrapped explosives around their bodies and blew themselves up' would have been as understandable and interesting then as now. For the essential quality of news does not change much. Only the personalities, the mechanics, the terms and attitudes in which it is reported alter with time.

Even old political issues sometimes survive or are resurrected. The schools question, for instance, in Manitoba: 'Manitobans should not be deceived. The men who are supporting the government are the men who are pledged to maintain national schools. They are the men to be trusted. . . .' Thus the *Tribune* on January 14, 1896, the day before the Greenway government almost wiped out the Conservative opposition on the question of separate schools. Six years earlier the province had removed denominational schools from its public educational system. Five months later, efforts by federal Conservatives to override the province would contribute to their fall – and paradoxically the victory of the Catholic Laurier. The Manitoba school question, it seemed, was settled. 'That this assumption was to prove wrong in the minds of many citizens', said Premier Duff Roblin in 1964, 'is a fact that history was subsequently to establish. The issue still smoulders explosively beneath the surface of our political and community life.'

Already when Roblin won office in 1958 (heading the first Conservative government in Manitoba since his grandfather's fall in 1915) a royal commission had Manitoba's school system under study. Late in 1959 it recommended, among other things, direct grants to private schools, most of which were Roman Catholic parochial schools supported by parents who also paid public school taxes. A couple of years earlier the *Tribune* had deserted the long-ago stand of Richardson and questioned whether a school should be disqualified for public assistance merely because it attempted to meet educational requirements and provide something more. Of the 1959 recommendation it said: 'Private schools may fairly expect some financial support from public funds, provided this does not harm the public school system.'

What Roblin came up with was something else. On February 11, 1964, he announced an offer of shared services. Direct provincial aid would have made an election or plebiscite necessary that would probably have split the province. But under his plan all services in the public school system, from free text books to bus transportation, could be made available to private schools.

The *Tribune* commented that it was unusual to find a new approach in a seventy-year-old controversy, but this was what Roblin had done. The new policy 'should appeal to moderate elements in the community.'

To some it appealed and to some it did not. But free school books worth $60,000 went to 10,000 private school students on September 1, 1965. On the same day the government proclaimed legislation permitting public school boards to provide transportation, instruction, and use of public school workshops and gymnasiums to private schools, under arrangements by which the province would meet extra costs involved. Agreements were concluded in most districts having parochial schools in a position to take advantage of the plan.

Perhaps the *Tribune*'s founder, by that time, would have come to agree with his paper's modern editorial stand on the school question. Certainly he would have cheered a piece of news enterprise in the spring of 1964: there are few more satisfying operations to a lively newspaper than the exposure by its own efforts of sharp practice or plain skulduggery.

On Saturday, May 2, the *Tribune* devoted most of its front page to the plight of a fifty-seven-year-old baggage porter from St. Vital. The baggage-man's mail one day had included a folder captioned 'Do you need money? Look inside!' He needed money. Of his $296 monthly take-home pay, $157 went into mortgage payments, instalments on a car, deep-freeze, house repairs, and clothing, leaving him and his family $139 to live on. He looked inside. The folder contained an invitation to visit an institution described as a financial federation. He accepted the invitation, hoping to renegotiate a first mortgage and consolidate his debts at a monthly pay-off of $75 or so. What he wound up with was a $3,500 second mortgage at 12 per cent – granted after he had agreed to make $1,215 of home improvements, material for which came from building-products companies housed in the same building as the 'financial federation' and the corporation taking the second mortgage.

Tribune probing turned up the fact that the president of the financial federation also headed the mortgage company and two of the building-products companies. The paper hired a reputable supply company to appraise the $1,215 in improvements. It came up with a figure of $463.03. Recapitulating, the *Tribune* found that the baggage porter had received $1,601.30 in paid-off debts and home improvements – in return for an obligation to pay, over five years, more than $4,500 in principal and interest on the second mortgage.

A week later the paper detailed the story of a four-plex owner who needed $1,500, went through an even more elaborate wringing-out, and wound up in a rooming-house on $50.60 a month welfare.

No one was more tickled with this piece of *Tribune* enterprise than the city's reputable mortgage companies. The provincial government appointed a commissioner to look into mortgage-loan deals and that summer passed an Unconscionable Transactions Act to block abuses.

12

Vancouver:
The Lively Coast

Through the years of *Province-Sun* rivalry in the evening field, Vancouver readers were treated to some of the liveliest newspaper cut-and-thrust of modern times.

Key personalities differed as widely as the papers. Frank Burd, massive and kindly, embodied long newspaper experience and a native but orthodox astuteness without innovational flair: 'A high-minded man with instincts of the best,' in the words of one *Province* contemporary. R.J.Cromie once inspired this character sketch by a weekly newspaper editor:

> New lines of thought are his delight, and his impatience and ruthlessness when convention and tradition block the way are apparent. It may be that in his search after the new and the unusual more than a hint of the bizarre and the fantastic will be and has been featured. No one knows better than that astute publicist the value of shock effect, and he sees that the readers of the Sun do not go short.*

Burd and the *Province* proceeded at a normal pace while Cromie rode the *Sun* at a multi-directional gallop.

The gallop carried it sometimes into front-page forays in which its enthusiasm for anything that might heighten the glory of Vancouver (to which in Cromie's view the western edge of the continent and a good deal of the interior were tributary) combined with thrusts at the *Province*'s habit of looking at two or more sides of everything. The hacking as such was largely one way, the *Province* seldom replying directly to the *Sun*'s assaults on it as a newspaper but continuing unperturbed to discuss the merits of propositions for which its lively

*W.S.Harris in the Vernon *News,* March 15, 1930.

rival often went on flamboyant crusade.

The papers' contrasting treatment of the Pacific Great Eastern question in 1928 is perhaps typical. Sixteen years and $50,000,000 after conception, the railway's separate sections – North Vancouver to Horseshoe Bay and Squamish to Quesnel – still plagued the treasury. Prior to the provincial election that year the *Sun* mounted a campaign: let the provincial government complete the PGE and push it on to give the Peace River country, straddling the B.C.–Alberta border, an outlet through Vancouver.

The *Province* sent reporter Hugh Savage to the Peace to report on conditions at first hand. He returned with conclusions thus set out by the paper: The Peace River district wasn't suffering from lack of rail service to market its grain, though it needed branch lines into remote sections. Even with the PGE built into the Peace, the best freight rate to the Coast could scarcely be less than the existing rate for grain shipped to Vancouver via Edmonton, and already 65 per cent of the Peace crop turned west from Edmonton for Vancouver export. Alberta, whose government lines were just beginning to pay, would resent competition that divided between two railroads business scarcely sufficient for one.

The *Province* held that building of further main lines into the Peace could be justified only by the prospect of a great increase in business, a large increase in wheat-growing, which would mean a bigger population. Since building must depend on settlement, and this must depend on immigration, development of the PGE hinterland was a job for railway and immigration experts, not provincial politicians; for the Dominion government and one, or both, of the national railways. It suggested that Premier MacLean (Liberal leader after Honest John Oliver's death) should be showing the CNR the advantages of the development of northern B.C. and the Peace area through intelligent extension and operation of the PGE, rather than trying to get elected on the ground that as a Liberal he was the only one who could put over sale of the railway at Ottawa.

Conservative S.F.Tolmie won in British Columbia, nobody bought the PGE (to be completed by a provincial government a generation later), and the *Sun* nailed up the *Province*'s position on the Peace River outlet as one of a long list of crimes to be deplored through the years.

In that good summer of 1928, however, there were some things – including certain events in Amsterdam – for which even competing newspapers could raise a concerted cheer.

A Turn of Speed

In 1924 King Edward High School had a couple of track-men on whom coach Bob Granger kept a special eye. One was a senior, Bob Elson, who won the 880 Olympic trial for British Columbia that spring. The other was a sixteen-year-old freshman with a turn of speed in the sprints. His name was Percy Williams.

By 1928 Williams, then in the High School of Commerce, was equalling Olympic records in trials and high school meets. Elson – American-born, he couldn't run for Canada – had gone on to other things. He had joined the *Province* as office boy and moved up to junior reporter in the city-room, covering track and field on the side. Few experts apart from Granger and the *Province* reporter rated Williams as anything exceptional in a track world that included the American sprinters Frank Wykoff, Bob McAllister, Jackson Scholtz, and the veteran Charley Paddock, and such Europeans as Helmut Koernig and George Lammers. But the Amsterdam Olympics were coming up and he was probably the best sprint bet Canada had.

The *Province* then had a Sunday magazine edited by Lukin Johnston, soon to become the Southams' first staff man in Europe. Johnston, born in England but steeped in western Canadian life, believed in travel as a developer of young reporters. He encouraged an idea already sprouting in Elson's mind. This was somehow to get to Amsterdam to cover Williams. Spurred by Johnston, Elson put his dream in the form of a proposition to Roy Brown: if the *Province* would pay half his expenses he would put up the rest. Brown agreed, and with $750 from the paper and $750 borrowed from his father, the twenty-two-year-old Elson set out for Europe. The deal paid off for all concerned.

On July 30 the telegraph sounders clicked out the news:

AMSTERDAM – A Canadian schoolboy from Vancouver, Percy Williams, sprang from obscurity to fame today by beating the world's greatest sprinters in the Olympic final in 10 4/5 seconds. . . .

Williams hit the tape a yard in front of Britisher Jack London in the 100 metres. Wykoff and McAllister finished fourth and sixth. The *Province* threw a four-column spread into the front page, including a foot-deep picture captioned 'Percy Williams Puts City On Map by Olympiad Victory'.

Bobby Robinson of the Hamilton *Spectator*, a power among track-and-field entrepreneurs and already working toward the first Empire Games held at Hamilton two years later, was No. 1 Southam Olym-

EXPLORERS REACH BAY
John Schooners Are Heading for Chesterfield Inlet —Page 2.

RICHEST MAN IN WEST DIES
Thomas Barlow Walker Reputed to Be Worth $100,000,000—Page 22.

U.S. Part HELPS CHINA'S HAND
With Nationals May Encourage Them to Resist Japan.—Page 3

Riot of Cheers Swept Stadium As Percy Won

edlam Broke Loose At Canada's Great Victory.

ARVELLOUS SHOW OF SPEED

rovince Staff Correspondent Describes Contest

By ROBERT T. ELSON

THIRTY POOL SHIPS FIXED FOR LOADING

Report Says Many Wheat Vessels Coming to Vancouver.

ALL TO TAKE FULL CARGOES

Early Predictions Indicate Record Grain Traffic Here.

FRENCH RETAIN TENNIS TROPHY

ROLAND GARROS STADIUM, Paris, July 29.

Williams of Vancouver Wins World's Sprinting Title at Olympic Games

Williams Won in Sensational Finish to Brilliant Race.

CITY IS AGOG WITH PRIDE

Canada, Free State and England Take Three Championships.

AMSTERDAM, July 30

PERCY WILLIAMS PUTS CITY ON MAP, BY OLYMPIAD VICTORY

GET $25,000 FROM BANK MESSENGERS

Five Desperadoes Hold Up Couriers in Winnipeg Streets and Escape.

THOUGHT TO BE AMERICANS

Car Used by Holdup Men Believed to Have Been Stolen Machine.

WINNIPEG, July 30—(CP)

Three Canadian Girls Out of Four Enter Final.

RUN FAST IN 100 METRES

Lord Burghley Gains Striking Victory in Hurdle Event.

AMSTERDAM, July 30

CANADIAN MEN SEMI-FINAL

GIRLS QUALIFIES In 100 METRES.

CITY MILL WORKER HIT BY TRAIN

SUCCESSION DUTIES WILL BE UNIFIED

VICTORIA, July 30

GAME BIRD SEASON FIXED

Willow Grouse Protected Throughout B.C. to Prevent Extermination.

TWO DIVISIONS

VICTORIA, July 30

"I Just Pushed Ahead With Every Ounce I Had"

By ROBERT T. ELSON
Correspondent of the Daily Province.
AMSTERDAM, July 30

ANGLICAN RECTOR HAS PASSED AWAY

REV. HAVELOCK DEACHAM

JACK MILLER, RUM AGENT, IS 'BROKE'

SAN FRANCISCO, July 30—AP

Tanner Will Retire

NEW YORK, July 30

PERCY WILLIAMS

A BOY, just out of his teens...

ALL Vancouver was thrilled...

Sonnysayings
By FANNY Y. CORY

Here I came...

pic reporter. But Elson had the inside track on Williams and made the most of it.

The 200 was still to come. Elson hedged a bit: 'Williams goes to fight again for Canada in the 200 metres, but what he can do after today's tests is problematic. . . . Canada may pray for one more victory, or at least points, if he is at his best.' He was. On August 1 lightning struck a second time. The *Province* widened its front-page spread to six columns. It already had started a fund to bring Bob Granger back first class. The coach had accompanied Williams to the final trials and got to Amsterdam third class, on a slow boat with $100 raised by the *Province* when he ran out of funds in Hamilton. He came back in style.

It was Canada's year of Olympic glory. Four girls – Fanny Rosenfeld, Myrtle Cook, Ethel Smith, and Jane Bell – won the 400 metres women's relay, Ethel Catherwood the high jump. But the top-line story was Williams. The *Province* was moved to a front-page editorial that urged: 'Let's hoist all the flags in Vancouver!' Most of them were already up.

For Elson the trip was a notable milestone. After the games he went on to Berlin, Rome, Venice, and Geneva (where Johnston was covering a League of Nations session), and later did chores for a month around the London office. In Montreal on the way back, F.N. Southam sent for him, talked the jaunt over, and issued a cheque for half the money Elson had spent personally on a trip that was half work and half a personal tour 'for to admire and for to see'.

Elson became sports editor and later news editor of the *Province*, before moving to Washington as Southam correspondent in 1941, and on to *Time* magazine a couple of years later. The 1928 trip remained in his mind as a rich experience for a young reporter: 'I had a taste of the world, I had seen an Olympics, I had been introduced to the League of Nations – and all it cost me was $375.'

Vancouver in the Thirties

In the spring of 1930 D.A.McGregor and Percy Rawling had a problem. A federal election loomed. Four years earlier the *Province* had come out strongly for Arthur Meighen; but the two editorial writers could get no word from publisher Frank Burd or editor Roy Brown as to how it stood on R.B.Bennett's challenge to the Mackenzie King régime. In an effort to force a choice McGregor wrote an editorial from the Liberal point of view and Rawling produced a Conservative one. They had them set in type and sent to Burd and Brown. Each was approved and the paper ran them both.

This habit of pro-and-con discussion rather than a downright choice of sides continued through the campaign. A story drifted out to Vancouver after the election. F.N.Southam, meeting Bennett at some eastern function, congratulated him on his victory. 'Yes,' R.B. said. 'No thanks to the Vancouver Province!'

Even the Southam brothers differed on just what the *Province*'s political position was or whether it had any. Early in 1932 in a letter to F.N., Harry referred casually to the paper as 'independent Conservative'. F.N. commented: 'In comparison with all of our other papers the Province is in the happy position of having no party affiliations either before elections, during elections, or after they are over.' To some extent it had inherited this situation from Walter Nichol, 'but the present management has greatly strengthened their editorial standing by either friendly comment or frank criticism of all political parties.' Harry wrote back that he still thought the independent Conservative label correct, though the *Province* admittedly was 'editorially freer than the rest of us'.

In any event the paper's editorial page had about it a special atmosphere, touched with warmth and sometimes a light-hearted scepticism. Along with its studied discussions of public affairs it carried columns ranging from the chatty to the irreverent, written by characters who had in their own way become *Province* institutions.

One was a gentle and bearded ancient named Bernard McEvoy, born in Birmingham in 1842, who wrote book reviews, art critiques, and a column headed 'Street Corners', and who had one final ambition: to do so until he was ninety. He made it with ten days to spare.

Another was Philip Winter Luce, the title of whose column 'The Odd Angle' accurately reflected its content. When Arthur Stringer suggested an exchange of Canadian and English authors, Luce proposed a trade of Hector Charlesworth for G.K.Chesterton – with, if England insisted, a minor female poet thrown in.

But the real collector's item was Jim Butterfield, a Cambridge and Heidelberg man who shared with church and farm editors a room that thus became known as Heaven, Earth, and Hades. Luce in a column of reminiscence once wrote of days when bar-tenders were important news-tipsters, and of a reporter who got fired trying to cover the saloon beat from a seat on the water wagon. No such fate could have overtaken Butterfield. Nevertheless, for nearly twenty years until his death in 1941 his column, 'The Common Round', devastating in its treatment of the stuffy and conventional, tickled and sometimes maddened *Province* readers. As one executive admitted (admitting also that Butterfield completely baffled him) it was a power on the page.

The war of words continued. In its role of aggressor from second place in circulation and advertising (the *Province* held first place with over 80,000, a bulge of 10,000 or so) the *Sun* bolstered its claim that it was the only authentic voice of Vancouver by making the *Province*'s ownership a point of attack. 'We want to make greater Vancouver a live city, a city owned, controlled, and run by our own local people, so that our sons and daughters will some day have a chance to own our Vancouver institutions instead of having to work for eastern owners,' it said in a letter to subscribers in 1930. 'This can only be done by developing a strong Vancouver spirit and a Vancouver-owned newspaper with no strings attached to its policy or ownership is the only paper which can honestly pretend to do this for you in a really conscientious way.'

F.N.Southam thought this 'quite legitimate and very interesting' and suggested to Frank Burd that he meet it with promotional material calling attention to the news services and other points of merit the *Province* could claim.

Cromie attacked on two levels and with a touch of inconsistency. Publicly the *Sun* blasted the *Province* as the expression of an 'eastern voice' that 'comes hurtling over 3,000 miles of space'. In Harold Weir the paper had an editorial writer whose special talent was converting the powder and ball of Cromie's ideas into mortar-bursts of words. A typical *Sun* editorial paragraph, inspired by arguments over specifications for the proposed First Narrows (Lions Gate) bridge: 'The intrigues, the journalistic machinations, the kite-flying and the stealthy innuendoes that have centred about this structure ever since it was first proposed constitute the most offensive and preposterous affront that has been offered to any self-contained community since the Babylonians came down and enslaved Jerusalem.' At the same time, by letter and wire, the *Sun*'s publisher kept urging F.N.Southam to inject his eastern voice into the *Province*'s conduct: to force Burd into co-operative arrangements between the papers.

Early in 1933 the *Province* and *Sun* did in fact agree to stabilize the circulation position in various classifications (city carrier, city total, and so on) with the *Sun* at 86 per cent of the *Province* over-all, the agreement providing that either paper making gains in any classification would cease efforts to get new subscribers while the other took steps to catch up. They couldn't get together on advertising. In May of 1934 when Vancouver department stores began distributing circular advertising independently of the newspapers, Cromie blamed the *Province*. Only co-operation on rates and plans could save mass advertising, he wired F.N., but so far as the *Province* was concerned 'co-operative spirit to protect this precarious advertising situation never started and from what I can observe of present crowd and present ideas never will.' F.N. should 'come out here and clean out half this Province gang or these two newspapers will be wrecked.'

Neither Burd nor F.N.Southam appears to have been particularly perturbed, though F.N., who was friendly with Cromie, occasionally entered a mild remonstrance against *Sun* editorial attacks, as when in August of 1934, the *Province* having questioned plans to build a new city hall at that time, the *Sun* again blistered it as the voice of St. James Street. To F.N.'s objection that St. James Street had no influence with himself or with the *Province*, Cromie replied that maybe this was true; the trouble with F.N. was that he sat there in Montreal delegating authority to Burd, 'a kindly incomprehensible individual'. Anyway, every bit of *Sun* influence and innuendo had been invited by 'Province innuendo and guile'.

The *Province* just occasionally picked a spot for a counter-thrust. In August of 1935 the *Sun* described a Mackenzie King radio speech as 'defining the true spirit of government . . . a refreshing breeze after five years of political drouth.' The *Province* dug up and quoted a *Sun* editorial of three years before that had accused King of being an 'accessory before the fact in the economic ruination of the country'. The *Sun* replied that it had often deprecated King's academic approach and probably would again, and fired a new salvo in which it accused the *Province* of furthering a 'Fascist program' to 'ensure the security of the Holts, the Bennetts and the Southam press.'

At one point – in October of 1935 – Harry Southam took a hand. The *Sun* sometimes quoted the *Citizen*, and whenever Charlie Bowman visited Vancouver lost no opportunity to refer to him as 'a great Liberal editor' and mention his views on Social Credit – its editors enjoying a chuckle at the expense of the *Province*, the views of which differed considerably from the *Citizen*'s. At this time the *Sun* was giving wide play to demands for monetary reform, and Cromie sent Harry, through Bowman, a tabloid section it had published giving the text of a Social Credit speech by Dean Hewlett Johnson, better known later as the Red Dean of Canterbury.

Congratulating 'Dear Robert' on this display by the *Sun*, Harry added a regretful rebuke:

> I wonder at times how you can bring yourself to write to me . . . in such a friendly spirit, notwithstanding the unkind, untrue, and I think wholly indefensible references which you on occasions make in the *Sun* about the Vancouver Province and its owners. I know you would

not say such things about us or to us personally and I should think you
would be happier in the fine work you are doing in so many directions
if you omitted from the Sun your sensational and, in my view, cheap
references to the ownership of the Vancouver Province. . . .

Cromie was not in a receptive mood. Back in August as a promotional venture the *Sun* had brought Will Durant to Vancouver to lecture. Under the subhead WINDMILL WILL, Jim Butterfield commented in the *Province*: 'There is something fascinating in watching
the gyrations of Mr. Will Durant, the well-known second-hand phi-
losopher. Every time he comes along on one of his lecture tours and
deflects himself from the land of the free for an adventure among the
wild Canadians he gives us something to laugh about. . . .' And just
before he got Harry's letter Cromie had invited Beverley Baxter out
from the East to talk to the Canadian Club. Once again Butterfield
inserted a rusty needle:

> Mr. Beverley Baxter, super-Canadian and adopted son of British
> films, with a newly-born Oxford accent and a carefully selected set of
> ideas about what is good for Canada, is now actually with us. . . . It is
> interesting to note the passionate adulation expressed by Mr. Pat
> Terry of the Sun in welcoming his ex-chief on the Daily Express. The
> Daily Express is perhaps the best conducted organ of opinion in Eng-
> land and at the same time conveys to the public the worst set of
> opinions yet known to civilized man.

In the light of such disreputable attacks, Cromie told Harry, anything the *Sun* called the *Province* was justified. The Southam brothers were all right, better than most. 'But I see no wings sprouting
from your shoulders, nor do I see any of you following Christ's advice of giving all your goods to the poor. . . . After your letter you
can be sure that I shall endeavor to keep my friendly spirit, as you
call it, out of your Christian path.'

There was no further correspondence between Harry and Robert.

This acrid jousting was of course a mere sidelight to the business of
publishing newspapers in a trying time.

The *Province* in an editorial December 3, 1931, remarked that in
normal times newspaper pages run to gloom and disaster because
these are unusual and therefore news; dark shadows on the bright
background of life. But now the pattern was reversed, the background dark: good news at last was news. The previous day for instance the *Province* had reported: 'National loan over-subscribed
. . . B.C. apple crop oversold . . . Orders for canned salmon diverted
to Vancouver . . . British Columbia boxes being used for African
oranges . . . Santa Claus fund grows. . . .' In other days these might

have so merged in their bright background as to be almost invisible. Now they showed up against the dark. The theme was over-simplified but had in it a core of truth.

One depression casualty was Odlum's morning *Star*. It appeared for the last time on February 12, 1932. Largely through the efforts of out-of-work *Star* men a replacement struggled into being in November: the Vancouver *News* (later the *News-Herald* and still later the *Herald*) born amid predictions of quick failure but due to last, at times precariously, a quarter-century. On June 6, 1933, with advertising too light to justify two weekend editions, the *Province* discontinued its Sunday edition, merging magazine material in its Saturday.

Late in 1932 as the depression lengthened Conservative Premier Tolmie (abetted by the *Province*) began to urge union government as the proper way to meet British Columbia's troubles, and was snowed under in a provincial election a year later – a vote that threw Thomas Duff Pattullo to the top of the heap, all but eliminated the Conservatives, and elevated the new C.C.F. to the status of official opposition.

At the beginning of 1935, Vancouver picked a mayor who would have caught the younger Walter Nichol's imagination but probably would have won nothing from the later and more conservative Nichol but a shake of the head. Outspoken and original (when an acquaintance mentioned his campaign habit of speaking to church groups he remarked: 'There's nothing like a shot of God!'), Gerry McGeer made startling copy as mayor and later in the federal Commons where his ideas on money and attacks on bankers shocked Liberals of an older school.

The *Province* thought McGeer's monetary ideas simply meant inflation, but in general regarded him as basically a good boy with bad manners: 'Very justly he has an enormous following. With great courage and ability he has accomplished much as mayor of Vancouver. If he would refrain from shaking his fist in the faces of people who should be the best friends of Vancouver, we can see enormous possibilities for good.' When relief campers poured into the city in April, forcing McGeer to read the Riot Act, the *Province* departed from its usual quiet style. Unemployment was a national matter, on a national scale. Vancouver was in the hands of an army of occupation, apparently 'quite beyond the vision of a complacent and dying government in Ottawa.'

And while we are giving advice to long-suffering camp-men who know from experience the destruction of the human spirit which enforced idleness brings [the paper continued] we should like, if it is not presumptuous, to despatch a little to that government on Parliament Hill which awaits its end with such dignity and fortitude. . . . It would make the Dominion happy and prosperous and secure – in the future. But while it dreams of the future there is a fire burning now that must be extinguished or there will be no future of the sort it dreams about.

The remedy could come only through applying the waiting labor to the millions of dollars of work that was crying to be done.

McGeer and the city council ran the editorial as a full-page advertisement in eastern newspapers as an expression of the city's view.

The early months of 1936 initiated a time of change in Vancouver's newspaper life. Frank Burd had reached retirement age at the *Province* and M.E.Nichols, himself approaching his sixty-third birthday, had come out from Winnipeg to take the paper in hand. In May, Robert J. Cromie, the restless and ambitious personal force at the *Sun*, died of heart failure at the age of forty-eight.

Nichols, always first of all a newsman, moved Bob Elson into the news editor's spot. Gradually the old order changed. Veterans like editor Roy Brown and managing editor Ronald Kenvyn retired. Brown, still under sixty and unhappy that no prospect existed of his taking over direction of the paper, shortly thereafter joined the *Sun*.

Through the late 1930s Nichols worked to improve the *Province* as a newspaper, holding to his conviction, often expressed, that in competition 'the content of the newspaper is the determining factor', that 'an ounce of content is worth a pound of direct circulation promotion.'

Content, to Nichols, meant first of all full news coverage. A *Province* colleague has described him as 'an editor of great breadth, profoundly conservative, but with a dedication to free speech.' One of his first orders at Vancouver assured full coverage of labor and the C.C.F., areas he felt the paper had slighted.

The period was one of curious ambivalence as the last troubled days of a fading depression came under the nightmare light evoked by a screaming voice in Europe. On Saturday, May 21, 1938, the *Province* carried two main headings of equal size: HITLER THREATENS COUP AS CZECHS KILL NAZIS and DEMAND OTTAWA ACTION ON TWO-DAY SIT-DOWN.

The day before, 1,200 jobless men, mostly from the Prairies, had marched into the art gallery, the post office, and the lobby of the Hotel Georgia to draw attention to their plight. Twenty-eight days later they were still there. But early Sunday, June 19, on orders from Ottawa, R.C.M.P. and city police moved on the art gallery and post office with tear gas. Jobless in the gallery left their stronghold without violence. At the post office it was a different story.

As reported in Monday's *Province*:

> Vancouver swung back into commercial stride this morning after a weekend marked by bitter street-fighting and destruction of $30,000 in private property. . . .
> Thirty-nine persons, including five constables, were injured in the brawling which followed the assault on the post office. Many others received superficial hurts.
> The fleeing jobless, maddened by gas and galvanized by blows from police truncheons, stormed east along Hastings and Cordova streets, smashing windows in business houses as they ran. . . .

Editorially the *Province* regretted that the jobless had damaged their cause by the outburst but reserved its sharpest words for government and its highest praise for Harold Winch, C.C.F. member of the legislature, for effective work in calming the strife.

Elson had been lucky. His reporters and photographers came back with reams of detail and dozens of startling pictures, including shots of police violence and of damage to stores that were among the *Province*'s biggest advertisers. He felt he must show them to Nichols for a view on the play they should get. The publisher's reaction was typical: 'Go up four pages and print them all.'

The Spirit of '42

On January 5, 1942, Paul Malone, a young Edmontonian who had got into newspaper work via the *Journal*, wrote for the *Province* an assessment of public opinion on a current possibility: 'Will Vancouver be bombed?' There were three schools of thought: optimists who believed the chances nil, pessimists certain that Japanese bombs would fall, and the rest – who hoped not but couldn't guess.

Bombing. Invasion. In the tension of the months that followed Pearl Harbor and Hong Kong, one special question worked on the emotions of British Columbians and disturbed certain minds at Ottawa: what of the more than 20,000 in the Coast province who had been born in Japan or of Japanese parents? Public feeling coalesced in a drive to clear them from the coastal area, a drive that had in it a mixture of reason, prejudice, and fear: the old responses of an earlier generation, but immeasurably sharpened by circumstance. This was no simple threat to a labor market; out there in the Pacific the warships ranged and the warplanes struck.

Even before Pearl Harbor the city had set up a standing committee to advise Ottawa. Now the tempo heightened. On January 3 the *Province* headlined: CITY MAY ASK JAP EXODUS FROM COAST. Editorially the paper took a moderate line: 'The Japanese situation . . . is serious enough . . . but not so serious as certain individuals and newspapers are endeavoring to make out.' It was strictly a federal matter. Federal authorities had information gathered for them by the military, the mounted police, and the standing committee. Let them deal with it promptly.

In mid-January Ottawa barred the Japanese from fishing or serving on any fishing vessel in Canadian waters and announced plans to move enemy aliens from the coast. On February 25 Torchy Anderson reported a radical tightening in the government's policy: a new order empowered the minister of justice to exclude persons from protected areas regardless of citizenship. The *Province* lined: OTTAWA PLANS TO MOVE 22,000 JAPS.

The necessity or otherwise of moving thousands of Japanese and Japanese-Canadians to points east of the Cascades remains controversial. There was nothing to ease the tension that caused it in the incident of Saturday night, June 20, when thirty shells from the sea, presumably fired by a Japanese submarine, fell round the wireless station at Estevan Point on Vancouver Island – the first attack on Canadian soil since Confederation.

Earlier that month United States planes and ships had blasted, at Midway, the greatest fleet Japan ever sent over the international dateline. But there was little of cheer in the Monday *Province* that headlined the shelling of Estevan Point. The front page looked like the face of doom: 'Egypt, Whole Mid-East Menaced'; '25,000 British Captured in Surrender of Tobruk'; 'Bids Non-residents Evacuate Hawaii'; 'Churchill Faces Crisis'; 'Russian Defenders Drop Back as Sevastopol Peril Grows'. . . .

All summer the movement of the Japanese went on, at a rate of about 800 a week, to work-camps, farms on the prairies, and towns farther east. In August 3,000 were encamped at Hastings Park, while 5,000 or so continued to live in their Vancouver homes, under curfew but free to work while they waited for evacuation. Small classified ads, which carry their own pathos when read in fading files, appeared in the *Province*: Experienced Japanese woman wants work; Japanese woman, experienced, clean, wash; Canadian Japanese girl, work, 30¢ hr., fare. . . .

Time changes perspectives. What might be regarded as a footnote to the long history of anti-Orientalism in British Columbia appeared in a *Province* editorial after the 1957 federal election – fifty years after that window-smashing raid through Chinatown and Japtown: 'Young Douglas Jung in Vancouver Centre defeated Defence Minister Campney. . . . This was the most significant upset in the province.' In June of 1965 Whistling Sea won the Queen's Plate – ridden by Tak Inouye, a Canadian-born Japanese, who in infancy was one of thousands moved inland from the coast. That spring British Columbia's premier headed a trade and goodwill mission to Japan. Millions of dollars in Japanese money continued to pour into the province's mines and mills.

Late in 1941 British Columbia had already begun a political transition. Before the October election the *Province* had returned to its ancient ground of non-party politics and suggested the voters think about candidates rather than party. When the vote turned up a stalemate (21 Liberals, 13 Conservatives, 14 C.C.F.) the paper urged a coalition – if possible a complete renunciation of party by all three; if not, a union of two.

The two-party coalition came into being, over objections from a disgruntled Pattullo. John Hart formed a government of Liberals and Conservatives, which in one form or another would hold power for ten years. The first coalition legislature brought to Victoria the individual destined to emerge eventually, from the confusion of its breakup, as head man. On the back benches a hardware merchant from the Okanagan named W.A.C.Bennett, then wearing a Conservative label, sat for the first time.

New hands were in charge at the *Sun*. Since R.J.Cromie's death, P.J.Salter, a long-time associate, had headed the paper. In mid-July of 1942 Don Cromie, son of the man who had been its driving force during his lifetime, took over as general manager. Up from the sports desk as managing editor came Hal Straight, built like a heavyweight wrestler and qualified by temperament and experience to bring the vigor of mat and ring to the gathering and display of news.

Nichols, an intensely interested observer of his competition, had noted in the late 1930s that at the time of R.J.Cromie's death the management, realizing the loss of a power they could not hope to replace, had reversed their policy: 'Instead of attempting to put out a newspaper with a Cromie personality and Cromie color, they proceeded to employ substance.' With Don Cromie now in charge and Hal Straight on news development, he saw the *Sun* as shaping again toward lines developed by the elder Cromie.

One of Nichols's last worrisome duties – he was to retire January

1, 1946 – involved negotiations with the International Typographical Union in co-operation with the *Sun* and the *News-Herald*. Existing agreements, identical in terms, expired March 1, 1945. Talks went on through the summer, the local insisting on the clause providing for non-arbitrability of the I.T.U.'s general laws. Finally the papers conceded the point. 'Wisely or unwisely,' Nichols wrote after the event, 'the Vancouver publishers felt they had to take the bitter medicine or stand a strike.' They signed November 2. At Winnipeg the publishers were even then refusing to accept the clause. Six days later began the Winnipeg strike that was to cause endless grief for the *Province*.

The Strike at the *Province*

> Lay that Province down, babe,
> Lay that Province down;
> That scab-run rag is blackballed
> In this union town. . . .

This neat little version of a current popular song appeared in October 1946, in a periodical issued by paper-makers at Ocean Falls, B.C. It might well have been the theme-song of the I.T.U. and its allies in a bitter battle of which the side-effects were more significant than the strife: they changed the balance of newspaper power in Vancouver.

The cloud hanging over the *Province* since the December threat of 'such action as they see fit . . . to bring about a settlement in Winnipeg' began to darken April 4. On that day I.T.U. local 226 (comprising printers at the three newspapers and commercial plants) gave two months' notice, as required by the labor regulations, of intention to end its collective agreement with the *Province*.

Publisher Leigh Spencer asked that the union negotiate for renewal. Because three identical contracts had been jointly arrived at, the two other members of the Vancouver publishers' committee, Don Cromie of the *Sun* and Clayton Delbridge of the *News-Herald*, were present when the union's local executive met with *Province* representatives April 30. The meeting accomplished nothing except to get on public record the fact that the move (a 'pressure play', the *Sun* called it) was designed to put the union back in at Winnipeg and that the international now controlled strategy.

As reported by the *Sun*:

Today the union spokesman said the existing contract was entirely satisfactory to the local and international union, and that cause of the termination was the union's dissatisfaction with the Winnipeg situation, where the papers employ non-union printers following the strike. . . .

Mr. Spencer stated that he had no authority or jurisdiction in the Winnipeg field and very little information on the situation there. He said the divisions of the company are entirely autonomous and that difficulties there could have no bearing on the Province's labor relations. . . .

Mr. Neelands [Harry Neelands, secretary of local 226] said that it was not the intention of the union to renew the contract and that the local union had no authority to make a new contract but that their committee would consider calling for an international representative to discuss the possibility.

From that point on it was a matter of going through the motions: the local demanding negotiations directly with The Southam Company, Spencer calling attention to the National Labor Relations Board's finding that it had no authority to interfere with the local plant basis, and his own inability to speak for anyone but the *Province*. On June 3 he applied for a conciliation officer, who saw both union and publisher during the next two days. On the afternoon of June 5 the union decided to strike the *Province*, an action the paper termed illegal since the conciliator hadn't had time to report. The night shift did not appear and picket lines formed.

Fifty-three members of the staff were out, a *Province* statement said, adding that 'staffs of the other two papers are not affected and they will publish as usual.'

Therein lay the seeds of tribulation. Publication by the morning *News-Herald* made little difference. Spencer rather welcomed it as providing a vehicle in which he could state the *Province*'s case. To see *Province* presses idle while the *Sun*'s rolled was something else.

Back in December when the threat first appeared, there had been definite signs of a united front. On December 14 Spencer wrote Fisher that he had the verbal undertaking of Cromie and Delbridge that on request they would order their printers to set type for the *Province*, which would have resulted in a refusal to handle struck work and a consequent walk-out. The papers at this point were considering some such joint publication as Winnipeg's. Three days later Cromie, as reported by Spencer, qualified the undertaking by advising that 'after further consideration of his whole situation, he was not prepared to leave me counting on his complete co-operation,' his chief point of doubt being how it would affect other unions, particularly the American Newspaper Guild, which was then established at the *Sun* but not yet in the *Province*.

At the end of May, Cromie told Spencer by letter that two considerations led him to amend his original position. One was the 'difficulties and slowness in arriving at measures for co-operation between the Sun and the Province in union matters, and even on meetings of the mind on principles and relatively urgent issues.' Another was uncertainty over 'the final degree of Southam domination over Province autonomy, an unknown which I had mentioned as disturbing at times and which I mentioned lightly as appearing greater in fact than it is advantageous for you to admit. . . .'

On June 1 the *Sun* noted:

> The Vancouver Sun and the News-Herald are drawn into the tangle because in accordance with standard practice for many years, all three Vancouver papers jointly negotiate collective agreements with local No. 226. One clause states that similar conditions shall prevail in the various plants. Consequently when the I.T.U. terminated the Province contract the Sun and the News-Herald were constrained to give notice of termination also. What the upshot will be is not yet clear. . . .

One aspect became clear on June 3. In Don Cromie's temporary absence Spencer met his younger brother Sam and business manager George Cran. 'They told me flatly', he wrote, 'that they would not go through with the original undertaking.' Spencer regarded this a simple breach of agreement. Cromie has attributed the situation to refusal by Spencer to agree on plans under which such an agreement could effectively be kept.

Eight years after the event Spencer said: 'I had an agreement . . . to the effect that, in case of either paper being unable to publish, either on account of accident, mechanical failure, labor trouble, being struck, and particularly in the case of labor trouble, that the other paper would put all its facilities at the disposal of the paper in difficulty . . . and publish for them. We both understood very well that in case of labor stoppage the paper undertaking to fill the breach would inevitably be struck also.' If this had occurred, he felt, the strike would probably have been a short one.

Cromie has said he was prepared, 'subject to certain conditions . . . to print the Province.' But differences between himself and Spencer supervened; he wanted advance preparations to publish every day if struck, but 'Spencer professed belief that a strike was not inevitable and that preparations by the papers might be provocative.' The *Sun* proceeded to research cold-type methods. 'Spencer minimized the value of such early preparations and rejected joint preparations.' There were other areas of disagreement, and collateral questions.

One was that of financial reserves. The *Sun* had been spending heavily on building changes. It lacked resources that the *Province*, as one of a group, might be expected to have. He could not, he said, get from Spencer 'evidence from Southam headquarters of their guarantee of any course agreed between Spencer and myself.' Twenty years later, and out of the daily newspaper business, Cromie summed up his point of view: 'What produced the papers' failure to unite, I suggest, was the *Sun*'s fear of going into mortal battle with an indifferent partner and no united battle plans.'

In any event, whatever the justice of Cromie's and Spencer's views of each other, when the printers went out on the night of June 5, 1946, the prospect of a common stand was gone.

Weeks of frustration began. Two days before the strike, Spencer and his executives had formed tentative plans to produce a makeshift paper. On the night of June 5 typewritten pages were pasted up. The *Province*'s engravers refused to handle them, and they went to non-union shops. Next morning stereotypers refused to cast the engravings.

Here perhaps was the key point. If the *Province* had been able to get out a paper – any kind of paper – within a day or two of the strike's start, and somehow keep it going until conventional production could be reorganized . . . The answer is of course a question mark.

The barriers were formidable. Vancouver labor was in ferment. A woods-workers strike and other walk-outs were under way. Unions set up a co-ordinating committee to force complete stoppage in all strike-bound industry in British Columbia. The city's labor council quickly put the *Province* on its 'do not patronize' list. A council of allied printing trades representing four newspaper unions, including the pressmen, did the same thing (an action not made more palatable by the fact that its chairman worked for the *Sun*). A quick resumption of publication might have brought on an early outbreak of the violence that occurred a month and a half later. Might this – a quick resumption, and the response to an earlier crisis – have stayed the slide?

The 'ifs' and 'mights' persist.

Meanwhile the *Sun* made hay. Whatever the considerations that brought the situation about, it obviously opened a business opportunity for the paper that continued to publish. On June 12 the *Sun* ran a front-page picture of news-hungry readers crowding round a circulation truck. An accompanying story said: 'All Vancouver is on a mad paper-chase nowadays, trying to catch up with a copy of the

Vancouver Sun, noon, home, or final edition. . . .' *Province* men
watched ruefully the *Sun*'s enlargement to twenty-six and thirty
pages from the normal sixteen (newsprint was short) and its pick-
up of all the classified advertising in sight.

Spencer had gradually been building up to resume publication if
all efforts to get the I.T.U. men back failed. W.W.(Peter)Southam,
recently transferred to Montreal as company executive assistant
after fifteen years on the *Province*, and fresh from a hand at getting
the Ottawa *Citizen* on the street again, flew back to Vancouver. Pete
Galbraith arrived from Calgary in July to help Spencer. A few printers were coming in, organized under the Canadian National Printing
Trades Union, a small group with its chief strength in Calgary.

On Friday, July 12, four Calgary printers arrived for work and
walked through to the elevator. Pickets followed, attacked, and
ejected the four. A couple of hours later, classified advertising super-
visor W.B.Mackie was grabbed in the lobby, pulled outside, and
beaten. The four printers made it into the building that afternoon,
one being beaten again. The picket line had grown to seventy-five
men, members of the International Union of Mine Mill and Smelter
Workers (itself on strike) and of the Canadian Seamen's Union
joining with the I.T.U.

Early Saturday eight printers arrived by plane from Winnipeg. At
the *Province*, pickets grabbed one and beat him up. The other seven
rescued him and all got in. Later a solid line of pickets blocked off
pressmen and mailers. That evening a tenant was seized, dragged
down the steps, and manhandled.

Through Saturday and Sunday, counsel for the paper took affidavits covering these incidents and on Monday, July 15, started proceedings that resulted in an immediate temporary injunction banning
I.T.U. picketing, and in eventual trial – more than a year later – of
a damage action against I.T.U. officials, which the company won.
The injunction checked I.T.U. picketing but plenty of militant union
men had time to spare. That night 200 boilermakers marched singing round the *Province*. On Tuesday morning 'protest' picket lines
included fishermen, steel-workers, boilermakers, metal and chemical
workers, and woods workers.

Preparations to publish continued. Amateur stereotypers had been
trained, including, incidentally, Gordon T. Southam who had rejoined the paper as promotion manager after wartime naval service.
At a meeting Wednesday the pressmen's union, under persuasion
from their international president, decided to return to work.

The shipwreck of these plans typifies the prolonged tension, frustration, and disappointment that dogged the *Province* staff in efforts to get the paper on the street. On Thursday the press-crew worked all morning. Both presses were ready for plating, the plates on their way from the stereo-room, when a committee of two from the press-room came to Spencer's office. Despite the fact that they had crossed the picket line they felt they could not carry on. Four of their men had gone to lunch and after contact with pickets had come back in a state of nerves bordering on collapse.

Spencer went down to the pressroom. His informants had not exaggerated: 'One of the men was so over-wrought that he was in tears and so nervous he could not talk and the others were in not much better condition. The upshot of it was the entire press crew was simply scared to death and just walked off the plant and I could not stop them.'

Next day, Friday, a crew gathered from other departments manned one press under Peter Southam's direction and ran off a few copies of a trial edition, but it was decided not to publish till continuity could be assured. Monday, July 22, would be it: a twelve-page paper for street sale.

On that day, at 2:35 P.M., without the aid of union pressmen, stereotypers or mailers, the *Province* published for the first time since June 5. The edition was small – 10,000 copies.

The paper ran a front-page editorial:

> After a period of difficulty, the Vancouver Daily Province greets its readers again. It and they have gone through the fires of labor troubles and both have happily survived. . . .

Next day's paper carried a boxed announcement. The pressroom crew were back again, recognizing the validity of their contract.

The paper carried some light-hearted human-interest stuff on its own reappearance. One woman had finished her downtown shopping with only seven cents left for carfare. She spent the nickel for a paper and put the coppers in the fare-box 'and the conductor was so pop-eyed looking at the Province in my hand that I got away with it.'

Any light-heartedness was premature. The fires of labor troubles were far from out. Within an hour of that second day's press-run – July 23 – copies of the *Province* were burning in the street.

The *Sun* led its final edition with the story:

POLICE ARREST
5 IN MOB SCENE
AT PROVINCE . . .

What happened was in fact a rousing riot. Union truckers had returned to work after they learned the pressmen were back. Three *Province*-laden trucks got away, harassed by pickets. Each truck's passage heightened the truculent excitement of a gathering crowd. Demonstrators seized the next truck, dragged out and beat the driver (who was rescued by a policeman), and upset it in the street. Strewn papers littered the battle-ground; 3,000 went up in flames. The crew of a fourth truck, laden with 25,000 papers, understandably declined to proceed. Police arrested seventeen rioters. None were printers. They included seamen, machinists, and foundry workers.

Next day – Wednesday – 75,000 papers went out on trucks manned by *Province* office workers in convoy with police protection. From this time on, except for one three-day hitch in September, the *Province* printed without a break.

Through August, as new employees trained, production rose and channels of distribution opened. Union truckers returned. Longshoremen on the various boats agreed to handle the papers.

But the road back was uphill and rocky. Picketing continued (I.T.U. picketing resumed July 30 under a modification of the injunction, not opposed by the *Province*) as did union pressure on readers and advertisers. In August, for instance, the Seattle I.T.U. local noted in its publication: 'Reports from Vancouver indicate that our sister union is putting up a terrific battle against the Southam chain. Wives of members, each taking a page from the telephone directory, are calling possible subscribers to present the union's case. Pressure is being brought against advertisers. . . .' Buttons appeared on coat lapels emblazoned I DON'T BUY DAILY PROVINCE.

The *Province* planned a twenty-eight-page paper for September 11. The atmosphere was cheerful; department store advertising had been lined up for the first time since the strike began. But on the night of September 10 a delegation from the trades and labor council's trial committee told the pressmen's local they faced expulsion unless they quit the *Province*. For three days the *Province* did not publish.

On Saturday, September 14, a volunteer crew from other departments manned one press and got a thirty-two-page paper rolling. Once again, with the pressmen out, union truckers refused to handle it. Office workers manned trucks; publication continued. Meantime president George Berry of the pressmen's international undertook to set up a chapel in the *Province* under a steward who would report solely to the international 'until we can reconcile the local union to its moral and contractual obligations.' On September 26 the pressmen came back to stay.

Sequels to the July violence occurred in court. The three pickets who attacked Mackie were fined. Nine of the seventeen arrested after the July 23 riot drew jail terms or fines.

Finally on October 18, 1947, the company's damage action against officials of the I.T.U. opened before Mr. Justice J.O.Wilson of the Supreme Court of British Columbia. Between that date and November 17 the story from both points of view went into the record. At the outset the *Province* lawyer announced that though the original claim was for $250,000 he had been instructed to propose that in the event of a favorable judgment the court assess 'not the full amount proven to have been suffered . . . but rather such amount as the court may deem appropriate to impose as a deterrent.'

Trial evidence gave some indication of the drubbing the *Province* took. Circulation in September 1947 was 96,112 compared to 127,-420 when the strike started. It had crawled up to the September figure from 90,000 in January. Using round figures, accountant Cecil Williams said that advertising and circulation revenue declined by $370,700 and expenses by $113,000 for a net loss of $250,000 in June and July 1946, when publication ceased for six weeks. The paper had spent $48,000 since then on special guards and watchmen.

The long-term effect, far more important than any immediate loss, was at that time still an intangible.

Throughout, union witnesses insisted that guidance from international headquarters was simply suggestion, and that their own action in striking the *Province* was voluntary and essentially one of self-defence against a possible effort to break down local I.T.U. conditions.

In the course of the trial a letter from international president Woodruff Randolph, written more than three months before the strike, got into the evidence. Randolph had suggested the local give notice of contract cancellation. 'The more we impress the Southam chain that all of their papers will be involved if they do not straighten out Winnipeg,' he wrote, 'the sooner we will be able to break the Southam paper away from the Sifton man in Winnipeg. If we can break him away I believe we can correct the situation as regards both papers in Winnipeg. . . .'

Leigh Spencer reiterated that local publishers' autonomy had been the policy of the company ever since his first association with it. He himself could not negotiate on behalf of any other Southam publication.

On February 18, 1948, Mr. Justice Wilson brought down his decision: the strike was illegal; the strikers had damaged the *Province* by unlawful acts. He ordered $10,000 to be paid by six Vancouver officers of the I.T.U., noting that the amount 'is under the circumstances purely nominal, bearing no relation to the actual loss. . . .' As relating to Randolph and his Canadian representatives, Harry Finch and James Davidson, he dismissed the action. While their advice and direction 'started the strike which led to all later events, there is no evidence before me that they joined in the conspiracy to strike unlawfully or to do unlawful acts.'

The judgment, a quietly-worded document, rejected certain contentions by both sides:

> It is suggested that the object of the strike was to injure the Province or the plaintiff company. I cannot accept this argument. The defendants were on the whole respectable craftsmen who had been employed by the Province for many years and had happy and harmonious relations. . . . Into this admirable picture of labor-management relations intruded the Winnipeg strike. . . . Suffice it to say that the international executive of the I.T.U., as represented by Mr. Randolph and his Canadian lieutenants, felt that the Winnipeg situation menaced the future of all I.T.U. printers in the employ of the . . . company. They envisaged the refusal of the Winnipeg papers to accept their terms, a refusal which might seem reasonable to many persons, as part of a plot by the plaintiff to eliminate the I.T.U. from employment by the Southams. Such a conception may seem to many, and does to me, fantastic.

Randolph had communicated his view to local 226 and the members of that union adopted it and chose to go on strike:

> I think they did so with an honest conviction that they were acting in their own interests and those of their union. True, they knew they would injure the Province and the plaintiff company. This, however, was not their predominant object, but, perhaps a means of obtaining their object. Their action has been disastrous to themselves, highly injurious to the plaintiff, and has achieved nothing for the Winnipeg strikers. Its wisdom, and particularly the wisdom of Mr. Randolph, appear doubtful. But their object was at worst the furtherance of their own interest (an object which the law accepts as legitimate) and at best an altruistic interest in the welfare of their Winnipeg brothers.
> . . .

At another point in his judgment Mr. Justice Wilson, referring to the October 3, 1945, minute of Southam company directors recording the general feeling that the I.T.U. laws were unreasonable and should be resisted, expressed his conviction that 'the general policy of the plaintiff company was to leave to its local management the whole question of labor relations and that each newspaper was free to conclude or refuse a bargain with the local unit of the I.T.U.'

Mr. Justice Wilson thus brought the issues down from conjectured motive to demonstrable fact.

He found for the company on two chief grounds: first, that the printers broke the labor law banning strikes until fourteen days after the report of a conciliation board; second, that picketing of the *Province* and news-stands went beyond the reasonable and into the area of unlawful intimidation. He absolved the I.T.U. of responsibility for the July 23 riot: 'I cannot escape from a strong suspicion that the defendants knew that the persons involved in this riot had taken over picketing duties ... but I do not believe that blame for the incidents of this day can or should be attributed to the defendants.' Other incidents however were evidence of 'a general scheme of intimidation of Province employees'.

> I can only say that the concerted nature of acts of the defendants, and particularly the acts of July 12 and 13, is not, in my mind, reconcilable with anything less than a general agreement and plan among members of local 226 to create a nuisance around the Province building by molesting and intimidating employees and others entering the building. . . . I must find that these acts were agreed on and done by the general membership of local 226 and that all defendants who have been served with the writ herein and who are members (except the non-voting apprentices) are responsible as conspirators.

He expressed relief at not having to assess actual damages, since 'proven damages during the shut-down period ran at the rate of about $300,000 per month', and hoped the $10,000 assessed against the officers (damages were not asked against the rank and file) would be sufficient 'to fix in the minds of parties to labor disputes the necessity for deliberation, moderation, and adherence to the law.' The company did not press for collection of the $10,000.

Ironically, the one paper most badly hurt by the 1946 strikes was the one to which the I.T.U. eventually returned. When Spencer retired at the beginning of 1948 Pete Galbraith succeeded him. He faced a rugged task. Just before the strike the *Province* enjoyed a circulation bulge of more than 25,000 over the *Sun*, which stood at just under 100,000. When Galbraith took over, the *Province* was down to 93,000, the *Sun* up to 129,000. For a year or two the *Province* merely held its own or a little better while the *Sun* surged. At September 30, 1949, the figures were 97,000 and 160,000. In that year it became known that the I.T.U. international had stepped down from its all-or-nothing stand on Southam newspapers. Sandy Bevis, a striking *Province* printer and an ambitious and dedicated union man – he afterwards became an official at I.T.U. headquarters

– talked with Galbraith. From this came an agreement under which the I.T.U. moved back into the *Province* at November 5, 1949, the C.N.P.T.U. printers being absorbed into the I.T.U. except for some who took cash settlements. Galbraith undoubtedly hoped that this move, in a highly unionized city, would help in the fight to restore *Province* prosperity. But as results in the next few years were to show, the *Province*'s slow gains were more than matched by the *Sun*. A reading habit had been formed.

Province Men Trap Suspect . . .

The period in which the *Province* waged its struggle to win back lost ground saw its staff pull off some of the most notable news beats in its history. Occasionally enterprise had a touch of the bizarre.

In the spring and summer of 1949 the secluded quiet of Stanley Park became unsafe for lovers. Night-time marauders made its by-ways sinister with the hazards of robbery and rape. Police were handicapped – short of men and faced with reluctance by victims to tell what happened.

The *Province* at the time had a photographer named Ray Munro, a newspaper man in the Ben Hecht tradition, only more so. Compared to this particular Munro, Hildy Johnson of *The Front Page* was a choir-boy.

Munro conceived the idea of setting out a decoy. Reporter Don McClean, a slightly built R.C.A.F. veteran, borrowed a red wig. In Munro's car the two embarked on an enterprise that had, as the *Province* said in a resulting picture caption, elements of both Keystone Cops and *Charley's Aunt*.

A preliminary run on the night of Wednesday, August 10, produced nothing. Thursday night Munro and McClean tried again. Near Brockton Point they began to feign a spooning session in dim moonlight. Beside Munro in the driver's seat lay an automatic. McClean clutched a borrowed policeman's billy. The right-hand door of the car flew open. A light flashed in their faces. A voice said: 'This is the morality squad.' McClean swung his billy against a head. Munro dived over him at the man behind the light.

In September the captive, a Port Coquitlam laborer, drew a year for impersonating police. In November, after a victim of an April attack had testified, he started a fifteen-year prison term for rape.

Another exclusive from the crime beat made headlines in 1956. At 2:45 P.M. on Monday, May 7, city editor Bruce Larsen answered his phone. The caller was warden Hugh Christie of Oakalla prison. Three prisoners held a guard – tied up, a razor at his throat. Their leader wanted Larsen. Could he get out there? Within a minute he was on his way.

The mission developed into a grim bargaining session. Robert Tremblay, Marcel Frenette, and Charles Talbot, sentenced to twenty years each for an attempted murder on False Creek flats, had just learned their appeals were lost. Returning from an exercise yard, they expressed a wish to shave, walked into the barbering space at the end of an open tier, picked up a straight-edge razor and shears, returned to the corridor, and seized guard Ernie Loveless. Within minutes the stalemate was set; the three convicts in the hostage room at one end of the corridor; Loveless bound to a mattress with a razor at his throat; warden and guards behind a steel gate 100 feet away.

Talbot was the messenger, memorizing what Tremblay said, walking down the corridor, and repeating it to Christie. It was incoherent stuff, but slowly Tremblay's design came through: to force publicity for his side of the attempted murder case, a case he called a frame-up. Larsen was the only newspaper name he knew. So he had asked for Larsen.

Larsen talked with Talbot. If Larsen would go down the corridor and listen to Tremblay and print his story, Loveless would go free when Tremblay's wife could buy a *Province* that displayed it.

Larsen called assistant publisher Ross Munro (no relation to Ray). Would the *Province* go extra? Munro said yes.

In the hostage room Tremblay and Larsen talked for an hour. What Tremblay sought was publication of the prisoners' position: their wish for a chance to get in the box – at the trial the lawyers had advised them, he said, to stay out; their wish for a study by the attorney-general of what they knew that hadn't got into the courts; and a decision as to whether he should intervene.

They released Loveless on Larsen's word that the extra would run. It did, under a banner head: THIS STORY FOR A LIFE.

Larsen's story won him a National Newspaper Award. Tremblay and Frenette got an extra year on the end of their twenty-year sentences.

A year later the *Province* profited for a second time from the fact that it had mountain climbers on its staff.

The first occasion was back in 1943. On Sunday, December 20, 1942, a CPA Lockheed Lodestar, flying in from Prince George with

364 News and the Southams

thirteen aboard, disappeared within minutes of Vancouver. Twin-engined bombers roared up and down the Fraser Valley under the overcast while seaplanes scoured Harrison Lake and Howe Sound. Nothing. It was not until August that Captain Dan Patry caught the gleam of metal from one of the peaks of Mount William Knight in the Cheam Range east of Chilliwack. Gullies and ridges and shale-like rock lay between the scattered wreck, 7,000 feet up, and the mountain's foot. One four-man party tried the climb and failed. On Saturday, August 14, Charles Woodsworth of the *Province* with Len Van Zuben and Charles McMillan, all members of the Alpine Club, left Vancouver shortly before noon. They camped on a ridge that night, began to climb early Sunday, and reached the wreck that afternoon. Late Monday they reached Vancouver with pictures and detailed descriptive.

The Mount William Knight exclusive remained in mind. Again on a December Sunday, tragedy broke in British Columbia's sea of mountains. On the evening of December 9, 1956, a Trans-Canada North Star headed east with sixty-two aboard, including five professional football players from the previous day's all-star game at Empire Stadium. Shortly after take-off it turned back reporting engine trouble. Then it vanished.

The *Province* had a climber in Paddy Sherman. Sherman started spending weekends in the mountains looking for the plane. He did not find it, but it was his association with the sport that gave the *Province* a beat when others did.

On Saturday, May 12, 1957, three acquaintances of Sherman – Elfrida Pigou, Geoff Walker, and David Cathcart – left Vancouver for the Chilliwack area, planning an attempt on the 7,910-foot peak of Mount Slesse, which Elfrida had reached the year before. They had no purpose except to make the climb, a hard one with a lot of rock-work and snow. After camping Saturday night 1,900 feet up, they resumed climbing Sunday. Clouds, down to 4,000 feet on the west face, obscured the mountain. The party took a gully Elfrida thought was the one she had followed before. It was not, but it led to something else. They had climbed for six hours when Walker picked a piece of paper from the snow – a scrap from a book of approach charts to Canadian airports. Farther up, at the 7,600-foot level, they began to find wreckage.

At 8:15 Monday morning Elfrida Pigou phoned Sherman in the *Province* city-room. The three climbers were swept up, rushed to the office, and hidden in the magazine department to tell their story. Bits of wreckage went to TCA. Editor Ross Munro alerted circulation.

Managing editor Bill Forst and city editor Larsen headed for Chilli-wack for clean-up coverage. By 9:45 TCA had confirmed that serial numbers on the scraps tallied with those of the lost North Star. At 10:30 the extra reached the street.

In this period big industry in B.C. progressed at speed: aluminum refining at Kitimat, natural gas, pulp and paper, mines. Back in 1950 coalition premier Byron Johnson had resumed work on the much-maligned PGE, work that Bennett's Social Credit régime carried on, until in 1956 trains ran between West Vancouver and Prince George and connection with the Peace River country was assured. The old white elephant had changed its hide.

'Nobody can deprive the present government of the great credit it deserves for taking its courage in its hands and deciding to complete the railway,' the *Province* said.

Early in February of 1957 Ross Munro heard of a new proposal that would dwarf anything so far projected. Checks with various sources proved the reports correct. On February 12 the *Province* had a one-edition beat – BILLION DOLLARS FOR NORTHERN B.C. – on the fantastic plans of Axel Wenner-Gren to develop timber, mines, and power of the Rocky Mountain trench.

Events, as it turned out, would change direction. When Wenner-Gren died four years later his proposed 400-mile monorail to the Yukon border remained a dream. The province itself had moved into the centre of the northern power picture with plans to develop the Peace under public ownership.

Pacific Press and a Morning *Province*

News enterprise was not enough. In seven of the ten years that fol-lowed the strike (1947-56) the *Province* lost money. In its best year, the last, it made $191,000, or less than three per cent of revenue, and faced a poor outlook for 1957. In the same period the *Sun*'s net rose from $100,000 to $950,000. Arthur Moscarella, who came out from Winnipeg to take over from the fatally-ill Galbraith in 1951, said later the effort to keep the *Province* in the black was like butting a stone wall.

Additional stonework kept buttressing the wall. New processes and techniques were invading newspaper pages. Color was one and the *Sun* was equipped to exploit it. There were other plant and build-ing necessities. To keep the *Province* competitive would cost some-thing like $5,000,000 in new money.

Actually the need for new plant faced both properties. Had both been content to let technology bypass them, to ignore the pressure of serving a growing population, then conceivably they could have continued in a kind of precarious balance as competing evening papers, the *Sun* out-weighing the *Province* and fighting to hold the edge. In the face of a changing newspaper industry, neither could afford to do that. New plant and buildings they must have. And though the *Sun* rode well in front, the *Province* had the central company behind it. It looked like a long and costly war.

As early as 1950 Don Cromie noted casually in a letter to Philip Fisher, dealing with the TV threat to ad revenue, high competitive costs, and other things: 'Perhaps you'll find it worth considering whether the Vancouver public would get its best newspaper service and value from a co-operating morning-evening operation.'

Nothing came of this at the time, but by 1955 principals of the two papers had reached one point of agreement: they would like to agree on *something*. Cromie and Clair Balfour hashed over the possibilities whenever newspaper gatherings brought them together: in hotel rooms, cocktail lounges, and aboard the Cromie yacht *Tempest IV* cruising Vancouver harbor between winter hills.

In September of 1956 they spent four days exploring Howe Sound and the possibility of joint production; in an outboard skimmer in the middle of the Sound the two shook hands on the principle of a deal. Later that fall Don and Sam Cromie* met the Southam executive committee at Edmonton. Finally, in a telephone conversation with Balfour in January of 1957, Don Cromie agreed to formation of 'Company X' to take over the physical assets of the *Province* and the *Sun*, the *Province* to switch to morning publication and profits to be shared equally.

In May, Company X became Pacific Press Limited, owned 50 per cent by Sun Publishing Company and 50 per cent by The Southam Company – which put in $3,850,000 as an equalization payment, a measure of the *Sun*'s surge to ascendancy. Each parent company would continue to appoint the publisher of the paper with which it had long been identified.

One matter remained to be resolved. The morning field was already occupied. The *Sun* had bought the *News-Herald* in 1951 to get its surplus newsprint, and sold it to Roy Thomson in 1952 – one of Thomson's few losing propositions. On June 15 the paper – it had

*Sam Cromie died tragically in February of 1957, drowned while testing an outboard in Halfmoon Bay.

been renamed the *Herald* – went out of existence and sold certain of its assets, including subscription lists, to Pacific Press. On Monday, June 17, the *Province* appeared as a morning paper and a new period in Vancouver publishing began.

The agreement under which the new deal was born noted that *Sun* and Southam had determined to make the arrangement 'as a means of practising and achieving economy in the mechanical production' of the newspapers 'while continuing to maintain the existing quality, character, and personality of each of the said newspapers and independence, freedom, and autonomy in the publishing thereof. . . .'

The deal caused considerable editorial discussion about newspapers' difficulties in modern times and some satirical comment. Columnist Scott Young wrote in the *Globe and Mail*: 'Each paper has assured its readers that it will retain its former character. Since the chief characteristic of each paper was its bitter competitive spirit toward the other, this character-retention will be quite a trick, something like watching a wrestling match between Siamese twins.'

Cromie wrote him that the Siamese-twins crack pointed up the dilemma nicely – 'But a chap wearies of the prospect of putting out a leading newspaper with an old pile of bricks and baling wire for 20 more years, with the prospect that someone will need a monopoly to justify a modern plant. . . . This way we avoid a monopoly – I can't envision the Vancouver Sun ever looking, thinking or acting like the Southams' Province – and get modern plant and equipment.'

Balfour mused on a slight element of paradox: 'I wonder if he [Young] stopped for even a second to think that his column only appeared because four Toronto newspapers* had been swallowed or married so that the Globe and Mail would be strong enough to survive, pay him a comfortable salary, allow him to write as he pleases.'

Before final agreements were even signed, a sharper worry had begun to overhang the enormously detailed job of planning the combined operation. On March 25 T.D.MacDonald, director of investigation and research for the Combines Investigation Act, wrote Fisher:

> I have been reading in the press about a rumored merger of the Vancouver Sun with the Vancouver Province. . . . I believe that such a merger would put me upon enquiry. . . . It simply means that I would consider it a case in which I should gather all the facts with a view to determining whether they should be placed before the Restrictive Trades Practices Commission. . . .

Mail, Empire, World, and *Globe*.

Various evidence-taking sessions followed, climaxed by a commission hearing in Vancouver in January of 1960.

The implication in much of the evidence was that continued full-scale competition in Vancouver would produce a trend *towards* newspaper monopoly rather than away from it, through the inevitability of one or the other eventually being forced to quit.

Commissioner Rhodes Smith's report, brought down in August, noted that 'the continued publication of separate newspapers, particularly when the individual papers are linked in a traditional way with separate publishing interests, does not immediately present as serious a danger to the public interest . . . as a newspaper monopoly in the hands of a single owner.' Nevertheless there was some immediate public disadvantage and the further danger of a more complete monopoly. Pacific Press seemed to have 'confined its activities to mechanical and financial matters and has left the determination of content and policy of the two newspapers to their respective publishers' – but changes in personnel could occur within a relatively short time.

The commission therefore recommended action to see that nothing happened to the status quo:

> In view of the absence of a sufficient safeguard to protect the public interest in the continuance of separate newspapers in the Vancouver area the commission considers that steps should be taken to ensure that no changes are made in the existing agreements which would reduce the degree of independence which now exists with respect to the publication of the Province and the Sun and that no action is taken under those agreements which would increase the disadvantage to the public which has resulted from the common ownership of the Province and the Sun.

It suggested a judicial order to restrain the parties from any alteration in the agreements without approval of a court, and a review of the requirement that national advertising be carried in both papers. No such order was ever issued, the recommendation being met by written assurance to the Combines Investigation Branch that it would be told of any proposed changes, and that the combination requirement for national advertising had been washed out.

The evening field was now the *Sun*'s alone, while the *Province* took on the job of building morning-paper readership in a city where no morning paper in modern times had ever known success. From the start it had been recognized that the bulk of Pacific Press profits would accrue from the *Sun*, flowing out into evening readership areas left bare by the *Province*. At the same time, continuance of a respected and respectable *Province*, editorially independent and vigorous in news enterprise, remained an absolute necessity to the combined operation. As an entity it might not make money; neither, as an entity, does the news content that justifies a newspaper's existence and distinguishes it from a simple advertising sheet. The *Province* was the readers' and advertisers' alternative that justified the Pacific Press set-up from a public-interest point of view.

By the time the papers moved into Pacific Press's new $10,000,-000 plant at Granville Street and Seventh Avenue on Christmas Eve of 1965, the *Sun's* circulation ran close to 250,000. The *Province* had established a morning circulation of around 110,000. Pacific Press's net earnings in 1965 crossed the $2,600,000 mark.

The years between produced some sensations in the Canadian newspaper world. In June of 1963 Max Bell lunched with Don Cromie and bought control of Sun Publishing Company for F.P. Publications, thus putting into partnership in Vancouver through Pacific Press two groups that were in competition in Ottawa, Winnipeg, and Calgary. And less than a year later Cromie, who stayed on at first as publisher and then as board chairman, walked out – protesting the 'policies, procedures, and manners' of the F.P. leadership.

Of wider interest was appearance of a new newspaper in Vancouver, dedicated to the proposition that the city would support a second evening paper. Conceived by a promoter named Val Warren, and with General Victor Odlum as a venerable figure-head, the *Times* ran its first edition September 5, 1964, with appropriate fanfare. Eleven months later $3,000,000 – largely put up by small investors – and the *Times* itself had gone down the drain.

There is an interesting footnote to financial aspects of the *Province-Sun* story. Back in 1955, a year and a half before Pacific Press, and as the result of a casual remark by Max Bell to Balfour, Southams had begun to 'hold a basket' under the market for *Sun* stock, buying for investment through an agent without the company's name appearing. When Pacific Press was formed, the Southam company held about 12 per cent of the *Sun's* voting stock and 8 per cent of the non-voting. At that time Balfour disclosed the position to Cromie and agreed not to buy further without informing him. Afterward, in agreement with Cromie and as possible assistance in safeguarding the *Sun* from falling into foreign hands (Cromie had already refused offers from the American Sam Newhouse and the Swedish industrialist Axel Wenner-Gren), Southams went back into the market. They held just over 18 per cent of the *Sun's* voting stock when Max Bell made his deal with Cromie in 1963. Since the *Sun* had come into strong Canadian hands, there was no point in hanging onto it but two years passed before they could agree on a price. When F.P. Publications finally bought the block in 1965 The Southam Company in seven years had done better than double its money.

Editorially the two papers turned out to be perhaps the most irascible Siamese twins ever joined by a common cartilage. A couple of random instances: When in March of 1960 the *Province* attacked the C.B.C. for its recurrent deficits and suggested sale of the public broadcasting system, the *Sun* remarked: 'To sell it to the Southams, and through them to the soap salesmen, would be a national disaster. Canadian TV and radio would then be giving us the same mealy-mouthed pap that the Southam papers peddle.' A year or so later the *Sun* made sensational hay concurrently with an abortion *exposé* and a new Berlin crisis. 'This week,' said the *Province*, 'we find ourselves ashamed of our own trade. At a time when big-circulation dailies should be striving to give their readers a balanced view of our community and our times, the newspaper that now enjoys undisputed occupancy of the evening field in Vancouver is exhibiting all the restraint of a small boy on a lavatory wall with a large piece of white chalk.'

The *Province* as a morning paper in fact jumped into controversy with an abandon that would have shocked conductors of earlier editorial-page discussions. 'Our editorial approach to a number of things has become sharper and more controversial,' remarked Fred Auger (who moved out from the Winnipeg *Tribune* to succeed Moscarella in 1959) in the course of a philosophical discussion of editorial pages with Balfour. This was putting it mildly.

In the 1960 provincial election the *Province* even went so far as to support W.A.C.Bennett's Social Credit government, as a business administration and the only alternative to the C.C.F. This despite a history of opposition to Social Credit and a certain friendliness to the C.C.F. position in federal politics; in 1948 it expressed satisfaction that a hard core of C.C.F. members remained at Ottawa 'functioning so often not only as the best old-school parliamentarians . . . but also as a kind of parliamentary conscience.'

The delayed honeymoon with Social Credit did not last. In March of 1962 the *Province* remarked that the Bennett government had been elected seventeen months before on a program of preserving investor-ownership and reducing public debt. Since then it had taken over the province's biggest investor-owned company, B.C. Electric, at an arbitrary price, dismissed private investors engaged in developing Peace River power, undertaken a Peace program that dwarfed even the national investment in the St. Lawrence Seaway – and done all this without settling the Columbia development, which might make Peace power unnecessary for twenty-five years.

Its suggested solution in 1963 recalled earlier days when the paper often urged the virtues of candidate rather than party. It drew up a slate of twenty-two Liberals and Conservatives – a 'third force' – whose election 'would guarantee balance and stability in the next legislature, whatever party wins the greatest number of seats.' Just five of its choices were elected as Bennett won again. The *Province* mourned: 'The moment of political truth is still afar off. It will come on the wings of some distant morning when British Columbians awaken from their dream.'

13
The Company

Years before the Southam company opened its ownership to the stock-buying public, the editor of one of its newspapers called attention to the singularity of his craft: 'The newspaper is a business, true enough – but this is the strange thing about it: the newspaper that is operated strictly as a business becomes, in a very few years, a business that isn't worth owning.'* There is a difference from the normal climate of the market-place. Essentially this lies in the nature of the stock in trade, the news itself: elusive, volatile, a thing that can never be stock-piled. And in the sense of personal adventure that stirs the best of the men and women who pursue it and get it into print. Fisher got to the core of the thing in a single sentence in the company's report for 1951: 'Each day's issue of each paper is a separate adventure and a new creation.'

Earlier, in its first yearly report to its wider ownership, the company touched on some aspects of the fascinating business in which these new shareholders were investing.

'Canadian newspapers in the main', it said, 'are the servants of the public, not published by men or organizations who have other private interests to serve, nor by men forwarding personal ambitions.' They were as accurate as they *could* be, consistent with human frailty and time pressure. Certainly not perfect – 'hardly any edition of any paper is ever produced that could not be legitimately criticized in some detail or other' – but relatively free from fault considering production speed, complexity of material, and 'the enormous diversity of human interest to which they cater'.

The report went into the relationship between the company's in-

*W.L.MacTavish in a radio talk, July 12, 1937.

372

dividual papers and head office: 'The editorial policies and the judgment governing the selection of news are individual to each paper, the responsibility of its publisher,' it said. However, this did not mean lack of interest in quality. The company believed in certain principles for any newspaper: accurate news content, fair editorial comment, availability of advertising space to any purchaser 'subject to considerations of truthfulness, decency and the public interest'. Each Southam newspaper tried to live up to the best traditions of newspaper publishing. So did the company – not by interference with the individual papers, but by establishing standards of personnel for each.

The company thus recorded formally the philosophy of group publication that had developed through the early days and had long been understood as basic. What it said in effect was that the papers conducted their own separate adventures in creation. Implicit in the statement was the assurance that public participation in ownership would bring no change in this practice.

One gradual change at the centre, however, was in the cards. For years Fisher had been suggesting broadening the directorate by bringing in men from outside the family and management. It was not a point of view that appealed to the elder Southams, instinctively reluctant to depart from earlier patterns. But one step had been taken in 1940 with selection of Glyn Osler. As close friend and legal adviser he could scarcely be called an outsider, but he was neither family nor management. Another came three years later when Ottawa lawyer Duncan MacTavish joined the board. MacTavish was a family connection, husband of H.S.Southam's daughter Janet, but had no ties with management. Nor had Eric Harvie, husband of F.N.'s daughter Dorothy, when selected to bring the board to its full strength of fifteen in 1946, though he had done legal work for the Calgary *Herald*.

It was time, Fisher felt, to give some general study to the kind of board the company should have eventually. Various interests were concerned: shareholders, management, and the public. He suggested to the executive committee that it might contemplate a board to include four or five large shareholders not in company employ, five or six divisional operating-men, two or three head-office men, and two or three independent or professional directors. Neither present nor future boards would fall neatly into such rigid categories, but their establishment would indicate a balance to aim at.

There were some special considerations. One was the family background. In looking at any younger member of the family for possible membership Fisher thought there were two tests: that either through share ownership or executive position, or both, he should have an interest in the company and an ability to contribute to its operation; and that his presence on the board would not upset the balance between different types of directors as outlined.

Twenty-two years after this discussion the board had evolved in a way that brought it close to the outline. Philip Fisher, Balfour, W.W. (Peter) Southam, and Gordon N. Fisher represented head office. Six divisional heads were also directors: R.W.Southam of the *Citizen*, Nichols of the *Spectator*, Dean of the *Journal*, Auger of the *Province*, James A. Daly of Southam Business Publications, and John D. Murray of Southam Printing. The group of individuals not concerned with management included some large shareholders and some who might be considered independent or professional directors: Gordon T. Southam and G. Hamilton Southam; J. Grant Glassco, Toronto business man; George L. Crawford, Calgary lawyer; W.C.Riley, Winnipeg insurance man; J. Jacques Pigott, Toronto builder; and B.B.Osler, carrying on in his father's tradition as legal adviser to the company. All groups included members of the Southam family. The family, some connected with company enterprises but many more following other careers as the generations proliferated, still held in aggregate just over half the stock.

The company thus has three interlocking echelons of operation: various divisions out on the firing line; a head-office staff exercising general supervision; a board of directors – which includes head-office men and divisional men – determining business (as distinct from editorial) policy. This last, of course, including questions of investment and expansion.

The Market

Probably no business possibilities have engaged the interest of the Southams (and their business emanation, the company) more keenly than those in which the prospect appeared of buying a newspaper. In the years after the moves into Calgary, Edmonton, Winnipeg, and Vancouver, they seemed a natural market to anyone wanting to sell such a property. Discussions were many. Few came down to the point of sale. One consideration was a disinclination on the part of the company with its small head-office staff to take on smaller newspapers, particularly in centres under the shadow of big-city dailies near by. Another was a hesitancy to buy in regions where the company already published. Another, a sensitivity about monopoly situations. Late in 1947 Southams refused to consider buying the Edmonton *Bulletin* for this reason.

As a result (except for the equity involved in Pacific Press), from the time of the *Province* purchase in 1923 up to 1967, the company added only two daily newspapers to its group and acquired less-than-half interests in two others. In 1948 it relaxed its practice in regard to smaller papers in buying the Medicine Hat *News*. In 1956 it picked up the somewhat larger North Bay *Nugget*. In 1953 it bought 47 per cent of the Kitchener-Waterloo *Record* and in 1967 an interest in the Brandon *Sun*.

The company grew, generally speaking, through build-up of newspaper and printing properties already owned, and involvement in other areas in the public communications field, rather than through newspaper purchases.

Some of the possibilities that came to nothing were of more than passing interest in their day.

After the western purchases a mild ambition grew to round out Canadian coverage with a paper in the Maritimes. Negotiations with W.H.Dennis of the Halifax *Herald* were already on when The Southam Publishing Company held its first operational directors' meeting in February of 1928. F.N.Southam reported in May, however, that he had been unable to reach an arrangement. Through the early 1930s Dennis continued to talk sale, but F.N. concluded that the Halifax publisher did so simply because he enjoyed the discussion. Experience with Howard Robinson of the Saint John *Telegraph-Journal* (annexed many years later to the empire of K.C.Irving) was much the same.

Though the company came to be associated chiefly with medium-sized centres in its newspaper enterprises, the urge to publish in one or both of Canada's two biggest cities has lurked in the thinking of its principals for more than sixty years.

Back in 1899 and 1902 and again in 1907 F.N.Southam dickered with the Whites for the Montreal *Gazette* in talks that petered out. In 1923 he discussed with Lord Atholstan possible purchase of the *Star*. Stories have circulated about how Southams 'just missed' getting it. The suggestion of a near miss is not backed by the record. Shortly after F.N. and Atholstan talked about it, F.N. left for Vancouver to buy the *Province*. With the *Province* to pay for and mortgage liabilities elsewhere, William Southam and Sons had all it could handle just then. The *Star* idea lapsed; and in 1925 Atholstan sold the paper to J.W.McConnell for $4,000,000 in a deal under which Atholstan kept possession until death or retirement.

Thinking this over later, Wilson Southam grew mournful. He blamed himself for not pressing for the *Star* purchase. F.N. told him to forget it. It would have been 'the height of folly' to consider such a thing. Having bought the *Province* he couldn't have been pressed into a commitment of any such amount as that required to buy the *Star*.

Rumors stirred in the Toronto newspaper community in 1930. Speculation had it that the *Globe*, none too strong financially and less potent editorially than in the days of George Brown, might be sold. I.W.Killam, the Montreal financier who had bought the *Mail and Empire* in 1927, was said to be on the trail, the idea being a merger to create one morning paper to flourish in a field where two could not. Complicating the situation was the religiosity of the current owner, W.G.Jaffray, and his wife Ethelwyn. Both were hesitant to deal unless given guarantees of the paper's continuance as the sort of publication it was, and as an entity; whereas no one was likely to buy without at least the prospect of a future merger. The *Globe* had its own set of standards. It didn't run routine news from the race-tracks. It carried ads for tobacco and cigars, but not cigarettes; theatre and patent-medicine advertising were closely screened.

The Southams began to check, through Glyn Osler, in the summer of 1930, the explorations reaching the point of contact between principals in December when F.N.Southam called on the Jaffrays and left with them the assurance that the company would be glad to talk at any time. Nothing developed. On June 4, 1931, Jaffray published a signed announcement saying rumors of sale or merger were false. This decision stood up for five years until in October of 1936 he sold to George McCullagh, backed by the mining money of W.H. Wright.

McCullagh bought the *Globe*, he told an assemblage at the National Club held in his honor, without even looking at a balance sheet: 'I was buying character and tradition.' In a curious letter read to this group, Jaffray, who was not present, noted that 'the new management's methods may not be the methods of the last 22 years' but he believed wholly in their sincerity and high ideals.

New methods were already evident. The issue reporting the celebration dinner carried a full page of entries and results from Pimlico, Narragansett, Arlington, and Churchill Downs. By late November the *Globe* would be the *Globe and Mail* as McCullagh achieved the design of a single morning paper in Toronto.

The story of the Southams and this newspaper was not over. The company bid $10,000,000 when the McCullagh and Wright estates sold the *Globe and Mail* in 1955, but saw the property go to Montreal financier Howard Webster at a figure reported as $800,000 higher.

There was one more postscript. From time to time reports cropped up that Webster planned to sell. The company let him know it was in the market. On a December day in 1965 word leaked out that the *Globe and Mail*'s owner and Max Bell were conferring in a Winnipeg hotel. A day or two later the story broke: the *Globe and Mail* had merged with Southams' chief rival, F.P.Publications, in a share-swapping deal that had special advantages through F.P.'s position as a private company.

Of all the deals considered by Southams none was more intriguing than one that actually got into a signed agreement in the fall of 1953. In early November Clair Balfour, helping navigate a friend's converted Fairmile to Florida, was intercepted by a phone call at Oswego. Philip Fisher wanted him at Ottawa where a deal was under way: a transaction that would bring the Winnipeg *Free Press*, newspaper core of the Sifton empire, into the Southam group. The proposition was not of Fisher's seeking. It grew from differences between the two surviving Sifton brothers, Clifford and Victor, over future ownership of the family company that held, among other things, the *Free Press*, the Regina *Leader-Post* and the Saskatoon *Star-Phoenix*. Death of a nephew, Clifford Maclean (Cliffie) Sifton, who ran the *Star-Phoenix*, brought matters to a climax.

Clifford had offered to let things go on as they were or to divide the properties leaving the *Free Press* with Victor. Victor held that one brother should buy out the other and run the whole show, and asked Clifford to name a buy-or-sell price. This the elder brother declined to do, whereupon Victor said he would set such a price himself. Clifford decided to buy. He could have raised the money through normal financial channels. But there was another consideration: the rather specialized newspaper experience needed to direct the *Free Press*. Clifford Sifton had been a lawyer and president of the family company, but had not himself directed the day-to-day operations of a newspaper. Why not solve the whole problem by selling it to Southams? He approached Philip Fisher who agreed to talk.

Fisher, Duncan MacTavish, and Balfour worked out with Sifton in Ottawa on November 7 an agreement to buy the *Free Press* for the lesser of two sums – $4,500,000 or eight times the average of net profits after taxes for the years 1948-53. It included a proviso that Clifford would 'put himself in a position prior to noon of November 23' to complete the deal. The arrangement made, Fisher said: 'Look:

is this the right thing? Shouldn't you and Victor both be in the news-paper business? If you can settle things on some basis that will keep you both in . . . well, we want you to feel free to do so.'

Victor asked for a division of the properties, as originally offered. Clifford complied and was released from the Southam arrangement.

The *Free Press*'s destiny was to become one of a newspaper group, but not Southams'. In 1959 it hoisted the flag of F.P.Publications Limited, the company set up by Victor Sifton and Max Bell to hold the Victoria *Colonist*, Victoria *Times*, Lethbridge *Herald*, Calgary *Albertan*, and Ottawa *Journal* – and which eventually would enfold the *Globe and Mail*.

Medicine Hat

In January of 1948 publisher John Southam and business manager Duncan Waines of the Calgary *Herald* got word from Medicine Hat that a situation there might be worth a close look. Death of a share-holder in the *News* had released for sale a block of stock. A contest for control was under way.

The history of the *News* went back to 1885. In October of that year Tom Braden and Andrew Armour, the two young men who had founded the Calgary *Herald* in a tent two years before, established a weekly at Medicine Hat in a box car. They called it the *Times*. In 1894 when a group of local businessmen and ranchers took over – after several changes of ownership – it became the Medicine Hat *Weekly News*. Two years later the paper moved out of the box car. Natural gas had been discovered. By 1904 The Hat was using it for heat and light. In 1907 it got from Rudyard Kipling its classic des-cription: the town with all Hell for a basement. By then the *News* was a flourishing twelve-page weekly with a circulation of 1,600 and a good deal of western flair. 'The News is the best weekly paper pub-lished in Alberta,' it informed its readers. Display ads cost 65 cents per inch a month, but there were no fast contracts: 'If it don't pay, pull out any time.' By 1909 real-estate fever had gripped the little city and the publishing company built its own two-storey home. In July of 1910 it began daily publication and in the following year a group of local Liberals, including most of its former shareholders, bought and reorganized it.

Meantime the community had grown quickly. Roy Osborne, who came out from Listowel, Ontario, in April of 1912 as circulation manager (and stayed on to retire as publisher forty-six years later), found an overflow of 1,500 living in tents. Circulation was no problem. Everybody bought a paper to check the price of lots: 'Business was a mere sideline at which you worked when not selling real estate.'

The boom produced some interesting situations for the *News*. Editor Alf Terrill, in Medicine Hat since 1909, was another Ontario man – he had written copy in Toronto, Woodstock, Barrie, and St. Catharines – who had followed the lure of the West. When real-estate promoters won a street-railway franchise, which the *News* had fought, they celebrated with a torchlight parade and threw an effigy of Terrill into the South Saskatchewan.

Less spectacular was day-to-day competition from the *Times*, a Conservative organ (no relation to the earlier *Times*, which had become the *News*) and the *Call*, a paper issued by enthusiasts who saw the *Times* and the *News* as too modest about the city's future and its natural gas. Neither rival could withstand such successive blows as the land boom's collapse, onset of the First World War, and years of drought. The *News* alone survived. Medicine Hat had long been a one-paper city when the small civil war over its ownership broke out in 1948.

John Southam advised head office of the apparent opportunity. The *News*, far enough away from bigger cities to make continued existence of a local paper fairly certain, was in a slightly different situation from other small newspapers. The company decided to buy.

This decision was not the last word. The local strife was still on. In the end it narrowed down to a contest in which there were some paradoxical elements. A Medicine Hat businessman who had major industrial interests outside the *News*, but already an influential stockholder, went after personal control. A group of long-time stockholders favored turning the paper over to Southams, an impersonal newspaper company, rather than see it become the adjunct of a local industrial complex.

One curious snag developed. Even when those acting for Southams had gathered up a stock majority it wasn't enough. Under the *News* company's charter the voting value per share diminished as an individual's shareholdings increased. The Southam block was hastily broken up and temporarily split among Calgary *Herald* employees to produce the necessary voting power. Eventually all shares were bought for $125,000.

For more than sixty years, as weekly and daily, the *News* had covered the south-east corner of Alberta, a land of ranch and wheat and antelope. On at least two occasions stories from the region tickled in a special way the news fancies of editors round the continent.

The Medicine Hat News

MEDICINE HAT, ALBERTA, THURSDAY, OCTOBER 20, 1966 — 14 Pages — 10 cents.

END OF AN ERA

Chuck and Iolene Meagher express their victory feelings to NEWS reporters John Stanley (second from right) and Myron Johnson. (NEWS photo)

Meagher takes over from Harry Veiner

By JOHN STANLEY
Of The NEWS

(See poll chart and photos on page eight)

Medicine Hat enters a new era Monday when 35-year-old Chuck Meagher takes over from its chief magistrate for the past 14 years, 63-year-old Mayor Harry Veiner.

The young hospital pharmacist ousted the rancher-businessman mayor from office Wednesday night in an unpredicted 1000-vote victory, 4,881 votes to 3,868. He will be the city's youngest mayor.

Mayor Veiner conceded the election to Mr. Meagher at 9.50 p.m., less than two hours after the polls closed. About 15 minutes earlier the city's longest serving mayor had commented, "well that finishes me," when he saw the Medicine Hat High School poll return.

NEWCOMER

As the new mayor Mr. Meagher is a newcomer to civic politics. He has never stood for municipal office before. Last November he was runner-up to local Socred MP Bud Olson as Progressive Conservative Candidate.

The man he replaces made three unsuccessful attempts at entering Parliament as a Liberal, in 1949, 1953, and 1957. But as Medicine Hat's leading citizen Mayor Veiner never lost a civic poll from the day he was first elected mayor back in 1952.

Since then a whole new generation has grown up. Mr. Meagher is part of this generation. In 1952 he was eligible for his first vote at the age of 21.

When Mayor Veiner entered City Hall in 1952 he had coasted to a comfortable victory over Harry Leinweber, now MLA, and outgoing Mayor Wilson Riley. History repeated itself yesterday in that Mayor Veiner found himself in the same position as Mayor Riley had done 14 years ago.

From then until his crashing defeat against Mr. Meagher, Mayor Veiner had been opposed twice — by Mr. Olson in 1958, and Karl Brucker in 1964.

RECORD

On Wednesday Mayor Veiner said he would break all North American records by heading the polls for eight consecutive terms in office if he won. He is the longest serving mayor in the city's history. The record was previously held by Isaac Bullivant from 1926-1938.

Mr. Veiner was born at Dysart, Sask., went into business in 1928 and came to Medicine Hat in 1936. During the war he was a major in the army holding the rank of Catering Inspector for all military and POW camps in Alberta.

Mr. Meagher was born at Delisle, Sask., and moved to Saskatoon with his parents in 1940. He attended school and university there and graduated in pharmacy in 1955. While at university he was a member of the Royal Canadian Navy Reserve and earned a Lieutenant's commission.

He practiced as Assistant Director of Pharmaceutical Services at the University of Saskatchewan Hospital until moving to Medicine Hat. At present he is pharmacist at the Medicine Hat General Hospital.

When Mr. Meagher arrived at City Hall last night he said he was definitely pleased and quite encouraged by the result of the election in which 58.7 per cent of the voters had turned out.

CHANGE

"I think it's the indication of the people in advocating me that they desire to have progressive change," he said.

He left shortly afterwards for an informal celebration with family friends.

His pretty blonde wife Iolene, a graduate nurse from the General Hospital, was asked if she was surprised at her husband winning the mayoralty.

"Behind every successful man there's a surprised woman. I'm very proud of Chuck," she replied.

She added that their four children Chuck (nine), Kevin (seven), Colleen (six) and Shaun (2) had all stayed up late to watch the results on television.

Mrs. Meagher said she is looking forward to being a mayor's wife but frankly doesn't know what her duties will be.

"I am used to Chuck being busy. He is happiest when busy," she said.

FIRST LOSS

Mayor Veiner had gone home by the time Mr. and Mrs. Meagher arrived on the scene. Shortly before he left the Riverside Scout Hall H-O ballot result had been phoned in to Returning Officer Bill Keith.

When the figures 120 for Meagher and 97 for Veiner were read out Mayor Veiner sadly shook his head and said, "It's the first one I ever lost."

He added, "I can see the younger people wanted a younger man. I gave the best I had for 14 years. Changes take place and a person has to accept them. As the old saying goes 'Men may come and men may go, but rivers go on forever'."

Newcomer George Renner heads aldermanic poll

Newcomer George Renner headed the polls yesterday in a 58.7 per cent turn out of voters that sent him, a former alderman, and two incumbents, to City Hall.

It was the second-highest polling in the City's history.

Mr. Renner led the field strongly with 4,537 votes and was followed to victory by Ald. Jack Edwards with 3,640, Pete Simpson with 3,514, and Ald. Earl Smith with 3,445.

Fifth place went to Rod Carry with 3,176, who was followed by George Maser, 3,041; Leslie Cluff, 2,875; Rod Ray, 2,846; Karl Brucker, 1,526; and Dave Oliphant, 1,217.

Mr. Renner, 35, said he was "real pleased" with the result.

"This was my first attempt to win a council seat. I'd like to say thank you to all who supported me. I don't know why I did so well. I did well at all the polls and had an even strength throughout the city," he said.

Ald. Edwards, who is recovering from an operation he recently underwent in Calgary, was unavailable last night for comment. He was first elected to City Council in 1958 and is Chairman of the Civic Finance Committee.

Mr. Simpson, a CPR yardmaster, said the result was something he had been striving for.

"I'd like to thank the people who voted for me. I thought I'd won after the vote from Connaught came in," he said.

Mr. Simpson was elected to council in 1963 and lost his seat in last year's elections. During his term as an alderman he was a member of the Public Works Committee.

Ald. Earl Smith is beginning his 17th year on council. He said last night he didn't know why he had ended up among the top four candidates.

"It may have been because of the independence of my activities on council. I never had a committee or machine on council. I had nothing to sell or buy," he said.

Mr. Carry and Mr. Maser both stated last night they will seek election again next year.

Mr. Cluff was unavailable for comment and Mr. Ray refused to make any comment on whether he will stand again.

Mr. Brucker, who stood against Mayor Harry Veiner in 1964, said he has no plans for next year.

"I'm quite happy this one is over. I'm pleased with the mayor's ballot," he said. He added he felt he had accomplished something.

Mr. Oliphant said he has plans to run for alderman again but not next year.

'Hatters say no to meters

Medicine Hat residents apparently do not want water meters.

A plebiscite in Wednesday's civic election on the issue of installing water meters was rejected by a resounding 4-1 vote.

A total of 1,586 "Yes" votes were cast, compared to 6,708 "No" votes.

Every poll reporting in the election recorded a majority of "No" votes over "Yes" votes, with one poll recording an outstanding 10-1 majority. That poll, at Elizabeth Street School, recorded a vote of 134-13 against meters.

The question of whether or not Medicine Hat will have water meters is still undecided, however. The plebiscite is not binding, and it will still be up to city council to make a final decision on the matter.

The issue has been vigorously debated, and many council candidates publicly took a stand against water meters during the election campaign.

First loss for Hawrelak; Edmonton returns Dantzer

EDMONTON (CP)—After 15 years, the people of Edmonton have finally said no to William Hawrelak.

Never beaten in seven previous tries for municipal office, the personable 52-year-old former mayor lost decisively Wednesday night to Vince Dantzer, who took over a year ago when Mr. Hawrelak was ousted by a judicial order.

Once before, in 1959, Mr. Hawrelak left office under a cloud, resigning after a royal commission accused him of "gross misconduct" in a land deal. When he ran for the mayoralty again in 1963, he was returned with a thumping majority.

When the first polls reported this time, Mr. Hawrelak was ahead. But his dreams of another comeback quickly faded.

The second report gave Mr. Dantzer a 13-vote lead. It increased steadily as the counting progressed and Mr. Hawrelak was more than 6,000 votes behind when he conceded less than two hours after the polls closed. A third candidate, political newcomer Alexander Latta, was never in the race.

The spotlight was on the Edmonton race and it shone squarely on the rugged features of Mr. Hawrelak, the onetime farm boy who first appeared in the council chamber in 1948 to appeal for better garbage collection, returned the following year as an alderman and won the first of his six terms as mayor in 1951.

A high school graduate at 15, he lost his chance to go to university when a hail storm wiped out the family crop and settled for night classes in commerce while he worked at a variety of jobs ranging from liquor store clerk to insurance salesman.

Eventually, Mr. Hawrelak owned his own soft-drink bottling plant and became associated with a number of real estate firms. But in his years in office, he always invited his most humble constituents to come to him at any hour of the day with their problems.

His conqueror was a quiet, 42-year-old lawyer and RCAF veteran who was an alderman in March, 1965, when Chief Justice C. C. McLaurin ruled that Mr. Hawrelak had violated the City Act in a land transaction and declared the mayor's post vacant. Mr. Dantzer's fellow-aldermen elected him to serve the remaining 19 months of the mayor's term.

He conducted a low-key campaign, stressing the achievements of his administration and refusing to be drawn into the controversy over Mr. Hawrelak's ouster.

The weather

Westerly winds will bring cooler and drier air to the prairies Friday resulting in more sunshine but temperatures will be 5 to 10 degrees lower. Modified arctic air will move into the Peace River region this afternoon with extreme cloudiness.

Sunrise	6:48
Sunset	5:28
Wind at noon	SW-28
Temperature at noon	60
Precipitation	Nil
Maximum yesterday	60
Minimum yesterday	41
Low tonight	35
High tomorrow	50
River today	8:61
River yesterday	7:79

Anderson on school board

When the votes were counted Wednesday, the Public School Board had only one new member, James Anderson.

Mr. Anderson placed fourth in the race with 3,242 votes, thus taking the last slot on the board and beginning a one-year term.

The first three winners were all incumbents.

Leading the race with 4,105 votes was present board chairman James Newton. The two other winning candidates, incumbents Joseph Levinson and Dr. Robert Gray, tied for second place, each polling 3,931 votes. These three top men now begin two-year terms.

The lead was held at various times by Newton, Gray and Levinson, and it was only when the last returns began to come in that Newton was assured of top spot.

The only challenge for the final seat was by Mrs. Amy Frank, who was neck and neck with Anderson until the final returns. Her total vote was 3,064.

The two other defeated candidates were Harry Larson with 2,272 votes and Gordon Krausher with 1,492 votes. None of the losing candidates has ever been on the school board, although Mrs. Frank and Mr. Krausher have both been active with Home and School Associations.

Of the 39 polling booths reporting, James Newton won 19 and tied for one. Mr. Levinson won eight and tied for two, and Dr. Gray captured seven and tied for two. One poll was taken by Mrs. Frank, while Mr. Anderson won one and tied for one.

Mr. Newton, most popular at the polls, has been a member of the board for the past 12 years and has just completed his second term as board chairman. Following his election last night, he said this: "I would like to thank everyone for what they've done. I have given freely of my time, knowledge and energy to help and improve our educational system. I will continue in the same for the next two years."

Dr. Gray, who has just completed his first term on the board, also thanked the voters. "I enjoyed my first term and I appreciate being given another chance. I'm glad to see we were all returned. The board is a matter of teamwork and co-operation. It's a very capable staff. The election went pretty well as I expected."

Mr. Levinson has been a member of the board for 14 years. He has been chairman and vice-chairman in previous years. Mr. Levinson was not available for comment following his victory.

The fourth candidate, Mr. Anderson, making his first attempt to gain a seat, said he was thrilled people would give him their confidence. He had a close race with Mrs. Frank. "I didn't feel safe until the last vote was in," he said. "I have to work twice as hard now to prove my worthiness. I am looking forward to working with th eother experienced members, but I will always reserve the right to make my own decisions."

Meters lose in Calgary

CALGARY (CP) — Calgary voters turned down two of three Wednesday and passed the third by a margin of better than two-to-one.

For the third time in nine years, voters defeated a bylaw which would have allowed the addition of fluorides to the city water supply. Also turned down was a plebiscite which would have made water meters compulsory to all users.

A bylaw allowing commercial sports on Sundays between 1:30 p.m. and 6 p.m. was passed.

The fluoridation plebiscite needed only a simple majority to win, but was defeated 40,706 to 33,923. In 1957 and 1961, the bill also failed to gain approval of 50 per cent of the public. In those years, a two-thirds majority was needed to pass the bylaw.

The water meter bylaw was defeated 61,651 to 13,028.

The Sunday Sport bylaw passed 51,298 to 24397.

Figures were for 446 of 451 polls.

'Tin cup medicare'

Tories target for jibes

OTTAWA (CP) — Conservative MPs were accused Wednesday of proposing "tin cup medicare" and of falling into the hands of "19th-century reactionaries."

The jibes were fired at the official Opposition by New Democratic Party Leader T. C. Douglas and Liberal Richard Cashin as the Commons debate on medical care insurance rolled on for the fifth straight day.

Conservative speakers replied that the government bill has "socialistic tendencies" and that they don't see any need to rush it through Parliament.

The deadlocked debate continues today with no sign of a vote on a Conservative amendment or on second reading—approval in principle—of the measure.

The minority Pearson government is assured of voting support from the 21 New Democrats and the five Social Credit MPs on second reading, but Opposition MPs can delay the vote indefinitely by continuing to talk.

Mr. Cashin, member for St. John's West, accused the Conservatives of conducting a filibuster by putting up 27 speakers. Another Conservative spoke later, bringing the total to 28.

"Some of the statements made by honorable gentlemen opposite struck me as reactionary, even for the 19th century."

He said Opposition Leader Diefenbaker, who has not entered the debate so far, is losing control of his party to the "true blue Tories" of the Ontario government.

Mr. Douglas said his party will use every parliamentary devise in the book to press the Liberals to implement medical insurance next July, as they had pledged during the 1965 election campaign.

The delay of the target date to July 1, 1968 had not been explained by the government and amounted to deception of the electorate. It was a "complete betrayal" of election promises. To blame the deferment on inflation was ridiculous.

Liquor store for Redcliff

Mayor Alf Dutton of Redcliff told The NEWS today that Redcliff will be getting a liquor store next year.

Mayor Dutton was advised by provincial authorities this morning that the government will purchase lots for a liquor store next year.

Mayor Dutton was advised by provincial authorities this morning that the government will purchase lots for a liquor store on Broadway, opposite the IGA store. The store will be constructed next year.

One concerned a drive to change the city's name; the other, an effort to beat persistent drought by calling in a rainmaker.

The place got its name, the story goes, when a Cree medicine man, fleeing from a battle with the Blackfoot, lost his head-dress in midstream. In 1910 a host of newcomers had invaded Medicine Hat on the crest of the land boom. They wanted something slick in the way of a name. Something that would look well on a letterhead. Something not associated with American jibes that Medicine Hat – site of the weather-reporting service for the area – supplied the bad weather for the continent. City council agreed to hold a plebiscite. Language at the Cypress Club took on new convolutions. Old-timers there decided to appeal to Kipling.

The imperial bard had spent a day in town in the course of his 1907 tour of Canada. Sunday, October 13, of that year was well remembered in Medicine Hat. The Kiplings arrived on the morning train, met by a civic committee. From there on the formality vanished. Hilarity replaced it as the guests visited the CPR roundhouse, a nearby farm, and the brick-works.

The *News* – still a weekly then – gave four of its seven front-page columns to the visit, including a detailed account of the sight-seeing tour, which brought out a full roster of Medicine Hat's early motorists: 'Brown with the Chinook, the judge with the Ladies' Friend, Harry Tweed with Everybody's, the Pingle brothers with the Mud Turtle and the Scarlet Runner, and Dr. Smith with Skidoo, all were there.'

After visits to the farm and the roundhouse, where natural gas was shown off to the poet, the convoy – 'a supply of lubricant having been laid in' – formed up for the six-mile run to Redcliff and the brick-works. The usual motoring calamities began. The Ladies' Friend suffered a puncture and 'the vocabulary of the legal gentleman not being equal to the occasion, Mr. Kipling was asked to assist, which he kindly did.' Chinook and Skidoo made the works without trouble, but Everybody's, carrying the guest, 'laid down on the hill'. However, all were delivered at last and the *News* reported Kipling as delighted. A motorist since the game commenced, he admitted to having been stuck in front of every saloon in Sussex.

It was in the course of this exhilarating day under bright October sunshine that Kipling coined his enduring label. As transcribed by the *News* reporter it read: 'This part of the country seems to have all Hell for a basement and the only trap-door appears to be in Medicine Hat.' He added the admonition: 'And don't ever think of changing the name of your town. It's all your own and the only Hat of its kind on earth.'

This was what the old-timers remembered when the campaign for a name-change gathered strength. They commissioned postmaster Frank Fatt to write the master. Fatt appealed for 'a few words of encouragement in combating the heretics'.

Kipling was prompt and emphatic. He saw no reason on earth why men should be bluffed out of their city's birthright by an imported joke: 'Accept the charge joyously and go forward as Medicine Hat – the only city officially recognized as capable of freezing out the United States and giving the continent cold feet.' People and not prospectuses made cities. The name of Medicine Hat echoed the tradition of red mystery and romance that once filled the Prairies. Above all it was 'the lawful, original, sweat-and-dust-won name of the city'.

What, Kipling asked, should a place be rechristened that has sold its name? . . . 'Judasville'.

Kipling's letter foiled the upstarts (the plebiscite was never held) and incidentally brought Medicine Hat a round of world-wide publicity. Even the Chicago *Tribune* for once agreed with something British: 'Kipling is right. . . . We have used the Medicine Hat brand of weather for a quarter of a century and we refuse to accept any other.'

The winter brand of Medicine Hat weather was what the continent feared. But on nearby farmlands the scourge was summer drought.

Out in California Charles Hatfield's prowess as a rainmaker became the subject of international speculation when floods followed his operations around San Diego. Late in 1920 a Medicine Hat delegation went to see him. At a standing-room-only meeting in February of 1921 the newly founded United Agricultural Association agreed on a contract. It called for operations from May 1 to August 1, with expectations of a doubled natural rainfall – Hatfield to get credit for one-half the precipitation, 'the maximum consideration being $8,000 for a four-inch rainfall' over a radius of 100 miles.

Hatfield arrived in April and set up an open-work tower topped by a mysterious box-like arrangement at Chappice Lake, north-east of the city. Operations started May 1. A shower occurred May 2, another May 4, and on Saturday, May 7, the *News* front-paged RAIN-FALL OVER WHOLE DISTRICT.

Two days later F.S.Ratcliff, secretary of the Agricultural Association, got a wire from a farmer in Dollard, Saskatchewan, seventy-five miles away: 'Rain enough. Stop for a few days.' Hatfield didn't like the advice. 'Let it rain,' he told a *News* reporter who questioned him about talk in some quarters that he should lay off and give the farmers a chance to finish seeding.

The skies dried up of their own accord. Hatfield blamed it on the location of his tower, cut his bill from $8,000 to $5,500, and agreed to come back next year for $4,000 an inch for everything over three inches, with anything over six thrown in. The *News* reported this agreement August 5 under an execrable pun: IT'S STILL MEDICINE HATFIELD. 'Mr. Hatfield and his brother expect to start for Los Angeles tomorrow morning,' the story said.

They never returned.

But water eventually came through more prosaic means. By the late 1950s irrigation ditches had reached the region, and sugar beets, tomatoes, potatoes, and corn grew where in some past seasons only the thistle thrived.

The *Nugget*

Early in 1956 a machinery salesman, in the course of a casual visit to Peter Southam's office, mentioned that he had heard the North Bay *Nugget* might be bought. Southam went north to find out.

The *Nugget* had a colorful history. Founded as the weekly Cobalt *Nugget* in 1907 – printed at first in North Bay but distributed in the silver country – it moved into a plant in Cobalt in the following year and on January 23, 1909, began daily publication in a town that was still very much a mining camp (a headline March 11 forecast 'Running Water for Cobalt Very Soon').

For a dozen years it got out its eight pages daily, with an extra four on Saturdays, as the fortunes of the region rose and fell. An early standing heading proclaimed 'Cobalt is the Greatest Silver Mining Camp in the World'. An editorial entitled 'Millionaires of Cobalt' noted: 'There are so many that one is lost in the maze of trying to enumerate them . . . and they are being made every week. . . . Yet only a year or two ago many of them were but laborers, having hard work to make both ends meet.' Local news crowded the front page: 'English Capital in South Lorrain' . . . 'La Rose Shows over Million Dollars Profit' . . . 'New Vein Found on Cobalt Central'.

The boom died. In 1921 publisher Harry Browning moved the paper back to North Bay, and there, on July 18, 1922, it came into possession of a proprietor as colorful as itself.

William Edge Mason, who started as a dollar-a-week printer's devil on the Walkerton *Telescope*, had come north in the early boom days as press foreman for an infant daily in Sudbury – the *Northern Star*. With local backing he took charge of that paper when it failed as a daily and turned it into a paying proposition as the twice-weekly Sudbury *Star*. In the summer of 1922 Mason bought the *Nugget* and repeated the process. A paper that had faltered as a daily thrived at twice a week.

The *Nugget*, with its corps of correspondents – trappers, station agents, and school-teachers – carried many a startling story from a territory that stretched to James Bay. None rated in initial impact and continuing interest with one that broke within fifteen miles of its own front door.

The day was Monday, May 28, 1934, a publication day at the paper, by then issuing three times a week. Shortly before 8 A.M. editor Eddie Bunyan answered the phone. The caller was Leon Dionne, who ran a garage at nearby Callander. Leon had just become an uncle again. Laughing, he wanted to know whether a birth notice for five nieces would cost more than an insertion for one.

Thus began the story of the Dionne quintuplets. It made the *Nugget*'s eight-column line that day and flowed out in story and picture around the world. Indirectly it affected the fortunes of the newspaper that first reported it; for it ignited an industry that would come to be the region's greatest source of revenue, the tourist trade. Mason turned the paper into a daily again in 1941, a step he had taken at Sudbury two years before.

By the late 1940s the publisher had begun to think of easing up and sticking to his home base at Sudbury. For the *Nugget* he had devised a novel plan: to turn it over to its staff and let them pay for it out of earnings. Arrangements were under way when in June of 1948 Mason died. His executors concluded the deal. The price was $225,-000. Every employee at the time of the transaction became a shareholder in a company headed by Jack Grainger, one-time compositor who had managed the paper since 1939. Directors included other veteran *Nugget* men: managing editor C.M.Fellman, news editor Britt Jessup, secretary-treasurer G.W.Justice, and job-printing manager J.A.Beatty.

They ran the show successfully. Giving themselves ten years to pay off the debt, they cleared it in six. They put up a new building. They produced a progressive paper: in 1955 a series of Fellman's editorials won the national award for editorial writing.

But by 1956 the paper needed new money for expansion and

Weather Forecast

Northern Ontario: Moderate to fresh southwest winds; partly cloudy tonight and Tuesday with scattered thunderstorms and continuing warm.

Georgian Bay: Moderate southwest winds; fine and warm.

Toronto—moderate to fresh southwest winds; partly cloudy, warm.

The Nugget

VOL. XXV—NO. 11   NORTH BAY, ONT., MONDAY, MAY 28, 1934   TEN PAGES   PRICE THREE CENTS

LATE EDITION

QUINTUPLETS BORN TO FARM WIFE

French Fliers at Brooklyn Field

24-Year Old Corbeil Mother Establishes Canadian Mark

Land Safely After Ocean Flight Today

Ross and Codos Establish Record for Western Crossing

3,700 MILE HOP

Two Bush Fires Sweeping Over Sudbury Area

Destructive Blazes Raging in Falconbridge, Moffatt Townships

EIGHT-MILE FRONT

Taking the saddle for the first time in years, King George presented this picture of sartorial elegance as he left for a canter in Hyde Park. He was said to be preparing for the trooping of the color, which falls on his 68th birthday on June 3.

$200,000 DAMAGE IN ROUYN REGION

World Nations Turn to Russia To Avert War

Soviet Delegates Expected to Produce Sane Arms Proposal

COLLAPSE FORESHADOWED

Establishes Canadian Mark

LATE WIRE FLASHES

Mrs. Oliva Dionne Eligible for King's Bounty; Dr. A. R. Dafoe Says all Five Baby Girls Healthy

WEIGH 13 POUNDS, 6 OUNCES

MOTHER WILL GET AT LEAST THREE POUNDS

MARKET SUMMARY

WASHINGTON REPORT BUOYS GOLD STOCKS

POLICE AT SPRAGGE NAB ROBBERS QUICK

Trio Behind Bars 15 Minutes After Burglarizing Gas Station

TAKEN TO SUDBURY

More Good Wishes For Young Mother

WANTS TO FORTIFY

Baseball Today

INTERNATIONAL LEAGUE

NATIONAL LEAGUE

AMERICAN LEAGUE

Corbeil Eclipses Maritime Record

CANADIAN FLIER FOR FLIGHT RECORD

G. I. Reid Announces Plan to Fly from Toronto to Bagdad

SUSPECT FOUL PLAY IN BELLEVILLE DEATH

Stove Explodes; Suspect Revenge

Serious Head Hurt Proves Fatal to 'T' Wrestler

POLICE INVESTIGATE

FLAPPER FANNY SAYS:

WRIGHT-HARGREAVES DECLARES DIVIDEND

FOUR MEN ATTEMPT LIFE OF AMBASSADOR TO CUBA

RIVER DRIVER DROWNS SLIPPED FROM LOGS

COLOMBO STILL FAVORED AS TURF CLASSIC NEARS

A SMILE

plant. Peter Southam's exploratory visit to North Bay resulted in discussions that wound up with sale of the *Nugget* to The Southam Company in June. In an editorial June 18 announcing the change the *Nugget* acknowledged a measure of sadness, frankly explained its need for working capital, and assured its readers that it would remain a community newspaper with management unchanged.

New Departures

At the end of 1955 the company moved its head office to Toronto to be nearer the country's centre of printing and publishing and its own over-all operations. Late in 1954 St. Clair Balfour, grandson of William Southam and of the original St. Clair Balfour of Hamilton, became executive vice-president and managing director.

Balfour had come back to the *Spectator* after five years in the Royal Canadian Naval Volunteer Reserve, a commander holding the D.S.C. for service in corvettes and frigates. After F.I.Ker's retirement in 1951 he had published the *Spectator*. Now he was moving up as logical successor to Fisher as president of the company, a transition that occurred in 1961 when Fisher became chairman of the board.

On a May day in 1960 Balfour thought he spotted two men deeply concerned with the magazine trade lunching together at the Toronto Club – Floyd Chalmers, president of Maclean-Hunter, and Andrew Dyas MacLean, chairman of Hugh C. MacLean publications.

Back in the 1880s John Bayne Maclean had pioneered the business of trade journals with a periodical called the *Canadian Grocer*. In the early days his brother Hugh C. worked with him in building up a string. In 1898 the brothers split up, even to the extent of spelling their names differently.

Balfour was intrigued. Were the two empires about to be united, long after the death of the brothers? More to the point: Except for the *Nugget* the company had not added a newspaper to the group in years. And recent efforts to increase its interests in radio and television had met with little success before the bodies regulating the transfer of such properties. Was there a chance here to branch out into another region of the communications field? Balfour telephoned Andrew D. MacLean to suggest that, if he had a sale in mind, they talk things over. MacLean said his luncheon companion had not been Chalmers, and he didn't plan to sell to anyone. But a week later he was back on the phone.

The result was a deal involving close to $2,000,000 that put Southams into the trade-magazine field with nineteen publications bearing such names as *Shoe and Leather Journal, Hospital Administration,* and *Canadian Metalworker.* The old MacLean firm became Southam Business Publications and picked up more trade periodicals and annuals until in 1966 it published more than fifty.

Late in 1961 The Southam Company bought the *Financial Times,* a Montreal weekly, and in 1962 purchased *Canadian Homes* from Maclean-Hunter for distribution as a monthly supplement with its newspapers. In 1965 in partnership with the Toronto *Star* it launched the *Canadian,* an ambitious adventure in weekly supplements.

Meantime, in 1964, in a move to express in its corporate name its field of activity – mass communications – The Southam Company became Southam Press Limited, adopting, in a wider sense, the name once used by the printing plants.

In the same period a reshuffling – what might almost be called a new approach – occurred in its printing business. This had begun somewhat earlier. The commercial printing trade was dull in the mid-1950s. Recognizing sales as the crux of the problem, W.H.Woolnough, then heading the Toronto plant, reported: 'We have decided to get bright young men and train them ourselves. The creative department has been reorganized and expanded to provide a better flow of ideas to the sales staff.' So-called 'creative printing', the planning and production of brochures and folders designed to present a client's particular sales pitch, had been for years a considerable part of the Southam printing business. Now it got further emphasis in the Southam Specialized Marketing Service.

In 1958 The Southam Printing Company was organized to administer the printing divisions. There were some new components. In 1955 Southams bought the Nicholson Printing Company in Vancouver, a plant producing for British Columbia and Alberta much the same kinds of tickets and specialties as Montreal, though in smaller volume. The new company also took over from Consolidated Press the right to use for a period the name and franchise of Saturday Night Press (not including the magazine *Saturday Night*) and integrated it into the Toronto operation.

In 1962 Montreal discontinued general printing to concentrate on its specialty business – tickets, tags, tokens, labels, milk-bottle caps. The St. Alexander and Bleury Street buildings were sold, the Southam plant remaining as a tenant until 1965, when it moved across the river to a new plant in suburban Candiac.

Allied with equipment problems is that of changing methods. For centuries no one thought of printing in any terms but those of striking raised surfaces of inked metal against paper. In recent years the development of what is known as offset printing or offset lithography has become a growing factor in the printing craft. The process differs from letterpress in that smooth-surface plates, photographically produced, transfer their images by specially-developed inks to rubber blankets which in turn reproduce them on paper. The Toronto plant began experimenting with offset in the early 1950s. It became an increasingly important element in production. Rotogravure – smooth-finish quality printing from copper cylinders etched from photographic plates – was another development. The most important event in the modern history of Southam printing was purchase of Murray Printing and Gravure, a family company with a long tradition in gravure, offset, and conventional letterpress.

Murray's got into the printing business in 1893, grew steadily, and in 1935 took over Canadian Gravure. In 1961 Southams bought for $700,000 the stock interest in Murray's of two estates, amounting to just over 23 per cent of the company. Three years later they bought the remainder for $3,564,000 and prepared to move the whole Toronto printing business to enlarged buildings on the Murray property at Weston, an operation completed in 1966.

Merging of the Southam-Murray interests was formalized in that year with J.D.Murray's appointment as president of The Southam Printing Company. E.M.Pritchard, Southams' managing director of printing since 1961, continued as such for the combined operation.

Acquisition of Murray's more than doubled Southam printing volume. Incidentally it brought the company back into the giant business of mail-order catalogues for the first time since it ceased to produce the Simpson book more than thirty years before. Murray's had a long-term contract with Eaton's.

Daily newspapers continued to be the backbone of the company's business with total revenue from this source of $39,000,000 in 1965. But with the Murray purchase, printing established itself firmly in second place with $17,000,000 (up $10,000,000 from 1964). Magazines accounted for $7,000,000. Of this $63,000,000 revenue from operations, plus about $1,100,000 income from investments, the company, after operating expenses and other costs of $53,500,-000 and income taxes of more than $5,000,000, showed profit on operations and investments of just over $5,500,000. Included in the income-from-investments figure (of which the bulk was $680,000 from Pacific Press) was the profit from minority newspaper holdings and scattered interests in radio and TV. Dividends from the broadcasting field were $137,500.

On the Air

Monday, March 13, 1922, was an average news-day at the *Province*. A gang in Cork threatened to shoot Michael Collins. In Johannesburg radicals from the Rand mine war fired at General Jan Smuts. India faced political disaster, Salmon Arm fruit-men were sore at low prices, and fire swept the main street of Summerland. Fatty Arbuckle went on trial for the third time at San Francisco, M.P.s welcomed Agnes MacPhail as the first woman to reach the House of Commons, and in Nova Scotia a Boston professor produced a new theory on the fire-setting Antigonish ghost. The weather was cloudy with rain.

That evening the possessors of 'crystal radiophones' in Vancouver were treated to something unusual. They heard about the day's events (and got a musical bonus) just by sticking to their sets. The *Province* was on the air.

Less than two years before, on November 2, 1920, the first voice program had been broadcast from a Pittsburgh garage – running returns from the Harding-Cox election. The medium was tentative and experimental. Listeners were still 'fans', devotees of an exciting novelty. Most of them built their own receivers.

There had been certain signs, however. It was estimated that 300,-000 heard a description of the Dempsey-Carpentier fight at Jersey City in 1921, the first broadcast of a great sports event. Not that 300,000 receivers existed; to reach that audience amateurs wired theatres – an early version of the closed-circuit television technique of forty years later. A few dailies, fascinated by promotional possibilities, began to spill music and news into the airwaves. One was the Seattle *Times*. Cromie of the *Sun* went down to see how it was done. Frank Burd sent Stewart Armour of the *Province* in his wake, and the *Province* – using Marconi Company equipment – was first on the air.

On May 1 in the same year, Edmonton Mayor D.M.Duggan called 'Hullo, hullo, hullo,' into a horn-shaped gadget in a corner of the *Journal*'s newsroom and wound up a fifty-word speech with the declaration: 'Edmonton leads the way in all Alberta. Calgary and others follow. That is all. Goodnight.' It was not quite all. A recorded concert followed the mayor as the *Journal*'s station CJCA reached out to its first slender audience through two seventy-five-foot masts on the roof. Twenty-four hours later Calgary trade board president Frank Freeze said the 'hullos' for the *Herald*'s new station CQCA (it became CFAC in August) and retired in favor of a recording of 'Kiss Me Again'.

At about the same time the Winnipeg newspapers also moved into broadcasting, Sifton's *Free Press* erecting towers on its roof, and the *Tribune* following suit.

Early in 1924 the *Spectator* bought the equipment – for $1,000 in advertising space – and took over the licence of a radio and auto supply company that owned the only broadcasting plant in Hamilton.

Up to this time radio had been an experimental enthusiasm. In surrounding towns the *Journal* set up receiving sets in halls, inviting all comers, to demonstrate its station. Shortly after the *Herald* began to broadcast, excitement mounted when reports came in that it had been heard at Vulcan, eighty miles away. It also lent out receiving sets – now to a local store, next week to one in Okotoks – to broaden listening opportunity. Fans formed the Alberta Radio Experimenters Association. Newspapers devoted columns to plans and diagrams. The *Journal* ran a series on 'how to build a radio set for $3'. The *Spectator* called itself the Pioneer Radio Newspaper: 'Fans who make sets or parts at their work-benches will find our instructions on how to wire and assemble the standard hook-ups the best in print.' To subscribers it offered a radio atlas at cost – 15 cents – showing locations and wave-lengths of stations all over the world.

It soon became evident that this engaging experiment had become a giant – from the newspaper standpoint not necessarily friendly. As receivers multiplied by hundreds of thousands, radio began to capture a growing slice of the advertising dollar. Not only that. Looking back, publishers could see an omen in the fact that the first Pittsburgh broadcast had been based on a prime news event. Part of the enticement that swelled the audience was drawn from the newspapers' reason-for-being: the news itself; news often lifted for the ear from the printed page where, at considerable expense in money and enterprise, it had been displayed for the eye. Publishers grew explosive. John Bassett of the *Gazette* used to say he could hear the newsprint crackling behind the voices of announcers as they read off his front page to the breakfast tables of Montreal.

Would radio do to the newspapers what trucks and buses had done to the railways? The infighting grew severe. The period was one of confusion – confusion in availability of air frequencies, confusion over property right in news, confusion in ownership and motives and attitudes. There were broadcasters with no newspaper connection, often hostile to newspapers; newspaper owners who stayed out of radio and tried to ignore it or to fight it; newspaper owners who had gone into broadcasting. And in this last group, several further divisions with differing motives: some were in radio as straight promotion for their newspapers, or in the hope of protecting the newspaper field in ways not clearly defined; others for profit as station operators. Some believed they could combine these desirable results.

The beginning of something like order in the industry began to appear with formation late in 1932 of the Canadian Radio Broadcasting Commission – forerunner of the Canadian Broadcasting Corporation – as a result of the Aird Royal Commission, which in 1929 had recommended for Canada a set-up close to that of the nationalized British system.

Active in pressing for action on the Aird report had been the Canadian Radio League, organized by the young Ottawa idealist Alan Plaunt. Personally F.N.Southam supported the League, as did some other members of the family. Wilson's daughter Margaret took an active part in its work in Ottawa. As a result of this and the fact that Charles Bowman had been a member of the Aird commission, an impression grew in some quarters that the company, as a company, had taken a stand. Early in 1931 at a meeting of Quebec and Ontario broadcasters F.I.Ker – present by virtue of operating the *Spectator* station – heard the company blasted by one broadcaster as the inspiration behind the League, the imputed motive being protection of newspaper advertising, since a fully nationalized system would reduce or eliminate ads on the air. Ker pointed out that the company had nothing to do with forming the League; at least one of its papers, the Edmonton *Journal*, had opposed nationalization.

The company in fact developed no special point of view on the relationship between publicly owned and privately owned broadcasting during these years. Talk at board meetings centred mainly on the medium's relationship to newspapers. A full-dress discussion at a directors' meeting in June of 1933 ended in a consensus that radio would develop along its own lines and become less and less an adjunct of the newspaper business. As early as 1930 F.N.Southam, commenting on a suggestion by Ker for an all-Southam hook-up, wrote:

> Broadly speaking I look on the broadcasting business as being quite distinct from the publishing business and I fail to see wherein our publishing interests can be helped to any appreciable extent through becoming directly interested in radio. I still feel that radio, billboards, and the publication of monthly magazines are distinctive businesses

of their own, and our decision to go into one of them should be on the merits of the proposition itself.

Brooding on the subject five years later, Philip Fisher made the point that newspaper ownership of competitive media could help or hinder newspapers as such only if run with that in mind rather than their own success: 'Newspaper ownership of radio would only help newspaper advertising if the radio stations were run for the benefit of the newspapers rather than for the benefit of the radio stations themselves. Such a technique would, in the long run, I think, defeat itself, even if we were prepared to embark on it ignoring the rights which the public might have in the matter.'

However, the general policy of operating radio stations by the company's newspapers was approved when this recurrent subject came up again in 1944. By that time of course the stations concerned – at Calgary and Edmonton – had long been run as self-contained business propositions, not adjuncts of anything.

At the fall board meeting in 1945 Fisher returned to the subject and read a prepared memorandum that posed three questions: Would radio ownership help to make the newspapers more profitable? Was it a necessary sheet anchor to windward because radio potentialities were so great as to threaten the very existence of newspaper profits? Or would it be just another possible investment? The minutes of the meeting note that 'while considerable discussion took place, no definite decision was reached.'

As things turned out the company's interests in broadcasting moved through various phases: establishment and operation of stations by individual newspapers, operation by company-controlled subsidiaries, and finally divestment of control in moves that left its interest largely one of simple investment – usually protected by representation on the boards of companies concerned. It had long since reached the status of a 'distinctive business' as suggested by F.N. in 1930, after early development among the Southam papers along individual and differing lines.

The *Spectator*'s venture in 1924 was straight promotion, part of its battle with the *Herald* during W.F.Herman's operation of the competing paper. It broadcast a nightly news bulletin and some special events – a Sault-Tigers hockey game or a speech by Howard Ferguson – but Ker admitted that his main purpose was to freeze the *Herald* out and 'clear the air for local fans' to pick up worthwhile broadcasting originating elsewhere. By 1930 there were three licences in Hamilton: CKOC, CHML, and the *Spectator*'s CHCS. But all shared hours on the same wave-length. CKOC used most of the

Spectator's time, and the paper in turn broadcast through CKOC when it wanted to. Ker, a supporter of nationalization, pulled out of the field when the C.R.B.C. came into existence in 1932. The *Spectator* returned to it in 1949 with a frequency modulation station (centred in the old Southam house on Jackson Street) later discontinued when integrated with CHCH-TV, the first television station in which the company had an interest.

In Winnipeg the Siftons' *Free Press* and the Southams' *Tribune* stayed in broadcasting as operators only a year or so and then agreed to turn the job over to the provincial government. The Siftons went back into it in 1940.

In Vancouver the *Province* developed its own station, CKCD, but on a shared frequency with CKWX, and as late as 1937 kept the station on the air only thirteen hours a week, its main interest being a nightly newscast and promotion for such activities as its model kitchen. It closed in January 1940.

In Alberta the tale was different. The motive in Hamilton, Winnipeg, and Vancouver had been largely promotional. In Calgary and Edmonton, though the story started that way, it developed otherwise.

There is almost a note of surprise in John Imrie's report to George Disher at head office in April of 1933, eleven years after CJCA opened:

> CJCA was established as an aid to the Edmonton Journal. Very little radio advertising was available then and it was used mainly as a service of the Journal to its readers. In recent years however a great deal of radio advertising has been secured. In March for example 61 local retail advertisers used CJCA – almost one-third of the number using the Journal. CJCA is becoming more and more a commercial proposition and less and less a builder of goodwill and prestige for the Edmonton Journal.

CFAC, Calgary, grew in much the same way. Frank (Tiny) Elphicke joined the station in 1931 and became manager in 1933. Others whose names would become well known in Canadian broadcasting worked for CFAC in those early years: Guy Herbert, Norm Botterill, Monica Mugan, Jack Dennett.

Both stations were getting too big and too busy to run as sideshows of the newspapers. Leigh Spencer called in a business friend, Harold Carson, who with James Taylor and Hugh Pearson was building up an extensive radio connection in the West. Early in 1934 Taylor, Pearson and Carson took over management of both stations on a profit-sharing basis. Both operated from new and more powerful plants. In a 1948 reorganization the operating company took on

40 per cent of actual ownership, Southams at that time keeping 60 per cent. By then the last shreds of any suggestion that these stations were 'adjuncts of the newspapers' – their original purpose – were gone. The Southam annual report said: 'It is the policy and practice of the company to keep its radio stations apart from and entirely independent of its newspapers.'

The association with Taylor, Pearson and Carson also put Southams into a related business – that of station representation. In the early 1930s the management firm organized United Broadcast Sales Limited, which soon became All-Canada Radio Facilities (later All-Canada Radio and Television) to get national advertising for the stations it represented and to provide a transcription service. Taylor, Pearson and Carson, the Siftons and the Southams each held one-third until their interests were reduced to 25 per cent when All-Canada's president, Stuart MacKay, bought in. Southams later acquired the Sifton holding. The interest of The Southam Company in broadcasting now had become chiefly an investment interest.

Another development in the never placid world of broadcasting was on the way. The word 'television' (coined in 1909) remained merely a word, for all practical purposes, until after World War II. TV came into production with a rerun of the excitement and apprehension and speculation that attended the growth of radio: it would cut the effectiveness of the printed word; destroy its own parent, radio; cripple motion pictures; steal all the advertising in sight. As in the case of earlier electronic developments the results did not quite match the speculation.

But in one sense the upsurge of TV differed widely from that of radio. In the early days, given a licence, a radio transmitter could be got going hurriedly and on the cheap; Ker put the *Spectator* on the air for $1,000 in 1924. When in 1953 Niagara Television – CHCH-TV – was set up in Hamilton by Ken Soble, The Southam Company, and Wentworth Broadcasting (of which the Clifford Sifton interests were the largest holders), the original investment by the three ran to $1,500,000 or so. For years surplus revenue went back into the business. It paid its first dividend in 1965.

This was the first Southam investment in television, a station built around the personality of a man who had been a broadcaster since boyhood. Soble, a product of the Spadina Avenue district in Toronto, got on the air as an announcer at eighteen. By the time television emerged in the early 1950s he owned radio station CHML. Soble put into CHCH-TV the same imaginative approach he had brought to radio. A typical move was to disaffiliate the station from the

C.B.C. in 1961, when network programs interfered with independent business, and to meet the Canadian-content requirement by developing shows of his own.

To the Fowler Commission in 1956 The Southam Company defined a position: Licensing should rest with the Department of Transport, with no interference from the C.B.C. in respect to private stations. Programs should be subject only to existing laws against sedition, treason, libel, slander, false advertising, and misbranding. Canadian culture should continue to be encouraged by the C.B.C., financed if necessary from the country's general revenues. Multiple ownership should be subject only to such restrictions as the Combines Act specifies.

Policy decisions of the C.B.C. and of the Board of Broadcast Governors after its formation in 1958 set up some roadblocks to any widespread controlling ownership of radio or TV.

In March of 1960 Balfour appeared before the B.B.G. to support an application, eventually unsuccessful, by Southams and a group of Toronto citizens headed by Henry Borden for the one available private TV licence in Toronto. Similar bids in Vancouver and Ottawa were also turned down. At the Toronto hearing he listed the company's radio holdings as control of two stations – CJCA, Edmonton, and CFAC, Calgary – and a minority interest in a third (London, held through the company's quarter-share of the *Free Press*). In television it had minority interests in three stations: Hamilton, Calgary (where it had picked up 20 per cent in CHCT-TV), and London.

At the same time he told the board his company had concluded it should not control radio stations in cities where its newspapers published. Accordingly it reduced its interest in Edmonton and Calgary radio to 40 per cent by selling 20 per cent to Selkirk Holdings, a Taylor, Pearson and Carson company, and embarked on a policy of increasing general investment in radio and television by going after minority interests in more stations. Through Castleton Investments, a company having the same shareholders as All-Canada, it got small shares in two Pacific Coast television stations – CHAN-TV, Vancouver, and CHEK-TV, Victoria. Later it took over directly the 38 per cent share in radio station CKOY, Ottawa, that had been held personally by the families of Harry and Wilson Southam.

Because of various factors, including the costs now involved in any considerable radio and TV operation, the ownership picture of some large stations can be an interesting jigsaw. Southams went into Niagara Television on a one-third basis with Soble and Wentworth Broadcasting. Later all three interests came down to 25 per cent when Paul Nathanson of Hamilton Theatre Properties bought in. Still later, in 1961, Southams picked up 19 per cent of Wentworth, which not only gave the company an interest in radio station CKOC but, indirectly, another small slice of Niagara. And in 1965, through some additional dealing when Selkirk Holdings bought All-Canada, Southams emerged with 28 per cent of Selkirk, which held 27.58 per cent of Wentworth. Its interest in CHCH-TV, therefore, was 25 per cent direct plus two smaller percentages through Wentworth at one remove and Selkirk at two.

After the Selkirk deal the company held, directly or indirectly, interests in radio and TV in Vancouver, Calgary, Hamilton, Lethbridge, Victoria, and London (the latter through its share in the *Free Press*); radio-only in Vernon, Grande Prairie, Ottawa, and Edmonton; TV-only in Kelowna.

In no case did it control or operate a station. Nor did it have an interest in any communications enterprise outside Canada. When Roy Thomson went into Scottish TV in 1955 he suggested to Harold Carson that All-Canada should invest $25,000 in the new venture. Carson consulted Balfour, who wrote: 'We are opposed to investing in a non-Canadian publication just as we have opposed, and will continue to oppose, foreign investment in Canadian forms of mass communications.'

This philosophy would find the company at the centre of controversy a few years later.

The Canadian Ownership Issue

In 1963 the company placed itself at the centre of a controversial issue on which the country's publishers differed in various ways. It came out for legislation to ensure Canadian ownership of Canadian newspapers and other forms of public communication.

In the Southam view, and that of some others, something more than a windmill was there to tilt at. The American Sam Newhouse and the Swede Axel Wenner-Gren had tried to buy the Vancouver *Sun*. Leading contenders for the *Globe and Mail*, when Howard Webster bought it in 1955, had been the New Englander William Loeb and the Englishman Lord Rothermere. Americans had cast envious eyes at the Toronto *Star*. The Southam Company itself might be open to invasion.

The proposal was bound to get a mixed reception: a blast from newspaper owners who viewed it as an encroachment on press freedom; approval from those who saw a greater danger in foreign control than in laws to prevent it. The Southam Company in its report to shareholders for 1963 held that 'the potential danger to our nation, if no action is taken, is greater than the danger inherent in government legislation in this instance.' It went on record by formal resolution:

> The Southam Company Limited supports the objective of the retention of control of communications media in Canada by Canadians and recommends the investigation of the best means of achieving this objective, and will collaborate with other publishers in making any necessary representations to government to explore the possibility of introducing legislation, should such action be deemed necessary.

Early in December Balfour saw Prime Minister Pearson and followed the visit with discussion by letter. Canada, he suggested, would not remain 'a viable national entity' unless control of its opinion-forming communications remained in Canadian hands. How could this be assured? He cited the company's own position:

'While The Southam Company itself remains in the control of the founding family, the directors are conscious of the awkward position in which they, and various trustees, would be placed if an offer were made to the shareholders by foreign nationals at a price substantially above the present market.' The only answer seemed to be legislation – legislation that might be considered neither necessary nor desirable in dealing with other businesses. Southam directors knew that prohibition of foreign ownership might be to the financial disadvantage of shareholders. Nevertheless, they favored it.

Montreal *Star*, Montreal *La Presse*, Quebec *Le Soleil* and *L'Evénement*, and Toronto *Star* made similar representations to cabinet ministers at about the same time.

A matter that tended to blur the central issue of prohibiting foreign ownership was a coincidental push for protection of the Canadian periodical press from inroads in their advertising revenue – their chief means of existence – by United States magazines aimed at the Canadian market. Split runs of Canadian-printed editions loaded with Canadian-aimed ads plugged in around the original American editorial content constituted, Canadian periodicals claimed, a form of dumping. Back in 1961 a royal commission headed by Grattan O'Leary had recommended disallowance of the cost of such advertising as a business expense in figuring income tax, a step that would have wiped out the large share of Canadian advertising dollars enjoyed by *Time* and *Reader's Digest*.

The first indication of possible government action on newspaper ownership came from Pearson early in 1964 in reply to a question on what he planned to do about magazines. There was, he said, an additional factor to think about: 'The desirability or otherwise of broadening the basis of any action that may have to be taken to include foreign control of Canadian newspapers.'

Reaction was sharp and immediate. Roy Thomson, newly created Lord Thomson of Fleet, and owner of a newspaper empire reaching into many lands, said he was appalled. The Toronto *Telegram* was equally vehement: 'The danger to publishing in this country is not one of foreign ownership, which is non-existent, but of the increase of monopoly ownership which is one of the significant factors in Canadian publishing.' It suggested that The Southam Company was not so much concerned with foreign ownership as with improving its own competitive position if more daily newspapers became available for sale. This was the only argument, in the course of months of discussion and dissent on the proposal, that angered Balfour: nothing in the company's record, he held, would support that charge.

The *Globe and Mail* also opposed the proposal. The Toronto *Star* and the Montreal *Star*, on the other hand, came out strongly in favor. 'The issue before us is not, thank God, government control or censorship in any form of what goes into Canadian papers or magazines,' the Montreal paper said. 'The issue is keeping them Canadian.' The Toronto *Star* posed the question: 'Suppose the *Star* was owned by Americans. Would you have faith in an editorial saying there were no disadvantages to American control of Canadian industry? Or an editorial saying Canada should not trade with Cuba and Red China? Or one that sided with the U.S. in a trade dispute with Canada? . . .'

Here its linking with the magazine advertising question confused the ownership issue in a rather special way. Both *Stars* favored ownership legislation and both also pressed for protection of Canadian periodicals. The fact that both published weekly magazines left them open to suggestion, in this particular area, that self-interest colored altruism. The two questions merged in a *Telegram* editorial:

> The Telegram does not suggest that the strong urging of the Montreal Star and the Toronto Star for the government to use its legislative powers to cripple Time and Reader's Digest is based on the mean motivation that each has, in Weekend and the Star Weekly, a competing publication. But it does suggest that the two newspapers should examine more closely the possibility that in advocating control of one section of mass media today, they might open the door to proposed restrictions on another section tomorrow. The same principle applies to proposed restrictions on foreign ownership of newspapers.

The Toronto *Star* said quite openly that it discussed the magazine matter 'from the standpoint of special interest because of its owner-ship of the Star Weekly', but held that 'the issue at stake goes far beyond the interest of any one firm into 'the survival of a genuinely Canadian periodical press.'

The Southam Company's position created a curious situation vis-à-vis its newspapers. Here was the company, as a company, taking a public stand on a public issue on which individual newspapers would be expected to speak editorially. Four members of the fifteen-man board of directors that made the decision were also publishers: R.W. Southam of the *Citizen*, Fred Auger of the *Province*, T.E.Nichols of the *Spectator*, and Basil Dean of the *Journal*. It was unlikely that any individual publisher, director or non-director, would quarrel with the desirability of keeping Canadian newspapers Canadian. But they might have differing views on seeking legislation to ensure it. Board discussion stuck strictly to the point at issue, not what the news-papers should say about it. Balfour sent round a memorandum:

> The company has always prided itself on the editorial independence of our newspapers. None of them has been asked, or will be asked, to support the company's stand on this question. If after reading the case which I have made, or after the proposed legislation is introduced, you, or any of our publishers, wishes to disagree editorially, then he should feel free to do so.

Among Southam newspapers that commented at this time, none disagreed with the desirability of legislation, but they obviously wondered what form it could take. Said the *Tribune*: 'The drafting of legislation to carry out this purpose, which at the same time would allay fears of future government control, poses a tough problem for the government. But the Tribune believes the effort should be made.' The *Spectator* encased its view in an editorial on the general subject of investment in Canada. The first step should be an easing of taxes to free Canadian investment money. Second, establishment of firm legislation 'to protect our banks, our insurance companies, trans-portation, electronic media, newspapers and periodicals from being taken over and controlled by outsiders.' The *Citizen* met head-on the possible suggestion that it was acting as a gramophone for the com-pany and proceeded to agree with the company's stand:

> Mr. Balfour speaks for the directors of The Southam Company and not for The Citizen or any other individual newspaper . . . and we do not necessarily subscribe to all the statements made by Mr. Balfour in the present controversy. On the central question however we be-lieve that legislation to prevent foreign takeovers is necessary. Pro-vided that a bill can be drafted with full respect for the constitutional right of press freedom, we will support it.

The Winnipeg *Free Press*, historic property of F.P.Publications, the Sifton-Bell group, came down hard for Canadian ownership: 'To say that they [aliens] have the right to own Canadian newspapers, and thus to influence Canadian policy, is like saying that they have the right to vote in Canada, though they are citizens and voters of another nation.' But the paper and the company rejected the idea of legislation. Eventually F.P.Publications – a private company – met its own problem by applying for supplementary letters patent setting up bylaws that would permit sale of voting shares only to Canadian citizens living in Canada. Proponents of legislation felt this didn't meet the case, since it would not work for a public company, could be applied only at the instance of willing owners, and could be revoked given a change of mind. The Montreal *Star* commented that this solution 'leaves in the single hands of individuals the protection of interests which are in every way national.'

Legal minds differed on the constitutional problem. Legislation on property and civil rights is a provincial matter. Could the Parliament of Canada forbid the sale of newspapers to foreigners? Some eminent lawyers thought it could under the 'peace, order and good government' clauses of the British North America Act, and cited Chief Justice Duff's decision on the Alberta press bill in 1938. The government's advisers apparently thought not; in any event it may be assumed that the minority federal government of the time had no wish to sponsor legislation that invited provincial challenge, especially from Quebec.

So, in the end, Finance Minister Walter Gordon used a single stone of another kind to bring down a couple of rather different birds. His budget in April of 1965 used the O'Leary gambit in modified form and extended it to apply to newspapers. It disallowed as a business expense advertising aimed at the Canadian market and placed in a non-Canadian-owned periodical or newspaper.

This made few people happy. The choler of magazine publishers rose because Montreal-printed editions of the American-owned *Time* and *Reader's Digest*, the chief beneficiaries of the advertising dollar in question, were exempted. (Mark Farrell of *Weekend* told M.P.s and senators in a mailed broadside: 'We might as well attempt to fight an outbreak of typhoid fever by making an exception of Typhoid Mary.')

And, though the provision undoubtedly would preclude any alien from buying into the Canadian newspaper field, most of those interested in this ideal disliked the indirect method adopted to get the result. It was unfortunate, Balfour remarked, that Gordon had used a tax method to achieve a perfectly proper objective.

Comment in Southam newspapers varied. The *Tribune* called the goal praiseworthy but the method confused and dangerous. The *Province* was blunt: 'If the government is afraid of foreign control it should simply pass legislation prohibiting it.' The *Spectator* in an early editorial said Gordon's 'inclusion of daily newspapers in his shopworn bag of magazine protectionism is dubious and unwanted . . . the first creeping traces of government control,' but came round later to admitting that Gordon 'even if he is doing the right thing the wrong way, found himself with no alternative.' The *Citizen* argued that all that was involved was a commercial restraint: 'It has nothing to do with the restriction of information.'

Basil Dean of the *Journal* was in perhaps the oddest position of all. Newspaper organizations, including the Canadian Daily Newspaper Publishers Association, opposed the tax method. As vice-president of the C.D.N.P.A. Dean voted for the resolution of protest and was one of a four-man delegation headed by Richard A. Graybiel of the Windsor *Star* that saw Prime Minister Pearson to press it – without effect.

Dean subsequently decided – and used his personal column 'The Publisher's Notebook' to state his view – that a sour loaf was better than no bread: 'I supported the resolution adopted by the publishers protesting it. But having heard the results of the government's study of the matter at first hand, I am now inclined to think that, distasteful as this method may be, it is perhaps the only one available. And I think the question important enough that it is better to use this method than to do nothing at all.'

Newspaper publishers remained divided and troubled.

C.D.N.P.A. directors in the fall of 1965 decided that 'whether or not it is in the best interests of Canada that the ownership of newspapers or any other news medium or industry should be governed by legislation is properly a subject on which individual newspapers should express their views rather than a subject for the views of this association.' They then decided to go on exploring alternatives to the tax measure.

The Commonwealth Press Union, meeting in November and December in the West Indies, heard a plea from Lord Thomson against legislation limiting foreign ownership of British, Canadian, and New Zealand newspapers. The union decided to appoint a committee to see whether such legislation was likely to restrict freedom of the press.

I. Norman Smith, editor of the Ottawa *Journal* and leader of the

Canadian delegation to the C.P.U., discussed the issue thoughtfully in an article on his return:

> Freedom of the press I take to be the freedom of a newspaperman to serve his community or country, and his ideals.
>
> I'm not sure it means freedom *as a right* of a man to serve another community or country.
>
> I dislike the method of the Canadian government in controlling press ownership by taxation. It has great potential danger and I hope a better way can be found. . . .
>
> If the power (and usefulness) of the press – the Fourth Estate – is what I like to think it is then it seems to me the Fourth Estate implies citizenship, no less than Sovereign, Lords, and Commons.

The issue and the clash of views remained. In the spring of 1967 the council of the Commonwealth Press Union approved a definition of press freedom including the statement that '. . . in countries enjoying the greatest freedom of the press, the law will encourage the publication and circulation of newspapers and periodicals, without regard to the nationality, race, politics or religion of those who publish, edit or write in them.'

'Nationality' was the key word. At the annual C.P.U. conference in June, Lord Thomson led an effort to have this specific approval of non-interference with foreign ownership adopted. He lost. The conference reaffirmed a previous definition declaring that freedom of the press 'derives from the fundamental right of every person to have full and free access to the facts in all matters that directly or indirectly concern him, and from his equal right to express and publish his opinions thereon and to hear and read the opinions of others.'

The Group

The young publisher of a Southam newspaper once remarked that in seven years on the job he had had one comment from Philip Fisher on an editorial: the then president didn't like the slang term 'booze'. The same publisher recalled that he had noted down twenty-three business problems for St. Clair Balfour, who was about to visit his plant. Balfour turned them all back to him as local questions for his own decision.

The Southam 'consultation list' – subjects on which publishers are expected to consult head office – does not, of course, include any aspect of news or editorial practice at all. Business matters run less than a double-spaced page. If a publisher contemplates any unusual change in procedure (such as dropping an edition, for instance) he must take it up with the president. Other matters that call for head-office approval include bonuses, unusual donations, salary changes for top executives. If he wants to change his body-type or spend more than $5,000 on plant at a shot, he consults Peter Southam, a vice-president and the company's mechanical expert. John S. Ward, another vice-president (in charge of marketing), will advise on circulation and advertising rates, secretary-treasurer Brian Shelley on insurance and variations under the company's retirement plan. Otherwise, unless he needs advice and asks for it, he is on his own.

But there is a sort of modern version of round-the-circuit. Balfour, who broke in on the editorial side, can be an interested and willing critic of editorial pages – their content and layout and writing quality – without questioning local policy. And a loose general discussion goes on between the eight daily publishers, and occasionally the president and chairman, through an exchange of memos when some question strikes the mind of one on which he wants the views of others. There are management problems in common.

For instance: should a publisher accept appointment to the boards of local institutions and organizations? Tom Nichols, raising the question in 1964, thought not. Two things inevitably happened: reporters and editors were inhibited; no matter how strongly assured that their publisher's identification with a civic group must make no difference, they couldn't write about it with objectivity and confidence. And sooner or later the publisher would find himself politically involved. Nichols's opening of this discussion turned up a variety of opinion and practice, most publishers recognizing the risk of embarrassment in joining any group that made news. One or two took the view that this was a calculated risk and that as members of their community they should contribute such talents as they had.

Should newspapers accept, as advertising, coupon ballots inserted by interested parties designed ostensibly to test public opinion? Discussion brought out a majority, though not unanimous, opinion that they could be accepted but that the papers should call attention editorially to the weakness of the practice if the findings were used to promote questionable conclusions. Ward expressed a personal view that write-in ballots were harmless in such stunts as beauty contests but not when directed to political or public welfare issues.

What are the pros and cons of charging for publishing wedding items and pictures? Can a paper in a fair-sized city afford the space to run all comers? Considering public relations, can it decide to print only those that are newsworthy? If it sets a charge as a brake on such copy, can it charge for routine submissions while running the newsworthy ones as straight news? Discussion on this in 1966 disclosed, again, varied opinions and practices.

Complete agreement on such matters with head office, or each other, is far from the rule. Balfour, speaking to an investment group in Montreal in 1966, remarked that the company might be considered a confederation: its publishers often acted like a bunch of provincial premiers.

The Southam company picks its local publisher and tells him to run the show. As far as editorial and news treatment go, its action as a company stops there. The publisher picks his staff and takes responsibility for how the show is run; for what his paper says. Under this practice the company's one recourse in the event of some persistently flagrant editorial campaign would be to fire the publisher. It has never had occasion to do so.

(Fisher, questioned as to where he would step in if a newspaper's opinions became patently outrageous, once ruminated: 'If the Vancouver Province, for instance, came out in support of British Columbia's joining the United States, I don't know how I would react.')

On the other hand on at least one occasion a local publisher fired an editor who followed an editorial line with which the publisher – ultimately responsible – disagreed. Early in 1955 R.W.Southam dismissed Charles Woodsworth as editor of the *Citizen* in an incident – exacerbated by a lack of rapport and communication between the two – that revealed some confusion in the public (and even the professional) mind over the terms publisher and editor and the relative responsibilities implied. Woodsworth, incidentally, went into External Affairs and eventually became ambassador to South Africa.

The extent to which the publisher's determination of editorial policy touches day-to-day operation varies. Most Southam publishers reached the position from a background of news and editorial work. Some occasionally write a signed article or an editorial on an issue on which they feel strongly or in which they take a special interest.

While at the Calgary *Herald*, Basil Dean chatted with the paper's readers in a column called 'A Publisher's Diary'. In a 1960 column he explained the system as it operated at the *Herald*. Editorials were planned at a conference usually directed by editor-in-chief Dick Sanburn at which Dean was sometimes present or to which he sent suggestions. Policy as it emerged from day to day was determined in part by the *Herald*'s historic attitudes, in part by the opinions of himself and Sanburn, in part by the opinions of the editorial writers themselves. 'Ultimately,' he wrote, 'my own opinions have an over-riding force,' though he couldn't recall when it had been necessary for him to lay down a policy-line in the face of objections from the editorial-page staff. One rule was that no editorial writer ever had to write a piece expressing a view he didn't believe in. A dissenter on any given subject would work on something else. Ultimate responsibility rested with Dean and his editor-in-chief.

Attacks by politicians sometimes give individual papers a chance to restate their independence. Shortly after Dean's explanatory column, Hazen Argue, then C.C.F. house leader but later a convert to Liberalism, told a Toronto audience that development of newspaper chains in Canada 'has robbed us of much of the power of judgment and has placed democracy and freedom itself in jeopardy.' The *Herald* invited Argue to come to Calgary at its expense and attend its daily news and editorial conferences, sit in on meetings between publisher and department heads, and see how its policies were arrived at. Argue declined and replied that bigness was bad in itself: he'd have been more impressed if the *Herald* had said it was prepared to send witnesses to appear before a parliamentary committee to 'inquire into operations of the Southam chain'. The *Herald* replied that it would be glad to obey any summons by a committee (if Argue could persuade Parliament to set one up) but couldn't testify concerning 'what he persists in calling the Southam "chain" ' because it wasn't equipped to discuss operations of other company divisions.

Three years later a blast came from another direction when Dr. Hugh Horner, Conservative M.P. for Jasper-Edson (the Edmonton *Journal* by this time was supporting the federal Liberals), asked the government: 'What kind of a deal have they made with the Southam press?' Were the Southams American-controlled? Were they going to get a big deal out of this government? The *Journal* didn't bother to comment. The *Citizen* pitched in with a reiteration of Southam operating philosophy.

Neither of the two aspects of independence asserted by Southam newspapers – local editorial autonomy and freedom from party ties – precludes tradition. Around them certain political traditions gathered: the *Spectator*, Conservative from the first; the *Citizen*, radical and variable but in modern times consistently Liberal at election time; the *Tribune*, the *Journal*, the *Herald*, and the *Province*, generally Conservative but with varying degrees of emphasis and a habit of knocking or commending according to circumstance. And the two newer and smaller members of the family: Medicine Hat, nourished on Liberalism, and North Bay, inheriting a Conservative touch.

Certain comings and goings at election time in recent years have shaken even tenuous traditions. The *Journal* commended the St. Laurent government to the voters in 1949 and later until the emergence of Diefenbaker. The Medicine Hat *News* supported the Conservatives in 1958. And as the federal election of 1962 approached, the *Journal* (previously for Diefenbaker) under Dean, a small-c conservative, swung to Pearson. Not only that – it kidded the *Herald* down in Calgary (sticking to Diefenbaker under Frank Swanson, a small-l liberal who had succeeded Dean there) for having 'all the firmness of an aspen leaf in a high wind'.

Events leading up to the election of the following March brought on two new defections. In Calgary on February 7 the *Herald* came out against the Conservative leader, largely on the nuclear issue. And in Hamilton Nichols and the old true-blue *Spectator* climaxed a month-long series of editorials with a rueful conclusion that 'the Diefenbaker administration has broken its coherent links with the Conservative tradition, and jeopardized principles for which the party has stood through the decades.'

Incidentally, the *Herald*'s swing in 1963 gave Swanson a chance to state again the old position: 'Our policies are made in Calgary. . . . Several questioners have inquired why the switch in "Southam policy" in regard to what we have been saying on the editorial page as to the shortcomings of the outgoing government in Ottawa. There is no such thing as a Southam policy as far as editorial viewpoints are concerned.' He could have proved his point without much trouble. Eleven days after the February 7 editorial the president of The Southam Company, hearing comment on it elsewhere, asked him if such an editorial had appeared.

Succeeding events drew a variety of reactions. On the flag question the *Citizen* came out for a maple leaf design. The *Herald* saw it as justified if it hastened genuine unity. The *Journal* thought Pearson's timing couldn't be much worse in forcing an issue that could only be settled emotionally. The *Province* called the design a glorified dishtowel, and the *Tribune* said that while this 'committee-made emblem' might in time take on meaning, 'for this generation the clumsy, divisive and even dangerous way in which it was thrust upon the nation will not soon be forgotten.' The Medicine Hat *News* arrived at a shorter estimate of the time necessary for acceptance: 'The rancor and strife which its approval generated on Parliament Hill will be forgotten within the next few months by all, save for those politically conscious persons and groups who will refer to it for what they hope will be their own political gains.'

In August of 1965 the *Journal* carried independence to the ulti-mate. In a leading editorial it accused the Prime Minister of 'casuis-try and tortured logic in arguing for the morality of a general election before effect is given to redistribution', and followed this up with a further plea to Pearson to wait. In an adjoining column its own man-aging editor, Andy Snaddon, dissented.

Both *Herald* and *Journal* stuck to the Liberals in the campaign – as the lesser of two evils. 'If there were an acceptable alternative,' the *Herald* said, 'a case could be made for concluding otherwise.'

In Hamilton Nichols concluded otherwise. Again the *Spectator* ran a series of studied editorials and reached a decision: 'We feel an over-all majority for the Liberal government is anything but desir-able, and that a Conservative administration would be preferable. . . . It is no longer a party in disarray.' The shades of Gus Freed, John Robson Cameron, and Bill Mulliss could resume their rest.

None of these three papers could be accused of riding a band-wagon. Diefenbaker made no dents in Liberal Hamilton. Nor Pear-son in Conservative Alberta.

The News Services

Apart from casual exchanges of view by memo and letter one double-barrelled forum brings Southam publishers together, usually at the time of board meetings. This consists of the advertising committee and the news services committee, whose memberships are the same – the eight publishers.

They meet without the president or chairman or directors present (except for those among themselves who are on the board). The news services committee's chief subject, as its name implies, is Southam News Services. Successive presidents have taken the posi-tion that this is the concern of the newspapers that use the copy.

By the middle 1960s the News Services had come some distance from the days of Lukin Johnston in London, Charlie Smith in Wash-ington, and Charlie Bishop in Ottawa. Charles Lynch, formerly with Reuters and the C.B.C. in many parts of the world, headed a staff of eleven with headquarters at Ottawa. Ottawa bureau, once embodied in Bishop alone, now numbered five. Two men reported from Wash-ington and two from London. In 1965, with Quebec's so-called quiet revolution much in the news, the Services set up a bureau in Quebec City. These bureaus constituted command-posts from which a corre-spondent could be dispatched anywhere in the world when a news-break or a situation seemed to justify coverage beyond that provided by the regular wire services: Russia, China, Africa, Viet Nam ...

Development of the Services has been gradual. One milestone date is 1946. In that year John Bird came down to Ottawa from the Winnipeg *Tribune* as full-time manager. Previously an editor at one or other of the papers had done the managing, Bird since 1944. Another significant year was 1960 when Lynch, then senior Ottawa correspondent, became chief of Southam News Services, a new coordinating position.

More often in newspaper work than in most other pursuits, mercurial and inventive characters emerge. Bird, born in Pietermaritzburg, educated at Oxford and Harvard and William Allen White's Emporia *Gazette*, once startled his liaison committee (Fisher, Jim O'Neil of the *Spectator*, and Torchy Anderson of the *Province*) by signing a telegraphed message JUBJUB – taking it for granted they would recognize the sender from the lines of Lewis Carroll:

> As to temper the jubjub's a desperate bird
> Since it lives in perpetual passion.

(Anderson himself achieved some memorable effects. For a newly organized junior chamber of commerce he once suggested the motto: 'No shirt too young to stuff' – a slogan later lifted by a novelist for use by a fictional reporter. When his old friend of Calgary days, Hughie Campbell, joined the CPR as a public relations man, Torchy labelled him a 'presstitute'.)

That transition year of 1946 also marked the close of a notable incumbency in London. A.C.Cummings moved out of his bomb-wrecked flat to spend three years, until his retirement, as editor of the Ottawa *Citizen*.

Though no light-hearted coiner of *bon mots*, Cummings was certainly one of the most individualistic practitioners who ever trod a beat. A West of Ireland man, he got into news-work in Dublin 'in default of anything better'. After coming to Canada in 1909 he worked in Vancouver on the *Province*, the *News-Advertiser*, and the *World*, and when early mergers shook up the field there, took off for Hawaii and Fiji, New Zealand, Australia, India, Ceylon, and French Somaliland. He had worked his way round to London and a job with British United Press when Johnston opened the Southam bureau in the *Times* building, and in 1929 Johnston took him on to help handle the growing report. After Johnston's death in 1933 he carried on alone.

He proved to be dedicated, cranky, opinionated, and in the long run indomitable. Cummings's wartime copy sometimes seemed to indicate that Hermann Goering had aimed the *Luftwaffe* at him personally. But nothing drove him out of London. For that matter it had taken the combined efforts of six Southam publishers to get him to Canada for a trip in 1937 – and then only when he was ready.

At the time, H.S.Southam was chairman of the news services committee, with W.L.MacTavish at Winnipeg handling details. Early in January of 1937 MacTavish wrote H.S. suggesting Cummings come to Canada and visit the papers because 'if he were a little more closely in touch with all our offices he would not strike quite the doctrinaire note he does at times.' On the abdication, for instance, he had been 'actively taking sides with Beaverbrook, Rothermere, Wedgewood, and Cripps in attacking the government.' (From the diplomatic point of view, MacTavish might have cited a better example. The Ottawa Southams had come to the defence of the former king as well.)

'The trouble is not with Cummings's work,' H.S. wrote, 'nor his attitude on occasions, but rather with the unavoidable fact that he has to write for six papers widely dispersed geographically, and each of them having divergent views as to what he should send. . . . If this is the trouble a visit to Canada will hardly correct it.'

M.E.Nichols took much the same view: 'It is doubtful if we could make our group position known to him because I am not sure that we know it ourselves.'

However, H.S. favored bringing the crusty little correspondent over. So did most of the others – not for a change of doctrine but to take a holiday, visit the newspapers casually, and get used to Canada again. They sent the invitation.

Cummings was horrified. A coronation and an imperial conference were coming up. Among other things, he recalled that the *Province* in 1911 had profaned the coronation of that year by running American-written copy on it. He could not leave London that spring. Nor did he. He came over in September. He would not see Canada again for eight years.

Differences over the type of copy he should send kept cropping up as he worked in wartime London. But as seen by Cummings the chief hazards were the roadblocks in the way of sending anything at all; particularly a tough and inconsistent censorship.

One frustration he documented at length. Early in 1940 Allen Bill of the *Tribune* crossed to cover Canadian troops in England. In mid-December word came of the torpedoing of the *Western Prince* with C.D.Howe aboard. Cummings spent all day (a Sunday) arranging to get Bill to the 'northern port' to interview survivors, and then bethought himself. Since the papers would be covered through The Canadian Press, he'd better see what was wanted. He devised a cable: DO YOU WANT SPECIAL STORY SURVIVORS WESTERN PRINCE AS CANADIAN PRESS COVERING FULLY AT NORTHERN PORT.

A censor at the cable office stopped it because, he said, the survivors had not yet arrived. Another, appealed to at the Ministry of Information with an air-raid in progress, refused to pass it, not because the survivors were still at sea, but because Cummings mentioned 'a northern port' – a term, as Cummings pointed out, that took in the coast from Greenock round to Leith and could give no useful information to the enemy. Must he wait for survivors to arrive at an unknown port on an unknown day before sending any message at all? Discussion can hardly have been smoothed by Cummings's prefacing successive revisions with 'stupidity of censorship' as a reason for their lack of clarity. Eventually he got a scarcely intelligible message through (still carrying the 'stupidity' preface). Four hours later the ministry censor phoned to say a mistake had been made in applying the original strictures. By that time it was too late.

Flying bombs followed the blitz, and rockets followed the flying bombs. Cummings remained, a familiar daytime figure tenaciously questioning the brass at briefings of every description. Asserting blandly that 'I leave my personal opinions on the doormat every morning' and turning out copy in which personal opinion was obvious to all but himself. And at night a helmeted gnome, fire-watching in his home district of Worcester Park, which lay on the *Luftwaffe*'s bus-route. When the blackout lifted late in 1944 Bird cabled him that all would raise a cheer now that curtains were off. Cummings responded: 'Thousand thanks. But our curtains not coming off. We have no windows left.' As Nichols once remarked to Imrie: 'Cummings is Cummings. He cannot be changed and the more you try to change him the more he persists in being himself.'

Though much had changed since Cummings's time, some of the problems noted then were still there in the days of a larger staff and sharper organization.

The reporter for an orthodox wire service (such as The Canadian Press) turns out copy from round the world that aims to be, first of all, factual and objective. His personality may show in turn of phrase or crispness of style, but the copy must be 'straight down the line', acceptable as a factual report in any or all of 100 newspapers. The correspondent for a single metropolitan daily has just one paper to think of. Knowing it will be covered by the agencies on the facts of all important news, he can be selective; and if he wishes to plant a floral bed of prose in interpreting events he need only make sure that his blooms blend with his paper's landscape. The separation of news from editorial comment is as complete in Canada as anywhere, but it would be naïve to contend that there are not differences of tone, emphasis, and selection. Or to deny that a kind of personal comment brings many by-lined news stories closer to the world of the columnist than that of the reporter.

The correspondent for Southam News Services is in a different spot from either the wire service man or the single-paper man. Expected to provide the personal touch, he writes for eight papers. In theory at least they may have different ideas on what should be covered and on that elusive thing called tone. It may go even farther than that. In the 1930s H.S.Southam noted that Cummings had to write for six papers with views that possibly diverged. Discussing Bird's job in the 1950s, Fisher remarked that 'actually he had to try to reconcile the conflicting opinion of different people even on individual newspapers.'

Discussions on whether or not Services correspondents were too free with personal opinion continued to develop from time to time. When Walter MacDonald in 1956 complained about one man's writing, Tom Nichols responded with the view that 'if they are to please all and offend none then we might as well not bother with correspondents.' The company enjoyed a unique reputation for the editorial independence of its newspapers. Any idea that the newspapers as a group stepped on their correspondents' toes would do it no good. To which MacDonald replied that he didn't think it was ever intended that liberty should extend to expressing personal bias. Bob Southam came in with the suggestion that there is no set pattern of interpretative writing that can satisfy a variety of points of view; a good prospect could be spoiled by too much direction.

In any event the Services continued to grow and their correspondents to report from various parts of the world with a considerable personal flavor. Several reporters profited from experience in the Services on their way to highly responsible positions, including publishers Dean of the *Journal*, Swanson of the *Herald*, Munro of the *Tribune* (later of the *Canadian*), and Michael Barkway of the *Financial Times*; and on the editorial pages, Dick Sanburn of the *Herald*, Chris Young and Charles King of the *Citizen*, and Bill Gold of the *Spectator*. The traffic is two-way: in 1966, for instance, George Brimmell, who had come to the Services from the *Tribune*, took charge of the Washington bureau.

In the years down through 1965, News Services writers won six

National Newspaper Awards (roughly a Canadian equivalent of the Pulitzer prizes) in staff corresponding. In 1966 a Services man picked up another prize in conditions that had overtones of irony. In the 1950s Paul Kidd had come out from England and joined the *Spectator* after a term at Windsor. In 1958 a reporting trip to Cuba, where he found conditions close to Nazism under Batista, wakened a special interest in Latin America and its people. Castro's police held him for a day while on a visit for the *Spectator* in 1961. In September of 1966 – he was then spending a year for the Services in Latin America – a bit of picture-taking (or perhaps more precisely an 'incorrect attitude toward the revolution') during another tour of Cuba got him expelled from the country. The touch of irony came a few days later when Columbia University awarded him the Maria Moors Cabot prize of $1,000 for achievements in journalism contributing to greater inter-American understanding.

The Fellows

In the impulse that takes young men and women into news-work and the bent that makes them good at it there is still a touch of the mysterious: an urge, realized or not, toward a sharing in adventure of a special kind.

Curiously enough many newspaper publishers in their emphasis on training for the job ignore the essential difference that is its special appeal. Publishers, who (one would think) should be the first to resist the chromium word and the academic cliché, acquiesce in calling a term a semester and a study group a seminar. In some United States news-rooms they actually refer to reporters-in-training as interns. Despite this tendency to blur out the difference, newspaper work remains an adventure in dealing with the unforeseen.

But (chromium and clichés aside) education is increasingly important in the complex modern business that exploiting the adventure has become. Journalism schools can develop aptitudes and teach techniques if the urge and the bent are there. Scientific study is a must for writers specializing in that fascinating field. A general grounding in the liberal arts deepens the insight of anyone concerned with the day-to-day story of humanity.

In 1961 the Southam company came up with a plan that was new in Canada. There were already courses in journalism for students aiming to get into the craft through that particular door. There were also a multitude of scholarships for general students. The Southams had set up some themselves – notably at Upper Canada College and

University of Toronto in memory of Gordon, and at Carleton in honor of Mercy, the immigrant mother. This was something else: fellowships at University of Toronto under which working newspaper men and women with five years or more of experience, and preferably under forty, could get a year of study with fees paid plus a tax-free allowance, based on salary, of up to $7,500 for a university year.

'We had been aware for some years', Balfour wrote in the University magazine, 'that there was a shortage of first-rate talent in the newspaper business and that some of the good material was handicapped in dealing with the increasingly complex problems of today's life by lack of formal education.'

Ross Munro reflected on the fellowships from another angle: 'In the news-rooms across the land there are always young reporters and editors who dream of a year away from bosses, pressures, and deadlines to think and study and delve into specialized subjects in a reflective atmosphere. Few of them ever achieve it on their own, and the dream mists over. . . .'

In the first six years of the plan twenty-eight journalists won Southam fellowships. They came from backgrounds as widely different as the three Toronto dailies, Quebec *Le Soleil*, and the Dufferin *Leader*, a weekly in Carman, Manitoba. The subjects they studied ranged from the Canadian party system to the Chinese language.

Appendices

Directors of the Company 1927-67

For directors concerned with management, areas of executive service are shown after their names. Other service in Southam enterprises, whether by management or non-management directors in the past, is indicated in parentheses. Dates give period on the board.

RICHARD SOUTHAM Toronto printing	1927-37
F.N.SOUTHAM Southam Company administration	1928-46
W.M.SOUTHAM Ottawa *Citizen*	1928-47
H.S.SOUTHAM Ottawa *Citizen*	1928-54
W.J.SOUTHAM Hamilton *Spectator*	1928-41
F.I.KER Hamilton *Spectator*	1928-59
M.E.NICHOLS Winnipeg *Tribune*; Vancouver *Province*	1928-51
J.M.IMRIE Edmonton *Journal*	1928-42
J.H.WOODS Calgary *Herald*	1928-41
F.J.BURD Vancouver *Province*	1928-53
P.S.FISHER Southam Company administration	1928-
HON. W.C.NICHOL, Vancouver	1928

W.J.WATSON Southam Company (Calgary *Herald*)	1930-48
O.L.SPENCER Calgary *Herald*; Vancouver *Province*	1936-51
WILLIAM WALLACE SOUTHAM Toronto printing	1937-50
WILLIAM WAUGH SOUTHAM Montreal printing	1938-54
GLYN OSLER, Toronto	1940-9
WESLEY MCCURDY Winnipeg *Tribune*	1943-51
D.K.MACTAVISH, Ottawa	1943-63
ERIC L. HARVIE, Calgary	1946-59
W.H.WOOLNOUGH Toronto printing; Southam Company	1946-58
JOHN D. SOUTHAM Calgary *Herald* (Ottawa *Citizen*)	1947-54
A.A.COGHILL Montreal printing	1948-56
WILLIAM WATSON SOUTHAM Southam Company (Vancouver *Province*)	1950-
JOHN F. HAYES Toronto and Montreal printing	1950-61
K.G.SOUTHAM Toronto printing (Winnipeg *Tribune*)	1951-2
A.W.MOSCARELLA Winnipeg *Tribune*; Vancouver *Province*	1951-60
K. LE M. CARTER, Toronto	1951-61
W.A.MACDONALD Edmonton *Journal* (Vancouver *Province*)	1952-62
ST. CLAIR BALFOUR Hamilton *Spectator*; Southam Company administration (Winnipeg *Tribune*)	1953-
R.W.SOUTHAM Ottawa *Citizen*	1954-
F.S.AUGER Winnipeg *Tribune*; Vancouver *Province*	1954-
GORDON T. SOUTHAM (Ottawa *Citizen*, Vancouver *Province*)	1955-
B.B.OSLER, Toronto	1956-
J. GRANT GLASSCO, Toronto	1958-
GEORGE L. CRAWFORD, Calgary	1959-
T.E.NICHOLS Hamilton *Spectator* (Vancouver *Province*, Winnipeg *Tribune*)	1960-
W. CULVER RILEY, Winnipeg	1960-

J.A.DALY   1961-
   Business publications
BASIL DEAN   1962-7
   Calgary *Herald*; Edmonton *Journal*
   (Southam News Services)
J. JACQUES PIGOTT, Toronto   1962-
G. HAMILTON SOUTHAM   1964-
   (Ottawa *Citizen*)
GORDON N. FISHER   1967-
   Southam Company administration
J.D.MURRAY   1967-
   Toronto printing

The Family

Of the six sons and one daughter born to William Southam and his wife, Wilson McNeilage Mills, only one son – Gordon, killed in action in 1916 – died without children. The families:

> Wilson Mills Southam, m. Henrietta Cargill (November 7, 1899)
> *Their children:*
> Margaret Wilson Southam (Mrs. Margaret Brinckman)
> William H. C. Southam, b. March 28, 1902; d. May 28, 1924
> Ethel Jean Southam (Lady Jean Brinckman)
> John David Southam, b. April 12, 1909; d. November 28, 1954
> Donald Cargill Southam
> Gordon Hamilton Southam

> Frederick Neal Southam, m. Agnes Henderson Linton (September 24, 1894)
> *Their children:*
> Dorothy Jean Southam (Mrs. Eric L. Harvie)
> Amy Wilson Southam (Mrs. Frederick I. Ker), b. October 30, 1896; d. January 6, 1942
> Margaret Linton Southam (Mrs. Philip S. Fisher)

> Richard Southam, m. Edna Irene Zimmerman (October 31, 1900)
> *Their children:*
> William Wallace Southam, b. September 11, 1901; d. April 1, 1950
> Ethel Jean Southam (died in infancy)
> Richard Southam, b. May 31, 1904; d. July 21, 1929
> Elizabeth Southam (Mrs. G. Donald McMurrich)
> Kenneth Gordon Southam, b. September 9, 1909; d. September 12, 1952

> Harry Stevenson Southam, m. Lilias Ahearn (December 1, 1909)
> *Their children:*
> Gordon Thomas Southam
> Janet Southam (Mrs. D.K.MacTavish)
> Robert Wilson Southam
> Ethel Southam (Mrs. Fred Toller)

William James Southam, m. Annie Beatrice Watson (May 27, 1907)
Their children:
William Watson (Peter) Southam
Beatrice Wilson Southam (Mrs. J.W.Thomson)
Mary Southam (Mrs. John Taylor)
Frederick Morris Southam
Basil Gordon Southam

Ethel May Southam, m. St. Clair Balfour (January 21, 1909)
Their children:
St. Clair Balfour
Wilson Elizabeth Balfour (Mrs. H.A.Baxter)
Alice Mary Balfour (Mrs. Colin Glassco)
Ethel Joan Balfour (Mrs. Joan McColl)
William Southam Balfour
Elizabeth Somerville Balfour (Mrs. J.A.Campbell)

A Genealogical Note

All Southam families, in the opinion of the amateur genealogist who made their histories a lifelong enthusiasm, take their surname from the old district of Southam in Warwickshire. Thence they spread to various parts of England and some of them, eventually, farther afield. The Southam family whose one male descendant came to Canada in 1843 had been established at Kingsthorpe, a village on the northern outskirts of the county town of neighboring Northamptonshire, for three generations.

The genealogist was Colonel Herbert Southam of Shrewsbury (later of Woking, Surrey). Somewhere around 1900 he noticed in *The Times* a reference to the Southams of Hamilton, Canada, and wrote William Southam for information. William sent him what he knew, which was little beyond the fact that his parents had come from Kingsthorpe.

Harry Southam, in England in 1904, looked up the genealogist and through the years a desultory correspondence continued. Desultory is perhaps an understatement: in 1920 Wilson, at the colonel's request, filled in a partial family tree and sent it to W.J. for additions, relay to Fred and Dick, and transmission back to Woking. It lay in W.J.'s files for seven years.

When correspondence resumed in 1927 the colonel got down to business in cold vestries in and around Kingsthorpe. Registers yielded the information that one John Southam married Susannah Walden of nearby Dallington on October 10, 1776, and died in March of 1814. He was thought to have been a tailor. Colonel Southam (there was no evidence of relationship between him and Southams in Canada) was unable to find records in this particular line earlier than those of John and Susannah.

Their first child, born in 1777, was a son Richard who married Anne Jayes of Moulton, another near-by parish, in 1800. Subsequently they had four girls, two boys who died young, and another who disappears from the records.

Richard became a dealer in bacon, a man apparently of some small prosperity until cut down by illness. When he died in 1819 his only son was William, then ten years old, who grew up to become a mason, bricklayer, and builder, the trade of his grandfather Jayes. He owned a house in a lane called Parson's End and voted Whig. In the summer of 1843, with four daughters and a pregnant wife, he sailed for North America: the voyage climaxed by the birth at Lachine on August 23 of 'Billy Southam again' – the youngster who would grow up to establish a family and the beginnings of the company that bears his name.

William was apparently the last male Southam in Kingsthorpe. In the census of 1851 the name was not listed in the parish and though earlier Southam daughters married there, there is no evidence of later contacts between relatives separated by the Atlantic.

More was known about the Mills than about the Southam side of the family in the Old Country. An aunt of Mrs. William Southam was the mother of John Mills McCallum (he became Sir John in 1912), Liberal M.P. for Paisley from 1906 until his death in 1920, whom various Southams met on trips to the United Kingdom. J.F.Lymburn, Attorney-General in the Farmer government of Alberta, was another cousin, his father's mother having been a sister of James Mills, the cabinet-maker immigrant of 1854.

A Note of Acknowledgment

Much of the material for this narrative has come from people who worked or still work on Southam newspapers, and from the files of the newspapers themselves. There were of course many other sources:

> Members of the Southam family by birth and marriage, in and out of the business, to whom I am indebted for much family incident and background;
>
> The company archives. In the 1950s the late Bruce McKelvie of the *Province* organized this collection, which includes correspondence going back to the start of the century, and tran-

scribed interviews with old-timers;
Current company correspondence;
Officers of the company and present and former publishers of the newspapers.

Apart from head office people and the present publishers, all of whom co-operated in making information available, individuals who eased the way, and the divisions about which their information proved particularly valuable, included:

Spectator: F.I.Ker, A.G.Muir, J.G.O'Neil, Frank Keen, Milford Smith, T.W.D.Farmer.

Citizen: Christopher Young, C.A.Bowman, Charles Bishop, L.W. Gates, Fred Johnstone, Joe Finn, Ronald Grantham, E. Leigh.

Tribune: Fred J. O'Malley, Tom Green, R.W. Queen-Hughes, Margaret Robinson, A.G.Mahon.

Herald: H.H.C.Anderson, Gerald Brawn, Bruce Boreham, Mrs. Fran Fraser (whose *Herald* story on Buffalo Child Long Lance provided much of the material on that colorful character), Fred Kennedy, Parker Kent.

Journal: Don MacDougall, Walter MacDonald, George Cooper, Mrs. John Imrie, Grace Williams, Andrew Snaddon.

Province: Bruce Ramsey, D.A.McGregor, R.T.Elson, W.T.Robertson, Stan Sutherland, Jim Coleman.

News: Fred McGuinness, Peter Mossey, Patrick Roe.

Nugget: C.M.Fellman.

Printing: Katherine Finn, Alice Mae Sullivan, Charles and William Keates, J.F.Hayes, Norman Nicol, Bert Williams, E.M.Pritchard, J.D. Murray, Guy Fisher.

Business Publications: J.A.Daly.

I address a special word of thanks to librarians at the newspapers, particularly Jean Tebbutt at the *Spectator*, Ron Tysick at the *Citizen*, Betty Hall at the *Tribune*, Reg Titcombe at the *Herald*, Diana Taschuk at the *Journal*, and Syd Williamson and Sybil Sundman at the *Province*.

Acquaintances in newspaper work generally whose help I gratefully acknowledge: I. Norman Smith of the Ottawa *Journal*; R.S.Malone of F.P.Publications; Don Cromie, former publisher of the Vancouver *Sun*; Clifford Sifton; the late H.A. and R.A.Graybiel of the Windsor *Star*; L.N.Bronson of the London *Free Press*; Edgar Collard of the Montreal *Gazette*; Robert Hanson and Elmer Ferguson of the Montreal *Star*; Pat Kelly; W.A.Craick; Greg MacDonald;

Miles Patrone of the American Newspaper Publishers Association; Harris Holmes and Margaret McMillan of the Canadian Daily Newspaper Publishers Association.

Thanks are due also to many former colleagues in The Canadian Press: Jean Thompson, head office librarian, and her assistant Kathy Harrison; William Stewart at Montreal, Fraser MacDougall, Graham Trotter, and Ken Ward at Ottawa; Fred Chafe at Winnipeg; Andy Garrett at Edmonton; Ken Metheral at Vancouver; Harold Morrison at London; Ian Munro, Mary Kibblewhite, and Yolande Kilby at Toronto.

I am also grateful for assistance to many people outside the newspaper craft. These included: Dr. Kaye Lamb and Pierre Brunet of the Archives of Canada; Hugh Dempsey and T.R.McCloy of the Glenbow Foundation, Calgary; Elizabeth Hunter of the reference department, Ottawa Public Library; Maud Godfrey of the Kenilworth Avenue branch, Hamilton Public Library; R.H.Hubbard of the National Gallery; Eric J. Hanson, Edmonton; C.F.Harrington, Montreal; Edith Lorentsen of the Department of Labor, Ottawa; H.B.Cowan, Ottawa; R.A.Laidlaw, Toronto; Wilson Wyllie, Vancouver. On family matters, the recollections of Mrs. St. Clair Balfour (Ethel Southam), daughter of William Southam, and of the late Mrs. R.A.Wyllie (Maude Southam), a niece, were particularly valuable. Mrs. Margaret Brinckman lent personal papers left by her father, Wilson M. Southam, which included reminiscences of boyhood days in Hamilton. W.W. (Peter) Southam provided correspondence left by his father, W.J. Mrs. James Eccles (Mary McGibbon Southam) also gave valuable help.

Because of the essential involvement of newspaper men and women and newspapers themselves in the compilation of this record, it has been put together under a pleasant difficulty, the hazard of constant temptation. It is impossible to stick to a specific subject in correspondence with people like Torchy Anderson and Bruce Boreham and Bob Elson – or in talks with Jim O'Neil and Dan McGregor and Fred O'Malley. And it is next to impossible to hew to the business in hand – tracking through microfilmed pages, say, for some particular news climax – when a hundred provocative stories lie in wait to trap you down the interminable byways of events.

It may be true that there is nothing as dead as yesterday's newspaper. It is certainly true that after thirty and forty and fifty years it is again wonderfully alive. So at times I have yielded to temptation and pursued what may seem to be irrelevant. For this I make no apology. It was part of the life of its time and to image that life was the newspapers' business.

Index